A History of Utilitarian Ethics

In this landmark volume, Samuel Hollander presents a fresh and compelling history of moral philosophy from Locke to John Stuart Mill, showing that a 'moral sense' can actually be considered compatible with utilitarianism. The book also explores the link between utilitarianism and distributive justice.

Hollander engages in close textual exegesis of the works relating to individual authors, while never losing sight of the intellectual relationships between them. Tying together the greatest of the British moral philosophers, this volume reveals an unexpected unity of eighteenth and nineteenth century ethical doctrine at both the individual and social level.

Essential reading for advanced students and researchers of the history of economic thought, political economy, history of ethics, history of political thought and intellectual history.

Samuel Hollander is University Professor Emeritus at the University of Toronto, Canada, and an Officer in the Order of Canada.

Routledge Studies in the History of Economics

214. Money, Finance and Crises in Economic History
The Long-Term Impact of Economic Ideas
Edited by Annalisa Rosselli, Nerio Naldi and Eleonora Sanfilippo

215. Macroeconomic Theory and the Eurozone Crisis
Edited by Alain Alcouffe, Maurice Baslé and Monika Poettinger

216. The Economic Thought of Friedrich List
Edited by Harald Hagemann, Stephan Seiter and Eugen Wendler

217. Economic Crisis and Economic Thought
Alternative Theoretical Perspectives on the Economic Crisis
Edited by Tommaso Gabellini, Simone Gasperin and Alessio Moneta

218. Schumpeter's Capitalism, Socialism and Democracy
A Twenty First Century Agenda
Edited by Leonardo Burlamaqui and Rainer Kattel

219. Divine Providence in Early Modern Economic Thought
Joost Hengstmengel

220. Macroeconomics without the Errors of Keynes
The Quantity Theory of Money, Saving, and Policy
James C.W. Ahiakpor

221. The Political Economy of the Han Dynasty and Its Legacy
Edited by Cheng Lin, Terry Peach and Wang Fang

223. A History of Utilitarian Ethics
Studies in Private Motivation and Distributive Justice, 1700–1875
Samuel Hollander

222. The Economic Thought of Michael Polanyi
Gábor Biró

For more information about this series, please visit
www.routledge.com/series/SE0341

A History of Utilitarian Ethics

Studies in Private Motivation and Distributive Justice, 1700–1875

Samuel Hollander

LONDON AND NEW YORK

First published 2020
by Routledge
2 Park Square, Milton Park, Abingdon, Oxon OX14 4RN

and by Routledge
52 Vanderbilt Avenue, New York, NY 10017

Routledge is an imprint of the Taylor & Francis Group, an informa business

© 2020 Samuel Hollander

The right of Samuel Hollander to be identified as author of this work has been asserted by him in accordance with sections 77 and 78 of the Copyright, Designs and Patents Act 1988.

All rights reserved. No part of this book may be reprinted or reproduced or utilised in any form or by any electronic, mechanical, or other means, now known or hereafter invented, including photocopying and recording, or in any information storage or retrieval system, without permission in writing from the publishers.

Trademark notice: Product or corporate names may be trademarks or registered trademarks, and are used only for identification and explanation without intent to infringe.

British Library Cataloguing in Publication Data
A catalogue record for this book is available from the British Library

Library of Congress Cataloging-in-Publication Data
Names: Hollander, Samuel, author.
Title: A history of utilitarian ethics : studies in private motivation and distributive justice, 1700-1875 / Samuel Hollander.
Description: Abingdon, Oxon ; New York, NY : Routledge, 2019. | Series: Routledge studies in the history of economics ; volume 223 | Includes bibliographical references and index.
Identifiers: LCCN 2019011770| ISBN 9780367243876 (hardback) | ISBN 9780367243890 (ebk.)
Subjects: LCSH: Utilitarianism--Great Britain--History. | Philosophy, English--18th century. | Philosophy, English--19th century. | Distributive justice--Moral and ethical aspects.
Classification: LCC B1571 .H59 2019 | DDC 171/.509--dc23
LC record available at https://lccn.loc.gov/2019011770

ISBN: 978-0-367-24387-6 (hbk)
ISBN: 978-0-367-24389-0 (ebk)

Typeset in Bembo
by Taylor & Francis Books

Printed and bound in Great Britain by
TJ International Ltd, Padstow, Cornwall

Dedicated to the memory of Haim Chertok z"l
(1938–2018).

And for Maggie Davidson-Chertok in friendship.

Contents

Foreword	xii
Introduction	xiv

PART 1
John Locke   1

1 John Locke, utilitarian ethics and the moral sense   3

    1.1 Introduction 3
    1.2 Locke's 'Benthamite' categories: pleasure, pain and happiness 5
    1.3 Utilitarian ethics: theological and secular features 10
    1.4 Locke's rejection of innate moral sense elaborated 14
    1.5 'Of faith and reason' 22
    1.6 Concluding remarks 25

PART 2
Eighteenth-century moral-sense literature   29

2 Lord Shaftesbury, utilitarian ethics and the moral sense   31

    2.1 Introduction 31
    2.2 The public good as the 'main end' of virtue 32
    2.3 The 'moral sense' or 'sense of right and wrong' 38
    2.4 The moral sense and the public interest 39
    2.5 Summary and conclusion 44

3 Two Shaftesbury critics: Bernard Mandeville and John Brown   47

    3.1 Introduction 47
    3.2 Bernard Mandeville 49

3.3 John Brown 54
3.4 Concluding remarks 60

4 Francis Hutcheson and the Hutcheson–Locke relationship 64

4.1 Introduction 64
4.2 Propaedeutics: 'on human nature: reflections on our common systems of morality' (1724) 68
4.3 Inquiry concerning moral good and evil (1729), Essay on the nature and conduct of the passions and affections (1728, 1769), and related documents 71
4.4 'Inaugural Lecture on the Social Nature of Man' (1730) 86
4.5 A System of Moral Philosophy (1755) 89
4.6 A Short Introduction to Moral Philosophy (1747) 100
4.7 On Agrarian laws: Implications for distributive justice 105
4.8 On the Hutcheson–Locke relationship 109

5 David Hume, utilitarian ethics, the moral sense and distributive justice 115

5.1 Introduction 115
5.2 Humean utilitarianism and the moral sense 116
5.3 Distributive justice 124
5.4 Concluding note 129

6 C.A. Helvétius and David Hartley, utilitarian ethics, and the moral sense 132

6.1 Introduction 132
6.2 Mill's perspective on Helvétius 133
6.3 De L'Esprit 134
6.4 Helvétius on policy 139
6.5 Helvétius on ethical progress 141
6.6 Helvétius and Locke 143
6.7 Hartley 144

PART 3
Adam Smith 149

7 Utilitarian ethics in *The Theory of Moral Sentiments* 151

7.1 Introduction 151
7.2 A literature review 152

7.3 On motivation versus consequences: the 'moral sense' and sympathy 156
7.4 More on 'propriety' and utility 159
7.5 On justice and punishment 163
7.6 Smith's 'greatest happiness' principle 166
7.7 Concluding note: Smith in relation to Hume, Hutcheson and Bentham 169

8 Utilitarian ethics and distributive justice in *The Wealth of Nations* 174

8.1 Introduction 174
8.2 Smithian utilitarianism and natural rights 180
8.3 The ethics of class distribution 181
8.4 Distributive justice and reform proposals 190
8.5 Happiness and population size 193
8.6 Wage differentials 194
8.7 On the 'lower ranks' and the pauper population 196
8.8 Summary and conclusion 204

PART 4
Jeremy Bentham   213

9 Bentham, utilitarian ethics and distributive justice 215

9.1 Introduction 215
9.2 On benevolent motivation 216
9.3 Benevolence elaborated 221
9.4 Prospects for ethical progress 225
9.5 On self-regarding liberty and individuality 227
9.6 On economic equality 228
9.7 Summary and conclusion 233

10 Bentham in relation to Locke and the eighteenth-century literature 237

10.1 Bentham on Locke 237
10.2 On the charge against Shaftesbury, Hutcheson and Hume 238
10.3 Bentham and Smith 245
10.4 Bentham and Helvétius 246

PART 5
Thomas Robert Malthus — 253

11 Malthus and the utilitarians — 255

11.1 Introduction 255
11.2 Malthus's theological utilitarianism 258
11.3 Malthus's 'natural theology' 260
11.4 Population control: 'moral restraint' 265
11.5 Population control: 'prudence' 266
11.6 On happiness and virtue 270
11.7 Ricardo and J.S. Mill on virtue: a digression 273
11.8 Did Malthus strengthen the theological foundations of his work? 277
11.9 Conclusion 279

12 Malthus, distributive justice and the equality issue — 283

12.1 Introduction 283
12.2 Income distribution and the equality issue 284
12.3 Distributive 'fairness' 289
12.4 Distribution and aggregate demand: more on the equality issue 291
12.5 Trade policy: implications for real wages 294
12.6 Poor relief 297
12.7 Summary and conclusion 301

PART 6
John Stuart Mill — 305

13 Mill, distributive justice and reform — 307

13.1 Introduction 307
13.2 On distributive justice and the stationary-state analysis 309
13.3 Of property, competition and income distribution 314
13.4 The labour market and the role of the state 318
13.5 Reform proposals: public finance 324
13.6 Land reform 329
13.7. Summary and conclusion 332

14 Mill, ethical progress and personal liberty   340

   14.1 Introduction 340
   14.2 Ethical progress: Mill and Bentham compared 340
   14.3 The 'inviolability' of self-regarding actions 342

15 Mill and the 'moral sense': The return to Bentham
   (and Hutcheson)   346

   15.1 Introduction 346
   15.2 The 1830s: Mill's moral sense allowances 349
   *15.3 'Whewell on moral philosophy' (1852) and the return to
       Bentham 359*
   15.4 Utilitarianism (1861) 366
   15.5 Commentaries on James Mill's Analysis of the Phenomena of
       the Human Mind *and* Fragment on Mackintosh *368*
   15.6 On Professor Rosen's Mill *and the 'return to Bentham' 374*
   15.7 Utilitarianism and the moral sense reconciled 376
   15.8 Mill and Hutcheson 379
   15.9 Summary and conclusion 381
   Appendix: on Mill's eighteenth-nineteenth century contrast 384

Index   395

Foreword

This book concerns, in the first place, classic eighteenth-century contributions to utilitarianism as an ethical doctrine pertaining to individual conduct with an eye to motivation, and particularly the treatment of the so-called 'moral sense'. A second general theme relates to utilitarianism as an ethical doctrine pertaining to social policy, primarily distributive justice and the equality issue.

I do not attempt a comprehensive treatment, but limit myself to a series of studies focusing, insofar as concerns the first general theme, on Shaftesbury, Hutcheson, Hume, Helvétius, and Hartley in the light of the special attention accorded to these writers by Jeremy Bentham and John Stuart Mill; and on Hutcheson, Hume, Smith, Bentham, Malthus, and Mill regarding distributive justice and related matters. I thus avoid entirely, for example, the proto-history of utilitarianism, an issue explored by Rosen in his *Classical Utilitarianism from Hume to Mill*, and make only a passing reference to Richard Cumberland, considered by Albee in *A History of English Utilitarianism* as 'the true founder' of the doctrine.

My analysis of eighteenth-century writers is preceded by a chapter on John Locke, who famously rejected the moral sense notion; however my interpretation of the post-Lockean literature turns on a demonstration of the compatibility of the greater-good principle defining utilitarianism with a 'moral sense' understood as dictating *sympathy* as the key to ethical conduct. The post-Lockean literature thus turns out to be effectively at one with Locke, rather than in opposition as has often been supposed. While this compatibility was noted over a century ago by James Bonar and Elie Halévy, and more recently by others, I do claim to have provided a detailed justification for such a viewpoint and to have demonstrated its adoption by Adam Smith in his *Theory of Moral Sentiments* as well as by the aforementioned authorities. Bentham's failure to appreciate the consistency in question may well have misled later interpreters including Mill, although Mill finally accepted that the dictates of conscience relate specifically to the intended consequences of actions for the 'greatest happiness', and increasingly came to appreciate Bentham's contribution to utilitarian ethics, thereby confirming the *unity* of eighteenth- and nineteenth-century utilitarian ethical doctrines pertaining to the individual. I am heartened to find much common ground with Frederick Rosen regarding this central matter.

Each chapter may be read as an independent unit, but it is a prime objective of this work to establish the relationships between authors. A subject may therefore be discussed at length in more than one chapter: Locke for example appears in his own right in Chapter One but is referred to throughout; Chapters Four and Five treat Hutcheson and Hume respectively and they also figure in later chapters entailing comparisons with Smith and Bentham; and, as indicated, Mill and Bentham provide key points of reference throughout.

Regarding the second general theme I find that much of the literature establishes a case for 'satisfactory' wages based on the quantitative superiority of the labouring class in line with the 'greater good' criterion, while at the same time exercising caution, though still from a perspective sympathetic towards labour's interest, when evaluating the equality question. My analysis of utilitarianism as ethical doctrine pertaining to individual conduct demonstrates the consistency of the moral sense with concern for the *public good*, and this provides the formal link between the two general themes. But in addition I note instances where an author tasks public policy with the correction or enhancement of the moral sense itself, as Hutcheson did when he conceded that its *effective* operation may require education directed at instilling 'proper ends', as is certainly true of Mill.

The Introduction to this book provides a brief overview of its major arguments. More detailed summaries, including my engagement with some of the secondary literature, are given in the Introductions to the individual chapters.

I appreciate the helpful advice offered by the three referees of my manuscript, and the permission to reprint, with small modifications, two of my articles granted by their publishers: Springer Nature (for Chapter 7): 'Ethical Utilitarianism and *The Theory of Moral Sentiments*: Adam Smith in Relation to Hume and Bentham', *Eastern Economic Journal* 42, 2016: 557–80; and Taylor and Francis Ltd (for Chapter 11): 'Thomas Robert Malthus and the Utilitarians', *History of Economics Review* 64, 2016: 2–26.

Introduction

This Introduction provides a brief survey of the book. As demonstrated in the first chapter, comprising Part I, John Locke undermined the notion of innate ideas, including that of an in-born 'moral sense', and spelled out the essential building blocks of the hedonic structure entailing the quest for 'happiness' as governing human conduct. In addition, he elaborated an ethical doctrine approving the individual who engages in *other-regarding* conduct to the benefit of the 'greater good'. J.S. Mill wrote of 'the philosophy of Locke, Bentham, and the eighteenth century', but Bentham himself – and for that matter Hume too – was silent regarding Locke's positive contribution to ethical utilitarianism as sympathetic conduct in the public interest, and this even if such conduct were motivated by the promise of worldly advantage to the individual. Modern secondary commentaries cover a range of sometimes conflicting interpretations but often lack sufficient recognition of Locke's identification of morality with other-regarding conduct favouring general happiness. Now Locke sought to enhance sympathetic or socially-advantageous conduct by advising individuals not to discount a future life when considering the consequences of conduct for their personal 'happiness'; the central role he accorded to 'reason' was designed to counter appeals to revelation on the part of charlatans rather than *genuine* appeals. But this 'theological' consideration does not render Locke a 'theological utilitarian' in the strict sense of one who posits the hope of future rewards and the fear of future punishments as a *necessary* condition both for good social behaviour and for ethical commendation.

Rendering the post-Locke story particularly interesting, if more complex, is Bentham's presumption that moral-sense reasoning and the utility perspective are inherently contradictory. This presumption, I shall argue, is unjustified, although it was adopted lock, stock, and barrel by Mill. It will prove convenient to have Bentham's stance on hand at the outset since we shall revert to it frequently. The most influential of the principles Bentham rejected in the *Principles of Morals and Legislation* is that which 'approves or disapproves of certain actions, not on account of their tending to augment the happiness, nor yet on account of their tending to diminish the happiness of the party whose interest is in question, but merely because a man finds himself disposed to approve or disapprove of them: holding up that approbation or disapprobation as a sufficient reason for itself, and disclaiming the necessity of looking out for any extrinsic ground' (Bentham 1982 [1789]: 21, 25). Insertions made in 1819 into a note to the *Principles* – the insertions were first printed in the Bowring edition of *The Works* (Bentham (1843 [1789]: 8n) – specify the author's intended: 'One man (Lord Shaftesbury, Hutchinson [sic], Hume, &c.) says, he has a thing made on purpose to tell him what is right and what is wrong; and that it is called a *moral sense*: and then he goes to work at his ease, and says, such a thing is right, and such a thing is wrong – why? "because my moral sense tells me it is"' (Bentham 1982 [1789]: 26).[1]

Now Shaftesbury, Hume, Hutcheson, and Helvétius maintained, as I shall show in Part II, both the moral sense and utilitarian perspectives and did so consistently, considering that the character they ascribed to the moral sense specifically recommends a conscious *concern with the public welfare*, or the general good to the individual. Locke rejected the notion of a moral sense but those who came after and allowed for it narrowed down its dictates to reflect the value judgment that virtue consists in the concern for the public good, rendering it perfectly consistent with the Lockean perspective and indeed consistent with Mill's notion of 'general utility as the foundation of morality' (Mill 1969 [1838]: 86).

Shaftesbury enters our picture in Chapter Two with Bentham's presumption in mind that he championed a 'moral sense' *opposed to utilitarian ethics*. Mill viewed Shaftesbury in the same light. Some later commentators also imply that Shaftesbury opposed the general utility doctrine relying on an in-born 'sense of right and wrong'. There may be some justification for such a reading, but I shall show that when engaged in practical application Shaftesbury considers the moral sense as recommending to the individual a conscious *concern with the public welfare* – reflecting his perception of 'virtue' – as Locke had already established, as Hutcheson and Hume were later to do, and consistently with Mill's notion of 'general utility as the foundation of morality'. Furthermore, Shaftesbury emphasized that '*Virtue* and *Interest* may be found at last to agree', drawing on an argument from 'reason' whereby private advantage harmonizes with the public good, namely the individual's realization of his dependency on society which encourages him to be concerned for its welfare. *This is fully in line with Locke*. Shaftesbury's appeal to a built-in psychological capacity to distinguish good from evil was merely intended to reinforce his value judgment that virtue consists in the concern for the public good, albeit to private advantage (but this was scarcely essential to the argument). These features will surprise readers impressed by Shaftesbury's neglect of Locke in his printed writings and indeed the positive hostility expressed towards Locke in his private correspondence, although whether Shaftesbury realized how much he conceded to Lockean ethical utilitarianism I am unable to say. An important observation by James Bonar that Hume left the moral sense with 'little to do' once it is traced to commendation of other-regarding sympathy, therefore also applies to Shaftesbury.

Chapter Three concerns two critics of Shaftesbury's *allegedly* unrealistic faith in the widespread actuality of *strict* altruism – 'allegedly' since (as shown in Chapter 2) sympathetic behaviour always entailed for Shaftesbury some estimate of private advantage. Now Mandeville, I show, relies in his discussion of *pity* on a *sympathetic* natural sentiment satisfied by other-regarding conduct – implying in effect a Shaftesbury-like moral sense. Because of the personal satisfaction derived from being endowed by nature with other-regarding sentiment and because to act against nature would be psychologically painful, Mandeville regards such conduct as *ethically neutral*, ethical conduct requiring *no personal advantage whatsoever*. And yet he approaches Shaftesbury when he admits that the other-regarding act reflecting pity bears 'the greatest Resemblance to Virtue' – even that 'without a considerable mixture of it the Society could hardly subsist'. He is silently conceding a great deal to Shaftesbury by this blunting of the rigorist perception of virtue.

As for John Brown, I demonstrate his keen appreciation of Shaftesbury's ethical utilitarianism as entailing a concern for the public good – which provides support for my reading in Chapter 2 – although he, like Mandeville, mocked Shaftesbury's alleged faith in the actuality of pure altruism. I confirm in this manner Halévy's position – which is very much in line with that of Bonar mentioned above – that '[s]ince the principle of sympathy can ... be regarded as a special form of the principle of utility, the eighteenth-century moralists – such as John Brown – who are responsible for the "moral sense" theory may in many cases be already considered "utilitarians"'. To complete the picture, I take account of Brown's own perception of Mandeville.

Hutcheson's utilitarian status is carefully established in Chapter Four since to this day the matter remains the subject of heated debate. Mill had little to say about Hutcheson, whereas Bentham represents him as a moral-sense author opposed to the utilitarian principle, although – as shown in Chapter 10 – he himself emerges as far closer to Hutcheson than he apparently imagined. I understand the numerous and complex Hutcheson texts as maintaining that while moral approval derived from an innate feeling, from the 'heart', this sense was incapable of automatically yielding ethical verdicts *independent of consequences* – or, rather, of *intended* consequences. For conduct is approved as virtuous provided it is motivated by a concern for the happiness of others – by 'sympathy' or 'fellow-feeling' rather than by 'self-love' – extending in the best case to 'benevolent' conduct directed at advancing the welfare of *anonymous* beneficiaries, namely advancing 'the greatest Happiness for the greatest Numbers'. Bonar's remark regarding Hume that the moral sense was left with little to do once it is reduced to other-regarding sympathy may therefore be also said of Hutcheson. It is presumed that mankind, *pace* Mandeville and Clarke, was indeed 'susceptible of affections truly disinterested in the strictest sense, and not directly subordinated to self-interest, or aiming at private interest of any kind'. Allowance is made for ethically-neutral or '*innocent*' self-love but where selfish passions are 'too strong' and impinge on other-regarding sentiment the ethical quality of conduct is correspondingly reduced by the moral sense. Hutcheson was, however, unconcerned by self-satisfaction on the part of the actor who enjoys a 'sympathetic' character since such satisfaction does not enter into his motivation. Motivation in fact takes precedence over consequences in two respects: conduct properly motivated which, through no fault of the agent, does not yield the expected advantageous results does not diminish ethical merit; and conversely where the *intention* of the agent does not entail the public good, his action must be considered morally defective even if social advantage happened to result from his action.

By proposing a moral sense, Hutcheson sought to explain *why* disinterested conduct in the public interest is conventionally judged to be ethically meritorious – it was because a *feeling* approves of such conduct. Hutcheson's allowance for disinterested benevolence would appear antithetical to Lockean doctrine involving prudential calculation of the prospective advantage (mundane and/or other-worldly) to an individual of other-regarding conduct; but his attempt at *proving* the existence of a moral sense which approves disinterested conduct does not extend beyond a very general appeal to universal experience and introspection, while he (as with Shaftesbury) personally expressed doubts regarding its reliability as the 'faculty of perceiving moral excellence' or as 'an immediate undefinable perception', and therefore required spiritual reinforcement. Recognition of weaknesses in the operation of the moral sense coupled with the fact that Locke also did not rely entirely on divine reward and punishment as stimulus to ethical conduct, with the promise of purely mundane reward playing a part, greatly reduces the contrast between the two writers.

Also addressed is Hutcheson's application of the greater-good principle to the question of distributive justice, as reflected in his qualified support for Agrarian Laws limiting the concentration of (landed) wealth with an eye to the welfare of landless labour. Adam Smith, we shall later see, understood Hutcheson as forwarding a case for *equality* although this turns out to be an unjustified attribution.

Chapter Five reviews the position of David Hume. Here I draw attention to Bonar's opinion, mentioned above, that Hume explained the moral sense away, the sentiment of *sympathy* providing the key. Now Bonar's account of Hume is, I believe, accurate. I show that while Hume writes of the morality of actions 'felt by an internal sense, and by means of some sentiment, which the reflecting on such an action naturally occasions', he denies that such a sense operates as an automatic index of what is ethically good or bad independently of the tendency of an action to augment happiness, and applauds conduct motivated by concern for the general good. Indeed, despite a certain ambiguity it would seem that Hume prioritized motivation in the manner of Hutcheson. Hume, however, said nothing of Locke's having already designated *other-regarding* conduct as ethically meritorious despite such conduct being in the individual's interest, and was highly critical of Locke's 'loose' use of the word *idea* 'as standing for any of our perceptions, our sensations and passions, as well as thoughts'. Hume's perspective on distributive justice, entailing *inter alia* a case made out for increased equality, will also engage us. Details of the Hume–Smith and Hume–Bentham relationships are addressed in later chapters.

C.A. Helvétius – admired by Bentham for contributing 'a standard of rectitude for actions' – is shown in Chapter Six to be, like Shaftesbury, Hutcheson, and Hume, a utilitarian writer basing himself on the moral sense understood as *feelings of morality* entailing specifically *other-regarding* sentiment directed towards enhancing the general happiness. Those sympathetic feelings are ascribed by Helvétius to 'personal-' or 'self-interest', although when addressing policy issues, he considered most men to be governed in their 'personal interest' by crude *selfishness*. The ascription of feelings of morality to a *sense of interest*, while at the same time representing morality in terms of *other-regarding* sentiment, is precisely *Locke's* position. More generally, and unlike Hume, Helvétius admired Locke's 'genius' including his elaboration of the notion that our ideas are not in-born or innate but are rooted in actual experience and reflect our sensations or senses. I see no evidence in Helvétius of Lockean theological utilitarianism incorporating future reward and punishment as entering into 'personal interest', but Locke himself was scarcely naïve regarding mankind's capacity to take under consideration such distant prospects.

My account is organised around Mill's perspective which follows Bentham in crediting Helvétius – along with Hume – for the doctrine that general utility is the foundation of morality, and understands his utilitarianism as turning on purely 'selfish' calculation and without comprehension of the full character of man. Also taken under consideration is Mill's commendation of David Hartley, perceived as utilitarian, for recognizing 'the feelings of "the moral sense"' as a fact of life, thereby weakening Mill's own eighteenth-nineteenth century contrast dating largely to the 1830s between moral-sense adherents opposed to the utility doctrine and utilitarians (see Appendix to Chapter Fifteen).

Part III concerns Adam Smith, Chapter Seven treating his *Theory of Moral Sentiments*. Here I note Bentham's silence regarding *TMS* when he designates as the most influential of principles opposed to that of utility that which 'approves or disapproves of certain actions ... merely because a man finds himself disposed to approve or disapprove of them'. Would Bentham not have mentioned Smith amongst the *non-utilitarian* ethicists if he understood *TMS* in this manner, especially since he never hesitated to protest Smith's appeals in *WN* to 'natural liberty'? This possibility will immediately be discounted by those who maintain that Smith rejected 'ethical utilitarianism' while several of those who do allow the presence in Smith of a utility dimension insist on its secondary character. My own approach emphasizes the qualifications Smith and also Hume made to their respective doctrines, the utility dimension to *TMS* emerging clearly as a result. Partly responsible for the view of Smith as 'non-Utilitarian' is an understanding of *Bentham* as opposed to the idea of moral sentiments as the foundation of morals, when in fact it is a 'moral sense' understood as precluding the utility criterion of ethics that he dismissed.

Chapter Eight, devoted to the *Wealth of Nations*, expands the representation of Adam Smith as utilitarian. I shall seek to clarify how Smith's notions of 'natural liberty and justice' and 'equity' relate to his utilitarianism, having in mind a strict dichotomy sometimes discerned between Bentham's utilitarian principles and Smithian natural rights. It it is one of my objectives here to show how it is fair to view Smith as coherent in this regard provided we attribute to him the view – it is the position attributed by J.S. Mill to Bentham himself – that 'natural liberty and justice' and 'equity' are to be *tested* by their contributions to happiness so that a moralist can deduce from utility as a standard 'his whole system of ethics'.

A particular concern in Chapter 8 will be distributive justice and the declaration that 'no society can surely be *flourishing and happy*, of which the greater part of the members are poor and miserable', suggesting that the welfare of the working classes – the greatest happiness of the majority or the well-being of the median – constitutes the appropriate index of national 'happiness'. This generalization however requires qualification. Labour's wellbeing is only a *necessary* condition since there are other components of the utilitarian maximand; and the 'majority' is not an undifferentiated mass of poor but is subject to a distinction between the unskilled 'labourer' and the better-paid skilled 'artisan' within the 'lower ranks'. Nevertheless, the evidence I adduce reinforces the case that Smith's primary concern was the welfare of the working classes *as a whole*, although Smith did adopt a somewhat cavalier attitude towards the unemployed and unemployable.

I also make clear that the objective of improving the wellbeing of the 'lower ranks' might be satisfied *even if the wage share should decline*. Indeed, Smith's case for the commercial society on grounds of its contribution to the amelioration of poverty turned on 'the *paradox of inequality*' that equality would drag down rather than raise living standards. Nevertheless, this theme was not pushed to an extreme. The notion that for Smith income distribution should be entirely determined by the market is unacceptable, considering his allowances for state intervention – in particular in education and the credit market. And distributive justice also enters the picture here to some, rather limited, extent, as is clear from recommendations regarding taxation. Furthermore, quite apart from the question of productivity there is a perception of inequality as a necessary condition for social investments of a general order. Finally, there is the little noticed consideration that the superior weight placed by Smith on efficiency relative to 'fair' distribution partly reflected the existence, under contemporary British circumstances, of 'a graduall descent of fortunes' to which he attributed the absence of pressure emanating from the propertyless to reduce inequality.

Note is also taken of Smith's insistence on wage differentials reflecting training costs, provided these are not artificially enhanced. The correction of pay differentials reflecting fortuitous differences in mental and physical ability is a matter avoided by the Enlightenment presumption that the street-porter and philosopher are *constitutionally* indistinguishable. Whether in the event that experience undermined his overwhelming weight accorded to nurture Smith would have adopted the position of Mill, that (ideally) differentials of this order should be corrected by state intervention, or of Marx, who insisted upon their maintenance in the first stage of communism, it is difficult to say.

xx   *Introduction*

The two chapters comprising Part IV are devoted to Jeremy Bentham. It has been said that the ethics of the ordinary man was of little concern to Bentham; and that if the agent's intentions and habitual behaviour are studied it is only so that they may be controlled, with weight placed on a form of 'rational selfishness'. A related contrast between Bentham and J.S. Mill proposes that Bentham, unlike Mill in *On Liberty*, represents 'security' solely in terms of rights versus 'malefactors' and abuses of government' but not as protection of '*self-regarding* liberty and individuality'. In Chapter Nine I demonstrate to the contrary three related propositions: firstly, the positive role Bentham – no less than Smith and Hume – in fact accorded *motivation* in ethical evaluation; secondly, his allowance by his 'utilitarianism' for *ethical progress* entailing enhancement of other-regarding motivation; and, thirdly, his notion of justice as a basic right to 'security' encompassing *protection of personal liberty and individuality*. Finally, as in our investigation of Smith, we shall look closely at Bentham's perspective on the equality question, particularly his preference for stating the *desideratum* of policy to be the reduction of inequalities subject to the avoidance of damage to real incomes. Here we shall find that 'justice' features in the account in a manner consistent with the overall utility maximand.

Our understanding of Bentham's general position regarding ethics is further enriched in Chapter Ten by attending to his relationship with the main authors encountered in earlier chapters: Locke, Shaftesbury, Hutcheson, Hume, Smith, and Helvétius. A number of difficult issues arise. Firstly, Bentham by-passed Locke's ethical utilitarianism, whether the theological or the secular version, crediting Helvétius alone with establishing general happiness as '*a standard of rectitude for actions*', and also – by focusing (in the same contrast with Helvétius) specifically on Locke's analysis of '*ideas*' – he neglected Locke's perception of the quest for 'pleasure' and avoidance of 'pain', or the 'happiness' objective, as governing actual conduct. Secondly, he included both Shaftesbury and Hutcheson amongst the culprits *opposed* to the utilitarian perspective, failing in particular to recognize Hutcheson's reiterated contention that the moral sense approved conduct motivated, in Hutcheson's own terms, by the intention to enhance 'the greatest Happiness for the greatest Numbers'. Nonetheless, apparently unwittingly, by proposing – as shown in Chapter Nine –'an order of pre-eminence among motives' turning on 'the tendency which they have to unite, or disunite', an agent's interests and those of other members of the community, with 'good-will' ranked first considering that its 'dictates taken in a general view, are surest of coinciding with those of the principle of utility', Bentham was effectively adopting rather than refuting Hutcheson's position. And thirdly, Bentham included Hume amongst those appealing to a moral sense *opposed to* utilitarian ethics while at the same time viewing Hume's account 'Of Morals' as the text from which he had learned 'that the foundations of all *virtue* are laid in *utility*'. It is, I shall suggest, because Bentham was so attracted by the Humean utility doctrine that he so deeply regretted the features of Hume's account that *seemed* to be in conflict with this, whereas Hume had in fact firmly denied that the moral sense defined what is ethically good or bad *independently of the tendency of an action to augment general welfare*. Once again, we find Bentham on the same wavelength as his predecessors without it appears realizing it.

Part V concerns Thomas Robert Malthus. Chapter 11 is my response to Sergio Cremaschi's position in his *Utilitarianism and Malthus's Virtue Ethics* (2014), which distinguishes between a distinctive, theologically-based utilitarianism attributed to Malthus and the utilitarianism of the Philosophical Radicals. Here I restate and reinforce the case made out in the *Economics of Thomas Robert Malthus* (1997) for a coalescence of the Malthusian and secular utilitarian perspectives. For, while seeking to reconcile theology and welfare Malthus effectively undermined the former by radically reinterpreting the scriptures to justify a reduced birth rate. The theological dimension is absent from his adoption in the 1820s of the Ricardian vision of industrial development which turned on perceived changes in the empirical and legislative environment. And while Malthus at times perceived virtue as divorced from consequences for happiness, so also did Ricardo and J.S. Mill, it is easy to show, even when at odds with the wealth and happiness components of the utilitarian maximand.

A second Malthus chapter focuses on his views regarding income distribution. In the *Essay on Population* Malthus perceives inequality as essential to emulation, *but only within strict bounds*. For greater equality is there recommended on the strict utilitarian grounds of 'greater happiness', to be attained by 'an increase in the relative proportions of the middle parts', both by way of improved real wages assured by appropriate adjustment of labour supply, and by transfer of labour into the middle classes. In the *Principles* the utilitarian case for higher wages emphasizes the quantitative superiority of the labouring class in standard classical fashion. But from the perspective of positive economics the primary case for greater equality turns on the importance of a strong middle class with an eye to the propensity to spend, while Malthus discerns at least the potential of increased aggregate demand emanating from a wealthier working class thus reinforcing the desirability of greater equality. I reject a common belief that Malthus revealed an undue harshness towards the poor by his notorious declaration that 'no person has any claim of *right* on society for subsistence, if his labour will not purchase it'. Taken at face value, Malthus's declaration that he would welcome significant income redistributions were it not that the 'greatest happiness' rule broke down with a promise of open-ended population increase regardless of the depressing effects on *per capita* wages.

Features pertaining to distributive justice emerge during the post-Napoleonic debates on trade, especially regarding the effects of an altered price level on class distribution. The matter of 'fairness' also arises conspicuously in the early 1820s which were also witness to a transformation in Malthus's attitude towards landlords which set the stage for his abandonment of agricultural protectionism. The notion of 'Fairness' features in the analysis of primogeniture and is implied by a contention that 'the representative system … [secures] to the lower classes of society a more equal and liberal mode of treatment from their superiors'.

The three chapters of Part VI are devoted to John Stuart Mill. Chapter 13 is on distributive justice and reform and has in mind a contention that 'throughout the classical economics there runs a strong argument against assigning to greater equality of income a primary role in social ethics'. It is my position that whereas Mill placed little emphasis on larger *aggregate* income, he was preoccupied, wholly in the classical tradition, with high average *wages* on the grounds of the numerical significance of the labouring class; and while a higher average wage might be consistent with a falling wage share in national income Mill, I maintain, sought both higher absolute and relative wages. I complete the discussion by comparing Mill and Marx regarding distribution. Marx's main objection to the focus on distributive justice in the Gotha Programme was its option of reform within a capitalist arrangement designed to correct gross distributional defects, a prospect he ruled out as conflicting with the principle that the pattern of distribution is the *necessary* outcome of the 'mode of production' rendering 'unfairness' an irrelevant consideration (see Hollander 2008: 390–6.) Here of course resides the fundamental contrast with Mill, whose practical reform proposals in the interest of fairness were intended to be of immediate relevance, subject however to their acceptability considering the questionable state of public opinion.

Mill's perceptions of ethical progress and personal liberty are treated in Chapter 14. Here I have in mind Bentham's caution against 'the chimerical' in reform programs. As for Mill, I draw attention to his own profound cautiousness reflected in a warning given in 1849 against 'overrat[ing] the ease of making people unselfish' and in an observation as late as 1870 that 'the feeling of security of possession and enjoyment … could not (in the state of advancement mankind have yet reached) be had without private ownership'. The perspectives of Mill and Bentham regarding prospects for ethical progress are thus not so easy to distinguish. Chapter 14 proceeds to elaborate Mill's perception of 'security' encompassing the *protection of personal liberty and individuality* which (in Chapter Nine) we already found in Bentham. I also take account of the 'border line' between the *self-* and *other-regarding* categories established in *On Liberty*, finding Mill ambiguous in some of his formulations, and demonstrate that Mill would, under extreme conditions, have justified state intervention even in purely self-regarding acts.

The final chapter, Chapter 15, examines Mill's perception of the role played by the 'moral sense' in ethical evaluation and its relation to the 'happiness' criterion of utilitarian ethics, taking us full circle back to the primary issues discussed earlier in this book. In the present account I confirm the conclusions reached in *John Stuart Mill: Political Economist* (Hollander 2015) regarding a 'Return to Bentham' discernible in modifications made between the 1830s, 1840s, and 1850s. The present elaboration provides a closer analysis of alternative notions of the 'moral sense' in the Mill texts, with Mill shown to be finally engaging in a reconciliation of utilitarianism with the moral sense by adopting the notion that *conscience* prioritizes other-regarding sentiment such that the dictates of conscience relate specifically to the intended consequences of actions for 'greatest happiness' rather than any other end. In this manner Mill was unwittingly adopting the stance of Hutcheson, a linkage which is not surprising if the proximity of Bentham to Hutcheson – argued in Chapter Ten – is accepted. For Mill himself, after much soul searching, came to appreciate Bentham's contribution to utilitarian ethics confirming the unity of eighteenth- and nineteenth-century utilitarian ethical doctrines pertaining to the individual. There was, he finally came to recognise, no need to escape the eighteenth century; the 'reaction' of the nineteenth against the eighteenth he had once welcomed had gone too far.

My analysis renders more precisely the case for a 'return to Bentham' by taking account of Mill's abandoning in the early 1850s earlier objections to Benthamite 'sympathy'. The 'return', I thus demonstrate, occurred in two stages – in the first place, Mill came to appreciate that the character attributed to the eighteenth century had been something of a straw man, Bentham himself having in fact diluted the 'ratiocinative' dimension; and secondly, the so-called 'reaction' of the nineteenth century entailing enhanced once called for (see the Appendix to Chapter 15), Mill came to believe in the 1860s, had gone too far.

More generally, the evidence I bring in this final chapter and in earlier chapters, points away from the view that 'any history of the social sciences which fails to confront the discontinuity marked by the transition from Scottish moral philosophy and its associated histories of civil society on the one side, to Benthamism on the other, would be guilty of sidestepping one of the most intriguing problems in that history' (Winch 1978: 184). There is too much overlap to justify this strong dichotomy.

Note

1 To my knowledge, this insertion is the sole extant reference to Hutcheson by Bentham. Beattie, Price, Clarke, and Wollaston are also listed as culprits.

References

Bentham, J. 1843 (1789). *An Introduction to the Principles of Morals and Legislation, The Works of Jeremy Bentham* 1, ed. John Bowring. Edinburgh: William Tait: 1–154.

Bentham, J. 1982 (1789). *An Introduction to the Principles of Morals and Legislation* ed. J.H. Burns and H.L.A. Hart. London and New York: Methuen.

Mill, J.S. 1969 (1838). 'Bentham', *Collected Works of John Stuart Mill* 10. Toronto: University of Toronto Press: 75–115.

Cremaschi, S. 2014. *Utilitarianism and Malthus's Virtue Ethics: Respectable, Virtuous and Happy*. London and New York: Routledge.

Hollander, S. 1997. *The Economics of Thomas Robert Malthus*. Toronto: University of Toronto Press.

Hollander, S. 2008. *The Economics of Karl Marx: Analysis and Application*. Cambridge: Cambridge University Press.

Hollander, S. 2015. *John Stuart Mill: Political Economist*. Singapore: World Scientific.

Winch, D. 1978. *Adam Smith's Politics: An Essay in Historiographic Revision*. Cambridge: Cambridge University Press.

Part 1
John Locke

1 John Locke, utilitarian ethics and the moral sense

1.1 Introduction

In his *Essay Concerning Human Understanding*, John Locke contributed to utilitarian doctrine by specifying the building blocks of the hedonic structure governing analysis of human conduct in terms of a quest for 'happiness'.[1] In addition, he rejected the notion of an in-born 'moral sense', and more generally that of innate ideas. The 'true ground of morality' Locke identified rather with the *other-regarding* rule of conduct 'Do unto others…', and he may, I suggest, be fairly represented as engaged in an *essay in persuasion* designed to enhance such sympathetic or socially-advantageous conduct by advising self-interested individuals not to discount the distant future when considering the consequences of conduct for 'happiness', but rather to supplement the mundane calculations adopted by most men by recognizing 'a God, who sees men in the dark, has in his hand rewards and punishments, and power enough to call to account the proudest offender'. This perspective is suggestive of 'theological utilitarianism' although not in the strictest sense of that term which posits 'the hope of future rewards and the fear of future punishments [as] the *only* effective and rational support for good social behavior' (Viner 1972: 70; emphasis added).

Locke recognized mankind's ignorance of 'the true ground of morality', admitting even that the very concept of God was not an 'innate' idea, so that it was understandable (if not excusable) that so many failed to properly take into account the prospect of 'future' reward and punishment when contemplating action. Moreover, the scripturally-based ethical rule 'Do unto others…' was a 'truth', Locke maintained, amenable to trained reasoners drawing on observation, and he relies on reason when, in a discussion 'Of Faith and Reason, and their distinct Provinces', he raises doubts regarding belief based on revelation, thereby weakening the theological reinforcement provided for ethical or other-regarding conduct: 'if any thing shall be thought revelation which is contrary to the plain principles of reason, and the evident knowledge the mind has of its own clear and distinct ideas; there reason must be hearkened to, as to a matter within its province….; and so [one] is bound to consider and judge of it as a matter of reason, and not to swallow it, without examination, as a matter of faith'.

Bentham says nothing of Locke's positive contribution to ethical utilitarianism perceived in terms of actions advancing the 'greater good' or social welfare. Hume too was silent regarding Locke's designating *other-regarding* conduct as ethically meritorious despite such conduct being in the individual's interest. As for the secondary literature, we encounter disparate interpretations. Macpherson represents Locke's appeal to 'traditional natural law' as a 'façade' which 'could be removed, [as] by Hume and Bentham, without damage to the strong and well-built utilitarian structure that lay within' (Macpherson 1962: 270). This summary statement appears to apply to policy rather than ethics, as also seems to be true of Fraser's account in his edition of the *Essay*, which discerns 'a spirit of prudential utilitarianism' pervading Lockean social policy, although his evidence is not drawn from the *Essay* itself (Fraser 1894: xxi). Fraser makes no mention here of the theological–utilitarian category, but his *Locke* provides an analysis of papers dating to 1677, when 'the Essay was in the process of formation', and there he writes of '[t]he germ of the theological utilitarianism into which Locke's ethical and political philosophy resolved itself', without however providing supportive documentation even of this understated attribution (Fraser 1890: 51–2). For Carey, 'Locke had effectively tied [religion and morality] together, at least for Christians who relied on the only sure source of moral truth and guidance – the revealed word of Scripture' a stance opposed by Shaftesbury, writing 'in a deist vein' (Carey 2006: 99). Stephen, to the contrary, concluded that Locke cannot be counted amongst the 'theological utilitarians' considering the primacy accorded to reason in any clash with revelation (Stephen 1902: 84). Viner does not cite Locke amongst the 'theological utilitarians', his definition applying to those who represent the prospect of future reward and punishment as a *necessary condition* for proper conduct, leaving open where Viner stood regarding a less strict version.

The theological dimension, runs my argument, must be taken seriously in so far as Locke's prime objective in underscoring the role of reason was to counter appeals to revelation on the part of charlatans and 'enthusiasts' leaving untouched *genuine* appeals. But it is also true that Locke diluted the theological perspective in major ways. Thus, he based his exercise in persuasion on prudential grounds holding good even if only the *possibility* of a future life with its rewards and punishments is recognized, an unorthodox perspective suggesting Pascal's Wager whereby a sane person should conduct himself *as though* God exists. It is important to recognize that such qualifications do not affect the proposition that ethical conduct itself lies in essentially *other-regarding* considerations, and only weaken the motive for such comportment by placing reliance entirely on the worldly advantages promised by such conduct. And the *Essay* does in fact propose a wholly secular variety of ethical utilitarianism, the individual induced to behave in the social interest with an eye solely upon such mundane benefits as may be expected to flow from 'other-regarding' conduct.

Leslie Stephen affirms that though Locke stated the utility principle, and opposed the notion of 'innate ideas', he 'was not a consistent Utilitarian' (Stephen 1900: 237n). Stephen does not elaborate, but from his *English Thought in the Eighteenth Century* it is probable that he intended to refer to Locke's proposition that morality is capable of demonstration no less than mathematics, which cannot be 'reconciled with his general utilitarianism' (Stephen 1902: 85–6). Nonetheless, Stephen's theme in his *English Thought* remains that Locke provided the 'primary impulse' for later utilitarians, referring to the case against the ethical application of 'innate' ideas which presuppose the existence of self-evident or innate moral axioms (80). But this, on Stephen's account, amounted only to ground clearing. For he finds that the 'one universal motive' for Locke remains 'a desire of happiness and an aversion to misery', and that when we come to ask 'what then is morality?' all we are left with is the proposition that 'virtue is approved because visibly conducive to happiness' – it is all a matter of self-interest – Locke thereby failing to provide an alternative to so-called conscience, indeed 'never think[ing] to supply its place' (81). (Mandeville is said to carry this line to its logical conclusion by actually denying the 'real existence of virtue' and maintaining that virtue – or 'God's will' – is 'a mere arbitrary fashion'; 83–4.) It seems to me that a proper recognition of Locke's identification of morality with *other-regarding conduct favouring general happiness* is lacking here, as in several other accounts, even if such conduct should be motivated by self-interested considerations whether mundane or other-worldly. Stephen does mention the moral rule 'doing as we would be done by', but neglects to emphasize that this was regarded by Locke as the *overriding* ethical rule, not merely one amongst a variety.

The hedonic categories of pain, pleasure, and happiness as treated by John Locke will be addressed in Section 1.2. Section 1.3 presents the evidence on which I base my case to envisage Locke as an ethical utilitarian both in the general sense and in the more specific theological, albeit highly qualified, sense. An elaboration of Locke's objections to innate ideas follows in Section 1.4 and here we encounter the archetypal, perhaps the original, enlightenment figure appealing for evidence-based *reasoning*, rather than faith or tradition or mere habit, to justify ethical principles. Section 1.5 elaborates the 'distinct provinces' of faith and reason.

1.2 Locke's 'Benthamite' categories: pleasure, pain and happiness

Three chapters of the first volume of the *Essay Concerning Human Understanding*, Chapter VII ('Of Simple Ideas of both Sensation and Reflection'), Chapter XX ('Of Modes of Pleasure and Pain') and Chapter XXI ('Of Power') spell out Locke's stance regarding the characteristically 'Benthamite' categories of pleasure, pain, and happiness. The first of the chapters describes the role of the 'ideas' of pleasure and pain in stimulating action thus:

> By pleasure and pain I would be understood to signify whatsoever delights or molests us most; whether it arises from the thoughts of our minds, or any thing operating on our bodies. For whether we call it satisfaction, delight, pleasure, happiness, &c. on the one side; or uneasiness, trouble, pain, torment, anguish, misery, &c. on the other; they are still but different degrees of the same thing, and belong to the ideas of pleasure and pain, delight or uneasiness; which are the names I shall most commonly use for those two sorts of ideas ... It has ... pleased our wise Creator to annex to several objects, and the ideas which we receive from them, as also to several of our thoughts, a concomitant pleasure, and that in several objects, to several degrees; that those faculties which he had endowed us with might not remain wholly idle and unemployed by us. Pain has the same efficacy and use that pleasure has, we being as ready to employ our faculties to avoid that, as to assure this.
>
> (Locke 1823 [1700] 1: 112–13)

The second chapter goes a step further and asserts that

> [t]hings are good or evil only in reference to pleasure and pain. That *we call good*, which is apt to cause or increase pleasure or diminish pain in us; or else to procure or preserve us the possession of any other good, or absence of any evil. And, on the contrary, *we name that evil*, which is apt to produce or increase any pain or diminish any pleasure in us; or else to procure us any evil, or deprive us of any good' (231; emphasis added). And the third chapter elaborates the theme that 'we constantly desire happiness' (261); and '[i]f it be farther asked, what is that moves desire? I answer, Happiness, and that alone. Happiness, then, in its full extent, is the utmost pleasure we are capable of, and misery the utmost pain ... [W]hat has an aptness to produce pleasure in us is what *we call good*, and what is apt to produce pain in us *we call evil*, for no other reason but for its aptness to produce pleasure and pain in us, wherein consists our happiness and misery
>
> (262; emphasis added).

We note here that while Locke rejected 'innate' ideas of virtue he readily allowed at the outset of his *Essay* that it is *nature* that 'puts into man a desire for happiness, and an aversion to misery', thus accounting for the primary stimulus to action (36). (The allowance for *nature* will be elaborated in Section 1.4).

The qualifying '*what we call*' good and evil in the last two citations allows for the fact that the pleasure someone obtains from entirely anti-social actions he may yet call 'good'. In the second volume this qualification is omitted: 'Good and evil, as hath been shown [1823 [1700] 1: 231, 262] ... are nothing but pleasure or pain, or that which occasions or procures pleasure or pain to us' ('Of Moral Relations'; Locke 1823 [1700] 2: 97). However Locke immediately alters the proposition by adding when summarizing the case: 'Moral good and evil then is only the conformity or disagreement of our voluntary actions to some law, whereby good or evil is drawn on us by the will and power of the law-maker; which good and evil, pleasure or pain, attending our observance or breach of the law, by the decree of the law-maker, is that we call reward or punishment' (emphasis added) thereby distinguishing in effect between what may be treated as *true* morality or rules of conduct emanating from God – which we shall presently show is seen primarily as obedience to the rule 'Do unto others...' – and rules of conduct emanating from the civil law and from public opinion, especially the latter, which may deviate therefrom albeit that the conduct in question may popularly be labelled 'good' or 'evil' and perceived as such by the actor.

The common occurrence of conduct designated as 'good' but which, in some objective sense, is in fact 'evil' is much emphasized in the chapter 'Of Power': 'though all men desire happiness, yet their wills carry them so contrarily, and consequently some of them to what is evil ... [T]he various and contrary choices that men make in the world do not argue that they do not all pursue good, but that the same thing is not good to every man alike' (Locke 1823 [1700] 1: 272). Essentially, 'evil' conduct appears good to some because it adds to their happiness *as they perceive it*: 'the greatest happiness consists in the having those things which produce the greatest pleasure, and in the absence of those which cause any disturbance, any pain. Now these, to different men, are very different things' (273).[2] Such errors Locke maintains are inexcusable and merit punishment: 'though it be certain that in all the particular actions that he wills he does, and necessarily does, will that which he then judges to be good. For, though his will be always determined by that which is judged good by his understanding, yet it excuses him not; because by a too hasty choice of his own making, he has imposed on himself wrong measures of good and evil; which, however false and fallacious, have the same influence on all his future conduct as if they were true and right' (275).

Of high interest is Locke's concern to account for 'wrong measures of good and evil': 'since men are always constant, and in earnest, in matters of happiness and misery, the question still remains, How men come often to prefer the worse to the better; and to choose that which, by their own confession, has made them miserable (Locke 1823 [1700] 1: 275). 'By their own confession', it transpires, reflects a certainty on Locke's part that *sooner or later* men will come to realize their failure of judgment (278–9). As for the false choice in the first place, Locke points to two sources both entailing improper allowance for the prospects of reward and punishment in a *future life*, and this discussion proves essential to our case elaborated in Section 1.3 that Locke is to be considered a 'theological utilitarian'.

The first type of 'wrong judgment' reflects the circumstance that '[o]bjects near our view are apt to be thought greater than those of a larger size that are more remote; and so it is with pleasures and pains; the present is apt to carry it, and those at a distance have the disadvantage in the comparison ... But that this is a wrong judgment every one must allow, let his pleasure consist in whatever it will: since that which is future will certainly come to be present; and then, having the same advantage of nearness, will show itself in its full dimensions, and discover his willful mistake, who judged of it by unequal measures' (Locke 1823 [1700] 1: 279–80). The passage of time will 'bring it home upon himself, and consider it as present, and there take its true dimensions!' (280). The problem is exacerbated by the fact that 'absent good, or, what is the same thing, future pleasure, especially if it of a sort we are unacquainted with' – reflecting a concern with 'the happiness of another life'– 'seldom is able to counter-balance any uneasiness, either of pain or desire, which is present' (281–2).

So much for false judgment reflecting a realization of the evil character of the action in question but undervaluation of what is currently 'absent', namely the future consequences. The second source of error is a complete failure to recognize the evil of the act in question namely 'the wrong judgment, whereby the absent are not only lessened, but reduced to perfect nothing; when men enjoy what they can in present, and make sure of that, concluding amiss that no evil will thence follow. For that lies not in comparing the greatness of future good and evil, which is what we are here speaking of, but in another sort of wrong judgment, which is concerning good or evil, as it is considered to be the cause and procurement of pleasure or pain, that will follow from it' (Locke 1823 [1700] 1: 280). As to the 'things good or bad in their consequences and by the aptness in them to procure us good or evil in the future', the causes of wrong judgment are said to include ignorance and inadvertence (282–4), much of the problem reflecting bad 'habits' (285–6). Nonetheless, Locke allows for the possibility of some correction:

> it will be possibly entertained as a paradox, if it be said, that men can make things or actions more or less pleasing to themselves; and thereby remedy that, to which one may justly impute a great deal of their wandering. Fashion and the common opinion having settled wrong notions, and education and custom ill habits, the just values of things are misplaced, and the palates of men corrupted. Pains should be taken to rectify these; and contrary habits change our pleasures, and give a relish to that which is necessary or conducive to our happiness
>
> (286).

A further source of the second category of corrupted calculation is the painful effort required to achieve *genuine* happiness, or 'the real or supposed unpleasantness of the actions which are the way to this end', which render it 'so preposterous a thing to men, to make themselves unhappy in order to happiness, that they do not easily bring themselves to it' (Locke 1823 [1700] 1: 284). In his elaboration Locke takes for granted that there is indeed a *true* 'happiness' and a 'right way' of acting to achieve it which puts 'just values' on actions, and also that people understand this and finally admit it: 'This every one must confess he can do; and when happiness is lost, and misery overtakes him, he will confess he did amiss in neglecting it, and condemn himself for it: and I would ask every one, whether he has not often done so' (286). What follows confirms that the preeminent end is happiness in a *future life,* 'a good life here' constituting the means to arrive at that end. One notes, firstly, that Locke does not at this juncture specify in what a 'good life here' amounts to, presumably taking for granted what he had established at the outset of the *Essay* regarding the 'true ground of morality' as other-regarding conduct (see Section 1.4 below); and, secondly, that Locke asserts that even the *possibility* of a future life should suffice to sway any 'rational' individual:

> [M]orality, established upon its true foundations, cannot but determine the choice in any one that will but consider: and he that will not be so far a rational creature as to reflect seriously upon infinite happiness and misery, must needs condemn himself as not making that use of his understanding he should. The rewards and punishments of another life, which the Almighty has established as the enforcements of his law, are of weight enough to determine the choice, against whatever pleasure or pain this life can show, when the eternal state is considered but in its bare possibility, which nobody can make any doubt of. He that will allow exquisite and endless happiness to be but the possible consequence of a good life here, and the contrary state the possible reward of a bad one, must own himself to judge very much amiss if he does not conclude, that a virtuous life, with the certain expectation of everlasting bliss, which may come, is to be preferred to a vicious one, with the fear of that dreadful state of misery, which it is very possible may overtake the guilty; or at best the terrible uncertain hope of annihilation.
>
> (286–7)

Locke at this juncture avoids definitively committing himself to the existence of a future life,[3] and this he does by focusing, during the course of his exercise in persuasion, on prudential grounds which held good even if only the *possibility* of a future life is recognized: 'I have forborn to mention anything of the certainty or probability of a future state, designing here to show the wrong judgment that any one must allow he makes upon his own principles, laid how he pleases, who prefers the short pleasures of a vicious life upon any consideration, whilst he knows, and cannot but be certain, that a future life is at least possible' (287). This perspective suggests Pascal's Wager whereby a sane person should conduct himself *as though* God exists, since if he exists there are infinite rewards and if not little is lost.[4] The absence of certainty in a future life, extending to the very existence of the Deity himself, plays a part in the denial of 'innate' ideas (see Section 1.4).

1.3 Utilitarian ethics: theological and secular features

In his Introduction to the *Essay* John Locke asserts that God has provided men with sufficient knowledge to assure not only a 'comfortable provision' in this life but salvation in the next by dint of practicing *virtuous conduct*, the components of which – 'their own duties' – are no secret:

> Men have reason to be well satisfied with what God hath thought fit for them, since he hath given them (as St. Peter says) … whatsoever is necessary for the conveniences of life and *information of virtue*; and has put within the reach of their discovery the comfortable provision for this life, and *the way that leads to a better*. How short soever their knowledge may come of an universal or perfect comprehension of whatsoever is, it yet secures their great concernments, that they have light enough to lead then to the knowledge of their Maker, *and the sight of their own duties* … We shall not have much reason to complain of the narrowness of our minds, if we will but employ them about what may be of use to us; for of that they are very capable.
> (Locke 1823 [1700] 1: 4; emphasis added).

That proper application of the readily-available knowledge would be 'of use to us' relates both to mundane wellbeing or 'the comfortable provision for this life' and the route to salvation in the world-to-come, 'the way that leads to a better'. But in what *precisely* did Locke perceive virtuous conduct to consist? To answer this question, we turn to his early chapter 'No Innate Practical Principles' which firmly denies that moral 'principles' are known to mankind by an innate sense, innateness involving, in Fraser's terms an 'actual realization in the consciousness of each individual from birth' (Fraser 1894: 86n). That moral principles required a 'proof' Locke considered in itself *a priori* evidence that they could not be innate: 'I think there cannot any one moral rule be proposed, whereof a man may not justly demand a reason: which would be perfectly ridiculous and absurd, if they were innate, or so much as self-evident; which every innate principle must needs be, and not need any proof to ascertain its truth, nor want any reason to gain it approbation' (Locke 1823 [1700] 1: 36–7). And just here a, or rather, *the* prime moral rule is specified: 'But should that most unshaken rule of morality, and foundation of all social virtue, "that one should do as he would be done unto", be proposed to one who never heard it before, but yet is of capacity to understand its meaning, might he not without any absurdity ask a reason why?' (37). Locke in fact discerned (as we shall see) a variety of moral rules although the primary one is in no doubt; and he concludes that 'the truth of all these moral rules plainly depends upon some other antecedent to them, and from which they must be deduced; which could not be, if either they were innate, or so much as self-evident'.

That Locke should assign as rationale for the primacy of the moral rule 'Do unto others…' that it constitutes the 'foundation of all *social* virtue' – when coupled with what follows (as we shall presently see), namely an assertion that private 'virtue' and *public* happiness' are providentially 'joined' – points unmistakably to the positive effect on social welfare of private conduct which takes into account the interests of others by treating them as one would oneself wish to be treated.[5] (Relevant here is a journal entry from 1678 to the effect that 'vertue is but the name of such actions as are most conduceing to the good of the society & are therefore by that society recommended by all meanes to the practise of the people'; Carey 2006: 76, citing MS Locke f.3, pp.266–7.) There is some indication – in the chapter 'Of the Improvement of our Knowledge' in the third volume of the *Essay* – suggesting a moral dimension to a broad range of activities that raise society's real income and reduce mortality:

> I would not … be thought to disesteem or dissuade the study of nature. I readily agree the contemplation of his works gives us occasion to admire, revere, and glorify their Author: and, if rightly directed, may be of greater benefit to mankind than the monuments of exemplary charity, that have at so great been raised by the founders of hospitals and alms-houses. He that first invented printing, discovered the use of the compass … did more for the propagation of knowledge, for the supply and increase of useful commodities, and saved more from the grave, than those who built colleges, work-houses, and hospitals.
>
> (Locke 1823 [1700] 3: 87–8)

Now conduct of an order which might fairly be designated as '*other-regarding*' is said to be in the actor's own interest: 'Virtue generally approved, not because innate, but because *profitable*' (Locke 1823 [1700] 1: 38; emphasis added). Wherein lies the 'profitability' is of the first importance for a proper appreciation of Locke's status as 'utilitarian ethicist'. Locke sets out his case by affirming the 'true ground of morality' in *theological* terms as reflecting God's will and, accordingly as subject to divine judgment, and asserting that recognition of God's existence and legitimate authority was apparent to many as a 'law of nature' discernible 'in the light of reason', a position to be expected from the author of the *Reasonableness of Christianity, as delivered in the Scriptures*: 'The view of Heaven and Hell, will cast a slight upon the short pleasures and pains of the present state; and give attractions and encouragements to Virtue, which reason, and interest, and the Care of ourselves, cannot but allow and prefer. Upon this foundation, and upon this alone, Morality stands firm, and may defy all competition' (Locke 1695: 288–9). (In Section 1.4 we shall elaborate Locke's insistence that to deny innate ideas is not to deny 'that there is a law knowable by the light of nature'.) Mautner suggests that Locke's emphasis on the role of self-interest in his ethical theory reflects the influence of Pufendorf on the fear of divine punishment: 'no one would practise works of mercy or friendship without having the assurance of glory or reward' (from *De officio*, cited in Mautner 1993: 18–19). But Locke's position extends much further.

For he allowed that 'several moral rules may receive from mankind a very general approbation, without either knowing or admitting the true ground of morality', and this resulting from the wholly *mundane* consequences promised by ethical conduct – alluding to the circumstance, mentioned above, that private 'virtue' and 'public happiness' are joined, Providence having so arranged matters that it was 'profitable' to each individual to follow the rule 'Do unto others…', such conduct benefiting society as a whole, and playing back on the actor to his worldly advantage:

> I grant the existence of God is so many ways manifest, and the obedience we owe him so congruous to the light of reason, that a great part of mankind give testimony to the law of nature; but yet I think it must be allowed, that several moral rules may receive from mankind a very general approbation, without either knowing or admitting the true ground of morality; which can only be the will and law of a God, who sees men in the dark, has in his hand rewards and punishments, and power enough to call to account the proudest offender: for God having, by an inseparable connexion, joined virtue and public happiness together, and made the practice thereof necessary to the preservation of society, and visibly beneficial to all with whom the virtuous man has to do, it is no wonder that every one should not only allow, but recommend and magnify, those rules to others, from whose observance of them he is sure to reap advantage to himself.
>
> (Locke 1823 [1700] 1: 38)

The private advantage referred to might reflect the return favours to be expected from others by following the rule 'Do unto others…', but the weight placed on conduct which advances *'public happiness'* suggests more general benefits to the individual arising from the advanced social wellbeing encouraged by his virtuous conduct. (To my knowledge, nowhere does Locke allude to the complexities created by the free-riding phenomenon.) In either case, that the individual derives benefit from what we have called 'other-regarding' conduct' – indeed that they are stimulated to so conduct themselves by the promise of advantage – does not, it should be clear, detract for Locke from the ethical merit attached to such conduct, a stance which is in line with that of other hedonic utilitarian authors who 'insisted that there was no moral obligation on man to act contrary to his own nature, that it was natural for man always to seek his own happiness, and that there was therefore no obligation to disinterested benevolence' (Viner 1972: 71). Viner, we have already noted, does not cite Locke amongst the 'theological utilitarians', his definition including only those who represent the prospect of future reward and punishment as a *necessary condition* for proper conduct. This is a fair interpretation provided we also recognize that although ethical conduct may not *require* conscious appreciation of other-worldly consequences Providence has so arranged matters that it was in fact 'profitable' even from a purely worldly perspective for each individual to follow the rules of moral conduct. A theological dimension is to that extent always at play, if only indirectly acting as it were as an 'invisible hand'.

Theology of the aforementioned variety would have the character of a nominal allowance. A somewhat stronger theological foundation for Lockean ethical utilitarianism will be found in the second volume of the *Essay* in Chapter XXVIII, 'Of Moral Relations', treating three categories of 'laws that men generally refer their actions to, to judge of their rectitude or obliquity', namely the divine law, the civil law and the law of opinion or reputation:

> First, the divine law, whereby I mean that law which God has set to the actions of men, *whether promulgated to them by the light of nature, or the voice of revelation*. That God has given a rule whereby men should govern themselves, I think there is nobody so brutish as to deny. He has a right to do it; we are his creatures: he has goodness and wisdom to direct our actions to that which is best; and *he has power to enforce it by rewards and punishments, of infinite weight and duration, in another life*; for nobody can take us out of his hands. This is the only true touchstone of moral rectitude; and by comparing them to this law it is that men judge of the most considerable moral good or evil of their actions: that is, whether as duties or sins, they are like to procure them happiness or misery from the hands of the Almighty.
>
> (Locke 1823 [1700] 2: 98; emphasis added)

Missing here is a formal reference to the first principle of morality established in the first volume of the *Essay*, namely 'Do unto others...'; but if we permit ourselves to take this for granted, since there is no reason why we should suppose that Locke ever abandoned that principle, we have strongly implied here that feature characterizing theological utilitarianism whereby reliance on reward and punishment *in a future life* directs the individual towards conduct in the social interest. For all that, while belief in an afterlife provided the 'true touchtone of moral rectitude', it does not follow that individuals cannot conduct themselves ethically in its absence. And we have seen that Locke is explicit in his first volume that they may, and even usually, do so.

The theological dimension is, however, strengthened when the third category of laws – that of opinion or reputation – is introduced, whereby although virtue and vice vary according to local differences in 'temper, education, fashion, maxims, or interests of different sorts of men ... as to the main, they for the most part [are] kept the same every where' (Locke 1823 [1700] 2: 101–2). That this should be the case is said to be no accident, insofar as 'nothing can be more natural than to encourage with esteem and reputation that wherein every one finds his advantage, and to blame and discountenance the contrary', so that 'it is no wonder that esteem and discredit, virtue and vice, should in a great measure every where correspond with the unchangeable rule of right and wrong, which the law of God hath established: there being nothing that so directly and visibly secures and advances the general good of mankind in this world as obedience to the laws he has set them; and nothing that breeds such mischiefs and confusion as the neglect of them' (102–3). Accordingly, 'men, without renouncing all sense and reason, and their own interest, which they are so constantly true to, could not generally mistake in placing their commendation and blame on that side that really deserved it' (103).

That ethical standards should in the large 'correspond with the unchangeable rule of right and wrong, which the law of God hath established' is an unjustified assertion and does not fit well with the *differences* over time and place stressed in the first volume where Locke presents proofs against 'innateness' of moral principles, a matter we shall take up next. Viner was right to imply that Locke should be excluded from the theological-utilitarian category, for while calculation of other-worldly reward and punishment was certainly viewed as enhancing the motive to proper conduct, the *uncritical* adoption of supposedly moral principles on the basis of their alleged 'innateness' was firmly rejected. Indeed, even the Scriptures are not treated as a final court of appeal, Locke referring, as we have seen, to 'that law which God has set to the actions of men, whether promulgated to them by the light of nature' – by use of our natural faculties – 'or the voice of revelation'.

1.4 Locke's rejection of innate moral sense elaborated

If natural reasoning ability rather than faith in revelation as such is underscored it is certainly not because Locke himself doubted the veracity of the Gospels but because of a concern with the *misuse* of faith. In Chapter Three of Book One of his *Essay* 'No Innate Practical Principles' Locke sought to avoid misunderstanding on this score by establishing that to deny the *innateness* of ideas in general, and ideas of morality in particular, is not to deny that there *are* laws or rules of morality accessible by use of our natural faculties independently of revelation. This theme plays an important role in the demonstration that moral rules cannot reflect *innate* ideas since '[a]n evident indubitable knowledge of unavoidable punishment, great enough to make the transgression very ineligible, must accompany an innate law; unless, with an innate law, they can suppose an innate gospel too' (Locke 1823 [1700] 1: 46); as we know, such indubitability was the exception not the norm, Locke seeking to account for mankind's *typical* failure when contemplating action to make accurate calculations of true happiness. It is just here that he cautions:

> I would not here be mistaken, as if, because I deny an innate law, I thought there were none but positive laws. There is a great deal of difference between an innate law, and a law of nature; between something imprinted on our minds in their very original, and something that we

being ignorant of may attain to the knowledge of by the use and due application of our natural faculties. And I think they equally forsake the truth, who, running into contrary extremes, either affirm an innate law, or deny that there is a law knowable by the light of nature, i.e., without the help of positive revelation.[6]

Related grounds are advanced against the notion of innate moral rules. These include 'the great variety of opinions concerning moral rules which are to be found among men, according to the different sorts of happiness they have a prospect of, or propose to themselves: which could not be if practical principles were innate, and imprinted in our minds immediately by the hand of God' (Locke 1823 [1700] 1: 38). Similarly: 'The difference there is amongst men in their practical principles is so evident, that, I think, I need say no more to evince that it will be impossible to find any innate moral rules by this mark of general assent' (46). That people appealed to the 'sacredness' of certain rules should fool no one: 'outward acknowledgment ... proves not that they are innate principles' since 'self-interest, and the conveniences of this life, make many men own an outward profession and approbation of them whose actions sufficiently prove that they very little consider the lawgiver that prescribed these rules, nor the hell that he has ordained for the punishment of those that transgress them' (38–9). (In any event, Locke did not trust either the 'knowledge or charity' of those 'declaring that God has imprinted on the minds of men the foundations of knowledge, and the rules of living' since they were not typically forthcoming in specifying clearly what those rules were; 46–7.) His suspicions applied to the majority, men on the whole having 'no such internal veneration for these rules, nor so full a persuasion of their certainty and obligation. The great principle of morality, "to do as one would be done to", is more commended than practised' (39). As for those who might urge *conscience* 'as checking us for such breaches, and so the internal obligation and the establishment of the rule be preserved', Locke would have none of it: 'Conscience no proof of any innate moral rule', for there were all sorts of ways people 'come to assent to several moral rules', including 'education, company and customs', all of which 'will serve to set conscience on work, which is nothing else but our own opinion or judgment of the moral rectitude or pravity of our own actions'. But 'if conscience be a proof of innate principles, contraries may be innate principles; since some men, with the same bent of conscience, prosecute what others avoid'. In fact, Locke could not envisage men transgressing moral rules 'with confidence and serenity, were they innate, and stamped upon their minds' (39–40). And citing anthropological and historical studies he asks: 'Where then are those innate principles of justice, piety, gratitude, equity, chastity? Or, where is that *universal* consent, that assures us that there are such inbred rules? (41; emphasis added). 'He that will carefully peruse the history of mankind, and look abroad into the several tribes of man, and with indifferency survey their actions, will be able to satisfy himself that there is scarce that principle of morality to be named, or rule of virtue to be thought on (those only excepted that are absolutely necessary to hold society together, which commonly, too, are neglected betwixt distinct societies), which is not, somewhere or other, slighted and condemned by the general fashion of whole societies of man, governed by practical opinions and rules of living quite opposite to others' (41–2).

Locke proceeds to the possible objection from supporters of innate ideas that just because a rule is broken does not mean that it 'is not known' (Locke 1823 [1700] 1: 42). He responds that were there a rule of morality inbred or innate then *everyone* must be aware of it – not merely an individual transgressor – in which case it would be incomprehensible that there existed entire societies which openly denied it: 'Whatever practical principle is innate cannot but be known to every one to be just and good. It is therefore nothing less than a contradiction to suppose that whole nations of men should, both in their professions and practice, unanimously and universally give the lie to what, by the most invincible evidence, every one of them knew to be true, right, and good. This is enough to satisfy us that no practical rule, which is any where universally, and with public approbation and or allowance, transgressed, can be supposed innate' (43). Evidence to this effect respecting the allegedly innate rule of morality such as 'it is the duty of parents to preserve their children' is drawn from societies past and present where even the civil law tolerated all kinds of brutalities towards children.

At this point Locke allows God back into the picture, but in a surprising manner which is to insist that the very idea of God is not innate. The case runs as follows: An allegedly innate rule of morality, of universal applicability, necessarily implied a law and a law-maker with authority to reward and punish; but it was 'impossible that this ["preserve your children"], or any other practical principle, should be innate, *i.e.*, be imprinted on the mind as a duty, without supposing the ideas of God, of law, of obligation, of punishment, of a life after this, innate: for that punishment follows not in this life, the breach of this rule, and consequenctly, that it has not the force of a law in countries where the generally allowed practice runs counter to it, is in itself evident' (Locke 1823 [1700] 1: 44). Locke evidently found it impossible to believe that people would break God's law knowing that due punishment was to come in some future existence, so that the very fact that a rule was commonly broken, and this by entire societies, proved that it could not be innate. But beyond this the ideas in question – 'of God, of law, of obligation, of punishment, of a life after this' – are 'so far from being innate, that it is not every studious or thinking man, much less every man that is born, in whom they are to be found clear and distinct: and that one of them, which of all others seems most likely to be innate, is not so (I mean the idea of God) I think, in the next chapter, will appear very evident to any considering man'.

The reference is to the exposition in the Chapter 'Other Considerations Concerning Innate Principles': '"That God is to be worshipped", is, without doubt, as great a truth as any can enter into the mind of man, and deserves the first place amongst all practical principles' – this presumably because a thinking person must arrive at the idea of a wonderful creator; 'yet it can by no means be thought innate, unless the ideas of God and worship are innate' and they are not or else children would have such ideas let alone grown men who many of them do not (Locke 1823 [1700] 1: 60). By the same token, the idea itself of God was not innate: 'If any idea can be imagined innate, the idea of God may, of all others, for many reasons be thought so; since it is hard to conceive how there should be innate moral principles without an innate idea of a Deity: without a notion of a law-maker, it is impossible to have a notion of a law, and an obligation to observe it'. And yet atheists did not believe in a God and newly-encountered native tribes had no such idea.

We have noted already Locke's distrust of those who maintained the reality of innate moral principles – implying that 'God has imprinted on the minds of men the foundations of knowledge, and the rules of living' – and this partly because they characteristically failed to spell out what specifically they intended thereby. But he goes further by opining that if people did set out a list it would just be in support of 'the doctrines of their particular schools or churches' (Locke 1823 [1700] 1: 47); indeed, by specifying what is doctrinally acceptable, they would be 'denying freedom to mankind, and thereby making men no other than bare machines'. Consequently, 'they take away not only innate but all moral rules whatever, and leave not a possibility to believe any such, to those who cannot conceive how any thing can be capable of a law that is not a free agent and, upon that ground, they must reject all principles of virtue, who cannot put morality and mechanism together; which are not very easy to be reconciled, or made consistent' (47). Two related themes are expressed here, firstly, that freedom to obey a 'law', or fulfill a duty, is essential to ethical conduct, and secondly, that such choice is only open to those who 'put morality and mechanism together' apparently intending those who undertake reasoned calculations of the effects of the rules in question rather than take them uncritically at face value. There were of course ancient thinkers who maintained that 'virtue' was innate to man. But Locke had particularly in mind his contemporary Lord Herbert of Cherbury in *de Veritate* (1650) several innate practical principles but missed 'do as thou wouldest be done unto' which had a better claim to be an innate principle than those Herbert listed including 'virtue joined with piety is the best worship of God' (Locke 1823 [1700] 1: 47–9). While Locke found Herbert unhelpful since 'virtue' was too ambiguous a term, he actually went some way with Herbert provided 'virtue' was properly constrained: 'If virtue be taken for actions conformable to God's will, or to the rule prescribed by God, which is the true and only measure of virtue, when virtue is used to signify *what is in its true nature right and good*; then this proposition, "that virtue is the best worship of God", will be most true and certain, but of very little use in human life: since it will amount to no more than this, viz. "that God is pleased with the doing of what he commands"; which a man may certainly know to be true, without knowing what it is that God doth command; and so be as far from any rule or principle of actions as he was before' (49). Similarly, the proposition which reduces to 'God is pleased with the doing of what he himself commands' would not be accepted as an 'innate moral principle writ on the minds of all men (however true and certain it may be,) since it teaches so little' (50). Herbert also has 'men must repent of their sins', to which Locke objected that it was inconceivable that 'God should engrave principles on men's mind' of this unhelpful, because so general, an order.

Locke himself, we already know, *does* claim to know what God requires of man. It is encapsulated for him by the primary rule of ethics: 'Do unto others...', which 'had a better claim to be an innate principle' than anything listed by Herbert, but which Herbert had actually missed. Writing to William Molyneux on 30 March 1696 Locke affirmed in fact that '[t]he Gospel contains so perfect a Body of Ethics, that Reason may be excused from that Enquiry' — a proposed book on Moral philosophy suggested by Molyneux to supplement the *Essay* — 'since she may find Man's Duty clearer and easier in Revelation than in herself' (Locke, in Anon. 1742: 114). *But this is not the line adopted in the Essay itself.* Although the primary rule of ethics is evidently scriptural Locke insisted there that it could be arrived at by the use of reason — since there are no innate principles upon which to rely. Locke underscores reason rather than faith not to cast doubt on the Gospels but because of a concern with the *misuse* of faith and a wish to avoid opening the door to charlatanry, dangers revealed by taking a universalist perspective historically and spatially rather than focusing on the admittedly 'true' religion. Both the notion of an ethical 'truth' *amenable to trained reasoners* on the one hand and the character of 'divinity' typically stamped upon 'absurdities and errors' are nicely encapsulated in a passage following an account of how people typically arrive at their opinions:

> It is easy to imagine how by these means it comes to pass that men worship the idols that have been set up in their minds; grow fond of the notions they have long been acquainted with there; and stamp the characters of divinity upon absurdities and errors, become zealous votaries to bulls and monkeys; and contend too, fight, and die in defence of their opinions ... For since the reasoning faculties of the soul, which are almost constantly, though not always warily or wisely, employed, would not know how to move, for want of a foundation and footing, in most men; who through laziness or avocation do not, or for want of time, or true helps, or for other causes, cannot penetrate into the principles of knowledge, and trace truth to its fountain and original; it is natural for them, and almost unavoidable, to take up with some borrowed principles: which being reputed and presumed to be the evident proofs of other things, are thought not to need any other proofs themselves. Whoever shall receive any of these into his mind, and entertain them there, with the reverence usually paid to principles, never venturing to examine them, but accustoming himself to believe them, because they are to be believed, may take up from his education,

and the fashions of his country, any absurdity for innate principles; and by long poring on the same objects, so dim his sight, as to take monsters lodged in his own brain for the images of the Deity, and the workmanship of his hands.

(Locke 1823 [1700] 1: 55–6)

It is then upon *reason* that Locke relies in the *Essay* to confirm our knowledge of morality. But reason, we should have in mind, is itself God-given: 'The infinitely wise contriver of us, and all things about us, hath fitted our senses, faculties, and organs, to the conveniencies of life, and the business we have to do here ... We are furnished with faculties (dull and weak as they are) to discover enough in the creatures, to lead us to the knowledge of the Creator, and *the knowledge of our duty*' (Chapter XXIII: Our Ideas of Substances, Volume 2, Book Two; Locke 1823 [1700] 2: 16). And on at least three occasions Locke goes as far as to propose that 'morality is capable of demonstration, as well as mathematics', though unfortunately, Locke does not in these contexts formally restate his own perception of the primary rule of ethics, namely 'Do unto others'. But this proposition should not perhaps be taken too seriously. The first occasion purports to explain that the affirmation follows 'since the precise essence of the things moral words stand for may be perfectly known; and so the congruity and incongruity of the things themselves certainly discovered; in which consists perfect knowledge' (Chapter XI: 'Remedies of the Imperfection', Volume 2, Book Three; Locke 1823 [1700] 2: 298). But the concern that emerges here is the rather less ambitious one of merely countering 'the negligence or perverseness of mankind' in undertaking ethical discourse without due care regarding definition of terms (299). The second occasion (Chapter III: 'Extent of Human Knowledge', Volume II, Book 4) although more forthcoming, nevertheless qualifies the proposition as valid only in *principle* rather than as an actuality:

> The idea of a Supreme Being, infinite in power, goodness, and wisdom, whose workmanship we are, and on whom we depend; and the idea of ourselves, as understanding rational beings, being such as are clear in us, would, *I suppose*, if duly considered and pursued, afford such foundations of our duty and rules of action, as might place morality amongst the sciences capable of demonstration: wherein I doubt not but from self-evident propositions, by necessary consequences, as incontestable as those in mathematics, the measures of right and wrong *might* be made out to any one that will apply himself with the same indifferency and attention to the one, as he does to the other of these sciences.

(368–9; emphasis added)

As for the third instance, a chapter in Volume Three, 'Of the Improvement of our Knowledge', confirms that this discussion is merely a 'conjecture' whereby, '*if a right method were taken*, a great part of morality might be made out with that clearness, that could leave, to a considering man, no more reason to doubt than he could have to doubt of the truth of propositions in mathematics, which have been demonstrated to him' (Locke 1823 [1700] 3: 84; emphasis added). In fact, Locke pointed out in a response to strictures by Thomas Burnet against his moral theory that he had *not* claimed in his *Essay* to having actually demonstrated morality, but only to have proposed that it is '*capable* of demonstration as well as mathematics' – in principle as it were ([Locke] 1697: 4; emphasis added).[7] A 'right method' may be a matter of 'principle' and 'conjecture' but, on the basis of the earlier demonstration regarding the linkage between social welfare and other-regarding conduct reflected in the rule 'Do unto others…' – such conduct providentially arranged to be profitable to the individual actor – I conjecture that the 'reasoning' that would serve Locke *in practice* relates precisely to the enhanced general happiness expected to result from conduct of this order.

Returning now to the main theme, it is the characteristically *uncritical* adoption of certain alleged moral principles, reflected in appeals made to their innateness, that particularly irked Locke: 'if it be the privilege of innate principles to be received upon their own authority, without examination, I know not what may not be believed, or how any one's principles can be questioned' (Locke 1823 [1700] 1: 56). Here Locke approaches what was to be Bentham's complaint that appeal to a 'moral sense' is no more than asserting such and such an ethical principle to be true because I say it is.

Locke proceeds to elaborate his case: while 'the variety of opposite principles held and contended for by all sorts and degrees of men' was evidence of their unreasoned adoption, even universal consent did not prove innateness: 'If they may, and ought to be examined, and tried, I desire to know how first and innate principles can be tried; or at least it is reasonable to demand the marks and characters, whereby the genuine innate principles may be distinguished from others; that so, amidst the great variety of pretenders, I may be kept from mistakes, in so material a point as this. When this is done, I shall be ready to embrace such welcome and useful propositions; and till then I may with modesty doubt, since I fear universal consent, which is the only one produced' – by those who claim innateness – '"will scarce prove a sufficient mark to direct my choice, and assure me of any innate principles' (Locke 1823 [1700] 1: 56). In his next chapter Locke repeats that '[i]f anyone thinks there are such innate ideas and propositions, which by their clearness and usefulness are distinguishable from all that is adventitious in the mind, and acquired, it will not be a hard matter for him to tell us which they are, and then every one will be a fit judge whether they be so or no; since if there be such innate ideas and impressions, plainly different from all other perceptions and knowledge, every one will find it true in himself' (76). And he also appeals for people to use their *God-given* brains and not to take things simply on faith or authority, warning that peddlers of such notions often wish to use them to their own advantage. All in all, 'ideas and notions are no more born with us than arts and sciences … God having fitted men with faculties and means to discover, receive, and retain truths, according as they are employed' (76–7).

Locke sums up Chapter Three of the first volume by asserting that 'from what has been said, I think it past doubt that there are no practical principles wherein all men agree, and therefore none innate' (Locke 1823 [1700] 1: 56). This summary is misleading since it implies that universal agreement *would* provide the requisite evidence. And this Locke had denied. He was willing to concede that were certain specific rules universally accepted and practised as 'part of the worship of God' – such as do not murder, do not practice abortion, do not expose children, do not steal, and 'relieve and supply wants' and a thousand other rules – then 'there would be more reason for admitting these and the like for common notions and practical principles', but since knowledge of such rules could be arrived at 'by other means', it 'would scarce prove them to be innate; which is all I contend for' (50–1). The 'other means' intended are particularly well explained in Chapter Four where he explains why, 'had all mankind, every where, a notion of a God (whereof yet history tells us the contrary), it would not from thence follow, that the idea of him was innate' (62). This was because:

> The visible marks of extraordinary wisdom and power appear so plainly in all the works of the creation, that a rational creature, who will but seriously reflect on them, cannot but miss the discovery of a Deity. And the influence that the discovery of such a being must necessarily have on the minds of all, that have but once heard of it, is great, and carries such a weight of thought and communication with it, that it seems stranger to me that a whole nation of men should be any where found so brutish as to want the notion of a God, than that they should be without any notion of numbers or fire.
>
> (65).

For 'the goodness of God hath not been wanting to men without ... original impressions of knowledge, or ideas stamped on the mind: since he hath furnished man with those faculties, which will serve for the sufficient discovery of all things requisite to the end of such a being. And I doubt not but to show that a man, by the right use of his natural abilities, may, without any innate principles, attain a knowledge of a God, and other things that concern him.' (67). Nevertheless, 'right use' of one's natural abilities is represented as the exception rather than the rule, since it was only the 'wise men of all nations [who] come to have true conceptions of the unity and infinity of the Deity', which very fact proved that there was 'no universality of consent' since wise men were so uncommon; and it proved too that such notions were not 'imprinted' but 'acquired by thought and meditation, and a right use of their faculties; since the wise and considerate men of the world, by a right and careful employment of their thoughts and reason, attained true notions in this as well as other things; whilst the lazy and inconsiderate part of men, making far the greater number, took up their notions by chance, from common tradition and vulgar conceptions without much beating their heads about them' (70).

Locke continues his argument by asserting: 'And if it be a reason to think the notion of God innate, because all wise men had it, virtue too must be thought innate, for that also wise men have always had' (Locke 1823 [1700] 1: 70). It would have helped had Locke reiterated that 'virtue' implied for him conduct satisfying the rule 'Do unto others…', its primacy rationalized by its character as the 'foundation of all *social* virtue' which, when coupled with the notion that private 'virtue' and '*public* happiness' are providentially 'joined', suggests the positive effect on social welfare of 'other-regarding' private conduct.

1.5 'Of faith and reason'

The foregoing extracts may have given an impression of a simple Lockean dictum to 'take *nothing* on faith'. This would, however, be too strong a conclusion considering the formal discussion of the *legitimate* scope of faith which is given in Chapter 18: 'Of Faith and Reason, and their distinct Provinces' in the third volume. Nonetheless, the role allowed faith it is so restricted that the traditional believer would scarcely be appeased.

The categories in question are spelled out thus: 'Reason … here, as contradistinguished to faith, I take to be the discovery of the certainty or probability of such propositions or truths, which the mind arrives at by deductions made from such ideas which it had got by the use of its natural faculties, viz. by sensation or reflection. Faith, on the other side, is the assent to any proposition, not thus made out by the deductions of reason; but from the credit of the proposer, as coming from God, in some extraordinary way of communication. This way of discovering truths to men we call revelation' (Locke 1823 [1700] 3: 138). Revelation may be either 'original' referring to 'that first impression, which is made immediately by God, on the mind of any man, to which we cannot set any bounds'; or 'traditional' referring to 'those impressions delivered over to others in words, and the ordinary ways of conveying our conceptions one to another', the second evidently referring to biblical texts and sermons and the like (139–40). The former class 'to which we can set no bounds' is illustrated by the 'things … discovered by St. Paul, when he was rapt up into the third heaven', that cannot be transferred to others by words or any other means of communication any more than can a vision received by an individual of some extra-terrestrial creature with a sixth sense: 'whatsoever impressions he himself' – referring to the 'man inspired by God' – 'may have from the immediate hand of God, this revelation, if it be of new ideas, cannot be conveyed to another, either by words or any other signs'.

The impossibility of further transmission would seem to render the case of original revelation entirely academic. This is particularly so given a caution that 'where God immediately reveals [something] to us … our assurance can be no greater than our knowledge is, that it is a revelation from God' and not, so Locke implies, wholly a figment of the imagination (Locke 1823 [1700] 3: 141).

In any event, he insists that 'faith can never convince us of any thing that contradicts our knowledge' (142), for to suppose it otherwise would imply a severe inconsistency on the behalf of the Deity who is supposed to be responsible for our knowledge and reasoning capacity:

> Because though faith be founded on the testimony of God (who cannot lie) revealing any proposition to us; yet we cannot have an assurance of the truth of its being a divine revelation greater than our own knowledge: since the whole strength of the certainty depends upon our knowledge that God revealed it; which in this case, where the proposition supposed revealed contradicts our knowledge or reason, will always have this objection hanging to it, viz. that we cannot tell how to conceive that to come from God, the bountiful Author of our being, which, if perceived for true, must overturn all the principles and foundations of knowledge he has given us; render all our facilities useless; wholly destroy the most excellent part of his workmanship, our understandings; and put a man in a condition, wherein he will have less light, less conduct, than the beast that perishes.
>
> (142)

Here we take note of Locke's caution at the beginning of his chapter regarding *limitations* to reason: 'It has been above shown, 1. That we are of necessity ignorant, and want knowledge of all sorts, where we want ideas. 2. That we are ignorant, and want rational knowledge, where we want proofs. 3. That we want certain knowledge and certainty, as far as we want clear and determined specific ideas. 4. That we want probability to direct our assent in matters where we have neither knowledge of our own, nor testimony of other men, to bottom our reason upon' (Locke 1823 [1700] 3: 137–8). Clearly then his argument in the present context extracts from this limitation. And indeed, his reliance on reason is said to apply to 'propositions ... whose certainty is built upon the clear perception of the agreement or disagreement of our ideas, attained either by immediate intuition, as in self-evident propositions, or by evident deductions of reason in demonstrations' (141). It is in such cases that 'we need not the assistance of revelation, as necessary to gain our assent, and introduce them into our minds'. Indeed, in such cases nothing can 'shake or over-rule plain knowledge; or rationally prevail with any man to admit it for true, in a direct contradiction to the clear evidence of his own understanding'.

This insistence upon reason, which applied 'even in immediate and original revelation, where it is supposed to be made to [an individual] himself', extended *a fortiori* to traditional revelation by way of scripture or word of mouth where 'reason has a great deal more to do, and is that only which can induce us to receive them' (Locke 1823 [1700] 3: 143). He had earlier elaborated the superfluous character of much traditional revelation. For such revelation entailed the transmission of 'simple' – and necessarily familiar – ideas, ideas which 'are the foundation and the sole matter of all our notions and knowledge', and for which 'we must depend wholly on our reason, I mean our natural faculties; and can by no means receive them, or any of them, from traditional revelation' (139); indeed, where 'the same truths may be discovered, and conveyed down from revelation, which are discoverable to us by reason, and by those ideas we naturally may have ... there is little need or use of revelation, God having furnished us with natural and surer means to arrive at the knowledge of them' (140). Reason in fact has the advantage: 'For whatsoever truth we come to the clear discovery of, from the knowledge and contemplation of our own ideas, will always be certainer to us than those which are conveyed to us by traditional revelation', since 'the knowledge we have, that this revelation came at first from God, can never be so sure, as the knowledge we have from the clear and distinct perception of the agreement or disagreement of our own ideas' – an argument paralleling that used in the case for original revelation. But at a deeper level there is an objection that the case for its supposedly divine origin of Scripture must satisfy *reason*: 'faith, as we use the word (called commonly divine faith) has to do with no propositions but those which are supposed to be divinely revealed. So that I do not see how those, who make revelation alone the sole object of faith, can say, that it is a matter of faith, and not of reason, to believe that such or such a proposition, to be found in such or such a book, is of divine inspiration; unless it be revealed, that the proposition, or all in that book, was communicated by divine inspiration. Without such a revelation' – and Locke implies that revelation cannot be taken for granted – 'the believing or not believing that proposition or book to be of divine authority can never be a matter of faith, but matter of reason; and such as I must come to an assent to only by the use of my reason, which can never require or enable me to believe that which is contrary to itself: it being impossible for reason ever to procure any assent to that, which to itself appears unreasonable' (143).

Locke again cautions, when summarizing, that 'reason is the proper judge' only regarding matters 'where we have clear evidence from our ideas, and those principles of knowledge I have above-mentioned' – alluding presumably to the absence of the four-fold constraints upon knowledge noted above; and then 'revelation', though it may in consenting with it confirm its dictates, yet cannot in such cases invalidate its decrees: nor can we be obliged, where we have the clear and evident sentence of reason, to quit it for the contrary opinion, under the pretence that it is matter of faith; which can have no authority against the plain and clear dictates of reason' (Locke 1823 [1700] 3: 143). But matters where 'by the natural use of our faculties, we can have no knowledge at all' – such as resurrection – are '*when revealed*, the proper matter of faith' (144; emphasis added). Here our natural faculties, which allow only *probable* rather than certain judgment, must give way: 'revelation, where God has been pleased to give it, must carry it against the probable conjectures of reason. Because the mind not being certain of the truth of that it does not evidently know, but only yielding to the probability that appears in it, is bound to give up its assent to such a testimony; which it is satisfied, comes from one who cannot err, and will not deceive'. But while the authority emanating from revelation must be accepted in such cases, Locke immediately repeats his warning that what presents itself as a revelation is really such; and here he allows reason back into the picture: 'But yet it still belongs to reason to judge of the truth of its being a revelation, and of the signification of the words wherein it is delivered. Indeed, if any thing shall be thought revelation which is contrary to the plain principles of reason, and the evident knowledge the mind has of its own clear and distinct ideas; there reason must be hearkened to, as to a matter within its province…; and so [one] is bound to consider and judge of it as a matter of reason, and not to swallow it, without examination, as a matter of faith' (144–5). This caution is applied to 'any traditional revelation', Locke affirming that '[t]here can be no evidence' that any such 'is of divine original, in the words we receive it, and in the sense we understand it, so clear and so certain as that of the principles of reason: and therefore nothing that is contrary to, and inconsistent with, the clear and self-evident dictates of reason, has a right to be urged or assented to as a matter of faith, wherein reason has nothing to do' (146).

1.6 Concluding remarks

Locke's primary target is underscored at the close of the chapter 'Of Faith and Reason' – 'those extravagant opinions and ceremonies that are to be found in the several religions of the world' engaged in the 'crying up of faith, in opposition to reason' and generating 'those absurdities that fill almost all the religions which possess and divide mankind' (Locke 1823 [1700] 3: 146). The chapter closes on a welcome light note in this regard: '"Credo, quia impossibile est;" I believe, because it is impossible, might in a good man pass for a sally of zeal; but would prove a very ill rule for men to choose their opinions or religion by' (147). We should also keep in mind Locke's position suggesting Pascal's Wager that the mere *possibility* of an after-life with its rewards and punishments should suffice for rational individuals to extend their time horizon when calculating the happiness promised by their actions. But, most importantly, even to reject belief in an after-life would leave untouched the Lockean proposition that *other-regarding* consideration constitutes the essence of ethical conduct, though it weakens the *motive* for such conduct by placing reliance entirely on the worldly advantages promised thereby.

I am not sure that Ryan does not go too far when he avers that, for Locke, 'a man who does not believe in God cannot regard himself as *morally* obliged to behave in any particular way' (Ryan 2012: 465). But Locke's great caution regarding appeal to Scriptural revelation certainly restricts severely the scope for orthodox theology allowed in support of his ethical utilitarianism. Indeed, drawing primarily on Locke's political writings Ryan puts particular emphasis on his deism: 'Like Hobbes, Locke believed that law was law because it was the command of a superior; to believe that natural law was strictly law required a belief in God as lawgiver. It did not require a belief in any particular religion or in a deity with any particular qualities, or the illumination of any particular revelation. Natural theology grounded natural law' (Ryan 2012: 465; see also

Harris 1994: 186–9). Yet, for whatever reason, posterity seems not always to have viewed Locke in this fashion: *The Reasonableness of Christianity* was later recommended to undergraduates in an effort to reinforce orthodoxy against Deism (Waterman 1991: 92–3); and it is Lord Herbert who 'has come down to us as the father of English deism' (Carey 2006: 57).

We recall, in closing, the Burnet–Locke episode (above, p. 20). Jaffro writes that by stressing 'the immediacy of our "inward sense" of good and evil Burnet foreruns moral sense theories', while 'Locke's argument against the claim to immediate evidence in matters of faith … debars moral judgment from being by itself the standard of value', taking us 'very close to Jeremy Bentham's criticism of Shaftesburian and Hutchesonian moral sense theories as "ipso-dixitism"' (Jaffro 2014: 93–4). I would wish to add the caveat that Locke's rejection of a moral sense does not distinguish him sharply from Shaftesbury and Hutcheson (or for that matter from Hume and Helvétius), for in all these cases the moral sense reduces to commendation of 'sympathy' or other-regarding conduct which is in line with Locke's conception of what constitutes proper moral conduct.

Notes

1 First edition imprinted as 1690. I use the three-volume 1823 edition, which prints the last edition published during Locke's lifetime (1700). Locke died in 1704.
2 Locke refers mockingly in this context to 'the philosophers of old [who] did in vain inquire, whether the *summum bonum* consisted in riches, or bodily delights, or virtue, or contemplation'. The marginal principle is not adduced as an objection to such an inquiry.
3 Elsewhere Locke is more forthcoming, referring for example in his third volume to 'that sort of knowledge, which is most suited to our natural capacities, and carries in it our greatest interest, i.e., the condition of our eternal estate' (Locke 1823 [1700] 3: 87).
4 For a detailed study of Pascal's position, see Jordan 2006.
5 Samuel Clarke's Boyle lectures of 1705 similarly specifies as the essentials of ethical conduct the Scriptural dictum together with a concern for the general 'welfare and happiness': 'In respect to our *Fellow-creatures*, the Rule of Righteousness is; *that* in particular *we so deal with every Man, as in like Circumstances we could reasonably expect he should deal with Us*; and *that* in general *we endeavour, by an universal Benevolence, to promote the welfare and happiness of all Men*. The former Branch of this Rule, is *Equity*: the latter, is *Love*' (Clarke 1716 [1705]: 67).
6 Viner includes Locke together with Shaftesbury, Hume and Hutcheson as adhering to a 'naturalistic philosophy' (Viner 1958: 270). But see Macpherson for the complications surrounding Locke's version (Macpherson 1962: 230, 239, 258–9).
7 Relevant here is Locke's annotation in a copy of Burnet's criticisms of the *Essay* (see Carey 2006: 166–7). Burnet supposes an immediate capacity to distinguish between good and evil by means of a 'natural conscience' existing prior to the exercise of reason and thus, as Jaffro observed, 'foreruns moral sense theories' (Jaffro 2014: 93). Locke in his marginal note recognizes a capacity 'to find out in time the moral difference of actions', and this by use of *reason*, and explained: 'I never denied such a power to be innate' but that any 'ideas or any connection of ideas was innate'.

References

Anon. 1742. *Familiar Letters between Mr. John Locke and Several of his Friends*, 4th ed. London: F. Noble.

Carey, D. 2006. *Locke, Shaftesbury, and Hutcheson*. Cambridge: Cambridge University Press.

Clarke, S. 1716 [1705]. 'A Discourse Concerning the Unalterable Obligations of Natural Religion'. (Boyle Lecture.) 4th ed. London: W. Botham.

Fraser, A.C. 1890. *Locke*, Edinburgh and London: Blackwood.

Fraser, A.C. 1894. 'Introduction' to John Locke, *Essay Concerning Human Understanding* vol. 1. Oxford: Clarendon Press: xi–cxl.

Harris, I. 1994. *The Mind of John Locke: A Study of Political Theory in its Intellectual Setting*. Cambridge: Cambridge University Press.

Jaffro, L. 2014. 'Burnet, Thomas (c. 1635–1715)', in *The Bloomsbury Companion to Locke*, eds. S.-J. Savonius-Wroth, P. Schuurman and J. Walmsley. 2014. London: Bloomsbury.

Jordan, J. 2006. *Pascal's Wager: Pragmatic Arguments and Belief in God*, Oxford: Clarendon.

Locke, J. 1695. *Reasonableness of Christianity, as delivered in the Scriptures*. London: Awnsham and John Churchill.

[Locke, J.] 1697. *An Answer to Remarks Upon an Essay Concerning Humane Understanding*. London: Wotton.

Locke, J. 1823 (1700). *Essay Concerning Human Understanding*. London: T. Tegg.

Macpherson, C.B. 1962. *The Political Theory of Possessive Individualism: Hobbes to Locke*. Oxford: Oxford University Press.

Mautner, T. 1993. Introduction to Francis Hutcheson: On human nature. Ed. Thomas Mautner. Cambridge: Cambridge University Press: 3–87.

Ryan, A. 2012. *On Politics: A History of Political Thought from Herodotus to the Present*. London: Allen Lane.

Stephen, L. 1900. *The English Utilitarians*. London: Duckworth.

Stephen, L. 1902. *English Thought in the Eighteenth Century*. 3rd ed. London: John Murray.

Viner, J. 1958. *The Long View and the Short: Studies in Economic Theory and Policy*. Glencoe, Il. The Free Press.

Viner, J. 1972. *The Role of Providence in the Social Order: An Essay in Intellectual History*. Philadelphia: American Philosophical Society.

Waterman, A.M.C. 1991. *Revolution, Economics and Religion*. Cambridge: Cambridge University Press.

Part 2
Eighteenth-century moral-sense literature

Part 2

Eighteenth-century moral-sense literature

2 Lord Shaftesbury, utilitarian ethics and the moral sense

2.1 Introduction

Our approach towards the third Earl of Shaftesbury (Anthony Ashley Cooper) has in mind both Bentham's presumption that Shaftesbury championed a 'moral sense' *as opposed to a utilitarian ethics*, informing the individual 'such a thing is right, and such a thing is wrong – why? "because my moral sense tells me it is"', and John Stuart Mill's reading to the same effect. Some later commentators similarly imply that Shaftesbury opposed the general utility doctrine relying on an innate 'sense of right and wrong', as Bentham had explicitly maintained; thus, in a contrast made by Kaye between Shaftesbury and Mandeville, it is pointedly Mandeville alone who is designated as 'utilitarian' (Kaye 1924: lxxiv; see also lix–lxi). While there is some justification for such a reading, I shall show that when engaged in practical application Shaftesbury considers the moral sense not as a built-in index of the ethical quality of conduct, but specifically as recommending to the individual conscious a *concern with the public welfare* – reflecting Shaftesbury's perception of 'virtue' – as Locke had spelled out, as Hume and Hutcheson were later to do and consistently with what Mill designates as the principle that 'general utility is the foundation of morality' (Mill 1969 [1838]: 86). In brief, Shaftesbury's appeal to a built-in psychological capacity to distinguish good from evil was merely intended to reinforce his value judgment that virtue consists in concern for the public good, albeit to private advantage, but was scarcely essential to the argument. For Shaftesbury agreed in his *Inquiry concerning Virtue or Merit* 'that Goodness by which he is useful to others [is] a real Good and Advantage to himself' so that '*Virtue and Interest* may be found at last to agree'. Here he draws on an argument from *'reason'* whereby private advantage harmonizes with the public good, namely the individual's realization of his dependency on society which encourages him to be concerned for its welfare. *This is fully in line with Locke.* I shall show also that Shaftesbury even allows both in the *Inquiry* and *The Moralists* that the moral sense alone – indicating the purely ethical merit of other-regarding conduct – was far from wholly reliable. In any event, as I will later show, Bonar remarked of Hume that the moral sense was left with little to do once it is reduced to other-regarding sympathy (see Chapter 5). I shall maintain here that this may also be said of Shaftesbury (and, as we later argue, of Hutcheson too).

The Lockean correspondence may come as a surprise to those impressed by Shaftesbury's neglect of Locke in his printed writings, notwithstanding Locke's firm insistence in the *Essay* upon a '*true*' moral rule – that of 'Do unto others…' – the neglect of which implied for Locke either perversity, in Christian communities, or error, even if the error was explicable in terms of alternative cultural patterns, as well as Locke's recognition of the ethical merit attached to *other-regarding* conduct even when motivated by expected personal benefit. Also surprising is the harshness expressed towards Locke in Shaftesbury's private correspondence, 'the explicit statements of Shaftesbury's maturity reveal[ing] mostly intellectual hostility' (Klein 1999: xxvii). As Carey puts it: 'Locke appeared to him as a dangerous exponent of relativism, content to advertise human variation without identifying departures from the norm as instances of error, vice, or depravity' (Carey 2006: 99).

I proceed by considering in Section 2.2 Shaftesbury's perception of 'virtue' as *benevolence* apart from the alleged psychological capacity directing the individual towards such conduct, apart that is from a 'moral sense'. After demonstrating Shaftesbury's perception of virtue and virtuous motivation as the individual's concern for public welfare I raise the issue of how Shaftesbury would have responded to the question: 'how do you know?' and presume he would have responded 'my moral sense tells me so'. Sections 2.3 and 2.4 consider Shaftesbury's moral sense, the first *as interpreted by Bentham*, which does not directly allude to the public good and may have lead him to render Shaftesbury's 'moral sense' as evidencing a hostility towards utilitarianism, and also induced Mill to classify him as an opponent; and the second being Shaftesbury's actual reduction of the moral sense to a concern for the public interest.

2.2 The public good as the 'main end' of virtue

I shall first elaborate the utilitarian component in Shaftesbury's *Inquiry Concerning Virtue, or Merit* without explicit reference to the moral sense or 'sense of right and wrong', and with particular attention accorded the relation between private and public interest.[1] This procedure will help establish our contention that the moral sense for Shaftesbury was much ado about nothing just as it was for Hume.

It will clear the ground if we first take note of Adam Smith's classification of Shaftesbury's 'system' as having in common with those of Clarke and Wollaston the perception of virtue as 'propriety' or 'the suitableness of the affection from which we act, to the cause or object which excites it' – in Shaftesbury's specific case 'plac[ing] it in maintaining a proper balance of the affections, and allowing no passion to go beyond its proper sphere'

(Smith 1976 [1759]: 293). Now the *Inquiry* indeed formally defines virtue in these terms and it is to this that Smith presumably alludes: 'The Nature of VIRTUE consisting (as has been explain'd) *in a certain just Disposition, or proportionable Affection of a rational Creature towards the Moral Objects of Right and Wrong*' (Shaftesbury 1714a: 40).[2] Now while this requirement is indeed much emphasized by Shaftesbury it is not as an *end* for its own sake but as a condition to be satisfied by the 'moral Objects of Right and Wrong'; and this, we shall show, entails primarily – if not uniquely – concern for the *public interest* with the 'the proper balance of the affections' satisfied by taking *private interest* appropriately into account.

My argument runs as follows. As clarified in the *Inquiry*, motivation provides the key to ethical standing, with the highest merit accorded to the individual concerned for the public good, 'the main End' no less, although the (prospective) consequences of any action thus motivated also matter: 'When in general, all the Affections or Passions are suted to the publick Good, or good of the Species ... then is the *natural Temper* intirely good. If, on the contrary, any requisite Passion be wanting; or if there be any one supernumerary, or weak, or any-wise disserviceable, or contrary to that main End; then is the natural Temper, and consequently the Creature himself, in some measure corrupt and *ill*' (Shaftesbury 1714a: 26–7). By the latter qualifications Shaftesbury intends *excessive* concern with 'private interest' to be indicative of 'selfishness', excessive with respect to the (presumably *prospective*) outcome of the actions thus motivated:

> If the Affection be then only injurious to the Society, when it is immoderate, and not so when it is moderate, duly temper'd, and allay'd; then is the *immoderate* degree of the Affection truly vitious, but not *the moderate*. And thus, if there be found in any Creature a more than ordinary Self-Concernment, or Regard to private Good, which is inconsistent with the Interest of the Species or Publick; this must is every respect be esteem'd an ill and vitious Affection. And this is what we commonly call SELFISHNESS, and disapprove so much, in whatever Creature we happen to discover it.
>
> (22–3).

But, to the contrary, self-interested motivation that is consistent with the public interest merits approval – although it is unjustifiably 'deemed' selfish by some: 'On the other side, if the Affection towards private or Self-Good, however *selfish* it may be esteem'd, is in reality not only consistent with publick Good, but in some measure contributing to it ...'tis so far from being ill, or blameable in any sense, that it must be acknowledg'd absolutely necessary to constitute a Creature *Good*' (23).

Are we to understand from this latter comment that self-interested motivation is rendered ethically meritorious as soon as the prospectively beneficial social consequences of actions thus motivated come into the picture? In that case, as an obvious instance, profit-maximizing conduct in the market would be considered ethical in the light of benefits to society that may be expected therefrom. This in fact could not have been Shaftesbury's stance, since he goes on to maintain that socially-beneficial consequences following accidentally from self-interested motivation do *not* justify ethical approval of such motivation:

> Whatsoever ... is done which happens to be advantageous to the Species, thro an Affection merely towards Self-Good, does not imply any more Goodness in the Creature than as the Affection it-self is good. Let him, in any particular, act ever so well; if at the bottom, it be that selfish Affection alone which moves him; he is in himself still vitious. Nor can any Creature be consider'd otherwise, when the Passion towards Self-Good, tho ever so moderate, is his real Motive in the doing that, to which a natural Affection for his Kind ought by right to have inclin'd him.
>
> (Shaftesbury 1714a: 25).

More generally, a conscious intention to advance the public interest is essential for ethical commendation: 'we call any Creature *Worthy* or *Virtuous,* when it can have the Notion of a publick Interest, and can attain the Speculation or Science of what is morally good or ill, admirable or blameable, right or wrong ... So that if a Creature be generous, kind, constant, compassionate; yet if he cannot reflect on what he himself does, or sees others do, so as to take notice of what is *worthy* or *honest*; and make that Notice or Conception of *Worth* and *Honesty* to be an Object of his Affection; he has not the Character of being *virtuous*' (31).

It would follow that, in our instance, profit-maximizing conduct only acquires ethical status if the maximizer *intends* to render a social benefit. This reading is subsequently confirmed thus: 'We have found, that to deserve the name of *Good* or *Virtuous,* a Creature must have all his Inclinations and Affections, his Dispositions of Mind and Temper, sutable, and agreeing with the Good of his *Kind,* or of that *System* in which he is included, and of which he constitutes a PART. To stand thus well affected, and to have one's Affections *right* and *intire,* not only in respect of one's self, but of Society and the Publick: This is *Rectitude, Integrity* or VIRTUE' (Shaftesbury 1714a: 77). (One notes incidentally an implicit allusion to the condition of a 'proper balance of affections'.) And that an *intention* to advance public welfare is a condition for the establishment of 'virtuous' private interest is confirmed by an assurance that Nature has arranged for the consistency of such motivation and the public good:

> Everything which is an Improvement of Virtue, or an Establishment of right Affection and Integrity, is an Advancement of Interest, and leads to the greatest and most solid Happiness and Enjoyment.
>
> Thus the Wisdom of what rules, and is FIRST and CHIEF *in Nature,* has made it to be according to the *private Interest* and *Good* of every-one,

to work towards the *general Good*; which if a Creature ceases to promote, he is actually so far wanting to himself, and ceases to promote his own Happiness and Welfare. He is, on this account, directly his own Enemy: Nor can he any otherwise be good or useful to himself, than as he continues good to Society, and to that *Whole* of which he is himself a *Part*. So that Virtue ... *that single Quality*, thus beneficial to all Society, and to Mankind *in general*, is found equally a Happiness and Good to each creature *in particular*.

(175–6).

A passage in *The Moralists* nicely encapsulates the principle of a *virtuous* self-interest: ' If ... every *particular Nature* be ... constantly and unerringly *true* to it-self, and certain to produce only what is good for it-self, and conducing to its own right State; shall not, the *general-one, The NATURE of the Whole*, do full as much? ... And what is for the good of all in general, is *Just* and *Good*' (Shaftesbury 1714b: 360).

I do not find in Shaftesbury the naive observation that an individual's other-regarding concern *necessarily* reflects his own selfish interest insofar as he takes pleasure from being endowed with other-regarding sentiments. There would be little purpose in elaborating this proposition since whatever one chooses to do, however other-regarding, is necessarily 'pleasurable' or one would not do it. But this commonplace can be accepted without necessarily implying that the individual acts *because of* such personal satisfaction.[3] Much more interesting is the individual who acts in the public interest because of some positive personal benefit perceived to derive from a healthy society – which is in fact Locke's position. While Shaftesbury, as we know, detracts from his ethical merit, or rather designates him as 'vicious', if his *'real motive'* for concern with the public is *entirely* of a 'selfish' order – confirming that all is a matter of degree in line with the above-mentioned condition of a 'just Disposition, or proportionable Affection' – at the same time, as we have seen, he heartily applauds the individual's perception of personal benefit deriving from advancing the societal interest. (A relevant consideration, albeit of a negative order, would be fear of reprisal in the event of anti-social conduct: 'no Creature can maliciously and intentionally *do ill*, without being sensible, at the same time, that he *deserves ill*. And in this respect, every sensible Creature may be said to have *Conscience*. For with all Mankind, and all intelligent Creatures, this must ever hold, "That *what* they deserve from every-one, *that* they necessarily must fear and expect from all"' (1714a: 120–1.)[4] Shaftesbury is in fact emphatic 'how much NATURAL AFFECTION is predominant; how it is inwardly join'd to us, and implanted in our Natures; how interwoven with our other Passions; and how essential to that regular Motion and Course of our Affections, on which *our Happiness and Self-enjoyment so immediately depend*' (138–9; emphasis added). We have already noted that man's greatest satisfaction is said to derive from enhancement of the general good, 'which if a creature ceases to promote, he is actually so far wanting to himself, and ceases to promote his own Happiness and Welfare', alluding partly to loss of the personal benefit derived from social enhancement: 'Nor can he any otherwise be good or useful to himself, than as he continues good to Society, and to that Whole of which he is himself a Part'. Indeed, at the outset of the *Inquiry* we have the resounding declaration — the Lockean declaration — 'that Goodness by which he is useful to others [is] a real Good and Advantage to himself' so that '*Virtue* and *Interest* may be found at last to agree' (16).

The matter of proper degree or balance of affections arises conspicuously in an allowance that since self-protection is essential to the public good *up to a point*, no moral stigma is attached to some minimum of pure 'private Affection':

> *Publick Affection*, on the one hand, may be *too high*; so *private Affection* may, on the other hand, be *too weak*. For if a Creature be self-neglectful, and insensible of Danger; or if he want such a degree of Passion in any kind, as is useful to preserve, sustain, or defend himself; this must certainly be esteem'd vitious, in regard of the Design and End of Nature ... And thus the Affections towards private Good become necessary and essential to Goodness. For tho no Creature can be call'd good, or virtuous, merely for possessing these Affections; yet since it is impossible that the publick Good, or Good of the System, can be preserv'd without them; it follows that a Creature really wanting in them, is in reality wanting in some degree to Goodness and natural Rectitude; and may thus be esteem'd vitious and defective.
> (Shaftesbury 1714a: 89–90).

Listed as 'Home-affections which relate to the private Interest or separate Oeconomy of the Creature' are '*Love of Life;—Resentment of Injury;—Pleasure, or Appetite towards Nourishment and the Means of Generation;—Interest,* or *Desire* of *those Conveniences*, by which we are well *provided for*, and *maintain'd;— Emulation,* or *Love of Praise and Honour, — Indolence,* or *Love of Ease and Rest*' — these are the Affections which relate to the private System, and which constitute whatever we call '*Interestedness* or *Self-love*', and which, if 'they are moderate, and within certain bounds, are neither injurious to social Life, nor a hindrance to Virtue', but when carried too far turn into '*Cowardice.—Revengefulness.—Luxury.— Avarice.—Vanity and Ambition.—Sloth*', becoming 'vitious and ill, with respect to human Society' (139–40). What is of especially economic interest is further elaborated:

> Now as to that Passion which is esteem'd peculiarly *interesting*; as having for its Aim the Possession of Wealth, and what we call a *Settlement* or *Fortune* in the World: If the Regard towards this kind be moderate, and in a reasonable degree; if it occasions no passionate Pursuit, nor raises any ardent Desire or Appetite, there is nothing in

this Case which is not compatible with Virtue, and even sutable and beneficial to Society. The publick as well as private System is advanc'd by the Industry, which this Affection excites. But if it grows at length into a real *Passion*; the Injury and Mischief it does the Publick, is not greater than that which it does to the Person himself. Such a one is in reality a Self-oppressor, and lies heavier on himself than he can ever do on Mankind.

(155)

Shaftesbury also recognized instances of virtuous self-interest *beyond the norm*: 'whatsoever is the occasion or means of more affectionately uniting a rational Creature to his PART in Society, and causes him to prosecute the Publick Good, or Interest of his Species, with more Zeal and Affection than ordinary; is undoubtedly the cause of more than ordinary Virtue in such a person' (Shaftesbury 1714a: 75). The requirement for a proper 'balance of the affections' – in Smith's rendition (above, p. 33) – does not seem to bother Shaftesbury in such a case, perhaps because his primary concern is excessive *selfishness*, and the degenerative effects of excessive 'passion' and 'ardour': 'A *separate End* and *Interest* must be every day more strongly form'd in us; *Generous Views* and *Motives* laid aside: And the more we are thus sensibly disjoin'd every day from Society and our Fellows; the worse Opinion we shall have of those uniting Passions which bind us in strict Alliance and Amity with others. Upon these Terms we must of course endeavour to silence and suppress our natural and good Affections: since they are such as wou'd carry us to the Good of Society, against what we fondly conceive to be our private Good and Interest' (162). It is an important feature of Shaftesbury's account that virtuous self-interest, entailing a conscious concern with the public welfare, was prone to be undermined in favour of 'selfishness' by 'zealous' religious doctrine regarding reward and punishment in a future life:

> It may be consider'd withal; That, in this religious sort of Discipline, the Principle of *Self-Love*, which is naturally so prevailing in us, being no-way moderated or restrain'd, but rather improv'd and made stronger every day, by the exercise of the Passions in a Subject of more extended Self-Interest; there may be reason to apprehend lest the Temper of this kind shou'd extend it-self in general thro all the Parts of Life. For if the Habit be such as to occasion, in every particular, a stricter Attention to Self-Good, and private Interest; it must insensibly diminish the Affections towards Publick Good, or the Interest of Society… and introduce a certain Narrowness of Spirit, which (as some pretend) is peculiarly observable in the devout Persons and Zealots of almost every religious Persuasion.

(58)

'As some pretend' is not to be taken too seriously, since Shaftesbury himself warns against an 'over-sollicitous regard to private Good expected from [God]' and a 'violent Affection towards *private* Good', attitudes which fortunately were not encouraged by 'the generality of civiliz'd or refin'd Worshippers' (58–9). In his *Advice to an Author* Shaftesbury lamented that the typical religious instruction of the young turning on the Catechism, had damaged the chances for genuine educational progress at later ages: 'whatever Manner in Philosophy happens to bear the least resemblance to that of *Catechism*, cannot, I'm persuaded, of it self, prove very inviting. Such a smart way of questioning our selves in our Youth, has made our Manhood more averse to the expostulatory Discipline' (Shaftesbury 1710: 148).

2.3 The 'moral sense' or 'sense of right and wrong'

I have demonstrated Shaftesbury's perception of virtue and virtuous motivation as the individual's concern for public welfare. If he had been asked, 'how do you know?' he would doubtless have replied 'my moral sense tells me so'. But before elaborating the reduction of the moral sense to concern for the public interest I shall consider Shaftesbury's moral sense *as interpreted by Bentham*. His reading has some substance insofar as Shaftesbury indeed draws a parallel between the physical senses – assumed silently to be in full working order – and the moral, the latter sensitive to the ethical status attaching to observed actions and character with no particular reference to the general good:

> The case is the same in the *mental* or *moral* Subjects, as in the ordinary *Bodys*, or common Subjects of *Sense*. The Shapes, Motions, Colours, and Proportions of these latter being presented to our Eye; there necessarily results a Beauty or Deformity, according to the different Measure, Arrangement and Disposition of their several Parts. So in *Behaviour* and *Actions*, when presented to our Understanding, there must be found, of necessity, an apparent Difference, according to the Regularity or Irregularity of the Subjects.
>
> The MIND, which is Spectator or Auditor of *other Minds*, cannot be without its *Eye* and *Ear*, so as to discern Proportion, distinguish Sound, and scan each Sentiment or Thought which comes before it. It can let nothing escape its Censure. It feels the Soft and Harsh, the Agreeable and Disagreeable, in the Affections; and finds a *Foul* and *Fair*, a *Harmonious* and a *Dissonant*, as really and truly here, as in any musical Numbers, or in the outward Forms or Representations of sensible Things. Nor can it withhold its *Admiration* and *Extasy*, its *Aversion and Scorn*, any more in what relates to one than to the other of these Subjects. So that to deny the common natural Sense of a SUBLIME and BEAUTIFUL in Things, will appear an *Affectation* merely to any one who considers duly of this Affair.
> (Shaftesbury 1714a: 28–9).

Shaftesbury refers readers to a convenient summary at the close of *The Moralists* as printed with the *Inquiry*:

> No sooner the Eye opens upon *Figures*, the Ear to *Sounds*, then straight the *Beautiful* results, and *Grace* and *Harmony* are known and acknowledg'd. No sooner are ACTIONS view'd, no sooner the *human Affections* and *Passions* discerned (and they are most of 'em as soon discern'd as felt) than straight *an inward* EYE distinguishes, and sees *the Fair* and *Shapely*, the *Amiable* and *Admirable*, apart from the *Deform'd*, the *Foul*, the *Odious*, or the *Despicable*. How is it possible therefore not to own "That as these *Distinctions* have their Foundation *in Nature*, the Discernment it-self is *natural*, and from NATURE *alone*?"
>
> (Shaftesbury 1714b: 414–15).

There are remarks aplenty in the *Inquiry* which imply a moral sense as an index of ethical status regarding 'right' and 'wrong' without explicit reference to the general interest. For example, one lacking a sense of Right and Wrong would have 'no *Liking* or *Dislike* of Manners; no Admiration, or Love of any thing as morally Good; nor Hatred of any thing as morally ill; be it ever so unnatural and deform'd' (Shaftesbury1714a: 41–2). That such a sense is 'as natural to us as *natural Affection* it-self, and being a first principle in our Constitution and Make' assured its resilience, implying that 'there is no speculative Opinion, Persuasion or Belief, which is capable *immediately* or *directly* to exclude or destroy it' (44). The moral sense is identified at one juncture with what is 'Fair, Noble, and Deserving' (46). And we encounter general references to 'the truly just and good' (50) and to '*Goodness it-self*, or any good and deserving Object, worthy of Love and Admiration for its own sake; such as GOD is universally acknowleg'd, or at least by the generality of civiliz'd or refin'd Worshippers' (59).

2.4 The moral sense and the public interest

Reliance on formulations such as the aforementioned which do not allude directly to the public good may have lead Bentham to render Shaftesbury's 'moral sense' as evidencing hostility towards utilitarianism, and Mill to also perceive him as an opponent. But the fact is that, when engaged in specific application, Shaftesbury does not treat 'what is natural and honest' as some open-ended category in the manner of formal statements, but reduces this to concern for the social, public or general good, or the public or general interest – all terms that he used – fully in line with the perception of 'virtue' I outlined above in Section 2.2. This becomes apparent when we follow Shaftesbury as he descends from the upper stratosphere to provide actual content to the 'good and virtuous', specifying that '*Temperance, Modesty, Candour, Benignity*' (Shaftesbury 1714a: 62–3) all – except for the last – entail typically *personal* qualities; and also *other-regarding* or social affections including '*Kindness, Gratitude, Bounty, or Compassion*' (39). More elaborately: 'Tis impossible to suppose a mere sensible Creature originally so ill-constituted, and unnatural, as that from the moment he comes to be try'd by sensible Objects, he shou'd have no one good Passion towards his Kind, no Foundation either of Pity, Love, Kindness, or social Affection. 'Tis full as impossible to conceive, that a rational Creature coming first to be try'd by rational Objects, and receiving into his Mind the Images or Representations of Justice, Generosity, Gratitude, or other Virtue, shou'd have no *Liking* of these, or *Dislike* of their Contrarys' (43). As noted, to these 'Benignity' should be added. 'Benevolence' also appears in the *Moralists* (Shaftesbury 1714b: 334.) While Shaftesbury does not use the term 'sympathy', so prevalent in the later literature, the notion itself is implicit in the range of terms he does use.

Shaftesbury's repeated representation of the moral sense or 'sense of right and wrong' as dictating and approving a concern for the public interest implies a predominant concern with the second category of affections. We have, for example, encountered the affirmation that 'we call any Creature Worthy or Virtuous, when it can have the Notion of a publick Interest...' (Shaftesbury 1714a: 31; above, p. 34); the 'Natural Sense of Right and Wrong' relates specifically to '*the Notion of what is* good *or ill in the Species, or Society*' and we are assured that to 'the Reality of such a *Good* and *Ill*, no rational Creature can possibly be insensible. Every-one discerns and owns a publick Interest, and is conscious of what affects his Fellowship or Community' (41). With regard to the 'social passion' as essential to the moral sense we read: 'Let us suppose a Creature, who wanting Reason, and being unable to reflect, has, notwithstanding, many good Qualitys and Affections; as Love to his Kind, Courage, Gratitude or Pity. 'Tis certain that if you give to this Creature a reflecting Faculty, it will at the same instant approve of Gratitude, Kindness, and Pity; be taken with any shew or representation of the social Passion, and think nothing more amiable than this, or more odious than the contrary. And this is *to be capable of* VIRTUE, *and to have a sense of* RIGHT *and* WRONG' (53). In some instances passages which take for granted a non-specific 'knowledge of right and wrong' proceed to indicate that the 'natural affection by which the Species or Society is upheld' is actually presupposed: 'And thus we find how far Worth and Virtue depend on a knowledge of *Right* and *Wrong*, and on a use of Reason, sufficient to secure a right application of the Affections; that nothing horrid or unnatural, nothing unexemplary, nothing destructive of that natural Affection by which the Species or Society is upheld, may, on any account, or thro any Principle or Notion of Honour or Religion, be at any time affected or prosecuted as a good and proper Object of Esteem' (35). Similarly, in a general context dealing with *corrupted* ethical evaluations concern for the public interest is nonetheless specifically designated: 'Thus the several Motions, Inclinations, Passions, Dispositions, and consequent Carriage and Behaviour of Creatures in the various Parts of Life, being in several Views or Perspectives represented to the Mind, which readily discerns the Good and Ill towards the Species or Publick; there arises a new Trial or Exercise of the Heart: which must either rightly and soundly affect what is just and right, and disaffect what is contrary; or, corruptly affect what is ill, and disaffect what is worthy and good' (30–1).

The social dimension is particularly conspicuous in the religious context where 'the Good of our Species or Publick' is designated to be the 'End or Aim' of a true 'Sense of Right and Wrong':

> ... nothing can more highly contribute to the fixing of right Apprehensions, and a sound Judgment or Sense of right and Wrong, than to believe a God who is ever, and on all accounts, represented such as to be actually a true Model and Example of the most exact Justice, and highest Goodness and Worth. Such a View of divine Providence and Bounty, extended to *All*, and express'd in a constant good Affection to *the Whole*, must of necessity engage us, within our Compass and Sphere, to act by a like Principle and Affection. And having once the Good of our Species or Publick in view, as our End or Aim, 'tis impossible we shou'd be misguided by any means to a false Apprehension or Sense of Right and Wrong.
> (Shaftesbury 1714a: 51)

In discussing the dangers of religious fanaticism the focus is again placed on the sense of right and wrong as designating the public good as proper 'end or aim'. Here the specific danger is that religion, if excessively 'zealous', tends to encourage 'selfishness' and a correspondingly diminished concern for social interest, a matter we encountered at the close of Section 2.2.

A particularly striking extract binds the moral sense with concern for the public interest by identifying the 'natural' and 'social' affections, and reinforcing our understanding that the character accorded *virtue* allows for, indeed emphasizes, the satisfaction deriving from enhancement of public welfare considering the individual's dependency on society: 'How wretched must it be ... for MAN, of all other Creatures, to lose that *Sense*, and *Feeling*, which is proper to him *as a* MAN, and sutable to his Character, and Genius? How unfortunate must it be for a Creature, whose dependence on Society is greater than any others, to lose that *natural Affection* by which he is prompted to the Good and Interest of his Species, and Community?' (Shaftesbury 1714a: 136). Shaftesbury concludes strongly as we have noted earlier: 'Thus it may appear, how much NATURAL AFFECTION is predominant ... how essential to that regular Motion and Course of our Affections, on which our Happiness and Self-enjoyment so immediately depend' (139; cited above, p. 35). That man is naturally sociable is a highly pertinent consideration: 'Nor will any-one deny that [the] Affection of a Creature towards the Good of the Species or common Nature, is as *proper* and *natural* to him as it is to any Organ, Part or Member of an Animal-Body, or mere Vegetable, to work in its known Course and regular way of Growth' (78).[5]

Now even though the formal identification of the moral sense with the physical senses, which attributes to the former an in-born capacity (on a par with the physical senses) to distinguish good from evil without specific reference to the notion of virtue as benevolent or other-regarding concern (see above Section 2.3), it is likely that such an ability was extended to virtue thus understood. This seems to have been Viner's view since he identifies Shaftesbury's moral sense as 'an innate capacity for distinguishing virtue from vice' presuming that 'virtue consisted solely in the exercise of benevolence for its own sake, *without regard to temporal or future rewards*' (Viner 1972: 68–9; emphasis added). This points away from the Lockean perspective. And there can be little doubt that Shaftesbury stressed benevolent rather than anti-social sentiments as 'natural' to man – this matter takes on high significance considering John Brown's objections to Shaftesbury's allegedly naive idealism – so that 'the wrong Sense or false Imagination of Right and Wrong' could only reflect 'the Force of Custom and Education in opposition to Nature' (Shaftesbury 1714a: 45–6) rather than any innate tendency. (Shaftesbury did not believe that *atheism* could, at least 'directly', be blamed; 'corrupt religion or superstition' was the greater danger.)

This is, however, only half the picture. The psychological faculty – however any defect in its operation might have originated – was deemed fit to approve ethical conduct only 'in some measure', and even then only in 'disinterested Cases': 'In these vagrant Characters or Pictures of *Manners*, which the Mind of necessity figures to it-self, and carries still about with it, the Heart cannot possibly remain neutral; but constantly takes part one way or other. However false or corrupt it be within it-self, it finds the Difference, as to Beauty, and Comeliness, between one *Heart* and another, one *Turn of Affection*, one *Behaviour*, one *Sentiment* and another; and accordingly, in all disinterested Cases, must approve in some measure of what is natural and honest, and disapprove of what is dishonest and corrupt' (Shaftesbury1714a: 30). This entails a defective moral sense of a general order. That Shaftesbury also recognized defectiveness pertaining specifically to virtue as *benevolence* is clear from the allowance that – despite a concern lest the inculcation of the doctrine of reward and punishment in a future life encourages 'selfishness' (above, Section 2.2) – 'in many Circumstances' concern for the Next World might serve a good purpose: 'notwithstanding the Injury which the Principle of Virtue may possibly suffer, by the Increase of the selfish Passion … 'tis certain, on the other side, that the Principle of *Fear of future Punishment*, and *Hope of future Reward*, how mercenary or servile soever it may be accounted, is yet, in many Circumstances, a great Advantage, Security, and Support of *Virtue*', by opposing various 'Passions' opposed to the ' real Sense of Right and Wrong, a real good Affection towards the Species or Society' (Shaftesbury 1714a: 60).[6] Shaftesbury refers in the *The Moralists*, as early as 1709, to future reward and punishment encouraging motivation directed at the 'Good of Mankind and of the World' (Shaftesbury 1714b: 273; 1709: 89). And the positive effects of reward and punishment on motivation directed towards furthering the public good are extended in the *Inquiry* to the secular domain: 'Thus in a *civil* STATE or PUBLICK, we see that a virtuous Administration, and an equal and just Distribution of Rewards and Punishments, is of the highest service; not only by restraining the Vitious, and forcing them to act usefully to Society; but by making Virtue to be apparently the Interest of every-one, so as to remove all Prejudices against it, create a fair reception for it, and lead Men into that path which afterwards they cannot easily quit' (Shaftesbury 1714a: 63).

The moral sense alone was thus not wholly reliable as an assurance of ethical or socially-motivated conduct. Shaftesbury's recognition of the need for reinforcement by reference to an afterlife promising reward for good conduct and punishment for bad takes Shaftesbury close to the theological utilitarians, whose stance was maintained by Locke, albeit not in the strictest sense. Carey however places much emphasis on Shaftesbury as an opponent of Locke regarding the matter of 'innateness' and of the view that 'morality depended on some form of law and method of enforcement', the most important being the divine law which 'had the backing of rewards and punishments in the afterlife to make it effective' (Carey 2006: 98, 116–19, 129–30), although he recognizes that 'Shaftesbury did allow some role for rewards and punishments ... when things went wrong and people needed to be recalled to virtue' (139). That Shaftesbury was uncomfortable with what is in effect a concession to Locke is suggested by his insistence that in the *ideal* case reinforcement of this order is not required: 'whatever be decided as to a future Life, or the Rewards and Punishments of hereafter; he who, as a sound *Theist*, believes a reigning Mind, sovereign in Nature, and ruling all things with the highest perfection of Goodness, as well as of Wisdom and Power, must necessarily believe Virtue to be naturally good and advantageous' (Shaftesbury1714a: 72); and a summary statement makes no formal mention of concern with the hereafter although it may be silently intended: 'whatever is the occasion or means of more affectionately uniting a rational Creature with his PART in Society, and causes him to prosecute the Publick Good, or Interest of his Species, with more Zeal and Affection than ordinary; is undoubtedly the cause of more than ordinary Virtue to such a Person' (74–5). Our final evaluation of the Locke–Shaftesbury nexus thus depends on an essentially empirical evaluation of typical conduct.

A further detail requires clarification. In *Sensus Communis* Shaftesbury questions the common notion that '*Interest governs the World*', on the grounds that '*Passion, Humour, Caprice, Zeal, Faction*, and a thousand other Springs, which are counter to *Self-Interest*, have as considerable a part in the Movements of this Machine ... There are more Wheels and *Counter-Poises* in this Engine than are easily imagin'd. 'Tis of too complex a kind, to fall under one simple View, or be explain'd thus briefly in a word or two. The Studiers of this *Mechanism* must have a very partial Eye, to overlook all other Motions besides those of the lowest and narrowest Compass' (Shaftesbury 1999 [1711]: 54). This formulation reduces the weight accorded to *self-regarding* motivation in practice, but it also implicitly does the same to *other-regarding* motivation and thus the key notion insisted upon by Shaftesbury of a natural tendency towards disinterested benevolence since there are numerous forms of conduct touching on the irrational which reflect neither the one nor the other.

I close with a problem posed by a passage in *The Moralists* which seems to conflict with the aforementioned denial that 'Interest governs the World' by representing rational calculation – maximizing behaviour – as the rule. The context relates to 'Philosophy' understood as 'the Study of Happiness': '*This*, still, is PHILOSOPHY; "To inquire Where, and in what respect one may be most a *Loser*; Which are the greatest *Gains*, the most profitable *Exchanges*"; since every thing in this World goes by *Exchange*. Nothing is had for nothing' (Hutcheson 1714b: 439). The text continues to apply the rule to the quest for favour, interest, honours, riches, learning and accomplishments and much else, what Viner designates 'the routine business of life' (Viner 1972: 70). This too seems to undermine the weight placed by Shaftesbury upon other-regarding sentiment as a primary natural force.

2.5 Summary and conclusion

The function of the 'moral sense' for Shaftesbury is to reinforce the value judgment that virtue is to be understood as concern for the public interest. His adherence to the notion of a moral sense does not amount to a refutation of utilitarianism such as Bentham attributed to him, for his utilitarianism is reflected in the commendation he affords to other-regarding sentiment, in effect *sympathy*, precisely as with Locke and later with Hutcheson and Hume. Had Shaftesbury been asked *why* he himself maintains this perception he would doubtless have responded 'my moral sense' tells me so. But what Shaftesbury says of the moral sense is often assertive and rhetorical, and, in any event, he allows that the moral sense may be corrupted by faulty cultural influences such that the notion of virtue itself remains intact without its assistance.

Whether Shaftesbury himself realized how much he had conceded in his publications to a Lockean ethical utilitarianism – even extending to reinforcement of the motive to proper conduct from concern with an afterlife – is unlikely considering the sharp hostility towards Locke expressed in a letter of 3 June 1709, only a few months after the publication of the *Moralists* with its (silent) concession to Locke regarding the prospect of future reward and punishment encouraging motivation directed at the 'Good of Mankind and of the World' – virtue rendered very much a matter of prudential calculation – where Shaftesbury objects that Locke 'struck at all fundamentals, threw order and virtue out of the world, and made the very ideas of these (which are the same as those of God) *unnatural* and without foundation in our minds' (Rand 1900: 403). Shaftesbury's complaint extends to the misuse of the term 'innateness':

> *Innate* is a word he poorly plays upon; the right word, though unused, is *unnatural*. For what has birth or the progress of the foetus out of the womb to do in this case? The question is not about the time the ideas entered, or the moment that one body came out of the other, but whether the constitution of man be such that, being adult and grown up, at such and such a time, sooner or later (no matter when), the idea and sense of order, administration, and a God, will not infallibly, inevitably, necessarily spring up in him.

In any event, it would seem fair to qualify Carey's contention that 'Shaftesbury provided a powerful and influential … alternative to Locke' (Carey 2006: 99).

This account of Shaftesbury also shows that he does not hold self-interest as such, but only *anti-social* 'selfishness', to be inconsistent with virtue understood as other-regarding concern. Accordingly, he applauds the role played by self-regarding interests in economic development, although such activity would not be considered 'virtuous' unless a desirable impact on social welfare was actually *intended*. This position however is in line with that of Locke. While Locke maintained that the ethical merit of other-regarding consideration is not weakened by expected benefit, it would be consistent for him to accept that socially-beneficial consequences resulting from profit-seeking business activity does not justify according moral credit to an agent since those consequences are wholly incidental to the agent's objective.

Notes

1 An edition of *An Inquiry Concerning Virtue or Merit*, unauthorized by Shaftesbury, was published by John Toland in 1699. For the status of this version, see Walford's editorial introduction to Shaftesbury 1977 (1699); and Gill 2006: 83. After 1705 Shaftesbury reworked the *Inquiry* and completed *The Moralists; a Philosophical Rhapsody*, the latter published in January 1709. An authorized edition containing both works comprising Volume II of *Characteristicks of Men, Manners, Opinions, Times* appeared in 1711, and a revised second edition in 1714 after Shaftesbury's death the previous year.
2 In John Brown's apt rendition of this formulation, virtue consists in 'a perfect Conformity of our Affections and Actions with this supreme Sense and Symmetry of Things' (Brown 1752: 114).
3 Hume made the point effectively. Philosophers had been 'led astray' when they 'found, that every act of virtue or friendship was attended with a secret pleasure; whence they concluded, that friendship and virtue could not be disinterested. But the fallacy of this is obvious. The virtuous sentiment or passion produces the pleasure, and does not arise from it. I feel a pleasure in doing good to my friend, because I love him; but I do not love him for the sake of that pleasure' (Hume 1994 [1777]: 85–6). An edition of the *Essays* appeared in 1742.
4 This may perhaps be seen as an implication of the rule: 'Do unto others…' so much stressed by Locke.
5 In *Sensus Communis, an Essay on the Freedom of Wit and Humour*, first published in 1709, what is designated the 'herding principle' is said to easily account for the establishment of civil government and society, disputing those who made them appear as 'a kind of invention and creature of art' (Shaftesbury 1999 [1711]: 51–2).
6 The unauthorized 1699 edition of the *Inquiry* already contains this passage (Shaftesbury 1977 [1699]: 36).

References

Brown, J. 1752. *Essays on the Characteristics of the Earl of Shaftesbury*. Third edition. London: C. Davis.
Carey, D. 2006. *Locke, Shaftesbury, and Hutcheson*. Cambridge: Cambridge University Press.
Gill, M.B. 2006. *The British Moralists on Human Nature and the Birth of Secular Ethics*, Cambridge: Cambridge University Press
Hume, D. 1994 (1777). 'Of the Dignity or Meanness of Human Nature', *Essays Moral Political and Literary*, ed. E. F. Miller. Indianapolis: Liberty Fund: 80–86.

Kaye, F.B. 1924. Introduction to Bernard Mandeville, *The Fable of the Bees*. Oxford: Clarendon Press: xvii–cxlvi.

Rand, B. 1900. *The Life, Unpublished Letters, and Philosophical Regimen of Anthony, Earl of Shaftesbury*, ed. Benjamin Rand. London: Swan Sonnenschein.

Shaftesbury, A. 1709. *The Moralists; a Philosophical Rhapsody*. London: John Wyat.

Shaftesbury, A. 1714a. *An Inquiry Concerning Virtue, or Merit*, in *Characteristicks of Men, Manners, Opinions, Times*, Vol. II. Second ed. London: 5–176

Shaftesbury, A. 1714b. *The Moralists; a Philosophical Rhapsody*, in *Characteristicks of Men, Manners, Opinions, Times*, Vol. II. Second ed. London: 181–443.

Shaftesbury, A. 1977 (1699). *An Inquiry Concerning Virtue, or Merit*, with an Introduction and selection of materials from Toland's 1699 edition [unauthorized], ed. David Walford. Manchester: Manchester University Press.

Shaftesbury, A. 1999 (1711). *Sensus Communis, an Essay on the Freedom of Wit and Humour*. In *Characteriticks of Men, Manners, Opinions, Times*, ed. L.E. Klein. Cambridge: Cambridge University Press: 29–69.

Smith, A. 1976 (1759). *The Theory of Moral Sentiments*, edited by David D. Raphael and A.L. Macfie. Oxford: Clarendon Press.

Viner, J. 1972. *The Role of Providence in the Social Order: An Essay in Intellectual History*. Philadelphia: American Philosophical Society.

Walford, D. 1977. Editorial Introduction to Shaftesbury 1977 (1699): vii-xix.

3 Two Shaftesbury critics
Bernard Mandeville and John Brown

3.1 Introduction

Chapter Three concerns two of Shaftesbury's critics: Bernard Mandeville and John Brown. I give equal billing to Bernard Mandeville, even though he is rarely mentioned by Mill in his essays on ethics (see Chapter 15). A convenient formulation of Mandeville's understanding of Shaftesbury is given in an essay added to the second edition (1723) of the *Fable of the Bees* entitled 'A Search into the Nature of Society' directed, primarily, against the notion of man as essentially 'virtuous' and so concerned with the public interest:

> The Generality of Moralists and Philosophers have hitherto agreed that there could be no Virtue without Self-denial; but a late Author, who is now much read by Men of Sense, is of a contrary opinion, and imagines that Men without any Trouble or Violence upon themselves may be naturally Virtuous ... This Noble Writer (for it is the Lord *Shaftesbury* I mean in his Characteristicks) Fancies, that as Man is made for Society, so he ought to be born with a kind Affection to the whole, of which he is a part, and a Propensity to seek the Welfare of it. In a pursuance of this Supposition, he calls every Action perform'd with regard to the Publick Good, Virtuous; and all Selfishness, wholly excluding such a Regard, Vice.
> (Mandeville 1924 [1732] 1: 323–4)[1]

Mandeville rejects such notions regarding human nature as unfortunately 'not true' and 'inconsistent with our daily Experience' (324). He goes on to call for recognition 'not only that the good and amiable Qualities of Man are not those that make him beyond other Animals a sociable Creature; but moreover that it would be utterly impossible either to raise any Multitudes into a Populous, Rich and Flourishing Nation, or when so rais'd, to keep and maintain them in that Condition, without the assistance of *what we call Evil* both Natural and Moral' (325; emphasis added).

Now Mandeville errs by attributing to Shaftesbury an unrealistic faith in the widespread actuality of pure altruism, rigorously perceived as in no way linked to personal benefit. Sympathetic behaviour for Shaftesbury, as we have seen in Chapter 2, did in fact turn on expected personal advantage (largely mundane since the promise of reward and punishment in an after-life is played down). Mandeville in effect has set up a straw man to attack.

This chapter shall also review Mandeville's perception of an obligation to save a child from death as reflecting a wish *to avoid the pain caused by failing to act,* such 'painful sense' implying an other-regarding or sympathetic natural sentiment on the part of the observer, the intervention providing him or her with personal satisfaction and to that extent rendering the intervention ethically neutral. Yet while attaching the designation of 'ethical' to conduct required the absence of all *personal advantage*, this was only 'strictly speaking' and Mandeville approaches Shaftesbury by admitting that pity bears *'the greatest Resemblance to Virtue'*, indeed, that it is a widespread characteristic, averring that 'without a considerable mixture of it the Society could hardly subsist'. In so doing he is conceding more than perhaps he realized.[2] And he is right to feel uncomfortable since the personal satisfaction derived from other-regarding conduct which is said to undermine the 'ethical' character of such conduct is far removed from what is normally implied by personal advantage. Kaye thus exaggerates when he draws a sharp distinction between Shaftesbury for whom, he says, 'the coincidence of public and private good was due to an enlightened benevolence, whereas [for] Mandeville it was the result of narrow self-seeking – Mandeville believing men completely and inevitably egoistic, Shaftesbury thinking them endowed with altruistic and gregarious feeling' (Kaye 1924: lxxiii). Viner insisted against Kaye that Mandeville's profession of an extreme rigorist doctrine whereby whatever is not virtue is vice was not sincere for otherwise 'the whole satirical structure of his argument, its provocative tone, its obvious fun-making gusto, would be incomprehensible, and there would be manifest inconsistency between his satirical purposes and his purposes as a writer', expressing a 'rigorism too austere and too grim ... for the ordinary run of orthodox Anglicans or Catholics of his time ... for the Calvinists, and for the Jansenists' (Viner 1958: 335–7). The account given here therefore brings to the fore Mandeville's own admission that while acts motivated by pity might not merit the designation 'ethical' because they are tainted by self-interest, nevertheless pity bears *'the greatest Resemblance to Virtue'* a fudging of the issue reflecting appreciation that the rigorist view is untenable.

John Brown – like so many later readers – was unaware of Mandeville's concession, and presumed that the public affections in general are for Mandeville selfish without qualification and thus wholly at odds with Shaftesbury's idealisation of human nature – again his alleged idealisation. Brown, critical though he was of Shaftesbury thus interpreted, nonetheless himself brought to the fore Shaftesbury's utilitarian concern in practical application with the public welfare – very much in line with my own account of Shaftesbury in Chapter 2 – although he could not desist from ascribing to him an essentially incoherent position. In brief, Brown's main objection to Shaftesbury is not – as Mill was later to maintain – that Shaftesbury rejected the utilitarian standard of virtue but that he accepted it in an oblique manner by representing the moral sense as the ultimate standard governing what is right and wrong whereas his actual reference point with respect to virtue is enhancement of social happiness. I shall show furthermore that Brown, like Mandeville, mocked Shaftesbury's alleged faith in the actuality of altruism.

3.2 Bernard Mandeville

Mandeville of course had much to say in the *Fable of the Bees* of the self-regarding basis for sympathetic conduct which excluded strictly-defined altruism, namely other-regarding conduct wholly independent of personal advantage of any kind to the actor. There is in the first place the commonplace, that 'in the Choice of Things Men must be determin'd by the Perception they have of Happiness; and no Person can commit or set about an Action, which at that then present time seems not to be the best to him' (Mandeville 1924 [1729]: 178). Of greater substance is the essay 'An Enquiry into the Origin of Moral Virtue' which takes for granted that since sympathetic or other-regarding affections are foreign to most of mankind, private and social goods could only be reconciled by *bribing* men to deviate from their basic selfish instinct. Thus Mandeville asserts that '[a]ll untaught Animals are only solicitous of pleasing themselves, and naturally follow the bent of their own Inclinations, without considering the good or harm that from their being pleased will accrue to others'; that 'no Creature besides [Man] can ever be made sociable'; that 'Lawgivers and other wise Men, that have laboured for the Establishment of Society, have endeavor'd … to make the people they were to govern, believe, that it was more beneficial for every body to conquer than indulge his Appetites, and much better to mind the Publick than what seem'd his private Interest', and sought effective means to induce men to 'disapprove of their natural Inclinations, or prefer the Good of others to their own' (Mandeville 1924 [1732]: 41–2). Specifically: 'Those that have undertaken to civilize Mankind … thoroughly examin'd all the Strength and Frailties of our Nature, and observing that none were either so savage as not to be charm'd with Praise, or so despicable as patiently to bear Contempt, *justly concluded*, that Flattery must be the most powerful Argument that cou'd be used to Human Creatures' (42–3; emphasis added). His overall conclusion from an excursion into conjectural history is 'that it was not any Heathen Religion or other Idolatrous Superstition, that first put Man upon crossing his Appetites and subduing his dearest Inclinations, but the skilful Management of wary Politicians; and the nearer we search into human Nature, the more we shall be convinced, that the Moral Virtues are the Political Offspring which Flattery begot upon Pride' (51). It is to be emphasized here that *'Self-denial and Publick-spiritedness'* are taken for granted as constituting the *Moral Virtues,* however they may originate – whether artificially, as Mandeville insisted, or naturally (45).

Now John Brown condemned Mandeville for irreligion by conveying a 'pernicious Falsehood' which glorified private vice: 'For if *private Vices* be *public Benefits*, then private *Virtues* are public *Mischiefs*', so that (for example) 'if all people were strictly honest, half the Smiths of the Nation would want Employment' (Brown 1752: 158, 146, 152). This sort of charge had been made out against Mandeville in 1723 in a 'Presentment of the Grand Jury for the County of Middlesex' as part of a condemnation of various books and pamphlets allegedly directed against the Church representing the Fable as a 'public nuisance' (Kaye 1924: xxxiv). Brown might have been less critical had he taken into account Mandeville's 'A Vindication of the Book', an immediate response to the Middlesex Grand Jury later added to the 1732 edition, clarifying that the *Fable* was not intended as a commendation of private vice. Here Mandeville sets out by reproducing an explanation of his intentions by the choice of title, which he had already provided in his essay 'A Search into the Nature of Society' printed at the close of the first volume of the *Fable*: 'that neither the Friendly Qualities and kind Affections that are natural to Man, nor the real Virtues he is capable of acquiring by Reason and Self-Denial' – these, it should be carefully noted, he does not dispute insisting only that such kind affections were so uncommon that they could not be relied upon as the foundation of societal relations – 'are the Foundation of Society; but that what we call Evil in this World, Moral as well as Natural, is the grand Principle that makes us sociable Creatures; the solid Basis, the Life and Support of all Trades and Employments without Exception: That there we must look for the true Origin of all Arts and Sciences; and that the Moment Evil ceases, the Society must be spoiled, if not totally dissolved' (Mandeville 1924 [1732]: 369, 402). His critics had simply failed to realize what should have been self-evident, that he intended to convey, dramatically, the simple dictum that Necessity is the Mother of Invention, 'evil' designating something *lacking* which deficiency encourages the effort and inventiveness required to overcome it to the benefit of society and social cohesion: 'that every Defect, every Want was an Evil; that on the Multiplicity of those Wants depended all those mutual Services which the individual Members of a Society pay to each other; and that consequenctly, the greater Variety there was of Wants, the larger the Number of Individuals might find their private Interest in labouring for *the good of others*, and united together, compose one Body' (402–3; emphasis added). Mandeville insists that his theme was in no sense at odds with 'Probity and Virtue' since the 'good of others' – or the 'common good' – is designated as the social end (404–5).

A similar line appears in the Preface to the *Fable* in a protest against 'the wrong Inferences' drawn from the title that he provided a justification for Vice: 'When I assert, that Vices are inseparable from great and potent Societies, and that it is impossible their Wealth and Grandeur should subsist without, I do not say that the particular Members of them who are guilty of any should not be continually reprov'd, or not be punish'd for them when they grow into Crimes' (Mandeville 1924 [1732]: 10). By 'continual' reproof is implied reproof of those guilty of vice *even if such conduct should enhance public welfare* (and deserve punishment apparently notwithstanding resultant social benefits, should vice extend to criminal acts). Motivation matters for ethical approval regardless of outcome.

The foregoing theme is confirmed by Mandeville's assertion whereby 'when we pronounce Actions good or evil, we only regard the Hurt or Benefit the Society receives from them, and not the Person who commits them' (Mandeville 1924 [1732]: 244). This cannot be read as indicating unconcern with personal ethics, in effect with motivation, for we know from 'A Search into the Nature of Society' and 'An Inquiry into the Origin of Moral Virtue' that 'probity and virtue' relating to personal qualities are a prime issue, virtue being identified with *other-regarding* concern – recall that Moral Virtues, however they originate, comprise 'Self-denial and Publickspiritedness' – suggesting a Mandevillian *ethical utilitarianism* consistent with that of Shaftesbury and indeed of Brown.

Here I note Kaye's position that:

> Mandeville decided upon the public results of private actions according to utilitarian standards. That which is useful, that which is productive of national prosperity and happiness, he called a benefit.[3] But he judged the private actions themselves according to an anti-utilitarian scheme, whereby conduct was evaluated, not by its consequences, but by the motive which gave it rise ... the actual effect of conduct on human happiness made no difference.
>
> (Kaye 1924: xlviii–xlix)

My only qualification is to insist that since by morally-praiseworthy motivation Mandeville intended specifically *concern for the public good* it is unhelpful to refer to such judgment of private actions 'according to an anti-utilitarian scheme' – it is very much a scheme reflecting the core of utilitarian ethics. Again we may conclude that, since it is intention that counts, should the act in question fail (by no fault of the actor) to yield desirable social consequences the morality of the act would not be diminished.

We come now to further responses to critics. After alluding to so-called 'noble actions' usually motivated – as he understood it – by *self-love* with an eye to the public applause accorded such conduct, Mandeville expects to be told that 'there are noble and generous Actions that are perform'd in Silence; that Virtue being its own Reward, those who are really Good have a Satisfaction in their Consciousness of being so, which is all the Recompence they expect from the most worthy Performance ... that Pride has no hand in spurring Man on to the highest pitch of Self-denial' (Mandeville 1924 [1732]: 55–6). His response is to say that 'it is impossible to judge of a man's Performance, unless we are thoroughly acquainted with the Principle and Motive from which he acts'– a response implying that only those few for whom 'virtue' is in fact 'its own reward', without hint of selfish motivation, merit the designation *virtuous*. Again, altruism required that 'virtue is its own reward' and those who 'can part from what they value themselves' and 'from no other Motive but their Love of Goodness, perform a worthy Action in Silence' merit praise for virtuous conduct (57). Here is a thoroughgoing 'rigorist' view that virtue requires the absolute expulsion of any hint of self-interest.

Mandeville elaborates this theme by reference to *Pity*, which he represents as 'the most gentle and the least mischievous of all our Passions ... the most amiable, and bears the greatest Resemblance to Virtue; nay, without a considerable mixture of it the Society could hardly subsist' (Mandeville 1924 [1732]: 56). To allow that society depends upon the sentiment of pity which bears 'the greatest resemblance to Virtue' would seem to concede a very great deal. But it is a qualified concession: since, because 'it is an Impulse of Nature, that consults neither the publick Interest nor our own Reason, it may produce Evil as well as Good', Mandeville giving examples of situations wherein pity generates socially undesirable outcomes. For all that, the response implies that should there be individuals who *are* motivated by the public interest, we would have identified virtuous conduct. It is where the agent appeals in justifying his conduct to the '*principle*' of pity that ethical merit is undeserved, notwithstanding any social benefit resulting therefrom: 'whoever acts from it as a Principle, what good soever he may bring to the Society, has nothing to boast of but that he has indulged a Passion that has happened to be beneficial to the Publick'. And there is also to consider nature's *modus operandi* or its exertion of influence by playing upon *selfishness*: 'There is no Merit in saving an innocent Babe ready to drop into the Fire; The Action is neither good nor bad, and what Benefit soever the Infant received, we only obliged our selves; for to have seen it fall, and not strove to hinder it, *would have caused a pain*, which Self-preservation compell'd us to prevent' (Mandeville 1924 [1732]: 56; emphasis added). All this not to say that Mandeville took lightly the avoidable death of a child. Rather, he insists only that the socially-desirable life-saving action is wholly instinctive, and since conduct satisfying the instinct is a matter of 'self-preservation' – namely, the avoidance of the psychological pain expected from remaining passive – it cannot be considered as virtuous since virtue requires that the action be one 'by which Man, contrary to the impulse of Nature, should endeavour the Benefit of others, or the Conquest of his own Passions out of a rational Ambition of being good' (Mandeville 1924 [1732]: 48–9). In brief, by acting sympathetically, the agent is acting not against but in support of his very nature and so cannot be said to be acting 'virtuously' – at least if we demand a rigorous definition of virtue, as spelled out explicitly in the *Origin of Honour*: 'no Practice, no Action or good Quality, how useful or beneficial soever they may appear in themselves, can ever deserve the Name of Virtue, *strictly speaking*, where there is not a palpable Self-denial to be seen' (Mandeville 1732: vi; emphasis added). Since personal satisfaction, rather than self-denial, is derived from obeying the natural instinct to act in a sympathetic manner such actions lack an ethical dimension '*strictly speaking*', the qualification implying that Mandeville is uncomfortable with denying an 'ethical' property to other-regarding conduct tainted by even the hint of personal advantage. And that this is not reading too much into the texts is confirmed by the admission in the *Fable* itself, encountered above, that an act reflecting the sentiment of pity bears '*the greatest resemblance to Virtue*'. Mandeville draws thereby closer to Shaftesbury than he might have realized by suggesting a grey area, something akin to if not actually virtue, which thereby undermines the extreme rigorist doctrine whereby whatever is not virtue is vice. The grey area is also implicit in a rather self-contradictory contention that even in the case of those few who act with compassion 'from no other Motive but their Love of Goodness, having acquir'd more refin'd Notions of Virtue than those I have hitherto spoke of', will be found 'no small Symptoms of Pride, and the humblest Man alive must confess, that the Reward of a Virtuous Action, which is the Satisfaction that ensues upon it, consists in a certain Pleasure he procures to himself by Contemplating on his own Worth' (Mandeville 1924 [1732]: 57).

******

I now turn to briefly consider the utilitarian dimension to Mandevillian social thought. Mandeville's assertion in the *Fable* that 'when we pronounce Actions good or evil, we only regard the Hurt or Benefit the Society receives from them, and not the Person who commits them' (above, p. 51), implies a utilitarian standard and is only misleading if read to imply total unconcern with personal motivation which we have shown to be far from the case. That it is too strongly stated on Mandeville's own terms is clear from his representation of the sentiment of pity as 'an Impulse of Nature, that consults neither the publick Interest nor our own Reason' and so may produce socially undesirable as well as good outcomes, implying that individuals who *do* 'consult' the public interest would qualify as engaging in virtuous conduct – subject of course to the condition that there be no personal benefit attached – a characteristic of ethical utilitarianism holding good whatever the actual outcome may turn out to be (above, p. 51). It is also the case that the determining criterion of *criminality* entails not individual motivation but the effect upon society, such that while 'vice' might have a beneficial social function, vice that is socially harmful is a crime meriting punishment (above, p. 51), entailing as Kaye points out 'a definite application of the utilitarian standard' (above, note 3).[4] As for actions by the State, there are no ethical standards to be considered other than consequences, Kaye (1924: xl) citing as Mandeville's 'most succinct' statement of the utilitarian dimension his *A Modest Defence of Publick Stews*: 'it is the grossest Absurdity, and a perfect Contradiction, in Terms, to assert, that a *Government* may not commit Evil that Good may come of it; for, if a Publick Act, taking in all its Consequences, really produces a greater Quantity of Good, it must, and ought to be term'd a good Act, although the bare Act consider'd in itself, without the consequent Good, should be in the highest Degree wicked and unjust' ([Mandeville] 1740: 48–9). 'No beneficial Laws', he concluded, 'can be sinful'.

A word is required on the role of self-interest in assuring a desirable social outcome. In this regard Mandeville's assertion that manifestations of pity not only bear 'the greatest Resemblance to Virtue' but that 'without a considerable mixture of it *the Society could hardly subsist*' is of the first importance since it implies that other-regarding sentiment is *required* to assure community welfare. This does not support the generally-accepted view that while, for Shaftesbury, 'enlightened benevolence' accounted for the coincidence of public and private good, Mandeville related it to 'narrow self-seeking' (Kaye 1924: lxxiii–lxxiv). Narrow self-seeking would not apparently suffice. It would not suffice for a second reason, insisted upon at the very close of 'A Vindication of the Book', and strangely neglected by Kaye, explicating the expression 'private Vices, publick Benefits', namely that the desirable social outcome to be attained by reliance on private interest requires for Mandeville state intervention: 'no Man of Sincerity will question the Innocence of [the words], that has read the last Paragraph, where I take my Leave of the Reader, *and conclude with repeating the seeming Paradox, the Substance of which is advanced in the Title Page; that private Vices by the dextrous Management of a skilful Politician may be turn'd into publick Benefits*' (Mandeville 1924 [1732]: 411–12; see Chapter 6, n. 5). 'Narrow self-seeking' would *not* do the job. As Viner put the matter, Mandeville was no champion of laissez-faire (Viner 1958: 341–2).

3.3 John Brown

John Stuart Mill wrote enthusiastically of John Brown's contribution to the utility doctrine in response to Shaftesbury: 'We never saw an abler defence of the doctrine of utility than in a book written in refutation of Shaftesbury, and now little read – Brown's *Essays on the Characteristics*' (Mill 1969 [1838]: 86–7; see also Mill 1969 [1852]: 170). Mill evidently understood Shaftesbury to be positively hostile to utilitarianism, a reading opposed to our own demonstration of Shaftesbury's conception of virtue as a sympathetic concern for the public good – albeit with qualifications regarding the role of legitimate self-interest – and of the moral sense as applauding such concern. Mill's reading of Brown is, I believe, correspondingly untenable. In fact, Brown's own account provides an *ex ante* confirmation of my own reading of Shaftesbury since, *pace* Mill, his objection to Shaftesbury is not that Shaftesbury rejects the utilitarian standard of virtue but that he accepts it in too oblique a manner, by setting out with the moral sense as the ultimate standard governing what is right and wrong whereas his actual reference point with respect to virtue is concern for the public interest or social happiness:

> And first, though the *noble* Writer every where attempts to fix an original, independent, moral Beauty of Action, to which every thing is to be referred, and which itself is not to be referred to any thing further: Yet when he comes to an Enumeration of those *particular* Actions, which may be called morally Beautiful, he always singles out such as have a direct and necessary Tendency to *the Happiness of Mankind*. Thus he talks of the Notion of *a publick Interest*, as necessary towards a proper Idea of Virtue: He speaks of public Affection in the same Manner; and reckons Generosity, Kindness, and Compassion, as the Qualities which alone can render Mankind truly virtuous. So again, when he fixes the Bounds of the social Affections, he evidently refers us to the same End, of human Happiness ... When he fixes the proper Degrees of the *private Affections*, he draws his Proof from this one single Point, 'that by having the Self-Passions too intense or strong, a creature becomes miserable'. Lastly, when he draws a Catalogue of such Affections, as are most opposite to Beauty and moral Good, he selects '*Malice, Hatred of Society − Tyranny − Anger − Revenge − Treachery − Ingratitude*'. In all these Instances, the reference to human Happiness is so particular and strong, that from these alone an unprejudiced Mind may be convinced, that the Production of *human Happiness* is the great universal Fountain, whence our Actions derive their *moral Beauty*
>
> (Brown 1752: 129–30).[5]

This view of Shaftesbury is largely confirmed by our detailed analysis according to which any apparent incoherence on Shaftesbury's part dissipates once we turn from his general declarations regarding the moral sense to the specific property entailing approval of other-regarding motivation or concern for the public interest. Here we will find how relevant to Brown's critique of Shaftesbury is Halévy's observation that '[s]ince the principle of sympathy can ... be regarded as a special form of the principle of utility, the eighteenth-century moralists who are responsible for the "moral sense" theory may in many cases be already considered "utilitarians" ... This is the meaning of John Brown in his essay, published in 1751, in which he discussed Lord Shaftesbury's treatise' (Halévy 1995 [1901] 1: 22).

Turning to the motivation inducing virtuous practice Brown reverts to the main issue − the character of virtue itself: 'And as it hath already been made evident, that the *Essence* of Virtue consists in the Conformity of our Affections and Actions, with the greatest *public Happiness*; so it will now appear' − composing a dictum − 'that "the only *Reason* or *Motive*, by which Individuals can possibly be *induced* or *obliged* to the Practice of virtue, must be the *Feeling* immediate, or the *Prospect* of future *private Happiness*"' (Brown 1752: 159). Brown mocks Shaftesbury's admirers who 'stigmatize' private happiness as 'selfishness' or 'self-love', and complains that 'the many ambiguous Phrases of their Master have contributed not a little to this *vulgar Error*'. Nonetheless, he does finally conclude that Shaftesbury himself rejected that position, citing *Sensus Communis*: 'For thus, after all, his Lordship explains himself: "That *Happiness* is to be pursued, and, in Fact, is always sought after; that the Question is not, who *loves himself*, and who *not*; but who *loves* and *serves himself* the *rightest*, and after the *truest Manner*. That 'tis the Height of *Wisdom*, no doubt, to be rightly Selfish"', so that Brown felt safe attributing to Shaftesbury the view that 'the Motives of Man to the Practice of Virtue, can only arise from a Sense of his *present*, or a Prospect of his *future Happiness*' (166–7; for the original, see Shaftesbury 1999 [1711]: 56). Brown draws on *Sensus Communis* but in fact the *Inquiry* itself confirms this interpretation, for there Shaftesbury designates the individual as 'vicious' only if his '*real motive*' for concern with the public is *entirely* of a 'selfish' order and applauds the individual's perception of personal benefit deriving from advancing the societal interest (Chapter 2, p. 35); correspondingly, when Shaftesbury elaborates the moral sense in terms of concern for the public welfare, he takes for granted the personal benefit deriving from enhancement of public welfare in light of the individual's dependency on society (Chapter 2, p. 41).

The proximity of Brown and Shaftesbury is close indeed notwithstanding Mill's emphasis on a sharp difference between them and Brown's self-representation as hostile critic. The proximity is further enhanced by the striking fact that, surprising though it may seem, Brown himself adhered to the notion of a moral sense of right and wrong, understanding thereby the version identified with the sentiment of benevolence in the manner of Shaftesbury; and here again is reaffirmed Brown's appreciation that Shaftesbury recognized self-interested motivation in the virtuous quest to satisfy the public good: 'Again, that the Pleasures arising from Benevolence, and the moral Sense, are strictly *Selfish*, in this Sense of the Word, like every other Enjoyment' – recall Brown's objections to those who '*stigmatize*' all private happiness – 'seems evident from parallel Concessions of the noble Writer. For these seemingly disinterested Pleasures he perpetually sets on a Level with the Perceptions of natural Beauty, Order, Harmony, and Proportion. These last are, by all, acknowledged to be of the selfish Kind; therefore the other are so too; being only a *higher Order of the same*, and expressly called so by the noble Writer' (referring to the *Moralists*, Part II) (Brown 1752: 164–5**).** Brown's faith in the reinforcement by religious instruction of 'Benevolence and the moral Sense' will be discussed further below.

The differences that do exist between Brown and Shaftesbury ultimately reduce to the empirical question regarding typical behaviour and the potential for its modification. Brown considers a broad range of different characters (Brown 1752: 167f) and points to what he considered Shaftesbury's forced attempt to reconcile his notion of the typical individual, blessed with other-regarding sentiments, with his recognition that there are those with base or weak motivations, by the optimistic contention that 'all mankind are naturally capable of attaining a *Taste* or

Relish for *Virtue*, sufficient for every Purpose of social Life' (187). Brown is willing to admit that only where the Moral Sense – identified as usual with other-regarding sentiments – is in full force, does Shaftesbury come into his own:

> On the contrary, where the amiable Affections of Hope, Candour, Generosity, and Benevolence predominate, in this best and happiest of Tempers, Virtue hath indeed all the Force and Energy, which the noble Writer attributes to her Charms. For where the Calls of Sense are weak, the Imagination active and refined, the public Affections predominant; there the moral Sense must naturally reign with uncontrouled Authority; must produce all the Self-Satisfaction, that Consciousness of merited Kindness and Esteem, in which, his Lordship affirms, the very Essence of our Motives to Virtue doth consist.
>
> (184–5)

But since empirically there was no good reason for optimism 'the Noble Writer's Scheme of Morals seems essentially defective. For … it appears, that a great part of the Species are naturally incapable of this *fancied* Excellence … That consequently, where the benevolent Affections and moral Sense are weak, the selfish passions and Perceptions headstrong, there can be no internal Motive to the *consistent* practice of Virtue' (187–8). Without providing a source he again cites the idea of potential:

> The most plausible Pretence I could ever meet with, amidst all the Pomp of Declamation "thrown out in Support of this *All-sufficiency* of a *Taste in Morals*, is this: "That although the Force and Energy of this Taste for Virtue appears not in every Individual, yet the Power lies dormant in every human Breast; and needs only be called forth by a *voluntary Self-discipline*, in order to be brought to its just Perfection. That the Improvement in our Taste in Morals is parallel to the Progress of the Mind in every other Art and Excellence, in *Painting, Music, Architecture, Poetry*: In which, a true Taste, however natural to Man, is not born with him, but formed and brought forth to Action by a proper *Study* and *Application*".
>
> (188–9)

I have been unable to find this citation in Shaftesbury's *Characteristicks* (see Klein's edition of the 1711 publications) and conceivably Brown was drawing from, or paraphrasing, writers he considered to be Shaftesbury's acolytes.[6] It is true enough that Shaftesbury does assert that '[h]owever false or corrupt [the Heart] be within it-self, it finds the difference, as to Beauty and Comeliness, between one *Heart* and another, one *Turn of Affection*, one *Behaviour*, one *Sentiment* and another; and accordingly, in all disinterested Cases, must approve in some measure of what is natural and honest, and disapprove of what is dishonest and corrupt' (Chapter 2, p. 42). Yet the qualification 'in all disinterested cases' diminishes the degree of optimism allowed and correspondingly the contrast maintained by Brown, who insisted that 'if, as it certainly is, the *Capacity* for a Taste in *Morals*, be similar to a *Capacity* for a Taste in *Arts*; 'tis clear, that the most assiduous Culture or self-Discipline can never make it even *general*, much less *universal*', for 'Where the benevolent Affections … are *weak* or *wanting*, there is in the same Proportion, *little* or *no Capacity* for a *Taste* in Virtue. To harangue, therefore, on the superior Happiness attending the Exercise of the public Affections, is quite foreign to the Purpose' (190). Furthermore, Brown continued, 'even supposing all Men capable of this refined taste in Morals, there would arise an unanswerable Objection against the Efficacy of this refined Theory. Though it were allowed, that all Mankind have the same delicate Perception of *moral*, as some few have of *natural* Beauty, yet the Parallel would by no Means hold, that "as the *Virtuoso* always pursues his Taste in Arts *consistently*, so the Man of *Virtue* must be equally *consistent* in *Action* and *Behaviour*"' (193). (No source is provided by Brown.) There were too many conflicting pressures playing even upon the 'man of Virtue', since he 'hath often a numerous Train of Passions, and these perhaps the most violent to oppose: He must labour through the surrounding Demands and Allurements of selfish Appetite: Must subdue the Sollicitations of every the most natural Affection, when it opposes the Dictates of pure Benevolence. Hence even supposing the most refined Taste for Virtue common to all, it must ever be retarded in its Progress, often baffled and overthrown amidst the *Struggle* of contending *Passions*' (194). Nevertheless, mankind had been given *reasoning* power, so that there were 'sufficient Notices of the *moral Government* of GOD' pointing to 'a perfect Coincidence of the *virtuous* Conduct and *Happiness* of every Individual'; accordingly, 'it implies no essential Defect of Wisdom in the Creator, to suppose that he hath not given this *universal* and *unerring* Bias towards Virtue to the whole human Species' (196).

In all this, it should be noted, Brown is far from disputing Shaftesbury's position that true personal happiness lies in a sense of concern for the public good as transmitted by the moral sense. His own primary concern however were the actual motives typically at play in virtuous action. Reflecting on his concern that too few individuals were blessed with the ideal '*benevolent Affection* and the *moral Sense*', which rendered untenable the '*Allsufficiency* of the *Relish* or *Taste* in *Morals*', Shaftesbury naively supposed that: 'Had human Nature been indeed that *uniform* and *noble* Thing, which he seems to have *thought* it, he had surely been right in fixing the *Motives* to *Virtue*, on so generous and amiable a Principle. But as on an Examination it appears, that he hath all along supposed his human Nature to be *what it is not*, his System is *visionary* and *groundless*' (Brown 1752: 204).

Brown, we again emphasize, expresses his agreement with Shaftesbury that where the moral sense – approving the benevolent affections – is active there are sufficient motives to virtuous action: 'in minds of a *gentle* and *generous* Disposition, where the sensual Appetites are weak, the Imagination refined, and the benevolent Affections naturally predominant; these very Affections, and the *moral Sense* arising from them, will in all the common Occurrences of Life secure the Practice of Virtue' (Brown 1752: 206); furthermore he also agreed that '[t]o these fine Tempers thus happily formed, the inward Satisfaction of a virtuous Conduct exceeds that of every outward Acquisition; and affords to its Possessor a more true and lasting Happiness than Wealth, or Fame, or Power can bestow' (206–7). All this is a prelude to the main conclusion that, since such paragons were few and far between, artificial motives to virtuous action were required, and this 'not only for the Perfection of *Virtue*, but the Welfare, nay, the very Being of *Society*' (208). And while he hastened to insist that although 'the Design of introducing an universal high *Relish* or *Taste* for Virtue be *visionary* and *vain*, yet still a lower, or a lower Degree may *possibly* be instilled', the main solution turned on the Law and Religion. The 'Force of human Laws; which being established by common Consent, for the Good of all, endeavour[s], by the Infliction of Punishment on Offenders, to establish the general Happiness of Society, by making the *acknowledged Interest* of every *Individual* to coincide and unite with the *public* Welfare' (209). But law did not suffice, for 'without some further Aids, some Motives to Action more *universally* interesting, Virtue must still be left betrayed and deserted'. It is Religion, with its promise of reward and threat of punishment in the hereafter, which assured a coincidence of private with public happiness, the individual identifying his own happiness with the public welfare (210). Brown lamented that Shaftesbury undermined the religious 'Motive or Principle of Action' required by the 'Bulk of Mankind' by his idealistic and impractical focus on the exceptional person who did not require moral indoctrination as a means to strengthen their benevolent sentiment. But his objection was in fact specifically to Shaftesbury's criticism of those who propagated an Afterlife as means of social control, for he admitted Shaftesbury's positive attitude towards religion as such:

> To prevent Misinterpretation, it may be proper to observe, that Lord Shaftesbury sometimes talks in earnest of the *Nobleness* and *Dignity* of *Religion*. But when he explains himself, it appears, he confines his Idea of it to that Part which consists solely in Gratitude to, and Adoration of the supreme Being, without any Prospect of future Happiness or Misery. Now, though indeed this be the noblest Part, yet it be beyond the Reach of all, save only those who are capable of the most *exalted* Degrees of Virtue. His Theory of *Religion* therefore is precisely of a Piece, with his Theory of the *moral Sense*; not calculated for Use, but Admiration; and only existing ... as the noble Writer well expresseth it, in a *Mind taken up in Vision*.
>
> (211)

Brown took particular exception to Shaftesbury's concern lest the religious doctrine regarding reward and punishment encourage selfishness *at the expense of benevolent* sentiment. This he could not fathom, and wrote mockingly that since

Shaftesbury allowed of religion that it 'proposeth true Happiness as the End and Consequence of virtuous Actions' it made little sense to affirm that 'by leading Self-Love into the Path of *true* Happiness, Religion will inevitably conduct it to a *false*; by commanding us to *cherish* our *public* Affections it will certainly *inflame* the *private* ones; by assuring us, that if we would be happy hereafter, we must be *virtuous* and *benevolent*, it will beyond Question render us *vile* and *void* of *Benevolence*. But this Mode of Reasoning is common with the noble Writer' (Brown 1752: 216–17). We could rest assured, from observation of human nature, 'that the Hope of a happy Immortality hath no Tendency to produce selfish Affection, but its contrary' (220). Accordingly Brown put much faith in religious education, complaining that 'as the noble Writer hath strangely attempted to ridicule and dishonour Religion in every Shape' – here he forgets his own recognition that Shaftesbury did *not* go so far – 'so here, he hath endeavoured to throw an Odium on this Method of religious Discipline, by representing it as the Enemy of true Morals and practical Philosophy, as it fetters the Mind with early Prejudices' (230). Religious inculcation based on reward and punishment in a future life would, to the contrary, raise the individual 'to his utmost Capacity of moral Perfection; will be a wide and firm Foundation, on which the whole Fabric of Virtue may rise in its just Proportions; will *extend* and *govern* his *Benevolence* and *moral Sense*; will strengthen them, if weak; will confirm them, if strong; will supply their Want, if naturally defective: In fine, will direct all his *Passions* to their proper *Objects* and *Degrees*; and, as the great *Master-spring* of Action, at once *promote* and *regulate* every Movement of his *Heart*' (235).

All in all, Brown held Shaftesbury responsible for a general 'Contempt of Religion' (Brown 1752: 235) and more generally for a state of affairs where, focused as he was on an imaginary world inhabited by paragons of virtue, nothing was done to strengthen benevolence and the moral sense, with actual and potential devastating moral and political consequences. 'This', he grandly concluded, 'must be my Apology for opposing the noble Writer's fantastic System; which by exhibiting a false Picture of human Nature, is, in reality, an *Inlet* to *Vice*, while it seems most favourable to *Virtue*. And while it pretends to be drawn from the *Depths* of *Philosophy*, is, of all others, *most unphilosophical*' (239).[7] All of this has the flavour of propagandizing based on an unfair representation of Shaftesbury's actual position which, we have found, Brown himself manages to convey in a calmer mood.

3.4 Concluding remarks

Adam Smith saw in Mandeville a reversion to 'some popular ascetic doctrines which had been current before his time, and which placed virtue in the entire extirpation and annihilation of all our passions' (Smith 1976 [1759]: 313), paraphrased by Kaye as a condemnation of Mandeville's 'moral nihilism, the absence of any criterion to distinguish between moral good and evil except the impracticable and repulsive one of identifying virtue with complete self-denial'

(Kaye 1924 2: 414–15). The charge has a counterpart in John Brown's objection that whereas Shaftesbury 'contending for the permanent *Reality* of Virtue, and not content to fix it on its proper Basis, attempts to establish certain *absolute* and *immutable* Forms of Beauty, without regard to any *further End*', Mandeville in an excessive reaction 'intent on destroying the permanent Reality of Virtue and Vice, and perceiving how weak a Basis the noble Writer had laid for their Establishment, after proving *this* to be imaginary, as wisely as honestly infers, there is no real one in Nature' (Brown 1752:145).This strong charge we have found to be overstated – there is *some* substance to Mandevillian 'virtue' – recall his perception of the *other-regarding* sentiment 'pity' as bearing '*the greatest Resemblance to Virtue*' (above, p. 52) which, by fudging the issue, suggests an appreciation that the rigorist view is untenable.

To turn, then, to the utilitarian dimension. Kaye maintains that Brown, believing that Mandeville lacked *any* test of moral truth, 'tried to supply the deficiency which he and Smith found in Mandeville by offering utility as the missing test of moral truth' (Kaye 1924 2: 415), setting up "the great End of public Happiness ... as the *one, uniform* Circumstance that constitutes the *Rectitude* of human Actions'" (citing Brown 1752: 140–1). Doubtless it was this stance that caught J.S. Mill's attention, although Mill had in mind Brown's objections to Shaftesbury rather than to Mandeville (above, p. 54). I have argued, however, that since by morally-praiseworthy motivation Mandeville intended, despite appearance, *concern for the public good* it is unhelpful to refer to such judgment of private actions 'according to an anti-utilitarian scheme' as Kaye does and as Brown seems to have believed – it is very much a scheme reflecting the core of utilitarian ethics; and, by implication, since intention counts, the morality of the act would not be diminished should it fail to yield the desirable social consequences intended (above, p. 51).

Recall Hume's insistence that notwithstanding the pleasure derived from a sympathetic act such an act may be described as *disinterested* since the 'virtuous Sentiment or Passion *produces* the Pleasure, and does not arise from it' (Chapter 2, note 3). Now to this John Brown objected that 'neither the *Passion*, nor the *Pleasure*, are either the *Cause* or the *Consequence* of each other', but 'are the *same Thing* under *different Expressions*' (Brown 1752: 164); and he pointed out that Shaftesbury had himself conceded that a benevolent act such as friendship is a 'selfish' act: 'For these seemingly disinterested Pleasures he perpetually sets on a Level with the Perceptions of natural Beauty, Order, Harmony, and Proportion. These last are, by all, acknowledged to be of the selfish Kind; therefore the other are so too; being only a *higher order of the same*, and expressly called so by the noble Writer' (164–5, citing *The Moralist*, Part ii). Now this is in line with Mandeville, who maintained 'that in the Choice of Things Men must be determin'd by the Perception they have of Happiness; and no Person can commit or set about an Action, which at that then present time seems not to be the best to him' – which would encompass *all* conceivable acts including benevolent acts of friendship. We have also seen the apparently harsh assertion in an analysis of *pity* that the action of saving a baby in danger lacks ethical merit since 'we only obliged our selves'. But it is also the case that Mandeville's full rationale for such obligation entails an act motivated by the wish to avoid the pain caused by failing to prevent the death of a child, and this takes him – surprising though it might seem – close to Shaftesbury, a 'painful sense' implying a *sympathetic* natural sentiment. Brown – like later readers of Mandeville – was unaware of this concession and presumed that for Mandeville the public affections in general are selfish without qualification, thereby conflicting with what was thought to be Shaftesbury's idealisation of human nature.

Notes

1 I cite from the Kaye edition of 1924 which uses the sixth (1732) edition of Volume I of the *Fable*, the last published during Mandeville's lifetime, and the 1729 edition of the second Volume (Kaye 1924: ix).
2 On moral conduct for Mandeville as conduct motivated by benevolent concern with public welfare, see Hont 2006: 390.
3 Again: 'the real thesis of the book is not that all evil is a public benefit, but that a certain useful proportion of it (called vice) is such a benefit (and … is on that account not really felt to be evil, though still called vicious). There is here a definite application of the utilitarian standard' (Kaye 1924: lx).
4 Presumably Kaye intended to attribute to Mandeville a utilitarianism standard for social policy, including crime and punishment, since he finds only nihilism regarding personal ethics.
5 The same view is taken by Brown of Clarke and Wollaston, both classified by Bentham as crude moral-sense adherents (see Introduction, note 1): 'As therefore these celebrated Writers give no Instances of moral Beauty [Shaftesbury], Fitness [Clarke], or Truth [Wollaston], but what finally relate to the Happiness of Man; so, if we appeal to the common Sense of Mankind, we shall see that the Idea of Virtue hath never been universally affixed to any Action or Affection of the Mind, unless where this Tendency to produce Happiness was at least *apparent*' (Brown 1752: 133). Again: 'Thus it appears, that those Actions which we denominate Virtuous, Beautiful, Fit, or True, have not any absolute and independent, but a relative and reflected Beauty: And that their Tendency to produce Happiness is the only Source from whence they derive their Lustre. Hence therefore we may obtain a just and adequate Definition of Virtue: Which is no other than "the Conformity of our Affections with the public Good": Or "the voluntary Production of the greatest Happiness"' (136–7).
6 Brown represents Hutcheson as the 'most ingenious' of Shaftesbury's followers (Brown 1752: 162).
7 Leslie Stephen in his celebrated account of English thought in the eighteenth century similarly represents Shaftesbury as resorting to 'flimsy rhetoric' in support of his perception of 'virtue' as being in line with 'a certain harmony pervading all the works of nature, and recognisable by the human intellect', and adding a 'fine coating of varnish' to his account of human nature in sharp contrast to the 'savage origin of man' as seen by Mandeville (Stephen 1902 2: 39–40).

References

Brown, J. 1752. *Essays on the Characteristics of the Earl of Shaftesbury*. 3rd. ed. London: Davis.
Halévy, E. 1995 (1901). *La Formation du radicalisme philosophiques 1: La jeunesse de Bentham 1776–1789*. Paris: Presses Universitaires de France.

Hont, I. 2006. 'The early Enlightenment debate on commerce and luxury', in *The Cambridge History of Eighteenth-Century Political Thought*, ed. Mark Goldie and Robert Wokler. Cambridge: Cambridge University Press: 379–418.

Kaye, F. B. 1924. Editorial Commentary to Mandeville 1924 (1732).

Mandeville, B. 1732. *An Enquiry into the Origin of Honour, and the Usefulness of Christianity in War*. London: John Brotherton.

Mandeville, B. 1740. *A Modest Defence of Publick Stews*. London: Thomas Read.

Mandeville 1924 (1729). *The Fable of the Bees, or Private Vices, Publick Benefits*, the Second Volume, ed. F.B. Kaye. Oxford: Clarendon.

Mandeville 1924 (1732). *The Fable of the Bees, or Private Vices, Publick Benefits*, the First Volume, ed. F.B. Kaye. Oxford: Clarendon

Mill, J.S. 1969 (1838). 'Bentham', *Collected Works* 10. Toronto: University of Toronto Press: 75–115.

Mill, J.S. 1969 (1852). 'Whewell on Moral Philosophy', *Collected Works* 10. Toronto: University of Toronto Press: 165–201.

Shaftesbury, A. 1999 (1711). *Sensus Communis, an Essay on the Freedom of Wit and Humour*. In *Characteriticks of Men, Manners, Opinions, Times*, ed. L.E. Klein. Cambridge: Cambridge University Press: 29–69.

Smith, A. 1976 (1759). *Theory of Moral Sentiments*, ed. D.D. Raphael and A.L. Macfie. Oxford: Clarendon Press.

Stephen, L. 1902. *English Thought in the Eighteenth Century*. 3rd ed. London: John Murray.

Viner, J. 1958. *The Long View and the Short: Studies in Economic Theory and Policy*. Glencoe, Ill: The Free Press.

4 Francis Hutcheson and the Hutcheson–Locke relationship

4.1 Introduction

Francis Hutcheson's utilitarian status remains to this day the subject of debate. A recent study finds that '[t]he most often cited first source for the utilitarian credo is Francis Hutcheson, academic mentor to Adam Smith and David Hume, and a key founder of the Scottish enlightenment' (Persky 2016: 27). This may be the case, yet Hutcheson's interpretation is far from easy going, and his 'incoherence' has often been noted, *inter alia* by Hume (see Moore 1990: 41, 58–9). Most significantly, Bentham represented Hutcheson as a moral-sense author *opposed* to the utility rule; and this understanding is implied by James Bonar who argued that Hume reduces the moral sense to 'sympathy' thereby establishing motivation by concern for the *general good* as a condition for moral commendation rejected the Shaftesbury–Hutcheson view whereby man distinguishes good from evil through a 'moral sense' (Bonar 1922: 109). More recently, Turco similarly contrasts Hutcheson with Hume for whom 'utility perceived through sympathy is the foundation of merit' (Turco 2007).[1] I shall argue to the contrary that what Bonar says of Hume applies also to Hutcheson.[2] Conduct motivated by a desire to advance the general good is of the essence for Hutcheson when ethical approval is in question.[3]

One frequently encounters commentaries on Hutcheson's 'Non-utilitarian Motivational Morality', taking it for granted that 'Utilitarian theories typically do not engage with agents' motivations' (Bacon 2016: 3). Along similar lines Leslie Stephen had earlier attributed to Hutcheson the view 'that virtue conduces to happiness without allowing that its dictates are to be deduced from its tendency to produce happiness' (Stephen 1900 I: 158–9). A designation of Hutcheson as a 'motivational utilitarian' also implies that he stands apart from the utilitarians proper (Strasser 1990; also Mousourakis 1997); and Frazer explicitly posits that Hutchesonian utilitarianism differs from the 'classical utilitarianism of the following century' in rejecting 'what is now known as consequentialism' (Frazer 2010: 35). This sort of contrast is perhaps going too far, any difference being one of degree rather than kind, partly because consequences are not set at naught by Hutcheson's concern with motivation –

agents, we shall see, are duty bound to take reasonable care to evaluate possible consequences of their actions, so that outcomes damaging to the general interest that should have been foreseen diminish moral standing – but also because motivation was to play a role for Bentham (see Chapter 10, p. 239). My case accords with Rosen's insistence that 'classical utilitarians have never confined themselves to assessing consequences, and take numerous other aspects of the human condition into consideration, such as motives, intentions…' (Rosen 2003: 5).

The Hutcheson texts that will concern us relate to both factual questions regarding the actuality of altruistic conduct uncontaminated by self-interest – an objective matter that can in principle be determined by observation and experience – and to the subjective matter of evaluating the ethical merit of such conduct by means of an alleged Moral Sense answering the question of why actions motivated by altruism should be considered morally praiseworthy. While moral approval derived from an innate feeling, from the 'heart' being a favourite rendition, this sense was incapable of automatically yielding ethical verdicts *independent of consequences*, more strictly, of *intended* consequences, as Bentham understood Hutcheson to maintain. For conduct is approved as virtuous provided it is motivated by concern for the happiness of others – 'sympathy' or 'fellow-feeling' – extending in the best case to 'benevolent' conduct directed at advancing the welfare of *anonymous* beneficiaries, that is advancing 'the greatest Happiness for the greatest Numbers' in Hutcheson's own terms. In brief, 'the disposition … which is most excellent, and naturally gains the highest moral approbation, is the calm, stable universal good-will to all, or the most extensive benevolence'. It is also presumed that mankind is *capable* of whole-hearted altruism, or 'susceptible of affections truly disinterested in the strictest sense, and not directly subordinated to self-interest, or aiming at private interest of any kind'. Where such is not the case ethical merit is reduced. To be stressed is the priority accorded to motivation over consequences with the significant proviso, noted above, that '[n]o distant effects or consequences of actions or omissions, affect their morality, if they could not have been foreseen by that diligence and caution we expect from good men; for then they are no indications of the temper of the agent'. Accordingly, proper conduct that fails to yield the hoped-for outcome through no fault of the agent would not reduce his or her ethical ranking. Conversely, by implication, the moral sense considers as defective actions which *unintentionally* result in social advantage.

A theme carried through all of Hutcheson's texts, to which I shall draw particular attention, is the ready allowance for a 'due proportion' of *legitimate* self-interest and the purported ability of the moral sense (at least when operating efficiently) to identify that proportion by distinguishing between ethically-neutral or *'innocent'* self-love and selfish passions which are 'too strong' thereby impinging negatively on other-regarding sentiment and reducing the moral quality of conduct. (There is even a more positive allowance that self-interest might be a stepping stone towards disinterested conduct.) Hutcheson refutes the contention by those such as John Clarke (see below, p.77) that personal satisfaction derived by the actor from the very circumstance that his character is one naturally sympathetic towards the public good cannot be said to diminish the ethical quality of such conduct, arguing that self-satisfaction of that order does not enter into motivation.

Now, for Bentham, the utility principle was a postulate which was not further reducible: 'that which is used to prove every thing else cannot itself be proved: a chain of proofs must have their commencement somewhere. To give such a proof is as impossible as it is needless' (Bentham 1982 [1789]: 13). By proposing a moral sense, Hutcheson sought in effect to go back one further stage, insisting on an instinct confirming that conduct reflecting 'sympathy' or 'fellow feeling' – ideally extending to benevolence – is in fact 'good'. While the moral sense was without question important to Hutcheson, he may be said to have added little in practice to what was to be Bentham's position, since *without* it the reality of disinterested conduct reflecting sympathy or fellow-feeling's extending to benevolence directed at enhancing general happiness would be unaffected, and *with* it Bentham's Greatest Happiness axiom is simply reinforced by an alleged mental state offering its approval of such a sentiment. Hutcheson certainly purports to *prove* the existence of a moral sense, but the largely informal, discursive, and anecdotal character of the 'proofs' – reminiscent of Shaftesbury – their heavy reliance on a general appeal to universal experience and introspection, suggests rather that he regarded the matter as *self-evident*, and in effect axiomatic. His preoccupation with the matter can, however, be appreciated as a response to those who attributed the high ethical status commonly accorded to conduct motivated by benevolence to reason, or culture and training, or obeisance to the Deity, in addition to those (such as Mandeville and Hobbes) who denied that disinterested conduct was an actuality borne out by daily experience.[4]

It follows from our account that differences between Hutcheson and Locke should not be exaggerated. While Hutcheson's recognition of disinterested benevolence or unadulterated altruism would appear wholly antithetical to the Lockean doctrine involving prudential calculation of the prospective advantage to an individual (whether in this or the next world) of other-regarding conduct, we shall see that even Hutcheson – like Shaftesbury – expressed doubts regarding the reliability of the moral sense as the 'faculty of perceiving moral excellence' or as 'an immediate undefinable perception', as it is sometimes expressed. Thus, he struggled in the *Inquiry Concerning Moral Good and Evil* (1729) to reconcile the allegedly 'natural' or 'instinctive' character of the moral sense, suggesting the 'universality' of 'benevolence' towards anonymous beneficiaries as the ultimate requisite for ethical approval, with the variety of ethical judgments actually encountered across time and space. By the same token, the Glasgow lecture of 1730 is clear that the moral sense does not operate in its full 'force and power' in the 'corrupt' world as we know it where self-interested motivation is so pervasive. The lecture recognizes the problem without offering a convincing resolution of the serious implication that, insofar as it pertained to reality and notwithstanding all his efforts, the moral sense was not actually such a central element in Hutcheson's overall scheme of things.[5] In particular, the *effective* operation of the moral sense may require education directed at instilling 'proper ends', contradicting Hutcheson's frequent downplaying of culture and training in ethical evaluation. As we shall see, this qualification is apparent in a *London Journal* article from 1724, in the Glasgow lecture of 1730, and perhaps in an alteration made to the 1742 edition of the *Essay on the Nature and Conduct of the Passions and Affections*. It is elaborated in the posthumously-published *System of Moral Philosophy*, already circulating informally in 1737. The complexity is equally clear in the *Short Introduction* (1747), perhaps more so, for there the necessity of 'revelation' and on-going heavenly support to activate and maintain the moral sense is particularly stressed – an implicit concession to what we have designated above as Locke's 'theological utilitarianism'. But Locke by no means relied entirely on divine reward and punishment as stimulus to ethical conduct, the promise of purely mundane reward playing a part; while Hutcheson also maintained in the *Essay* that 'particular actions may be innocent, nay, virtuous, where there is no actual intention of pleasing the Deity influencing the agent'. Indeed, Hutcheson's remarks were directed against the puritanical Presbyterian Church (the 'Kirk') and its aggressive propagation of fear of God from the pulpit (see Buchan 2003). Even if it was not the intention, this 'unorthodox' stance opens the door for a secular perspective on social policy, and would surely have pleased Bentham had he not misunderstood the 'moral sense' as implying a denial of utilitarian consequentialism. By the same token, Hutcheson is also at one in spirit with Thomas Robert Malthus who was later to recommend social policies on utilitarian grounds even when they contravened literal readings of the scriptures.

The present chapter takes great care to trace Hutcheson's views through the complex mass of his writings. Section 4.2 prefaces the main discussion by reference to an early article of 1724 on 'Human Nature'. The concern of Section 4.3 is the third (1729) edition of the *Inquiry Concerning the Original of our Ideas of Virtue and Moral Good,* and additions made in 1738. We also take account of his correspondence of 1725, and *An Essay on the Nature and Conduct of the Passions and Affections with Illustrations on the Moral Sense* (1728) written in response to criticism of the *Inquiry*. Section 4.4 proceeds to an important lecture delivered in November 1730 on the 'Social Nature of Man' summarizing and clarifying several of the main features of Hutcheson's system, and Section 4.5 is devoted to the *System of Moral Philosophy* published posthumously circulating, as mentioned above, in the late 1730s. These documents are followed in 1742 by the *Philosophiae Moralis Institutio Compendiaria*, revised in 1745 and published in English in 1747 as the *Short Introduction to Moral Philosophy*. This last version is introduced in Section 4.6, where although differences of detail between these works these are signalled, all in all a high degree of uniformity emerges regarding the main principles.[6]

Hutcheson's qualified support of the Agrarian laws, limiting the concentration of (landed) wealth with an eye to the welfare of landless labour, illustrates the greater-good principle and his recognition of a concern with defects of distributive justice. This demonstration, taken up in Section 4.7, corrects Adam Smith's reading of Hutcheson as forwarding a case for *strict equality*. In a final section I revert by way of a general summary to the Hutcheson–Locke relationship.

4.2 Propaedeutics: 'on human nature: reflections on our common systems of morality' (1724)

In Hutcheson's article for the *London Journal* issue of 14 November 1724, composed when the *Inquiry* was in preparation, there is no formal reference to a 'moral sense' approving conduct which displays *disinterested* fellow feeling. But 'conscience' does make an appearance and is represented as recommending 'the good of others, a real delight in their happiness' which amounts in effect to the moral sense and its function. The absence of the term itself has little significance.

Hutcheson sets out with a review of 'modern schemes of morals' (Hutcheson 1993 (1724): 96–7). In his rendering of 'modern' positions the importance attached to what is 'most beneficial to mankind' is especially to be noted, with corresponding reliance on the Deity to assure such an outcome: 'All virtue is allowed to consist in affections of love toward the Deity, and our fellow creatures, and in actions suitable to these affections. Hence we may conclude, 1st, "That whatever scheme of principles shall be most effectual to excite these affections, the same must be the truest foundation of all virtue: And, 2dly, Whatever rules of conduct shall lead us into a course of action acceptable to the Deity, and most beneficial to mankind, they must be the precepts of morality"' (97–8). Hutcheson goes on to refer specifically to Pufendorf who argued (in Hutcheson's paraphrase) that '(a)ll our worldly happiness depends upon society, which cannot be preserved without sociable dispositions in men toward each other, and a strict observation of any rules adapted to promote the good of society', while 'since belief in a Deity is effectual to achieve this end it is important to believe in and love the Deity' (98). Hutcheson was in full agreement with the first part of this position, objecting only 'that views of worldly interest are as unfit to beget love and reverence in our hearts, as to form opinions or belief in our understandings, however they may procure obsequiousness in our outward deportment, and dissimilation of our opinions' (98–9).

Hutcheson also found objectionable the representation by Hobbes, amongst others, of typical human nature as reflecting 'wickedness and corruption', for this was to neglect a raft of socially-oriented dispositions: 'They never talk of any kind instincts to associate; of natural affections, of compassion, of love of company, a sense of gratitude, a determination to honour and love the authors of any good offices toward any part of mankind, as well as those toward our selves; and of a natural delight men take in being esteemed and honoured by others for good actions: which yet all may be observed to prevail exceedingly in humane life' (Hutcheson 1993 [1724]: 100–101). For his part, Hutcheson posits that 'every action is amiable and virtuous, as far as it evidences a study of the good of others, a real delight in their happiness' – referring to what is later termed 'benevolence'; but that 'innocent self-love, and the actions flowing from it, are indifferent', that is *morally neutral*, while 'nothing is detestably wicked, but either a direct study and intention of the misery of others, without any further view, or else such an entire extinction of the kind affections, as makes us wholly indifferent and careless how pernicious our selfish pursuits may be to others' (101). Furthermore, everyday instances of 'sympathetic' conduct conflicted with the Hobbesian view of mankind, and suggested the high potential for behavioural improvement. Were this appreciated, then men would be roused 'into another kind of love to their country, and resolution in its defence, than the mere considerations of terror either in this world or in the next' (103). As to the narrower 'private offices of virtue', observation of charity revealed 'that gratitude, compassion, and the appearance of virtuous dispositions, do move us most effectually. And how little many of our moralists employ of their labours, in giving us such representations of motives, every one sees who is not a stranger to their writings' which posit *fear of the Deity* as a *primary* motive. Reward and punishment had a role, Hutcheson conceded, but this was limited to the control of extreme deficiencies, namely 'altering a corrupted taste of life; of restraining the selfish passions when too strong, and turning them to the side of virtue; and of rousing us to attention and consideration, that we may not be led into wrong measures of good from partial views, or too strong attachments to parties' (103–4). But, he adds, external control of conduct did not suffice: 'there must be much more to form a truly great and good man' (104).

Hutcheson believed his rendition of the issues would contribute to a sort of re-education, the effect of which would be to enhance social harmony, and this essentially because of the high *potential* for truly moral conduct on the part of the general body of mankind. This theme is well expressed in a 'Smithian' remark regarding the unimportance for happiness of the quest after high income: 'The covetous and ambitious must surely feel the uneasiness of their passions, and yet they still continue slaves to them, till once you convince them, that the enjoyments of the highest stations and fortunes, are very little above those which may be obtained in very moderate circumstances' (Hutcheson 1993 [1724]: 104). But the proper ends themselves must be convincingly *taught* to assure reform of the 'passions', or else all efforts at improvement must fail: 'Unless just representations be given of the objects of our passions, all external arguments will be but rowing against the stream; an endless labour, while the passions themselves do not take a more reasonable turn, upon juster apprehensions of the affairs about which they are employed' (104–5).

Here we note the clear presumption that the ultimate object of activity is *general happiness* and that moral conduct is actions which are conducive to that end. Increase in aggregate wealth was no guarantee of increased general happiness since it was consistent with a skewed income distribution, an indication that higher incomes for the lower strata were not despised by Hutcheson (any more than they were to be despised by Adam Smith): 'The later moralists ... have very much left out of their systems, all enquiries into happiness, and speak only of the external advantages of peace and wealth in the societies where we live. But this is, no doubt, a great omission, since amidst peace and wealth, there may be sullenness, discontent, fretfulness, and all the miseries of poverty' (Hutcheson 1993 [1724]: 105). 'As to our duty towards others', Hutcheson adds, 'our later moralists hurry over all other things till they come to the doctrine of rights, and proper injuries; and like the civilians (ed. an expert in civil law, a jurisprudentialist), whose only business is to teach how far refractory or knavish men should be compelled by force, they spend all their reasonings upon perfect or external rights (legal rights of a creditor towards a debtor). We never hear a generous sentiment from them any further'. Hutcheson admits that 'there are bad men who need compulsion to their duty. But may not better sentiments prevail with a great many? All men are not incorrigible villains. There are still a great many who can be moved with sentiments of honour and humanity'. Now here, once again, we see allusion to proper training in ethics. But a concern that education might be *inappropriate* emerges in the course of discussing 'many weaknesses in humane nature' – including 'self-love' which is 'apt to grow too strong by bad habits ... overcoming the kind affections in the more remote attachments', and 'too much rashness in receiving bad notions, concerning those whose interests are opposite to our own, as if there were men so opposite to the publick good that it were a good deed to oppress them' (101). In this latter respect he adds – sarcastically, as I understand him: 'But for this goodly effect we are often indebted to education, and to many a grave lesson which nature would never have taught us'.

There remains a further detail of importance relating to self-interest. We have noted that 'innocent self-love, and the actions flowing from it' are seen as morally neutral. But that Hutcheson is rather more positive emerges in the course of a criticism of the Schoolmen for being too visionary and operating too much in the upper stratosphere when it came to the *Highest Good* in ethical conduct. Ethical advantage, Hutcheson opined, might attach to 'the earthly subjects of laborious diligence in some honest employment' (Hutcheson 1993 [1724]: 105). Thus the Scholastics 'seldom mention the delights of humanity, good nature, kindness, mutual love, friendships, societies of virtuous persons' – the 'kind affections' as these traits are sometimes referred to – and 'scarce ever spend a word upon the earthly subjects of laborious diligence in some honest employment; which yet we see to be the ordinary step, by which we mount into a capacity of doing offices'. Self-interest, in brief, might be – indeed is likely to be – a stepping stone towards disinterested conduct.

Where in all this, if at all, does the 'moral sense' appear? Hutcheson, we have seen, reveals his value judgment that the proper ends of our 'passions' entails 'the good of others, a real delight in their happiness', and provides an assurance that '(t)he covetous and ambitious must surely feel the uneasiness of their passions'. Now this 'feeling' evidently entails a sense of guilt which amounts in substance to *conscience* or a *moral sense* self-critical of ethically questionable conduct. That the term itself is not may seem odd since it figures so conspicuously in the *Inquiry* then in preparation. At the same time, we have also encountered Hutcheson's caution that education directed at instilling 'proper ends' was essential for assuring the reform of the 'passions', implying that in the absence of such reform the moral sense would be far from providing an automatic ethical directive.

4.3 *Inquiry concerning moral good and evil* (1729), *Essay on the nature and conduct of the passions and affections* (1728, 1769), and related documents

I commence by pointing to the strong declaration in the *Inquiry* (Treatise II, Section IV) regarding the universality of the moral sense, namely that 'All Mankind agree in this General Foundation of their Approbation of Moral Actions' perceived as other-regarding and in the limit as general *benevolence*: 'To shew how far Mankind agree in that which we have made the universal Foundation of this moral Sense, viz. BENEVOLENCE, we have observ'd already [170–1], that when we are ask'd the Reason of our Approbation of any Action, we perpetually alledge its Usefulness to the Publick, and not to the Actor himself' (Hutcheson 1729: 199).[7] Explaining the *apparent* diversity of moral principles across time and space, Hutcheson allows initially only for error: 'We may perhaps commit Mistakes, in judging that Actions tend to the publick Good, which do not; or be so stupidly inadvertent, that while our Attention is fix'd on some partial good Effects we may quite over-look many evil Consequences which counter-balance the Good. Our Reason may be very deficient in its Office, by giving us partial representations of the Tendency of Actions; but it is still some apparent Species of Benevolence which commands our Approbation' (200–1). But at a deeper level he accounts for the diversity of moral principles by 'Different Opinions of Happiness, or natural Good, and of the most effectual Means to advance it' (203); by 'Diversity of Systems, to which Men, from foolish Opinions, confine their Benevolence', thus restricting its scope from 'stronger Benevolence, toward the morally good Parts of Mankind, who are useful to the Whole ... toward the useless or pernicious', alluding to factions or cabals (208); and by 'false Opinions of the Will or Laws of the Deity' (213). The implications of these allowances, which raise more difficulties for Hutcheson's position than solutions, will be addressed presently.

The significance attached to the moral sense in the *Inquiry* is to be understood as part of an effort to subvert two features of contemporary opinion: a failure to take account of disinterested sympathy or fellow-feeling – in the limit pure benevolence or the greatest-good – as an observable feature of conduct, and the attribution of the high ethical status accorded by *disinterested* conduct to reason, or culture and training, or obeisance to the Deity. There is, I shall argue, no need in all this for an approving 'moral sense' insofar as, even in its absence, the possibility of disinterested conduct is (allegedly) confirmed by observation, eliminating the reliance on *fear* to assure against possible damage to the public interest by self-interested conduct.

The Preface to the *Inquiry* draws a parallel between ethics and aesthetics: 'all he is solicitous about' Hutcheson explains, citing the text of the first Treatise comprising the *Inquiry*,

> is to shew 'That there is some Sense of Beauty natural to Men; that we find as great an Agreement of Men in their Relishes of Forms, as in their external Senses, which all agree to be natural; and that Pleasure or Pain, Delight or Aversion, are naturally join'd to these Perceptions'. If the Reader be convinc'd of such Determinations of the Mind to be pleas'd with Forms, Proportions, Resemblances, Theorems; it will be no difficult matter to apprehend another superior Sense, natural also to Men, determining them to be pleas'd with Actions, Characters, Affections. This is the moral Sense, which makes the Subject of the second Treatise.
> (Hutcheson 1729: xvi).

Now this generalization is easy to misunderstand. The motivation of which the moral sense approves is not an *unknown* requiring identification as desirable, as the citation might be understood to maintain; rather the moral sense specifically approves those actions, characters, and affections which are expected to enhance the *General Good* – *benevolent* actions, characters and affections – and as such, reasoned evaluations might be made of the best course of action to assure that end. This is splendidly rendered in the body of the book in a pseudo-mathematical passage, worthy of Bentham, expressing the 'greatest Happiness' formula, although there is a distinctly non-Benthamite weighting of numbers by the 'moral importance of persons'. It is particularly noteworthy that Hutcheson specifies the '*expected*' result of the conduct, confirming that it is intention that counts in evaluating ethical merit:

> In comparing the moral Qualitys of Actions, in order to regulate our Election among various Actions propos'd, or to find which of them has the greatest moral Excellency, we are led by our moral Sense of Virtue to judge thus; that in equal Degrees of Happiness, expected to proceed from the Action, the Virtue is in proportion to the Number of Persons to whom the Happiness shall extend; (and here the Dignity, or moral Importance of Persons, may compensate Numbers) and in equal Numbers,

the Virtue is as the Quantity of the Happiness, or natural Good; or that the Virtue is in a compound Ratio of the Quantity of Good, and Number of Enjoyers. In the same manner, the moral Evil, or Vice, is as the Degree of Misery, and Number of Sufferers; so that, that Action is best, which procures *the greatest Happiness for the greatest Numbers*; and that, worst, which, in like manner, occasions Misery.

(179–80; emphasis added)

Consistently, Hutcheson contended that should the *intention* of the agent be 'interested', his action would be morally defective, even when social advantage resulted therefrom: 'A Covetous Man shall dislike any branch of trade, however useful soever it may be to the Publick, if there be no gain for himself in it; here is an Aversion from Interest. Propose a sufficient Premium, and he shall be the first who sets about it, with full Satisfaction in his own Conduct' (119). The observer, it is clearly implied, would have a very different opinion.

Explicitly ruled out is Bentham's interpretation whereby the moral sense acts independently of social-welfare consequences as an automatic index of what is good or bad in any specific conduct: 'the Approbation' – offered by the Moral Sense – '*is founded on Benevolence, because of some real, or apparent tendency to the publick Good*. For we are not to imagine, that this Sense should give us, without Observation, Ideas of complex Actions, or of their natural Tendencys to Good or Evil: it only determines us to approve Benevolence, whenever it appears in any Action, and to hate the contrary' (Hutcheson 1729: 204; emphasis added).

Several formulations, read in isolation, might be understood – as Bentham understood Hutcheson – as perceiving the moral sense at play without reference to benevolence or the General Good. In addition to the passage cited above from the Preface, Hutcheson entitles Section I proper: 'Of the moral Sense, by which we perceive Virtue and Vice, and approve, or disapprove them in others' (Hutcheson 1729: 110). But the text itself insists that moral approval is distinguished from the pleasure derived from natural objects precisely by the former's specific concern with the *public* advantage: 'For let it here be observ'd, that those Senses by which we perceive Pleasure in natural Objects, whence they are constituted Advantageous, could never raise in us any Desire of publick Good, but only of what was good to our selves in particular. Nor could they ever make us approve an Action merely because of its promoting the Happiness of others' (113). To the same effect: 'the Actions we approve in others' – indicated by the moral sense – 'are generally imagin'd to tend to the natural Good of Mankind, or that of some Parts of it', and are thus manifest in instances where self-interest is wholly irrelevant, as in evaluating distant historical episodes (114); similarly: 'Self-Interest will recommend Men to us only according to the Good they do to our Selves, and not give us high Ideas of public Good, but in proportion to our Share of it ... Unhappy would it be for Mankind, if a Sense of Virtue was of as narrow an Extent, as a Capacity for such Metaphysics' – referring to moralists 'who will rather twist Self-Love into a thousand Shapes, than allow any other Principle of

Approbation than Interest' (117–19). Again, Section I closes in on terms that can be easily misunderstood, for there Hutcheson writes of the Author of Nature 'who has given us a MORAL SENSE, to direct our Actions…', whereas the full context makes clear that this is not open-ended but takes for granted 'nobler Pleasures' than 'our own greatest private Good' (127–8). Throughout, the Moral Sense is consistently said to have the function of evaluating conduct, approvingly or otherwise. The term 'direct' in the present context suggests a function beyond evaluation but may also be read as referring to the guidance towards proper ethical conduct resulting from evaluation. In any event, we do not approve of conduct or dispositions simply because the moral sense says so independently of the enhanced happiness of mankind or sections thereof – as Bentham understood Hutcheson to maintain.

Now Hutcheson might have conveyed the principle theme emerging from his comprehensive, as distinct from his abbreviated accounts, *without formal appeal to the moral sense*, by merely observing that mankind (at its best) appreciates social happiness and is capable of acting to enhance it, independently of personal advantage. This was to be Bentham's position and later that of Ricardo as is clear from his discussion of Parliamentary competence (Hollander 2015: 438–9). But, as we have already intimated, because of the prevalence of the 'interest' notion Hutcheson felt obliged to reinforce his objection by introducing a moral sense. He did not always find it necessary to reiterate that the moral sense intends the Greatest Happiness, for this could be taken as self-evident precisely because it is the cynical view to the contrary that he is combating. Unfortunately, this presumption turns out to have been foolhardy. Nothing can be taken for granted regarding readership, even if the reader should happen to be one Jeremy Bentham.

There are revealing alterations to the 1729 edition compared with earlier editions. Two pages are added to Section I 'Of the Moral Sense' emphasizing that 'the Quality approved by our moral Sense is conceived to reside in the Person approved, and to be a Perfection and Dignity in him … Virtue is then called Amiable or Lovely, from its raising Good-will or Love in Spectators toward the Agent; and not from the Agent's perceiving the virtuous Temper to be advantageous to him, or desiring to obtain it under that View' (Hutcheson 1729: 129). Here Hutcheson is responding silently to John Clarke's rejection of the notion of *disinterested sympathy* (see Turco 1999: 87–8). A reworking of materials in Section 2 ('Concerning the immediate Motive to virtuous Actions') seeks to reinforce the response, and concludes with a plea to accept the notion of disinterested benevolence by extension from parental affection: 'If then the observing a moral Capacity [in children] can be the occasion of increasing Love without Self-Interest, even from the Frame of our Nature; pray, may not this be a Foundation of weaker degrees of Love where there is no preceding tie of Parentage, and extend it to all Mankind' (Hutcheson 1725: 146; 1729: 161). Similarly added to the *Inquiry* in 1738 is a firm rejection of 'sympathy' as a matter of 'private Advantage':

As Mr. Hobbes explains all the Sensations of Pity by our Fear of the like Evils, when by Imagination we place ourselves in the Case of the Sufferers; so others explain all Approbation and Condemnation of Actions in distant ages or nations, by a like Effort of Imagination: We place ourselves in the Case of others, and then discern an imaginary private Advantage or Disadvantage in these Actions. But as his Account of Pity will never explain how the Sensation increases, according to the apprehended Worth of the Sufferer, or according to the Affection we formerly had of him; since the Sufferings of any Stranger may suggest the same Possibility of our suffering the like: so this Explication will never account for our high Approbation of brave unsuccessful attempts, which we see detrimental both to the Agent, and to those for whose Service they were intended; here there is no private Advantage to be imagined. Nor will it account for our Abhorrence of such Injuries as we are incapable of Suffering.

(cited Turco 1999: 99–100)

Turco rightly sees this passage as proving the 'reduction of moral sense to sympathy' (99).

We return to the perception of moral good – incorporating concern with the general good as with Bentham – as a matter of *instinct*. There are two particularly important features to be noted here. Firstly, because instinctive, the moral good is divorced from environmental influences:

If what is said makes it appear, that we have some other amiable Idea of Actions than that of Advantageous to ourselves, we may conclude, 'That this Perception of moral Good is not deriv'd from Custom, Education, Example, or Study'. These give us no new Ideas: They might make us see private Advantage in Actions whose Usefulness did not at first appear; or give us Opinions of some Tendency of Actions to our Detriment, by some nice Deductions of Reason, or by a rash Prejudice; when upon the first View of the Action we should have observ'd no such thing: but they never could have made us apprehend Actions as amiable or odious, without any Consideration of our own Advantage.

(Hutcheson 1729: 127)

We shall find that in his posthumously-published rendition in the *System* of 1755 this optimistic stance is modified with potentially grave consequences for the main lines of the argument (below, pp. 98-9). But the recognition of a diversity of moral principles in the *Inquiry* itself, alluded to above, is equally problematic for the notion of a purely 'natural' moral sense.

Secondly, there is a related theme that 'reasoning' cannot be the *foundation* of ethical calculation. In his correspondence with Gilbert Burnet (*nom de plume* 'Philaretus'), published in the *London Review* immediately after the appearance of the *Inquiry*, Hutcheson ('Philanthropus') (referring to himself as a third party) focuses on this feature: 'Now Philaretus seems to me to maintain that there is some exciting reason to virtue, antecedent to all kind affections or instinct toward the good of others, and that in like manner there are some justifying reasons or truths antecedent to any moral sense causing approbation. The author of the *Inquiry*, I apprehend, must maintain that desires, affections, instincts must be previous to all exciting reason and a moral sense antecedent to all justifying reasons' (9 October 1725; Hutcheson 1971 [1725]: 227). It emerges particularly clearly from this correspondence that for Hutcheson both the 'instinct toward the good of others' – namely 'sympathy' which may extend to fully-fledged 'benevolence' relating to *general* happiness (see below, p. 78) – and the 'approbation' afforded by the moral sense accorded conduct thus conducive to general welfare are effectively considered as axioms *not further reducible*, and thus not reducible to 'exciting reason'. For example: 'If this being have also public affections, what are the exciting reasons for observing faith or hazarding his life in war? He will assign this truth as a reason, such conduct tends to the good of mankind. Go a step further, why does he pursue the good of mankind? If his affections be really disinterested, without any selfish view, he has no exciting reasons; the public good is an ultimate end to this series of desires' (1971 [1725]: 228). We see here how strikingly close Hutcheson comes to what was to be Bentham's stance regarding the utility principle whereby 'that which is used to prove every thing else cannot itself be proved'.

******

The aforementioned perspectives are elaborated in *An Essay on the Nature and Conduct of the Passions and Affections with Illustrations on the Moral Sense.*[8] Section IV of the *Illustrations* is devoted to 'Shewing the Use of Reason concerning Virtue and Vice, upon *Supposition* that we receive these Ideas by a moral Sense' (Hutcheson 1728: 275; 1769 (1742): 250), and asserts that 'without a moral Sense there is no Explication can be given of our ideas of Morality; nor of that Reasonableness supposed antecedent to all Instincts, Affections, or Sense' (281; 255). Similarly, Section V concerns 'Shewing that Virtue may have whatever is meant by Merit; and be rewardable upon *the Supposition* that it is perceived by a Sense, and elected from Affection or Instinct' (285; 259). Reason does enter the picture but only to determine the technical question: 'What Actions do really evidence kind Affections, or do really tend to the greatest publick good?' (276; 251). As for 'the Motives which, even from Self-Love, would excite each Individual to do those Actions which are publickly useful', Hutcheson insists that there was no source anchored in reason for such motives, but all turned on the *assumed* existence of the instinctive 'kind affections' supplemented by approval from the moral sense. It is true that concern for the 'publick good' was shown by a raft of considerations including authority, religion, 'universal experience', and 'inward consciousness', and 'self-approbation'; and these might be said to imply a quest for 'exciting reason' to account for such concern, but their general and universalist character suggests rather that the matter was seen by Hutcheson to be *self-evident* – at least to any man 'who considers these things' — and this notwithstanding the complications created by the presence of the self-interest motive:

> Yet since all Men have naturally Self-Love as well as the kind Affections, the former may often counteract the latter, or the latter the former. In each Case the Agent is uneasy, and in some Degree unhappy. The first rash Views of human Affairs often represent private Interest as opposite to the Publick: When this is apprehended, Self-Love may often engage Men in publickly hurtful Actions, which their moral Sense will condemn; and this is the ordinary Cause of Vice. To represent these Motives of Self-Interest, to engage Men to publickly useful Actions, is certainly the most necessary Point in Morals. This has been so well done by the antient Moralists, by Dr. Cumberland, Puffendorf, Grotius, Shaftesbury; t'is made so certain from the divine Government of the World, the State of Mankind, who cannot subsist without Society, from universal Experience and Consent, from inward Consciousness of the Pleasure of kind Affections, and Self-Approbation, and of the Torments of Malice, or Hatred, or Envy, or Anger; that no Man who considers these things, can ever imagine he can have any possible Interest in opposing the publick Good; or in checking or restraining his kind Affections ...
> (277; 251–2)

Hutcheson even speculated that 'if he had no kind Affections, his very Self-Love and Regard to his private Good might excite him to publickly useful Actions and dissuade from the contrary' (277–8; 252) — although he does not posit self-interest as a *necessary* condition for such actions — unlike Mandeville who requires state intervention to induce self-interested citizens to act in the social interest (see Chapter 3, p. 54). And he found it improbable that a man 'would approve as virtuous an Action publickly useful, to which the Agent was excited only by Self-Love, without any kind affection' (276; 251).

Differences between editions may be noted here. Firstly, in the first version Hutcheson proceeds to minimize the self-interest drive thus: "Tis also probable that no view of Interest can raise that kind Affection, which we approve as virtuous; nor can any Reasoning do it, except that which shews some moral Goodness, or kind Affections in the Object; for this never fails, where it is observed or supposed in any Person, to raise the Love of the Observer; *so that Virtue is not properly taught*' (Hutcheson 1728: 276; 1769 [1742]: 251; emphasis added). The concluding assertion is omitted in 1742, perhaps indicating a softening of position regarding the sense of virtue as *entirely* instinctive — virtue *can* be taught. But it may also be no more than removal of a conclusion that does not strictly follow from the preceding text.

Relevant here is the response to John Clarke's position that the notion of *disinterested sympathy* was self-contradictory insofar as the actor takes pleasure from the happiness of others. Hutcheson has no patience at all with those who actually denied a 'publick Sense', but is less harsh towards Clarke, who recognised such a sense 'especially in natural Affection, and Compassion; by which "the Observation of the Happiness of others is made the necessary Occasion of Pleasure, and their Misery the Occasion of Pain to the Observer'", but identified its source in self-love. His answer turns on the instinctive character of sympathy, the fact that such pleasure is unsought: 'That this Sympathy with others is the Effect of the Constitution of our Nature, and not brought upon ourselves by any Choice, with view to any selfish Advantage whatever' (Hutcheson 1728: 14; 1769 [1742]: 13–14).

Secondly, what should we make of the removal in 1742 of a striking assertion of 1728 regarding 'the more extensive calm Desire of the universal Good of all sensitive Natures' – an allusion to *general benevolence* – 'which our moral Sense approves as the Perfection of Virtue' (Hutcheson 1728: 8)? Does this not imply the abandonment of a main plank of Hutcheson's position? I think not. This deletion must be seen in its context which relates to a 'class of public desires' incorporating a variety of 'Affections' extending in the limit to *general benevolence* or the 'perfection of virtue' as approved by the moral sense: '[This] Class of publick Desires contains many very different sorts of Affections, all those which tend toward the Happiness of others, or the removal of Misery; such as those of Gratitude, Compassion, Natural Affection, Friendship, or the more extensive calm Desire of the universal Good of all sensitive Natures, which our moral Sense approves as the perfection of Virtue, even when it limits, and counteracts, the narrower Attachments of Love' (7–8).

There is nothing I can see in this passage to imply that the moral sense is, as it were, 'contaminated' by the pleasure enjoyed at observing the happiness of others engendered by the actor's virtuous conduct. But Hutcheson may have feared otherwise, for the passage is rewritten in the third edition to carefully distinguish the 'Public Sense' – understood as the 'determination to be pleased with the happiness of others' – from the Moral Sense which identifies and approves virtuous conduct *independently of pleasure derived from observing the happiness generated thereby*:

> The next [third] class of perceptions we may call a Public Sense, viz. "our determination to be pleased with the happiness of others, and to be uneasy at their misery" ... The fourth class we may call the Moral Sense, by which "we perceive virtue or vice, in ourselves, or others." This is plainly distinct from the former class of perception, since many are strongly affected with the fortunes of others, who seldom reflect upon virtue or vice, in themselves, or others, as an object: as we may find in natural affection, compassion, friendship, or even general benevolence to mankind, which connect our happiness or pleasure with that of others, even when we are not reflecting on our own temper, nor delighted with the perception of our own virtue.
>
> (Hutcheson 1769 [1742]: 5–6)

By implication, it would be a defective moral sense which, in evaluating *virtue*, did 'connect our happiness or pleasure with that of others'. And that the deletion in

1742 was indeed an unnecessary deviation is confirmed by the key fact that the utilitarian dimension to the moral sense remains identical across both editions with their emphasis on specifically *benevolent* intention, which of course excludes self-satisfaction:

> The greatest and most perfect Good is the whole Series, or Scheme of Events, which contains a greater Aggregate of Happiness in the whole, or more absolute universal Good, than any other possible Scheme, after subtracting all the Evils connected with each of them.
> An Action is good, in a moral Sense, [1742: An action is morally good,] when it flows from benevolent Affection, or Intention of absolute Good to others. Men of much Reflection may actually intend universal absolute Good; but with the common rate of Men their Virtue consists in intending and pursuing particular absolute Good, not inconsistent with universal Good.
> (Hutcheson 1728: 37; 1769 [1742]: 34–5).⁹

******

I return to the *Inquiry* itself and various refinements of the main themes, particularly the relationship between the primary motives. Notwithstanding his objection to Mandeville's denial of the actuality of wholly disinterested benevolence (see in particular Hutcheson 1729: 124–5.) Hutcheson admitted that 'Reason and calm Reflection may recommend to us, from Self-Interest, those Actions, which at first View' – before any such calculation, or 'immediately' as it is sometimes phrased – 'our moral Sense determines us to admire, without considering this Interest' (126). The *instinctive* character of the recommendations admired by the moral sense is of the essence, and contrasts with the evaluation of circumstances based on reasoned calculation entailed by personal interest: 'We are not to imagine, that this moral Sense, more than the other Senses, supposes any innate Ideas, Knowledge, or practical Proposition: We mean by it only a Determination of our Minds to receive the simple Ideas of Approbation or Condemnation, from Actions observed, antecedent to any Opinions of Advantage or Loss to redound to our selves from them' (128).

Hutcheson next engages in a calculus entailing various combinations of the two motive forces, confirming thereby that the sequential order of an immediate instinct reflecting benevolence or concern for the public interest, followed perhaps by reasoned evaluations of personal interest, was designed to establish the contrast but not necessarily to be understood temporally. He points out that even when the two principles act supportively *pure* benevolence may still be meaningful requiring, so to say, no reduction in the ethical quality accorded to conduct: 'Thus, if a Man have such strong Benevolence, as would have produc'd an Action without any Views of Self-Interest; that such a Man has also in View private Advantage, along with publick Good, as the Effect of his Action, does no way diminish the Benevolence of the Action' (Hutcheson 1729: 136). While Hutcheson rejected Mandeville's norm where no individual would ever act in the public interest unless he expected to derive some personal benefit, he did allow that '[w]here he would not have produc'd so much publick Good, had it not been for the Prospect of Self-Interest, then the Effect of Self-Love is to be deducted, and his Benevolence is proportion'd to the remainder of Good, which pure Benevolence would have produc'd' (136–7). Conceivably the meritorious balance *exceeds* what is strictly due to benevolence, for 'our Benevolence is not always accompanied by Pleasure, nay 'tis often attended with Pain when the Object is in Distress' (139), in which case 'the Benevolence is proportion'd to the Sum of the Good produc'd, added to the Resistance of Self-Love surmounted by it' (137). One notes the implicit mechanical analogy.

A summary formulation in *An Essay on the ... Passions and Affections with Illustrations on the Moral Sense* further clarifies the allowance made for *legitimate* self-interest in determining 'what is most noble, generous and virtuous in Life', which 'consists in sacrificing all positive Interests, and bearing all private Evils for the publick Good: and in submitting also the Interests of all smaller Systems to the Interests of the whole: Without any other Exception or Reserve than this, that every Man may look upon himself as a Part of this System, and consequently not sacrifice an important private Interest to a less important Interest of others' (Hutcheson 1728: 313;1769 [1742]: 284). Hutcheson admits that the balance was 'perhaps impossible precisely to determine'.

A further elaboration in the *Inquiry* relates to the immediate stimulus for 'virtuous' action. 'Benevolence' designates a concern to enhance 'the natural Good of Mankind or that of some Parts of it' (above, p. 73). But in practice, 'the immediate Motive to virtuous Actions' or 'the Springs of the Actions which we call virtuous' – notice the Benthamite term – resides not in benevolence as such but rather in a range of more specific 'affections' manifesting 'moral goodness' (Hutcheson 1729: 131). These are listed variously as 'Honesty, Faith, Generosity, Kindness'; 'Love, Humanity, Gratitude, Compassion'; 'Humanity, Mercy, Faithfulness'; 'Honour, Faith, Generosity, Justice' – provided no personal advantage is expected from such conduct (105, 114, 115, 121). The *Illustrations on the Moral Sense* elaborates why *general* benevolence – which implies anonymity or 'indifferent persons' as it is sometimes designated – is typically insufficient as an immediate motive to ethical conduct:

> But our Understanding and Power are limited, so that we cannot know many other Natures, nor is our utmost Power capable of promoting the Happiness of many: our Actions are therefore influenced by some stronger Affections than this general Benevolence. There are certain Qualities found in some Beings more than in others, which excite stronger Degrees of Good-will, and determine our Attention to their Interests, while that of others is neglected. The ties of Blood, Benefits conferred upon us, and the Observation of Virtue in others, raise much

more vigorous Affections, than that general Benevolence which we may have toward all.
(Hutcheson 1728: 303; 1769 [1742]: 276)

The various 'kind affections' are said in the *Inquiry* to reinforce benevolence, the primary affection. Thus Hutcheson envisaged 'a Benevolence ... in some degree extended to all Mankind', but only 'where there is no interfering Interest, which from Self-Love may obstruct it' (Hutcheson 1729: 163). Accordingly, any 'apparent want of natural Affection among collateral Relations' could be accounted for by the fact that 'these natural Inclinations ... are overpower'd by Self-Love, where there happens any Opposition of Interests' (164). But in the absence of such conflict, 'we shall find all Mankind under its Influence, but with different degrees of Strength, according to the nearer or more remote Relations they stand in to each other; and *according as the natural Affection of Benevolence may be join'd with and strengthen'd by* Esteem, Gratitude, Compassion, or other kind Affections; or on the contrary weaken'd by Displicence, Anger, or Envy' (emphasis added).

As we would expect, individuals possessed of 'kind affections' attract, instinctively *by way of their moral sense*, the *approval of observers* as reflected in 'Complacence, Esteem, or Good-liking'. I transcribe both the 1725 and 1729 versions:

> [1725: Love of] Complacence, Esteem, or Good-liking, at first view appears to be disinterested, and so [1725: the Hatred of] Displicence or Dislike; and are entirely excited by some moral Qualitys, Good or Evil, apprehended to be in the Objects, which Qualitys *the very frame of our Nature* determines us [1725: to love or hate,] to approve or disapprove, *according to the moral Sense* above explained ... [R]epresent a Character as generous, kind, faithful, humane, tho in the most distant Parts of the World, and we cannot avoid [1725: loving it with] Esteem and Complacence.
> (Hutcheson 1725: 128; 1729: 134–5; emphasis added)

The Introduction to the Second Treatise closes in similar terms, but clarifies well that the matter of approval relates to the observation of actions by oneself as well as by others, and the 1729 version omitting an earlier reference to the self-interested 'pleasure' derived from the undertaking benevolent actions: 'That some Actions have to Men an immediate Goodness; or, that by *a superior Sense, which I call a Moral one*, we approve the Actions of others, and perceive them to be their Perfection and Dignity; a like Perception we have in reflecting on such Actions of our own, [1725: we perceive Pleasure in the Contemplation of such Actions in others, and are determin'd to love the Agent (and much more do we perceive Pleasure in being conscious of having done such Actions our selves)] without any View of further natural Advantage from them' (1725: 106; 1729: 109; emphasis added). It seems to have been

Hutcheson's intention to silently counter the force of Clarke's insistence on *interested* sympathy (see above, p. 74).

A later statement is more precise, carefully distinguishing – as in Hutcheson's letter to Burnet cited above (p. 75) – between 'some Determination of our nature' to focus upon the welfare of others, and the Moral Sense itself represented as *source of approval* of such actions: 'Having remov'd these false Springs of virtuous Actions' – alluding to those who relate virtuous action to some form or other of self-interest – 'let us next establish the true one, viz. some Determination of our Nature to study the Good of others; or some Instinct, antecedent to all Reason from Interest, which influences us to the Love of others; even as the moral Sense, above explain'd, determines us to approve the Actions which flow from this Love in our selves or others' (Hutcheson 1729: 158–9). The moral sense in effect is said to answer the question *why* we should approve actions motivated by the instinctive 'Determination of our Nature to study the Good of others'.

It emerges from all this that there are *two* categories of approval by the moral sense, one appropriate for the *kindly affections* and one relating specifically to *general benevolence*: 'The Affections which are of most Importance in Morals, are commonly included under the names LOVE and HATRED. Love toward rational Agents, is subdivided into Love of Complacence or Esteem, and Love of Benevolence' (Hutcheson 1729: 133). Now although the benign affections are approved by the moral sense the discussion sometimes proceeds without formal mention of their social consequences. Even so, this scarcely supports Bentham's reading of Hutcheson as divorcing that sense from the general good. For the *cardinal virtues* of Temperance, Courage, Prudence, and Justice are so designated precisely 'because they are Dispositions universally necessary to promote publick Good, and denote Affections toward rational Agents; otherwise there would appear no Virtue in them'. In brief, the cardinal virtues are *necessary conditions* for sympathetic conduct or conduct governed by fellow-feeling or, indeed, concern for the 'Good of Mankind' – benevolence, the prime natural affection – as is clarified in an elaboration: 'Prudence, if it were only employ'd in promoting private Interest, is never imagin'd to be a Virtue; and Justice, or observing a strict Equality, if it have no regard to the Good of Mankind, the Preservation of Rights, and securing Peace, is a Quality properer for its ordinary Gestamen [Latin: That which is borne or worn, a burden, load, ornaments, accoutrements, arms, etc], a Beam and Scales, than for a rational agent' (132–3). On the other hand, a comment regarding *temperance* renders the moral quality rather elastic by adding to 'Service of Mankind' both 'obedience toward the Deity' and 'search after Truth': 'Ask the most abstemious Hermit, if Temperance of it self wou'd be morally good, supposing it shew'd no Obedience toward the DEITY, made us no fitter for Devotion, or the Service of Mankind, or the Search after Truth, than Luxury; and he will easily grant, that it would be no moral Good, tho still it might be naturally good or advantageous to Health' (132). *Justice* – defined as 'observing a strict Equality' – also introduces elements apart from the 'Good' or 'Service' of mankind as such, namely 'the Preservation of Rights, and securing

Peace', although these might well have been regarded as sub-categories. And in fact, elsewhere Hutcheson posits that provided *social advantage* can be demonstrated, claims to 'rights' are approved by the moral sense: 'From this Sense too we derive our Ideas of Rights. Whenever it appears to us, that a Faculty of doing, demanding, or possessing any thing, universally allow'd in certain Circumstances, would in the whole tend to the general Good, we say that one in such Circumstances, has a Right to do, possess, or demand that Thing. And according as this Tendency to the publick Good is greater or less, the Right is greater or less' (277–8).

******

One complexity arises in the suggestion by Hutcheson that 'benevolence' extends not to concern for the *general good* but only to those themselves possessed of the kindly dispositions. For, commenting on local and national connections and the accompanying 'Associations, Friendships, Familys, natural Affections, and other humane Sentiments', Hutcheson remarks that 'our moral Sense determines us to approve these lovely Dispositions where we have most distinctly observ'd them', and adds that '*our Benevolence concerns us in the Interests of those Persons possess'd of them*' (Hutcheson 1729: 163–4; emphasis added).

But what to make of this restriction is open to debate. It is pertinent that, after positing in the *Illustrations on the Moral Sense* 'stronger affections' than 'general benevolence' entailing anonymity, as primary stimulus to ethical conduct (cited above), Hutcheson points out that while the former 'are very different from the general Benevolence toward all, yet it is very probable, that there is a Regularity or Proportion observed in the Constitution of our Nature; so that, abstracting from some acquired Habits, or Associations of Ideas, and from the more sudden Emotions of some particular Passions, that Temper which has the most lively Gratitude, or is the most susceptive of Friendship with virtuous Characters, would also have the strongest general Benevolence toward indifferent Persons' (Hutcheson 1728: 303–4; 1769 [1742]: 276). Conversely, 'where there is the weakest general benevolence, there we could expect the least gratitude, and the least friendship, or love toward the virtuous'. And, in fact, he again proceeds to weigh heavily the role of *general* benevolence – which seems to be coming back into its own:

> Every kind Affection, if it be considered only with relation to its own Object, is indeed approved; such as natural Affection, Gratitude, Pity, Friendship: And yet when we take a more extensive View of the Tendency of some Actions proceeding even from these Affections, we may often condemn these Actions when they are apprehended as pernicious to larger Systems of Mankind ... Mankind is capable of large extensive Ideas of great Societies. And it is expected of them, that their general Benevolence should continually direct and limit, not only their selfish Affections, but even their nearer Attachments to others: that their Desire of publick Good, and Aversion to publick Misery, should overcome at least

> their Desire of positive private Advantages either to themselves or their particular Favourites; so as to make them abstain from any Action which would be positively pernicious or hurtful to Mankind, however beneficial it might be to themselves, or their Favourites.
>
> (310–11; 282)

We now introduce a further qualification in the *Illustrations* to the contention that the immediate motive to virtuous conduct resides not in general benevolence but rather in the more specific 'affections' manifesting 'moral goodness'. The problem is raised that the particular affections can become dangerously unstable and unreliable and capable of generating perverse outcomes: 'it is often observed, that the very best of our particular Affections or Desires, when they are grown violent and passionate, thro' the confused Sensations and Propensities which attend them, make us incapable of considering calmly the whole Tendency of our Actions, and lead us often into what is absolutely pernicious, under some Appearance of relative or particular Good' (Hutcheson 1728: 278; 1769 [1742]: 253). Confirming a proper, if limited, place for 'reason' in ethical calculation, Hutcheson distinguished between 'passionate' action and action reflecting 'calm desire and affection' the latter alone 'employ[ing] our Reason freely', but without implying any conflict with actions arising from 'Instinct, Desire or Affection', for this he saw as a false dichotomy. Importantly, he concludes 'that the most perfect Virtue consists in the calm, un-passionate Benevolence, rather than in particular Affections', which can be reconciled with the generalization in the *Inquiry* if the latter is understood as relating to virtue falling somewhat short of perfection.

★★★★★★

Finally, I return as promised to the ethical significance attached to 'obedience toward the Deity'. The *Illustrations* heavily qualifies this feature. Certainly Hutcheson posits that the 'Affections of Love and Gratitude' toward the Deity 'would necessarily raise frequent Attention and Consideration of our Actions; and would engage us, if we apprehended any of them to be offensive to him, or contrary to that Scheme of Events in which we apprehended the DEITY to delight, to avoid them with a more firm Resolution than what we had in any other Affairs' (Hutcheson 1728: 314; 1769 [1742]: 285). Yet more positively, such affections would encourage 'with the greatest Vigor to do whatever we apprehend as positively pleasing, or conducive to those Ends in which we apprehend the DEITY delights'. But whence the comprehension of God's wishes? Revelation as a source of instruction implies that 'the Omission of what we know to be required is positively evil: so that by a Revelation we may be obliged to farther Services than were requisite previously to it, which we could not innocently omit, after this Revelation is known' (315; 286). But Hutcheson immediately points out that 'we are here only considering our moral Sense' independently of revelation, leading him to 'inquire how far simple Ignorance of a DEITY, or unaffected Atheism, does evidence an evil

Disposition, or Defect of good Affections below Innocence'. His answer is positively liberal: There is no 'innate Idea of a DEITY so imprinted, that no Person could be without it; or ...so disposed, as necessarily to receive this Idea as soon as we can be called moral Agents' (316–17; 287). And while notions regarding the goodness of God might be acquired by 'Tradition or Reflection', he concludes by warning 'how cautious Men ought to be in passing Sentence upon the Impiety of their Fellows, or representing them as wicked and profane, or hateful to the DEITY, and justly given over to eternal Misery' (321; 291). And he firmly rejects those who 'assert, against universal Experience, that we approve no Actions which are not thus intended toward the DEITY. T'is plain, a generous compassionate Heart which, at first view of the Distress of another, flies impatiently to his Relief, or spares no Expence to accomplish it, meets with strong Approbation from every Observer who has not perverted his Sense of Life by School-Divinity or Philosophy' (326; 296). He goes so far in the first edition as to assert that virtue is *greater* when benevolent conduct is *not* founded on external support: 'more Virtue is evidenced by any given Moment of Beneficence from good Affections only toward our Fellows, or particular Persons, than by the same Moment produced from the joint Considerations of the DEITY, or of a general System or Species' (323). This strong statement is modified subsequently, but the conclusion stands: 'if the Moment produced by the Conjunction of these Motives' – including the religious – 'be not greater than that produced with unaffected Neglect of these Motives, from particular good Affection, there is less virtue in the former than the latter' (325–6; 295).

Hutcheson was sensitive to the charge that he was undermining orthodoxy. Thus, he found inexcusable John Clarke's 'raising such an Outcry against him as *injurious to Christianity*, for Principles which some of the most *zealous Christians* have publickly maintained' (Hutcheson 1728: xii–xiii). (Mention of Clarke is omitted in 1742 but the protest itself is reiterated in similar terms, in 1769 [1742]: xi.) Fearing that he would be misunderstood, he added a conspicuously orthodox note to the effect that strong support for benevolent conduct was to be derived from traditional religion:

> 'Tis also plain from universal Experience that a Regard to the DEITY, frequent Reflection on his Goodness, and consequent Acts of Love, are the strongest and most universally prevailing Means of obtaining a good Temper. Whatever Institution therefore does most effectually tend to raise Men's Attention, to recall their Minds from the Hurry of their common Affairs, to instruct them in the ways of promoting publick Good farther than the busy Part of the World without Assistance would probably apprehend, must be so wise and good, that every honest Mind would rejoice in it, even tho it had no other Authority than human to recommend it. Every one will understand that by this is meant a publick Worship on set Days, in which a stop is put to Commerce, and the busy part of Mankind instructed in the Duties of Piety and Humanity.
> (Hutcheson 1728: 326n; 1769 [1742]: 295n)

For all that, the final conclusion firmly reiterates the possibility of virtuous conduct divorced from any religious underpinning: 'To conclude this Subject. It seems probable, that however we must look upon that Temper as exceedingly imperfect, inconstant, and partial, in which Gratitude toward the universal Benefactor, Admiration and Love of the supreme original Beauty, Perfection and Goodness, are not the strongest and most prevalent Affections; yet *particular Actions may be innocent, nay virtuous, where there is no actual Intention of pleasing the DEITY, influencing the Agent*' (332–3; 301; emphasis added). Here is a wide opening for secularism notwithstanding the orthodox caution.[10]

4.4 'Inaugural Lecture on the Social Nature of Man' (1730)

Our next port of call is the 'Inaugural Lecture on the Social Nature of Man' delivered at the University of Glasgow in November 1730, regarded by some as providing a more careful and detailed exposition than the later works (Mautner 1993: 108). This lecture is certainly of high importance in explicitly recognizing that the moral sense does not operate properly in the world as we know it. Raising the issue of 'what kind of things can rightly be called natural to man as far as morality is concerned' (Hutcheson 1993 [1730]: 127), Hutcheson elaborates a contrast between the 'corrupt' world as it is with what it could ideally become: 'If we are to care at all about our use of words, the "state of nature" ought to denote either that condition to which men are for the most part brought through the exercise of all the natural appetites and powers, or else that most perfect condition to which men can rise by the most sagacious use of all their powers and faculties, a use that seems to be enjoined by the innate desire for the greatest happiness and by whatever benevolent and kind affections that may be natural to man' (131). He then opts for the 'perfect state' as meriting the term 'state of nature', and the 'moral sense' – the term is used explicitly and identified with 'natural conscience' – is said to be working at full capacity *only* in that state:

> [W]hen we consider the entire structure of human nature, no matter how perturbed or corrupted it may have become, as well as its several parts; and above all the public and benevolent affections, and again that moral sense that we also call natural conscience, we also see clearly that the vices do not belong to our nature; and we discern those parts which ought to restrain and govern the lower appetites. Therefore, however much the force and power of this sense or conscience may have been reduced, so as often to be incapable of ruling over the lower impulses, it is nevertheless seen to be fit to rule by its very nature and it is in fact … the ruling principle, to which, in the uncorrupted state of out nature, everything was subjected and rightly so.
>
> (131–2)

The closing remark, which alludes to Stoic doctrine (Mautner 1993:132n), leads to the conclusion that 'the true structure of our nature and the true condition of our nature that God instituted cannot indeed be restored until conscience, reinstated on her throne, shows her dominion over the bodily appetites' (132). As we have indicated, the moral sense operates properly only in an ideal world.

The main concern of the lecture is the sense in which social life can be said to be natural to man, and the question is raised: 'Does all that benevolence toward the general public, which is concerned with the protection and welfare of whole nations, spring from everyone's poverty, weakness, and need; namely, that there be those through whom everyone can obtain what he needs, so that, by giving and receiving what is due, everyone can receive from another what he is unable to obtain by himself? Or does benevolence rather arise by nature, and do we have a natural inclination to beneficence, not for the sake of favours, and without any thought of how much advantage may be gained from it?' (Hutcheson 1993 [1730]: 134). Hutcheson opts for the second position (that of Cumberland and Shaftesbury) on the grounds that the alternative, proposed by Pufendorf, omitted the 'many appetites immediately implanted by nature, which are not directed towards physical pleasure or advantage but towards certain higher things which in themselves depend on associating with others. These higher pleasures do not affect the external senses, and there is no conceivable way in which they can be pursued outside society' (135). Indeed, 'even if we were to suppose that everyone seeks his own pleasure or advantage, nevertheless, such is the nature of most pleasured and of the greatest ones, of such a kind are most of our desires, that they induce us to seek social life for its own sake almost without any reasoning, and to make the offices of social life in themselves joyful and agreeable' (136). In fact, however, '(i)t is not only because of some pleasure or advantage to oneself that human nature is sociable ... but human nature is also in itself, directly and in a primary sense benevolent, kind and sociable, even in the absence of any calculation of advantage or pleasure to oneself'.

Now, as offered by Cumberland and Shaftesbury, the explanation turns partly on 'kind and benevolent affections and passions' implanted by nature – intending what are more commonly referred to as 'moral sentiments' – which, 'in the longer view, have regard to the happiness of others' such that 'when things of a certain kind appear before it, particular affections will arise by the guidance of nature alone without any artifice or deliberation and indeed without any prior decree of the will' (Hutcheson 1993 [1730]: 137). 'Nor', Hutcheson adds, 'is this concern for the situation of others to be seen only when they are present and perceived by our external senses ... but whenever we calmly imagine other persons ... even in very distant countries or ages where no advantage of ours is involved we have a strong interest and concern for the fortunes of all virtuous individuals and societies'. And certainly it was not the case that people act benevolently solely from fear of Deity, as some maintained (139). But this is only part of the picture. There is in addition the *moral sense*, though the term itself is not used: 'These writers further postulate a sense, natural to man, of what is right and becoming. It is because of this sense that we seek to honour all kindness, loyalty, mildness, and friendliness and therefore also embrace with much greater willingness and love those who possess these virtues' (138).

Hutcheson readily admitted that we 'have keen appetites craving for private pleasure and advantage' in addition to 'virtuous affections, which render us sociable', generating an internal struggle, 'desire urging one thing, reason another' (Hutcheson 1993 [1730]: 140–1). But, relying here on 'introspection', he finds 'a certain part of [man's] nature to be … well suited to bring peace between these competing, affections … Divine Providence, which we often call nature [having] given us reason and a keenness of judgment which easily discerns that it is by means of a life in society and in friendship that we can most effectively procure and retain all pleasures, including the private and sensuous ones' (141). A 'Smithian' element is introduced regarding the relation of genuine satisfaction to the accumulation of wealth: 'Reason also teaches that the enjoyment of modest and restrained pleasures is most advantageous and most agreeable to us and does not produce an unsettling effect on human society. Conversely, there is no reason to believe that any man needs for the sake of an agreeable and secure life to hoard unlimited stores of goods or to indulge in continuous exquisite sensual pleasures, in the obtaining of which others are harmed or morally proper action is neglected'. Reason and keen judgment are of the essence in all this. Yet 'reason' is played down when Hutcheson goes on to assert that '[t]his does not require any lengthy or laborious deduction', alluding to the supplement provided by, in essence, the *moral sense*, to which he adds a 'sense of shame' and 'incentives of praise': 'God has given us a sense of what is becoming and beautiful; conjoined with it is a sense of shame, by which all the more lowly pleasures are restrained. Likewise, He has given us the keen incentives of praise'. (These senses supplementing the moral sense are also spelled out in the *Short Introduction*; below, 4.6.) 'All this', we are assured, 'leads to a kind and social life, and gives rise to virtuous actions which benefit others and which are most useful and most pleasant to the agent. There also arises that self-love of our nature which, although innate, is in no manner in conflict with our public and benevolent affections' the latter again referring to the moral sentiments.

We return finally to the difficulty that the moral sense, identified with 'conscience' does not operate in its full 'force and power' in the 'corrupt' world as we know it. How does Hutcheson reconcile this alleged fact with the weight placed elsewhere on the fully-functioning 'natural' moral sense? In the first place, he simply *reasserts* that 'benevolence is immediately and in itself natural, whilst ill-will arises only secondarily and often only by chance or through ignorance' (Hutcheson 1993 [1730]: 141–2). Secondly, he relies heavily on rhetoric, asserting further 'without any doubt' that the moral sense 'is destined by nature to govern, and that the bodily appetites are born to serve': 'Does anyone think that natural conscience, that sense of what is beautiful and becoming, every honourable affection and even that power of the mind that we call reason, are only handmaids to those desires that are commonly said to be merely sensual, and only pander to pleasure? On the contrary, we discern without any doubt that this conscience and sense of virtue, which has human reason as its permanent counsellor, is destined by nature to govern, and that the bodily appetites are born to serve' (142).

Doubtless it is the case, as Mautner maintains, that Hutcheson, in appealing to 'natural teleology' as the basis for his confidence in the overriding force of 'benevolence', was writing in opposition to Locke (Mautner 1993: 46–7, 121). But Hutcheson's case is not well made out. For, despite his strong assertions, he was troubled by recognition of defects in the moral sense which required correction and control. This emerges from his response to those – Hobbes and Mandeville fit the bill – who 'make much of education and statecraft, which, they say, explains this actual human sociality and those affections, which either seem or actually are kind'. He agrees that 'civilized manners can result from respect for the law and the efforts of those in authority; everyone's thought of his own interest can be relevant to this extent and can have that effect', but he yet firmly denies that controls resulting from 'hope for advantage, education or custom' rendered obsolete the essential functioning of the moral sense, asking: 'is it really possible that hope for advantage, education or custom can induce new inner affections and new senses contrary to one's natural constitution?' (Hutcheson 1993 [1730]: 143). There are rather 'senses antecedently implanted in us by nature; no new senses or affections come into being', which is proven by the fact that 'we do find that men judge most acts to be virtuous, praiseworthy, beautiful, and becoming, even when no advantage of their own is involved; likewise, we find a solicitous concern for others and a great willingness to help them even though all appearance of private advantage has been entirely removed'. This response, which *takes for granted* the existence of a moral sense, can scarcely be said to deal convincingly with the dilemma that in the real world the alleged sense does not in fact operate properly, opening the road for education and custom to provide support.

4.5 A *System of Moral Philosophy* (1755)

The posthumously-published *System of Moral Philosophy* – in circulation already in the late 1730s – explicitly rules out Bentham's interpretation of the Hutchesonian moral sense as providing an automatic specification of what is 'good' or 'bad' in any action independently of welfare consequences: 'Our having a *moral sense* does not infer that we have innate complex ideas of the several actions; or innate opinions of their consequences or effects upon society: these we discover by observation and reasoning, and we often make very opposite conclusions about them' (Hutcheson 1755: 97). This extract is from Book One, Chapter V. Now it is true that the title to Chapter IV taken in isolation – 'Concerning the Moral Sense, or faculty of perceiving moral excellence, and its supreme objects' (53) – might be said to support Bentham's reading, but those 'supreme objects' of 'moral excellence' turn out to be specifically goodwill towards others, moral conduct reflecting our 'kind affections ultimately aimed at the good of others' thereby confirming the 'reduction of moral sense to sympathy' established in the *Inquiry* (above, p. 75). Leslie Stephen understood the chapter, to the contrary, as maintaining that the moral sense 'is an independent faculty, as proven by the fact that 'none of the methods hitherto applied have resolved it into simpler elements. It cannot be analysed into sympathy, for we approve the virtues of our enemies' (Stephen 1902: 59). But, as we shall presently see, that we approve the virtues of our enemies is in fact adduced by Hutcheson as evidence that 'our approbating moral conduct is very different from liking it merely on the occasion of pleasure to ourselves in gratifying these kind affections' (Hutcheson 1755: 53).

If we should ask *why* disinterested sympathy is generally considered praiseworthy, the answer is quite simply that we *know* it to be so by a moral sense, having in mind that the enhancement of general welfare and the motives directed to that end constitute the very criteria of what is 'good'. Hutcheson assures the reader of the existence of a moral sense: 'In general, all descriptions of moral goodness by conformity to reason if we examine them well, must lead us to some immediate original sense or determination of our nature. All reasons exciting to an action will lead us to some original affection or instinct of will; and all justifying reasons, or such as shew an action to be good, will at last lead us to some original sense or power of perception' (Hutcheson 1755: 57). (Notice again the *two* stages entailed, first expressed in the correspondence of 1725 as, firstly, the 'instinct towards the good of others' and, secondly, the 'approbation' afforded by the moral sense of conduct thus conducive to public welfare; above, p. 76.) Again we have an *assurance* regarding the moral sense: 'There is ... as each one by close attention and reflection may convince himself, a natural and immediate determination to approve certain affections, and actions consequent upon them; or a natural sense of immediate excellence in them, not referred to any other quality perceivable by our other senses or by reasoning' (58). One might engage in a reasoned attempt to justify the designation of an action reflecting fellow-feeling as 'good' but any such attempt, we are promised, will necessarily lead back to an original moral sense designating such action as good. For '*reason is only a subservient power to our ultimate determinations either of perception or will* ... Reason can only direct to the means; or compare two ends previously constituted by some other immediate powers'. Hutcheson would agree that in practice – and of course taking the end for granted – reason plays a necessary if subsidiary role.

The irreducible character of the verdict provided by the moral sense whereby the instinct to act for the welfare of others is recognised as 'good' implies that such a verdict is in effect *axiomatic*. This conclusion is strongly reinforced by Hutcheson's rejection of the argument whereby moral goodness is proven by '*conformity to the divine will or laws*' on the grounds that this might justify evil should the divine will so dictate. That it does not do so indicates that what is intended is 'conformity to (God's) goodness, holiness, justice', namely to 'moral perfections that *must be previously known*' (Hutcheson 1755: 56; emphasis added). An explanation in Book One, Chapter V of observed differences between individuals in their sentiments towards actions in terms of 'different opinions about what God has commanded' (94), implies a moral sense dictating how God is to be properly understood: 'No man can have sufficient humanity of soul, and candour, who can believe that human sacrifices, or the persecution of his fellow-creatures about religious tenets which hurt not society, can be duties acceptable to *God*' (97). The *effective* downplaying of the theological dimension encountered in the earlier formulations outlined above is thus confirmed, notwithstanding the extensive discussions in Chapter IX regarding 'The Duties toward God', and Chapter X regarding 'The Affections, Duty, and Worship to be exercised toward the Deity'. It must however be said that Hutcheson wants to have his cake and eat it: 'The external advantages we procure to each other by our active virtues, *God* could have immediately conferred by his power without any action of ours; but, such was his goodness, he chose that we should enjoy some share of that divine and honourable pleasure of doing good to others; and, by the exercise of our kind affections and by our *moral faculty*, we do partake of it' (212).

Hutcheson likewise rejects evaluations of what is good based on 'fitness, congruity, agreement', on the grounds that '(t)he fitness of means or subordinate ends, does not prove them to be good, unless the ultimate end be good', while '(a)ll ultimate ends are settled by some of the original determinations of our nature' here referring readers to the *Illustrations on the moral sense* (Hutcheson 1755: 56).

Hutcheson's stance also dispenses with the argument alleging 'instruction, education, custom, or association of ideas as the original of moral approbation', since opinion can always be traced 'to an original principle' (Hutcheson 1755: 57-8). Nevertheless, Hutcheson did in fact allow that '(a)s some others of our immediate perceptive powers are capable of culture and improvement, so is this moral sense, without presupposing any reference to a superior power of reason to which their perceptions are to be referred' (59). The moral sense – approving, it should be noted, an 'extensive affection, a love to society, a zeal to promote general happiness' – stands sentinel independently of reason and actually governs all practical calculations relating to ethical ranking:

> A judge, from the motions of pity, gets many criminals acquitted: we approve this sweet tenderness of heart. But we find that violence and outrages abound, the sober, just, and industrious are plagued, and have no security. A more extensive view of a publick interest shews some sorts of pity to occasion more extensive misery, than arises from a strict execution of justice. Pity of itself never appears deformed; but *a more extensive affection, a love to society, a zeal to promote general happiness*, is a more lovely principle, and the want of this renders a character deformed.

> This only shews ... that among the several affections approved there are several degrees; some much more lovely than others. 'Tis thus alone we correct any apparent disorders in this, even as we correct our reason itself.
> (60; emphasis added)[11]

Here we find confirmed the Benthamite dimension to the argument – that the very essence of approval by the moral sense relates to conduct directed at the enhancement of general happiness, with reasoned adjustments required in the light of *experience* to assure accurate calculation of the maximand. It is precisely this facet that Bentham did not allow for in his interpretation of Hutcheson.

Were it only the sort of adjustment just alluded to that is intended by 'improvement' to the moral sense there would be no problem: what is judged 'good' must take into account real-world effects. But, as we shall presently see, there are far more disruptive forms of 'culture and improvement' affecting the moral sense itself (below, p. 98).

Returning to the actual existence of the moral sense, we have suggested earlier that Hutcheson regarded the phenomenon as self-evident. This he now confirms when he refers to mere *introspection* as 'proof' of the existence of a moral sense and of the superiority of moral good 'in kind and in dignity': 'This moral sense from its very nature appears to be designed for regulating and controlling all our powers. This dignity and commanding nature we are immediately conscious of, as we are conscious of the power itself. *Nor can such matters of immediate feeling be otherways proved but by appeals to our hearts* ... [W]e immediately discern moral good to be superior in kind and dignity to all others which are perceived by the other perceptive powers' (Hutcheson 1755: 61; emphasis added). Of the same order is 'proof' entailing appeal to universal experience: 'That some sort of benevolent affections, or some dispositions imagined to be connected with them, are the natural objects of approbation ... will be plain from almost all our reasonings in praising or censoring, applauding or condemning, the characters and actions of mankind. We point out some kind or beneficent intention, or some beneficent purposes proposed by the agent in what we praise, or would vindicate from censure' (63; also 89–92). The contention that the moral sense is 'naturally destined to command all the other powers' Hutcheson supports by distinguishing between self-directed and other-directed motivation, an exercise we have already encountered in the *Inquiry*:

> [I]n sacrificing ease, or health, or pleasure, to wealth, power, or even to the ingenious arts; their pleasures gain no dignity by that means; and the conduct is not more alluring to others. But in moral good, the greater the necessary sacrifice which was made to it, the moral excellence increases the more, and is the more approved by the agent, more admired by spectators, and the more they are roused to imitation. By this sense the heart can not only approve itself in sacrificing every other gratification to moral goodness, but have the highest self-enjoyment,

and approbation of its own disposition in doing so: *which plainly shews this moral sense to be naturally destined to command all the other powers.*

(62; emphasis added)

Noteworthy here is the suggestion that the moral sense not only acts as a source of approbation but might actually, at least indirectly by the high merit accorded to such conduct, *encourage* sympathetic conduct.

In this context Hutcheson confirms the prime message of his earlier expositions, namely that the moral sense approves above all actions enhancing the '*happiness of others*', now insisting strongly on the condition that such action be properly motivated:

> Let us next consider the several powers or dispositions approved or disapproved by this faculty. And here t'is plain that the primary objects of this faculty are the affections of the will, and that the several affections which are approved, tho' on very different degrees, yet all agree in one general character, of tendency to the happiness of others, and to the moral perfection of the mind possessing them. No actions, however in fact beneficial to society, are approved of as virtuous if they are imagined to flow from no inward good-will to any person, or from such dispositions as do not naturally suppose good-will in the agent, or at least exclude the highest selfishness.
>
> (Hutcheson 1755: 62–3)

Accordingly, 'the desires of glory, or even of rewards in a future state, were they supposed the sole affections moving an agent in the most beneficial services', would disqualify an apparently virtuous act. But here is added an important precondition: that such disqualification holds good assuming the agent is 'without any love to God, esteem of his moral excellencies, gratitude to him, or good-will to men' (63). Here 'love to God' is placed on a par with 'good-will to men', such that *a socially-beneficial act would be accorded some ethical status even if not motivated by sympathy towards mankind.* That this equation is seriously intended seems clear since the text goes on to assert that 'mere desire of one's own happiness, *without any love to God, or man*, is never the object of approbation' (emphasis added).

The essentially secular character of the general scheme emerging in the earlier works, and until this point in the *System* itself, may seem to have been abandoned. Nevertheless, a reconciliation may be affected: Even if 'love to God' suffices by itself as an adequate motive for the designation of ethical conduct, so by the same token does 'love to man' by itself. 'Love to God' is thus not a *necessary* condition for ethical approval. And the fact is that Hutcheson closes by reasserting that the 'disposition ... which is most excellent, and naturally gains the highest moral approbation, is the calm, stable universal good-will to all, or the most extensive benevolence' (1755: 69).[12] Notice that this assertion regarding the 'most excellent' of all dispositions itself concludes with the assurance: 'And this seems the most distinct notion we can form of the moral excellency of the Deity', which statement does not actually represent obedience to God as the source of, or stimulus for, moral conduct.

Also relevant is an account of 'another disposition inseparable' from that ranked highest – namely, the 'relish or approbation' accorded to high moral excellence, represented as 'a pretty different affection from benevolence or the desire of communicating happiness; and [which] is as it were in another order of affections', although 'never in opposition to benevolence, nay always conspiring with and assisting it. This desire of moral excellence, and love of the mind where it resides, with the consequent acts of esteem, veneration, trust, and resignation, are the essence *of true piety toward God*' (Hutcheson 1755: 69–70; emphasis added). This statement does not necessarily imply that 'the desire of moral excellence, and love of the mind where it resides' reflects a response to divine command – only that a person thus desirous and appreciative would be manifesting 'true piety'; nor does it detract from the conclusions at which we have arrived regarding benevolence as such.

✶✶✶✶✶✶

We come now to various nuances appearing in Book I of the *System* relating to moral approbation. I preface the discussion by citing a later formulation (in Book II) establishing not merely the high importance accorded to *motivation* as distinct from the desirable outcome of an action but also its (conditional) priority:

> No distant effects or consequences of actions or omissions, affect their morality, if they could not have been foreseen by that diligence and caution we expect from good men; for then they are no indications of the temper of the agent. For the same reason any prosperous effects which are not intended, do not increase the moral goodness of an action...
> (Hutcheson 1755: 230)

> Where kind affections alone are the springs of action, the good effected by any agent is as the strength of these affections and his ability jointly ... [W]hen the good done by two persons is equal, while their abilities are unequal, he shews the better heart, whose abilities are smaller. Where men are also excited by views of private interest, the effect of their selfish desires is to be deducted, and the remainder shews the effect of the virtuous disposition. Where motives of private interest dissuaded from some good action performed, the virtue appears the higher by surmounting these motives.
> (238)

With these generalizations in mind, we proceed to the analysis provided in Book I. Here Hutcheson sets out from so-called 'indifferent affections and actions (which) are such as pursue the innocent advantages of the agent without any detriment to society, and yet without any reference made by the agent to any good of others. Such are the necessary and moderate gratifications of appetite, and many trifling actions' (Hutcheson 1755: 64). To such actions unmotivated by fellow-feeling – 'pursuits of the ingenious arts and of knowledge', 'patience of labour', 'spirit in business' are mentioned – there nonetheless attaches 'a relish or sense of a certain dignity or decency'. Similarly, he refers to 'the exercise of those more manly powers, which have no necessary or natural connexion with virtue, but shew a taste above sensuality and the lower selfishness: such as the pursuits of the ingenious arts, of the elegance of life, and speculative sciences' (68). And he avers that '[e]very one sees a dignity in these pleasures, and must relish the desires of them; and indeed they are far less opposite to virtue, or the public interest, than keen tastes or appetites of a lower kind'.

The same approval applies, more generally, even to 'the necessary and moderate gratifications of appetite' (Hutcheson 1755: 64). Hutcheson elaborates this perspective on the 'selfish affections' with the emphasis upon moderation:

> The calm desire of private good, tho' it is not approved as virtue, yet is far from being condemned as vice. And none of the truly natural and selfish appetites and passions are of themselves condemned as evil, when they are within certain bounds, even though they are not referred by the agent to any publick interest. It was necessary for the general good that all such affections should be implanted in our species; and therefore it would have been utterly unnatural to have made them matters of disapprobation even while they were not hurtful. Nay, as these selfish affections are aiming at an end necessary to the general good, to wit the good of each individual, and as the abilities of gratifying them are powers which may be very usefully employed in subserviency to the most generous affections, it was highly proper and benign in the Author of Nature to invite us to the culture of these powers by an immediate relish for them wherever we observe them, in ourselves or in others; tho' this relish is plainly different from moral approbation.
>
> (65)

There is then an 'immediate' inner sense of moral approval *relating even to the selfish affections*, though subject to a condition: 'We all have by consciousness and experience a notion of the human constitution, and of a certain proportion of affections requisite to an innocent character', provided that the 'selfish affections' do not 'exclude or over-power the amiable affections', that is, provided that general welfare is not damaged.

A step beyond the 'indifferent affections' takes us to 'another set of dispositions and abilities still of a finer nature, tho' distinct from both the calm universal benevolence and the particular kind affections' (Hutcheson 1755:

66). According to the contrast as posited in the *Inquiry*, the former relates to the highest moral rank entailing concern for society as a whole, and the latter 'affections' entailing inter-personal connections such as love, honesty, faithfulness, generosity, kindness, gratitude, humanity, compassion, mercy, honour, and justice, with the proviso that the actors 'expect no Benefit from these admir'd Qualitys', both categories approved by the moral sense (above, pp. 80-1). The *Illustrations* emphasizes the relevance for the particular affections of blood ties earlier (above, p. 80). So too does the *System*, our present concern, which refers also to love of country:

> But to come to the more immediate objects of moral approbation, the kind affections themselves, 'tis certain that, among affections of equal extent, we more approve the calm stable resolute purposes of heart, than the turbulent and passionate. And that, of affections in this respect alike, we more approve those which are more extensive, and less approve those which are more confined. Thus, the stable conjugal and parental love, or the resolute calm purpose of promoting the true happiness of persons thus related to us, is preferable to the turbulent passionate dispositions of tenderness. And the love of a society, a country, is more excellent than domestick affections.
>
> (68–9)

As we know, benevolence stands at the head of the orders of ethical merit: 'that disposition ... which is most excellent, and naturally gains the highest moral approbation, is the calm, stable universal good-will to all, or the most extensive benevolence'.

The category said to be distinct from both benevolence and the 'kind affections' includes fortitude, candour, openness of mind, sincerity, veracity, courtesy and good manners, and a strong sense of honour (Hutcheson 1755: 66–7, 68). I have some difficulty in discerning the precise dividing line intended between the latter and the 'kind affections', but we need not be held up by this since a close link is anyway conceded. For Hutcheson perceives the category to be 'naturally connected with such affections, natural evidences of them, and plainly inconsistent with the highest sorts of selfishness and sensuality', and therefore 'immediately' approved by the *moral sense*, approved that is 'even before we think of this connexion with disinterested affections, or imagine directly that the agent is referring them to beneficent purposes ... As all these abilities and dispositions are of great importance in life, highly beneficial to mankind when exerted in consequence of kind affections, and are naturally connected with them, or exclude the opposite extreme, 'tis with the highest goodness and wisdom that they are immediately recommended to our approbation by the constitution of our moral faculty' (66–7). Here we have a helpful rendition of the '*immediacy*' of the approval accorded by the moral sense encountered throughout all the Hutcheson texts. Particularly noteworthy is the fact that, at the end of the day, approval after all relates to conduct directed towards enhancement of the *general good* even when the goodwill characterising *pure* benevolence is lacking.

When discussing the *Inquiry* we found that the moral sense is said '*to direct*' actions towards the enhanced happiness of mankind or sections thereof (above, p. 74). This term, I there suggested, probably refers to the guidance towards proper ethical conduct resulting from the evaluation rather than to a distinct function. The same may be said of a restatement in the *System*, which proposes that the 'moral faculty' identifies and *acts to encourage* a 'universal benevolence' – the epitome of moral excellence – the 'generous affections' and, yet more inclusively, our 'selfish affections', implying guidance regarding appropriate categories and degrees of self-interest, namely those which do not conflict with 'universal benevolence', thereby bringing order to the conflicting pressures playing on the individual:

> Without a distinct consideration of this moral faculty, a species endowed with such a variety of senses, and of desires frequently interfering, must appear a complex confused fabrick, without any order or regular consistent design. By means of it, all is capable of harmony, and all its powers may conspire in one direction, and be consistent with each other. 'Tis already proved that we are capable of many generous affections ultimately terminating on the good of others, neither arising from any selfish view, nor terminating on private good. This moral faculty plainly shews that we are also capable of a calm settled universal benevolence, and that this is destined, as the supreme determination of the generous kind, to govern and control our particular generous as well as selfish affections …'.
>
> (Hutcheson 1755: 74)[13]

Hutcheson forcefully denies that 'calm self-love' constitutes the 'supreme principle': 'To acknowledge the several generous ultimate affections of a limited kind to be natural, and yet maintain that we have no general controlling principle but self-love which indulges or checks the generous affections as they conduce to, or oppose, our own noblest interest' is a false idea, though one maintained by 'excellent authors and strenuous defenders of the cause of virtue' (75). Leslie Stephen, surprisingly, maintained that 'Hutcheson had spoken slightingly of sympathy … as means of explaining our moral judgments. Sympathy was, in his eyes, merely a variety of selfishness' (Stephen 1902: 63). Certainly Hutcheson argues against those who 'plead that our most generous affections are subordinate to private interest by means of *sympathy*, which makes the pleasures and pains, the happiness or misery of others, the constant causes of pleasure or pain to ourselves' (Hutcheson 1755: 47).[14] But this is not to 'slight' sympathy since the evidence, Hutcheson concluded, 'may suffice to establish that important point, that our nature is susceptible of affections *truly disinterested in the strictest sense, and not directly subordinated to self-interest, or aiming at private interest of any kind*' (49; emphasis added). Subsequently, he refers to instances of known self-sacrifice and acts undertaken entirely without thinking of any reward or praise and he concludes: 'There is therefore another ultimate determination which our souls are capable of, destined to be also an original spring of the calmest and most deliberate purposes of action; a desire of communicating happiness' – Hutcheson's term for benevolence – 'an ultimate goodwill, not referred to any private interest, and often operating without such reference' (76–7).

******

Hutcheson seems to have created a dilemma for himself. For while he proceeds to assert that the moral sense 'recommends the generous part by an immediate undefinable perception', at the same time he avers that it only functions properly when '*in its full vigour*', which is usually not the case:

> In those cases where some inconsistency appears between the two determinations, the moral faculty at once points out and recommends the glorious the amiable part; not by suggesting prospects of future interests of a sublime sort by pleasures of self-approbation, or of praise. *It recommends the generous part by an immediate undefinable perception*; it approves the kind ardour of the heart in the sacrificing even life itself, and that even in those who have no hopes of surviving, or no attention to a future life in another world. And thus, where the moral sense is in its full vigour, it makes the generous determination to publick happiness the supreme one in the soul, with that commanding power which it is naturally destined to exercise.
> (Hutcheson 1755: 77; emphasis added)

And he goes on to confirm the qualification by focusing on the potentiality of what can be achieved by culture and training: 'It must be obvious we are not speaking here of the ordinary condition of mankind, as if these calm determinations were generally exercised, and habitually controlled the particular passions; but of the condition our nature can be raised to by *due culture*; and of the principles which may and ought to operate, when *by attention* we present to our minds the objects or representations fit to excite them' (emphasis added). It is difficult to understand how the moral sense can be represented as an innate basic feeling immediately operative, if it only functions fully when 'raised ... by due culture'.[15] By this qualification, Hutcheson silently admits that his attempt to distinguish his own from alternative perceptions of the source of ethical sentiment has failed. For he declares that since the moral sense cannot be relied on, '*reasoning and reflection*' must take its place as means of approval, which is wholly at odds with his earlier position stressing the *constrained* role of reason in ethical evaluation (see above, pp. 72, 75–6):

> But as the selfish principles are very strong, and by custom, by early and frequent indulgencies, and other causes, are raised in the greatest part of men above their due proportion, while the generous principles are little cultivated, and the moral sense often asleep; our powers of reasoning and

comparing the several enjoyments which our nature is capable of, that we may discover which of them are of the greatest consequence to our happiness; our capacity, by reasoning, of arriving to the knowledge of a *Governing Mind* presiding in this world, and of a moral administration, are of the highest consequence and necessity to preserve our affections in a just order and to corroborate our *moral faculty*.

(Hutcheson 1755: 78)

The closing assertion loses its meaning if the moral faculty is typically 'asleep'. And there can be no doubt from what follows that a primary function attributed hitherto to the moral sense – that of resolving what is described as the apparently 'complex confused fabrick, without any order or regular consistent design' (above, p. 97), intending largely the relation between private and social motives – has been transferred to the *rational* dimension: 'by such reasoning and reflection we may discover a perfect consistency of all the generous motions of the soul with private interest, and find out a certain tenor of life and action the most effectually subservient to both these determinations' (78–9).

It is of considerable interest that Hutcheson should insist in his next chapter (Chapter V) that the moral sense did in fact yield, though only *in theory*, reliable verdicts on conduct and motive and also on the ranking thereof: 'Were nothing more requisite in laying the foundation of *morals*, but the discovering in theory what affections and conduct are virtuous, and the objects of approbation, and what are vicious, the account now given of the constitution of our *moral faculty* would be sufficient for that purpose; as it points out not only what is virtuous and vicious, but also shews the several degrees of these qualities in the several sorts of affections and actions' (Hutcheson 1755: 98). But again, there arise obstacles to the true path – 'however we may be conscious of its dignity' – created by self-interest:

> But ... we have also a strong determination toward private happiness, with many particular selfish appetites and affections, and these often so violent as not immediately to submit to the *moral power*, however we may be conscious of its dignity, and of some considerable effect it has upon our happiness or misery; as strong suspicions may often arise, attended with great uneasiness, that in following the impulse of our kind affections and the moral faculty we are counteracting our interest, and abandoning what may be of more consequence to our happiness than either this self-approbation or the applauses of others.
>
> (98–9)

The solution was 'to establish well the foundations of morality, and to remove as much as may be, all opposition arising from the selfish principles, that the mind may resolutely persist in the course which the *moral faculty* recommends', which task necessitated 'a full comparison of all human enjoyments with each other', in order to 'discover in which of them our greatest happiness consists' (99).

This task is undertaken in Book I, Part II: 'An Inquiry into the Supreme Happiness of Mankind' where we find amply confirmed the notion of the moral sense as recommending first and foremost *general benevolence* and providing the means of evaluating the more restricted affections: 'As the several narrower affections may often interfere and oppose each other, or some of them be inconsistent with more extensive affections to whole societies, or to mankind; our *moral sense* by its stronger and warmer approbation of the more extensive, both points out the affection which should prevail, and confirms this nobler affection by our natural desire of moral excellence' (Hutcheson 1755: 101). Again: 'The course of life ... pointed out to us by our *moral sense*' entails 'a constant study to promote the most universal happiness in our power, by doing all good offices as we have opportunity which interfere with no more extensive interest of the system; preferring always the more extensive and important offices to those of less extent and importance; and cautiously abstaining from whatever may occasion any unnecessary misery in this system' (222; also 138–9, 149, 158).

Hutcheson touches already at the close of Part I on the problem that differing perceptions of 'happiness' pertain across communities, a matter raised by critics as evidence that there could be no *uniform*, or commonly-experienced, moral sense such as one might expect were there such a 'natural' entity. He admits '[d]ifferent notions of happiness and the means of promoting it', but regarding 'different notions of happiness' he notes the contrast between underdeveloped societies with their simplistic notions of an adequate real income and more advanced societies, positing progress in that regard with 'civilization' (Hutcheson 1755: 92). The main problem related rather to 'reasoning' with regard to 'the means of promoting' given ends: 'Now almost all our diversities in moral sentiments, and opposite approbations, and condemnations, arise from opposite conclusions of reason about the effects of actions upon the publick, or the affections from which they flowed. The *moral sense* seems ever to approve or condemn uniformly the same immediate objects, the same affections and dispositions; tho' we reason very differently about the actions which evidence certain dispositions or their contraries (93). Unfortunately this was not understood by critics of the moral sense: 'And yet reason, in which all these errors happen is allowed to be the natural principle; and the *moral faculty* is not, because of the diversities of approbation; which yet arise chiefly from the diversity of reasonings'. Once again, 'reasoning' is accorded a much more important role – albeit in this context a distorting role – than his numerous formal claims to the contrary allow.

4.6 *A Short Introduction to Moral Philosophy* (1747)

The *Short Introduction to Moral Philosophy* [16] provides a convenient summary of the main themes up until this point. In particular, we find restated the contrast between 'disinterested affections', entailing inter-personal relations, and true benevolence involving the 'calm general good-will to mankind'. As for the former, '(t)hat there is among men some disinterested goodness, without any views to interests of their own, but pursuing ultimately the interests of persons beloved, must be evident to such as examine well their own hearts, the motions of friendship or natural affection; and the love and zeal we have for worthy and eminent characters' (Hutcheson 1747: 10–11). What we have found elsewhere described as 'the immediate undefinable perception' afforded by the moral sense, is here described thus: 'These particularly kind passions are quite different from any calm general good-will to mankind, nor do they all arise from it. They naturally arise, without premeditation or previous volition, as soon as that species or occasion occurs which is by nature adapted to raise them' (11). As for general benevolence, we are given a helpful summary of the role accorded to the moral sense, though the term is not used:

> ... there is deeply rooted in the soul a steady propensity or impulse toward its own highest happiness, which every one upon a little reflection will find, by means whereof he can repress and govern all the particular selfish passions, when they are in any way opposite to it; so whosoever in a calm hour takes a full view of human nature, considering the constitutions, tempers, and characters of others, will find a like general propension of soul to wish the universal prosperity and happiness of the whole system.
> (12)

In both instances the proof of the propositions are of an informal or homely nature, a characteristic to which we have become accustomed.

Referring to the 'noble senses' Hutcheson uses the term '*sympathy* or fellow-feeling, by which the state and fortunes of others affect us exceedingly, so that by the very power of nature, previous to any reasoning or meditation, we rejoice in the prosperity of others, and sorrow with them in their misfortunes' (Hutcheson 1747: 14). This refers to *general* benevolence entailing anonymity. However, the paragraph ends by reference to 'such as are dear to him [whose] misery or distresses will necessarily disturb his own happiness'. Doubtless 'sympathy' here covers both categories.

We also encounter the detail that the moral sense might actually play on decision-making favouring general benevolence by the individual's meditating on its evaluations of merit: 'And whosoever by frequent impartial meditation cultivates this extensive affection, which the inward sense of his soul constantly approves in the highest degree, may make it so strong that it will be able to restrain and govern all other affections, whether they regard his own happiness or that of any smaller system or party' (Hutcheson 1747: 12). More generally: 'by this sense, a certain turn of mind or temper, a certain course of action, and plan of life is plainly recommended to us by nature ... What is approved by this sense we count *right* and *beautiful*, and call it virtue; what is condemned, we count *base* and *deformed* and *vitious*' (17). Virtue, Hutcheson insists, 'is not approved under the notion of its *being profitable to the agent*. Nor is it approved under the notion of *profitable to those who approve it* ... Nor can it be alleged that the notion under which we approve actions is their tendency to obtain applause or reward' (18–19). And here the Deity enters the picture as in the earlier works: 'None can hope for Rewards from God without owning that some actions are acceptable to God in their own nature; nor dread divine punishments except upon a supposition of a natural *demerit* in evil actions' (19). In brief, *the moral sense takes precedence even over God's command*: 'When we praise the divine Laws as holy, just and good, 'tis plainly on this account, that we believe they require what is antecedently conceived as morally good, and prohibit the contrary, otherwise these Epithets would import nothing laudable'.

Now Hutcheson wants to have his cake and eat it. For he goes on to reflect – and doubtless to avoid criticism by the orthodox – that it is God who instilled the sense into us in the first place, so that 'the nature of virtue is … as immutable as the divine Wisdom and Goodness' (Hutcheson 1747: 21). Indeed, he even refers to 'this Divine Sense or Conscience naturally approving these more extensive affections', in reference to fulfillment of 'duty toward … friends … country, or the general interest of all' (24). Nevertheless, so far as true virtue is concerned what counts is conduct obeying the moral sense or conscience *automatically*, not as a matter of obedience to God and certainly without thought of reward in a future life. And equally important for our theme, even if God should be the ultimate source feeding the moral sense, the fact remains that *forwarding the general good* constitutes the epitome of virtue as far as concerns mortal beings.

There are other themes in the *Short Introduction* summarizing earlier perspectives, including the 'relish or approbation' accorded high moral excellence (above, p. 94). Here too is expressed the *self-consciousness* of which the moral sense, or 'soul' as it is here rendered, is capable:

> It was already observed that our esteem of virtue in another, causes a warmer affection of good-will toward him: now as the soul can reflect on all its powers, dispositions, affections, desires, senses, and make them the objects of its contemplation; a very high relish for moral excellence, a strong desire of it, and a strong endearment of heart toward all in whom we discern eminent virtues, must itself be approved as a most virtuous disposition; nor is there any more lovely than the highest moral excellency.
> (Hutcheson 1747: 22)

Hutcheson explains what he intends by the highest form this 'relish' can take: 'Since God must appear to us as the Supreme excellence, and the inexhaustible fountain of all good, to whom mankind are indebted for innumerable benefits most gratuitously bestowed, no affection of soul can be more approved than the most ardent love and veneration toward the Deity, with a steady purpose to obey him … and a constant purpose of imitating him as far as our weak nature is capable'.

We have seen that in the *System* the 'relish' or 'approbation' in question is described as 'a pretty different affection from benevolence or the desire of communicating happiness; and is as it were in another order of affections', though never opposed to it (above, p. 94). There is no reason to be believe that Hutcheson's silence regarding this detail in the *Short Introduction* implied a change of mind. Moreover, we have observed that the high moral weighting attached to *'approbation' of the Deity* does not necessarily detract from that attached to 'benevolence' towards mankind. In any event, the general theme is repeated that '[o]ur inward conscience of right and wrong ... prefers *the most diffusive goodness* to all other affections of soul, whether of a selfish kind, or of narrower endearments' (Hutcheson 1747: 25; emphasis added). And so too is the observation that private costs incurred in the general interest actually *enhances* merit: 'all these losses sustained increase the moral dignity and beauty of virtuous offices, and recommend them the more to our inward sense'.

The account in the *Short Introduction* is complicated – as in the 1830 Glasgow lecture (above, p. 88) – by what is referred to as the sense of 'Honour and Shame' which 'makes the approbations, the gratitude, and esteem of others who approve our conduct, matter of high pleasure; and their censures, and condemnation, and infamy, matter of severe uneasiness; even altho' we should have no hopes of any other advantages from their approbations, or fears of evil from their dislike' (Hutcheson 1747: 26). Hutcheson refers to 'these two senses, of moral good and evil, and of honour and shame', yet he also says that the latter is 'founded indeed upon our moral sense, or presupposing it, but distinct from it and all other senses' (27).[17] Like the moral sense it too may play upon conduct, having the effect of 'frequently exciting men to what is honourable, and restraining them from every thing dishonourable, base, flagitious, or injurious'.

Recall next from the earlier documents Hutcheson's concern with the *deficiency* of the moral sense which threatened the immediacy attributed to it in approving meritorious conduct. In the *Short Introduction* the concern re-emerges that only a few individuals manifest 'the kind affections, and compassion toward the distressed and beneficence, with their constant attendants and supporters, an high sense of moral excellence and love of virtue', whereas '(i)n the present state of mankind which we plainly see is depraved and corrupt, sensuality and mean selfish pursuits are the most universal: and those enjoyments which the higher powers recommend, the generality are but little acquainted with, or are little employed in examining or pursuing them' (Hutcheson 1747: 24, 34–5). It is surprising then that Hutcheson should go on to assert that 'every one find in himself the notion of a *truly good man*, to which no man ever comes up in his conduct' (35). In any event, there is allowance for the 'cultivation and improvement' of the moral sense motivated by a desire to realize its potential (24), severely tempered however by the opinion that *without divine help such efforts would be to little avail*: 'a full and certain account of the original of these (moral) disorders, and of the effectual remedies for them ... will never be given by any mortal without a divine revelation' (35; emphasis added).

An important summary elaborates the potential inherent in an awakened moral sense – *explicitly assuming support from 'God and kind nature'* – that can be tapped into by simple introspection without recourse to 'long dissertations and reasoning' (Hutcheson 1747: 36). Here we encounter once more those dual features which are approved by the moral sense to which we have become accustomed, namely the 'kind affections' and general 'benevolence'; and also the proper resolution of the relation between self- and other-regarding interests:

> Of this we may have some notion from what is above explained about that moral Power, that sense of what is becoming and honourable in our actions. Nor need we long dissertations and reasoning, since by inward reflection and examining the feelings of our hearts, we shall be convinced, that we have this moral power or Conscience distinguishing right and wrong, plainly destined and fitted to regulate the whole of life; which clearly discovers to us that course and conduct, which alone we can entirely approve; to wit, *that in which all kind affections are cultivated, and at the same time an extensive regard maintained toward the general happiness of all*; so that we pursue our own interests, or those of our friends, or kinsmen, no further than the more extensive interests will allow; always maintaining sweetness of temper, kindness, and tends affections; and improving all our powers of body and mind with a view to serve God and mankind.
>
> (37; emphasis added)

That the moral sense approves service of God as well as benevolence towards mankind is also a theme encountered earlier.

As before, *reason* is allowed a place though certainly not as the source of moral good as some supposed: 'We have already shewed that whatever is ultimately desirable must be the object of some immediate sense. But as men are naturally endued with some acuteness, forethought, memory, reason, and wisdom, they shall also naturally desire whatever appears as the proper *means* of obtaining what is immediately desirable; such means are riches and power, which may be subservient to all our desires whether virtuous or vitious, benevolent or malitious; and hence it is that they are universally desired' (Hutcheson 1747: 33). However, Hutcheson is now rather more generous, allowing the illumination by reason of the conciliation of 'general prosperity' – alluding to the consequences of benevolent conduct – and *private happiness* even with regard to material prosperity, provided it is of the order appropriate for 'a good mind': 'Nay our reason too reviewing the evidence exhibited to us in the whole order of nature, will shew us that the same course of life which contributes to the general prosperity, procures also to the agent the most stable and most worthy felicity; and generally tends to procure that competency of external things which to a good mind is in its kind the most joyful' (37).

Hutcheson closes by further extending the play of reason to demonstrating 'that the world is governed by the wisest and best Providence', thereby reinforcing the sort of conduct approved by the moral sense: 'We shall thence conclude that all these practical truths discovered from reflection on our own constitution and that of Nature, have the nature and force of divine Laws pointing out what God requires of us, what is pleasing to him, and by what conduct we may obtain his approbation and favour' (Hutcheson 1747: 37–8). To act with an eye to reward would presumably be a debit in the moral balance as Hutcheson had always insisted. A proper understanding of these principles, Hutcheson reiterates in conclusion, would assure that 'both our social and selfish affections will harmoniously recommend to us one and the same course of life and conduct' (38). Such reconciliation was evidently his prime objective.

4.7 On Agrarian laws: Implications for distributive justice

Francis Hutcheson in the *Inquiry*, as we have seen (above, p. 82), defined Justice — one of the four *'cardinal virtues'* — in commutative terms, as 'observing a strict Equality' to the end of assuring 'the Good of Mankind, the Preservation of Rights, and securing Peace' (Hutcheson 1729: 132–3). But we have touched briefly on Distributive Justice in Section 4.2 relating to the 1724 article for the *London Journal* (above p. 70) and devote the present section to the support in the *System of Moral Philosophy* (1755) for legal limitations on the accumulation of landed property, a case incorporating an ethical component, namely satisfaction of the greater-good welfare criterion, and to that extent concern for Distributive Justice. Hutcheson does not, we shall see, go so far as to justify equality, as Adam Smith seems to have understood him (see Chapter 8).

The argument is introduced in a manner suggesting that national expediency — 'the publick interest' — is at issue: 'as we shall shew hereafter … some publick interests of societies may justify such Agrarian Laws as put a stop to the immoderate acquisitions of private citizens which may prove dangerous to the state, tho' be made without any particular injury', the qualification referring to the absence of proof that 'immoderate acquisitions' entailed damage to specific individuals (Hutcheson 1755: 327). An elaboration (in Volume 2) confirms that strict equality is not countenanced, the problem relating only to assuring a diffusion of property which suffices to disallow the 'oppression' by the few against 'the whole body of the people', whereby the danger inherent in too great a concentration of property lay in its preventing the removal of the ruling 'cabal' even when 'oppressive':

> A Democracy cannot remain stable unless the property be so diffused among the people that no such cabal of a few as could probably unite in any design, shall have a fund of wealth sufficient to support a force superior to that of the rest … [W]hen power has its natural foundation of property it will be lasting, but may, in some forms, be very *pernicious and oppressive to the whole body of the people*; and it must be the more pernicious that it will be very permanent, there being no sufficient force to overturn or controul it. And this shews the great care requisite in settling a just plan, and a suitable division of property, and in taking precautions against any such change in property as may destroy a good plan: this should be the view of Agrarian laws.
>
> (Hutcheson 1755 2: 247; emphasis added)

The 'preservation' of the democratic component, Hutcheson reiterates, dictated that its strength as reflected in the distribution of property *supersedes* that of the rest – alluding to the monarchical and aristocratic components of the constitution – the assurance of which might require legal intervention: 'And consequently when the situation of the people, their manners and customs, their trade or arts, do not sufficiently of themselves cause such a diffusion of property among many as is requisite for the continuance of the Democratick part in the constitution; there should be such Agrarian laws as will prevent any immoderate increase of wealth in the hands of a few, which could support a force superior to the whole body' (248).

Although formally the focus throughout is on constitutional arrangement, the argument recognizes a problem in distributive justice requiring correction and takes for granted the *greater good* principle as the underpinning ethical rationale for its solution. Thus while the 'democratic' component includes not only propertyless labourers (the 'plebeians') but also farmers and even (presumably) the landed gentry in possession of *moderate* holdings, Hutcheson's particular concern appears to have been the welfare of the labourer. This dimension is reflected in the aforementioned reference to the welfare of 'the whole body of the people' as *desideratum*. A remark regarding farming tenancy with an eye to 'plentiful' wage disbursements is similarly suggestive: "Tis of great advantage in every form that the common farmers or husband-men have good tenures; not such as shall maintain them in sloth or afford servants to do all labour for them; but yet such as will yield *a plentiful support to the laborious and industrious; that they may live happy*, and have strength of body and mind for defence of themselves and their country against domestick tyrants or foreign invaders' (Hutcheson 1755 2: 259–60; emphasis added). And the same orientation is apparent in the firm rejection of a case against intervention as restricting the liberty of the rich even where only the *moderate* or 'just' acquisitions by the few is at issue – such that the income therefrom suffices only to finance the 'innocent enjoyments and pleasures of life' but does not extend to 'vain ambition' or 'unjust pleasures' – on grounds of a clash with *'the liberty and safety of thousands or millions'*:

> 'Tis in vain to talk of invading the liberty of the rich, or the injury of stopping their progress in just acquisitions. No publick interest hinders their acquiring as much as is requisite for any innocent enjoyments and pleasures of life. And yet if it did, *the liberty and safety of thousands or millions is never to be put in the balance with even the innocent pleasures of a few families*; much less with their vain ambition, or their unjust pleasures, from their usurped powers or external pomp and grandeur.
>
> (248; emphasis added)[18]

Hutcheson's sympathy for labour may be further illustrated by his insistence on coverage for sickness within the wage contract even when not explicitly spelled out – the context happens to relate to manufacturing – as a matter of simple justice: 'The hired labourer, as he is bound faithfully to execute his work, so he is not to be defrauded of his hire. If he is hired for a long tract of time, the hirer cannot in humanity make any deduction on account on account of smaller interruptions given to his service by transient fits of sickness. Such fits are incidental to the firmest constitutions; and the hirer is justly presumed to have precluded himself from such exceptions, or deductions from the price agreed to, by hiring for a tract of time' (70–1).

We should not, however, go overboard. In the light of Smith's apparent understanding that Hutcheson supported strict equality it is worthwhile reinforcing the demonstration that this was in fact far from his position. Reference may be made, for example, to the following considerations. The principle of 'natural equality' relates specifically to 'the laws of *God* and nature [which] prohibit the greatest or wisest of mankind to inflict any misery on the meanest, or to deprive them of any of their natural rights, or innocent acquisitions, when no public interest requires it … If great occupation and much labour employed, intitles the vigorous and active to great possessions; the weak and indolent have an equally sacred right to the full possessions they occupy and improve' (Hutcheson 1755 1: 299–300). The 'foundation' of private property is to resolve the problems created by *differential* motivation: 'If the goods procured, or improved by the industrious lye in common for the use of all, the worst of men have the generous and industrious for their slaves. The most benevolent temper must decline supporting the slothful in idleness, that their own necessities may force them to contribute their part for the publick' (321–2). In discussing the optimal composition of legislative assemblies the wealth (as well as the numbers) of voters in each electoral district is to be taken into account (1755 2: 260). Unequal ability is taken for granted both generally and in matters relating to governance:

> ''Tis well known how hard it is to make the vulgar quit their own customs for such as are far better in agriculture or mechanick arts. And how much more difficult must it be to obtain their concurrence in any great and noble designs of distant advantage to whole nations, when they cost much present labour and expence. As there are in our species men of superior genius and penetration, and of more extensive views, nature points them out as fit to direct the actions of the multitude for the general good, upon proper security given by them for their using faithfully the powers committed to them'
>
> (214).

The principle that the distribution of happiness does not correspond to the distribution of wealth – all but universally attributed to Adam Smith as originator by his famously striking reference to the beggar happily sunning himself by the roadside – also needs to be taken into account:

> Men placed in the higher conditions of life, enured to ease and softness, may imagine the laborious state of the lower, to be a miserable slavery, because it would be so to them were they reduced to it with their present

habits of soul and body. But in the lower conditions, strength of body, keen appetites, sweet intervals of rest, moderate desires, and plain fare, make up all their wants in points of sensual pleasure. And the kind affections, mutual love, social joys, friendships, parental and filial duties, moral enjoyments, and even some honour, in a narrower circle, have place in the lower conditions as well as the higher; and all these affections generally more sincere.

(Hutcheson 1755 1: 196)

This proposition evidently did not imply for Hutcheson – any more than it did for Smith – a denial of the importance of tolerably good standards of material earnings.

I return to our main theme, and Hutcheson's concern with the *ethics* of land accumulation and the resultant pattern of income distribution. The same preoccupation with distributive justice comes conspicuously to the fore in a continuation of the passage cited earlier rejecting the case against intervention on grounds of 'invading the liberty of the rich, or the injury of stopping their progress in just acquisitions': 'For the same reason, all those groundless partition-walls among citizens, confining places of power and profit to certain families and certain orders, ought to be prevented or broke down; as they are both the occasions of immoderate and dangerous wealth in these orders; and give the justest causes of indignation, resentment, and setting up of a separate interest, to all those who are thus unjustly excluded. Thus we see that Rome was never at rest till the brave and popular among the plebeians obtained access to the highest offices in the state, contrary to their old unreasonable laws' (Hutcheson 1755 2: 248–9). Summing up, Hutcheson declares roundly: 'The general good of all is the end of associating, and not the grandeur of a few' (249).

In making his case for Agrarian laws Hutcheson takes care to avoid fixed rules regarding the maximum socially-desirable accumulation of landed property in the hands of an individual or a 'few'. In this elaboration it again becomes apparent how far Hutcheson was from arguing in favour of strict equality; it was *excessive* accumulation that he reprobated: 'To preserve the Democratick part, we observed above the use of some agrarian law, or some contrivance that would prevent any dangerous degree of wealth coming into the hands of a few. No precise sum can be fixed as the highest. Different states may admit of different degrees of wealth without danger. If the agrarian law limits men to too small fortunes; it discourages the industry of the more able hands in trade or manufactures. If it allows too much wealth, some cabal of potent families may enslave the rest' (Hutcheson 1755 2: 259). The caution regarding the effect of too low a permissible concentration may refer to a reduced motive to industry arising from inadequate expenditure by landowners on manufactures, or it may allude to a reduced motive to manufacturing activity undertaken with an eye to acquiring land.

It will be noted that while the case for an Agrarian law relates by definition specifically to *landed* property Hutcheson frequently refers to 'wealth' without qualification, as in the present instance, raising the question as to whether the limitation to landed property is a matter of principle or reflects the particular circumstances of the day, with manufacturing and commerce assumed to be of secondary importance. (Recall too that Hutcheson himself alludes to the circumstance of the original Agrarian laws having been an ancient Roman institution.) An important concession points to the latter option, namely that legal constraints on concentration might not be required at all. Two conditions are mentioned: 'Without any such laws some mixed states are safe, provided the lords can sell their estates', implying the absence of primogeniture and similar arrangements restricting the sale of property; and provided also that 'trade and manufactures flourish among the plebeians; and they have access to the places of greatest profit and power. By these means, without any law, wealth may be sufficiently diffused'. Since Hutcheson believes Agrarian laws *are* required, he must assume that trade and manufacturing were empirically of secondary significance. Winch is therefore correct to point out that Hutcheson 'does not deal with the special characteristics of a form of society deeply penetrated by commerce and manufacturing' (Winch 1978: 66). While Hutcheson's considered position assuming a significant industrial sector remains an open question, there seems no reason to rule out in principle a concern that excessive accumulation of wealth in general might in some circumstances pose a threat requiring state intervention.

4.8 On the Hutcheson–Locke relationship

We recall Hutcheson's concern in the first edition of *An Essay on the Nature and Conduct of the Passions* to respond to John Clarke by offering 'a farther illustration of *disinterested Affections*, in answer to his scheme of deducing them from *Self-Love*, which seem'd more ingenious than any which the Author of the *Inquiry* ever yet saw in print' (Hutcheson 1728: xii; above, note 8). Hutcheson at various junctures also addressed this and related issues with an eye to Locke.

We have encountered in the *Short Introduction* of 1747, and elsewhere, a recognition that the 'natural' moral sense can not always be relied upon to assure ethical conduct but requires reinforcement to 'cultivate' and 'improve' its operation. This in itself is an implicit concession to the Lockean viewpoint. But beyond this we have Hutcheson's observation that such reinforcement would be hampered without divine help – that 'a full and certain account of the original of these (moral) disorders, and of the effectual remedies for them … will never be given by any mortal without a divine revelation' (above, p. 103). The necessity of 'revelation' and on-going heavenly support to activate and maintain the moral sense suggests a step towards the Lockean 'theological utilitarianism' discussed in our first chapter, although it must be recalled that Hutcheson also maintained, in the *Essay,* that 'particular actions may be innocent, nay, virtuous, where there is no actual intention of pleasing the Deity influencing the Agent' (above, p. 86). There is still this difference, that Locke could fall back upon the promise of *worldly* advantages arising from benevolent conduct as an adequate stimulus whereas Hutcheson's admission is consistent with the view that other-regarding conduct being 'natural' to the actor requires no promise of advantage of *any* kind — at least in the ideal case where the moral sense operates without 'disorder'.

The evidence until this point suggests a greater degree of agreement between Hutcheson and Locke than might be expected. There is a little more to be said along these lines. I draw attention to a reference in the Preface to the *Essay on the Nature and Conduct of the Passions and Affections*, in both the 1728 and 1742 versions, to the celebrated proposition in the *Essay Concerning Human Understanding* that 'all Ideas arise from *Sensation* and *Reflection*'. Here Hutcheson seeks to turn Locke's formulation to his own advantage by strengthening his position that 'internal perception' — referring to the moral sense — is as 'natural and necessary' as external sensation, slyly suggesting that a little more thought on Locke's part would have yielded this perception:

> It were to be wish'd, that those who are at such Pains to prove a beloved Maxim, that 'all Ideas arise from *Sensation* and *Reflection*', had so explain'd themselves, that none should take their Meaning to be, that all our Ideas are either *external Sensations*, or *reflex Acts* upon *external Sensations*: Or if by *Reflection* they mean an *inward Power of Perception*, as I fancy they do, [1742: as Mr. Locke declares expressly, calling it internal sensation,] they had as carefully examin'd into the several kinds of internal *Perceptions*, as they have done into the *external Sensations*: that we might have seen whether the former be not as natural and necessary as the latter.
> (Hutcheson 1728: x–xi; 1769 [1742]: x)

The *Inquiry* similarly protests against the 'very different Judgments concerning the *internal* and *external* Senses', adding that '[n]othing is more ordinary among those, who after Mr. LOCKE have rejected *innate Ideas* than to alledge, "That all our Relish for *Beauty*, and *Order*, is either from prospect of *Advantage, Custom*, or *Education*", for no other Reason but the *Variety* of *Fancys* in the World' (Hutcheson 1729: 78). To this is further added the charge of neglecting other-regarding sentiment, attributable to invalid preconceptions: 'Had they in like manner consider'd our *Affections* without a previous Notion, that they were all from *Self-Love*, they might have felt an *ultimate Desire* of the Happiness of others as easily conceivable, and as certainly implanted in the human Breast, tho perhaps not so strong as *Self-Love*'. Hutcheson's aside at the close that 'self-love' is the strongest motive probably does not express his own estimation, but rather the most that could be expected from a modified Lockean perspective. Were it his own view he would be ceding the game to Locke (and also to John Clarke).

In the *Essay*, Hutcheson briefly mentions Locke in the course of a discussion of Samuel Clarke's explication, in his Boyle lectures of 1705, of morality in terms of the 'fitness or unfitness' of actions (Hutcheson 1728: 247; 1769 [1742]: 226).[19] But this notice does not relate to the main theme entailing inter-personal relations where alone issues of morality arise, so that I am inclined to understand a declaration that follows immediately regarding 'that ingenious Author' to refer to Clarke rather than to Locke, notwithstanding a confusing ambiguity: "Tis plain, that ingenious Author says nothing against the Supposition of a *moral Sense*: But many do imagine, that his Account of moral Ideas is independent upon [sic] a *moral Sense*, and therefore are less willing to allow that we have such an immediate Perception, or *Sense* of Virtue and Vice. What follows is not intended to oppose his Scheme, but rather to suggest what seems a necessary Explication of it; by shewing that it is no otherwise intelligible, but upon Supposition of a *moral Sense*' (247–8; 226). While the reference to 'moral Ideas' might suggest Locke, Clarke also had much to say on this matter, while the interpretation of 'fitness' implies that Clarke is intended.

Whoever is intended, the substantive argument amply confirms the centrality to Hutcheson's thought of the 'public good' as the ultimate end: 'Perhaps the *virtuous Fitness* is that of *Ends*. The Fitness of a *subordinate End* to the ultimate, cannot constitute the Action good, unless the *ultimate End* be good … The *moral Fitness* must be that of the *ultimate End* itself: The *publick Good* alone is a *fit End*, therefore the *Means* fit for this *End* alone are good' (Hutcheson 1728: 250; 1769 [1742]: 228). As for the existence of a moral sense, that (as we have found so often to be the case) is merely *asserted* by Hutcheson: 'What means the *Fitness of an ultimate End*? For what is it fit? Why, 'tis an *ultimate* End, not fit for any thing farther, but *absolutely fit*. What means that Word *fit*? If it notes a *simple Idea*' – which Hutcheson believes to be the case – 'it must be the *Perception of some Sense*: thus we must recur … to a moral Sense' (250; 228–9). Alternatively, by 'fitness' might be intended that 'certain *Affections* or *Actions* of an Agent, standing in a *certain Relation* to other Agents, is *approved* by every *Observer*, or raises in him a *grateful Perception*, or moves the Observer to *love* the Agent' (252; 230). It is unclear whether Hutcheson is here paraphrasing or citing an author, and if that author is Clarke. But again he concludes assertively: 'This Meaning is the same with the Notion of pleasing *a moral Sense*'.

I shall return to Hutcheson in Chapters Seven and Ten to consider the Hutcheson–Smith and Hutcheson–Bentham relationships. Adam Smith's perspective on Hutcheson will emerge as consistent with the main lines of our interpretation, but I remain mystified both by Bentham's apparent unawareness of Hutcheson's formulation of the Greatest Happiness principle that pre-dated Hume's much admired version, and by his misattribution to Hutcheson of a 'moral sense' *opposed* to the enhancement of the 'greatest happiness'.

Notes

1 Turco elsewhere contrasts Hutcheson with both Hume and Smith; and does Frazer (Turco 2003; Frazer 2010: 24–5).
2 Albee raises several difficult issues regarding the relationship between the moral sense and utilitarian doctrines in Hutcheson's system (Albee 1902: 58–63), and also that of Shaftesbury (56–8).

3 For this reading of Hutcheson, see Moore 2006: 299, although the common ground with Hume is not there explored.
4 Turco 1999 draws special attention to John Clarke (1726) and Archibald Campbell (1733) amongst those prioritizing self-love, thereby rendering 'disinterested sympathy' a contradiction in terms.
5 For a similar position, see Leidhold 1985: 21, cited Mautner 1993: 6n. See also Strasser on the 'fallibility' of the Moral Sense (1990: 27–48).
6 Turco 2007 takes issue with Scott 1900 who perceived different influences at play from work to work, in favour of variations in form according to the intended readership.
7 Four editions of the *Inquiry* appeared during Hutcheson's lifetime: 1725, 1726, 1729, and 1738. I focus largely on the third taking some account of modifications between editions and additions made in 1838. That Mandeville is the prime target is indicated on the title page of the first edition only: 'An Inquiry into the Original of our Ideas of Beauty and Virtue; in Two Treatises. In which the Principles of the Late Earl of Shaftesbury are Explain'd and Defended, against the Author of the *Fable of the Bees*'.
8 I shall cite both the 1728 edition and the posthumous edition of 1769 which incorporates changes made by Hutcheson in an edition of 1742. This work was Hutcheson's response to John Clarke's criticisms of the *Inquiry* in his *Foundation of Morality* (1726): 'The principal Objections offer'd by Mr. Clarke of Hull, against the second Section of the second *Treatise*, occurr'd to the Author in Conversation, and had appriz'd him of the necessity of a farther illustration of *disinterested Affections*, in answer to his scheme of deducing them from *Self-Love*, which seem'd more ingenious than any which the Author of the *Inquiry* ever yet saw in print' (Hutcheson 1728: xii). This comment does not appear in the 1742 version (see Hutcheson 1769 [1742]: xi).
9 For a perspective on the 1742 deletion emphasizing the motivation to action, see Turco 1999: 85–6, 100–101.
10 Archibald Campbell (1733) was concerned that the *Essay* would have the unintended effect of sowing doubt against religious orthodoxy (Turco 1999: 92; also 97–8).
11 Regarding Hutcheson's ethical rankings with attention to Aristotelian origins, see Bonar 1930: 98; Riley 2008: 275–8.
12 Our interpretation of Hutcheson regarding this particulary accords with Frankena 1955: 374.
13 Yet Hutcheson accepts that 'in the order of selfish affections, our self-love, or our calm regard to the greatest private interest, controls our particular selfish passions' (Hutcheson 1755: 74). Presumably then the moral sense provides *further* control where necessary.
14 Hobbes, Bayle, Mandeville, and Rochefoucault are mentioned specifically in a related context (Hutcheson 1755: 88, 111). Locke, whose ethics turned on prudential calculation taking account of prospective rewards and punishments, is a candidate, and we have earlier referred to Clarke and Campbell.
15 On 'correction of the moral sense', see Peach 1971: 47–58.
16 First published in Latin in 1742 and revised in an edition of 1745. For analysis of variations between editions, see Turco 2007. I place the Short Introduction after the 1755 System since the latter was already circulating in the late 1730s.
17 Also referred are the 'sense of the *ridiculous*' – activated by the appearance of clashes occurring between the two aforementioned senses (Hutcheson 1747: 28.)
18 This formulation corresponds to that later adopted by Hume whereby increased wages, even if adverse to international competitiveness, are justified because pertinent to the 'happiness of millions'.
19 Regarding the Boyle Lecture, see Chapter 1, note 5.

References

Albee, E. 1902. *A History of English Utilitarianism*. London: Swan Sonnenschein.
Bacon, C. 2016. 'Calculating Benevolence: Hutcheson's Non-utilitarian, Motivational Morality'. www.academia.edu / 10182139. Downloaded 24 July 2016.
Bentham, J. 1859 (1776). *A Fragment on Government*. *The Works of Jeremy Bentham* I, edited by John Bowring. Edinburgh: William Tait: 221–295.
Bentham, J. 1859 [1789]. *An Introduction to the Principles of Morals and Legislation*. *The Works of Jeremy Bentham* I, edited by John Bowring. Edinburgh: William Tait: 85–154.
Bentham, J. 1982 [1789]. *An Introduction to the Principles of Morals and Legislation*, edited by J.H. Burns and H.L.A. Hart. London and New York: Methuen.
Bentham, J. 2015 (1824). *The Book of Fallacies*, edited by Philip Schofield. Oxford: Clarendon Press.
Bonar, J. 1922. *Philosophy and Political Economy*. London: Allen and Unwin.
Buchan, J. 2003. *Crowded with Genius: The Scottish Enlightenment*. New York: Harper Collins.
Campbell, A. (1733). *An Enquiry into the Original of Moral Virtue*. Second edition. Edinburgh.
Carey, D. 2006. *Locke, Shaftesbury, and Hutcheson: Contesting Diversity in the Enlightenment and Beyond*. Cambridge: Cambridge University Press.
Clarke, J. (1726). *The Foundation of Morality in Theory and Practice*. York: Thomas Gent.
Clarke, S. 1716 (1705). 'A Discourse Concerning the Unalterable Obligations of Natural Religion'. Boyle Lectures. 4th edition, London: W. Botham.
Frankena, W. 1955. 'Hutcheson's Moral Sense Theory', *Journal of the History of Ideas* 16(3): 356–375.
Frazer, M. 2010. *The Enlightenment of Sympathy: Justice and the Moral Sentiments in the Eighteenth Century and Today*. Oxford: Oxford University Press.
Hollander, S. 2015. *John Stuart Mill: Political Economist*. Singapore: World Scientific.
Hutcheson, F. 1725. *An Inquiry into the Original of our Ideas of Beauty and Virtue in Two Treatises: Treatise II: An Inquiry Concerning the Moral Good and Evil*. First edition. London: J. Darby.
Hutcheson, F. 1728. *An Essay on the Nature and Conduct of the Passions and Affections with Illustrations on the Moral Sense*. London: J. Darby and T. Browne.
Hutcheson, F. 1729. *An Inquiry into the Original of our Ideas of Beauty and Virtue in Two Treatises: Treatise II: An Inquiry Concerning Moral Good and Evil*. Third edition, corrected. London: J. and J. Knapton.
Hutcheson, F. 1747. *A Short Introduction to Moral Philosophy. Book I. The Elements of Ethics*. Chapter I. 'Of Human Nature and its Parts'. Second edition. Glasgow: R. Foulis: pp. 1–38. [Translated from 1742 Latin edition.]
Hutcheson, F. 1755. *A System of Moral Philosophy*. London: Millar and Longman.
Hutcheson, F. 1769 (1742). *An Essay on the Nature and Conduct of the Passions and Affections with Illustrations on the Moral Sense*. ['The Third Edition'.] Glasgow: R. & A. Foulis.
Hutcheson, F. 1971 (1725). The Correspondence between Gilbert Burnet ('Philaretus') and Francis Hutcheson ('Philanthropus'). Appendix to *Illustrations on the Moral Sense*, Bernard Peach ed. 1971:195–247.
Hutcheson, F. 1971 [1769]. *Illustrations on the Moral Sense*. Bernard Peach ed. Cambridge, MA: The Belknap Press of Harvard University Press: 103–194. [The 'third edition' 1742.]

Hutcheson, F. 1993 (1724). *On Human Nature: Reflections on our common systems of morality. London Journal* (14 November 1724; signed 'Philanthropus'). In *Francis Hutcheson: Two texts on human nature*, Thomas Mautner ed. Cambridge: Cambridge University Press: 91–106.

Hutcheson, F. 1993 [1730]. Inaugural lecture on the 'Social Nature of Man', November 1730. *Francis Hutcheson: Two texts on human nature*, Thomas Mautner ed. Cambridge: Cambridge University Press: pp. 107–147.

Leidhold, W. 1985. *Ethik und Politik bei Francis Hutcheson*. Munich: Alber.

Mautner, T. 1993. *Francis Hutcheson: Two texts on human nature*. Cambridge: Cambridge University Press.

Mill, J.S. 1969 [1852]. 'Whewell on Moral Philosophy', *Essays on Ethics, Religion and Society, Collected Works* X: pp. 165–201.

Moore, J. 1990. 'The Two Systems of Francis Hutcheson', in M.A. Stewart ed. *Studies in the Philosophy of the Scottish Enlightenment*. Oxford: Oxford University Press: 37–59.

Moore, J. 2006. 'Natural Rights in the Scottish Enlightenment', in Mark Goldie and Robert Wokler, *The Cambridge History Eighteenth-Century Political Thought*. Cambridge: Cambridge University Press: 291–316.

Mousourakis, G. 1997. 'Utility and Rights in Francis Hutcheson's Ethical Theory', *Indian Philosophical Quarterly* 24: 527–542.

Peach, B. 1971. Editor's Introduction. *Frances Hutcheson: Illustrations on the Moral Sense* [1769]. Cambridge, MA: The Belknap Press of Harvard University Press: 1–100.

Persky, J. 2016. *The Political Economy of Progress: John Stuart Mill and Modern Radicalism*. Oxford: Oxford University Press.

Riley, J. 2008. 'Millian Qualitative Superiorities and Utilitarianism, Part I'. *History of Political Economy* 20: 257–278.

Rosen, F. 2003. *Classical Utilitarianism from Hume to Mill*. London and New York: Routledge.

Scott, W.R. 1900. *Frances Hutcheson: His Life, Teaching and Position in the History of Philosophy*. Cambridge: Cambridge University Press.

Stephen, L. 1900. *The English Utilitarians*. London: Duckworth.

Strasser, M.P. 1990. *Francis Hutcheson's Moral Theory: Form and Utility*. Wakefield, NH: Longwood Academic Press.

Turco, L. 1999. 'Sympathy and Moral Sense: 1725–1740'. *British Journal for the History of Philosophy* 7(1): 79–101.

Turco, L. 2003 'Moral Sense and the foundations of merit', *The Cambridge Companion to the Scottish Enlightenment*, ed. A. Broadie, Cambridge: Cambridge University Press: 136–156.

Turco, L. 2007. Introduction to *Francis Hutcheson, Philosophiae moralis institutio compendiaria with a Short Introduction to Moral Philosophy*, Indianapolis: Liberty Fund. (On-line.)

Winch, D. 1978. *Adam Smith's Politics: An essay in historiographic revisionism*. Cambridge: Cambridge University Press.

5 David Hume, utilitarian ethics, the moral sense and distributive justice

5.1 Introduction

If it can be shown that eighteenth-century utilitarianism is consistent with 'moral-sense' allowances, then Mill's concern in the 1830s with a 'hard' and 'stern' Benthamism, turning on 'selfish' calculation and lacking a comprehension of the full character of man, loses much of its force. Chapter Five considers from this perspective David Hume, greatly admired by Bentham as a utilitarian predecessor but a cause of bemusement given his allowances for a moral sense. I draw particular attention to Bonar's proposition according to which Hume, 'by showing the elements into which the alleged "sense" may be analyzed', rejects the view of Shaftesbury and Hutcheson whereby man distinguishes moral good from moral evil through a 'moral sense' (Bonar 1922:109), or yet more strongly, that the moral sense 'fared ill at the hands of Hume, its professed defender', who 'explained [it] away', leaving it 'with little to do', the sentiment of *sympathy* – implying concern for the general interest – providing the key (Bonar 1930: 241,16, 131, 134). Bonar's account of Hume is I believe accurate (although, as explained in earlier chapters, what he says of Hume applies equally to Shaftesbury, Hutcheson, and Helvétius). Thus, while Hume writes of the morality of an action 'felt by an internal sense, and by means of some sentiment, which the reflecting on such an action naturally occasions', he at the same time denies that such a sense operates as an automatic index of what is ethically good or bad independently of the (expected) tendency of an action to augment happiness; rather to the contrary, as we show in Section 5.2, Hume – very much like Hutcheson – reduces the moral sense to 'sympathy' establishing motivation by concern for the general good as a condition for moral commendation. Now Hutcheson, we recall from Chapter 4, prioritized motivation in the sense that a benevolent intention which, for no fault of the actor, failed to yield desirable consequences, did not diminish the ethical ranking accorded by the moral sense; and conversely that an action not intended by the agent to advance the public good must be considered morally defective even if social advantage should happen to result. Hume we shall see is not so clear. He may be cited as focussing *solely* on consequences, but it seems most unlikely that this was his considered position and we shall argue that the weight of evidence confirms that for him, as for Hutcheson, 'private vices might be public benefits, and yet remain vices' (to cite James Bonar).

Rosen contrasts Hume with Hutcheson in this context: 'One important theme for Hume was benevolence to which he gave a prominent, but unlike Hutcheson, not a foundational role in human affairs ... Hume discussed benevolence in four brief examples where he showed that on its own benevolence could not form the basis of morality but required guidance and supplementation from the principle of utility' (Rosen 2003: 39–40). But this stance does not in fact distinguish Hume from Hutcheson for whom, as we have found, conduct reflecting benevolent intentions but not based on a thorough estimate of all likely consequences would not merit ethical commendation should the outcome of such conduct prove to be hostile to the public interest; furthermore, the moral sense Hutcheson maintained may require reinforcement by education and the like.

Among the classical contributors, Bentham is no exception in by-passing Locke's contribution towards establishing a 'standard of rectitude for actions'. In this regard Leslie Stephen's placement of Hume within 'Locke's school' (Stephen 1902: 86) requires qualification, as we shall show.

Hume's perspective on private property and hence on Distributive Justice will play a part in the story and is addressed in Section 5.3. Of particular interest is a case advanced for greater equality, welfare perceived as rising with redistribution from rich to poor, while at the same time inequalities reflecting differential effort and skill are justified.

This chapter offers a partial treatment of Hume. The Hume–Smith and Hume–Bentham relationships are examined in Chapters Seven and Ten respectively and these discussions round out our analysis.

5.2 Humean utilitarianism and the moral sense

As noted in the Introduction to this book, Bentham took David Hume to task, amongst others, for entertaining the 'moral sense' though at the same time he greatly admired Hume's utilitarian *bonâ fides*. James Mill charged Hume with inconsistency on precisely these grounds: 'they who ascribe the classification of acts, as moral, and immoral, to a certain taste, an agreeable or disagreeable sentiment which they excite (among whom are included the Scottish professors Hutcheson, and Brown, and David Hume himself, though on his part with wonderful inconsistency) – hold the same theory with those who say, that beauty is the source of the classification of moral acts' (*Analysis of the Human Mind*, cited by John Stuart Mill in Mill 1989 [1869]: 237). As we shall see, the Hume texts are exceedingly complex lending themselves, without due care, to misunderstanding and justifying to a degree Bentham's evident frustration.

We may illustrate the problem by reference to the heading of a section at the outset of Book III 'Of Morals' in *A Treatise on Human Nature* (1978 [1740]: 470) stating that '*Moral distinctions deriv'd from a moral sense*'. Taken at face value this bald summary might easily be read as affirming that version of a moral sense to which Bentham so much objected, telling man 'what is right and what is wrong' and when asked why responds in circular fashion 'because my moral sense tells me it is' (see Introduction, p. xv). But the formal declaration is misleading and it will become clear that Hume ought to have written, properly to convey his own stance, 'Moral distinctions derived from the *moral sentiment of sympathy*'.

Hume it must be recognised does not deny the existence of a 'sense of morals' – sometimes identified with 'conscience' (e.g. Hume 1978 [1740]: 458) – but he did insist that to conceive of it merely in terms of 'original instincts of the human mind' only went partway towards explaining moral judgment; a proper explanation required that the sense be traced back to – or 'accounted' for by – the sentiment of sympathy for mankind: 'Those who resolve the sense of morals into original instincts of the human mind may defend the cause of virtue with sufficient authority, but want the advantage which those possess, who account for that sense by an *extensive sympathy with mankind*' (619; emphasis added).

Again, Hume reiterates in the *Treatise* that 'sympathy' was 'the chief source of moral distinctions' (Hume 1978 [1740]: 618) – or as expressed in the *Enquiry Concerning the Principles of Morals* – 'benevolence in human nature, where no *real* interest binds us to the object' (Hume 1751: 19; 1927 [1777]: 300).[1] The unqualified version of a 'sense of morals' yielding self-evident verdicts regarding the 'multitude of precepts commonly designated as ethical' (1978 [1740]: 473) – precisely the version later attributed to him by Bentham and James Mill – entailed a serious methodological error as Hume elaborated in discussing the 'pain or pleasure, that distinguishes moral good and evil':

> 'tis absurd to imagine, that in every particular instance, these sentiments are produc'd by an original quality and primary constitution. For as the number of our duties is, in a manner, infinite, 'tis impossible that our original instincts should extend to each of them, and from our very first infancy impress on the human mind all that multitude of precepts, which are contain'd in the compleatest system of ethics. Such a method of proceeding is not conformable to the usual maxims, by which nature is conducted, where a few principles produce all that variety we observe in the universe, and every thing is carry'd on in the easiest and most simple manner. 'Tis necessary, therefore, to abridge these primary impulses, and find some more general principles, upon which all our notions of morals are founded.

'Sympathy with mankind' is the general principle intended, leaving the moral sense 'with little to do', as Bonar put it (above, p. 115). (Bonar introduces the qualifying 'alleged' moral sense whereas Hume did not himself deny its existence.)

Hume's *rejection* of what amounts to the Bentham–James Mill reading of his position can be seen in his discussion of 'Of virtue and vice in general' in Book III 'On Morals' of the *Treatise*. Specifically in a section entitled '*Moral distinctions not deriv'd from reason*' he rejects the notion of '[t]hose who affirm that virtue is nothing but a conformity to reason; that there are eternal fitnesses and unfitnesses of things, which are the same to every rational being that considers them; that the immutable measures of right and wrong impose an obligation, not only on human creatures, but also on the Deity himself: All these systems concur in the opinion, that morality, like truth, is discern'd merely by ideas, and by their juxta-position and comparison' (Hume 1978 [1740]: 456–7; cf. 465). To similar effect, Hume rejects 'an opinion very industriously propagated by certain philosophers, that morality is susceptible of demonstration; and though no one has ever been able to advance a single step in those demonstrations; yet 'tis taken for granted, that this science may be brought to an equal certainty with geometry or algebra' (463). There were in brief no 'eternal rational measures of right and wrong' (466), referring to allegedly self-evident opinion accepted by every sane individual on a par with a mathematical proposition. The *Enquiry* cites Malebranche as originator of the 'abstract theory of morals' which was then adopted by Cudworth, Samuel Clarke and others (Hume 1751: 55n; 1927 [1777]: 197n). This doctrine, Hume declares, 'excludes all sentiment, and pretends to found everything on reason'.

Now Hume declares that 'the question only arises among philosophers, whether the guilt or moral deformity of [an] action be discover'd by demonstrative reasoning, or be felt by an internal sense, and by means of some sentiment, which the reflecting on such an action naturally occasions. The question will soon be decided against the former opinion' (Hume 1978 [1740]: 466). Here again Hume, it may be said, appears to be opting for 'an internal sense' of what is right and wrong, so that it should come as no surprise that he devotes a second section to the theme: '*Moral distinctions deriv'd from a moral sense*'. But this reading is premature considering the necessity to bring 'sentiment' into play, by which is here intended 'our own sentiments of pleasure or uneasiness' (469). Correspondingly, the 'moral sense' in the title also concerns 'sensations' generated by observations of character and behaviour: 'Thus the course of the argument leads us to conclude, that since vice and virtue are not discoverable merely by reason, or the comparison of ideas, it must be by means of some impression or sentiment they occasion, that we are able to mark the difference betwixt them ... Morality, therefore, is more properly felt than judg'd of' (470).

Hume proceeds to the question: 'Of what nature are these impressions, and after what manner do they operate upon us?' by reference to sensations of pleasure and pain, such that we 'pronounce the impression arising from virtue, to be agreeable, and that proceeding from vice to be uneasy'. More specifically:

An action, or sentiment, or character is laudable or vicious; why? Because its view causes a pleasure or uneasiness of a particular kind. In giving a reason, therefore, for the pleasure or uneasiness, we sufficiently explain the vice or virtue. To have the sense of virtue, is nothing but to *feel* a satisfaction of a particular kind ... The very *feeling* constitutes our praise or admiration. We go no farther; not do we enquire into the cause of the satisfaction. We do not infer a character to be virtuous, because it pleases: But in feeling that it pleases after such a particular manner, we in effect feel that it is virtuous. The case is the same as in our judgments concerning all kinds of beauty, and tastes, and sensations. Our approbation is imply'd in the immediate pleasure they convey to us.

(Hume 1978 [1740]: 471).

The identification of a 'sense of virtue' with a 'feeling [of] satisfaction of a particular kind' – rendered more simply as 'virtue and vice [are] determin'd by pleasure and pain' – unfortunately lends itself to misunderstanding by apparently by-passing the entire matter of 'sympathy for mankind' or 'benevolence' *which Hume had himself represented as 'the chief source of moral distinctions'*. An alternative rendition is no less troublesome: 'virtue is distinguished by the pleasure, and vice by the pain, that any action, sentiment or character gives us by *the mere view and contemplation*' (Hume 1978 [1740]: 475; emphasis added). And Hume may once again be said to lay himself open to Bentham's objection to a crude interpretation of 'moral sense' when he later writes that '[t]he approbation of moral qualities most certainly is not deriv'd from reason, or any comparison of ideas; but proceeds entirely from a *moral taste* and from certain sentiments of pleasure or disgust, which arise upon the contemplation and view of particular qualities or characters' (581; emphasis added). Similarly, a discussion in the *Enquiry* 'Concerning moral Sentiment' asserts that 'crime or immorality is no particular fact or relation, which can be the object of the understanding, but arises entirely from the sentiment of disapprobation, which, by the structure of human nature, we unavoidably feel on the apprehension of barbarity or treachery' (Hume 1751: 209; 1927 [1777]: 292–3). Or that '[t]he ultimate ends of human actions can never ... be accounted for by *reason,* but recommend themselves entirely to the sentiments and affections of mankind, without any dependence on the intellectual faculties' (209–10; 293). Or again, that 'as virtue is an end, and is desirable on its own account, without fee and reward, merely for the immediate satisfaction which it conveys; it is requisite that there should be some sentiment which it touches, some internal taste or feeling, or whatever you please to call it, which distinguishes moral good and evil, and which embraces the one and rejects the other' (210–11; 293–4). We are only able to make sense of these and similar texts, and avoid charging Hume with incoherence, by assuming that he is silently taking for granted sympathy or benevolence as the 'chief source' of moral distinctions such that the 'pleasure' or 'satisfaction' to which he refers are to be understood as the *proximate* sensations generated by observation of certain actions, whereas the true source of such sensations resides in sympathetic or benevolent motivation.

Recall now Hutcheson's affirmation that where the *intention* of the agent did not entail the public good, his action must be considered morally defective even if social advantage happened to result (above, p. 115). Hume's position is not so easy to pin down. In his essay 'Of Refinement in the Arts' (first published in 1752) he objected to Mandeville that 'it seems upon any system of morality, little less than a contradiction in terms, to talk of a vice, which is in general beneficial to society' (Hume 1994 [1777]: 280); and in the *Enquiry* it is implied similarly that consequences alone matter by the contention that 'what promotes their happiness is good, what tends to their misery is evil, without any farther regard or consideration' (Hume 1751: 101; 1927 [1777]): 230). But Bonar has pointed out that 'Hume himself has to make similar concessions' to those made by Hutcheson, which 'seem fatal to his reply to Mandeville. Private vices might be public benefits, and yet remain vices' (Bonar 1922: 109).[2] Bonar did not elaborate on his assertion that for Hume an action is morally defective even if social advantage should result therefrom where the *intention* of the agent does not entail the public good, but that motivation takes precedence over consequences is established in the *Treatise* and Bonar may have had this in mind: ''Tis evident, that when we praise any actions, we regard only the motives that produced them, and consider the actions as signs or indications of certain principles in the mind and temper ... After the same manner, when we require any action, or blame a person for not performing it, we always suppose, that one in that situation shou'd be influenc'd by the proper motive of that action, and we esteem it vicious in him to be regardless of it' (Hume 1978 [1740]: 477). Hume implies as much also when he denies that 'the distinction betwixt moral good and evil, can be made by reason ... Reason and judgment may, indeed, be the mediate cause of an action, by prompting, or directing a passion: But it is not pretended, that a judgment of this kind ... is attended with virtue or vice' (462). Similarly, the *Enquiry* maintains that although 'reason' might indicate 'the pernicious or useful tendency of qualities and actions; it is not *alone* sufficient to produce any moral blame or approbation'; for, in addition, '[i]t is requisite a *sentiment* should here display itself, in order to give a preference to the useful above the pernicious tendencies,' namely a 'feeling for the happiness of mankind, and a resentment of their misery,' alluding of course to the benevolent sentiment of 'sympathy' (Hume 1751: 199; 1927 [1777]: 286; emphasis added).

There is a pervasive belief that, in evaluating merit, Hume focuses *entirely* on the end of utility, unlike Adam Smith whose concern was proper motivation (see Chapter 7.3). And Bentham famously described Hume's chapter 'Of Morals' in the *Treatise on Human Nature* as the text from which he had learned that, that 'utility was the test and measure of all virtue' apart from exceptional cases (see Chapter 10, p. 242). But to focus on utility as the 'end' in matters relating to ethical merit or to assert that 'the foundations of all *virtue* are laid in *utility*' is by no means to reject motivation in moral evaluation; the very contrary is true, since ethical merit turns on the motive of other-regarding 'sympathy' entailing an intention to enhance the general good. It is the *intended* utilitarian consequences that matter.

Several months before the publication of the *Treatise* Hume spelled out in correspondence with Hutcheson, who had the manuscript on hand, that 'tis on the Goodness or Badness of the Motives that the Virtue of the Action depends', and promised to render the notion more clearly in the forthcoming printed version (17 September 1739; Hume 1932: 35). And indeed in that version the high significance of *intended* utilitarian consequences can be easily shown by drawing a comparison with a source of ethical approval provided by 'particular *original* principles of human nature' (Hume 1978 [1740]: 590). Even if Hume did mean by this the direct appeal to a moral sense independently of intended consequences, as Bentham charged, this source is said to apply to 'cases of less moment', whereas in 'all the great lines of our duty,' consequences – 'their tendency to the happiness of mankind, and of particular persons' – have 'by far the greatest influence, and determine all the great lines of our duty', which evidently concerns conduct influenced, or motivated by, concern to advance general or at least particular 'happiness'.[3]

All this is reinforced in the remarks on *justice* in the *Enquiry* appearing in both the 1751 and the posthumously-published version. Whereas the 'necessity of justice to the support of society is the sole foundation of that virtue, and since no moral excellence is more highly esteemed, we may conclude that this circumstance of usefulness has, in general, the strongest energy, and most entire command over our sentiments. It must, therefore, be the source of a considerable part of the merit ascribed to humanity, benevolence, friendship, public spirit, and other social virtues of that stamp as it is the sole source of the moral approbation paid to fidelity, justice, veracity, integrity, and those other estimable and useful qualities and principles' (Hume 1751: 61; 1927 [1777]: 203–4); and similarly, '[t]he merit of benevolence, arising from its utility ... is, no doubt, the source of a *considerable* part of that esteem, which is so universally paid to it,' although not all, taking into account feelings and emotions (154; 257).[4]

The interpretation of *justice* as reflecting concern to advance the general or at least particular 'happiness' is reinforced by the perspective taken on property: 'With regard to justice ... the inference against this theory [the abstract theory of morals as adopted by Malebranche and Clarke] seems short and conclusive. Property is allowed to be dependent on civil laws; civil laws are allowed to have no object, but the interest of society: This therefore must be allowed to the sole foundation of property and justice' (Hume 1751: 55n; 1927 [1777]: 197n). Again: 'If we examine the *particular* laws, by which justice is directed and properly determined; we shall ... be presented with the same conclusion. The good of mankind is the only object of all these laws and regulations. Not only is it requisite, for the peace and interest of society, that men's possessions should be separated; but the rules, which we follow, in making the separation, are such as can best be contrived to serve farther the interests of society' (48; 192).

A passage appearing only in the posthumously-published version does not indicate a change of perspective, but rather its confirmation. Since 'the sentiment of justice' arises from 'reflecting' on the tendency of justice to 'promote public utility', rather than from a 'simple original instinct', it also provides the rationale underlying the *private-property* institution, the latter being 'of justice':

> As justice evidently tends to promote public utility and to support civil society, the sentiment of justice is either derived from our reflecting on that tendency, or like hunger, thirst, and other appetites, resentment, love of life, attachment to offspring, and other passions, arises from a simple original instinct in the human breast, which nature has implanted for like salutary purposes. If the latter be the case, it follows, that *property, which is the object of justice,* is also distinguished by a simple original instinct, and is not ascertained by any argument or reflection. But who is there that ever heard of such an instinct?
>
> (Hume 1927 [1777]: 201; emphasis added)

The role accorded conscious thought or 'reflection' is introduced at the outset of the *Enquiry Concerning Human Understanding* during the course of a sharp criticism of Locke that 'ambiguity and circumlocution seem to run through that philosopher's reasoning on this [the notion of "ideas"] as well as most other subjects' (Hume 1927 [1777]: 22n).[5] More specifically, 'the word *idea* seems to be commonly taken in a very loose sense, by LOCKE and others, as standing for any of our perceptions, our sensations and passions, as well as thoughts. Now in this sense, I should desire to know, what can be meant by asserting that self-love, or resentment of injuries, or the passion between the sexes is not innate?' Hume himself proposed that by '*innate*' should be understood 'what is original or copied from no precedent perception', from which it followed 'that all our impressions' – including *sensations* and *passions* – 'are innate, and our ideas not innate'. That our *ideas* are not innate we now see is applied to the sentiment of 'justice' – and extends therefrom to justify or account for private property – perceived as turning on '*our reflecting*' on its role in promoting public utility rather than as a matter of 'simple original instinct' implanted by nature albeit to advance that same end.

Considering Stephen's placement of Hume within 'Locke's school' (above, p. 116) it should be further pointed out that apart from the aforementioned objection to Locke, Hume in *Enquiry Concerning the Principles of Morals* remarked that – unlike Locke – Hobbes 'lay not under any restraint of religion which might supply the defects of his philosophy' (1751:13; 1927 (1777): 296). He there attributed to Locke and Hobbes 'the selfish System of Morals', saying nothing of Locke's designating *other-regarding* conduct as ethically meritorious despite such conduct being in the individual's interest, and again was highly critical of Locke's 'loose' use of the word *idea* 'as standing for any of our perceptions, our sensations and passions, as well as thoughts'.

******

As in the *Enquiry Concerning the Principles of Morals* two categories of 'moral duties' are spelled out in the essay 'Of the Original Contract' (first published in 1752), the first being 'those, to which men are impelled by a natural instinct or immediate propensity, which operates on them, independent of all ideas of obligation, and of all views, either to public or private utility. Of this nature are, love of children, gratitude to benefactors, pity to the unfortunate' (Hume 1994 [1777]: 479). But even in such cases 'natural instinct' is secondary to intended consequences since their *moral content* derives from expected social advantage: 'When we reflect on the advantage, which results to society from such human instincts, we pay them the just tribute of moral approbation and esteem,' notwithstanding that 'the person, actuated by them, feels their power and influence, antecedent to any such reflection.' We see, once again, a reconciliation of something akin to a moral sense with expected utilitarian consequences, contrasting with Bentham's reading of Hume.

The second category of moral rules entails *justice* with regard to property, *fidelity* with regard to the observance of promises, and 'obedience to magistrates' or *political allegiance*, and duties of this nature are said to be 'performed *entirely* from a sense of obligation, when we consider the necessities of human society, and the impossibility of supporting it, if these duties were neglected' (Hume (1994 [1777]: 480; emphasis added). The 'sense of obligation' may be understood as a particularly strong form of *social* sympathy, confirming the necessary condition for moral approval that conduct be governed by an intention to advance 'the necessities of human society'.

******

As we have seen, the *Enquiry Concerning the Principle of Morals* proposes that 'the sentiment of justice' underpinning the institution of private property arises from reflecting on its tendency to 'promote public utility' rather than from a 'simple original instinct' implanted by nature. As for the specifics of the justification of private property on utilitarian grounds, to which I turn next, all depends on circumstances, namely whether or not there exists a scarcity problem and whether or not the self-interest motive predominates (Hume 1751: 33–7; 1927 [1777]: 183–5). A summary statement elaborates:

Thus, the rules of equity or justice depend entirely on the particular state and condition in which men are placed, and owe their origin and existence to that utility, which results to the public from their strict and regular observance. Reverse, in any considerable circumstance, the condition of men: Produce extreme abundance or extreme necessity: Implant in the human breast perfect moderation and humanity, or perfect rapaciousness and malice: By rendering justice totally *useless,* you thereby totally destroy its essence, and suspend its obligation upon mankind.

The common situation of society is a medium amidst all these extremes. We are naturally partial to ourselves, and to our friends; but are capable of learning the advantage resulting from a more equitable conduct. Few enjoyments are given us from the open and liberal hand of nature; but by art, labour, and industry, we can extract them in great abundance. Hence the ideas of property become necessary in all civil society: Hence justice derives its usefulness to the public: And hence alone arises its merit and moral obligations.

(41; 188)

A Treatise of Human Nature illustrates Hume's appreciation of 'the circumstances in which an abdication of certain rights of individual action may be in the interest of all individuals' (Robbins 1952: 113). His rationale for public goods, which incorporates recognition of irrational time preference, and the complexity created by free-riding, is impressive indeed:

[G]overnment ... not contended to protect men in those conventions they make for their mutual interest, it often obliges them to make such conventions, and forces them to seek their own advantage, by a concurrence in some common end or purpose. There is no quality in human nature, which causes more fatal errors in our conduct, than that which leads us to prefer whatever is present to the distant and remote, and makes us desire objects more according to their situation than their intrinsic value. Two neighbours may agree to drain a meadow, which they possess in common; because 'tis easy for them to know each other's mind; and each must perceive, that the immediate consequence of his failing in his part, is, the abandoning the whole project. But 'tis very difficult, and indeed impossible, that a thousand persons shou'd agree in any such action; it being difficult for them to concert so complicated a design, and still more difficult for them to execute it; while each seeks a pretext to free himself of the trouble and expence, and wou'd lay the whole burden on others. Political society easily remedies both these in conveniences [...] Thus bridges are built; harbours open's; ramparts rais'd; canals form'd; fleets equip'd; and armies disciplin'd; every where by the care of government [...]

(Hume 1978 [1740]: 538)

5.3 Distributive justice

Assuming both scarcity and self-interest and the property institution, and provisionally taking aggregate wealth as given, how is it to be distributed?[6]

An equal distribution would be justifiable on something akin to, though by no means identical with, the later principle of diminishing marginal utility: 'It must, indeed, be confessed, that nature is so liberal to mankind, that were all her presents equally divided among the species, and improved by art and industry, every individual would enjoy all the necessaries, and even most of the comforts of life ... It must also be confessed, that, wherever we depart from this equality, we rob the poor of more satisfaction than we add to the rich, and that the slight gratification of a frivolous vanity, in one individual, frequently costs more than bread to many families, and even provinces' (Hume 1751: 49–50; 1927 [1777]: 193–4). The Roman Agrarian laws, referring to regulations entailing restrictions on land accumulation and land distribution among the plebeians, proceeded, Hume remarks, 'from a general idea of the utility of this principle' (50; 194).

The proposition whereby happiness increases with the redistribution from rich to poor – and the desirability of an Agrarian law – is, however, set aside once Hume introduces the implications for productivity, and thus for the total available to society for distribution, of neglecting differentials between individuals in skill and ability: 'Render possessions ever so equal, men's different degrees of art, care, and industry will immediately break that equality. Or if you check these virtues, you reduce society to the most extreme indigence', apart from the 'most rigorous inquisition ... requisite to watch every inequality on its first appearance; and the most severe jurisdiction, to punish and redress it' (Hume 1751: 51; 1927 [1777]: 194). Of interest here is the absence of any mention of the *unfairness* inherent in treating unequal individuals as if they are equal, such as Marx and J.S. Mill (not to speak of Hayek) were to insist upon in rejecting equality (see Chapter 13, pp. 332-3). Even the assertion that 'whatever is produced or improved by a man's art or industry ought, for ever, to be secured to him, in order to give encouragement to such *useful* habits and encouragements' (195) relates to motivation rather than fairness – which may not be surprising since 'fairness' is, strictly speaking, an extra-utilitarian value judgment.

By concentrating its focus on the case against *perfect* equality, the account in the *Enquiry* by no means conveys the full picture. In the essay 'Of Commerce' appearing in 1752 – one of a collection published originally under the title *Political Discourses* – Hume states his opposition to severe inequality. The general context is an account of the social and productivity advantages flowing from the existence of manufacturing and commercial sectors complementing agriculture which closes with a case against a 'too great disproportion' implying that welfare rises on balance with redistribution from rich to poor: 'as the multitude of mechanical arts is advantageous, so is the great number of persons to whose share the productions of those arts fall. A too great disproportion among the citizens weakens any state. Every person, if possible, ought to enjoy the fruits of his labour, in a full possession of all the necessaries and many of the conveniencies of life. No one can doubt, but such an equality is most suitable to human nature, and diminishes much less from the *happiness* of the rich than it adds to that of the poor' (Hume 1994 [1777]: 265). This is only part of the argument for greater equality: 'It also augments the *power of the state,* and makes any extraordinary taxes or impositions be paid with more cheerfulness. Where the riches are engrossed by a few, these must contribute very largely to the supplying of the public necessities. But when the riches are dispersed among multitudes, the burthen feels light on every shoulder, and the taxes make not a very sensible difference on any one's way of living'; Hume adds that 'where the riches are in few hands, these must enjoy all the power, and will conspire to lay the whole burthen on the poor, and oppress them still further, to the discouragement of all industry'.

The case proceeds with a celebration of England's status with respect to satisfactory real wages, evidently reflecting in part a situation approaching the distributive ideal: 'In this circumstance consists the great advantage of ENGLAND above any nation at present in the world, or that appears in the records of any story. It is true, the ENGLISH feel some disadvantages in foreign trade by the high price of labour, which is in part the effect of the riches of their artisans, as well as of the plenty of money: But as foreign trade is not the most material circumstance, it is not to be put in competition with the happiness of so many millions' (Hume 1994 [1777]: 265). The qualification playing down the significance of foreign trade – it reflects the notion expressed earlier that at least after a certain stage in economic development, foreign trade might be lost and any disadvantage compensated for by expansion for the domestic market (264) – in no way dilutes the striking implication of this famous passage that (as for Adam Smith) society cannot be said to be happy if the majority (median) class is miserable (see Chapter 8).

Hume's concern for labour's welfare is further confirmed by his satisfaction, expressed in 'Of Refinement in the Arts',[7] with that feature of the going system generating amongst an important 'middling rank of men', the effect of 'luxury': 'where luxury nourishes commerce and industry, the peasants, by a proper cultivation of the land, become rich and independent; while the tradesmen and merchants acquire a share of the property, and draw authority and consideration to that middling rank of men, who are the best and firmest basis of public liberty' (Hume 1994 [1777]: 277). It is to 'the middling rank' that Hume refers when he adds that '[t]he lower house is the support of our popular government; and all the world acknowledges, that it owed its chief influence and consideration to the increase of commerce, which threw such a balance of property into the hands of the commons' (278). One should also note the observation in 'Of National Characters' (appearing first in 1748) that 'the ENGLISH government is a mixture of monarchy, aristocracy, and democracy. The people in authority are composed of gentry and merchants' (1994 [1777]: 207). Now, as explained in 'Of Commerce', 'absolute monarchy' favours the rich and is adverse to 'the common people', although whether the going system of 'free government' works towards their betterment is by no means certain albeit more likely:

> The poverty of the common people is a natural, if not an infallible effect of absolute monarchy: though I doubt, whether it be always true, on the other hand, that their riches are an infallible result of liberty [...] Where the labourers and artisans are accustomed to work for low wages, and to retain but a small part of the fruits of their labour, it is difficult for them, even in a free government, to better their condition, or conspire among themselves to heighten their wages. But even where they are accustomed to a more plentiful way of life, it is easy for the rich, in an arbitrary government, to conspire against *them*, and throw the whole burthen of the taxes on their shoulders.
>
> (Hume 1994: [1777]: 265–7)

Since Hume's justification of wealth dispersal in 'Of Commerce' does not relate to *strict* equality, it allows in principle for earning inequalities which reflect differential effort and skill, so that we may perhaps understand why there is no mention of the effect of redistribution on motivation, as there is in the *Enquiry*. More broadly, there would be no pressing need for corrective action by the state considering Hume's general satisfaction with the degree of wealth dispersion in contemporary England envisaged as a mixed rather than an agricultural economy and characterized by a firm 'middling rank'. According to Winch there is 'similarity between Hume's position and that adopted by Smith in his *Lectures* when speaking about the redundancy of agrarian laws' (Winch 1978: 75). This evaluation appears valid. Smith was explicit regarding their redundancy where a substantial manufacturing sector exists and where there is '*a graduall descent of fortunes* betwixt these great ones and others of the least and lowest fortune' (see below, Chapter 8, p. 183); as for Hume, he refers in 'Of Commerce' to 'the great equality of fortunes among the inhabitants of the ancient republics, where every field, belonging to a different proprietor, was able to maintain a family, and rendered the numbers of citizens very considerable, even without trade and manufactures' (Hume 1994 [1777]: 259) and we have noted his favourable comment in the *Enquiry* regarding the Roman agrarian law which assured such equality (above, p.125). By implication, an economy such as Great Britain's would not require such measures. Recall that even Hutcheson, who did recommend agrarian laws, seems to have been prepared to modify his stance where a substantial manufacturing sector existed (see Chapter 4, p.109).

Hume's concern with labour's welfare also emerges in his proposition, in the essay 'Of Taxes', whereby '[t]he best taxes are such as are levied upon consumption, especially those of luxury; because such taxes are least felt by the people' (Hume 1994 [1777]: 345), which at least points towards Smith's proposals for a degree of income redistribution by way of the fiscal system (Chapter 8, p. 177). But Hume also observes in 'Of Public Credit', although rather enigmatically, that '[d]uties upon consumption are more equal and easy than those upon possessions' (Hume 1994 [1777]: 356). Hume's concern with an 'equal' burden arises also in a condemnation of 'arbitrary' taxes ('Of Taxes'; 1994 [1777]: 345).[8]

Hume goes yet further in 'Of Public Credit' by narrowing the legitimate range of consumption goods appropriate for taxation to protect the 'poorest' category of labour in particular, a matter that will preoccupy us when we consider a contention that Adam Smith's concern was largely with the *least* well off. This contention, I find, is more appropriately applied to Hume: 'In every country, there are always some methods of levying money more easy than others, agreeably to the way of living of the people, and the commodities they make use of. In GREAT BRITAIN, the excises upon malt and beer afford a large revenue; because the operations of malting and brewing are tedious, and are impossible to be concealed; and at the same time, *these commodities are not so absolutely necessary to life, as that the raising of their price would very much affect the poorer sort*' (Hume 1994 [1777]: 356; emphasis added). Hume in the same manner expresses concern regarding the National Debt that '[t]he taxes, which are levied to pay the interests of these debts, are apt either to heighten the price of labour, or be an oppression on *the poorer so*rt' (355; emphasis added), 'oppressive' both by obliging reduced consumption and increased effort since – as conveyed in 'Of Taxes' – labour is not in a good position to achieve compensatory wage increases: 'If a duty be laid upon any commodity, consumed by an artisan, he has two obvious expedients for paying it; he may retrench somewhat of his expence, or he may increase his labour. Both these resources are more easy and natural, than that of heightening his wages' (346). If this is the case of the artisan it would in principle be even truer of the common labourer.

Also noteworthy is Hume's approval in 'Of Commerce' of certain categories of luxury consumption as a stimulus to activity to all classes *including labour*, thus rejecting contemporary mercantilist attitudes: 'It is a violent method and in most cases impracticable, to oblige the labourer to toil, in order to raise from the land more than what subsists himself and family. Furnish him with manufactures and commodities, and he will do it for himself' (Hume 1994 [1777]: 262); similarly in 'Populousness of Ancient Nations' (first published in 1752): 'The most natural way, surely, of encouraging husbandry, is, first, to excite other kinds of industry, and thereby afford the labourer a ready market for his commodities, and a return of such goods as may contribute to his pleasure and enjoyment. This method is infallible and universal', (1994 [**1777**]: 419–20). It may be true, as Coates has pointed out, that Hume 'did not explicitly advocate an increase of real wages as a means of spurring the labourer to greater effort' (Coates 1992: 67), but to my mind such an effect seems to be at least implicit in the foregoing citations. There is, however, a complexity created by Hume's recognition in 'Of Taxes' of what is referred to by economists as a backward-bending labour supply curve such that an increase in the real wage *decreases* the labour supply, suggesting that 'artificial burdens' such as a commodity tax might encourage effort to the national benefit (Hume 1994 [1777]: 344). But Hume's concern not to 'oppress' labour – particularly the lower categories − by the taxation of necessaries remains largely intact, since he firmly warned against 'abuse' of the doctrine: "'Tis always observed, in years of scarcity, *if it be not extreme*, that the poor labour more, and really live better, than in years of great plenty, when they indulge themselves in idleness and riot … This doctrine, therefore, with regard to taxes, may be admitted in some degree. *But beware of the abuse*. Exorbitant taxes, like extreme necessity, destroy industry, by producing despair; and even before they reach this pitch, they raise the wages of the labourer and manufacturer, and heighten the price of all commodities' (635; emphasis added).

5.4 Concluding note

In summarising Humean utilitarianism, I take note of two particular features thus far left in abeyance. The first relates to Hume's contrast in 'Of Commerce' between the 'greatness of a state, and the happiness of its subjects' (Hume 1994 [1777]: 255; also 257), and his contention that 'according to the most natural course of things, industry and arts and trade encrease the power of the sovereign as well as the happiness of the subjects', whereas 'that policy is violent, which aggrandizes the public by the poverty of individuals' (260). The argument turns on the case for a mixed economy rather than a purely agricultural economy insofar as it concerns the motive for good cultivation and thus the agricultural surplus, which:

> [i]n times of peace and tranquillity … goes to the maintenance of manufacturers, and the improvers of liberal arts. But it is easy for the public to convert many of these manufacturers into soldiers, and maintain them by that superfluity, which arises from the labourer of the farmers … [T]o consider the matter abstractedly, manufactures increase the power of the state only as they store up so much labour, and that of a kind to which the public may lay claim, without depriving any one of the necessaries of life … In a state without manufactures, there may be the same number of hands; but there is not the same quantity of labour, nor of the same kind. All the labour is there bestowed upon necessaries, which can admit of little or no abatement.
>
> (261−2)

The public in meeting its war-time tax obligation in a mixed economy would 'retrench what is least necessary to their subsistence', referring to manufactures. Foreign commerce is of the first importance from this perspective:

> In short, a kingdom, that has a large import and export, must abound more with industry, and that employed upon delicacies and luxuries, than a kingdom which rests contented with its native commodities. It is, therefore, more powerful, as well as richer and happier. The individuals reap the benefit of these commodities, so far as they gratify the senses and

appetites. And the public is also a gainer, while a greater stock of labour is, by this means, stored up against any public exigency; that is, a greater number of laborious men are maintained, who may be diverted to the public service, without robbing any one of the necessaries, or even the chief conveniencies of life.

(263).

In normal times therefore the welfare of the state may be said to reflect that of the individuals, satisfying in effect the greater-happiness formula entailing a rough summation of individual happinesses, and *coincidentally* satisfying its defence needs by assuring a reserve of labour in the manufacturing sector at hand for emergencies. Smith also later maintained that '[t]he riches, and so far as power depends upon riches, the power of every country, must always be in proportion to the value of the annual produce, the fund from which all taxes must ultimately be paid' (Smith 1976 [1776]: 372), but he nonetheless justified the Act of Navigation on the grounds that 'defence … is of much more importance than opulence' (464–5). Hume's argument reinforces the essentially complementary nature of the two dimensions, though perhaps he would agree with Smith regarding such matters as national self-sufficiency with respect to key industries.

My second observation relates to Lord Robbins's comment that the standard utilitarian proposition whereby 'each man's capacity for happiness was to be counted as equal' is in 'an ethical postulate rather than a principle established by observation or introspection' (Robbins 1952: 179–80). This may be so, yet it is the case that Hume drew heavily on observation – as did Smith – to confirm the enlightenment view that differences between individuals reflected largely environmental factors rather than innate character. In these terms the essay 'Of Commerce' closes to explain 'why no people, living between the tropics, could ever yet attain to any art or civility, or reach any police in their government, and any military discipline; while few nations in the temperate climates have been altogether deprived of these advantages' (Hume 1994 [1777]: 267). The same liberal stance is affirmed in 'Of National Characters' (Hume 1994 [1777]: 207–8), although with an exception: 'I am apt to suspect the negroes to be naturally inferior to the whites' (208n). At the same time, to be noted is Hume's strong aversion to the institution of domestic slavery, as expressed in 'Of the Populousness of Ancient Nations', partly on grounds that slavery debases the slave masters no less than the slaves (Hume 1994 [1777]: 383f).

We are not done yet with Hume. Adam Smith found in him the idea of virtue as 'prudence' and this matter will be addressed in Chapter 7. Hume also reappears in Chapter 10 where his ideas are compared with those of Bentham.

Notes

1 Recall from Chapter 4 that Hutcheson regarded benevolence as a particularly strong form of sympathy entailing strictly *anonymous* beneficiaries. Hume here apparently adopts the same contrast.

2 For a critical discussion of similarities between Hume and Hutcheson regarding 'the 'good will' view of what constitutes rightness, see Prichard 2002: 160–2.
3 I find some difficulty with a remark in the letter to Hutcheson which puts *personal* good on a par with public good or at least the good of second parties: 'I desire you to consider if there be any Quality that is virtuous, without having a Tendency either to the public Good or to the Good of the Person who possesses it' (17 September 1739; Hume 1932: 34).
4 Hume observes that even natural-law writers recognized that the 'ultimate reason for every rule' from which they set out terminates with the effect on the 'convenience and necessities of mankind' (Hume 1751: 52; 1927 [1777]: 195).
5 The criticism appears in the original version of the *Enquiry* published as *Philosophical Essays Concerning Human Understanding* (Hume 1748: 29).
6 As with Adam Smith it is not always clear whether wealth or income is intended. 'Possessions' is the term Hume sometimes uses, and certainly where property is at issue, wealth is presumably intended, but the text that follows appears to refer to income and it may be safe to suppose that for the purposes of the discussion Hume presumed a one-to-one relation.
7 First published in 1752 under the title 'Of Luxury'.
8 The essays mentioned in this paragraph first appeared in 1752.

References

Bonar, J. 1922. *Philosophy and Political Economy*. London: Allen and Unwin.
Bonar, J. 1930. *Moral Sense*. London: Allen and Unwin.
Coates, A.W. 1992. *On the History of Economic Thought* I. London and New York: Routledge.
Hume, D. 1748. *Philosophical Essays Concerning Human Understanding*. London: Millar.
Hume, D. 1751. *Enquiry Concerning the Principles of Morals*. First edn. London: Millar.
Hume, D. 1927 (1777). *Enquiries Concerning Human Understanding and Concerning the Principles of Morals*, edited by A. Selby-Bigge. Posthumous ed. Oxford: Clarendon Press.
Hume, D. 1932. *The Letters of David Hume* I, edited by J.Y.T. Greig. Oxford: Clarendon Press.
Hume, D. 1978 [1740]. *A Treatise on Human Nature* III: *Of Morals*. Oxford: Clarendon Press: 455–639.
Hume, D. 1994 (1777). *Essays Moral, Political, And Literary*. Eugene F. Miller, ed. Indianapolis: Liberty Fund.
Mill, J.S. 1989 (1869). 'James Mill's *Analysis of the Phenomena of the Human Mind*', *Miscellaneous Writings, Collected Works* 31, ed. John M. Robson. Toronto: University of Toronto Press: 93–253.
Prichard, H.A. 2002. *Moral Writings*, edited by Jim MacAdam. Oxford: Clarendon Press.
Robbins, L.C. 1952. *The Theory of Economic Policy*. London: Macmillan.
Smith 1976 (1776). *The Wealth of Nations*. Oxford: Clarendon Press.
Stephen, L. 1902 1: *English Thought in the Eighteenth Century* 1. Third edition. London: John Murray.
Winch, D. 1978. *Adam Smith's Politics: An essay in historiographic revisionism*. Cambridge: Cambridge University Press.

6 C.A. Helvétius and David Hartley, utilitarian ethics, and the moral sense

6.1 Introduction

As we shall see in Chapter 10 Bentham expressed gratitude to Helvétius – and secondarily to Hartley – for instructing him to treat happiness as an 'aggregate or compound' of simple pleasures, however *apparently* irreducible the elements are to a common dimension, and both Helvétius and Hartley can indeed be cited to this effect. Our concern in the present chapter is however with more specific matters. As for Helvétius, he will be shown to be, like Hume, a utilitarian writer basing himself nonetheless on the moral sense understood as *feelings of morality* entailing specifically *other-regarding* sentiment directed towards enhancing the general happiness. Those sympathetic feelings are ascribed by Helvétius to 'personal-interest' or 'self-interest' – with 'conscience' (the moral sense) prioritizing such sentiment – although when addressing policy issues he considered most men not to be virtuous, governed as they tended to be in their 'personal interest' by narrow *selfishness*. The ascription of feelings of morality to a sense of interest, while at the same time representing morality in terms of other-regarding sentiment, is precisely Locke's position. More generally, and unlike Hume, Helvétius admired Locke's 'genius' including his elaboration of the notion that our ideas are not in-born or innate but rooted in actual experience and reflect our sensations or senses. On the other hand, I see no evidence in Helvétius of Lockean theological utilitarianism incorporating future reward and punishment as entering into 'personal interest', but Locke himself, as we know, was far from naïve regarding mankind's capacity to take account of such distant prospects.

My account is organised around John Stuart Mill's perspective which follows Bentham in crediting Helvétius – along with Hume – for establishing the doctrine that *general utility* is the foundation of morality, and understands his utilitarianism as turning on a purely 'selfish' calculation lacking comprehension of man's full character. This latter perspective we shall show does not do justice to Helvétius's actual position, namely that virtuous sentiment – albeit a matter of 'personal interest' – implies *other-regarding sympathy*, in line with Hume and Hutcheson who both formally adopt the idea of a 'moral sense' while reducing it to the sentiment of *sympathy*.

Also taken under consideration is Mill's commendation of David Hartley, perceived as a utilitarian who while rejecting a moral sense as the test of right and wrong acknowledged it as a 'fact in human nature'. By noting this acknowledgement Mill weakened his own eighteenth–nineteenth century contrast between moral-sense adherents opposed to the utility doctrine and utilitarians. In any event, we shall see that Mill's perspective on Hartley requires correction.

6.2 Mill's perspective on Helvétius

While in 1838 Mill commended Bentham's method, he doubted whether he had contributed anything novel regarding the expediential doctrine itself: 'The generalities of his philosophy itself have little or no novelty: to ascribe any of the doctrine that *general utility is the foundation of morality*, would imply great ignorance of the history of philosophy, of general literature, and of Bentham's own writings. He derived the idea, as he says himself, from Hume and Helvétius' ('Bentham'; Mill 1969 [1838]: 86; emphasis added). Mill also refers to Helvétius's ascription of 'a *selfish* origin to the feelings of morality, resolving them into a *sense of interest*' ('Coleridge'; 1969 [1840]: 131; emphasis added).[1] Mill does not at this point state explicitly that Helvétius's resolution of feelings of morality into a 'sense of interest' – understood as *selfishness* – was adopted by Bentham, but that is the impression we have from a further feature of his account of Bentham's obligation to his predecessors, namely the dangers of excessive, even distorted, manifestations of selfish motivation. Mill here intended Bentham's 'illustrations of what he terms "interest-begotten prejudice" – the inherent [1867:common] tendency of man to make a duty and a virtue of following his self-interest', manifested in particular as 'selfish interest in the form of class-interest and the class morality founded thereon … the manner in which any set of persons who mix much together, and have a common interest, are apt to make that common interest their standard of virtue, and the social feelings of the members of the class are made to play into the hands of their selfish ones' (1969 [1838]: 109–10). This notion was not novel to Bentham, but 'given to him by Helvétius, whose book, *De l'Esprit*, is one continued and most acute commentary on it' (110).[2]

Mill's reading of Helvétius, we may note, is remarkably long-lived. It was expressed by A.R.J. Turgot immediately on the appearance of *De l'Esprit*:

> Nulle part il ne s'appuie sur une connaissance approfondie du coeur humain: nulle part il n'analyse les vrais besoins de l'homme qu'il semble ne faire consister que dans celui d'avoir des femmes; il ne se doute nulle part que l'homme ait besoin d'*aimer*. Mais un homme qui auroit senti ce besoin n'auroit pas dit que *l'intérêt est l'unique principe qui fait agir les hommes*. Il eut compris que dans le sens où cette proposition est vraie, elle est une

puérilité et une abstraction métaphysique d'où il n'y a aucun résultat pratique à tirer, puisqu'alors elle équivaut à dire que *l'homme désire que ce qui'il désire.*

(Turgot 1810 [1760]: 290–1).

'Nowhere does he base himself on a profound knowledge of the human heart: nowhere does he analyze the true needs of man which he apparently identifies entirely with that of having women; nowhere does he appreciate that man has a need *to love*. But someone who did appreciate this need would never have said that *interest is the sole principle that governs man's actions.* He would have understood that the only sense in which this proposition holds good is puerile and a metaphysical abstraction without practical implications since it is equivalent to saying that *man only desires what he desires.*'

(Author's own translation)

And this is precisely the position taken by Schumpeter. Discussing 'the utilitarian point of view' and the underlying notion of 'individual self-interest [as] oriented on rational expectation of individual pleasure and pain ... defined in a narrowly hedonist sense', Schumpeter distinguishes between the Scholastics, who limited the doctrine to 'the sphere of stable, barn, shop, and market', and eighteenth-century expositors including Helvétius and Beccaria – but also Priestley, Paley, and Hume – who 'reduced the whole world of human values to the same scheme, ruling out, as contrary to reason, all that matters to man', thereby creating 'the shallowest of all conceivable philosophies of life' (Schumpeter 1954: 130–3). Such a system, Schumpeter lamented, was 'incapable of taking account of the facts of political life and of the way in which states, governments, parties, and bureaucracies actually work', although 'its preconceptions did little harm in fields such as that of economics where "its logic of stable and barn" may be considered as a tolerable expression of actual tendencies' (429).

6.3 *De L'Esprit*

I turn now to *De L' Esprit* itself in order to evaluate Mill's representation of eighteenth-century utilitarianism illustrated by Helvétius as turning on 'selfish' calculation and wanting the comprehension of a person's full character. I shall argue that while Mill accurately represents Helvétius's position regarding the principle that *general utility is the foundation of morality*, it is difficult to understand how the resolution of feelings of morality into 'a sense of interest', intending thereby a 'selfish' origin to such feelings, relates to that primary principle. The problem dissipates once we appreciate that Helvétius in fact perceived *other-regarding* sentiment – albeit a manifestation of 'self-interest' – to comprise moral feelings, 'conscience' prioritizing such sentiment. But here we must pause. What I have said relates entirely to matters of *principle*. When Helvétius addresses *policy* he focuses on practicalities and estimates that the vast majority are not in fact 'virtuous'. In this context, which involves the problem of assuring the public wellbeing by way of legislation, 'personal interest' is indeed identified with selfishness, supporting the Mill–Schumpeter reading.

I turn now to justify these assertions. General utility as the foundation of morality is, as Mill says, a pervasive theme: '[public] utility is the principle on which all human virtues are founded, and the basis of all legislations. It ought to inspire the legislator with the resolution to force the people to submit to his laws' (Helvétius 1759 [1758]: 41); or again with regard to principles of legislation:

> It is … on the uniformity of the legislator's views, and the dependence of these laws on each other, that their excellence consists. But, in order to establish this dependence, it would be necessary to refer them all to one simple principle, such as that of the public utility; or, to that of the greatest number of men, subject to the same form of government: a principle more extensive and more fruitful than imagination can conceive: a principle that includes all the morality and all the legislations, of which many men discourse without understanding them, and of which the legislators themselves have yet had but a very superficial idea, at least if we may judge from the unhappiness of almost all the nations upon earth.
>
> (88)

But we can be more precise. Some formulations of morality focus on *motivation*, as for example: 'Real Probity' relates to 'regard to the public' (Helvétius 1759 [1758]: 25); 'by the word Virtue can only be understood, a desire of the general happiness' (67); '[b]y a hypocrite, I mean him who, in the study of morality, is not animated by a desire of procuring the happiness of mankind, being too much taken up with himself' (82). Others focus on actions: 'a Man is just, when all his actions tend to the public welfare' (39); and this is extended to justice and the enforcement of proper action: '… man is made to be virtuous; and in fact, if force essentially resides in the greater number, and justice consists in the practice of actions useful to the greater number, it is evident that justice is in its own nature always armed with a power sufficient to suppress vice, and place men under the necessity of being virtuous' (116).[3] Other formulations focusing on utilitarian consequences take for granted that a virtuous man can, *at least in principle*, be recognized by his intentions even prior to action. Thus: 'virtue is only the desire of the happiness of mankind, and … probity, which I consider as virtue put into action, is among all people, and in all the governments of the world, only the habit of performing actions useful to our country' (70); or again: 'the actions personally advantageous to … virtuous men are so truly just, that they tend to promote the general welfare, or, at least not to lessen it' (26). In principle only, considering the difficulty of discerning motivation even by the individual in question: 'I say of actions, because we cannot judge of intentions ... Now if a man be, in general, ignorant himself of the motives of his generous action, how can the public be acquainted with them? Thus it is only from the actions of men, that the public can judge of their probity' – referring to 'intentions'. There is the further complexity that actions may not accurately reflect sentiment since 'the virtue of man greatly depends on the circumstances in which they are placed. Virtuous men have often sunk under a strange series of unhappy events'. Nonetheless, any sharp contrast between motive and action is effectively erased when Helvétius writes that 'the humane man is he to whom the sight of another's misfortunes is insupportable, and who to remove this afflicting spectacle, is, as it were, *forced* to relieve the wretched' (27n; emphasis added); and similarly that 'the virtuous man is not ... he who sacrifices his pleasures, habits, and strongest passions to the public welfare, since it is impossible that such a man should exist; but he whose strongest passion is so conformable to the general interest, that he is almost constantly *necessitated* to be virtuous' (188; emphasis added). This notion of a quasi-obligatory response, as it were, to virtuous motive is further reinforced by the rational offered to explain why 'some men have seemed to sacrifice their interest to the public welfare', namely that 'in a good form of government, the idea of virtue is so united to that of happiness, and the idea of vice to that of contempt, that they are hurried away by a lively sensation, the origin of which is not always to be discovered; and from this motive perform actions, that are often contrary to their interest' (188n).

The primary difficulty with Mill's account relates, as I have said, to the alleged 'selfish' origin to feelings of morality. Certainly it is easy to cite formulations that can be read in that fashion. Thus Helvétius famously declared that '[i]f the physical universe be subject to the laws of motion, the moral universe is equally so to those of interest'; and 'personal interest' is relevant to the virtuous man since both he and the cruel man 'so very opposite, both equally tend to their pleasures, and are actuated by the same spring' (Helvétius 1759 [1758]: 27, 27n); and he concludes 'that personal interest is the only and universal estimator of the merit of human actions; and, therefore, that Probity, with regard to an individual is, according to my definition, nothing more than the habitude of actions *personally advantageous* to this individual' (28; emphasis added). But to leave the matter here is to neglect Helvétius's cautions against representations of 'interest' or 'self-love' as vice or even as 'love of money':

> When the famous M. De la Rochefoucault, said, that Self-love is the principle of all our actions, what invectives, occasioned by the ignorance of the word Self-love, were thrown out against that illustrious

> author! Self-love was considered as pride and vanity; and therefore M. Rochefoucault was said to consider vice as the source of all the virtues. Yet it was easy to perceive, that Self-love was nothing more than a sentiment implanted in us by nature; that in every individual this sentiment becomes vice or virtue, according to his dispositions and passions; and that Self-love, differently modified, was equally productive of pride and modesty.
>
> (19)

> The word Interest is generally confined to the love of money; but the intelligent reader will perceive that I use it in a more general sense; and that I apply it in general to whatever may procure us pleasure or exempt us from pain.
>
> (24n)

'Interest', or a man's regard for his own happiness, is *pace* Mill and Schumpeter a neutral fact of life consistent with an entire range of 'passions and tastes' some of which – such as the 'passion for virtue' and the 'love for justice and virtue' – favour the 'public interest'; and 'the actions *personally advantageous to … virtuous men* are so truly just, that they tend to promote the general welfare, or, at least not to lessen it' (26–7; emphasis added). A man's 'interest' or 'personal advantage' may thus dictate *disinterested* concerns – dictate in an almost literal sense considering the tight nexus between motive and action noted above:

> virtues and vices are wholly owing to the different modifications of his personal interest; that all equally tend to their [sic] happiness; that it is the diversity of the passions and tastes, of which some are agreeable and others contrary to the public interest, which term our actions either virtuous or vices. Instead of despising the vicious man, we should pity him, rejoice in our own happy disposition, thank heaven for not having given us any of those tastes and passions, which would have forced us to have sought our happiness in the misery of another. For, after all, interest is always obeyed.
>
> (27)

It followed that *soi-disant* 'moralists' motivated by self-interest *in the narrow sense* were 'no more than mere egotists', for 'it is only by an absolute detachment from personal interest, by a profound study of the science of legislation, that a moralist can become serviceable to his country. He is then able to weigh the advantages and disadvantages of a law or custom, and to judge whether it should be abolished or continued' (82). Here a form of cost–benefit calculus is applied.

In all this we find amply confirmed Viner's succinct observation that the individual's 'sovereign masters' for Bentham and other eighteenth-century utilitarians, were not identified with self-interest, but with 'whatever men are interested in' (Viner 1958: 312). Taking a broader view, it emerges from the discussion so far that virtuous sentiment – albeit a matter of 'personal interest' – implies for Helvétius *other-regarding sympathy*, even if he never used this term, fully in line with the proposition that 'general utility is the foundation of morality'. Helvétius, it may therefore be said, has much in common with writers such as Hume and Hutcheson who adopt the idea of a 'moral sense' but reduce it to the sentiment of *sympathy*, rejecting the crude version positing a mental sense of the same order as the physical senses and capable of yielding automatic and unambiguous verdicts regarding the ethics of every conceivable motive and action, independently of consequences or indeed any other rational consideration. It is significant that Helvétius should have firmly opposed 'innate ideas' in favour of 'natural sensibility and personal interest' which suggests Locke's position although Helvétius cites no authority at this point (Helvétius 1759 [1758]: 139). It was this general orientation – coupled with the Humean methodological principle established in his Preface: 'It is by the facts that I have ascended to causes. I imagined that morality ought to be treated like all the other sciences, and founded on experiment, as well as natural philosophy' (iii) – that attracted the displeasure of the religious establishment (see Forget 1999: 46–7).

Helvétius does not use the term *moral sense* but does refer to *conscience* or *soul* or *heart* encouraging an attention to those passions and tastes which favour promotion of the public welfare, such as the 'passion for virtue' and the 'love for justice and virtue'. But he is not starry eyed. Conscience does not declare itself unambiguously, and he seeks to understand 'why, in any government whatsoever, man, variable in his conduct, is determined by his passions sometimes to good, and at others to bad actions; and why, his heart is an amphitheatre, always open to the contests between virtue and vice' (Helvétius 1759 [1758]: 186). This 'moral problem' he proposes to resolve by 'search[ing] into the cause of the successive disquietude and sleep of conscience, into the source of those confused and various emotions of soul'. The resolution he finds in the fact 'that men are not moved by one single species of sensations; that none of them are completely animated by those solitary passions, that fill the whole capacity of the soul; that, drawn by turns by different passions, some of which are comfortable, and others contrary to the general interest, every man is subject to two different attractions; one of which leads him to virtue, and the other to vice' (187). In any event, 'a good conscience is often indolent' (309). Furthermore, 'greatness of soul' is said – the context is the court – not to be the only 'gift of nature' requisite for virtue:

> It is ... certain, that there can be no method of preserving there a virtue constantly firm and uncorrupt, without having constantly present to the

mind, a principle of public utility; without being thoroughly acquainted with the true interest of the public, and consequently without moral and political knowledge. Perfect probity never falls to the lot of the stupid: for probity without knowledge, is only probity of intention, for which the public neither have nor can have any regard; both because they cannot judge of the intention, and because in the judgment they form, they consult nothing but their own interest.

(40–1)

The principle is extended to the individual: 'We ought then, in order to be virtuous, to blend the light of knowledge with greatness of soul. Whoever assembles within himself these different gifts of nature always directs his course by the compass of the public utility' (41).

Here we may take note of Helvétius's preoccupation with small societies, remarked on by Mill, particularly the danger of their diverting the individual member's 'interest' from concern with public utility: 'I am sensible that an honest man, apprehensive of the ascendency of the opinion of the society in which he lives may have over him, may justly be afraid of being frequently turned from the path of virtue' (Helvétius 1759 [1758]: 39). The concern is that the individual will come to identify his own interest not with the public good, but with the interest as perceived by the society. Some societies may 'appear to lay aside their own interest to judge the actions of men, in conformity to the interest of the public; but in this they only gratify the passion of which an enlightened pride gives them for virtue; and consequently ... obey the law of personal interest' (37).

6.4 Helvétius on policy

In Helvétius's judgment – and here we may discern a difference with Hume and Hutcheson – the virtuous man was the exception, their number being 'so small, that I only mention them in honour of humanity. And the most numerous class, which alone comprehends the far greater part of mankind, is that of men so entirely devoted to their own interest, that they never consider the welfare of the whole. Concentrated, if I may be allowed the expression, in their own happiness, these men call those actions only honest, which are advantageous to themselves' (Helvétius 1759 [1758]: 26–7). Here, where the concern is with the majority, or average, 'interest' is indeed identified with *selfishness*, as Mill had it, whereas ethical motivation is identified with other-regarding or sympathetic sentiment. And this is the case too when Helvétius writes in the same context that it is 'to the habitude of actions *advantageous to him*, that an individual gives the name of Probity' (26; emphasis added), for here he refers to the 'hypocrite' who 'in the study of morality, is not animated by a desire of procuring the happiness of mankind, being too much *taken up with himself*, and not to the man characterized by 'real probity' entailing 'regard to the public' (above, p. 135).

This alteration in the sense given to the term 'interest' is central to Helvétius's concern with policy entailing the problem of 'how to render men virtuous' as the matter is often phrased, at least with regard to his actions. Helvétius might be charged with serious self-contradiction unless we say that he adopts for this purpose a *working assumption of selfish motivation for practical purposes* having in mind his empirical estimate that most individuals are not naturally virtuous. (Or – it comes to the same thing – he takes for granted the selfish–sympathetic mix whatever that might be, and posits the need for policy makers to concern themselves only with the selfish category.) Thus we find that, when discussing sensible policy, Helvétius deviates from the neutral sense of terms such as 'interest' or 'self-love' – whereby both the virtuous and the cruel man 'equally tend to their pleasures, and are actuated by the same spring', as Viner maintained. For he cautions that 'all men tend only towards their happiness; that it is a tendency from which they cannot be diverted; that the attempt would be fruitless, and even success dangerous' (Helvétius 1759 [1758]: 81) and this appears to relate to the futility of policies opposing *selfish* motivation – intending perhaps the uselessness of exhortation – since to divert men from acting upon their *other-regarding* or sympathetic sentiment would be to no purpose. On the other hand, encouraging selfishly-motivated agents to work for socially-desirable ends would encourage *actions* that are in the public interest. This may be what is intended by the conclusion that 'it is only by incorporating personal and general interest, that [men] can be rendered virtuous', at which point Helvétius puts theoretical ethics as such into the shade by asserting that '[t]his being granted, morality is evidently no more than a frivolous science, unless blended with policy and legislation'. As the matter is phrased subsequently: 'It is ... only by good laws that we can form virtuous men. All the art therefore of the legislator consists in forcing them by self-love to be always just to each other' (120–1). Again, there would be no need for legislation if men were by and large naturally virtuous such that 'personal interest' in the first extract and 'self-love' in the second are understood as accommodating *other-regarding* motivation. In brief, when policy is the concern, virtuous action must be *forced* on individuals since in most individuals the motive as such is and remains selfishness. Indeed, in the present context regarding 'good laws' the claim that men have other-regarding as well as selfish sentiments is quite distinctly set aside by the assertion that men have 'sensibility for themselves, and indifference with respect to others':

> Now, in order to compose such laws, it is necessary that the human heart should be known, and in the first place that we should be convinced that *men having sensibility for themselves, and indifference with respect to others,* are neither good nor bad, but ready to be either according as a common interest unites or divides them; that self-love, a sensation necessary to the preservation of the species, is engraved by Nature in a manner not to be erased ... By contemplating these preliminary ideas ... a legislator discovers the means of laying men under a

necessity of being virtuous, and causing the passions to bear no other fruit but probity and wisdom.

(121)

Notice the parallel terminologies. Whereas the 'strongest passion' of the *naturally* virtuous man – other-regarding motive – 'is so conformable to the general interest, that he is almost constantly *necessitated* to be virtuous' (above, p. 136), in practice reliance must be placed on the legislator to induce even selfish people – the vast majority – to assure this outcome: 'a legislator discovers the means of laying men under a necessity of being virtuous'. We recall also the affirmation that public utility, as the basis both for human virtue and legislation, 'ought to inspire the legislator with the resolution to force the people to submit to his laws' (above, p. 135).

Helvétius thus emerges as an exponent of state intervention to harmonize private with public interest since self-interested individuals could not be relied upon to bring about such reconciliation: 'a philosopher … ought to give virtue a foundation on which all nations may equally build, and consequently erect it on the basis of personal interest. He should the more closely adhere to this principle, as the motions of temporal interest, *managed with address by a skilful legislator,* are alone sufficient to form virtuous men' (Helvétius 1759 [1758]: 117–18; emphasis added).[4] Viner has brought to our attention that here Helvétius is 'echoing [Mandeville] even as to language' (1958: 342; see also 316), the French original of the italicized phrase reading: 'maniés avec adresse par un législateur habile' (Helvétius 1758: 232), which corresponds to the concluding proposition of the *Fable of the Bees* that 'Private Vices by *the dextrous Management of a skilful Politician* may be turned into Publick Benefits' (Mandeville 1924 [1732]: 369; emphasis added), in the French: 'Que les Vices des particuliers *ménagés avec dextérité par d'habiles politiques,* peuvent être tournés à l'avantage du public' (*La fable des abeilles*, Tome Second. London: Jean Nourse 1750: 261).[5] Helvétius in fact goes a step further and maintains that conduct may provisionally be assumed ethically neutral until the state decides otherwise: 'we ought to consider actions as indifferent in themselves … it is the business of the state to determine those that are worthy of esteem or contempt; and … it is the office of the legislator, to fix, from his knowledge of the public interest, the instant when an action ceases to be virtuous, and becomes vicious' (1759 [1758]: 84–5).

6.5 Helvétius on ethical progress

Nothing in our analysis so far of *De l'Esprit* suggests a possibility of *genuine* ethical progress extending beyond assuring socially-desirable conduct on the part of the selfishly motivated to allowance for modification of character favouring other-regarding motivation. For considerable attention is paid to the reward system characterising different societies and governments, the fact that 'great rewards produce great virtues [so] that the wise distribution of honours is the strongest band, which legislators can use to unite the private and general interest, and so form good citizens' (Helvétius 1759 [1758]: 213), whereas '[t]astes and passions' themselves appear at times to be taken as natural data and by implication unchangeable: 'Instead of despising the vicious man, we should pity him, rejoice in our own happy disposition, thank heaven for not having given us any of those tastes and passions, which would have forced us to have sought our happiness in the misery of another' (above, p. 137).

There is some counter-evidence. The passions themselves are at one point represented not as natural data but as the *outcome* of 'self-love', Helvétius writing 'that a physical sensibility has produced in us a love of pleasure and a hatred of pain; that pleasure and pain have at length produced, and opened in all hearts the buds of self-love, which by unfolding themselves give birth to the passions; whence spring all our virtues and vices' (Helvétius 1759 [1758]: 121). Moreover, in discussing obstacles to general welfare on the part of powerful cabals, he points to the necessity, especially on the part of the elite, to *cultivate* the sentiments characterizing a virtuous man, suggesting the potential malleability of character traits:

> A person solely subject to reason and virtue, might ... brave every prejudice, and *arm himself with those many and courageous sentiments that form the distinguishing character of a virtuous man*: sentiments desirable in every citizen, and which we have the right to expect from the great. How shall the person, raised to the highest posts, remove the obstacles to the general welfare, which certain prejudices raise against it, and resist the menaces and cabals of men in power, often interested in the public misfortune, if his soul is not accessible to all kinds of solicitations, fears and prejudices?.
>
> (84; emphasis added)

That 'character' is not fixed in stone may be suggested by the enlightenment view taken of the essential equality of men, observable differences in mental capacity reflecting not an irrevocable nature but environment and accident: 'The great inequality of mind, observable in mankind ... only depends on the different education they receive, and the unknown and varied chain of circumstances in which they are placed' (220; see also 240).[6] There were in fact no limits, in principle, to what the individual might achieve in the right environment and given the right opportunities. Not only is the enlightenment perspective applied to the historical and geographical incidence of *genius*, it is applied also to that of *virtue* – our present concern.

Yet on balance malleability of character as such cannot be said to constitute a prime theme; as we have noted it is the reward system that takes centre stage. As for education as a 'means of rendering men better', Helvétius was profoundly pessimistic regarding the practical prospects given 'the actual manners of the people': 'After having considered the mind in so many various relations, I ought, perhaps, to trace out the plan of a good education, and perhaps a complete treatise on this subject should have been placed at the conclusion of this work. If I avoid this labour, it is because, supposing that I could really point out the means of rendering men better, it is evident, that, from the actual manners of the people, it would be almost impossible to make use of them' (Helvétius 1759 [1758]: 324). Apart from the low ethical standard of the majority which is here alluded to, there was the further problem that 'the art of forming men is in all countries so strictly connected with the form of the government, that, perhaps, it is impossible to make any considerable change in public education, without making the same in the constitution of states' (325). The task was not to be underestimated.

6.6 Helvétius and Locke

We have pointed out that Helvétius opposed 'innate ideas' in favour of 'natural sensibility and personal interest' (above, p. 138). This suggests Locke's position and, while Helvétius cites no authority at this particular point, it is Locke he commends elsewhere in his text – sharply differing from Hume's evaluation – for having 'so happily discussed' the 'abuse of words' (Helvétius 1759 [1758]: 17), and above all for the notion that our ideas are not in-born or innate but are rooted in actual experience reflecting our sensations: 'Aristotle, [Petri] Gaffendi, and Montaigne, had a confused view, that we owe all our ideas to our sensations: Locke cleared up, searched into this principle, and established its truth by an infinite number of applications; and hence Locke is a genius' (243); alternatively: 'all our ideas, as Mr. Locke has shown, proceeds from our senses' (231; also 133).[7]

I find nothing in de *L'Esprit* regarding Lockean theological utilitarianism with its basis in future reward and punishment as relevant to 'happiness'. Helvétius does refer to Locke's advice to the legislature of Carolina – in his *Two Treatises on Government* – to be flexible in response to changing circumstances with regard to its constitution, advice which Helvétius applied to religion in the following terms:

> If we apply Mr. Locke's ideas to the false religions, we shall be soon convinced of the folly of their inventors, and their followers. Whoever, in fact, examines the religions, (all of which, *except ours*, are formed by the hand of man) must perceive, that none of them was ever contrived by the great genius of a legislator, but by the narrow mind of an ordinary person; that consequently a false religion was never founded on the basis of the laws, and *a principle of public utility:* a principle always invariable, but pliable in its application to all the various situations in which a people can successively be placed.
>
> (Helvétius 1759 [1758]: 85–6, emphasis added)

The qualification 'except ours' maintains that the Christian religion carries with it a principle of public utility, but the context does not entail or even imply private ethics as concerned with the public good. More broadly, it seems fair to conclude that Helvétius, like Bentham (and Hume), neglected the positive contribution of Locke's *Essay* to theological utilitarianism.[8]

6.7 Hartley

In 'Remarks on Bentham's Philosophy' (1833) Mill commended David Hartley (1749) for recognizing the 'the moral sense': 'In this Mr. Bentham differs widely from Hartley, who, although he considers the moral sentiments to be wholly the result of association' – that is to say the effect of social living extending back to formal and informal learning processes of early childhood – 'does not therefore deny them a place in his system, but includes the feelings of "the moral sense" as one of the six classes into which he divides pleasures and pains' (Mill 1969 [1833]: 13). And also in 'Bentham' Mill applauded certain unnamed Bentham 'disciples' for offering a meaningful treatment of the moral sense: 'They may have followed [Bentham] in his doctrine of utility, and in his rejection of a moral sense as the test of right and wrong: but while repudiating it as such, they have, with Hartley, acknowledged it as a fact in human nature; they have endeavoured to account for it, to assign its laws: nor are they justly chargeable either with undervaluing this part of our nature, or with any disposition to throw it into the background of their speculations' (Mill [1838]: 97; emphasis added). Although he does not here express an opinion regarding Hartley as a utility doctrinaire, the retrospect provided in the *Autobiography* describes his 'Sedgwick's Discourse' (1835) as a 'defence of *Hartleianism* and *utilitarianism*' (1981 [1873]: 209; emphasis added) suggesting that Mill did not regard it as self-contradictory to maintain both the utility doctrine and the meaningfulness of a 'moral sense' – at least in some manner if not 'as the test of right and wrong' – and to that extent may be said to have somewhat diluted his contrast between the eighteenth and nineteenth centuries. (See Appendix to Chapter 15.)

Mill's commendation of Hartley – as well as of Bentham himself and unnamed Bentham 'disciples' – for rejecting a moral sense as the test of right and wrong while acknowledging it as a 'fact in human nature' requires correction. Firstly, Hartley does in fact attribute to the moral sense – at least when it operates near full force – the ability to offer instantaneous verdicts regarding the ethics of actions and motivations: 'When the moral sense is advanced to considerable Perfection, a Person may be made to love and hate, *merely because he ought; i.e.* the Pleasures of moral Beauty and Rectitude, and the pain of moral Deformity and Unfitness, may be transferred, and made to coalesce, almost instantaneously' (Hartley 1749: 497–8; emphasis added). It may not have been Hartley's intention to represent the moral sense as commending actions automatically without reference to their expected social consequences –

such consequences may perhaps be silently taken into account considering his remarks regarding happiness to be noted presently – but even so this form of expression invites the sort of objections by Bentham to those who contrived to avoid 'appeal to any external standard' of right and wrong, namely the utility standard (Bentham 1982 [1789]: 25).

A second qualification relates to Hartley's designation of the moral sense as a matter of 'association', as Mill emphasized. Although Hartley indeed insists that there is no 'moral Instinct' and no 'Determination of the Mind, grounded on the eternal Reasons and Relations of Things', or 'Disposition producing in us moral Judgments concerning Affections and Actions … independently of 'prior Associations determining thereto', he nonetheless allows that 'some Associations are formed so early, repeated so often, riveted so strong, and have so close a Connexion with the common Nature of Man, and the Events of Life which happen to all, as, in a popular way of speaking, to claim the Appellation of original and natural Dispositions' (Hartley 1749: 498–9).

Thirdly, and of particular interest to us, Mill's account is not quite accurate in that Hartley has seven classes: sensation, imagination, ambition, self-interest, sympathy, theopathy and the moral sense, with the last represented as the 'sum total' of the first six:

> And thus we may perceive, that all the Pleasures and Pains of Sensation, Imagination, Ambition, Self-interest, Sympathy, and Theopathy, as far as they are consistent with one another, with the Frame of our Natures, and with the Course of the World, beget in us a Moral Sense, and lead us to the Love and Approbation of Virtue, and the Fear, Hatred, and Abhorrence of Vice. This Moral Sense therefore carries its own Authority with it, inasmuch as it is the Sum total of all the rest, and the ultimate Result from them; and employs the Force and Authority of the whole Nature of Man against any particular Part of it, that rebels against the Determinations and Commands of the Conscience or moral Judgment.
>
> (Hartley 1749: 497)

Now although the moral sense is not explicitly reduced by Hartley to, or identified with, other-regarding or sympathetic or benevolent sentiment in particular – as it was by Hume and Hutcheson and, as we have confirmed earlier in this chapter, Helvétius – each of the elements after the first ('sensation') is built upon the one preceding, so that – setting aside for the moment 'Theopathy' and the further complication that each class reacts back upon its predecessors generating complex 'reciprocal Influences' (369) – the moral sense turns proximately on *sympathy*, the sixth class, for 'the mere Pleasures of Imagination and Beauty are … of a kind much inferior to those of *Sympathy and the Moral Sense*' (441; emphasis added). Sympathy for its part follows upon 'self-interest' in that notwithstanding the pleasant feelings generated by possession of ethical or benevolent sentiment – by way of the multifold processes of 'association' – such sentiment comes to be a desired quality for its own sake: 'there may be no direct, explicit Expectation of Reward, either from God or Man, by natural Consequence, or express Appointment, not even of the concomitant Pleasure which engages the Agent to undertake the benevolent or generous Action. And this I take to be a proof from the Doctrine of Association, that there is, and must be, such a Thing as pure disinterested Benevolence' (474; see also 493, 496). Here is implied a gradual ethical progress entailing the internalizing of benevolent sentiment such that the interest of the individual becomes identified with that of the community (on which matter see Halévy 1995 [1901]: 26). This perspective is consistent with the general view of ethical progress we shall later encounter in Bentham and Mill.

The foregoing scheme does not emphasize the utilitarian consequences entailing the 'greatest happiness' in the manner of Hume and Hutcheson. Increasing 'happiness' approaching asymptotically some undefinable maximum is certainly represented as the outcome of the entire associationist process assuring increasingly the identification of interests: 'Thus Association would convert a State, in which Pleasure and Pain were both conceived by turns, into one in which pure Pleasure alone would be perceived; at least, would cause the Beings who were under its Influence to an indefinite Degree, to approach to this last State nearer than by any definite difference' (83). But what is intended here is the *theological* rather than the social dimension to fully-fledged ethical progress: 'That our ultimate Happiness appears to be of a spiritual, not corporeal Nature; and therefore that Death, or the shaking off the gross Body, may not stop our Progress, but rather render us more expedite in pursuit of our true End: That Association tends to make us all ultimately similar; so that if one be happy, all must: And, lastly, That the same Association may also be shewn to contribute to introduce pure ultimate spiritual Happiness, in all' (84). All this is implied by the placing of the moral sense immediately after the class of Theopathy in the ordering of pleasures and pains, such that 'the Moral Sense carries us perpetually to the pure Love of God, as our highest and ultimate Perfection, our End, Centre, and only Resting-place, to which yet we can never attain' (497). Any worldly consequences flowing from sympathetic conduct are, in effect, relegated to second place.

Halévy observed that Joseph Priestley freed Hartley's 'theory ... from the theological elements which had complicated it with him' (1995 [1901]: 26). Certainly Priestley appealed for civil and religious liberty with only a nominal bow to 'the doctrine of an over-ruling providence' in support (Priestley 1771: xiii); and he related progress to the superiority of man's intellectual powers – illustrated by the discovery and application of the division of labour and proper government – such that 'the happiness of man, as he advances in intellect, is continually less dependent on temporary circumstances and sensations' to the benefit of the 'common good' (1, 4–6). Priestley's abridged edition of Hartley's *Observations* reproduces the sections 'of

Theopathy' and the 'Pleasures and Pains of the Moral Sense' including the passage describing the Moral Sense as carrying us 'perpetually to the pure Love of God, as our highest and ultimate Perfection, our End, Centre, and only Resting-place' (Priestley 1775: 331). But Bentham was not distracted by these theological features and – discussing the influence of habit in *Morals and Legislation* – commended Hartley's account of the association principle which he encountered in the Priestley edition (Bentham 1982 [1789]: 119). Furthermore, as we noted at the outset of this chapter, much later he expressed his gratitude to Hartley – and even more to Helvétius – for instructing him to treat happiness as an 'aggregate or compound' of simple pleasures, however apparently irreducible the elements are to a common dimension. We shall return to this matter in Chapter 10.

Notes

1 This perspective, Mill explains, was at odds with that of the French 'Philosophes' who 'trusted too much to those feelings; believed them to be more deeply rooted in human nature than they are; to be not so dependent, as in fact they are, upon collateral influences. They thought them the natural and spontaneous growth of the human heart; so firmly fixed in it, that they would subsist unimpaired, nay invigorated, when the whole system of opinions and observances with which they were habitually intertwined was violently torn away'.
2 Mill here adds a second idea of Helvétius – the influence of circumstances on character. He does not, however, cite Bentham himself as expressing a debt to Helvétius for the two features.
3 This, of course, is in principle only, as a comment implying the typically unfair distribution of gains from technological progress makes clear: 'The progress of a science does not solely depend on its being of use to the public: every citizen of which a nation is composed ought to reap some advantage from its improvement. Now in the revolutions that have taken place among all the nations of the earth, the public interest, which is that of the majority, among whom the principles of sound morality ought to find its improvement, not being always agreeable to the interest of those most in power, the latter being indifferent with respect to the progress of all sciences, must effectually oppose that of morality' (Helvétius 1759 [1758]: 112).
4 It emerges in this context that the concern was as much with ignorance as with the 'crimes of self-love' (Helvétius 1759 [1758]: 116).
5 Mandeville's annoyance is entirely understandable: 'These are the last Words of the Book, printed in the same large Character with the rest' (Mandeville 1924 [1732]: 412). I here call attention to the fact that the 1750 French rendition of the title leaves precisely the impression Mandeville disowned: '*La fable des abeilles .... Où l'on prouve que les vices des Particuliers tendent à l'avantage du Public.*
6 For a succinct discussion of 'Helvétius and Egalitarianism', evaluating his reception in this regard by other Enlightenment figures including Adam Smith, see Persky 2016: 10–15.
7 Helvétius also commended Locke's analysis 'Of Liberty' with an eye to the multifold influences acting upon man (Helvétius 1759 [1758]: 20–1), and his concern with 'man in general' (97).
8 Viner, in commenting on theological utilitarian, makes no mention of Helvétius (Viner 1972: 70f).

References

Bentham, J. 1982 (1789). *An Introduction to the Principles of Morals and Legislation*, ed. J.H. Burns and H.L.A. Hart. London and New York: Methuen.

Forget, E.L. 1999. *The Social Economics of Jean-Baptiste Say: Markets and Virtue*. London and New York: Routledge.

Halévy, E. 1995 [1901]. *La formation du radicalisme philosophiques*. Paris: Presses Universitaires de France.

Hartley, D. 1749? *Observations on Man, His Frame, His Duty, and His Expectations*. London: Hitch and Austen.

Helvétius, C.A. 1758. *De l'esprit*. Paris: Durand.

Helvétius, C.A. 1759 (1758). *De L'esprit: or Essays on the Mind and its Several Faculties*, London: Dodsley.

Mandeville, B. 1750. *La fable des abeilles*, vol. 2. London: Jean Nourse.

Mandeville, B. 1924 (1732). *The Fable of the Bees or Private Vices, Publick Benefits*. 6th edition. Oxford: Clarendon Press.

Mill, J.S. 1969 (1833). 'Remarks on Bentham's Philosophy', *Collected Works* 10. Toronto: University of Toronto Press: 3–18.

Mill, J.S. 1969 (1838). 'Bentham', *Collected Works* 10. Toronto: University of Toronto Press: 75–115.

Mill, J.S. 1969 (1840). 'Coleridge', *Collected Works* 10. Toronto: University of Toronto Press: 117–163.

Persky, J. 2016. *The Political Economy of Progress: John Stuart Mill and Modern Radicalism*. Oxford: Oxford University Press.

Priestley, J. 1771. *Essay on the First Principles of Government*, 2nd ed. London: J. Johnson.

Priestley, J. 1775. *Hartley's Theory of the Human Mind, on the Principle of the Association of Ideas*. London: J. Johnson.

Schumpeter, J.A. 1954. *History of Economic Analysis*. New York: Oxford University Press.

Turgot, A.R.J. 1810 (1760). 'A Monsieur de C[ondorcet] sur le livre De l'esprit'; in *Oeuvres*, IX: 288–298. Paris: Delance: 288–298.

Viner, J. 1958. *The Long View and the Short: Studies in Economic Theory and Policy*. Glencoe: The Free Press.

Viner, J. 1972. *The Role of Providence in the Social Order: An Essay in Intellectual History*. Philadelphia: American Philosophical Society.

Part 3
Adam Smith

7 Utilitarian ethics in *The Theory of Moral Sentiments*

7.1 Introduction

The third part of this book is devoted to Adam Smith, with Chapter Seven concerning *TMS* and Chapter Eight the *WN*. Bentham designated the most influential of principles opposed to that of utility as being that which 'approves or disapproves of certain actions, not on account of their tending to augment the happiness, nor yet on account of their tending to diminish the happiness of the party whose interest is in question, but merely because a man finds himself disposed to approve or disapprove of them: holding up that approbation or disapprobation as a sufficient reason for itself, and disclaiming the necessity of looking out for any extrinsic ground' (Bentham 1982 [1789]: 21, 25). Bentham does not mention *TMS* amongst the *non-utilitarian* ethicists, but one might expect that he would have mentioned Smith in that context had he read *TMS* in this manner, especially since he never hesitated to protest Smith's appeals in *WN* to 'natural liberty'. This possibility will doubtless be discounted by those who maintain that Smith in fact rejected 'ethical utilitarianism' in *TMS*, while several of those who do allow the presence of a utility dimension insist on its secondary character. My own approach emphasizes both the qualifications Smith (and also Hume) made to their respective doctrines, with the utility dimension to *TMS* then emerging clearly as a result. Partly responsible for the view of Smith as 'non-Utilitarian' is an understanding of *Bentham* as rejecting the idea of moral sentiments as the foundation of morals, when in fact it is a 'moral sense' understood as precluding the utility criterion of ethics to which he objected.

In Section 7.2 I set the stage by reviewing a selection of modern commentaries which deny or minimize the presence in TMS of 'ethical utilitarianism', a necessary preliminary to considering the allusion to a 'fairly standard view among philosophers that *TMS* is a book in the Utilitarian tradition' (Witztum and Young 2013: 573).

Section 7.3 questions the validity of sharply contrasting Hume's focus in evaluating ethical merit on the end of utility – on consequences – and Smith's on proper motivation. In this context we encounter Smith's perspective on the 'moral sense' as dictating benevolence or sympathy. Section 7.4 evaluates the passages where Smith formally relegates 'utility' to second place in favour of 'propriety', or what is 'right ... accurate ... agreeable to truth and reality'; whilst Section 7.5 elaborates the importance to Smith of motivation by reference to his concern with public welfare – implying the consequential dimension – under the rubrics of 'justice' and 'punishment'. Our argument culminates in Section 7.6 with a demonstration of Smith's adoption of the 'greatest happiness' principle itself.

7.2 A literature review

Lionel Robbins expressed reticence regarding the utilitarian component in *TMS* insofar as it concerns personal ethics, for he clearly had his doubts as to this interpretation. Robbins attributed the Utilitarian doctrine itself – 'the habit of judging actions and policies by their consequences rather than by reference to some intuitive norm', contrasting with that of the Continental metaphysicians – to the entire classical school 'from its beginnings in Hume's *Essays* right through to Cairnes and Sidgwick', holding good 'even for Adam Smith whose explicit moral philosophy had a somewhat different complexion' (Robbins 1970: 56). Adam Smith is singled out as 'the only possible exception' to the general run of 'classical' economists, for he 'had a moral philosophy of his own which in some respects appears to be in contrast with the utilitarian outlook' (Robbins 1952:178). With the terminology in mind of 'Deistic philosophy' and of *Naturrecht* embellishing even the analysis of the market in the *Wealth of Nations*, Robbins cautioned against judging that work by reference to the *Theory of Moral Sentiments* 'rather than by examining the merits of the arguments by which they are supported in the contexts in which they appear' (25; also 48).

Bonar maintained that 'Adam Smith is less Utilitarian than Hume; regard for consequences is always secondary to immediate regard to virtue for its own sake' (Bonar 1922: 169); and 'immediate sympathy is ... antecedent to any consideration of utility, personal or social' (165). Macfie argued to a similar effect that: 'So far ... as Smith defined intrinsic value, he placed it especially in virtue and beauty. Utility itself had only instrumental value, except in so far as it partook of the beautiful in the "system". And the exercise of any virtue had "many agreeable effects". In this sense, good or pleasing consequences were essentially associated with and coloured by the exercise of the values from which they were derived' (Macfie 1967: 48). 'Smith then', Macfie concludes, 'was not a utilitarian, even in Hume's sense. Utility for him was not basic'. More recently, Montes has elaborated this theme, his purpose being 'to show that if Hutcheson and Hume prepared the ground for Bentham, Smith paved the road for some of Kant's ideas on ethics', referring to evaluation of moral good by reference to *intention* rather than *consequences* (Montes 2004: 114). He prefers, however, to say that Smith 'is not a proto-utilitarian' rather than that he is an 'antiutilitarian', while allowing that 'some passages in the *TMS* definitively have a pre-utilitarian tone', and that 'the importance (Smith) attributes to motives does not necessarily exclude the significance of effects' (115–17). It is Smith's position whereby 'the sentiment of approbation always involves in it a sense of propriety quite distinct from the perception of utility' that 'completely invalidates any attempt to describe Adam Smith as a forbear of utilitarianism' (117).

Raphael asserts strongly that 'far from being a utilitarian, Adam Smith was a severe critic of utilitarianism in many parts of his ethics and Jurisprudence' (Raphael 2007: 46). Similarly, 'Hume is by and large a utilitarian. Adam Smith is an anti-utilitarian, indeed a natural-law theorist …' (Raphael 1972/73: 88); and he reiterates the theme that while Smith 'was prepared to allow that moral actions do in fact tend, as a whole, to promote the general happiness, and that this is the end intended by God', he opposed Hume's view 'that utility is the one and only standard of right action. In practice, he argued, the thought of utility has a subordinate role in the formation of moral judgement'; for while 'the pleasure which attends the thought of utility' is taken into account, it is the least important 'in its contribution to the final judgement of approval' (Raphael 1985: 38). In brief, 'we do not in practice decide what is right by reference to utility'. Along these lines, Raphael and Macfie wrote in their bicentenary edition of *TMS*: 'Smith continually insists that considerations of utility are the last, not the first, determinants of moral judgement. Our basic judgment of right and wrong is concerned with the agent's motive, not with the effect of his action. Our more complex judgements of merit and demerit, justice and injustice, depend on the reactions of gratitude and resentment to benefit and harm respectively, not simply on the benefit and harm themselves' (Smith 1976 [1759]: *13*). Moreover, 'even though the pleasant or painful effects of action are relevant to the moral judgement passed upon it, they are primarily the effects of this particular action upon particular individuals, not the more remote effects upon society at large. Considerations of general social utility are an afterthought, not a foundation' (12–13). Elsewhere in their commentary the editors represent Smith simply as 'an opponent of utilitarianism' (305n).

Whereas Haakonssen allows that utility in *TMS* 'is a real source of moral judgement, although a secondary one', which, only when afterwards recognized, 'comes to have an influence on moral judgment and behaviour' (Haakonssen 1981: 73), he also insists that 'Smith's concept of utility cannot be taken in any Benthamite sense of uniform happiness' (135). He allows too that, for Smith, 'the laws of justice are *useful* in the sense that they serve as a *means to an end*, the end being the public interest', but maintains that 'this idea of "means-utility" … is clearly different from the idea of utility which we find in the later utilitarian theorists. For them utility is more or less identified with pleasure or happiness of a kind, and is thus the end towards which actions should aspire' (40–1). Thus, utility considerations are recognized in the context of justice, but 'do not form the foundation of justice (since) social utility is rarely thought of by the bulk of mankind' but pertains rather to 'how philosophers ... interpret human morality' (88). To the same effect, Witztum and Young conclude that 'under no circumstances can Smith be considered as part of the Utilitarian tradition. For this to happen we should have seen the search for happiness as a motivator of human actions and of human moral judgment. We found neither' (Witztum and Young 2013: 600). For what Smith intended by 'utility' was either 'the simple colloquial notion of usefulness or, the more complex notion of social usefulness or, a pleasure from harmony' – alluding to Smithian 'propriety' – 'rather than the idea of "happiness" in any form'. These authors further maintain that colloquial 'utility' is 'foreign to utilitarianism' (602). They allow that 'utility maximization is (for Smith) appropriate in some cases', although – like Haakonssen – only as a matter of 'philosophical judgment', and this they take to be 'consistent with Smith's non-utilitarian moral theory and non-utilitarian theory of individual motivation' (p. 596; on the 'philosophical spectator', see also 600). Muller too perceives a fundamental clash here with Bentham: 'While Smith's deistic humanism had judged commercial society according to the standards of the civilizing project, Bentham's utilitarianism eliminated the possibility of standards beyond sensual pleasure for judging character. Indeed, it tended to discredit qualitative distinctions, to make them appear as intellectually suspect and morally sinister, and promoted a model of moral thinking which tries to do without them altogether' (Muller 1993: 190).

It is a feature of Raphael's account that 'utilitarianism' supposes right behaviour by an individual to be behaviour motivated by a desire to enhance *social* happiness: 'the proper standard is maximum promotion of the general happiness', not his own (Raphael 1985: 38). McCloskey also perceives Smith as opposed to Hume and utilitarianism, but her conception of the category is diametrically opposed to that of Raphael. Thus she contends that Smith 'sharply opposed the reduction of what is good to what causes pleasure, that is, utilitarianism', though 'not quite in the form of the "chaos of precise ideas"' (McCloskey 2009: 4).[1] This opposition, however, was to the opinion of those – including Hume as Smith understood him – who maintained that 'virtue consists in prudence' or, more precisely, 'prudence only'. McCloskey in fact regards 'prudence suffices' and 'greed is good' as synonymous; and she represents nineteenth-century utilitarianism – and later the 'new' welfare economics – as 'attempting to build judgments about the economy' on the basis of an identification of virtue with 'prudence only', with justice taken as sheer taste: 'If all people are benefited, or could be benefited, the proposed policy is good. That is all ye know of ethics, and all ye need to know' (4–5). Her perception of utilitarianism incorporates the simplistic textbook reading of the *Wealth of Nations* whereby people guided by self-interest nonetheless act (unwittingly) to enhance social well-being, for she cites Smith's 'book on prudence' to the effect that 'what is prudence in the conduct of every private family can scarce be folly in that of a great kingdom' (Smith 1976 [1776]: 457). Other virtues, she writes, are recognized by Smith elsewhere, especially 'temperance' and 'justice' in Smith's *Lectures*; while *TMS* allows a range of 'moral sentiments' divorced from any sort of self-interest, and there Smith's 'grounds for opposing utilitarianism' are based on observed behaviour similarly divorced (McCloskey 2009: 7).

In much the same vein Hanley refers to Smith's 'argument against utilitarianism' in *TMS* designed 'not simply to counter the claim that the proper standard for evaluating actions is their capacity for utility-maximizing effects', since 'Smith does not deny the goodness of utility maximization, but rather suggests that to posit utility maximization as either the sole or the ultimate standard of ethical value … precludes a comprehensive understanding of the multiple phenomena involved in moral judgment' (Hanley 2009: 68–9). Smith's concern, in brief, was 'to resist the reductionism characteristic of utilitarianism', since – in Smith's terms – 'it seems impossible that the approbation of virtue should be a sentiment of the same kind with that by which we approve of a convenient and well-contrived building; or that we should have no other reason for praising a man than that for which we commend a chest of drawers' (Smith 1976 [1759]: 188); again: 'any theory of our admiration of (men's) virtue must not only account for their utility, but also for 'the unexpected, and on that account the great, the noble, and exalted propriety of such actions' (192). Posner asserts firmly that 'Adam Smith, who was not a utilitarian or a "welfare economist", thought people were deluded in believing that they would be happier if they were richer' (Posner 1981: 64). He apparently allows himself to be seduced by Smith's remark in *TMS* regarding the happy 'beggar who suns himself by the side of the highway' (see below, p. 182).

Concessions in the aforementioned commentaries to a utility dimension to *TMS* insist on its secondary character for Smith whereas the utility dimension emerges in much stronger colours according to my approach which emphasizes the qualifications both Hume and Smith made to their respective doctrines – as well as the complexity of Bentham's position. My results corroborate Raynor's position 'that there is much in *TMS* that Hume could heartily accept. It is not so very surprising that Hume composed a complimentary notice of Smith's book' for the *Critical Review* of 1759 (Raynor 1984: 64). Other commentators forwarding this sort of reading, if not in every detail, would include: Rawls, who places Smith within a Shaftesbury–Hutcheson–Hume–Bentham tradition (Rawls 1999 (1971): 20n); Campbell, according to whom '(d)espite all that Smith has to say against utility as the explanation for the ordinary person's moral and political attitudes, his own normative moral and political philosophy turns out to be, in the end, a form of utilitarianism … Utility, or the production of happiness, is … the principle by reference to which he judges that both the natural moral sentiments and the system of natural liberty are desirable' (Campbell 1971: 205–6), or again: 'Utility is … very much *the* meta-principle for Smith. It is to be found at the basis of his whole moral outlook', although Campbell opines that 'it operates most typically at the level of contemplation, when men adopt a God's-eye-view of society, enter into His universal benevolence and feel admiration and approval for what they observe' (219; also Campbell 1975: 76–7); Schneewind, who argues that, notwithstanding his criticisms of Hume, '(u)tility does play a major part in Smith's view of morals' (Schneewind 1998: 390–1); and Alvey who recognizes the utilitarian dimension in Smith's discussion of 'the virtue of prudence' (Alvey 2003: 60). Finally, my study amply confirms Rosen's case for a close Hume–Smith connection (Rosen 2000; 2003), including his denial that whenever Smith in *TMS* 'discusses utility, he intends to diminish its importance' (Rosen 2000: 82). Indeed, Rosen properly maintains that 'in several respects Smith gives greater scope and importance to utility than Hume'.

Of prime importance, of course, is the 'utilitarian' standard itself. As for the alleged absence in *TMS* of the Benthamite idea of 'happiness', we shall show that the '*real happiness of human life*' constitutes Smith's justification for population expansion – implying no less than the *greatest happiness of the greatest number* – although subject to the condition that worker's living standards are satisfactory, recognizing in brief that distribution matters. In any event, when Smith talks of the 'welfare of society' it is (we shall show) frequently 'happiness' that he intends, as with Bentham who made use of synonyms for happiness, including 'public interest' and 'general good'. And the remarks in *A Table of the Springs of Action* relating to '*self-regarding* prudence' – considered as a virtue when perceived in terms of pleasure and pain – in response to 'want, need, demand, exigency, necessity' (Bentham 1859 (1815): 208, 211) point away from the contention, noted above, that the 'colloquial' notion of 'utility' as 'usefulness' is 'foreign to utilitarianism', since the colloquial version would fall within 'necessity' and perhaps even 'exigency'. Furthermore, the view of Smith as 'non-Utilitarian' reflects in many instances an unjustifiably narrow reading of Bentham, while Muller's view of Bentham is a caricature (Hollander 2015: 34–42). And while confirming Rosen's interpretation of the Smith–Hume relation I would qualify his reading of the Smith–Bentham relation, which asserts, following Schneewind, that 'Bentham firmly rejected the idea of moral sentiments as the foundation of morals' (Rosen 2000: 101; 2003: 81). It is a 'moral sense' understood as precluding the utility criterion of ethics that Bentham firmly rejected, as will be amply confirmed in the fourth part of this book.

7.3 On motivation *versus* consequences: the 'moral sense' and sympathy

I turn now to the substantive issues, commencing with the contention that, in evaluating merit, Hume focuses on the end of utility and Smith on proper motivation. This contrast is to be avoided since there is too much common ground. I have considered Hume in Chapter Five and will devote this section to Smith.

Smith too (like Hume) objected to strict renditions of the 'moral sense' such as he attributed to Hutcheson:

> According to some the principle of approbation is founded upon a sentiment of a peculiar nature, upon a particular power of perception exerted by the mind at the view of certain actions or affections; some of which affecting this faculty in an agreeable and others in a disagreeable manner, the former are stamped with the characters of right, laudable, and virtuous; the latter with those of wrong, blamable, and vicious. This sentiment being of a peculiar nature distinct from every other, and the effect of a particular power of perception, they give it a particular name, and call it a moral sense.
>
> (Smith 1976 [1759]: 321)

Smith's 'confutation' of Hutcheson covers only the 'moral sense', since he approves the exclusion of 'self-love' and of 'reason' as foundations for the principle of approbation, on Humean grounds.[2] And we shall presently confirm Smith's appreciation that Hutcheson's 'moral sense', despite first appearance, in fact went hand in hand with the position that 'virtue consists in benevolence' and hence with concern for social welfare, Smith objecting only that Hutcheson went too far by asserting that virtue consists in benevolence *alone* (below, p. 163). On this reading Hutcheson himself, and not only Hume as Bonar maintained, 'showed the elements into which the alleged "sense" may be analysed' (Bonar 1922: 109).[3] And, of course, disinterested 'benevolence' famously dictated for Hutcheson '(a)ction ... which procures the greatest Happiness for the greatest Numbers' (Hutcheson 1729: 180).

Now in an anonymously-written review of *TMS* in May 1759 Hume writes in accommodating fashion that '(i)t is sufficient to (Smith's) purpose, if sympathy, whence ever it proceeds, be allowed to be a principle in human nature, which surely, without the greatest obstinacy, cannot be denied' (Hume 1984 (1759): 67). For his part, Smith credited Hume with 'attempt(ing) to account for the origin of our moral sentiments from sympathy', but distinguished between their perceptions of sympathy (Smith 1976 [1759]: 327).[4] For Hume's system 'places virtue in utility, and accounts for the pleasure with which the spectator surveys the utility of any quality from sympathy with the happiness of those who are affected by it', whereas his own system entailed two categories: 'that by which we enter into the motives of the agent, and ... that by which we go along with gratitude of the persons who are benefited by his actions'. Hume's was 'the same principle with that by which we approve of a well-contrived machine', whereas 'no machine can be the object of either of those last two mentioned sympathies'. I question whether we are justified in discerning in these objections to Hume a substantive contrast regarding the tendencies of actions relative to the motives of agents.

Firstly, as we indicated in Chapter 5, for Hume an action is morally defective even if social advantage should result therefrom where the *intention* of the agent does not entail the public good. As for Smith, good motivation accompanied by 'disagreeable' consequences would not merit wholehearted approval. This emerges at several junctures in his account.

The section 'Of the Sense of Propriety' defines 'two different aspects' of moral approval or disapproval, one relating to *motive* and the other to *consequences*:

> In the suitableness or unsuitableness, in the proportion or disproportion which the affection seems to bear to the cause or object which excites it, consists the propriety or impropriety, the decency or ungracefulness of the consequent action.[5] In the beneficial or hurtful nature of the effects which the affection aims at, or tends to produce, consist the merit or demerit of the action, the qualities by which it is entitled to reward, or is deserving of profit.
>
> (Smith 1976 [1759]: 18)

In a recapitulation Smith insists on the satisfaction of *both* 'aspects' to justify whole-hearted applause:

> We do not ... thoroughly and heartily sympathize with the gratitude of one man towards another, merely because this other has been the cause of his good fortune, unless he has been the cause of it from motives which we entirely go along with ... If in the conduct of the benefactor there appears to have been no propriety, how beneficial soever its effects, it does not seem to demand, or necessarily to require, any proportionable recompense.
>
> But when to the beneficent tendency of the action is joined the propriety of the affection from which it proceeds, when we entirely sympathize and go along with the motives of the agent, the love which we conceive for him upon his own account, enhances and enlivens our fellow-feeling with the gratitude of those who owe their prosperity to his good conduct.
>
> (73)

Motivation satisfying 'propriety' does not therefore alone suffice since consequences are no less relevant for full moral approval. Even a passage (added in 1790) sometimes said (as by Montes 2004: 77) to prove the centrality of motivation rather than consequences can be read as insisting upon the latter:

> But in our approbation of the virtues of self-command, complacency with their effects sometimes constitutes no part, and frequently but a small part of that approbation. Those effects may sometimes be agreeable, and sometimes disagreeable; and though *our approbation is no doubt stronger in the former case*, it is by no means altogether destroyed in the latter. The most heroic valour may be employed indifferently in the case either of justice or

of injustice; and *though it is no doubt much more loved and admired in the former case*, it still appears a great and respectable quality even in the latter.

(264; emphasis added)

Evidently consequences *do* matter for moral evaluation – even apparently for the general run of humanity and not merely an elite – approbation being 'stronger', and 'much more loved and admired' where the effects are 'agreeable'. It must be admitted, however, that Smith seems to be riding two horses since he immediately goes on to maintain that '(i)n that, and in all the other virtues of self-command, the splendid and dazzling quality seems always to be the greatness and steadiness of the exertion, and the strong sense of propriety which is necessary in order to make and to maintain that exertion. The effects are too often but too little regarded'.

7.4 More on 'propriety' and utility

Two particular passages in *TMS* objecting to Hume – frequently said to demonstrate a *non-utilitarian* ethical stance – must be addressed. The first is from the outset of the work discussing judgments made by an individual of the 'propriety of other men's affections', where Smith relegates 'utility' to second place in favour of what is 'right … accurate … agreeable to truth and reality' and, furthermore, fits in with the observer's prejudices:

> The utility of those qualities (judgments generally considered eminently praiseworthy), it may be thought, is what first recommended them to us;[6] and no doubt, the consideration of this, when we come to attend to it, gives them a new value. Originally, however, we approve of another man's judgment, *not as something useful, but as right, as accurate, as agreeable to truth and reality*: and it is evident we attribute those qualities to it for no other reason but because we find that *it agrees with our own*.
>
> (Smith 1976 [1759]: 20; emphasis added)[7]

Smith extends to 'taste' the general complaint that Hume had neglected the 'propriety' component of moral approval: 'Taste, in the same manner, is originally approved of, not as useful, but as just, as delicate, and as precisely suited to its object. The idea of the utility of all qualities of this kind, is plainly an after-thought, and not what first recommends them to our approbation'. We read similarly of 'the suitableness of the affection from which we act to the object which excites it' (267). For future reference we note here that Smithian 'propriety' has a sense understood as that which is 'just … delicate, and … precisely suited to its object', would accommodate Humean 'fitness' (below, p. 166).

In our extract treating *utility* as a secondary consideration Smith defines the term as 'something useful'. Now the so-called water–diamonds 'paradox' of *The Wealth of Nations* may easily be misunderstood as rejecting a 'utility' dimension to price formation for, to the contrary, it asserts the relevance for value determination of 'desirability' – which may, but need not, entail 'usefulness' in the sense that water is 'useful' (Hollander 1973: 137–8). Correspondingly, in the present context Smith does not necessarily downplay 'utility' except in the popular sense of *'usefulness'*. Indeed, elsewhere we shall find Smith explicitly admitting into the moral calculus 'utility' identified quite generally as 'agreeableness' or 'advantageousness'.

The second extract, from Part IV, 'Of the Effect of UTILITY upon the Sentiment of Approbation', points out that 'the same ingenious and agreeable author who first explained why utility pleases' resolves 'our whole approbation of virtue into a perception of this species of beauty which results from the appearance of utility. No qualities of mind, he observes, are approved of as virtuous, but such as are useful or agreeable either to the person himself or to others; and no qualities are disapproved of as vicious but such as have a contrary tendency' (Smith 1976 [1759]: 188).[8] What should be underscored here is the fact that Smith does not dispute the *principle of utility* as such, since he goes on immediately to affirm that '(n)ature, indeed, seems to have so happily adjusted our sentiments of approbation and disapprobation, to the conveniency both of the individual and of the society, that after the strictest examination it will be found, I believe, that this is universally the case'; and he further allows that the sentiments of approval and disapproval 'are no doubt enhanced and enlivened by the perception of the beauty or deformity which results from this utility or hurtfulness'. His point of contention is that 'it is not the view of this utility or hurtfulness which is either the first or principal source of our approbation and disapprobation'. What precisely we are to understand by this declaration requires a consideration of the importance Smith accords 'propriety'.

In the first place, Smith objects to identifying the 'approbation of virtue' with that of a building or piece of furniture – in the manner attributed to Hume (Smith 1976 [1759]: 188). Different sentiments are at play, and in the case of character evaluation, 'the sentiment of approbation always involves in it *a sense of propriety quite distinct from the perception of utility*. We may observe this with regard to all the qualities which are approved of as virtuous, both those which, according to this system, are originally valued as useful to ourselves, as well as those which are esteemed on account of their usefulness to others' (188–9; emphasis added).

Consider next Smith's assumption that Hume limits his utility argument to qualities 'valued as useful to ourselves' or 'to others'. The first category Smith identifies with the virtue of 'prudence', prudential conduct entailing two primary components: 'superior reason and understanding, by which we are capable of discerning the remote consequences of all our actions, and of foreseeing the advantage or detriment which is likely to result from them'; and 'self-command, by which we are enabled to abstain from present pleasure or to endure present pain, in order to obtain a greater pleasure or to avoid a greater pain in some future time' (Smith 1976 [1759]: 189).[9] The first component of 'prudence' entails qualities 'originally approved of as just and right and accurate' – approved of, we understand, as satisfying the 'propriety' sense – 'not merely as useful or advantageous'; and the second component is said similarly 'to be approved of, *as much under the aspect of propriety, as under that of utility*' (emphasis added). When we act prudentially 'the sentiments which influence our conduct' – pre-eminently that of propriety – 'seem exactly to coincide with those of the spectator (who) does not feel the solicitations of our present appetites' (190). For the natural power of time preference is so strong that it would always prevail in practice '*unless it was supported by the sense of propriety*, by the consciousness that we merited the esteem and approbation of every body, by acting in the one way, and that we become the proper objects of their contempt and derision by behaving in the other' (emphasis added).

'Propriety' intrudes even with respect to qualities 'approved of as virtuous', and 'originally valued as usefulness to others' – 'Humanity, justice, generosity, and public spirit' are the prime candidates. For, Smith explains, 'our admiration is not so much founded upon the utility, as upon the unexpected (sacrifices made), and on that account the great, the noble, and exalted propriety of such actions' (Smith 1976 [1759]: 192). He allows that 'utility, when we come to view it, bestows upon them, undoubtedly, a new beauty, and upon that account still further recommends them to our approbation', but adds the qualification that '(t)his beauty ... is chiefly perceived by men of reflection and speculation, and is by no means the quality which first recommends such actions to the natural sentiments of the bulk of mankind'. It should be noted that this restriction is very flexible, since *in the final resort* even the 'bulk of mankind' is not immune.

What seems to have been frequently overlooked in the commentaries on Smith's *Theory of Moral Sentiments* is that notwithstanding Smith's declaration that 'the sentiment of approbation always involves in it a sense of propriety *quite distinct from the perception of utility*', he himself admitted in the 1790 edition that '(i)n our approbation of all those virtues (prudence, justice, and beneficence), our sense *of their agreeable effects, of their utility*, either to the person who exercises them, or to some other persons, *joins with our sense of their propriety*', and '*constitutes always a considerable part of that approbation*' (Smith 1976 [1759]: 264; emphasis added). There is certainly no rejection of the utility component governing ethical merit.[10]

Smith goes yet further, maintaining a '*coincidence*' of utility and propriety, and underscoring a proper *balance* of ethical considerations, no single one going too far (or falling short) of the 'proper degree':

> That system which places virtue in utility, coincides too with that which makes it consist in propriety. According to this system, all those qualities of the mind which are agreeable or advantageous, either to the person himself or to others, are approved of as virtuous, and the contrary disapproved of

as viscous. But the agreeableness or utility of any affection depends upon the degree which it is allowed to subsist in. Every affection is useful when it is confined to a certain degree of moderation; and every affection is disadvantageous when it exceeds the proper bounds. According to this system therefore, virtue consists not in any one affection, but in the proper degree of all the affections.

(Smith 1976 [1759]: 305–6).

Now Smith is happy with the so-called 'propriety' view – here said to 'coincide' with the utility view – subject to one qualification: 'The only difference between (the 'propriety' system) and that which I have been endeavouring to establish, is, that it makes utility, and not sympathy, or the corresponding affection of the spectator, the natural and original measure of this proper degree' (306).

What does all this imply for the validity of Smith's critique of Hume? The principle that '(e)very affection is useful when it is confined to a certain degree of moderation; and every affection is disadvantageous when it exceeds the proper bounds' – a feature of 'propriety' – is in fact conveyed by Hume's contention that even a meritorious 'public spirit', such as alms giving, might be taken too far rendering the excess no longer 'useful' (Hume 1927 [1751]: 180). As for Smith's qualification that the utility system 'makes utility, and not sympathy, or the corresponding affection of the spectator' the measure of the requisite balance of affections, recall that Smith himself in fact credited Hume with 'attempt(ing) to account for the origin of our moral sentiments from *sympathy*' (above, p. 157), and that the distinction there drawn between his own and Hume's perception of 'sympathy' – the former focusing on the *motives* of agents and the latter on the *consequences* or tendencies of actions – does not, so I have argued, indicate a definitive contrast between the two systems. And, needless to say, Hume's system, no less than Smith's, accords the spectator a central role.[11]

We turn to the matter of 'self-command'. That 'superior reasoning', incorporating 'prudence', by which 'we are capable of discerning the remote consequences of all our actions' – identified by Smith as 'originally approved of as just and right and accurate', a feature of 'propriety' – had been expressed by Hume when he wrote of 'views of utility or of future beneficial consequences' as 'enter(ing) into this sentiment of approbation' (Hume 1927 [1751]: 260). It is confirmed by a comment on the esteem for natural ability: 'The principal reason why natural abilities are esteem'd, is because of their tendency to be useful to the person, who is possess'd of them. 'Tis impossible to execute any design with success, where it is not conducted with *prudence and discretion*; nor will the goodness of our intentions alone suffice to procure us a happy issue to our enterprizes' (Hume 1978 [1740]: 610; emphasis added). There is no substantive difference between the Smith and Hume formulations.

The complaint that Hume identified the 'approbation of virtue' with that of a building or piece of furniture – or that Hume's principle was the same as 'that by which we approve of a well-contrived machine' – has little justification. For Hume had responded to this sort of objection: 'We ought not to imagine, because an inanimate object may be useful as well as a man, that therefore it ought also, according to this system, to merit the appellation of *virtuous*. The sentiments, excited by utility, are, in the two cases, very different; and the one is mixed with affection, esteem, approbation, &c, and not the other' (Hume 1927 [1751]: 213n). The same point is made in his anonymously-written contribution to the *Critical Review* (Hume 1984 (1759): 74). Again, there are no differences between Hume and Smith regarding this particular.

What though of Smith's relegation of the utility component of merit to an elite? We would mark this as an important contrast with Hume were it not that Smith himself qualified the restriction, allowing that even the 'bulk of mankind' is affected in the final resort.

Finally, whereas Smith understood that for Hume 'utility' is the *sole* source of moral approval, Hume's position is actually more complex. In a narrow range of cases, he recognized a source of approval provided by 'particular *original* principles of human nature' (above, p. 121). And as indicated above, he represented utility as the *sole* source of moral approbation regarding 'fidelity, justice, veracity, integrity and those other estimable and useful qualities and principles', but only as the source of 'a *considerable part* of the merit ascribed to humanity, benevolence, friendship, public spirit, and other social virtues of that stamp' (emphasis added).

7.5 On justice and punishment

As we have seen, motivation enters into Smith's view of ethical merit as it does for Hume. We now focus on the importance to Smith of motivation reflecting concern with public welfare. Thus man is 'naturally endowed with *a desire of the welfare and preservation of society*', although 'the Author of nature has not entrusted it to his reason to find out that a certain application of punishments is the proper means of attaining this end; but has endowed him with an immediate and instinctive approbation of that very application which is most proper to attain it' (Smith 1976 [1759]: 77; emphasis added). Now we must not overlook that concern for public welfare is said *to supersede all others*, as becomes clear in a case against Hutcheson's proposition that virtue consisted in benevolence alone (265). It was not true, Smith maintained, that 'a regard to the welfare of society should be the *sole* virtuous motive of action, *but only that, in any competition, it ought to cast the balance against all other motives*' (304–5; emphasis added). Now to this Raphael and Macfie append the editorial comment: 'The view expressed in the last clause of this sentence is an unusual one for an opponent of utilitarianism to accept' (305n). Unusual indeed. Surely a more natural reaction would be to conclude that Smith clearly reveals himself *not* to be an opponent.

All this must be kept in mind when we consider Smith's reaction to Hume's strong proposition in the *Enquiry* that 'public utility is the *sole* origin of justice, and ... reflections on the beneficial consequences of this virtue are the *sole* foundation of its merit' justifying private property where scarcity rules (Hume 1927 [1751]: 183).[12] Now Smith agreed that 'society cannot subsist unless the laws of justice are tolerably observed' (Smith 1976 [1759]: 87), but he denied that 'consideration of this necessity ... was the ground upon which we approved of the enforcement of the laws of justice by the punishment of those who violated them'.[13] A reformulation reiterates the concern with social stability, but (as always) not as man's 'first' consideration, as: 'it is seldom this consideration which *first* animates us against (licentious practices). All men, even the most stupid and unthinking, abhor fraud, perfidy, and injustice, and delight to see them punished. But few man have reflected on the necessity of justice to the existence of society, how obvious soever that necessity may appear to be' (89). And he proceeds: 'that it is not a regard to the preservation of society, which *originally* interests us in the punishment of crimes committed against individuals, may be demonstrated by many obvious considerations', including the fact that 'when a single man is injured, or destroyed, we demand the punishment of the wrong that has been done to him, not so much from a concern for the general interest of society, as from a concern for that very individual who has been injured' (90; emphasis added).

But we must allow here for considerations that radically affect the interpretation of Smith. In cases where particular persons are directly hurt by a crime, Smith seeks to prove that punishment is not justified 'merely' in utilitarian terms, that is 'on account of the order of society', by suggesting that any such appeal does not provide a sufficient guarantee that it will achieve the desired objective. This he does by pointing to the reinforcement provided by religion: 'Nature teaches us to hope, and *religion, we suppose*, authorizes (editions 1, 2: *religion authorizes*) us to expect, that it will be punished, even in a life to come' (Smith 1976 [1759]: 91, emphasis added). The textual amendment suggests a weakening of Smith's religious conviction. Similarly: 'The justice of God, *we think*, still requires, that he should hereafter avenge the injuries of the widow and the fatherless, who are here so often insulted with impunity. In every *religion, in every superstition*, there is a hell as well as a paradise' (emphasis added). The last sentence appears in 1790 at the end of a chapter considering to what extent the sense of justice depends upon utility. It replaces a lengthy text in the first five editions *rejecting*, as unacceptable and indeed unnatural, the opinion that the Deity loves virtue and hates vice because the former promotes the happiness of society and the latter misery, rather than for their own sakes: it 'is not the doctrine of nature, but of an artificial, though ingenious, refinement of philosophy. All our natural sentiments prompt us to believe' in a sort of 'perfect virtue ... for its own sake' (91n).

The omission in 1790 of this strong assertion would appear to strengthen the utility component allowed by Smith, and also to weaken the appeal to something rather close to a 'moral sense' dictating what is self-evidently virtuous. In any event, elsewhere in all editions Smith himself confirms his adherence to the Deity's utilitarian objective, and this he also ascribes to *the man in the street*: 'by acting according to the dictates of our moral faculties, we necessarily pursue the most effectual means for promoting the happiness of mankind, and may therefore be said, in some sense to co-operate with the Deity, and to advance as far as in our power the plan of Providence' (Smith 1976 [1759]: 166).[14]

Smith's editors, we may conclude, correctly allow that 'Smith gives partial support to a utilitarian theory of justice' (Smith 1976 [1759]: 398). But such support is yet stronger than has appeared thus far. For Smith has been concerned with the motive behind approval of punishment in cases where *crimes affecting particular persons* are involved and the moral sentiments are awakened by sympathy with those persons. Justice is required to preserve society, but in cases of this sort such utilitarian grounds are secondary in men's moral evaluations. However, where crimes are involved which 'do not immediately or directly hurt any particular person' then, Smith allows, *extra-utilitarian considerations become irrelevant or at the least are overwhelmed*:

> Upon some occasions, indeed, we both punish and approve of punishment, *merely from a view to the general interest of society, which, we imagine, cannot otherwise be secured*. Of this kind are all the punishments inflicted for breaches of what is called either civil police, or military discipline. Such crimes do not immediately or directly hurt any particular person; *but their remote consequences, it is supposed, do produce, or might produce, either a considerable inconveniency, or a great disorder in the society* ... When the preservation of an individual (sentinel) is inconsistent with the safety of a multitude, nothing can be more just than that the many should be preferred to the one.
>
> (90; emphasis added)

Thus, while an observer might feel pity for a sentinel who sleeps while on duty, 'the interest of the many' is to his mind the overriding consideration and the sentinel must bear the consequences (91). This case is said by Raphael to have been considered by Smith himself as the exception that proves the rule (Raphael 1972/73: 95).[15] But the entire domain of 'civil police' can scarcely be said to be quantitatively insignificant. For it is greatly broadened, and with it application of the utility criterion in the guise of the promotion of public welfare, when account is taken of '(t)he perfection of police, the extension of trade and manufactures', as part of 'the great system of government' (Smith 1976 [1759]: 185).[16] Rosen, with the present case in mind, similarly points out that 'justice was concerned with more than responding to particular injuries and must take into account public utility as well as private injury' (Rosen 2003: 64).

7.6 Smith's 'greatest happiness' principle

In discussing a person's judgment of his fellow's actions, Smith, we have seen, underplays utilitarian considerations but only where *particular individuals* are affected by those actions. The topic is expanded in Part IV: 'Of the Effect of Utility upon the Sentiment of Approbation', and in the course of this discussion it becomes clear that whatever the character of approbation, the end of social intercourse and activity is *happiness*. All this has a bearing upon social policy, and Robbins's concerns regarding the place of *TMS* within the classical utilitarian tradition in this regard, as well as those more recently of Witztum and Young, seem to be overstated.

The first chapter of Part IV concerns aesthetics or 'the productions of art' and cites Hume's position that 'the utility of any object pleases the master by perpetually suggesting to him the pleasure or conveniency which it is fitted to promote' (Smith 1976 [1759]: 179). Smith might here be referring to the discussion of 'Why Utility Pleases' in the *Enquiry* or to the formulations in the *Treatise*. But he points out – the context clarifies that his concern extends beyond aesthetics to moral approval generally – that 'the fitness of any system or machine to produce the end for which it was intended, bestows a certain propriety and beauty upon the whole, and renders the very thought and contemplation of it agreeable, is so very obvious that nobody has overlooked it'. Smith thus maintains that the sense of 'propriety' requires that 'fitness' should complement utility, implying that *the means must take account of the end* – as Hume maintained. He then famously raises the need to explain why:

> this fitness, this happy contrivance of any production of art, should often be more valued, than the very end for which it was intended; and that the exact adjustment of the means for attaining any conveniency or pleasure, should frequently be more regarded, than that very conveniency or pleasure, in the attainment of which their whole merit would seem to consist ... That this however is very frequently the case may be observed in a thousand instances, both in the most frivolous and in the most important concerns of human life.
> (179–80)

Smith's explanation for the phenomenon in question runs in terms of the attraction exerted by love of 'system' as such, independently of any particular end or purpose, *'fitness' taking on a life of its own*. For all that, Smith does not turn his back on 'utility' and Humean 'fitness' with its focus on the final end; for the final end is taken for granted throughout, which must necessarily be the case since any pleasure derived from observing, for example, the workings of a highly sophisticated watch (one of Smith's 'trivial' instances) would evidently be erased if the timepiece failed to tell the time accurately. *Presupposing* an end purpose, Smith simply adds the complexity that the machinery employed in its achievement is admired for its own sake in some cases – 'often', 'frequently, even 'very frequently', but also, we shall see, 'sometimes'.

We turn now from aesthetics and 'trivial' applications to Smith's primary application. It is his contention that wealth is admired and sought after not to the end of achieving 'happiness', but because of the attraction exerted by the devices at play in the quest for happiness:

> If we examine … why the spectator distinguishes with such admiration the condition of the rich and the great, we shall find that it is not so much upon account of the superior ease or pleasure which they are supposed to enjoy, as of the numberless artificial and elegant contrivances for promoting this ease or pleasure. He does not even imagine that they are really happier than other people; but he imagines that they possess more means of happiness. And it is *the ingenious and artful adjustment of those means to the end for which they are intended, that is the principle source of his admiration.*
> (Smith 1976 [1759]: 182; emphasis added)

Here, as the italicized phrases indicate, Smith amply confirms that 'fitness' cannot be understood independently of end purpose – namely 'happiness', albeit an *imaginary* happiness. It is an imaginary happiness since '(i)f we consider the real satisfaction which all these things (accommodation, possessions) are capable of affording, by itself and separated from the beauty of that arrangement which is fitted to promote it, it will always appear in the highest degree contemptible and trifling' (183). 'But', Smith proceeds, 'we rarely view (wealth) in this abstract and philosophical light. We naturally confound it in our imagination with the order, the regular and harmonious movement of the system, the machine or oeconomy by means of which it is produced. The pleasures of wealth and greatness, when considered in this complex view, strike the imagination as something grand and beautiful and noble, of which the attainment is well worth all the toil and anxiety which we are so apt to bestow upon it'. Here 'the pleasures of wealth and greatness' with an eye to happiness – the end point – ultimately proves illusory, a providential 'deception' assuring that people are motivated to effort: 'it is well that nature imposes upon us in this manner. It is this deception which rouses and keeps in continual motion the industry of mankind'.

The social advantage referred to relates specifically to population increase, the aforementioned 'deception' assuring 'a new fund of subsistence' and the means 'to maintain a greater multitude of inhabitants' (Smith 1976 [1759]: 183–4). If we ask *why* a large population is desirable the answer provided is that the '*real happiness of human life*' is thereby expanded, presumably referring to the units capable of happiness. But here we must stress an assurance that the 'invisible hand' assures an egalitarian 'distribution of the necessaries of life' if not of its luxuries (184–5; emphasis added).[17] Numbers alone, in brief, are *not* a sufficient condition for expansion of the 'greatest happiness of the greatest number'.

This outcome gainsays the view that Smith's notion of 'deception' in the quest for wealth proves the secondary status accorded the utilitarian standard (Witztum and Young 2013: 575).[18] In addition, we recall what Smith himself apparently missed – that 'deception' is equally a feature of Hume's *Enquiry*, which posits that 'the honest man, if he has any tincture of philosophy, or even common observation and reflection, will discover that they themselves are, in the end, the greatest dupes, and have sacrificed the invaluable enjoyment of a character, with themselves at least, for the acquisition of worthless toys and gewgaws. How little is requisite to supply the *necessities* of nature?' (Hume 1927 [1751]: 283). This accords with the representation of 'vanity' in *A Treatise of Human Nature* – albeit a 'secondary satisfaction' – as 'the chief reason why we either desire (riches) for ourselves, or esteem them in others' (Hume 1978 [1739]: 365).

Now Bonar maintained that '(u)nlike Adam Smith, Hume by no means regarded the desire of wealth as a force which shaped society, in any good sense. It is rather a disintegrating influence which needs to be counteracted' – the latter an allusion to rules of justice (Bonar 1922: 116). But provided the quest for wealth was effectively 'counteracted' Hume did discern the beneficial social effects of such 'deception'. And Smith too did not conceive of social benefit as deriving from *unregulated* activity, arguing the case for usury laws as essential to growth (Hollander 2013). Furthermore, there is of course the broad case for justice, for while '(s)ociety may subsist among different men … from a sense of its utility, without any mutual love or affection' – without, that is, 'beneficence' – 'the prevalence of injustice must utterly destroy it' (Smith 1976 [1759]: 86).

The notion of 'deception' is further extended. Smith takes for granted that '(a)ll constitutions of government … are valued only in proportion as they tend to promote the happiness of those who live under them. This is their sole use and end' – to assure, he continues, that the people are 'are better lodged, that they are better clothed, that they are better fed' (1976 [1759]: 185–6). Fortunately, he avers, 'the same love of system, the same regard to the beauty of order, of art and contrivance', as described earlier, 'frequently serves to recommend those institutions which tend to promote the public welfare'. The main illustration of the theme whereby 'we sometimes seem to value the means more than the end' pertain to economic policy programmes designed to increase real income by the removal of mercantilist-type obstacles,[19] Smith advising the reformist politician to base his argument rather more by reference to 'the great system of public police which procures these advantages' – 'explain(ing) the connections and dependencies of its several parts, their mutual subordination to one another', than by explicit promotion of societal happiness (186). Even so, a persuasive campaign would culminate in explaining to the public 'their general subserviency to the happiness of society'. The end is to be kept in sight – even of the public, and not merely of 'philosophers' as is sometimes asserted.

A final observation: 'The greatest possible quantity of happiness' as the objective of 'that great, benevolent, and all-wise Being, who directs all the movements of nature' is set up in the sixth (1790) edition as a sort of model for emulation by the 'virtuous' individual albeit on a comparatively modest arena limited to family, friends and nation (Smith 1976 [1759]: 235).

7.7 Concluding note: Smith in relation to Hume, Hutcheson and Bentham

In this chapter I have not sought to *identify* the different ethical perspectives of Hume and Smith – allowing, for example, for their alternative perceptions of 'sympathy' – but have instead shown how the major contrasts perceived between the two in the literature, with Smith allegedly markedly playing down the utility component in ethical evaluation compared to Hume, do not survive a careful examination of the extensive qualifications and elaborations made by each party to his own doctrine. Even when Smith designates utility as a 'secondary' consideration, it constitutes an *essential* ingredient in ethical evaluation – a necessary condition. And Smith emerges in *TMS* as more 'Benthamite' than Hume by applauding a large population in terms of an increased mass of 'happiness'. (Bentham's own perspectives on Hume and Smith will be addressed in Part IV.)

Our analysis has also confirmed Smith's recognition that Hutcheson's 'moral sense' was consistent with the position that 'virtue consists in benevolence' and hence with concern for social welfare. Smith objected to what he believed to be Hutcheson position that virtue consists in benevolence *alone*, although he himself affirmed that a natural 'desire of the welfare and preservation of society ... ought to cast the balance against all other motives' (above p. 163). Now although Smith erred, since Hutcheson in fact accorded benevolence the *primary* and not the sole requirement for moral approval, the former's appreciation that concern for public welfare in Hutcheson's scheme was not displaced by, or opposed to, the Hutchesonian moral sense – as Bentham seems to have believed – remains unaffected. This appreciation strongly supports the reading of Hutcheson I have here offered. It also rather weakens a contention that 'the direct chain from Hutcheson to Bentham is, in effect, broken by Smith's reluctance to explicitly advocate the greatest-happiness principle' (see below, p. 239).

Notes

1. The expression was coined by Oakeshott 1993 [1935]: 454.
2. On the doctrine which 'excludes all sentiment, and pretends to found everything on reason', see Hume 1927 (1751): 197n. On 'the deduction of morals from self-love or a regard for private interests', see p. 215.
3. See also Brown 1994: 32n4. The same contrast between Hutcheson and Hume was much earlier drawn by Dugald Stewart 1980 [1793]: 279.
4. Valuable commentaries on Smithian 'sympathy', and the related 'impartial spectator', include Morrow 1923: 28–44; Bonar 1922:164–8; Raphael 1985: 29–45; Raphael 2007; Raphael and Macfie: 5, 7, 9–10, 12–13, 15–16; Wilson 1976; Skinner 1979.
5. On 'propriety' as relating to *motive*, see Bonar 1922: 165–6. When commenting on 'modern systems, according to which virtue consists in propriety', Smith complains that '(n)one of these systems either give, or even pretend to give, any precise or distinct measure by which this *fitness or propriety of affection* can be ascertained or judged of', which 'can be found nowhere but in the sympathetic feelings of the impartial and well-informed spectator' (Smith 1976 [1759]: 294).
6. Smith intended Hume (see Smith 1976 [1759]: 188–9).

7 This passage raises the complexity that by relating approval to coincidence with 'propriety' understood as what is 'right, accurate, agreeable to truth and reality' Smith appears to be entertaining self-evident criteria of ethical evaluation of the sort he himself condemned. Problematic too is the supplementary 'because we find that it agrees with our own' as the condition 'first' attracting us, for this contravenes the objectivity in moral assessment implied by recourse to the 'spectator'.
8 Smith intended the following Hume passages: 'every quality of the mind, which is *useful* or *agreeable* to the *person himself* or to *others*, communicates a pleasure to the spectator, engages his esteem, and is admitted under the honourable denomination of virtue or merit … [P]ersonal merit consists entirely in the usefulness or agreeableness of qualities to the person himself possessed of them, or to others, who have any intercourse with him' (Hume 1927 [1751]: 277–8; see also 266, 270.). And: 'Every quality of the mind is denominated virtuous, which gives pleasure by the mere survey; as every quality, which produces pain, is call'd vicious. This pleasure and this pain may arise from four different sources. For we reap a pleasure from the view of a character, which is naturally fitted to be useful to others, or to the person himself, or which is agreeable to others, or to the person himself' (Hume 1978 [1740]: 591).
9 Elsewhere 'prudence' is designated as entailing 'the habits of caution, vigilance, sobriety and judicious moderation' (Smith 1976 [1759]: 307).
10 One notes here the adoption of an unrestricted understanding of 'utility' as 'agreeable effects'.
11 See, for example, Hume 1978 (1739): 364; 1978 (1740): 576; 1927 (1751): 230–1, 250n, 287–9.
12 On this text see the editorial comment to Smith 1976 [1759]: 87. Smith's editors refer to the account of justice in the *Treatise* (Hume 1978 [1740]: 484f), finding there a lesser emphasis on utility.
13 In the *Lectures* regarding writers – including Grotius and Pufendorf – who 'commonly alledge as the originall measure of punishments, viz. the consideration of the publick good', Smith commented that this 'will not sufficiently account for the constitution of punishments' (Smith 1978 [1762–3]: 104).
14 All this brings to mind the affirmation that 'the Author of nature has not entrusted it to his reason to find out that a certain application of punishments is the proper means of attaining this end' – 'the welfare and preservation of society' – 'but has endowed him with an immediate and instinctive approbation of that very application which is most proper to attain it' (above, p. 163).
15 We have also noted Raphael and Macfie's opinion that 'considerations of general social utility' were for Smith little more than an 'afterthought' (above, p. 153).
16 On this matter, as indicating that in some contexts Smith took the utility principle yet further than Hume, see Rosen 2000: 82, 93–4, 100.
17 The desirability of a large population on grounds of the happiness enjoyed by a large number, does not appear in the *Wealth of Nations*. On this matter see Ricardo 1951 (1817): 348–9.
18 Our position coincides with that of Rosen 2000: 96.
19 In the space of a few pages Smith has altered his stance on the desirability of real income increase, if – as seems to be the case – he now refers to average rather than aggregate income.

References

Alvey, James E. 2003. *Adam Smith: Optimist or Pessimist?* Aldershot: Ashgate.
Bagolini, Luigi. 1975. 'The Topicality of Adam Smith's Notion of Sympathy and Judicial Evaluations', *Essays on Adam Smith*, edited by A.S. Skinner and T. Wilson. Oxford: Clarendon Press, 100–113.

Bentham, Jeremy. (1776) 1859. *A Fragment on Government. The Works of Jeremy Bentham* I, edited by John Bowring. Edinburgh: William Tait, 221–295.
Bentham, Jeremy. (1789) 1859. *An Introduction to the Principles of Morals and Legislation. The Works of Jeremy Bentham* I, edited by John Bowring. Edinburgh: William Tait, 85–154.
Bentham, Jeremy. (1789) 1982. *An Introduction to the Principles of Morals and Legislation*, edited by James H. Burns and H.L.A. Hart. London and New York: Methuen.
Bentham, Jeremy. (1795)1952. 'Supply Without Burthen'. *Jeremy Bentham's Economic Writings* I, edited by Werner Stark. London: Allen and Unwin, 279–367.
Bentham, Jeremy. (1801)1954. 'Defence of a Maximum'. *Jeremy Bentham's Economic Writings* III, edited by Werner Stark. London: Allen and Unwin, 247–302.
Bentham, Jeremy. (1801–4) 1954. 'Institute of Political Economy'. *Jeremy Bentham's Economic Writings* III, edited by Werner Stark. London: Allen and Unwin, 303–380.
Bentham, Jeremy. (1815)1859. *A Table of the Springs of Action. The Works of Jeremy Bentham* I, edited by John Bowring. Edinburgh: William Tait, 195–219.
Bentham, Jeremy. (1817) 1843. *Plan for Parliamentary Reform, The Works of Jeremy Bentham* III, edited by John Bowring. Edinburgh: William Tait, 433–557.
Bentham, Jeremy. (1824) 2015. *The Book of Fallacies*, edited by Philip Schofield. Oxford: Clarendon Press.
Bentham, Jeremy. (1830) 1843. *Constitutional Code. The Works of Jeremy Bentham* IX, edited by John Bowring. Edinburgh: William Tait.
Bonar, James. 1922. *Philosophy and Political Economy*. London: Allen and Unwin.
Bonar, James. 1930. *Moral Sense*. London: Allen and Unwin.
Brown, Charlotte. 1994. 'From Spectator to Agent: Hume's Theory of Obligation', *Hume Studies* 20(1): 19–36.
Campbell, Tom D. 1971. *Adam Smith's Science of Morals*. London: Allen and Unwin.
Campbell, Tom D. 1975. 'Scientific Explanation and Ethical Justification in the *Moral Sentiments*', *Essays on Adam Smith*, edited by Andrew S. Skinner and T. Wilson. Oxford: Clarendon Press, 68–82.
Evensky, Jerry. 2007. *Adam Smith's Moral Philosophy*, Cambridge: Cambridge University Press.
Fitzgibbons, Athol. 1995. *Adam Smith's System of Liberty, Wealth and Virtue*. Oxford: Clarendon Press.
Haakonssen, Knud. 1981. *The Science of a Legislator: The Natural Jurisprudence of David Hume and Adam Smith*. Cambridge: Cambridge University Press.
Hanley, Ryan P. 2009. *Adam Smith and the Character of Virtue*. Cambridge: Cambridge University Press.
Hart, Herbert L.A. 1982. Introduction. *An Introduction to the Principles of Morals and Legislation*, edited by James H. Burns and H.L.A. Hart. London and New York: Methuen, xxxiii–lxx.
Hollander, Samuel. 2013. 'Adam Smith: market-failure pioneer and champion of "Natural Liberty"', *Essays on Classical and Marxian Political Economy*. London and New York: Routledge, 3–41.
Hollander, Samuel. 2015. *John Stuart Mill: Political Economist*. Singapore: World Scientific.
Hume, David. (1739) 1978. *A Treatise of Human Nature* II: *Of the Passions*. 2nd ed. Oxford: Clarendon Press, 275–454.
Hume, David. (1740) 1978. *A Treatise of Human Nature* III: *Of Morals*. Oxford: Clarendon Press, 455–639.

Hume, David. (1751) 1927. *An Enquiry Concerning the Principles of Morals*. In *Enquiries concerning human understanding and concerning the principles of morals*, edited by Lewis A. Selby-Bigge. Oxford: Clarendon Press, 166–346.

Hume, David. (1759) 1984. Review, *The Theory of Moral Sentiments. Critical Review*, May 1759. In Raynor 1984, 65–79.

Hume, David. (1777) 1994. *Essays Moral, Political and Literary*. Revised edition, edited by Eugene F. Miller. Indianapolis: Liberty Fund.

Hutcheson, Francis. 1729. *An Inquiry into the Original of our Ideas of Beauty and Virtue. Treatise II: Concerning Moral Good and Evil*. 3rd ed. London: Knapton.

McCloskey, Deirdre. 2009. 'Adam Smith, the last of the former virtue ethicists', *Elgar Companion to Adam Smith*, edited by J.T. Young. Cheltenham UK: Edward Elgar, 3–24.

Macfie, A.L. 1967. *The Individual in Society: Papers on Adam Smith*. London: George Allen & Unwin.

Mill, John S. (1859)1969. Preface to *Dissertations and Discussions. Essays on Ethics, Religion and Society. Collected Works of John Stuart Mill* X. Toronto: University of Toronto Press, 493–494.

Montes, L. 2004. *Adam Smith in Context: A Critical Reassessment of Some Central Components of His Thought*. London: Palgrave Macmillan.

Morrow, Glenn R. 1923. *The Ethical and Economic Theories of Adam Smith*. New York: Longmans Green.

Muller, Jerry Z. 1993. *Adam Smith: In His Time and Ours*. Princeton: Princeton University Press.

Oakeshott, Michael. 1993 (1935). 'The New Bentham'. *Jeremy Bentham: Critical Assessments* I, edited by Bhikhu C. Parekh. London and New York: Routledge, 443–456.

Posner, R.A. 1981. *The Economics of Justice*. Cambridge: Harvard University Press.

Raphael, David D. 1972/73. 'Hume and Adam Smith on justice and utility', *Proceedings of the Aristotelian Society*, 73: 87–103.

Raphael, David D. 1975. 'The Impartial Spectator', *Essays on Adam Smith*, edited by Andrew S. Skinner and T. Wilson. Oxford: Clarendon Press, 83–99.

Raphael, David D. 1985. *Adam Smith*. Oxford: Oxford University Press.

Raphael, David D. 2007. *The Impartial Spectator: Adam Smith's Moral Philosophy*. Oxford: Clarendon Press.

Raphael, David D. and A.L. Macfie. 1976. Introduction to Adam Smith (1759) 1976. *The Theory of Moral Sentiments*, edited by and A.L. Macfie. Oxford: Clarendon Press, 1–52.

Rawls, John. 1999 (1971). *A Theory of Justice*. Revised edition. Cambridge, Mass: Belknap Press of Harvard University Press.

Raynor, David R. 1984. 'Hume's Abstract of Adam Smith's Theory of Moral Sentiments', *Journal of the History of Philosophy*, 22(1): 51–79.

Ricardo, David. (1817) 1951. *Principles of Political Economy and Taxation. Works and Correspondence*, edited by P. Sraffa. Cambridge: Cambridge University Press.

Robbins, Lionel C. 1952. *The Theory of Economic Policy in English Classical Political Economy*. London: Macmillan.

Robbins, Lionel C. 1970. *The Evolution of Modern Economic Theory*. London: Macmillan.

Rosen, Fred. 2000. 'The Idea of Utility in Adam Smith's Theory of Moral Sentiments', *History of European Ideas*, 26(2): 79–103.

Rosen, Fred 2003. *Classical Utilitarianism from Hume to Mill*. London and New York: Routledge.

Schneewind, Jerome B. 1998. *The Invention of Autonomy: A History of Modern Moral Philosophy*. Cambridge: Cambridge University Press.

Sidgwick, Henry. 1877. 'Bentham and Benthamism in Politics and Ethics', *Fortnightly Review*, 21 (125): 627–652.
Skinner, Andrew S. 1979. 'Moral philosophy and Civil Society', *A System of Social Science: Papers relating to Adam Smith*. Oxford: Clarendon Press, 42–67.
Smith, Adam.(1759) 1976. *The Theory of Moral Sentiments*, edited by David D. Raphael and A.L. Macfie. Oxford: Clarendon Press.
Smith, Adam (1762–3) 1978. Report of 1762–1763, *Lectures on Jurisprudence*, edited by Ronald L. Meek, D.D. Raphael, and P.G. Stein. Indianapolis: Oxford: Clarendon Press, 45–394.
Smith, Adam (1776) 1976. *An Inquiry into the Nature and Causes of the Wealth of Nations*, edited by Roy H. Campbell, A.S. Skinner and W.B. Todd. Oxford: Clarendon Press.
Stephen, Leslie 1900. *The English Utilitarians* I. London: Duckworth.
Stewart, Dugald (1793) 1980. 'Account of the Life and Writings of Adam Smith, LLD'. In Adam Smith, *Essays on Philosophical Subjects*, edited by William P.D. Wightman, J. C. Bryce and I.S. Ross. Oxford: Clarendon Press, 263–351.
Viner, Jacob 1958. *The Long View and the Short*. Glencoe, Ill: The Free Press.
Wilson, Thomas 1976. 'Sympathy and Self-Interest', *The Market and the State: Essays in Honour of Adam Smith*, edited by Andrew S. Skinner and T. Wilson. Oxford: Clarendon Press, 73–99.
Winch, Donald. 1978. *Adam Smith's Politics: An Essay in Historiographic Revision*. Cambridge: Cambridge University Press.
Witztum, Amos and Young, J.T. 2013. 'Utilitarianism and the Role of Utility in Adam Smith', *European Journal of the History of Economic Thought*, 20(4): 572–602.

8 Utilitarian ethics and distributive justice in *The Wealth of Nations*

8.1 Introduction

The representation of Adam Smith as a utilitarian is advanced in Chapter Eight with primary attention now accorded to the *Wealth of Nations* (hereon *WN*) and with particular reference to distributive justice. We recall first that Adam Smith accepted the effect on human happiness, as the appropriate index in evaluating institutions and policy, is manifest at a general level in the *Theory of Moral Sentiments*: 'All constitutions of government … are valued only in proportion as they tend to promote the *happiness* of those who live under them', and to assure that the people are 'are better lodged, that they are better clothed, that they are better fed' (Smith 1976 [1759]: 185–6 emphasis added; cited in Chapter Seven, p. 168). In the *Lectures on Jurisprudence* Smith comes close to stating the 'greatest happiness' principle in so many words albeit with a fascinating twist: 'The greater the freedom of the free, the more intolerable is the slavery of the slaves. Opulence and freedom, the two greatest blessings men can possess, tend greatly to the misery of this body of men, which in most countries where slavery is allowed makes by far the greatest part. A humane man would wish therefore if slavery has to be generally established that these greatest blessings, being incompatible with *the happiness of the greatest part of mankind*, were never to take place' (Smith 1978 [1762–3]: 185; emphasis added). And he raises the question in the *Wealth of Nations*: 'Is [the] improvement in the circumstances of the lower ranks of the people to be regarded as an advantage or as an inconveniency for the society? The answer seems at first sight abundantly plain. Servants, labourers and workmen of different kinds, make up the far greater part of every great political society. But what improves the circumstances of the greater part can never be regarded as an inconveniency to the whole. No society can surely be *flourishing and happy*, of which the greater part of the members are *poor and miserable*' (Smith 1976 [1776]: 96; emphasis added). This passage may be understood as asserting that 'the welfare of the working classes constituted Smith's index of national "happiness"' (Hollander 2013: 23), or as Levy phrased it, as proposing 'the doctrine that one ought to seek the greatest happiness of the majority, that is maximize the wellbeing of the median' (Levy 2001: 65–6). (Levy represents Smith as an instance of 'pre-Benthamite utilitarianism', whereas in fact Hume, Malthus and Ricardo can also be cited to the same effect.)

A dramatic formulation in the Draft of the *Wealth of Nations* dating to c. 1763 renders with splendid clarity the identification of social welfare with that of the labouring class: 'The high price of labour is to be considered not meerly as a proof of the general opulence of Society which can afford to pay well all those whom it employs; it is to be regarded as what constitutes the expence of public opulence, or as the very thing in which public opulence properly consists … National opulence is the opulence of the whole people, which nothing but the great reward of labour, and, consequently the great facility of acquiring, can give occasion to' (Scott 1937: 332). That society as a whole cannot reasonably be said to be 'happy' if its main quantitative component is miserable might seem to be so patently self-evident as not to deserve mention, were it not required by the mercantilist *exclusion* of the working class in its entirety from the welfare maximand. In any event, what matters on this view as an index of economic welfare is not *per capita* income but the *average wage* such that to condemn high wages is 'to lament over the necessary effect and cause of the greatest publick prosperity' (Smith 1976 [1776]: 99).

The foregoing representation of Smith's utilitarian maximand, though accurate, may nonetheless mislead without due care. In the first place, it implies that labour's wellbeing is a *sufficient* condition for assuring social welfare whereas in fact it is only a *necessary* condition since there are other components of the utilitarian maximand, including cultural investment relating to the 'state' or the 'community' in general. Secondly, it leaves the impression that the 'majority' was one undifferentiated mass of the poor. This perception extends to a voluminous body of recent literature amounting to a 'synthesis' that 'Smith was dedicated to the alleviation of poverty' (Hanley 2009: 15 and note; also Rasmussen 2016: 342–3). One commentator is more precise and perceives Smith's prime policy norm to be the well-being of the 'worst off' or 'least advantaged' implying at the time the majority (Young 2018: 506, 519). The matter is of considerable interest when we consider Rawls's stress in our own day on the welfare of those worst off – his 'difference principle' (Rawls 2001: 42–3). Now J.S. Mill was dissatisfied with the outcome of political organization in his day, both for the least advantaged and the representative member of society which weighs heavily the working class *as a whole* (Persky 2010: 142; 2016: 192). Where did Smith stand?

I propose to take into account Smith's distinction between the unskilled 'labourer' and the better-paid skilled 'artisan' within the 'lower ranks', with an eye to his own and contemporary or near-contemporary estimates of the quantitative significance of these categories. Considering Smith's doubts as to whether the higher earnings of the skilled worker in contemporary Britain were always wholly justified, one might expect the contrast to affect the initial generalization regarding the welfare index which relates to the working classes as a whole. Nevertheless, the evidence I shall adduce reinforces the case that

Smith's primary concern – as a matter of principle relating to his index of national 'happiness' – was the welfare of the working classes *as a whole* including better-paid skilled 'artificers' as well as lower-paid unskilled 'labourers'. The least advantaged were of particular interest insofar as faulty institutional arrangements depressed the relative earnings of unskilled labourers relative to artisans. But this distortion was corrigible by the abolition of the Settlement and Apprenticeship laws, after which concern for the skilled artisans as well as the poorer-paid 'labourers' comes back into its own, for Smith opposed wage differentials not on principle but only if they were unwarranted. In any event, the faulty institutions also acted to the detriment of the skilled worker during periods of downturn. Our exercise also highlights the fact that Smith's index of social welfare applies, formally at least, to the *employed* workforce – skilled and unskilled – and did not extend to the very lowest category in society, the 'pauper' and 'vagrant' classes towards whom Smith adopted a somewhat cavalier attitude.

I shall also seek to clarify how Smith's notions of 'natural liberty and justice' and 'equity' relate to his utilitarianism. I shall have in mind here a strict dichotomy which can sometimes be discerned between 'the utilitarian principles of Bentham' and 'the natural rights of Adam Smith' (Fay 1964: 20), and a contrary view, that of Lionel Robbins, regarding Smith 'who so frequently uses the terminology of the *Naturrecht*, but whose arguments are so consistently utilitarian in character', or again: 'Whatever the nature of the *Theory of Moral Sentiments*, the tests of policy applied throughout the entire *Wealth of Nations* are, in fact, consistently utilitarian in substance' (Robbins 1961: 48, 178). When a writer insists as strongly as does Smith on both 'natural liberty and justice' and 'equity' while at the same time adopting the happiness criterion in evaluating policy and institutions, there is a presumption that he would not have pleaded guilty to a gross contradiction. In this regard we might cite J.S. Mill's insistence, spelled out in his 'Whewell' (1852), that 'secondary or middle' principles defining the precise constituents of 'greatest happiness' are as essential as the primary principle itself; Bentham's achievement, Mill explained, was to use the utility principle as the foundation for 'secondary or middle principles, capable of serving as premises for a body of ethical doctrine not derived from existing opinions, but fitted to be their test', so that a moralist can deduce from utility as a standard 'his whole system of ethics' (Mill 1969 [1852]: 172–4; see Hollander 2015: 33, 59). If we may attribute this perspective to Smith, then his notions of 'natural liberty and justice' and 'equity' are to be *tested* by their contributions to happiness – so that a moralist can deduce from utility as a standard 'his whole system of ethics' – rather than constituting an indigestible intrusion into an essentially utilitarian framework. It will be one of our objectives to show that it is fair to make such an attribution of *coherence* to Smith.

A more specific objective will be to discern whether, when treating the return to labour, a quest for *equality* was a desideratum on utilitarian grounds. I shall have in mind here an assertion regarding 'the egalitarian nature of Adam Smith's economics', which he found reflected in the circumstance 'that even the analytical core of the *Wealth of Nations* ... shows that Adam Smith's book is aimed at aiding the large number of working poor' (Schliesser 2008: 228). It is no exaggeration to say that Smith's purpose in writing the *Wealth of Nations* as concerns policy was to relieve the poor by the abolition of institutions inimical to their interest, for mercantilist regulation is famously said to be 'the industry ... which is carried on for the benefit of the rich and the powerful, that is principally encouraged by our mercantile system. That which is carried on for the benefit of the poor and the indigent, is too often, either neglected, or oppressed' (below p. 192). Nevertheless, Smith cannot fairly be classified as 'egalitarian' on the grounds of his concern to enhance the wellbeing of the 'lower ranks', for this objective might be satisfied *even if the wage share declined*. We shall confirm Hanley's helpful rendition whereby 'Smith's first defense of commercial society might be said to rest on the *paradox of inequality* as a contributor to the amelioration of poverty' since equality would depress rather than raise living standards (Hanley 2009: 19; emphasis added). And moreover there were steps to be taken to assure that workers indeed enjoyed 'tolerable' living standards, reflecting in part a perception of aggregate labour demand as a valid subject for state action to the end of enhancing the rate of accumulation and thus the general wage. Bald generalizations to the effect that for Smith income distribution should be determined by the market (Stigler 1982 [1981]: 11) must be firmly qualified.

But the question of whether Smith was an egalitarian cannot end with the 'greatest happiness' issue's dictating tolerable living standards for the largest class, without making reference to distributive justice. Hont and Ignatieff go too far when they maintain that Smith 'effectively excluded "distributive justice" from the appropriate functions of government in a market society ... Distributive Justice, which deals with the allocation of superfluity according to claims of need, or desert, or merit, was not properly in the domain of law, but of morality' (Hont and Ignatieff 1983: 24–5). I allow that Smith can be quoted in support of this stance, as in the lectures where he describes distributive justice as a matter of 'imperfect rights ... not belonging properly to jurisprudence, but rather to a system of moralls as they do not fall under the jurisdiction of the laws' (Smith 1978 [1762–3]: 9). But the fact that there were productivity advantages deriving from inequality even from labour's perspective was not taken to an extreme, as is clear from the recommendations regarding taxation in the *Wealth of Nations*; such advantages might be reaped even if the degree of inequality is reduced by introducing a degree of progression.[1] At the same time, while the taxation proposals can be read as pregnant with implications for a fully-fledged policy of redistribution, we shall also note the almost apologetic hesitancy with which Smith himself proceeds, and the limitation of the legitimate degree of progression to only 'something more than in proportion'. This sort of reticence confirms Lord Robbins's contention that Smith 'laid down the rule that the just tax was proportionate to ability to pay – that is to say, should be roughly proportionate to income. He was prepared to tolerate minor deviations from this rule and even to recommend them. But, in the main, this was his canon and this was the Classical prescription' (Robbins 1961: 66).

It is no easy matter to accurately capture the balance Smith sought to establish. But that in contemporary British circumstances he placed a greater weight on efficiency than on 'fair' distribution seems to be confirmed by his justification of the broad lines of contemporary distribution – subject of course to the case for government intervention to assure the working classes a tolerable living standard – on the grounds that there existed in the Britain of his day 'a graduall descent of fortunes' (below, p. 183), which accounted for the absence of significant pressure emanating from the propertyless to reduce inequality, and this notwithstanding a vast differential between the highest and lowest incomes in society. And quite apart from Smith's rejection of equality as inimical to working-class living conditions there is a wholly different justification for inequality perceived as a *sine qua non* for social investments of a general order, including the development of the arts and sciences (below, p. 184; see also Smith 1967 [1795]: 49-50). In summary, once the proposed reform programme, including the interventionist proposals, had been undertaken there yet remains a residuum of *inequality* which Smith found acceptable, indeed necessary, to assure both good working-class standards and social investment more broadly.

Equality might also refer to the eradication of wage differentials, and here one may point to Smith's insistence on those differentials reflecting training costs, provided these are not artificially enhanced. Smith avoided the matter of so-called 'luck egalitarianism' – the correction of pay differentials reflecting fortuitous differences in mental and physical ability (Persky 2016: 206) – by his Enlightenment presumption that the street-porter and the philosopher are *constitutionally* indistinguishable. It is difficult to say whether, in the event that experience undermined the overwhelming weight he accorded to nurture, Smith would have adopted the position of Mill that (ideally) differentials of this order should be corrected by state intervention or of Marx, who insisted upon their maintenance in the first stage of communism. (On this contrast, see Chapter 13, p. 332-3.)

Section 8.2 below takes note of a contrast between 'the utilitarian principles of Bentham' and 'the natural rights of Adam Smith' (Fay 1964: 20) and argues for their reconciliation. Sections 8.3 and 8.4 concern 'The ethics of class distribution' and 'Distributive justice and reform proposals', the former based upon a perception of income from property as a 'defalcation' of labour, although we also note that when discussing the origins of property Smith adopts a justification in terms formally suggestive of Locke. Setting aside this complexity we review in the first of the duo a series of texts revealing Smith's willingness to tolerate the *essential inequity* of class distribution on the grounds of the higher earnings that labour earns in general relative to those theoretically available in an egalitarian society where labour receives its entire product. Of high interest is Smith's justification in the British case of major differentials in annual income from property ranging from £40,000 to £200 on the grounds 'that there is *a graduall descent of fortunes* betwixt these great ones and others of the least and lowest fortune'. This condition is not formally applied to other income categories, but the principle might be generalized. The existence of a manufacturing sector creating an option for the landless is another feature of the justification. But, as explained in the second of our two sections, the approval accorded to the institution of private-property held good only if subjected to institutional reform. Here a range of proposals is outlined, including the abolition of the existing Laws of Settlement, Apprenticeship and Corporation and modifications to public finance and trade policy, demonstrating a concern for distributive justice which qualifies – although it does not eliminate – the primary concern with efficiency.

Section 8.5 – 'Happiness and Population Size' – reverts briefly to the notion expressed in *TMS* entailing the adherence to the 'Greatest Happiness of Greatest Number' in the *literal* sense of the expression by implying that social benefit attaches to high population size (see Chapter 7, p 167). This position which is found also in the 1790 edition would conflict diametrically with the *Wealth of Nations* were it not for an explicit assumption that the larger population benefits from adequate real wages, implying that numbers alone do not in fact guarantee greater national happiness.

Sections 8.6 and 8.7 on 'Wage Differentials' and on 'The "Lower Ranks" and the Pauper Population' detail the difficulties which arise from adopting the view found in the literature that Smith identified the workforce with the *least advantaged members*, particularly the problem of specifying who were the 'least advantaged'. I certainly do not suggest that Smith was unconcerned by the poorest class amongst the employed – namely the unskilled 'labourers' – for these were the most affected by faulty institutional arrangements. Here I pay particular attention to the Draft of *WN* (composed c. 1763) which extends the charge of inequity from class distribution and the 'defalcations' made from wages to the distribution of the wages component itself, by affirming that *'those who labour most get least'* alluding to the excessive earnings of skilled artisans due to unjustifiable immobility imposed by the Settlement and Apprenticeship laws. For all that, even the skilled suffered in years of economic downturn from the effects of institutionally-imposed immobility. A correction of this anomaly re-establishes the primary objective of enhancing the real earnings of the labouring class as a whole. Smith's remarks regarding the indigent who fall below 'the lowest rate which is consistent with common humanity' will also be taken into account and here I propose that his tendency to somewhat play down the magnitude of the problem may be explained, partly at least, by an expectation that vagrancy and pauperism would tend to resolve themselves should all the reforms he proposed be successfully undertaken.

In my Conclusion I draw on the foregoing materials to emphasize that the 'exploitative' character ascribed to property income is more of a theoretical than a practical matter, the facts of life dictating that in the absence of private property and with strict equality, living standards would fall to unacceptably low levels. Accordingly, the proposed correction of the distributional inequities of the prevailing system – including the 'progressive' taxation proposals – fall far short of a case *for equality*. The same holds good of the case for wage differentials, even those reflecting differential natural ability, in respect of which Smith seems in discernibly closer proximity to Marx than to Mill. I further argue that Smith's stance regarding 'equity and justice' may be considered as a coherent deduction from utilitarian principles rather than a manifestation of the severe contradiction implied by Fay's contrast between 'the utilitarian principles of Bentham' and 'the natural rights of Adam Smith'.

8.2 Smithian utilitarianism and natural rights

We take note in this preliminary section of a strict dichotomy sometimes discerned between 'the utilitarian principles of Bentham' and 'the natural rights of Adam Smith' (Fay 1964: 20). For his part, Lionel Robbins – who rightly maintained that the 'greatest happiness' formula referred broadly to evaluations of institutions and policy by reference to their effects on 'human happiness', with the 'felicific calculus' being the 'shop window' (Robbins 1961: 181) – allowed that Smith 'had a moral philosophy of his own which in some respects appears to be in contrast with the utilitarian outlook', referring here to the *Theory of Moral Sentiments*, yet insisted that 'the tests of policy applied throughout the entire *Wealth of Nations* are, in fact, consistently utilitarian in substance' (178). This overview does not, however, formally address the fact to which Fay doubtless referred: that the *Wealth of Nations* itself protests institutional arrangements which constrain labour's freedom of movement and choice of occupation as 'an evident violation of natural liberty and justice', on the grounds that '[t]he property which every man has in his own labour, as it is the original foundation of all other property, so it is the most sacred and inviolable ... [a] most sacred property. It is a manifest encroachment upon the just liberty both of the workman, and of those who might be disposed to employ him'. As we shall see, Smith also appealed simply to 'equity' in discussing the return due to labour.

To insist as strongly as Smith does upon both 'natural liberty and justice' and 'equity' while at the same time he adopts the happiness criterion in evaluating policy and institutions does not neccesarily imply self-contradiction, for there is no reason why an adherent to the happiness rule should not regard free movement and choice of occupation as requisite conditions defining a happy community. If J.S. Mill's approach to this sort of issue is valid (see above, p. 176) then Smith's notions of 'natural liberty and justice' are to be tested by their contributions to happiness.

There is one obvious caveat to Mill's position that a moralist can deduce from utility as a standard 'his whole system of ethics', namely that it does not logically apply to the selection of those whose 'happiness' is to be taken into account, the basic unit of the entire structure. That is an independent value judgment. With this in mind I return to the test of social welfare provided for Smith by the *average wage*, and note that his index would register an increase even with a *reduced wage share* in national income should wages rise at a slower rate than incomes in general, at least provided minimum ethical requirements are met once labour is assured an acceptable living standard. It is true that Smith continues in the passage which proposes that '[n]o society can surely be flourishing and happy, of which the greater part of the members are poor and miserable' by asserting: 'It is but equity, besides, that they who feed, cloath and lodge the whole body of the people, should have *such a share of the produce of their own labour* as to be themselves tolerably well fed, cloathed and lodged', taking for granted that property income is a deduction from labour's product (Smith 1976 [1776]: 96); emphasis added). We are not obliged to understand Smith here as denying that the inclusion of labour, as the primary component in the utilitarian maximand, is itself a fundamental value judgment and indeed the foundation of the utilitarian structure. Rather, to insist on a 'tolerable' return to labour *when labour is responsible for the entire product* – that property income is *robbery* or a 'defalcation' as Smith phrased it – is a further elaboration of the ethical dimension based upon an implied technical proposition that landowners and capitalists – as distinct, it should perhaps be added, from land and capital – do not contribute to national income. But if non-wage income is indeed an exploitation income, then labour on the grounds of equity should receive the *entire* product, whereas Smith insists only that the worker receives a fraction of his own product assuring him a 'tolerably' high real wage, a formulation consistent even with a *reduced* wage share should acceptable wage earnings be assured.

8.3 The ethics of class distribution

I shall consider in temporal sequence various statements of principle by Smith before turning to his proposed corrective interventions. Two famous interrelated propositions appearing in the *Theory of Moral Sentiments*, serve effectively to downplay the unfairness of inequality in terms amounting to an apologia. Concerning '*riches*' in general, the distribution of happiness is not to be identified with the (class) distribution of income, for wealth and greatness are illusionary (Smith 1976 [1759]: 182). By implication, inequality does not pose a serious ethical dilemma since the poor lose nothing meaningful and in fact save themselves a lifetime of useless effort by avoiding the rat race. As for *necessaries*, again there was no serious inequality and by implication no ethical problem created, since distribution was, providentially, much fairer than appeared to be the case. I touch on one of the celebrated 'invisible hand' applications:

> The produce of the soil maintains at all times nearly that number of inhabitants which it is capable of maintaining ... [The rich] are led by an

invisible hand to make nearly the same distribution of the necessaries of life which would have been made had the earth been divided into equal portions among all its inhabitants; and thus, without intending it, without knowing it, advance the interest of society and afford means to the multiplication of the species. When Providence divided the earth among a few lordly masters, it neither forgot nor abandoned those who seemed to have been left out in the partition. These last, too, enjoy their share of all that it produces.

(184–5)

We shall elaborate presently the implicit suggestion here that social happiness rises with population size.

At this point the text reverts to the question of real happiness: 'In what constitutes the real happiness of human life, they are in no respect inferior to those who would seem so much above them. In ease of body and peace of mind, all the different ranks of life are nearly upon a level, and the beggar, who suns himself by the side of the highway, possesses that security which kings are fighting for' (Smith 1976 [1759]: 185). Was Smith unaware that the sun is not always shining and that poverty entails suffering? Were we to leave the matter with his philosophical musings regarding the nature of true happiness, it would be difficult to escape the conclusion that he was engaged in an unconvincing apology for inequality. But astute commentators have been unwilling to take him at his word. Thus Bonar opines that for Smith, as for Hume and Hutcheson, while wealth does not make a man happy he still cannot as a rule be happy without it and therefore requires a certain minimum equipment of external goods to realize 'internal' happiness (Bonar 1922: 113). Lionel Robbins pointed out that the assertion regarding the beggar need not conflict with the view that *ceteris paribus* he would benefit from increase in real income (Robbins 1968:164). They are right not to take Smith at his word, since he goes on to applaud the fact that mankind is fooled into believing that their happiness *does* hinge on material wellbeing: 'It is well that nature imposes in this manner. It is this deception which rouses and keeps in continual motion the industry of mankind' (Smith 1976 [1759]: 183).

A more measured justification of inequality is to be found in a case, recorded in the *Lectures*, against Francis Hutcheson's support of Agrarian Laws to limit the accumulation of landed property. In his account of the matter Donald Winch maintains that Hutcheson, in arguing for Agrarian laws, 'does not deal with the special characteristics of a form of society deeply penetrated by commerce and manufacturing' (Winch 1978: 66). Perhaps so, but Hutcheson does allow that to the extent that good manufacturing opportunities existed the need for agrarian laws was less urgent (see Chapter 4, p. 109). Now Smith says much the same thing as we shall see. Furthermore, he not only opposed strict equality – which is not in fact Hutcheson's objective since he was undecided regarding the desirable degree of equality – but also vast wealth differentials between the highest and the lowest *should the difference be discrete*, that is where there is a great 'leap' from one to the other.

The argument commences by the observation that a strictly egalitarian society would necessarily be poor, and incapable of generating a surplus for emergencies: '[T]ho an agrarian law would render all on an equality, which has indeed something very agreable in it, yet a people who are all on an equality will necessarily be very poor and unable to defend themselves in any pressing occasion. They have nothing saved which can give them relief in time of need' (Smith 1978 [1762–3]: 195). Such was not the case even presuming inequality where a significant manufacturing sector existed: 'But when goods are manufactured, a very small quantity of them will procure an immense one of the unmanufactured produce of another country ... [I]n a country where manufactures are carried on a small part of this manufactured produce will bring a great quantity of unmanufactured, which may supply their present necessities or employ their industry so as to procure more in futurity' (195–6). And here the second condition is introduced: 'So that in the present state of things a man of a great fortune is rather an advantage than dissadvantage to the state, providing that there is *a graduall descent of fortunes* betwixt these great ones and others of the least and lowest fortune. For it will be shewn hereafter that one who leaps over all his country men is of real detriment to the community' (196; emphasis added).

The 'real detriment' of vast differentials alludes to social tensions extending to (understandable) incursions by the poor against property, normally protected by the 'rules of justice' (Smith 1978 [1762–3]: 197–8). The condition of a 'graduall descent of fortunes' refers to income from property, Smith specifying that under ruling British conditions legislation against 'overgrown fortunes' was unjustified, for 'we have fortunes gradually descending from £40,000 [sic] to [200] or 300' (196), alluding to annual incomes with a minimum of approximately £200.^{2} The student note taker is silent regarding Smith's sources, but £40,000 is wholly out of line with contemporary estimates and is probably a misreporting of the lecture which perhaps specified £4,000.^{3} In any event, Mingay's account confirms a 'graduall descent of fortunes' when he distinguishes the 'great landlords' owning estates producing 'at least five or six thousand pounds a year at the end of the eighteenth century', from lesser landlords or 'wealthy gentry' with incomes of £3,000 or £4,000, from 'small country gentlemen' or 'lesser gentry' with incomes from £1,000 to £3,000, and these from 'modest gentlemen, only barely gentry [with] incomes of some hundreds of pounds' (Mingay 1963: 10, 21–2). Perkin observes that inequality in the eighteenth century was 'mitigated by a wide diffusion of wealth' and cites Colquhoun to that effect; this feature is also apparent in the fact that '[b]etween the landowners and the labouring poor stretched the long, diverse, but unbroken chains of the "middle ranks"' (Perkin 1969: 22). Perkin further explains that '[e]ven domestic service formed a separate hierarchy which curiously typified the rest ... Domestic service like every other occupation was marked by internal differences of status greater than any which separated it from those outside' (23–4; see also Mingay 1963: 227–8.)

According to the account in the lectures, the earnings of a working household amounted to no more than £10 (Smith 1978 [1762–3]: 194), an order of magnitude confirmed in *WN* which notes that £10 is the minimum rental that must be paid by a tenant to establish residence in a parish, 'a thing impossible for one who has nothing but his labour to live by' (Smith 1976 [1776]: 154). The reference is almost certainly to *unskilled* labour and seems to be an understatement.[4] Intervention to restrict the size of land holdings was also inappropriate for a second reason, namely the alternative employment opportunities available to the landless, a circumstance to which the tolerant attitude towards private property on the part of the general public is attributed. Thus, whereas in ancient Rome the wealthy 'consumed what should have supported a great number of free citizens', and freemen called justifiably for the confiscation of property and redistribution, '[w]e never hear of any such demands as these at this time ... the poor people now who have neither a land estate nor any fortune in money can gain a livelihood by working as a servant to a farmer in the country, or by working to any tradesman whose business they understand' (Smith 1978 [1762–3]: 196–7). 'We may see from this', Smith concludes, 'that slavery amongst its inconveniencies has this very bad consequence, that it renders rich and wealthy men of large properties of great and real detriment, which otherwise are rather of service as they promote trade and commerce' (198).

The lectures are of further interest for a distinction drawn between two categories of inequality. The first is that 'usefull inequality in the fortunes of mankind which naturally and necessarily arises from the various degrees of capacity, industry, and diligence in the different individualls', a category protected, to society's advantage, by law and government:

> All most all laws and regulations tend to the encouragement of these arts, which provide for those things which we look upon as the objects of the labour of the vulgar alone, meat, drink, and cloathing. Even law and government have these as their finall end and ultimate object. They give the inhabitants of the country liberty and security [in the cultivation of the] land which they possess in safety, and their benign influence gives room and opportunity for the improvement of all the various arts and sciences. They maintain the rich in the possession of their wealth against the violence and rapacity of the poor, and by that means preserve that usefull inequality in the fortunes of mankind which naturally and necessarily arises from the various degrees of capacity, industry, and diligence in the different individualls.
>
> (Smith 1978 [1762–3]: 337–8)

Here wealth and inequality are justified as reflecting *differential merit*. The category of inequality which is less 'usefull' reflects the exploitative character of an institution allowing forcible extraction from labour's product, a system subjecting labour to 'oppression and tyranny' on the part of landlords, usurers, and tax gatherers (339). Smith elaborates:

> The labour and time of the poor is in civilized countries sacrificed to the maintaining the rich in ease and luxury. The landlord is maintained in idleness and luxury by the labour of his tenants, who cultivate the land for him as well as for themselves. The moneyd man is supported by his exactions from the industrious merchant and the needy who are obliged to support him in ease by a return for the use of his money. But every savage has the full enjoyment of the fruits of his own labours; there are there no landlords, no usurers, no tax gatherers ... Thus he who as it were supports the whole frame of society and furnishes the means of the convenience and ease of all the rest is himself possessed of a very small share and is buried in obscurity.
>
> (340–1)

Now all this is a prelude to expounding the positive effect on productivity of private-property arrangements by way of the division of labour such that the earnings of labour exceed the maximum available in a system where 'every one has the full fruits of his own labours' (Smith 1978 [1762–3]: 339). It is difficult to escape the impression that Smith deliberately exaggerates the dark side of the private-property institution in order to bring out dramatically for his students the compensating advantages for labour: 'In what manner then', Smith asks rhetorically, 'shall we account for the great share he and the lowest of the people have of the conveniencies of life', referring to one 'who bears on his shoulders the whole weight of mankind, and unable to sustain the load is buried by the weight of it and thrust down into the lowest parts of the earth, from whence he supports all the rest' (341).

Earlier in the lectures we find similarly strong accusations against the inequities of private property: 'Laws and government may be considered ... as a combination of the rich *to oppress the poor*, and preserve to themselves the inequality of goods, which would otherwise be soon destroyed by the attacks of the poor, who if not hindered by the government would soon reduce the others to an equality with themselves by open violence' (Smith 1978 [1762–3]: 208; emphasis added). Yet once again we are obliged to question how seriously to take such statements recalling the estimate that the propertyless in contemporary Britain – unlike those of ancient Rome – posed no threat. In any event, the injustice of inequality reflecting property distribution is, we have also seen, qualified by the proposition that law and government 'maintain the rich in the possession of their wealth against the violence and rapacity of the poor, and by that means preserve that usefull inequality in the fortunes of mankind which naturally and necessarily arises from the various degrees of capacity, industry, and diligence in the different individualls', or again by the affirmation that '[t]he government and laws hinder the poor from ever acquiring the wealth by violence which they would otherwise exert on the rich; *they tell them they must either continue poor or acquire wealth in the same manner as they have done*' (208–9; emphasis added), implying that the acquisition of wealth reflected not force or good fortune but valid merit of some order. Indeed, in an earlier lecture on the origins of property which accords primary consideration to 'occupation' the moral justification in the eyes of the impartial spectator is based on the consideration that the occupier has 'bestowed ... time and pains' in its acquisition (17).[5]

A similar duality is to be found in the second set of students' notes. On the one hand, a critical view is expressed of the inequality characterizing the property institution: 'In a civilized society, tho' there is indeed a division of labour there is no equal division, for there are a good many who work none at all. The division of opulence is not according to the work ... [H]e who, as it were, bears the burden of society, has the fewest advantages' (Smith 1978 [1766]: 489–90). But in the very same context a more positive view emerges according to which inequality is the natural outcome of flourishing activity: 'Law and government ... seem to propose no other object but this, they secure the individual who has enlarged his property, that he may peaceably enjoy the fruits of it. By law and government all the different arts flourish, and that inequality of fortune to which they give occasion is sufficiently preserved' (489; see Winch 1978: 68). And by thus emphasizing inequality as a necessary, and implicitly permanent, feature, the matter of unfairness is rendered academic: 'They who are strongest and in the bustle of society have got above the weak, must have as many under as to defend them in their station; from necessary causes, therefore, there must be as many in the lower stations as there is occasion for. There must be as many up as down, and no division can be overstretched' (492). In an exercise in Conjectural History Smith declares that '[t]he appropriation of herds and flocks, which introduced an inequality of fortune, was that which first gave rise to regular government. Till there be property there can be no government, the very end of which is to secure wealth, and to defend the rich from the poor' (404).

The distribution problem is also elaborated in a passage appearing in a draft of the *Wealth of Nations* dating to c. 1763, the same period as the first set of lectures and bearing the same complex message, namely: (1) *Property income perceived as exploitation or deductions from the produce due to labour, contrasting with primitive societies*: 'In a Civilized Society the poor provide both for themselves and for the enourmous luxury of their Superiors. The rest, which goes to support the vanity of the slothful Landlord, is all earned by the industry of the peasant ... Among savages, on the contrary, every individual enjoys the whole produce of his own industry. There are among them, no Landlords, no usurers, no taxgatherers' (Scott 1937: 326). (2) *The 'unfairness' of income distribution characterizing civilized society reflecting institutions guaranteeing income from property by force and law*, a formulation suggesting that such unfairness is inevitable:

Supposing ... that the produce of the labour of the multitude, was to be *equally and fairly divided*, each individual, we should expect, could be little better provided for than the single person who laboured alone. But with regard to the produce of the labour of a great Society *there is never any such thing as a fair and equal division*. In a society of an hundred thousand families, there will perhaps be one hundred who don't labour at all, and who yet, either by violence, or by the more orderly *oppression of law*, employ a greater part of the labour of the society than any other ten thousand in it. (327; emphasis added)

And (3) *Higher real wages notwithstanding the 'oppressive inequality' reflecting an unequal distribution of property*: 'Superior affluence and abundance' are enjoyed by the 'lowest and most despised member of civilized society' despite 'so much oppressive inequality' (328). Wages are not only high 'compared with what the most respected and active savage can attain to', but also absolutely: 'It is the immense multiplication of the productions of all the different arts, in consequence of the division of labour, which, *notwithstanding the great inequalities of property, occasions,* in all civilized societies, *that universal opulence which extends itself to the lowest ranks of the people*. So great a quantity of every thing is produced, that there is enough both to gratify the slothful and oppressive profusion of the great, and at the same time *abundantly to supply the wants of the artisan and peasant*' (328, 331; emphasis added).

The notion of exploitation, or deductions by landlords and capitalists from a product due to labour, is confirmed in the published version of the *Wealth of Nations*: '[the] original state of things, in which the labourer enjoyed the whole produce of his own labour, could not last beyond the first introduction of the appropriation of land and the accumulation of stock' (1976 [1776]: 82); and landowners are represented as 'demand[ing] a share of almost all the produce which the labourer can either raise or collect from it', while '[t]he produce of almost all other labour is liable to the like deduction of profit' (83), since the labourer 'must share [his produce] with the owner of the stock which employs him' (67). The '*oppressive inequality*', '*the oppression of the law*', the '*slothful and oppressive profusion of the great*' of the Draft has a counterpart in the contention that in countries other than new colonies 'rent and profit eat up wages, and the two superior orders of people *oppress* the inferior one' (565; emphasis added).

In the discussion of 'justice' in Book V the essential unfairness of the inequality characterizing the property system seems to be taken for granted: 'Wherever there is great property, there is great inequality. For one very rich man, there must be at least five hundred poor, and the affluence of the few supposes the indigence of the many' (1976 [1776]: 710),[6] and Smith reaffirms that 'civil government, so far as it is instituted for the security of property, is in reality instituted for the defence of the rich against the poor, or of those who have some property against those who have none at all' (715). Nevertheless, as we found to be the case in the Lectures, this apparently critical tone towards property ownership is countered, in the very same context, by the contention that the acquisition of property is itself a result of honest effort – as before I leave open the question of a Lockean connection – whereas it was those who *threatened* property who were truly guilty of injustice, their enmity reflecting 'avarice and ambition in the rich, in the poor the hatred of labour and the love of present ease and enjoyment' (709). In brief: 'It is only under the shelter of the civil magistrate that the owner of that valuable property, which is acquired by the labour of many years, or perhaps of many successive generations, can sleep a single night in security. He is at all times surrounded by unknown enemies, whom, though he never provoked, he can never appease, and from whose injustice he can be protected only by the powerful arm of the civil magistrate continually held up to chastise it' (710).[7]

While for the foregoing reasons it is doubtful whether the *inherent* unfairness of income distribution mirroring that of private property is consistently carried through to the *Wealth of Nations*, what is certainly retained is the insistence that, because of relatively high productivity, even in a society characterized by exploitation and inequality real wages exceed what they would otherwise be in an egalitarian society where labour's produce is not subject to deduction, indeed that labourers '*are often abundantly supplied*' implying high real wages absolutely and not only compared to what would be available in a 'savage' state: 'Among civilized and thriving nations ... though a great number of people do not labour at all, many of whom consume the produce of ten times, frequently of a hundred times more labour than the greater part of those who work; yet the produce of the whole labour of the society is so great, *that all are often abundantly supplied,* and a workman, even of the lowest and poorest order, if he is frugal and industrious, may enjoy a greater share of the necessaries and conveniencies of life than it is possible for any savage to acquire' (Smith 1976 [1776]: 10; emphasis added). What matters most for Smith is the absolute wage, whereas the comparison with what could be earned by a 'savage' is rhetorical, for a subsequent aside indicates that historical comparisons with 'original', non-exploitative, states are of a conjectural order and not to be pressed too far: 'this original state of things, in which the labourer enjoyed the whole produce of his own labour, could not last beyond the first introduction of the appropriation of land and the accumulation of stock. It was at an end, therefore, long before the most considerable improvements were made in the productive powers of labour, and it would be of no purpose to trace farther what might have been its effects upon the recompence or wages of labour' (82–3).[8]

******

That real wages are 'tolerably' high in a private-property system notwithstanding an *inherently* unjust distribution of property and income – setting aside the passages which modify the harsh notion of 'oppressive inequality' – would be of little comfort if we take seriously the downplaying of material well-being with respect to happiness elaborated in the *Theory of Moral Sentiments* and occasionally in the *Wealth of Nations*: 'happiness and misery, which reside altogether in the mind, must necessarily depend more upon the healthful or unhealthful, the mutilated or entire state of the mind, than upon that of the body' (Smith 1976 [1776]: 787). Smithian cynicism is also apparent in a comment on the Corn Laws: 'The laws concerning corn may every where be compared to the laws concerning religion' – represented later in the book as 'more or less influenced by popular superstition and enthusiasm' (539, 793). 'The people feel themselves so much interested in what relates either to their subsistence in this life, or to their happiness in a life to come, that government must yield to their prejudices, and, in order to preserve the publick tranquility, establish that system which they approve of' (539). But these and similar remarks are wholly at odds with the notion that 'it is in the progressive state, while the society is advancing to the further acquisition, rather than when it has acquired its full complement of riches, that the condition of the labouring poor, of the great body of the people' – earning 'liberal' or 'high' real wages – 'seems to be the happiest and the most comfortable' (99).

We have found similar statements in *TMS* itself justifying the unwillingness of Bonar and Robbins to take very seriously the alleged discordance between wealth and happiness proposed by that work (above, p. 182). However a new rationale for inequality might seem to be introduced in Part VI, added in the 6th edition published in 1790 shortly before Smith's death (see Smith to Cadell, 31 March 1789, in Scott 1937: 309), touching on 'the greatly fortunate and the greatly unfortunate, the rich and the powerful, the poor and the wretched' (Smith 1976 [1759]: 226) but prioritizing stability over welfare:

> The distinction of ranks, the peace and order of society, are, in a great measure, founded upon the respect which we naturally conceive for the former. The relief and consolation of human misery depend altogether upon our compassion for the latter. The peace and order of society is of more importance than even the relief of the miserable ... Nature has wisely judged that the distinction of ranks, the peace and order of society, would rest more securely upon the plain and palpable difference of birth and fortune, than upon the invisible and often uncertain differences of wisdom and virtue.
>
> $(226)^9$

However, the *conditional* character of the secondary status accorded to welfare should be carefully noted. We have already encountered the proposition in *TMS* that '[a]ll constitutions of government ... are valued only in proportion as they tend to promote the happiness of those who live under them'. This takes on a striking urgency with the French Revolution under way, Smith recognizing that it is only in 'peaceable and quiet times' when '[t]he support of the established government seems evidently the best expedient for maintaining the safe, respectable, and happy situation of our fellow-citizens; when we see that this government actually maintains them in that situation' (231). By contrast, 'in times of public discontent, faction, and disorder ... even a wise man may be disposed to think some alteration necessary in that constitution or form of government, which, in its actual condition, appears plainly unable to maintain the public tranquility. In such cases ... it often requires, perhaps, the highest effort of political wisdom to determine when a real patriot ought to support and endeavour to re-establish the authority of the old system' – which considering the context implies severe inequality – 'and when he ought to give way to the more daring, but often dangerous spirit of innovation' (231–2). This remarkable allowance is consistent with the recognition in the *Lectures* of a right, under certain conditions, to resist established authority even if this implies the undermining of established inequalities (Smith 1978 [1762–3]: 320).

8.4 Distributive justice and reform proposals

The Smithian texts considered thus far indicate a willingness to tolerate the inequity of class distribution reflecting *'defalcations'* from labour's product, in large part on the grounds of the higher earnings earned by labour relative to those (theoretically) available in an egalitarian society where labour receives its entire product. I now turn to further qualifications to the approval of the private-property institution, which turn on the requirement that its operation be subjected to institutional reform including reforms playing on the distributive shares.

In the first place, Smith recommends direct transfers from 'rich' to 'poor' – intending from property to labour – objecting to various contemporary taxes on grounds of 'their inequality, an inequality of the worst kind, as they must frequently fall much heavier upon the poor than upon the rich' (Smith 1976 [1776]: 846). As a corrective he proposes reducing taxes on 'the wholesome and invigorating liquors of beer and ale' and the imposition of taxes on home-brewed liquors and beers, commonly produced by 'many middling and almost all rich and great families' (888–9, 891). He adds the indictment that '[i]t has probably been the interest of this superior order of people ... which has hitherto prevented a change of system that could not well fail both to increase the revenue and to relieve the people' (893). Commenting on road tolls Smith observes that 'a tax upon carriages in proportion to their weight, though a very equal tax when applied to the sole purpose of repairing the roads, is a very unequal one, when applied to any other purpose, or to supply the common exigencies of the state' (1976 [1776]: 728). But 'as the turnpike toll raises the price of goods in proportion to their weight, and not to their value, it is chiefly paid by the consumers of course and bulky, not by those of precious and light commodities. Whatever exigency of the state therefore this tax might be intended to supply, that exigency would be chiefly supplied at the expence of the poor, not of the rich; at the expence of those who are least able to supply it, not of those who are most able' (728). A further corrective entails the imposition of a disproportionately heavier road toll on luxury carriages than on freight wagons, in order that 'the indolence and vanity of the rich is made to contribute in a very easy manner to the relief of the poor, by rendering cheaper the transportation of heavy goods to all the different parts of the country' (725). The reduction in wage-goods prices here alluded to is reinforced by a proposal to grant a subsidy on coal transportation, coal being 'a necessary of life' as well as 'a necessary instrument of trade' (874). And the taxation of house rents is supported on distributional grounds, with account taken of the differential weighting of housing in the budgets of different classes and thus implied support for a degree of progression in taxation: 'A tax upon house-rents ... would in general fall heaviest upon the rich; and in this sort of inequality there would not, perhaps, be any thing very unreasonable. It is not very unreasonable that the rich should contribute to the publick expence, not only in proportion to their revenue, but something more than in proportion' (842). Maclean has summarized the matter by affirming that Smith's 'maxims of taxation warranted both progressive taxation and redistribution' (McLean 2007: 140–1).[10]

Apart from transfers from property to labour *via* the tax system a remarkably broad range of interventionist proposals would also work indirectly to labour's advantage. I allude first and foremost to Smith's striking case for *credit-market control*, manifested in support for Usury Laws, as a means of encouraging capital accumulation by closing off wasteful leakages of savings engendered by excessive risk taking (Hollander 2013: 23, 58–81). To the extent that accelerated accumulation is *particularly* beneficial to labour not only the absolute wage but also the wage share in national income will be increased, although of this we cannot be certain since Smith also maintains that the landowning class (as distinct from capitalists) has interests 'connected with the general interest of the society', insofar as rents rise with economic growth (Smith 1976 [1776]: 265).

The implications of an accelerated growth rate extend to market structure. Recall in particular one of the most celebrated declarations of the *Wealth of Nations* – that '[p]eople of the same trade seldom meet together, even for merriment and diversion, but the conversation ends in a conspiracy against the publick, or in some contrivance to raise prices' (Smith 1976 [1776]: 145), a lament applied to the labour market: 'whoever imagines ... that masters rarely combine, is as ignorant of the world as of the subject' and that 'in disputes with their workmen, masters must generally have the advantage' (84–5). It is notorious that Smith had his doubts as to what could be done directly to thwart conspiracy (145), but it is also certain that a rapid growth rate would tend to reduce elements of monopsony power and thereby raise the wage–profit share.

Reform of *internal and external trade laws* would also be to labour's advantage, thereby raising the wage–profit ratio. Although wage control at the national and county levels had been abandoned there were still attempts to regulate wages in particular trades and places, Smith observing that '[w]henever the legislature attempts to regulate the differences between masters and their workmen, its counselors are always the masters' (Smith 1976 [1776]: 157). Thus, recent legislation reinforced informal employer combinations to reduce the wage by fixing wage maxima (158). Various 'extortions' by cloth manufacturers from the legislature regarding foreign trade are similarly condemned in a passage introduced into the third edition of 1784, in a passage touched on above: 'They are as intent to keep down the wages of their own weavers, as the earnings of the poor spinners, and it is by no means for the benefit of the workman, that they endeavour either to raise the price of the compleat work, or to lower that of the rude materials. It is the industry which is carried on for the benefit of the rich and the powerful, that is principally encouraged by our mercantile system. That which is carried on for the benefit of the poor and the indigent, is too often, either neglected, or oppressed' (644). In other contexts, the focus is on the conduct of merchants and master-manufacturers directed against the 'general interest of the whole' or the 'publick' (144, 266–7). At the very least, legislation enhancing the advantage of employers over labour should be abandoned. In all this there can be no doubt of Smith's condemnation of employers' conduct on ethical, and not merely economic, grounds.

Removal of impediments to labour mobility created by the Corporation and Settlement Laws would similarly be to labour's benefit. For whereas '[t]he statute of apprenticeship obstructs the free circulation of labour from one employment to another, even in the same place', the 'exclusive privileges of corporations obstruct it from one place to another, even in the same employment', a form of obstruction relating 'to the labour of artificers and manufacturers only', that is to skilled labour (Smith 1976 [1776]: 151–2). Settlement laws were peculiar to England, consisting in 'the difficulty which a poor man finds in obtaining a settlement, or even being allowed to exercise his industry in any parish but that to which he belongs'. This matter – described as 'a disorder, the greatest perhaps of any in the police of England' – was of the highest ethical concern: 'To remove a man who has committed no misdemeanor from the parish where he chuses to reside, is an evident violation of natural liberty and justice' (157). Yet more forcefully:

> The property which every man has in his own labour, as it is the original foundation of all other property, so it is the most sacred and inviolable. The patrimony of a poor man lies in the in the strength and dexterity of his hands; and to hinder him from employing this strength and dexterity in what manner he thinks proper without injury to his neighbour, is a plain violation of this most sacred property. It is a manifest encroachment upon the just liberty both of the workman, and of those who might be disposed to employ him.
>
> (138).[11]

As we shall presently see, Smith ascribed part of the very problem of pauperism the system was intended to treat to the Corporation and Settlement Laws – especially the latter – by their impeding exit from contracting industries.

Much of what has been said by Smith applies also to the impact upon labour's wellbeing of the Statute of Apprenticeship, namely that it impeded transfer from declining to expanding industries generating pockets of unemployment which forced those affected either to have recourse to parish relief or accept minimum wages as unskilled labourers:

It frequently happens that while high wages are given to the workmen in one manufacture, those in another are obliged to content themselves with bare subsistence ... The linen industry ... can afford no general resource to the workmen of other decaying manufactures, who, wherever the statute of apprenticeship takes place, have no other choice but either to come upon the parish, or to work as common labourers, for which, by their habits, they are much worse qualified than for any sort of manufacture that bears any resemblance to their own. They generally, therefore, chuse to come upon the parish.

(Smith 1976 [1776]: 151–2).

Smith had in mind here *skilled* workers who are prevented from transferring to progressive industries and therefore are faced with the options of accepting unskilled work or going on relief, more likely choosing the latter.[12]

Working-class elementary education served, for Smith, as a means to enhanced earnings. For Smith recommended the partial finance by government of elementary schools, and that the state (as in Scotland) establish parish schools 'where children may be taught for a reward so moderate, that even a common labourer may afford it...' (Smith 1976 [1776]: 785). Now starting from an illiterate base, it is impossible to distinguish purely elementary from vocational training, so insofar as many workers initially received no, or very little, education, or education of a low quality, the introduction of adequate elementary training would tend to affect their ability to acquire specific skills. The economic advantages are clearly indicated in the elementary-school curriculum recommended, which included instruction in 'the principles of geometry and mechanics ... the necessary introduction to the most sublime as well as the most useful sciences' (786). All in all, state-supported education would enhance earnings and employment opportunities with positive effects on the real wage and perhaps on the wage share. Furthermore, the state's responsibility extends to countering the potentially stultifying effects of specialization, the danger being that the industrial worker would find it ultimately impossible to function 'in any other employment than that to which he has been bred' (782).[13]

8.5 Happiness and population size

As we have argued thus far, the index of social welfare for Smith is the *average wage*. Nonetheless, we have encountered the proposition of the *Theory of Moral Sentiments* whereby distribution, assuming private property, is fairer than it seems since no one is left out of the account, '[t]he produce of the soil maintain[ing] at all times nearly that number of inhabitants which it is capable of maintaining', presumably at a given subsistence wage. Here the *magnitude of population* rather than the *wage* is adopted as the index of social 'happiness' (cf. Viner 1968: 325).

This notion, apparently entailing adherence to the 'Greatest Happiness of the Greatest Number' in the *literal* sense of the expression, conflicts diametrically with the joint propositions in the *Wealth of Nations* that '[n]o society can surely be flourishing and happy, of which the far greater part of the members are poor and miserable' (Smith 1976 [1776]: 96; cited above, p. 175), while '[i]t is not the actual greatness of national wealth, but its continual increase, which occasions a rise on the wages of labour. It is not, accordingly, in the richest countries, but in the most thriving, or in those which are growing rich the fastest, that the wages of labour are highest' (87). Were population size the index of happiness, then China – 'long one of the richest, that is, one of the most fertile, best cultivated, most industrious, and *most populous* countries in the world' – would be ranked happiest, which for Smith is positively not the case (89–90; emphasis added).[14] We might be obliged to conclude that Smith must have altered his stance radically between 1759 and 1776, were it not for the assumption in the TMS account that Providence had so arranged matters to assure that the larger population enjoyed adequate real wages – Providence must have been unaware of the China case! – combined with the fact that the 1759 formulation is repeated in all editions including the last of 1790. It is nonetheless regrettable that Smith himself did not seek to avoid leaving even an impression of an 'Adam Smith problem' entailing the relation between his two primary works.[15]

8.6 Wage differentials

We have thus far been primarily concerned with *class distribution* and specifically Smith's identification of social happiness with the happiness of the labouring class as a whole. I turn now to Smith's explicit discussions of the wage structure.

In the Draft of 1763 the charge of inequity is extended from class distribution, and the 'defalcation' of income from labour's share, to *the distribution of the wages component itself*: 'The division of what remains too, after this enormous defalcation, is by no means made in proportion to the labour of each individual. On the contrary *those who labour most get least*' (Scott 1937: 327). This rule of thumb is applied to the 'Clerks and Accountants' of the 'opulent merchant'– who 'enjoy a much greater share of the produce, than three times an equal number of artizans, who, under their direction, labour much more severely and assiduously' – and thence to the 'poor labourers':

> The artizan again, tho' he works generally under cover, protected from the injuries of the weather, at his ease and assisted by the convenience of innumerable machines, enjoys a much greater share than the poor labourer who has the soil and the seasons to struggle with, and, who while he affords the materials for supplying the luxury of all other members of the common wealth, and bears, as it were, upon his shoulders the whole fabric of human society, seems himself to be pressed down below ground by the weight, and to be buried out of sight in the lowest foundations of the building.
>
> (327–8)

The important fact emerges that Smith sharply distinguishes here between the relatively high earnings of the artizan and those of 'poor labourers' who, incidentally, are identified with agricultural workers. As we shall now see, Smith in the *Wealth of Nations* recognizes, but does not exaggerate, the skilled–unskilled pay differential.

Considering the detailed attention the *Wealth of Nations* gives to the wage structure Smith could scarcely have countenanced a *strict* equality of pay; and in fact he expressly agreed that 'if all persons in the same kind of work were to receive equal wages, there would be no emulation, and no room left for industry or ingenuity' referring to one feature of the ancient Laws of Settlement (Smith 1976 [1776]: 157; citing Richard Burn 1764: 130). Indeed, he represents workers themselves as opposed to equal pay on motivational grounds: 'The complaint of the workmen, that it puts the ablest and most industrious upon the same footing with an ordinary workman, seems perfectly well founded' (158).

Now in elaborating '*Inequalities arising from the Nature of the Employments themselves*' Smith explores investment in training: 'The work which he learns to perform, it must be expected, over and above the usual wages of common labour, will replace to him the whole expence of his education, with at least the ordinary profits of an equally valuable capital', so that it was 'reasonable ... that in Europe the wages of mechanicks, artificers, and manufacturers should be somewhat higher than those of common labourers They are so accordingly... ' (1976 [1776]: 118–19).[16] Several empirical observations follow, one regarding the journeymen's daily or weekly earnings relative to those of common labour in the 'more common sorts of manufacture', with some allowance made for their steadier and more uniform employment, with Smith concluding that the differential is 'no greater than what is sufficient to compensate the superior expence of their education' (119); a second observation regards the [day] wages of a Newcastle pitman said to be generally double those of the labourer; and a third regarding the mason or bricklayer who received from 'one half more to double' those of his unskilled assistant (1976 [1776]: 120). Lindert and Williamson – drawing on Williamson 1982 – present *Estimates of Nominal Annual Earnings: Adult Males, England and Wales (in current £'s)* which confirm Smith's 'one half ... to double' ratio for two years that are relevant for us, namely 1755 and 1781 (Lindert and Williamson 1983: 4).

Smith allows that the daily or weekly pay differentials do not capture seasonal variation, and from the fact that 'no species of skilled labour ... seems more easy to learn than that of masons and bricklayers' it could be deduced that '[t]he high wages of those workmen ... are not so much the recompence of their skill, as the compensation for the inconstancy of their employment' (Smith 1976 [1776]: 120). Smith's appreciation that daily or weekly earnings data required supplementation by employment data is of high significance. While Deane and Cole indicate a daily money–wage differential over unskilled common labour in building of some 50% in favour of 'craftsmen' they make no allowance for the regularity of employment or number of hours worked (Deane and Cole 1967:

18–22). Lindert and Williamson (1983) seek to correct annual rates, usually based on daily or weekly data, for unemployment.

The professional class in Smith's analysis of the wage structure is treated as a category of skilled labour: 'Education in the ingenious arts and the liberal professions is still more tedious and expensive than those of mechanicks, artificers, and manufacturers. The pecuniary expense, therefore, of painters and sculptors, of lawyers and physicians, ought to be much more liberal: and it is so accordingly' (Smith 1976 [1776]: 119). But Smith's primary concern was with skilled industrial labour and specifically his objections to the apprenticeship laws that '[l]ong apprenticeships are altogether unnecessary. The arts, which are much superior to common trades, such as those of making clocks and watches, contain no such mystery as to require a long course of instruction' (139); indeed, '[t]here is scarce any common mechanick trade ... of which all the operations may not be as completely and distinctly explained in a pamphlet of a very few pages, as it is possible for words illustrated by figures to explain them' (143). And the ease of acquiring skills is further underscored by the Enlightenment view – shared with Hume – that '[t]he difference in natural talents in different men is, in reality, much less than we are aware of; and the very different genius which appears to distinguish men of different professions, when grown up to maturity, is not on many occasions so much the cause, as the effect of division of labour. The difference between the most dissimilar characters, between a philosopher and a common street porter, for example, seems to arise not so much from nature, as from habit, custom, and education' (28–9).[17] Nevertheless, all this is presumably a matter of degree since the discussion ends with mention of the 'respective talents' of 'the most dissimilar geniuses' (30). We have even encountered an allowance for differential 'capacity' in a justification of inequality (above, p. 184), and a lament that the settlement laws during downturns obliged skilled workers to either accept unskilled employment or, since this adjustment was usually found too difficult, to appeal to the parish (above, p. 193).

The reference to education reminds us of the case made for state funding of an elementary-school curriculum including 'the principles of geometry and mechanics ... the necessary introduction to the most sublime as well as the most useful sciences' (above, p. 193). Such a programme and also abolition of the Apprenticeship Laws would presumably go a long way towards reducing any *inordinate* superiority in the earnings of skilled relative to unskilled labour.

8.7 On the 'lower ranks' and the pauper population

Smith affirmed that – 'in every improved and civilized society' – 'the great body of the people' is composed of the 'labouring poor' (Smith 1976 [1776]: 782), a 'labourer' for Smith indicating specifically an *unskilled* worker.[18] Thus in his *Lectures* Smith asserted that '[t]he price of the work done by day labourers in time of peace when workmen are not scarce is very moderate in this country; I mean of such labours whose [exercise] requires no art but mere labour' (1978 [1762–3]: 192). The same usage is apparent in the *WN*, in fact in the very passage identifying social welfare with the welfare of the majority class – the 'lower ranks' – namely in Smith's response to the question whether the 'improvement in the circumstances of the lower ranks of the people [is] to be regarded as an advantage or as an inconveniency for the society': '[s]ervants, labourers and *workmen of different kinds*, make up the far greater part of every great political society' and '[n]o society can surely be flourishing and happy, of which the greater part of the members are poor and miserable' (above, p. 174). Here the distinction between mere 'labourers' and 'workmen of different kinds' is deliberate as is explicitly confirmed when Smith explains why 'labourers' are worse paid in Europe than 'mechanicks, artificers, and manufacturers'. Hume's 'Of Commerce' similarly refers to the 'common people' as wage recipients including skilled artisans as well as 'common' labourers, declaring that any damaging impact on foreign trade exerted by high wages 'is not to put in competition with the happiness of so many millions' (see Chapter 5, p. 126). (It is, however, my impression that Hume was rather more concerned than Smith with the very poorest – the paupers.)[19]

For both Smith and Hume, the objective of policy is thus to raise the real wages of the higher-paid skilled workers as well as simple 'labourers'. This needs to be appreciated since, as mentioned at the outset, Smith has been understood by some commentators as perceiving the purpose of the 'virtuous legislator' to be the improvement of 'the well being of the majority' where the majority is identified with the '*least advantaged*'. This view might be supported by the reference in TMS to one 'who bears on his shoulders the whole weight of mankind, and unable to sustain the load is buried by the weight of it and thrust down into the *lowest* parts of the earth, from whence he supports all the rest' (above, p. 185), and by Smith's quest to 'account for the great share and the *lowest of the people* have of the conveniencies of life'. This formulation seems even to imply that the *entire* class of propertyless workers is designated as the lowest and poorest, conflicting with the *Wealth of Nations*. There is, however, no necessary conflict, or evidence of a change of mind, if we appreciate that the question in TMS is posed rhetorically and should be understood in the context of affirming the exploitative character of property income as a 'defalcation', for which purpose there was no need to breakdown the constituent elements of those lacking property. It should at the same time be noted that proposed measures to raise the general wage would, at least in the long run, improve the lot of the unskilled at the bottom of the wage scale since relative wages are said to be unaffected by a general wage increase: 'The proportion between the different rates both of wages and profits in the different employments of labour and stock, seems not to be much affected ... by the riches or poverty, the advancing, stationary, or declining state of the society. Such revolutions in the publick welfare, though they affect the general rates both of wages and profit, must in the end affect them equally in all different employments' (Smith 1976 [1776]: 158–9; cf. 80).

Before proceeding further, we should note Smith's inclusion of 'servants' within the body of the 'lower ranks'. Gregory King's data of 1688 lacks an entry for the class of domestics, Deane and Cole drawing attention to the fact that '[t]he omission of the incomes of domestics is more serious if we want to make comparisons with later periods…' (Deane and Cole 1967: 1). Similarly, there is no such designation in the Massie data of 1759–60 or the Colquhoun data of 1803. But Smith's inclusion of the category is a mere formality since his discussion focuses on the so-called 'productive' sector – unskilled and skilled workers – presumably reflecting his standard presumption that unproductive or service workers are financed by a sort of transfer payment out of property income.

Although I am unconvinced that Smith identified the general workforce with the 'lowest of the people' the questions do arise as to precisely who Smith intended by the 'lowest' amongst those lacking property and what his attitude was towards them. We shall address these questions within a broader context regarding the structure of the propertyless class and the returns due to its various segments.

There can be no doubt that, for Smith, the unskilled outnumbered the skilled artisans, although it is unclear by how much. In calculating a general average of eighteenth-century money wages in the building sector, Deane and Cole give double weighting to a series relating unskilled *labourers* relative to skilled *craftsmen* (Deane and Cole 1967: 19). Lindert provides an estimate of the number of Household Heads in England and Wales for 1740 as follows: Industrial trades 245,000, Building trades 95,000, and Labourers and Paupers 572,000 (Lindert 1986: 1137–8). If the first two categories are identified with 'craftsmen' (as Lindert suggests) and we presume that 'labourers' refer to the unskilled, and neglect 'paupers' – a risky procedure indeed – we arrive at a ratio of unskilled to skilled of 1.66: 1, which is not too far distant from the rule of thumb used by Deane and Cole, (although Lindert himself notes especially the unreliability of data for 'labourers', and I would add the confusing combination of labourers with paupers). A comparison of the ratios of 'Labourers' to 'Artisans' – implying unskilled to skilled – in Gregory King's estimates of the Number of Families for 1688 and Patrick Colquhoun's estimates for 1803 yields a complete transformation from an overwhelming majority of unskilled in the workforce = 364,000: 60,000 = 6: 1 to a minority 380,000 [='laboring, people in mines, canals, etc' + 'laboring people in husbandry, including females']: 445,000 = 0.85:1 (see Perkin 1969: 20–1; Deane 1967: 8–9; Lindert and Williamson 1982: 400). What information was available to Smith presumably relates to a period when a quantitative transformation favouring skilled labour – assuming that so extraordinary an event actually occurred and is not a statistical mirage – would already be underway such that a 2:1 ratio of unskilled to skilled for his period cannot be excluded. (Massie's data confuses by comingling employers and employed under the designation of 'Master manufacturers'.)

We turn next to the wage differential between the unskilled and skilled, As for skilled workers, Smith's observation that '[w]here all other circumstances are equal, wages are generally higher in new than in old trades' is pertinent, for '[w]hen a projector attempts to establish a new manufacture, he must at first entice his workmen from other employments by higher wages than they can either earn in their own trades, or than the nature of his work would otherwise require, and a considerable time must pass away before he can venture to reduce them to the common level' (Smith 1976 [1776]: 131). This observation particularly pertains to skilled labour, as illustrated by the relatively high wages in Birmingham.[20] As to the pay scale itself, a complexity is raised in *WN* that '[w]hen the inconstancy of employment is combined with their hardship, disagreeableness and dirtiness of the work, it sometimes raises the wages of the most common labour above those of the most skilled artificers. A collier working by the piece is supposed, at Newcastle, to earn commonly about double, and in many parts of Scotland about three times the wages of common labour' (121).[21] We set aside such complexities and assume that, all things equal, the unskilled – constituting the majority of the workforce – are generally paid less than the skilled.

Although the general statement regarding the desirability of high wages refers to *all* categories of labour including skilled 'mechanicks, artificers, and manufacturers' as well as 'common labourers' can it perhaps be said that Smith nonetheless showed some preference for the majority comprising unskilled labourers? The passage from the Draft of *WN* encountered above expresses concern with a distortion in the wage scale against the poorest: 'The division of what remains too, after this enourmous defalcation, is by no means made in proportion to the labour of each individual. On the contrary *those who labour most get least* ... The artisan ... enjoys a much greater share than the poor labourer who ... bears, as it were, upon his shoulders the whole fabric of human society' (Scott 1937: 327). That the skilled artisan receives an *excessive* wage differential is also implied by the case made out against Apprenticeship laws which exaggerate the skill level typically required to be achieved by apprentices. But, paradoxically, a more sympathetic view is taken when Smith expresses his concern in *WN* that those same institutional constraints on mobility forced skilled artisans in declining trades either into the class of the unskilled or to a reliance on poor relief: 'wherever the statute of apprenticeship takes place, [those displaced in contracting industries] have no other choice but either to come upon the parish, or to work as common labourers, for which, by their habits, they are much worse qualified than for any sort of manufacture that bears any resemblance to their own. They generally, therefore, chuse to come upon the parish' (above, p. 193).

There is also the fact that Smith did not treat the unskilled category of labourers as an indistinguishable mass. As we have seen, he mentions £10 as the annual earnings of an unskilled labourer, but as Ashton emphasized, eighteenth-century wage earners were 'never ... a homogenous group' (1966: 217), and also to be noted is Smith's estimate that 'in every particular trade, the lowest common earnings may always be considered as those of the far greater number' (1978 [1762–3]: 121), with the term 'lowest common earnings' implying that the unskilled category is intended. That there was a range of earnings is confirmed when Smith writes in *WN* that 'the produce of the whole labour of the society is so great, *that all are often abundantly supplied,* and a workman, *even of the lowest and poorest order*, if he is frugal and industrious, may enjoy a greater share of the necessaries and conveniencies of life than it is possible for any savage to acquire' (above, p. 188). A further passage referring to '[t]he common complaint that luxury extends itself even *to the lowest ranks* of the people, and that *the labouring poor* will not now be contented with the same food, cloathing and lodging which satisfied them in former times' (1976 [1776]: 96; emphasis added) may perhaps be understood as *identifying* the 'labouring poor' with 'the lowest ranks' but suggests rather the lowest paid amongst 'poor' unskilled labourers.[22] The observation that the 'common people ... have little time to spare for education. Their parents can scarce afford to maintain them even in infancy. As soon as they are able to work, they must apply to some trade by which they can earn their subsistence' (784) also suggests the generality of workers as being at or very close to some minimum. But, as I shall explain, this perception does not accord well with the analysis of contemporary population growth which assumes above-subsistence wages for the labouring class as a whole in contrast to the lowest segment.

The latter perception emerges in the *Lectures* where Smith, discussing mortality rates, distinguishes 'the meaner and poorer sort, whose children are neglected and exposed to many hardships from the inclemencies of the weather and other dangers', from 'the better sort' (Smith 1978 [1762–3]: 193). The theme is elaborated in the *Wealth of Nations*:

> This great mortality ... will every where be found chiefly *among the children of the common people*, who cannot afford to tend them with the same care as those of better station. Though their marriages are generally more fruitful than those of people of fashion, a smaller proportion of their children arrive at maturity ... In civilized people it is only *among the inferior ranks of people* that the scantiness of subsistence can set limits to the further multiplication of the human species; and it can do so in no other way than by destroying a great part of the children which their fruitful marriages produce.
>
> (Smith 1976 [1776]: 97–8; emphasis added).

The terms '*among* the inferior ranks' and '*among* the children of the common people' suggest a sub-category of the poorest workers, *within* the general class of 'inferior ranks' or 'common people' and subject to particularly high infant mortality. This contrast between the *general* and the *lowest* wage is also implied by the assertion that 'though in disputes with their workmen, masters must generally have the advantage, there is however a certain rate below which it seems impossible to reduce, for any considerable time, the ordinary wages even of *the lowest species of labour*', which Smith – following the lead of Cantillon and Harris – defines as that real wage assuring an unchanged population, namely the subsistence wage of classical economics (85–6; emphasis added). This reading is further reinforced by the estimate that in contemporary Britain '[t]he real recompence of labour, the real quantity of the necessaries and conveniencies of life which it can procure to the labourer, has, during the course of the present century, increased perhaps in a still greater proportion than its money price ... [I]t is not the money price of labour only, but its real recompence, which has augmented' (95–6); and also with an extended demonstration that British population growth revealed wages to be 'evidently more than what is precisely necessary to enable the labourer to bring up a family', here identified with the 'lowest rate which is consistent with common humanity' (91; also 89). Although the excess did not compare with that of North America Britain is nonetheless classified as a moderately progressive state with the *general* wage above the minimum and, as mentioned, rising.[23] Smith's reading of British trends is similar to that given by Young 1774 in his general effort to counter claims of actual 'depopulation'.

Now Smith also affirms strongly that '[t]here are many plain symptoms that the wages of labour are *no-where* in this country regulated by [the] lowest rate which is consistent with common humanity' (Smith 1976 [1776]: 91; emphasis added). In some contexts he suggests that even the *poorest* can survive comfortably enough, although it is doubtful how seriously we should take this optimistic view considering the rhetorical context. I refer to the two extracts encountered earlier, in the *Lectures* regarding 'the great share ... the *lowest* of the people have of the conveniencies of life', and in *WN* regarding the circumstance that 'the produce of the whole labour of the society is so great, that all are often abundantly supplied, and a workman, even of *the lowest and poorest order*, if he is frugal and industrious, may enjoy a greater share of the necessaries and conveniences of life than it is possible for any savage to acquire'. In any event, these assertions conflict with the observation elsewhere that the operation of the Corporation Laws, Statute of Apprenticeship, and the Settlement Laws impeded transfers of labour from contracting to expanding industries thereby creating pockets of unemployment, the displaced either obliged to have recourse to parish relief or to '*content themselves with bare subsistence*'. Apparently, there are some who survive at the subsistence level even if the generality of the unskilled, and *a fortiori* the skilled, can earn above-subsistence wages. Recall too Smith's distinction in the *Lectures* when discussing mortality rates between 'the meaner and poorer sort' of worker 'whose children are neglected and exposed to many hardships' and 'the better sort'. Similarly there is an elaboration in the *Wealth of Nations* of the 'great mortality ... every where [to] be found chiefly among the children of the common people, who cannot afford to tend them with the same care as those of better station', all of which implies existence at the subsistence minimum. Only in 'foundling hospitals, and among the children brought up by parish charities' was the mortality 'still greater than among those of the common people' (Smith 1976 [1776]: 97) but abandonment of infants is in and of itself presumably an index of distress among the lowest strata of the 'common people'.

Thus far we have concluded that Smith's 'least advantaged' refers not to the mass of unskilled labourers but only to a sub-section thereof. But we can be yet more specific. His response to the question of whether the 'improvement in the circumstances of the lower ranks of the people [is] to be regarded as an advantage or as an inconveniency for the society', with its focus on 'servants, labourers, and workmen of different kinds', suggests a concern with the *employed*, although conceivably he silently allowed within these categories for those *temporarily* unemployed and therefore still part of the workforce. In the latter case any exclusion would be limited to the unemployable – truly the least fortunate in society – which would be surprising considering the data published by King (1688) and Colquhoun (1803) listing the Numbers of Families classified as 'Paupers, cottagers' as 400,000 and 260,179 respectively, the first estimate actually *exceeding* the 'Labouring People and Out Servants' (364,000), although the second falls slightly short (340,000) (Perkin 1969: 20–1). A further category is then to be added of 'Vagrants', given as 30,000 persons by King and as 234,000 by Colquhoun respectively. An order of this magnitude cannot be lightly dismissed. Where then did Smith stand regarding the truly lowest strata of society?

We cannot neglect the apologia advanced in *TMS* that even the beggar can survive happily; and a passage in the 1763 Draft of the *Wealth of Nations* suggesting that 'the very meanest person in civilized society' – presumably intending those on relief – is adequately provided for 'even in what we very falsely imagine, the easy and simple manner in which he is commonly accommodated' (Scott 1937: 325). There is an apparent satisfaction with the level of relief obtained by the needy under the parish system.[24] Himmelfarb rightly notes that Smith was not 'one of those who, in the years following the publication of the *Wealth of Nations*, expressed anxiety about the mounting costs of relief' (Himmelfarb 1984: 61). For Smith seems to deny there was a severe problem when he asserts that the demobilization of over one hundred thousand men with the peace of 1763 had been so easily accomplished that '[t]he number of vagrants was scarce anywhere sensibly increased by it, so far as I have been able to learn' (Smith 1976 [1776]: 470).[25] But although Smith presumably would have been aware of the three-fold increase in national poor relief expenditure between 1748/9 and 1783/5 from £689,971 to £1,943,649 recorded by officially recorded statistics (Rule 2014: 129) we can perhaps understand the apparent lack of urgency if Rule is right that '[b]efore the 1790s higher spending on poor relief, although it convinced many contemporaries that the incidence of poor relief was increasing, probably did not, except in particularly bad years, reflect much other than the increase in population and in food prices'. In any event, any concerns he might have had were mitigated by the expectation that problems of vagrancy and pauperism would at least partially resolve themselves should all the reforms he proposed be successfully undertaken. We may again refer to the representation of mercantilist regulation as entailing industry 'carried on for the benefit of the rich and the powerful' whereas that 'carried on for the benefit of the poor *and the indigent*, is too often, either neglected, or oppressed' (Smith 1976 [1776]: 644; emphasis added). Also suggesting that reform would mitigate the problem of indigence is the ascription to the Corporation and Settlement Laws –

especially the latter – of at least part of the very problem of pauperism that the relief system was intended to treat, and this by impeding exit from contracting industries: 'It frequently happens that while high wages are given to the workmen in one manufacture, those in another are obliged to content themselves with bare subsistence. The one is in an advancing state, and has, therefore, a continual demand for new hands: The other is in a declining state, and the super-abundance of hands is continually increasing' (151); and more generally: 'The scarcity of hands in one parish ... cannot always be relieved by the super-abundance in another ... [I]t is often more difficult for a poor man to pass the artificial boundary of a parish, than an arm of the sea or a ridge of high mountains' (156–7).[26] Accordingly: 'Let the same natural liberty of exercising what species of industry they please be restored to all his majesty's subjects, in the same manner as to soldiers and seamen ... so that a poor workman, when thrown out of employment in one trade or in one place, may seek for it in another trade or in another place' (470) rather than, it is implied, being forced to apply for parish relief.

The opinion expressed by Smith in 1790 that 'the peace and order of society is of more importance than even the relief of the miserable' (above, p. 189) does not imply the *rejection* of poor relief. Whatever Smith's expectations, Himmelfarb has rightly emphasized that when explaining his opposition to the Settlement Laws 'what Smith conspicuously did not do, was to challenge the poor law itself, the obligation to provide relief for those who could not provide for themselves (Himmelfarb 1984: 61). But Smith's further contention that 'the relief and consolation of human misery depend altogether upon our compassion' suggests charitable acts on the part of the public-spirited, including perhaps the parish, rather than the state. Hont and Ignatieff affirm that Smith looked solely to 'pity and compassion towards the unfortunate ... It was to this discretionary sentiment that [Smith and Hume] looked to the relief of the necessities of the poor in any emergency' (Hont and Ignatieff 1983: 24).

Elsewhere, Pack underscores the fact that '[n]owhere does [Smith] explicitly say that it is one of the functions of the state to aid the poor and indigent', which is '[i]n light of his concern for the poor ... quite a curious omission' (Pack 1991: 65). Pack promises, but does not provide, an explanation. We can only speculate upon Smith's attitude towards state responsibility for the unemployed and unemployable if 'pity and compassion' proved inadequate and the local authority unable to cope, as would have been the case if demobilization had proven overwhelming for the local services. I am prepared to venture a guess, basing myself on the extraordinary admission in 1790 that even revolution might be justified in dire circumstances (above, p. 190). If Smith was willing to go so far it would be reasonable to suppose that he would have seriously entertained measures by the state to accommodate the unemployed and unemployable not only on the grounds of justice but also to prevent unrest. After all, even Hayek, more recently, accepted the necessity for a safety net (Hayek 2007 [1944]: 148).

8.8 Summary and conclusion

Smith repeatedly represents the institution of private property as having an inherently exploitative character reflecting the 'defalcation' from wages. When discussing the *origin* of property, however, he adopts a far more positive perspective – emphasizing merit of some order, including effort, perhaps suggestive of the Lockean perspective. But the exploitative character ascribed to property income is seen to be an academic rather than a practical matter, in the sense that while it would be ideal were matters different, the facts of life dictated that in the absence of private property and with strict equality workers' living standards would be unacceptably low. Writing of J.S. Mill's famous Chapters on Property, Joseph Persky affirms that they were 'not Mill at his best' for he there adopts an abstract thought experiment to consider the usefulness of the institution setting out from an imaginary Eden and then seeking to reconcile property and equality, an exercise which 'does not produce a defense of private property as it exists in the real world' (Persky 2016: 69–70). Much of this might also be said of Smith who, it must be said, does not push the imaginary Eden very far.

Certainly, Smith did not accept the going pattern of income distribution as sacrosanct, his recommendations extending, albeit to a modest degree, to direct transfers from property to labour via the tax system. More conspicuous is his recommendation of state control of credit markets in an effort to encourage net accumulation to labour's advantage. And of course a primary practical purpose of the *Wealth of Nations* was to assure that markets operate efficiently by the weakening of institutional and legal impediments to growth and mobility, and of monopolistic and monopsonistic privileges – some of which would presumably involve measures requiring on-going state supervision to enforce – frequently with an eye to the wellbeing of the majority class. But Smith did not go beyond this, with his proposed correction of the distributional inequities of the prevailing system – including the 'progressive' taxation proposals – falling far short of a case *for equality*. It would be more accurate to say in fact that Smith presented a defence of the private-property institution *with its inevitable inequalities* and this even after the implementation of reforms to reduce their extent – on the grounds that it served as the best guarantee of economic development in the interest of the working classes, and also of cultural development. To summarize, there is the allusion to 'that usefull inequality in the fortunes of mankind which naturally and necessarily arises from the various degrees of capacity, industry, and diligence in the different individualls' (above, p. 184); the further justification that 'in the present state of things a man of a great fortune is rather an advantage than dissadvantage to the state, providing that there is a graduall descent of fortunes betwixt these great ones and others of the least and lowest fortune …' (p. 183); and even a representation of inequality as a necessary, and implicitly permanent, feature which seems to render the matter of unfairness academic: 'Law and government … seem to propose no other object but this, they secure the individual who has enlarged his property, that he may peaceably enjoy the fruits of it. By law and government all the different arts flourish, and that inequality of fortune to which they give occasion is sufficiently preserved' (Smith 1978 [1766]: 489).

While Smith viewed the contemporary pattern of relative wages as thoroughly unjust and requiring correction there can be no doubting his strong objections to 'equality' of pay as a general principle, on the grounds – citing Burn – that 'if all persons in the same kind of work were to receive equal wages, there would be no emulation, and no room left for industry or ingenuity' (above, p. 195). Workers themselves, he maintained, did not favour 'equality'. But what of the condition that inequality is justified provided there is 'graduall descent' from highest to lowest? This condition is applied formally to 'fortunes' from landed property, and nothing is reported regarding the wage structure in this context, while the twenty- or even thirty-fold differential between the lowest of property owners and the standard annual earnings of the common labourer is entirely passed by (at least by the student note-taker). Was this omission deliberate, or was it unintended and explicable by the context which involves historical parallels with ancient Rome? I can think of no good reason why the principle should not have been generalized; for even if a wage differential can be shown to reflect scarce talent of some order, public opinion might still find it unacceptable, which is no insignificant matter considering Smith's general view that the state is constrained in what it can do by what the public finds acceptable. Nevertheless, that all segments of the population portrayed a striking variety of earnings suggesting a generalized 'graduall descent' from highest to lowest, a fact often commented upon by modern social historians of the eighteenth century, should be taken into account.

There remains to consider a second condition for tolerating the inequality in incomes from (landed) property, in addition to that of 'graduall descent', namely the existence of *manufacturing* as an alternative option to the landless (above, p. 183). In principle, such opportunities would help to bridge the gap between earnings from labour and the 'fortunes' from landed property although there would doubtless be some overlap in the magnitude of returns from trade and from established landed property, especially since merchants are envisaged in the *Wealth of Nations* as being 'the best of all improvers' when they turn 'country gentlemen' (Smith 1976 [1776]: 411).

A fuller discussion would elaborate Smith's 'middling ranks' of society, including the observations in *TMS* regarding the 'patience, industry, fortitude, and application of thought' of a man of 'inferior rank' who wishes to advance in society, virtues not to be found among those born to 'rank and distinction' or to 'high stations' (Smith 1976 [1759]: 54–6). Although his focus here is upon the virtues required to achieve societal recognition and appointment to high administrative positions in government, Smith touches on the training to achieve these ends obtained in 'professional' activity and does not exclude commerce and manufacturing: 'He must acquire dependants to balance the dependants of the great, and he has no other fund to pay them from, but the labour of his body, and the activity of his mind. He must cultivate these therefore: he must acquire superior knowledge in his profession, and superior industry in the exercise of it…' (55).

I return now to the opening theme, namely Smith's utilitarian interest in the wellbeing of the largest class. Joseph Persky has recently demonstrated that J.S. Mill's reformism, extending to equality and fairness, derived from his utilitarianism in a 'coherent' manner, and that more was entailed than *ad hoc* value judgments that might also be maintained by *non-utilitarians* appealing directly to allegedly self-evident natural rights and the like (Persky 2016). In Smith's case the 'coherence' of his position, as I see it, relates to the justification of the *inequality* inherent in the private-property system as a necessary condition for economic and cultural development, such that even the 'natural right' of labour to which we referred at the outset – regarded by some as conflicting with utilitarianism – is merely an application of a view of property-in-general as an assurance of progress.

The difference between Mill and Smith regarding the character of the 'general good' is manifest in the fact that whereas Mill's *ideal* was the replacement of capitalistic organization by industrial co-operation and profit-sharing as a means towards enhanced equality and fairness, Smith accepted the 'exploitative' private-property system as a fact of life and did not explore the possibility of an alternative. Even his view of the system as essentially unfair insofar as labour did not receive the entire product was limited to a high level of abstraction and not even consistently maintained insofar as the acquisition of property is at times attributed to talent and effort. And, notwithstanding the hesitant allowances he makes for progressive taxation, he did not focus on the *share* of wages in national income but emphasized the absolute advantage reaped by labour from the system, subject of course to elimination by state intervention of institutional arrangements preventing the working classes from obtaining 'tolerable' real wages.

I reiterate here that it is the welfare of the working classes as a whole as index of social welfare – apart from cultural benefits – rather than specifically the lowest paid, as is sometimes suggested, that was Smith's primary concern. I certainly do not intend to affirm by this a *disinterest* with the lowest paid of the unskilled, for any such view conflicts with his ascription of responsibility for much of labourers' poverty to going institutions. Similarly, with respect to pauperism, while Smith does not exaggerate the poverty problem, expecting that it would be assuaged by institutional reform, he by no means proposed the abolition of poor relief. As for Mill, the complaint is often that he actually abandoned the lowest paid in favour of an elite amongst the workers. This charge cannot be substantiated. In his quest for distributive justice Mill was guided by the Smithian wage–structure analysis freed from institutional distortion (Hollander 2015: 204).

Turning now to the matter of pay differentials there is here a difference between Smith and Mill, that whilst the latter – in representing his ideal – objected, on grounds of justice, to differentials reflecting fortuitous differences in both mental and physical ability (Persky 2016: 206; Hollander 2015: 204–6), Smith downplayed his 'Enlightenment' denial of differential native talent *even as an ideal* objecting only to an exaggerated perception of them enforced by European apprenticeship regulations. Smith comes closer to Marx who, when discussing his future labour-certificate scheme, insisted against the Party Programme of 1875 that such differentials were *fully justified*: 'But one man is superior to another physically or mentally and so supplies more labour in the same time, or can work for a longer. time; and labour, to serve as a measure, must be defined by its duration or intensity ... This *equal* right is an unequal right for unequal labour ... *It is, therefore, a right of inequality*' (Marx 1989 [1875]: 86).

It may be of interest to speculative briefly regarding Smith's likely attitude towards the protests in our day against the 'obscenity' of vast earnings paid out to CEO's relative to the average of employees of their corporations, (a complaint recently extended to the higher administrators of British universities). If Smith's condition of 'graduall descent' from highest to lowest is generalized to incomes from all sources – and we have seen that this indeed was the eighteenth-century pattern – it would follow that he would have raised objections to payments of the order with which we are now familiar insofar as this condition is not satisfied. He would moreover certainly be suspicious of any exaggerated rationale turning on the uniqueness of those *favoured by nature* with the requisite managerial and entrepreneurial skills and responsibility for raising the company's (or the University's) profitability. This all the more so considering his famous perception of capitalists as an unreliable order when it comes to the public interest: 'The interest of the dealers ... in any particular branch of trade or manufactures, is always in some respects different from, and even opposite to, that of the publick' (Smith 1976: [1776]: 267). The matter is further complicated by the fact that Smith took public opinion seriously, which tends to find major differentials, where conspicuously discrete, to be objectionable even where they can perhaps be rationalized. Possibly he would be more tolerant of the argument that the differential reflected years of business-school training, but he would presumably wish to explore the source of finance behind such a long course of study – whether, for example, it reflected parental or state resources, and if the latter the obligation of the recipient to the taxpayer.

Notes

1 Rasmussen has recently elaborated Smith's concern that 'extreme economic inequality leads people to sympathize more fully and readily with the rich than the poor, and this distortion in our sympathies in turn undermines both morality and happiness' (Rasmussen 2016: 342; also 347–51).
2 It is of biographical interest that in 1763 Smith accepted a salary of £300 as travelling tutor of the Duke of Buccleugh (Rae 1895: 165).
3 King's estimate (1688) for the highest earning category of 'Peers' or 'Temporal lords' is only £2,800 per family and Colquhoun's estimate (1803) £8,000 (Perkin 1969: 20–1); Massie however has a figure of £20,000 for 1759–60 which Mathias finds 'more apposite' (Mathias 'The Social Structure...' 1957: 37, 42); see also Table 3 in Lindert and Williamson 1982: 396
4 The annual income per family is given by King (1688) as £15, for 'Labourers' or 'Labouring People and Out Servants', by Massie (1759–1760) as £12 10s. for

'country labourers' and £22 10s. for 'London labourers', and by Colquhoun (1803) as £31 for 'laboring people in husbandry (including females); as for 'Artisans' or 'Artizans and Handicrafts', £40 and £55 are the respective figures for King and Colquhoun (see Perkin 1969: 20–1; Wilson 1965: 239; Mathias 1957: 42–3; Lindert and Williamson 1982: 396). Massie lists £40 for both the lowest category of 'master manufacturers' and of 'tradesmen' and these may be the closest we come to 'artisans and handicrafts'. Waller's *General Description of All Trades* records the wages of a journeyman – one who has passed his apprenticeship – as ranging from £10 to £40 annually for those working for an Apothecary, from £20 to £30 in Birmingham hardware, from £50 to as much as £200 in Brewing, from £10 to £20 in School mastering, and from £20 to £30 in Tin Plate working (Waller 1747: 3, 18, 34–5, 187, 208).

5 An editorial note has it that 'Smith's explanation of the right acquired by occupation seems to be intended as an alternative to Locke's explanation', providing an unfortunately all-too-brief explanation for this opinion. In their Introduction the editors assert yet more strongly that Smith's account is 'evidently intended to be an alternative to a celebrated argument of Locke' (*33*). For an elaboration of the alleged disaccord between Smith's account and that of Locke, see Winch 1978: 58–9, 89–90.

6 Cf. Hume: 'Where the riches are in few hands, these must enjoy all the power and will readily conspire to lay the whole burthen on the poor' (see above Chapter 5, p. 126).

7 Although Smith sets out by explaining that it is in the shepherd stage of the celebrated four stages of progress when inequality of possessions creates new sources of subordination, the proposition in question appears to be generalized.

8 Other advantages of property-based commercial society are well analysed by Winch 1978: 93f.

9 Highly interesting is Boswell's account in 1773 of Samuel Johnson's reconciliation of his support for 'inequality and subordination with wishing well to the happiness of all mankind, who might live so agreeably, had they all their portions of land, and none to domineer over another' (Boswell 1999: 364). It is that 'mankind are happier in a state of inequality and subordination. Were they to be in this pretty state of equality, they would soon degenerate into brutes ... Sir, all would be losers, were all to work to all [sic]: they would have no intellectual improvement. All intellectual improvement arises from leisure: all leisure arises from one working for another'.

10 The reference to the 'vanity of the rich' suggests a qualitative rationale for income redistribution rather than Hume's quantitative rationale more akin to the principle of diminishing marginal utility: 'wherever we depart from ... equality, we rob the poor of more satisfaction than we add to the rich'; redistribution in favour of greater equality 'diminishes much less from the *happiness* of the rich than it adds to that of the poor' (see Chapter 5, pp. 125-6).

11 For an excellent account of the Law of Settlement and its dependency for enforcement on the Vagrancy Laws, and the replacement by 1720 of parish relief in the form of provision of materials for the able-bodied by a workhouse system, (see Fay 1964: 336–87).

12 Smith's qualifying remark 'wherever the statute of apprenticeship takes place' is significant. Lipson maintained that by Smith's day the system imposed by the Statute 'was not in general operation' (Lipson 1931: 263; also 290–1).

13 On this matter, see Fay 1964: 9.

14 But aggregate wealth does have significance for Smith from the perspective of national power (Smith 1976 [1776]: 372).

15 The lectures of 1762-3 also imply that significance is accorded a large population. I have in mind a case relating to 'a man of an overgrown or large estate' who 'we are apt to conceive of ... at first sight as a monster who destroys what might afford subsistence for *a vast number of the human species*', but who is in fact 'in no way prejudiciall to society but rather of advantage to it' Smith (1978 [1762–3]: 194;

emphasis added). The 'advantage' does not, however, entail the direct distribution of food but the indirect effect on manufacturing activity, as '[t]he produce of his estate' being 'wrought up to be worth altogether 1000 times its originall value. It will not however support more men than before; the rich man has not that effect. But he gives occasion to a greatly [sic] of work and manufacturing, such as is necessary to raise so much in its value' (195). This perspective is in line with Smith's objection to Agrarian Laws wherein a substantial manufacturing sector exists.

16 This is confirmed by Massie's data for 1759–60 (Rule 2014: 166); Matthias 1957: 43.
17 For a discussion of social bifurcation arising from the degrading effects of 'division of labour' at the plant level, see Hollander 1973: 214–5, 266.
18 In analyzing the origins of modern English society, Harold Perkin has posited that '[a]t the base of the [social] pyramid stood the "labouring Poor", the labourers, cottagers, seamen and soldiers, paupers and vagrants, with no property or special skill to shield them from the pressures of the daily struggle for existence. These amounted in 1688 to over half, in 1803 to over a third of the population, and received (apart from poor relief, charity, dishonest gains and other transfer payments), about one fifth (20.7 percent) and about one-sixth (16.5 percent) of the national income respectively' (Perkin 1969: 19–22). Here the 'labouring poor' excludes skilled artisans but includes paupers and vagrants.
19 A passage in Wallace 1758 raises a complexity relating to contemporary usage. Wallace refers to 'merchants, farmers, and artisans' as the 'inferior ranks' or 'commons' comprising 'the *whole* body of the people' omitting entirely *unskilled labour* unless they are included within 'farmers' which term seems rather to refer to small land owners: 'The gentlemen of this kingdom, no doubt, deserve great regard; but a greater regard still is due to the *whole* body of the people. The commons, consisting of merchants, farmers, and artisans, are indeed the glory of England' (Wallace 1758: 147). Now Wallace's silence regarding unskilled labour, if deliberate, would suggest he intended by the 'commons' a sort of middle-class – the inclusion of artisans implies perhaps an extension to lower middle-class – suggestive of fully-fledged mercantilism. On the other hand, Eden 1797 identifies the 'poor' with the 'labouring classes' while dealing most extensively with the *pauper* category.
20 See Ashton regarding impressive increases in the first half of the century in the money-wage rates paid unskilled labour in Lancashire and London, and his surmise, on Smithian lines, regarding the rapidity of increases in artisanal wages in industrially advancing areas such as Birmingham and the industrial north (Ashton 1966: 232).
21 In the Glasgow lectures the high wages of Scotch colliers and salters relative to their English counterparts are interpreted as compensation for their dislike of 'the vestiges of slavery', referring to conditions of bondage attached to those occupations (Smith 1978 [1762–3]: 191). John Millar argued similarly and provided wage data confirming Smith's position (Millar 1771: 238–40). For a general discussion of 'slavery' in the Scottish mines, see Viner 1965: 109–16.
22 John however understands contemporary complaints regarding 'luxury' as applying to English craftsmen and artisans rather than the unskilled (John 1962: 373).
23 Smith's account of rising *real* wages is considered accurate by John 1962: 365–6. Other evaluations are more complex. Gilboy's famous indices of real-wages in London and Lancashire show a slight rise for the first half of the century, then a decline for London but another sharp rise for the North (Gilboy 1936: 139, 141). The account by Deane and Cole, limited to the building trades in London, Kent, Oxfordshire, and Lancashire, record rising real wages in the 1720s and 1730s 'by amounts ranging from 10 per cent in the case of labourers in the southern rural districts to 45 percent or more for both labourers and craftsmen in the North'; the trend in the following two decades is 'generally downward' although the gains were not completely erased by 1760 in London, unlike in the rural South, whereas in the North real wages renewed their increase in the 1760s (Deane and Cole 1967: 21).

Wrigley and Schofield similarly suggest a downward real-wage trend after mid-century lasting for about a half century (Wrigley and Schofield 1981: 408, 432). Lindert and Williamson record a sharper fall in adult male real-wage trends 1755–1781 in the case of artisans than those of a 'middle group' of workers and 'farm labourers' (Lindert and Williamson 1983: 12); the former trend continues into the early years of the next century, but is reversed in the last two cases after 1781. Population trends are perceived as clearer: 'Taking the century as a whole … there were two periods in the eighteenth century in which the rate of population growth tended to accelerate, one from 1740 to 1760 and the other from 1780 onwards … It is reasonably certain that the rate of growth of English population accelerated markedly somewhere about the middle of the eighteenth century…' (Deane and Cole: 6–7; Wrigley and Schofield: 408).

24 King 1688 and Colquhoun 1803 ascribed respectively to 'Cottagers and Paupers' a yearly income per family of £6.10s. and £16.8s. which should be compared with Smith's estimate of £10 for unskilled labourers (Perkin 1969: 21–2).

25 Released servicemen enjoyed the special privilege 'to exercise any trade, within any town or place of great Britain or Ireland', and the same liberty created by abolition of the Settlement Laws should imply that 'neither the publick nor the individuals will suffer much more from the occasional disbanding some particular classed of manufacturer, than from that of soldiers' (Smith 1976 [1776]: 470–1).

26 Workers themselves, Smith observed, did not appreciate the damage to their interests created by the Settlement Laws (Smith 1976 [1776]: 157).

References

Ashton, T.S. 1966. *An Economic History of England: The 18th Century*. London: Methuen.
Bonar, J. 1922. *Philosophy and Political Economy*, 3rd edition. London: George Allen & Unwin.
Boswell, J. 1999. *The Life of Samuel Johnson*. Ware, Herts: Wordsworth Editions Limited.
Burn, R. 1764. *The History of the Poor Laws: With Observations*: London: Woodfall and Strahan.
Deane, P. 1967. *The First Industrial Revolution*. Cambridge: Cambridge University Press.
Deane, P. and W.A. Cole. 1967. *British Economic Growth 1688–1959: Trends and Structure*Cambridge: Cambridge University Press.
Eden, F. (1797). *State of the Poor: or, An History of the Labouring Classes in England*. London: J. Davis.
Fay, C.R. 1964. *Great Britain from Adam Smith to the Present Day: An Economic and Social Survey*, 5th ed. London: Longmans.
Gilboy, E.W. 1936. 'The Cost of Living and Real Wages in Eighteenth Century England', *Review of Economic Statistics* 18(3): 134–143.
Hanley, R.P. 2009. *Adam Smith and the Character of Virtue*. Cambridge: Cambridge University Press.
Hayek, F.A. 2007 (1944). *The Road to Serfdom: Texts and Documents*, ed. Bruce Caldwell. Chicago: University of Chicago Press.
Himmelfarb, G. 1984. *The Idea of Poverty: England in the Early Industrial Age*. New York: Knopf Alfred A.
Hollander, S. 1973. *The Economics of Adam Smith*. Toronto: University of Toronto Press.
Hollander, S. 2013. *Collected Essays/ IV. Essays on Classical and Marxian Political Economy*. London and New York: Routledge.
Hollander, S. 2015. *John Stuart Mill: Political Economist*. Singapore: World Scientific.
Hont, I. and M. Ignatieff. 1983. *Wealth and Virtue: The Shaping of Political Economy in the Scottish Enlightenment*. Cambridge: Cambridge University Press.

John, A.H. 1962. 'Aspects of English Economic Growth in the First Half of the Eighteenth Century', in *Essays in Economic History*, 2nd ed. E.M. Carus-Wilson. London: Edward Arnold: 360–373.
Levy, D. 2001. *How the Dismal Science Got Its Name*. Ann Arbor: University of Michigan Press.
Lindert, P.H. 1986. 'Unequal English Wealth Since 1670', *Journal of Political Economy* 94(6): 1127–1162.
Lindert, P.H. and J.G. Williamson. 1982. 'Revising England's Social Tables 1688–1812', *Explorations in Economic History* 19: 395–408.
Lindert, P.H. and J.G. Williamson 1983. 'English Workers' Living Standards During the Industrial Revolution: A New Look, *The Economic History Review* 36: 1–25.
Lipson, E. 1931. *The Economic History of England 3*. London: A.& C. Black.
Marx, K. 1989 (1875). 'Critique of the Gotha Programme'. *Marx–Engels Collected Works* 24: 81–99.
Mathias, P. 1957. 'The Social Structure in the Eighteenth Century: A Calculation by Joseph Massie', *Economic History Review* 10(1): 30–45.
McLean, I. 2007. *Adam Smith, Radical and Egalitarian: An Interpretation for the Twenty-first Century*. London: Palgrave Macmillan.
Mill, J.S. 1969 (1852). 'Whewell on Moral Philosophy', *Collected Works of John Stuart Mill*10th ed. J.M. Robson. Toronto: University of Toronto Press: 165–201.
Millar, J. 1771. *Observations Concerning the Distinction of Ranks in Society*. London: J. Murray.
Mingay, G.E. 1963. *English Landed Society in the Eighteenth Century*. London: Routledge and Kegan Paul.
Pack, S.J. 1991. *Capitalism as a Moral System: Adam Smith's Critique of the Free Market Economy*. Aldershot: Edward Elgar.
Perkin, H. 1969. *The Origins of Modern English Society: 1780–1889*. London: Routledge and Kegan Paul.
Persky, J. 2010. 'Rawl's Thin (Millian) Defense of Private Property', *Utilitas* 22: 134–147.
Persky, J. 2016. *The Political Economy of Progress: John Stuart Mill and Modern Radicalism*. Oxford: Oxford University Press.
Rae, J. 1895. *The Life of Adam Smith*. London: Macmillan.
Rasmussen, D.C. 2016. 'Adam Smith on What is Wrong with Economic Inequality', *American Political Science Review*, 110(2): 342–352.
Rawls, J. 2001. *Justice as Fairness: A Restatement*, ed. Erin Kelly. Cambridge: Harvard University Press.
Robbins, L.C. 1961. *The Theory of Economic Policy in English Classical Political Economy*. London: Macmillan.
Robbins, L.C. 1968. *The Theory of Economic Development in the History of Economic Thought*. London: Macmillan.
Rule, J. 2014. *Albion's people: English Society 1714–1815*. London: Routledge.
Schliesser, E. 2008. 'The Measure of Real price', in S. Peart and D. Levy (eds). *The Street Porter* 2008: 228–235
Scott, W.R. 1937. *Adam Smith as Student and Professor*. Glasgow: Jackson.
Smith, A. 1976 [1759]. *The Theory of Moral Sentiments*, edited by David D. Raphael and A.L. Macfie. Oxford: Clarendon Press.
Smith, A. 1976 [1776]. *An Inquiry into the Nature and Causes of the Wealth of Nations*, edited by R.H. Campbell, A.S. Skinner and W.B. Todd. Oxford: Clarendon Press.

Smith, A. 1978 (1762–1763) Report of 1762–1763, *Lectures On Jurisprudence*, eds. R.L. Meek, D.D. Raphael, and P.G. Stein. Indianapolis: Oxford: Clarendon Press, 45–394.

Smith, A. 1978 (1766). Report of 1766. *Lectures on Jurisprudence* eds. R.L. Meek, D.D. Raphael and P.G. Stein. Oxford: Clarendon Press: 395–554.

Smith, A. 1967 [1795]. *Essays on Philosophical Subjects in The Early Writings of Adam Smith*, edited by J. Ralph Lindgren. New York: Kelley: 29–223

Stigler, G.J. 1982 (1981). 'The Economist as Preacher', *The Economist as Preacher and Other Essays*. Chicago: University of Chicago Press: 3–13.

Viner, J. 1965. 'Guide to John Rae's *Life of Adam Smith*'. Introduction to John Rae, *Life of Adam Smith*. New York: Kelley: 5–145.

Viner, J. 1968. 'Adam Smith', *International Encyclopaedia of the Social Sciences* 14:322–329.

Wallace, R. 1758. *Characteristics of the Present Political State of Great Britain*. London: A. Millar.

Waller, T. 1747. *A General Description of All Trades*. London: Waller.

Williamson, J.G. 1982. 'The Structure of Pay in Britain, 1710–1911', *Research in Economic History* 7: 1–54.

Wilson, C. 1965. *England's Apprenticeship 1603–1763*. London: Longman

Winch, D. 1978. *Adam Smith's Politics: An Essay in Historiographic Revision*. Cambridge: Cambridge University Press.

Wrigley, E.A. and R.S. Schofield. 1981. *The Population History of England 1541–1871* Cambridge: Harvard University Press.

Young, J.T. 2018. 'Justice, Equity and Distribution: Adam Smith's Answer to Rawl's Difference Principle', eds. M. Knoll, S. Snyder and N. Simsek eds. *New Perspectives on Distributive Justice*. Berlin: De Gruyter: 505–522.

Part 4
Jeremy Bentham

Part 1

Jeremy Bentham

9 Bentham, utilitarian ethics and distributive justice

9.1 Introduction

Jacob Viner has affirmed that it was the ethics of moral leaders who were to attempt to influence legislators that mainly concerned Bentham rather than the ethics of the ordinary man (Viner 1958: 310). Robson in *The Improvement of Mankind* maintained that the priority Jeremy Bentham accorded to self-regarding over social motives implied for him 'the rejection of progress in individual morality, as commonly understood, for while reason can improve the individual's chances of success in the world, such improvement is not moral, and is certainly not without a final and not far-distant term … [F]or Bentham the agent's intentions and habitual behaviour are studied only so that they may be controlled' (Robson 1968: 13). The same heavy weighting accorded to 'rational selfishness' is attributed to Bentham by Riley (2016), on the basis of which Riley finds it difficult to understand 'why individuals will cooperate to construct a social code of equal rights instead of sacrificing one person's vital interests to promote the good of others' or what motivates reformers to pursue equal justice. Riley contrasts Bentham's position thus envisaged with 'Mill's enlarged utilitarianism' which 'also assigns importance to the cultivation of higher moral and aesthetic sentiments' – sentiments 'associated with higher kinds of pleasure' – and allows 'that humans can develop ideal virtuous characters'. Bentham, so the argument runs, 'does not recognize higher qualities of pleasant feelings in Mill's sense. Instead, for him, utilities are homogeneous in quality and differ only in terms of quantity such as intensity or duration'; or again: Bentham ignored the 'higher moral and aesthetic sentiments as motives', thereby missing 'the importance for general happiness of the individual's cultivation of a noble individuality'.[1] A related contrast between Bentham and Mill discerned by Riley is that Bentham represents 'security' solely in terms of rights versus 'malefactors' and '[abuses of] government' (1838–43 [1827]: 522), but not as protection of '*self-regarding* liberty and individuality' as it was regarded by Mill. The contrast perceived is between '*political liberty*' and '*personal liberty*'. It followed, Riley concluded, that an interpretation of justice as a basic right to security broadly perceived (as in Hollander 2015: 42) serves only for Mill but not for Bentham who 'does not explicitly defend rights of self-regarding liberty and individuality of the sort Mill defends in *On Liberty*'.

I find these alleged contrasts questionable. I shall demonstrate the positive role Bentham – no less than Smith or Hume – accorded to *motivation* in ethical evaluation; the allowances his 'utilitarianism' gave for *ethical progress* as entailing an enhancement of other-regarding motivation; and his notion of justice as a basic right to 'security' encompassing the *protection of personal liberty and individuality*.

As in my investigation of Smith I shall look closely at Bentham's perspective regarding the equality question, particularly his preference for stating the desideratum of policy to be the reduction of inequalities subject to the avoidance of damage to real incomes. Here we shall find that 'justice' features in the account without conflict with the overall utility maximand.

Sections 9.2 and 9.3 provide evidence of the importance for Bentham of benevolent motivation in according ethical credit. Considering Bentham's designation of benevolence or sympathy as ethical sentiments of a higher order, it is apparent how far removed his system is from the simple-minded 'reductionism' often attributed to it, and how questionable the commonly alleged contrast between Humean and Benthamite Utilitarianism is, the latter identified with James Mill's version. I note here the weight accorded by the editors of the modern *Collected Works* version of 'sympathy' in *Deontology* (1834): 'Although some elements of his discussion of sympathy in the theoretical part of the *Deontology* are to be found in *An Introduction to the Principles of Morals and Legislation* [1789], the later work contains a more fully developed thesis about its role in the moral life of the individual' (Bentham 1783: xxi). (The editors also discern an alteration in weighting in Bentham's informal notes after 1814.) While much is said of other-regarding sentiment in *Deontology*, Bentham's allowances in earlier works should not be played down and my case will largely turn on the *Principles of Morals and Legislation* and *A Table of the Springs of Action* (1817).

Section 9.4 proceeds to Bentham's evaluation of prospects for ethical progress. Bentham's stance with respect to self-regarding liberty and individuality follows in Section 9.5. A further issue, treated in 9.6, is that of Distributive Justice with particular reference to economic equality. We shall find that Bentham expresses himself firmly against equality in the strict sense ascribable to 'levelling' systems, while at the same time he recommends reducing inequalities if this is achievable without damage to national output and real incomes. An outstanding feature is his opposition to significantly *discrete* income differentials, a position maintained earlier by Smith.

9.2 On benevolent motivation

By way of background to the main theme I first note the remark in 1789 that the fallacious principle opposed to utility – designated as 'sympathy and antipathy' – which maintained in effect 'approbation or disapprobation as a sufficient reason for itself, disclaiming the necessity of looking out for any extrinsic ground' (Bentham 1982 [1789]: 28), extended from morals to politics: 'If a man is an infallible judge of what is right and wrong in the actions of private individuals, why not in the measures to be observed by public men in the direction of such actions? ... I have more than once known the pretended law of nature set up in legislative debates, in opposition to arguments derived from the principle of utility'. Surprising as it may seem, Bentham did not positively deny that there might be 'other considerations than those of utility [from which] we derive our notions of right and wrong', namely 'a moral sentiment ... originally conceived from any other source than a view of utility' – this was in fact a position Smith maintained against Hume – 'I do not know: I do not care' he declared. But he maintained that there was a moral 'duty' – appealing, ironically perhaps, to some *extra-utilitarian* reference point? – to avoid basing practical evaluations, whether relating to individuals or the community, upon essentially *speculative* considerations rather than upon utility. He was even prepared to allow that a defective 'moral sense' or 'natural equity' perspective in practical applications, as in the case of penal justice, frequently generated 'dictates' which 'coincide with those of utility' (29). (This we shall later see was also observed by John Stuart Mill.) In all events, Bentham did not object to the notion of a moral sense if defined to recommend the public good.

The principle of 'aestheticism' is listed as opposed to that of utility, but in the special sense that while it 'approves or disapproves of any action according to the tendency which it appears to have to augment or diminish the happiness of the party whose interests are in question', it does so 'in the adverse manner: approving of actions in as far as they tend to diminish his happiness; disapproving of them in as far as they tend to augment it' (Bentham 1982 [1789]: 17–18). The so-called '*theological* principle', or 'that principle which professes to recur for the standard of right and wrong to the will of God', entailed no 'distinct principle' since the scriptural texts required interpretation and interpretation entailing appeal to 'some other standard': 'We may be perfectly sure, indeed, that whatever is right is conformable to the will of God: but so far is that from answering the purpose of showing us what is right, that it is necessary to know first whether a thing is right, in order to know from thence whether it is conformable to the will of God' (31).

We note also the important admission that the greatest-happiness principle itself is not susceptible to direct proof: 'that which is used to prove every thing else, cannot itself be proved: a chain of proofs must have their commencement somewhere' (Bentham 1982 [1789]: 13). The general rule in brief was a postulate, a value judgment in effect (see Robbins 1970: 80). The axiomatic character of the general-good did not, however, preclude differences between adherents at any time, and changes over time, regarding its specific content. Who or what, for example, to include within the maximand? Bentham, for example, hoped that 'the day *may* come when the rest of the animal creation may acquire those rights which never could have been withheld from them but by the hand of tyranny' (1982 [1789]: 283n). That the axiom must itself be fleshed out, certainly implies recourse to *value judgment*. Moreover, there were, Bentham again observed, many who rejected the postulate while actually using it, their arguments proving 'not that the principle is *wrong*, but that, according to the applications ... to be made of it, it is *misapplied*' (15). Such opponents, who insist formally on some absolute sense of 'right', were themselves obliged to make reference to a criterion akin to utility.

The 1789 work was originally intended to serve as '*an introduction to a plan of a penal code*' (1982 [1789]: 4), and Bentham conceded that the final product placed too much weight on penal as distinct from civil law. He also somewhat played down the production as 'an introduction to the principles of *morals*', rather than of legislation, since 'in addition to the analysis it contains of the extensive ideas signified by the terms *pleasure, pain, motive,* and *disposition*, it ought to have given a similar analysis of the not less extensive, though much less determinate, ideas annexed to the terms *emotion, passion, appetite, virtue, vice,* and some others, including the names of the particular *virtues* and *vices*' (3). Nonetheless, the former provided the 'true ground-work' for the latter. We shall now see how much Bentham contributed to the 'less determinate' matter relating to private ethics.

******

Professor Persky has properly reminded us that the 'principle of utility', according to Bentham, extended to the ethical standard 'in the field of Morality in general' (2016: 30–1). But this does not go far enough. To be stressed is Bentham's insistence that *benevolent motivation matters in ethical evaluation*, writing that though 'antipathy' may be 'the cause of an action which is attended by good effects ... *this does not make it a right ground of action*' (1982 [1789]: 32; emphasis added).[2] By extension, it follows that a benevolent motive for an action that fails to yield the positive social benefits intended – 'ill-advised' as Bentham would say – nonetheless deserves some ethical credit.

The foregoing dimension is clouded by a common identification of Benthamite utilitarianism with *selfishness*. For Bentham, personal ethics certainly includes – as it did for Adam Smith – a moral duty towards oneself, a manifestation of the quality of '*prudence*' but it extended to a moral duty towards others – partly negative ('*probity*') to avoid reducing their happiness, and partly positive ('*beneficence*') to increase their happiness (1982 [1789]: 284). Allowing that 'the only interests which a man at all times and upon all occasions is sure to find *adequate* motives for consulting, are his own', Bentham raises the obvious query: 'What motives (independent of such as legislation and religion may chance to furnish) can one man have to consult the happiness of another?' The answer turns partly on 'the purely social motive of sympathy or benevolence', which applies 'on all occasions' and acts 'according to the *bias* of his sensibility'; and partly on the 'semi-social motives of love of amity and love of reputation', which apply 'on most occasions' depending upon the 'strength of his intellectual powers, the firmness and steadiness of his mind, the quantum of his moral sensibility, and the character of the people he has to deal with' (284–5).

If the 'social motive of sympathy or benevolence' is not the *only* motive directing conduct appropriately towards the general good, it is the most important. And this is reflected in Bentham's 'order of pre-eminence among motives', the ranking turning on 'the tendency which they appear to have to unite, or disunite' an agent's interests and those of the other members of the community, such that 'good will' or 'benevolence' or 'sympathy' are ranked first: 'On this plan [motives] may be distinguished into *social, dissocial,* and *self-regarding*. In the social class may be reckoned, 1. Good-will. 2. Love of reputation. 3. Desire of Amity. 4. Religion. In the dissocial may be placed, 5. Displeasure. In the self-regarding class, 6. Physical desire. 7. Pecuniary interest. 8. Love of power. 9. Self-preservation; as including the fear of the pains of the senses, the love of ease, and the love of life' (1982 [1789]: 116).[3] Now 'good-will' is ranked first considering that its 'dictates' – intending purposes – 'taken in a general view, are surest of coinciding with those of the principle of utility', for the dictates of utility itself are perceived to be 'neither more nor less than the dictates of the most extensive and enlightened (that is *well-advised*) benevolence. The dictates of the other motives may be conformable to those of utility, or repugnant, as it may happen' (116–17). (Bentham allows that an individual's good-will may be 'imperfect and confined' to particular groups only, 'not taking into contemplation the interests of all the persons whose interests are at stake'; 135.)

The representation of the principle of utility as satisfying *benevolent* sentiment – to the extent we have just seen of identifying the dictates or purposes of utility with those of benevolence – extends to the matter of Justice: 'justice, in the only sense in which it has a meaning, is an imaginary personage, feigned for the convenience of discourse, whose dictates are the dictates of utility, applied to certain particular cases' (Bentham 1982 [1789]: 120n). Justice, Bentham famously concludes, 'is nothing more than an imaginary instrument, employed to forward on certain occasions, and by certain means, the purposes of benevolence'. This conclusion *taken out of context* might easily be read as indicating a 'moral sense' of the sort Bentham rejected – namely, one maintaining 'approbation or disapprobation as a sufficient reason for itself, and disclaiming the necessity of looking out for any extrinsic ground' (above, p. 217).

The later *A Table of the Springs of Action* reiterates that in the absence of '*pleasures* and *pains*, not only *happiness*, but *justice*, and *duty*, and *obligation*, and *virtue* – all of which have been so elaborately held up to view as independent of them – are so many empty sounds' (Bentham 1843 [1817a]: 206). And regarding motivation, 'self interest' – in the strict sense of selfishness – is not *per se* a bad motive, for if weeded out 'the thread of life is cut, and the whole perishes' (216). True morality in short has its source in utility:

> A *virtuous disposition* is the disposition to give birth to *good*, – understanding always *pathological* [physical and mental] good, – or to prevent, or abstain from giving birth to, *evil*, understanding always *pathological* evil, – in so far as the production of the effect requires *exertion* in the way of *self-denial*: i.e. sacrifice of supposed lesser good to suppose greater good. In so far as the greater good, to which the less is sacrificed, is considered as being the good of *others*, the virtue belongs to the head of *probity* or *beneficence*: in so far as it is considered as being the good of *self*, to that of *self-regarding prudence*.
> (211)

The further analyses of compound or complex motivation and of the nature of 'interest' elaborate what Bentham had in mind. The complex pleasures of love of justice include justice for oneself ('self-preservation'), but also sympathy, intending justice for another party, and '*sympathy* for *the community* at large, in respect of the interest, which it has in the maintenance of *justice*: i. e. as being liable, in an indefinite extent, to become a sufferer by *injustice*' (210).

The frequent confusion of Benthamite utilitarianism with *selfishness* arises perhaps from too literal a reading of the assertion in the *Springs of Action* that one 'is said *to have an interest in any subject* in so far as that subject is considered more or less likely to be to him a source of pleasure or exemption [from pain]' (Bentham 1843 [1817a]: 207). For Bentham in fact explains that 'interest' simply entails efficient selection of means to some end 'whether that interest be of the *self-regarding* class, or of the *extra-regarding*; viz. of the *social* or of the *dissocial class*', such that to insist upon 'interested' behaviour is not to deny benevolence or to maintain 'all interest of the *self-regarding* class' (211–12). Accordingly, 'the most *disinterested* of men' – motivated by benevolence or 'the absence of all interest of the *self-regarding* class' even though pleasure is derived from it – 'is not less under the dominion of *interest* than the most *interested*' (212). (Bentham surmises that 'the only cause of his being styled *disinterested* is – its not having been observed that the sort of *motive* (suppose it *sympathy* for an individual or a class of individuals) has as truly a corresponding *interest* attached to it, as any other species of motive has'.) Elsewhere Bentham notes that the 'trite' proposition 'concerning man in general, that he is never governed by any thing but his own interest ... is indubitably true', but 'as comprehending all sorts of motives' (1945 [1782]: 154n). Again, in the *Constitutional Code*: 'Of action the sole efficient cause is interest, if interest be taken in its most enlarged sense: *i.e.* according to each man's perception of what, at the moment in question, is his most forcibly influencing interest: the interest determined by social sympathy and antipathy, as well as that which is of a purely self-regarding complexion, included' (Bentham 1843 [1830]: 46). As Viner expressed the matter, pleasure and pain – the individual's 'sovereign masters' for Bentham, and other eighteenth-century utilitarians – were not identified with self-interest, but with 'whatever men are interested in'; and while Viner found in Bentham a frequent emphasis on the selfish sentiments, it was James Mill who systematically argued that even the 'affectionate sentiments' reflect (consciously) the individual's *own* pleasures (Viner 1958: 312–13). The similarity with Francis Hutcheson may be noted.

As for the source of the meritorious status attached to 'extra-regarding acts of the social class', albeit that like all acts they are the product of so-called 'interest', in 1817 Bentham repeats the theme of 1789 that *there are no points of reference governing the morality of an action other than utility itself – the General Good*:

> As there are some motives, the force of which, they being either of the *self-regarding*, or of the *dissocial* class, is more liable than the force of those of the remaining class, viz. the *social* class, to operate in the breast of each particular individual, to the prejudice of the general good – of the interest of mankind at large; so, on the other hand, there are others, – and more particularly among those which belong to the *social* class, – which, in a particular degree, are capable of being employed, and with success, in checking the operative force of the above *comparatively* dangerous motives, and restraining it from applying itself with effect to the production of acts of the tendency just mentioned.
>
> (Bentham 1843 [1817a]: 215)

9.3 Benevolence elaborated

To better appreciate the Benthamite position, one should pay attention to the principle of utility as it relates to social arrangements and particularly to legislation, insofar as 'private ethics has happiness for its end: and legislation can have no other' (1982 [1789]: 285). Conspicuous here is Bentham's concern with 'sinister interest', or 'interest-begotten prejudice' as he sometimes expressed it. The reformist implications of this concern emerge clearly in an addition made in 1822 to the *Principles of Morals and Legislation* responding to Alexander Wedderburn who had objected to the formulation in *A Fragment on Government* (1776) of the 'all-comprehensive and all-commanding principle, the principle of *utility*':

> The *principle of utility* was an appellative, at that time employed – by me, as it had been by others, to designate that which, in a more perspicuous and instructive manner, may ... be designated by the name of the *greatest happiness principle*. 'The principle (said Wedderburn) is a dangerous one'. Saying so, he said that which, to a certain extent, is strictly true: a principle, which lays down, as the only *right* and justifiable end of Government, the greatest happiness of the greatest number – how can it be denied to be a dangerous one?

dangerous it unquestionably is, to every government which has for its *actual* end or object, the greatest good of a certain *one*, with or without the addition of some comparatively small number of others, whom it is matter of pleasure or accommodation to him to admit, each of them, to a share in the concern, on the footing of so many junior partners. *Dangerous* it therefore really was, to the interest – the sinister interest – of all those functionaries, himself included, whose interest it was, to maximize delay, vexation, and expense, in judicial and other modes of procedure, for the sake of the profit, extractable out of the expense.

(14–15n)

Here Bentham expresses his concern with manifestations on the part of legislators of self-interest of the 'self-regarding' order of the very narrowest sort.

To leave the matter at this point is to identify Bentham with James Mill who, in his *Essay on Government* (1820), 'setting out from the proposition that the sole proper purpose of government is to promote the greatest happiness of mankind ... proceeded by purely *a priori* analysis, without any reference to history or contemporary facts, from the premise that legislators served *only* their "sinister interests" ... to the conclusion that good government was therefore obtainable only by making it, through popular suffrage and frequent elections, the self-interest of the elected to serve the interests of the electors' (Viner 1958: 310). According to Viner, Bentham did not take this stance: 'Bentham always, but James Mill rarely, if ever, conceded that men, even legislators, could ... display a measure of pure benevolence'; furthermore it was the ethics of moral leaders, who were to attempt to influence legislators, that mainly concerned Bentham rather than the ethics of the ordinary man, an exercise to little purpose if legislators were perceived as governed *only* by their 'sinister interest'. But this contrast should not be drawn too strongly. Harrison has shown from a systematic study of a broad range of texts that with the passage of time Bentham's concern with sinister-interest scarcely abated (Harrison 1983: 195–224). Thus, the urgent problem as formulated, for example, in *The Book of Fallacies* was to assure that 'the will of the people' controls the 'ruling few' (Bentham 1824: 240). For 'in the ruling few there is most vice and corruption, because in their hands has been the power of serving their own private and sinister interest at the expense of the universal interest'; whereas 'in the subject many, there has been least of vice and corruption, because they have not been in so large a degree partakers of that sinister interest, and have thus been left free to pursue the track pointed out to them, partly by men who have found a personal interest in giving to their conduct a universally beneficial direction, – partly by discerning and uncorrupted men, who, lovers of their country and mankind, have not been in the way of having that generous affection overpowered in their breasts by any particular self-regarding interest' (284–5). More generally, 'it follows by the unchangeable constitution of human nature, that in every political community, by the hands by which the supreme power over all the other members of the community is shared, the interest of the many over whom the power is exercised, will on every occasion, in case of competition, be in act or in endeavour sacrificed to the particular interest of those by whom the power is exercised' (394). This orientation points to the case for representative democracy subject to certain safeguards such as a secret ballot, as already spelled out in the *Plan for Parliamentary Reform* (Bentham 1843 [1817b]: 451f.).[4]

Setting aside the latent problem of 'sinister-interest', I turn to an allusion in *Morals and Legislation* regarding the effect of government on men's 'sensibilities' which confirms not only Bentham's ample recognition of 'men's moral, religious, sympathetic, and anti-pathetic sensibilities', but also a belief that '[u]nder a well-constituted, or even under a well-administered though ill-constituted government, men's moral sensibility is commonly stronger, and their moral biases more conformable to the dictates of utility: their religious sensibility frequently weaker, but their religious biases less uncomfortable to the dictates of utility: their sympathetic affections more enlarged' (Bentham 1982 [1789]: 68). Here Bentham is describing an influence of a benign sort on moral sensibility itself emanating automatically rather than by design from good administration. But does he not leave scope for deliberate interference with private moral sentiments when he goes on to assert that 'the business of government is to promote the happiness of the society, by punishing and rewarding' (74)? Not if he is alluding to inducements to assure behaviour corresponding to that required by the greatest-happiness principle, even if such behaviour should not reflect the *natural* sentiments of the individual. And even so he took care to delimit the legislator's responsibility:

> There is no case in which a private man ought not to direct his own conduct to the production of his own happiness, and of that of his fellow-creatures: but there are cases in which the legislator ought not (in a direct way at least, and by means of punishment applied immediately to particular *individual* acts) to attempt to direct the conduct of the several other members of the community. Every act which promises to be beneficial upon the whole to the community (himself included) each individual ought to perform of himself: but it is not every such act that the legislator ought to compel him to perform. Every act which promises to be pernicious upon the whole to the community (himself included) each individual ought to abstain from of himself: but it is not every such act that the legislator ought to compel him to abstain from.
> (285)

Bentham's hesitancy suggests that Viner's attribution to Bentham of the position that 'man by living in society, by education, *and by acts of parliament*, could be made good' (Viner 1958: 312; emphasis added), may go too far with respect to the last. But it is true that Bentham saw a role for 'education and moral leaders to mould men's desires so that they spontaneously associate the happiness of others with their own happiness' (312–13).

By recognizing the existence of *natural moral sentiments*, here and elsewhere, was Bentham allowing for a 'moral sense'? Not if the term is read to imply the source of direct answers to questions of right and wrong in the manner of those who appealed, for example, to 'natural justice', for such appeals implied 'that approbation or disapprobation [is] a sufficient reason for itself ... disclaiming the necessity of looking out for any extrinsic ground', intending utilitarian consequences. This would of course be wholly out of character.

★★★★★★

A word next on Bentham's caution in *A Table of the Springs of Action* that it would be to carry on 'the business of *law* and *government* ... blindfold' were one to neglect his scheme of estimating the 'value of a pleasure' in terms of its intensity, duration, probability, propinquity, purity, fecundity and extent, when considering reward, punishment or compensation (Bentham 1843 [1817a]: 206). He had himself insisted that no more than a rule of thumb was intended by this: 'It is not to be expected that this process should be strictly pursued previously to every moral judgement, or to every legislative or judicial operation. It may, however, be always kept in view; and as near as the process actually pursued on these occasions approaches it, so near will such process approach to the character of an exact one' (1982 [1789]: 40). The use of quantification (the 'felicific calculus') in estimating social utility – interpersonal comparisons and arithmetical summations – is represented in a manuscript on the 'Dimension of Happiness' as a 'fictitious' but nonetheless necessary postulate:

> 'Tis in vain to talk of adding quantities which after the addition will continue distinct as they were before, one man's happiness will never be another man's happiness: a gain to one man is no gain to another: you might as well pretend to add twenty apples to twenty pears, which after you had done that could not be forty of any one thing but twenty of each just as there was before ... This addibility of the happiness of different subjects, however, when considered rigorously, it may appear fictitious, is a postulatum without the allowance of which all political reasoning is at a stand.
> (Halévy 1995 [1904]: 227: tr. Halévy 1955 [1928]: 495)

Similarly, the rule 'everyone to count for one, nobody to count for more than one' was a postulate which can be upheld by one who fully recognizes (as Bentham did recognize) the reality of differences in sensibility, character, and motivation between individuals. The postulates were intended for the purposes of rough 'welfare' calculation rather than to express a view of 'the whole world of human values' such as Schumpeter, as we have seen, imagined. In Robbins's judicious terms, the 'greatest happiness' principle was typically used as a working rule wherewith to judge legislative and administrative projects, that was in no way dependent upon the quantitative measurements implied by the unfortunate term 'felicific calculus' (Robbins 1961: 181; 1970: 80). Hume also, Robbins points out, 'never indulged in such flourishes' (Robbins 1961: 181).

9.4 Prospects for ethical progress

The social motive not only exists for Bentham but can be positively *encouraged* by appropriate education and opinion, taking us beyond mere recognition of the function of legislation to coerce or bribe individuals, to an assurance that their conduct coincides with the greatest-happiness. Thus, we find an allusion to the 'moral part' of education affecting 'the bent of [the student's] inclinations, the quantity *and quality* of his moral, religious, sympathetic, and antipathetic sensibility' (Bentham 1982 [1789]: 66; emphasis added). More elaborately, the 'circumstances influencing sensibility' which 'concern his mind ... concern either his *understanding* or his *affections*. To the former head belong the circumstances of quantity and quality of knowledge, strength of understanding, and insanity. To the latter belong the circumstances of firmness of mind, steadiness, bent of inclination, moral sensibility, moral biases, religious sensibility, religious biases, sympathetic sensibility, sympathetic biases, antipathetic sensibility, and antipathetic biases' (72). As Jacob Viner expressed it, we recall, for Bentham the function 'of education and moral leaders [was] to mould men's desires' in order to assure that individuals '*spontaneously* associate the happiness of others with their own happiness' (Viner 1958: 312, emphasis added). On this view, superior ethical merit attaches to conduct which *spontaneously* takes into account other interests than conduct which *calculates* the prospective advantages to oneself. Indeed herein, it may be said, lies ethical progress. As for 'the happiness of others', the potential for moral progress entailing reinforcement of the 'social motive' could not be made more apparent than by Bentham's declaration that the day *may* come when the utilitarian maximand would be extended to include the interests of animals (1982 [1789]: 283n).

Also taking us beyond mere recognition of the function of legislation to coerce or bribe individuals to assure that their conduct coincides with the greatest-happiness is Bentham's perception of the improved personal morality to be derived '[u]nder a well-constituted, or even well-administered government', since 'men's moral sensibility is commonly stronger, and their moral biases more conformable to the dictates of utility: their religious sensibility frequently weaker, but their religious biases less uncomfortable to the dictates of utility: their sympathetic affections more enlarged' (above, p. 223).

It is thus abundantly clear that 'moral sensibility' is for Bentham a meaningful category, and subject to reinforcement by a variety of means including, but also extending beyond, education narrowly perceived. I recognize that Bentham did not abandon the notion that consideration of the happiness of others reflected in the final resort the agent's self-interest. We have found it pithily expressed in the *Springs of Action*: '[T]he most *disinterested* of men is not less under the dominion of *interest* than the most *interested*' (Bentham 1843 [1817a]: 212). And it appears also in Bentham's Memoirs for 1822: 'If it be through the happiness of another, or others, in whatsoever numbers, that man pursues his own happiness, still the direct, and immediate, and nearest object of pursuit is not the less his own happiness: the happiness of others is but a means to that relatively universal end' (Bentham 1843 [1822a]: 532). But to rule out altruism in this absolutist sense did not lead Bentham to the other extreme of denying the possibility of ethical progress; indeed, on the contrary – and as Viner intimated – it is precisely by dint of such progress that 'man pursues his own happiness ... *through* the happiness of another, or others, in whatsoever numbers' (532, emphasis added).

The prospects envisaged for ethical progress *in practice* should not be overstated, for Bentham cautioned against 'the chimerical' in reform programmes on the grounds that '[p]erfect happiness belongs to the imaginary regions of philosophy, and must be classed with the universal elixir and the philosopher's stone ... Let us seek only for what is attainable: it presents a career sufficiently vast for genius; sufficiently difficult for the exercise of the greatest virtues' ('Influence of Time and Place'; Bentham 1843 [1782]:194). The matter is, however, complicated by passages which seem to negate *all* prospects for progress based upon a training of the moral sentiment of sympathy. Conspicuous amongst these is the following strong statement from the 'unfinished papers' published in 1824 under the title *The Book of Fallacies*:

> Taking the whole of life together, there exists not, *nor ever can exist*, that human being in whose instance any public interest he can have had, will not in so far as depends upon himself, have been sacrificed to his own personal interest. Towards the advancement of the public interest all that the most public-spirited, which is as much as to say the most virtuous of men can do, is to do what depends upon himself towards bringing the public interest, that is *his own personal share in the public interest*, to a state as nearly approaching to coincidence, and on as few occasions amounting to a state of repugnance, as possible *with his private interests.*
>
> (Bentham 1824: 363; emphasis added)

This statement denies that the public-interest – in the event of a clash – could ever be given priority by the agent, and yet contends that even a 'public-spirited' agent is merely concerned with his 'own personal share in the public interest', leaving little hope for the 'training' of sympathy, to use Mill's term. A further contention from the same work is equally uncompromising: 'In *every* human breast, rare and short-lived ebullitions, the result of some extraordinarily strong stimulus or incitement, excepted, self-regarding interest is predominant over social interest: each person's own individual interest, over the interests of all other persons taken together' (392–3; emphasis added). On this assumption regarding conduct it followed, 'by the unchangeable constitution of human nature, that in every political community, by the hands by which the supreme power over all the other members of the community is shared, the interest of the many over whom the power is exercised, will, on every occasion, in case of competition, be in act or in endeavour, sacrificed to the particular interest of those by whom the power is exercised' (394).

One solution is to simply ignore the problem, which is implicitly the line followed by Jacob Viner when he contends that Bentham '*always conceded*', unlike James Mill, 'that men, even legislators, could not only be influenced by the praise and blame of other men, but could even display some measure of pure benevolence' (Viner 1958: 310; emphasis added). Unfortunately, Bentham concedes *nothing* in these passages. It is more convincing to suggest that he simply went overboard with his generalizations regarding private behaviour in a work revealing 'fallacies in public debate' aimed 'to curb government corruption, expense, and opposition to reform on the part of both Whigs and Tories' (Rosen 1996: xlviii–xlix). His 'onslaught on the British establishment that preoccupied him from the summer of 1809' (Schofield 2015: xxi) made use of any weapon at hand including exaggeration of 'the unchangeable constitution of human nature'.

9.5 On self-regarding liberty and individuality

As noted at the outset of this chapter, Professor Riley perceives Bentham as representing 'security' solely in terms of rights versus 'malefactors' and '[abuses of] government' rather than as a protection of '*self-regarding* liberty and individuality' as in *On Liberty*. Bentham's concern was therefore with '*political liberty*' whereas Mill's extended to '*personal liberty*'. I do not find this contrast convincing since it may be shown that for Bentham, as well as for Mill, the societal control of predation is designed to protect individual security with respect to self-regarding matters.

As expressed in *Morals and Legislation*: '… the happiness of the individuals, of whom a community is composed, that is their pleasures and their security, is the end and the sole end which the legislator ought to have in view: the sole standard, in conformity to which each individual ought, as far as depends upon the legislator, to be *made* to fashion his behaviour' (Bentham 1982 [1789]: 34). Again, 'security' is provided by the law against the 'pains' inflicted by 'extra-regarding' acts entailing 'malevolence' (49). But state interference with purely 'self-regarding' conduct is all but ruled out, again indicating protection of individual liberty where second parties are not involved:

> It can only be through some defect on the part of the understanding, if a man be ever deficient in point of duty to himself. If he does wrong, there is nothing else that it can be owing to but either some *inadvertence* or some *missupposal*, with regard to the circumstances on which his happiness depends. It is a standing topic of complaint, that a man knows too little of himself. Be it so: but is it so certain that the legislator must know more? It is plain, that of individuals the legislator can know nothing: concerning those points of conduct which depend upon the particular circumstances of each individual, it is plain, therefore, that he can determine nothing to advantage.
> (Bentham 1982 [1789]: 289–90).

Even with respect to the poor conduct common to large numbers, such as drunkenness and fornication, the legislator 'must never expect to produce a perfect compliance by the mere force of the sanction of which he himself is the author. All he can hope to do, is to increase the efficacy of private ethics, by giving strength and direction to the influence of *the moral sanction*' (290; emphasis added); even 'in cases of notoriety', '[a]ll that he can do ... in the way of direct legislation, is to subject them ... to a slight censure, so as thereby to cover them with a slight shade of artificial disrepute'. Bentham laments that typically legislators are apt to go too far: 'The great difficulty here is, to persuade them to confine themselves within bounds. A thousand little passions and prejudices have led them *to narrow the liberty of the subject* in this line, in cases in which the punishment is either attended with no profit at all, or with none that will make up the expense' (291; emphasis added). 'The liberty of the subject' is thus unquestionably to be protected insofar as possible; and where in exceptional cases some intervention is justified it is to be limited to moral pressure. I conclude that Bentham was profoundly concerned with the protection of personal liberty. In this regard, and also with respect to his limitation of intervention in self-regarding matters to moral pressure at most, there is little to distinguish Bentham from Mill.

9.6 On economic equality

Although preceded by Hume, Bentham famously stated the axiom of diminishing marginal utility – an axiom of 'pathology' – from which he derived the desirability of strict income equality.[5] A formulation of this postulate and its consequences is found in the *Principles of the Civil Code*:

1. Each portion of wealth is connected with a corresponding portion of happiness.
2. Of two individuals, possessed of unequal fortunes, he who possesses the greatest wealth will possess the greatest happiness.
3. The excess of happiness on the part of the most wealthy will not be as great as the excess of his wealth.
4. For the same reason, the greater the disproportion between the two masses of wealth, the less the probability that there exists an equally great disproportion between the masses of happiness.
5. The more nearly the actual proportion approaches to equality, the greater will be the total mass of happiness.

(Bentham 1843 [1838]: 305)

But the deduction of strict equality is conditional on the assumption of *given wealth* as emerges in an elaboration of 'Distinct Objects of the Civil Law', or various 'subordinate ends' designed to enhance the primary end, namely 'the sum of social happiness': 'Subsistence, Abundance, Equality, Security' (302).[6] It was not possible, Bentham continues, 'to obtain the greatest good, but by sacrifice of some subordinate good', and specifically '[e]quality ought not to be favoured, except in cases in which it does not injure security; where it does not disturb the expectations to which the laws have given birth; where it does not derange the actually established distribution' (303). This formulation, taken literally, might seem to rule out *any* changes to a body of laws defining an 'actually established distribution'. But as I shall show this was far from Bentham's intention, and in any event he proceeds immediately from the case entailing the disappointment of expectations to a comparative statics comparison of two states with an eye to the lower productivity of that state characterized by 'equality': 'If all property were to be equally divided, the certain and immediate consequence would be, that there would soon be nothing more to divide. Every thing would be speedily destroyed. Those who had hoped to be favoured by the division, would not suffer less than those at whose expense it would be made. If the condition of the industrious were not better than the condition of the idler, there would be no reason for being industrious'.

A primary concern in all this was to demonstrate the deficiencies of 'levelling' systems on the grounds of their certain damage to 'subsistence' and 'abundance' due to the absence of incentives from which all would suffer, the intended beneficiaries no less than those targeted. This was coupled with a prediction that such systems could not in any event survive. Thus, after stressing the overriding importance of 'security' as an assurance of 'subsistence', 'abundance' and 'happiness', Bentham adds a further consideration, namely that the introduction of 'equality' – explicitly identified here with the abolition of property – could not possibly be permanently assured since 'if it could exist for a day, the revolutions of the next day would disturb it. The establishment of equality is a chimera: *the only thing which can be done is to diminish inequality*' (Bentham 1843 [1838]: 311; emphasis added). And focusing more specifically on proposals for the 'community of goods ... in which the whole belongs to everyone', Bentham objects on grounds of inefficiency in the absence of 'personal interest', but also because 'the apparent equality of this arrangement would only serve to hide a real inequality. The strongest would abuse his strength with impunity, the richest would enrich themselves at the expense of the poorest' (341). Bentham is careful not to extend his strictures to what we today label 'public goods' such as the public 'right of way, or right of water' (342).

Consistently with the analysis in the *Civil Code* Bentham elsewhere expresses a preference for the term 'inequality-minimizing principle' rather than 'equality-maximizing' to express the objective of 'securing the nearest approximation to absolute equality ... consistent with universal security ... for subsistence and maximization of the matter of abundance' ('Pannomial Fragments'; Bentham 1843 [nd]: 211–13). And here he also provides a particularly sharp rendition of the diminishing-utility postulate wherein, in reference to items 3 and 4 in the list cited above, Bentham writes:

> 3. But the quantity of happiness will not go on increasing in anything near the same proportion as the quantity of wealth ...Thus it is, that, 4. The effect of wealth in the production of happiness goes on diminishing, as the quantity by which the wealth of one man exceeds that of another goes on increasing: in other words, the quantity of happiness produced by a particle of wealth (each particle being of the same magnitude) will be less and less at every particle; the second will produce less than the first, the third less than the second, and so on.
> (229)

And this version also affirms 'that *if the effects of the first order were alone taken into account*, the consequences would be, that, on the supposition of a new constitution coming to be established, with the greatest happiness of the greatest number for its end in view, sufficient reason would have place for taking the matter of wealth from the richest and transferring it to the less rich, till the fortunes of all were reduced to an equality, or a system of inequality so little different from perfect equality, that the difference would not be worth calculating' (230; emphasis added). And here again, when it comes to policy in practice, the assumption of given wealth is abandoned and with it the support for 'levelling systems' on the grounds of the damaging effects on wealth creation which are exerted by the 'alarm' generated by a policy of equalization and the impact of 'the certainty of the non-enjoyment of the fruits of labour, and thence the extinction of all inducements to labour'.

I turn next to Bentham's actual policy recommendations having in mind the aforementioned conclusion in the *Civil Code* that '[t]he establishment of equality is a chimera: the only thing which can be done is to diminish inequality'. This general objective is elaborated in a discussion of 'property' perceived as 'an established expectation ... to derive certain advantages from the object'; since 'security consists in no shock or derangement being given to the expectation which has been founded on the laws of enjoying a certain portion of good. The legislator owes the greatest respect to these expectations to which he has given birth: when he does not interfere with them, he does all that is essential to the happiness of society; when he injures them, he always produces a proportionate sum of evil' (Bentham 1843[1838]: 308–9). As for specifics, Bentham offers a 'reconciliation' of the apparent clash between 'security' and 'equality' turning on the laws related to *inheritance*: 'Would you follow the counsels of equality without contravening those of security, wait for the natural period which puts an end to hopes and fears – the period of death' (312). More specifically: 'When property is vacated by the death of the proprietors, the law may intervene in the distribution to be made, either by limiting in certain respects the power of disposing of it by will, *with the design of preventing too great an accumulation of property in the hands of a single person*' or, in cases where relatives in the direct line do not exist and a man dies intestate, 'by making the right of succession *subservient to the purposes of equality*' such that the property 'passes ... to new possessors, whose expectations are not formed, and equality may produce good to all, without deceiving the expectations of any' (emphasis added). The objectives of legislation with regard to succession are later said to be '1st, To provide for the subsistence of the rising generation; 2*dly*, To prevent the pain of disappointment' and also '3*dly, To promote the equalization of fortunes*' (334; emphasis added). As Stark explains, Bentham's concern was to reduce social inequality subject to the accommodation of 'security', implying the liberty to accumulate wealth and provide for future generations, and legitimate expectations, and he found the solution in 'the partial disinheritance of *distant* relations' (Stark 1952a: 64).

Bentham's inequality-reducing proposals by restrictions on legacies were modest, Mill for one finding that Bentham did not go far enough by limiting himself to recommending that only *collateral* inheritance intestate should cease, the property in that case alone passing to the state (Mill 1965 [1848]: 220–1, 811). Stark refers to Bentham's notes including 'Laws providing security for the fruits of industry. 2. Laws gently tending to equalisation (general)' (Stark 1952a: 54). The term 'gently' is a fair description.

Apart from these limitations on legacies, Bentham proposed certain *exemption limits* to direct taxation: 'Rule 1. Insufficient income derived from profits and earnings of any description of individuals ought to be exempted altogether. Rule 2. Income little more than barely sufficient ought to receive an abatement gradually lessening up to the measure of full sufficiency. Rule 3. Sufficient and insufficient are evidently terms of reference. The reference I make is to the sum which, in the estimation of the world, would enable a man to maintain himself with decency in the station in which he is placed by the occupation from which his income is derived' (*Proposal for a Mode of Taxation*, Bentham 1952 [1794]: 388). Mill would later adopt Bentham's case for exemption limits – although he does not cite it chapter and verse – qualifying a general opposition to a progressive income tax on the grounds that any burden imposed on incomes below a certain minimum would entail a sacrifice 'entirely incommensurate' (Mill 1965 [1848]: 808–9). Mill argued his case in terms of equity, fairness, or justice embodied in the maxim of 'equal sacrifices', and though some commentators are uncomfortable with attributing such a concern to Bentham, finding it to be conflictory with his utilitarianism (see Harrison 1983: 244–5), on my reading Bentham – no less than Mill – found it quite consistent to absorb 'justice' and related concepts within his utilitarian frame of reference. This evaluation is confirmed by the rejection of objections to restrictions on succession as undermining aristocracy on the grounds that 'they keep up inequality, and all inequality that has no special utility to justify it is *injustice*' (from a manuscript relating to *Supply Without Burthen*, Bentham 1952 [1795]: 329; emphasis added).

The textual evidence thus far considered allows for a modest degree of income redistribution. On one occasion, however, Bentham declares much more strongly that '[e]quality requires, that *though it be at the expense of all the other members of the community*, the income of those whose income is composed of the wages of labour be maximized. Reason: Of these are composed the vast majority of the whole number of the members of the community' ('Pannomial Fragments'; Bentham 1843 [nd]: 230). But this affirmation is difficult to accommodate and the manuscript relating to the *Manual of Political Economy* emphasizes the objective of assuring 'that the poorer should be less poor rather than that the richer should be less rich' implying a primary concern with improved living standards for the less-well paid by means other than redistribution, an objective that would be consistent even with a reduction in *labour's share*: 'Equality is a [further] end which law ought to propose to itself, as far as [it] is consist[ent] with the others' – referring to 'subsistence, enjoyment, security, encrease', the last presumably referring to what in some places is designated as 'abundance': 'but what has been done, or may be done, with this view, will hardly be thought to come within the pale of political economy. As far as it concerns wealth, it will hardly be reckoned an object distinct from opulence: since the end in view, in whatever may be done in the design of favouring equality, is nothing but the making those who would otherwise be poorer richer, [or] rather that the poorer *should be less poor rather than that the richer should be less rich*' (Bentham 1952 [1793–5]: 226n; emphasis added). This position, we have found, is held in common to Smith. It comes as no surprise then that Bentham should reject subsidies on food 'in the character of a measure of equalization' on the grounds that the growth rate of the economy on which the real wage depends will be adversely affected (247–8). Unfortunately, there is some doubt as to Bentham's mature position regarding prospects for working-class living standards. Thus in his rough notes he states that '[t]he higher the wages of labour, the better consistent with national security', but also asserts '[t]he impossibility of raising the wages of ordinary labour beyond mere subsistence' (Stark 1952b: 482).

I have left for last a matter of great importance that has not been sufficiently recognised in the secondary literature on this topiv, namely the significance of income *gradation*. I allude to the following proposition in the manuscript relating to the *Institute of Political Economy*:

> But though security encreases in proportion as opulence encreases, and inequality is an inseparable accompaniment of opulence, security does not encrease in proportion as inequality encreases. Take away all ranks in respect of opulence between the highest and the lowest, the degree of inequality will be encreased, but the degree of [security] will be diminished … Large fortunes derived from trade rise one above another naturally in gentle and almost insensible gradations, that is *with very [little] inequality between any two contiguous classes*. Large fortunes consisting in land rise one above another in gradations which may be gentle or abrupt according to the distribution originally made of the land, and according to the disposition of the law favouring or disfavouring the condensation of it.
> (Bentham 1952 [1801–4]: 327–8; emphasis added)

What matters on this account is not so much the difference between the poorest and the richest but that between *contiguous classes*. Unequal income distribution, even of a major order, is acceptable provided that 'gradation [is] most regular and insensible', a point also spelled out in 'Pannomial Fragments': 'the plan of distribution applied to the matter of wealth, which is most favourable to universality of subsistence, and thence, in other words, to the maximization of happiness, is that in which, while the fortune of the richest – of him whose situation is at the top of the scale, is greatest, the degrees between the fortune of the least rich and that of the most rich are most numerous – in other words, the gradation most regular and insensible'

(Bentham 1843 [nd]: 230). That the degree of security is damaged by *vast* differentials implies a threat to civil order and consequences for social wealth and welfare. As for the underlying logic of the argument, it is difficult to escape the conclusion that *resentment* or *jealousy* enters the picture, with individuals only prepared to tolerate the advantageous positions of those in the 'class' immediately above their own if the differential is a limited one. Such a rationale may be said to be typically non-Benthamite (see Harrison 1983: 245), but I find it unconvincing to maintain that Bentham denied the existence of sentiments of this order and I can think of no other rationale for his case.

It is worth recalling here that Adam Smith had earlier opposed vast wealth differentials between the highest and the lowest where there is a great 'leap' from one to the other: 'in the present state of things a man of a great fortune is rather an advantage than dissadvantage to the state, providing that there is *a graduall descent of fortunes* betwixt these great ones and others of the least and lowest fortune ... [O]ne who leaps over all his country men is of real detriment to the community' (Smith 1978 [1762–3]: 196; emphasis added). Smith's argument turns on the social tensions created by significantly discrete differentials (197–8); Bentham's concern that security is adversely affected by vast differentials makes the same point.

9.7 Summary and conclusion

The main theme of this chapter relates to Bentham's allowance for other-regarding motivations in ethical evaluation. Our position accords with that of the Bentham-critic William Whewell in his *Lectures on the History of Moral Philosophy in England* whereby 'it would be unjust to Bentham not to allow that in that portion of Ethics in which his principle is really applicable, there is a great deal of felicity, and even of impressiveness, in the manner in which he follows out his doctrine. I speak of the virtues and duties which depend directly upon Benevolence' (Whewell 1852: 229).[7] I note that the version of *Deontology* edited from the manuscript by Bowring records Bentham firmly representing as a 'narrow and baneful sentiment' the perspective of those 'who deem all services done to others as something lost to themselves' (Bentham 1834: 190). This stance is reinforced in the text that follows: 'To *make* a favour of that which should be a spontaneous, or at all events a willing contribution to the happiness of another, is, in common parlance, to give evidence of a low-toned spirit of philanthropy, while, on the other hand, no beneficence looks so bright in the popular eyes, none is, in fact, so praiseworthy as that which avoids the parade of its sacrifices' The Bowring edition is however not always reliable (see Mill 1969 [1852]: 174; also Harrison 1983: xxi, 263–4). The modern *Collected Works* edition refers to an individual who '[e]ven without self-sacrifice in any shape' refuses 'to be the source of advantage or gratification to any one else without receiving an advantage equal at least in value...', and the disposition in question is simply said to have been 'productive of its natural effects' (Bentham 1983: 186). By the 'natural effects' are evidently intended effects of a negative order implying something akin to the moralistic tone of the Bowring version; and we recall the weight accorded to 'sympathy' in *Deontology*, as discerned by the editors (above, p. 216).

A further matter considered in the present chapter has been Bentham's position regarding equality, which we have found to be much the same as Smith's, namely that in the absence of private property and with strict equality, living standards would be unacceptably low and thus '*unjust*' precisely because hostile to the greatest happiness principle (Chapter 8). This conclusion may be placed in a broader context. Recall Mill's perspective on Bentham's achievement, which was to use the utility principle as the foundation for 'secondary or middle principles, capable of serving as premises for a body of ethical doctrine not derived from existing opinions, but fitted to be their test', so that a moralist can deduce from utility as a standard 'his whole system of ethics' (Mill 1969 [1852]: 173, 194) This perspective, we have argued, applies also to Smith, whose notion of 'equity and justice' may be considered as a coherent deduction from utilitarian principles rather than a manifestation of the severe contradiction implied by Fay's alleged contrast between 'the utilitarian principles of Bentham' and 'the natural rights of Adam Smith' (Fay 1964: 20).

Notes

1 The charge against Bentham of ignoring qualitative differences among social goods is difficult to dislodge. For a recent instance, see Sunstein 2014: 20.
2 'Antipathy' for Bentham bears a negative connotation because it is *generally* followed by social or other forms of disutility; the designation 'bad' is still attached in exceptional cases where the normal result does not follow; similarly with respect to benevolence. David Hume had similarly maintained that moral evaluation concerns general 'Tendencies of Qualitys, not their actual Operation, which depends on Chance' (letter to Hutcheson, 17 September 1739, in Hume 1932 I: 34–5).
3 Bentham nonetheless cautioned that 'there is no such thing as any sort of motive which is a bad one in itself: nor, consequently, any such thing as a sort of motive, which in itself is exclusively a good one'; and even as regards consequences 'it appears too that these are sometimes bad, at other times either indifferent or good' (1982 [1789]: 114). Concepts condemned by 'common-place morality', such as avarice, were therefore meaningless independent of utility and disutility (115).
4 Ricardo questioned James Mill's simplistic behavioural premise in the sphere of legislation as it emerges in the *History of British India*. It is unclear whether he would have applied the following objections to Bentham: 'You are I think a little too severe when you speak of the rare occurrence of parliamentary influence with knowledge and talent, in all places where much either of money or power is to be enjoyed. If money and power were the only things desirable to man your conclusion could not be denied, but while public opinion and public sympathy are so much valued by all ranks of men, sufficient motives exist for the acquirement of knowledge and talent independent of the power and money which they may chance to bring along with them. Would not theory lead us to expect that the sanction of public opinion would have most weight with those who had no other object of ambition?' (Ricardo to Mill, 30 December 1817; Ricardo 1952: 238–9).

Similarly, in the case of legal arrangement: 'Do you not give too much weight to the influence of fees on the administration of justice particularly when the fees do not increase the emoluments of the judge but of those who are appointed by the judge? – Is not the love of ease, which is natural to the judge as well as to others, a corrective against the multiplication of causes in which he (the judge) has no direct interest? The love of patronage so trifling in degree must be more than balanced by a fear of censure and the love of ease' (237–8).

5 I shall not distinguish here between income and wealth. Bentham we shall see was much concerned with private property but frequently can be read as concerned with income from property.

6 In the manuscript relating to the *Institute of Political Economy* (1801–4), 'Abundance' is defined both in *per capita* and aggregate terms: 'Abundance in respect of wealth [is] opulence. Abundance in respect of population [is] Populousness. These two branches of the common end run in direct opposition to one another. Given the quantity of wealth, the degree of abundance is inversely as the number of the sharers. The encrease of abundance in point of population is an object of the community in two points of view: to encrease the mass of comfort by increasing the numbers of those who enjoy comfort, and to encrease security as against aggression from without...' (Bentham 1952 [1801–4]: 310). Elsewhere Bentham similarly affirms that 'in a political community, the *extent* of a pleasure is as the *number* of the persons by whom it is experienced' (Bentham 1843 [1822b]: 540). In this regard Bentham is in line with the *Theory of Moral Sentiments* rather than the *Wealth of Nations* which denies merit in a large population as such. But a further comment on the *motive* to population increase does accord with Smith's later work: 'Abundance is the seed of populousness. Abundance is the means of multiplication: for the work of generation men want not any incitements but the means' (Bentham 1952 [1801–4]: 310).

7 Although Whewell also cautions 'that a great many of the precepts which he ... gives are rather rules of good manners than rules of morality' (Whewell 1852: 230).

References

Bentham, J. 1824. *The Book of Fallacies. From unfinished papers*. London: J. and H.L. Hunt.
Bentham, J. 1834. *Deontology; or the Science of Morality*. Vol. 1, ed. John Bowring. London: Longman, Rees, Orme, Browne, Green and Longman; Edinburgh: William Tait.
Bentham, J. 1843 (nd). 'Pannomial Fragments', *The Works of Jeremy Bentham* 3, ed. John Bowring. Edinburgh: William Tait: 211–230.
Bentham, J. 1843 (1782). *Essay on the influence of Time and Place in Matters of Legislation*. Works 1, ed. John Bowring. Edinburgh: William Tait: 169–194.
Bentham, J. 1843 (1817a). *A Table of the Springs of Action*. Works 1, ed. John Bowring. Edinburgh: William Tait: 195–219.
Bentham, J. 1843 (1817b). *Plan for Parliamentary Reform*. Works 3, ed. John Bowring. Edinburgh: William Tait: 433–557.
Bentham, J. 1843 (1822a). Extract from Memorandum-Book. *Memoirs of Jeremy Bentham*. Works 10, ed. John Bowring. Edinburgh: William Tait: 531–532.
Bentham, J. 1843 (1822b). *Codification Proposal*, Works 4, ed. John Bowring. Edinburgh: William Tait: 534–594.
Bentham, J. 1843 (1830). *Constitutional Code* [Book 1, Chapter VIII: 'Public-Opinion Tribunal']. Works 9, ed. John Bowring. Edinburgh: William Tait: 41–46.
Bentham, J. 1843 (1838). *Principles of the Civil Code*. Works 1, ed. John Bowring. Edinburgh: William Tait: 297–364.
Bentham, J. 1945 (1782). *Of Laws in General*, ed. H.L.A. Hart. London: Athlone Press.
Bentham, J. 1952 (1793–1795). *Manual of Political Economy. Jeremy Bentham's Economic Writings* 1, ed. W. Stark. London: George Allen and Unwin: 219–273.

Bentham, J. 1952 (1794). *Proposal for a Mode of Taxation. Jeremy Bentham's Economic Writings* 1, ed. W. Stark. London: George Allen and Unwin: 375–412.
Bentham, J. 1952 (1795). *Supply Without Burthen. Jeremy Bentham's Economic Writings* 1, ed. W. Stark. London: George Allen and Unwin: 279–367.
Bentham, J. 1952 (1801–1804). 'Institute of Political Economy'. *Jeremy Bentham's Economic Writings* 3, ed. W. Stark. London: George Allen and Unwin: 303–380.
Bentham, J. 1982 (1789). *An Introduction to the Principles of Morals and Legislation*, ed. J.H. Burns and H.L.A. Hart. London and New York: Methuen.
Bentham, J. 1983. *Deontology together with A Table of the Springs of Action and Article on Utilitarianism*. Oxford: Clarendon Press: ed. Amnon Goldworth. Oxford: Clarendon Press: 117–281.
Fay, C.R. 1964. *Great Britain from Adam Smith to the Present Day: An Economic and Social Survey*, 5th ed. London: Longmans.
Halévy, E. 1955 (1928). *The Growth of Philosophical Radicalism*. Boston: The Beacon Press.
Halévy, E. 1995 (1904). *La formation du radicalisms philosophique III: Le radicalisme philosophique*. Paris: Presses Universitaires de France.
Harrison, R. 1983. *Bentham*. London: Routledge and Kegan Paul.
Hume, D. 1932. *The Letters of David Hume* I, edited by J.Y.T. Greig. Oxford: Clarendon Press.
Hollander, S. 2015. *John Stuart Mill: Political Economist*. Singapore: World Scientific.
Long, D. 1988. 'Censorial Jurisprudence and Political Radicalism: A Reconsideration of the Early Bentham', *The Bentham Newsletter*, June (12): 4–23.
Mill, J.S. 1965 (1848). *Principles of Political Economy. Collected Works of John Stuart Mill* 2–3, ed. J.M. Robson. Toronto: University of Toronto Press.
Mill, J.S. 1969 (1852). 'Whewell on Moral Philosophy', *CWJSM* 10: 165–201.
Persky, J. 2016. *The Political Economy of Progress: John Stuart Mill and Modern Radicalism*. Oxford: Oxford University Press.
Ricardo, D. 1952. *Works and Correspondence of David Ricardo* 7, ed. Piero Sraffa. Cambridge: Cambridge University Press.
Riley, J. 2016. Review of Hollander 2015. *History of Political Economy* 48(4): 752–758.
Robbins, L.C. 1970. *The Evolution of Modern Economic Theory*. London: Macmillan.
Robbins, L.C. 1961. *The Theory of Economic Policy in English Classical Political Economy*. London: Macmillan.
Rosen, F. 1996. New Introduction to *The Collected Works of Jeremy Bentham: An Introduction to the Principles of Morals and Legislation*, edited by J.H. Burns and H.L.A. Hart. Oxford: Clarendon Press: xxxi–lxix.
Schofield, P. 2015. Editorial Introduction to Jeremy Bentham, *The Book of Fallacies. Collected Works of Jeremy Bentham*. Oxford: Clarendon Press: xix–lxxxv.
Schumpeter, J.A. 1954. *History of Economic Analysis*. New York: Oxford University Press.
Smith, A. 1978 (1762–1763). Report of 1762–1763, *Lectures on Jurisprudence*, eds. R.L. Meek, D.D. Raphael, and P.G. Stein. Indianapolis: Oxford: Clarendon Press: 45–394.
Stark, W. 1952a. Introduction, *Jeremy Bentham's Economic Writings* 1, ed. W. Stark. London: George Allen and Unwin: 11–78.
Stark, W. 1952b. *Jeremy Bentham's Economic Writings* 3, ed. W. Stark. London: George Allen and Unwin.
Sunstein, C.R. 2014. 'How do we know What's Moral?' *The New York Review of Books* 61, 24 April: 14–18.
Viner, J. 1958. *The Long View and the Short: Studies in Economic Theory and Policy*. Glencoe: The Free Press.
Whewell, W. 1852. *Lectures on the History of Moral Philosophy in England*. London: Parker.

10 Bentham in relation to Locke and the eighteenth-century literature

10.1 Bentham on Locke

Problematic in the first place is Bentham's neglect of Locke's ethical utilitarianism, whether the theological or the secular version which we have spelled out in Chapter 1. For while Bentham applauded Locke's denial of an innate 'moral sense', he said nothing of Locke's positive contribution to ethical utilitarianism perceived in terms of commendable actions enhancing the 'greater good' in the mundane sense of social welfare, and sometimes credited Helvétius and sometimes Hume rather than Locke with establishing as an *ethical standard* the impact of actions on the greater good: 'A digest of the Laws is a work that could not have been executed with advantage before Locke and Helvétius had written: the first establishing a test of perspicuity for ideas; the latter establishing *a standard of rectitude for actions ...* [whereby] a sort of action is a right one, when the tendency of it is to augment the mass of happiness in the community' (Bentham 1843 [1773–4]: 70; emphasis added). Similarly, a memorandum dating to 1776 reminisces regarding the year 1769 when 'I was beginning to get gleams of practical philosophy', that 'Montesquieu, Barrington, Beccaria, and Helvétius, but most of all Helvétius, set me on the principle of utility' (54); and in a draft letter to Voltaire of November 1776 he declared: 'I have built solely on the foundation of utility, laid as it is by Helvétius' (cited in Harrison 1983: 7; Long 1988: 7). Complicating the story of indebtedness is the fact that *A Fragment on Government* refers not to Helvétius but to Book III of Hume's *Treatise on Human Nature* 1740 ('Of Morals') as the text from which he had learned 'that the foundations of all *virtue* are laid in *utility*', that '*utility* was the test and measure of all virtue' (Bentham 1843 [1776]: 268–9n). In any event, in 'Conversations 1827–8', Locke's prime contribution is said – as in the 1770s – to have been 'to destroy the notion of innate ideas' and not the utility dimension for which Bentham claimed priority: 'What Bacon did was to proclaim – "*Fiat experimentum*"; but his own knowledge of Natural Philosophy was ignorance.– What Locke did, was to destroy the notion of innate ideas.– What Newton did, was to throw light on one branch of science.– But I have planted the tree of Utility.– I have planted it deep, and spread it wide' (Bentham, in Bowring 1843

X: 587–8). An observation in 1795 (in 'Supply Without Burthen') taking note of Locke, amongst others, in relation to the utility principle, is inconclusive: 'The principle of utility, with the united powers of Bacon, Locke, Hume, Smith [and] Paley to develop it, would be nothing against one Danton bawling out natural rights' (Bentham 1952 [1795]: 336).

Closely related to his neglect of Locke as ethical utilitarian is Bentham's underplaying of Locke's perception of the quest for 'pleasure' and the avoidance of 'pain', or the 'happiness' objective, as governing human conduct. Locke's effectively-argued case against innate ideas, to the extent that the so-called 'moral sense' was undermined, serving only as a necessary step towards the valid doctrine. Certainly, Locke traced *all* ideas – including amongst them those of pleasure and pain – to two experiential sources, sensation and reflection, but Bentham's commendation of Locke for 'first establishing a test of perspicuity for ideas' is very general and does not specifically pinpoint pleasure and pain. And yet as was shown in Chapter 1, the first volume of the *Essay Concerning Human Understanding* elaborates in detail the characteristically 'Benthamite' categories of pleasure, pain, and happiness including the role of the 'ideas' of pleasure and pain in stimulating action.[1]

10.2 On the charge against Shaftesbury, Hutcheson and Hume

Recall next Bentham's representation in 1819 of Shaftesbury, Hutcheson and Hume as moral-sense authors *opposed* to the utilitarian principle (see Introduction). Bentham's stance is problematic in each case and for the same reason. As for Shaftesbury, the function of the 'moral sense', as was shown in Chapter 2, is to reinforce the value judgment that virtue is to be understood as a concern for the public interest; his utilitarianism reflected precisely in the applause afforded to such other-regarding sentiment, in effect *sympathy*, as indeed with Locke – although Shaftesbury doubtless would not have admitted the common ground – and later with Hutcheson and Hume. I have surmised that if asked *why* he himself maintains this perception he would doubtless have responded 'my "moral sense" tells me so', but at the same time what he says of the moral sense is often assertive and rhetorical, and he himself cautioned that the moral sense may be corrupted by faulty cultural influences, the notion of virtue itself remaining intact without its assistance.

Bentham opposed moral-sense authors on the grounds that the *utility principle* is the axiom upon which all depends and for which no proof is possible or required: 'that which is used to prove every thing else, cannot itself be proved: a chain of proofs must have their commencement somewhere' (Bentham 1982 [1789]: 13). As will be seen below (p. 243), he shared this position with Hume. Is this not an ineluctable difference with Hutcheson? *No*, is my answer: despite his efforts at 'proof', Hutcheson regarded the moral sense as existing largely on the basis of general experience and introspection, its introduction adding little of substance to those positions which stopped short at utility. It is therefore best seen as an attempt to deny alternative explanations of the source of ethical merit, particularly religion and reason – not to speak of self-interest. I shall justify this assertion presently.

Elsewhere in this book we have encountered conflicting opinions in modern commentaries regarding Hutcheson's status as utilitarian, in particular a contention emphasizing Hutcheson's 'Non-utilitarian Motivational Morality' which presumes that 'Utilitarian theories typically do not engage with agents' motivations', and a designation of Hutcheson as a 'motivational utilitarian' implying that he stands apart from the utilitarians proper (see Chapter 4, p. 64). Were the latter contrast found to be valid, Bentham's stance would pose no difficulty: He simply objected to writers engaging with agents' motivation as providing an index of ethical approval. However, I do not believe this contrast holds water. Bentham has formulations which designate consequences as if they alone mattered for ethical approval – including the propositions that 'the foundations of all *virtue* are laid in *utility*' and that utility is 'the test and measure of all virtue' – but these must be understood as abbreviated statements, silently assuming proper motivation, since Bentham himself identified the 'most virtuous of men' with 'the most public spirited' and proposed 'an order of pre-eminence among motives' turning on 'the tendency which they have to unite, or disunite', an agent's interests and those of other members of the community, with 'good-will' ranked first considering that its 'dictates taken in a general view, are surest of coinciding with those of the principle of utility. For the dictates of utility itself are neither more nor less than the dictates of the most extensive and enlightened (that is *well-advised*) benevolence' (Chapter 9, p. 219). Benevolence and good-will mean nothing if not proper motivation. That Bentham should have included Hutcheson amongst the culprits rejecting utilitarian principles implies that he had somehow missed Hutcheson's reiterated contention that the moral sense approved conduct motivated by benevolence, or – in Hutcheson's own terms – the intent to enhance 'the greatest Happiness for the greatest Numbers'.

A recent account by Joseph Persky (2016) is pertinent to the issues at hand. Persky correctly points out that Bentham's utilitarian formula is not based on Hutcheson and offers a hypothesis: 'Hutcheson, Smith's mentor, is reasonably credited with inventing the greatest-happiness principle. Smith's self-proclaimed acolyte Bentham was to make that principle famous. Yet the direct chain from Hutcheson to Bentham is, in effect, broken by Smith's reluctance to explicitly advocate the greatest-happiness principle' (Persky 2016: 28–9, see Chapter 7, p. 169). This hypothesis does not however account for the absence of a *direct* reference by Bentham to Hutcheson's version that pre-dated Hume's – and is quite as explicit – which he so much admired. And why did Smith's failure to explicitly endorse the greatest-happiness rule not impede Bentham from applauding *Hume's* formulation? In any event, even had Hutcheson not coined the celebrated expression itself one would expect some appreciation on Bentham's part – in the manner of Smith – for the role Hutcheson accorded to benevolence, namely the public good, in ethical evaluation. It is after all substance not form that matters.

I find it difficult to imagine that Bentham could have been unaware of the greater-good formula as employed by Hutcheson or of the substance behind it; while the common terminology entailing the 'Springs' of human action engenders a suspicion that he may actually have had Hutcheson close at hand, in which case the question arises as to why he deliberately refused to cite Hutcheson's formulation. But for one objection I would propose that his decision reflects a disappointment with what he mistakenly believed to be Hutcheson's *rejection* of the greater-good principle by adhering to the moral sense. As for Bentham's misreading of Hutcheson's moral sense, that can be better understood if we suppose that his attention was drawn to various abbreviated formulations whereby, for example, the moral sense provides 'an immediate undefinable perception' of what is praiseworthy, or the identification of 'natural conscience' with 'that sense of what is beautiful and becoming', and of 'conscience' with the 'sense of virtue' (Chapter 4, pp. 88-9). For it is easy enough to neglect the elaborations explaining that the intention to contribute to the public good constitutes the essential ingredient of ethical conduct. Thus, an action would be morally defective for Hutcheson notwithstanding social advantage resulting therefrom should the agent's *intention* lack concern for the public good (pp. 65, 72). This is true of Bentham, although I do not claim an identity of position, insofar as Hutcheson's ethical utilitarian calculus weights the numbers expected to be affected by an action by the 'Dignity or moral importance' of the individuals involved, a procedure without (to my knowledge) a counterpart in Bentham.[2]

The objection to which I refer — it parallels my objection to Persky's hypothesis — is that Bentham, as is also clear from the 1819 annotations, misunderstood *Hume's* moral sense, yet nonetheless enthusiastically cited him regarding the greatest-happiness principle, in effect putting the objection aside. I am unable therefore to convincingly account for Bentham's silence regarding the Hutcheson contribution — why, that is, he did not make the same allowance here that he made for Hume. I am no less at a loss to understand John Stuart Mill's almost total silence regarding Hutcheson.

Hutcheson, I have said, was keen to reject various explanations of the source of ethical merit, particularly religion and reason. As for a religious source, the *Inquiry* certainly perceives the moral sense as a natural implant by the Deity and to that extent the source of morality. But it also recognizes virtuous conduct divorced from such underpinning, allowing that 'particular actions may be innocent, nay, virtuous, where there is no actual intention of pleasing the Deity influencing the agent' (Chapter 4, p. 86). This conclusion is strongly reinforced by a *denial* in the *System* that moral goodness is proven by 'conformity to the divine will or laws', for such conformity implies that moral qualities '*must be previously known*' (pp. 90-1). The secular dimension to the argument is thereby enhanced, taking it closer to Bentham in that regard. It is of the highest significance that Bentham made the same point, and in very similar terms: 'We may be perfectly sure that whatever is right is conformable to the will of God: but so far is that from answering the purpose of showing us what is right, that it is necessary to know first whether a thing is right, in order to know from thence whether it is conformable to the will of God' (Bentham 1982 [1789]: 31).

We now turn to Hutcheson's concession that the moral sense only functions properly when 'in its full vigour' which is usually not the case, thereby bringing into question the notion of a *natural instinct* yielding 'an immediate undefinable perception' of benevolent conduct, as it is phrased in the posthumous *System* (Chapter 4, p. 98). Hutcheson there confirms the qualification by focusing on the potentiality of what can be achieved by culture and training allowing for 'reasoning and reflection' and noting also a religious contribution. We have found in Chapter 4 earlier intimations of the problem in 1724, while the *Short Introduction* elaborates the necessity for 'cultivation and improvement' of the moral sense, and stresses that 'revelation' and on-going heavenly support required to activate and maintain it. But of particular interest is the 1830 Glasgow lecture, for there Hutcheson shows himself to be very much aware that the moral sense is under threat by the allowance that it is not necessarily, or even usually, fully alert or fully mature, necessitating measures to support it, and even proposes a half-hearted solution. The *System* also alludes to the problem. Closely related is the attempt in the *Inquiry* itself to reconcile the natural 'universality' of the moral sense with the observed *diversity* of moral principles over time and place.[3]

Hutcheson's continued reliance on the moral sense in the face of serious complications he himself recognized seems to reflect the urgency of undermining self-interest enthusiasts both secular and orthodox who found disinterested motivation to be inconceivable. In any event, had Bentham been familiar with Hutcheson's recognition of the malleability by way of education and culture of what was supposed to be a purely 'natural' instinct, and with the allowances made for different interpretations of the content of the 'benevolence' or general-good criterion of ethical approval it would surely have pleased him as constituting severe threats to the moral-sense conception. And, notwithstanding the link to the moral sense, he could scarcely have objected to Hutcheson's utilitarian perspective on 'rights' as expressed in 1729: 'From this Sense too we derive our Ideas of Rights. Whenever it appears to us, that a Faculty of doing, demanding, or possessing any thing, universally allow'd in certain Circumstances, would in the whole tend to the general Good, we say that one in such Circumstances, has a Right to do, possess, or demand that Thing. And according as this Tendency to the publick Good is greater or less, the Right is greater or less' (Hutcheson 1729: 277–8; cited Chapter 4, p. 83).

★★★★★★

Bentham's inclusion of Hume amongst those appealing to a moral sense *opposed to* utilitarian ethics is no less difficult to appreciate. For while Hume adhered to a moral sense, identified with 'conscience', he firmly denied that such a sense operates as an automatic index of what is ethically good or bad *independently of the tendency of an action to augment general welfare*. To the contrary, the moral sense applauds conduct motivated by the benevolent sentiment of 'sympathy for mankind', and to introduce sympathy is immediately to commit to a utilitarian perspective entailing concern for the advancement of the general good.[4] Stranger still is the fact that notwithstanding the objection to Hume's moral-sense we famously find in *A Fragment on Government* – where Bentham first stated the ethical axiom that '*It is the greatest happiness of the greatest number that is the measure of right and wrong*' (Bentham 1843 [1776]: 227) – him crediting Hume's chapter 'Of Morals' in the *Treatise on Human Nature* (1740) as the text from which he had learned 'that the foundations of all *virtue* are laid in *utility*', that 'utility was the test and measure of all virtue', notwithstanding 'a few exceptions' discerned by Hume which Bentham dismissed as such (268n). 'I felt', he declared, 'as if scales had fallen from my eyes'. It is doubtless this formulation that led J.S. Mill to describe Bentham's ethics as derived from Hume (Mill 1969 [1832]: 497), and Robbins in our day to see in Hume rather than Bentham the *originator* of utilitarianism as an ethical theory and not only a 'criterion of social arrangement' (Robbins 1961: 177).

An 'Article on Utilitarianism' dating to 1829 based on a series of manuscript notes, and now printed in the *Collected Works*, adds to the difficulty we have in pinning Bentham down with respect to his attitude towards Hume. For in a brief introductory overview of the early development of the notion 'principle of utility', we find him designating as 'the first work in which it ever made its appearance in the character of a subject of discussion was the work entitled *Essays* by David Hume' – apparently referring to the section 'Why Utility Pleases' in the *Enquiry Concerning the Principles of Morals* (see editorial note in Bentham 1983 (1829). 290n). But the commendation, if such was intended, is double edged and Bentham goes on to hint that Hume, while intending to set up the principle as 'corner stone' of a system opposed to 'moral sense' reasoning, had left the matter 'altogether vague' and of small practical value:

> In that work it is spoken of as the name of a principle which might be considered as the foundation or corner-stone of one of the systems of morals at that time known and embraced by a philosophical sect, the moral sense being the denomination of a different system and that in truth a very widely different one. In that work of David Hume's the idea attached to it was altogether vague: the idea not being followed up and by the means of any particular ideas exhibited as representative of so many species contained in the genus so denominated, liquidated as were and applied to practical use.
>
> (290).

Recall now Hume's position that '[t]hose who resolve the sense of morals into original instincts of the human mind, may defend the cause of virtue with sufficient authority; but want the advantage, which those possess, who account for that sense by an extensive sympathy with mankind' (above, Chapter 5, p. 117). We are asked, in brief, not to entertain a 'sense of morals' yielding immediate verdicts regarding that 'multitude of precepts' commonly designated as ethical. Rather, the benevolent sentiment of 'sympathy' must be stimulated by the pertinent social consequences relevant to each specific application and precept; conversely, that sentiment gives 'a preference to the useful above the pernicious tendencies'. This mutual relation assures the equivalence of the proposition that 'the foundations of all *virtue* are laid in *utility*' (in Bentham's rendition of Hume) and Hume's proposition that 'sympathy is the chief source of moral distinctions'. Bentham too, as shown in Chapter 9, treats benevolence as a natural sentiment, and the interpretation here offered of Hume applies equally to his account. The identification of Bentham's ethical utilitarianism with *selfishness* is certainly to be avoided, the latter identified with James Mill's version, which is sometimes said to distinguish it from the Humean version (Robbins 1961: 177–8; 1970: 56). For *both* authors 'sympathy' is recognized not casually but as a prime social motive; indeed, for Bentham even the 'semi-social' motives turn on the degree of 'moral sensibility' pertaining to each case.[5]

A further contrast can be dismissed. Robbins correctly emphasizes that the assumption that 'each man's capacity for happiness was to be counted as equal' was only 'a working rule for legislation' (in Maine's words), and that the 'felicific calculus' entailed 'rough judgments of the expediency of particular items of the penal law' in no way intending precise 'quantitative computations' (Robbins 1961: 180–1). But if by his assertion that Hume never used it in any other way, he intended to suggest by contrast that Bentham did so he would be in error since Bentham himself explicitly disassociated himself from literal quantitative computation (see Chapter 9, p. 224).

Other common features may be noted. For Bentham, of course, concepts condemned outright by 'common-place morality', such as avarice, had no meaning independent of utility and disutility (Bentham 1982 [1789] 1982: 114–15). For Hume, similarly, there were no absolutes so that there could be too much of a good thing even with respect to 'public utility', as in the case of alms-giving (see Chapter 7, p. 162).

Now Hume tried to understand why 'the difficulty of accounting for these effects of usefulness, or its contrary, has kept philosophers from admitting them into their systems of ethics, and has induced them rather to employ any other principle, in explaining the origin of moral good and evil' (Hume 1927 [1777]: 213). It was, he insisted, unjustified to reject 'any principle, confirmed by experience, that we cannot give a satisfactory account of its origin, nor are able to resolve it into other more general principles'. And, indeed, Hume perceived the quest for pleasure and avoidance of pain as 'an ultimate end, [which] is never referred to any other object' (293). Hence also his refusal to consider 'why we have humanity or a fellow-feeling with others. It is sufficient, that this is experienced to be a principle of human nature. We must stop somewhere in our examination of causes ... No man is absolutely indifferent to the happiness and misery of others. The first has a natural tendency to give pleasure; the second pain' (219–20n). Similarly, he assumed the sentiment of 'general benevolence, or humanity, or sympathy' to be 'real, from general experience, without any other proof' (298n). This general stance corresponds exactly to Bentham's position that the principle of utility is not susceptible of direct proof: 'that which is used to prove every thing else, cannot itself be proved: a chain of proofs must have their commencement somewhere' (Bentham 1982 [1789]: 13).[6] For both, The utility principle was axiomatic for both, a 'postulate'. In this regard Hume's elaboration of his second category of moral duties, which includes political allegiance or 'obedience to magistrates', could scarcely be more 'Benthamite' in its concern to escape circular reasoning:

> If the reason be asked of that obedience, which we are bound to pay to government, I readily answer, *because society could not otherwise subsist*. And this answer is clear and intelligible to all mankind. Your answer is, *because we should keep our word*. But ... you find yourself embarrassed, when it is asked, *why we are bound to keep our word?* Nor can you give any answer, but what would, immediately, without any circuit, have accounted for our obligation to allegiance.
>
> (Hume 1994 [1777]: 481)

All in all, the coincidence of the two ethical perspectives is so extensive that the high praise given to Hume in *A Fragment on Government* is easy to appreciate. We must then face the problem that in his annotations of 1819 to *Morals and Legislation* Bentham cited Hume along with Shaftesbury and Hutcheson as adopting the idea of a 'moral sense' as entailing the *rejection* of utility considerations.[7] This insertion, I surmise, must have been made carelessly in a reaction to features that *seemed* to be in conflict with Humean utility that was so much appreciated. As has been explained, Bentham was *unnecessarily* concerned, precisely because Hume did not intend by his 'moral sense' an innate ability to sense what is right and wrong independently of circumstances; to the contrary, the moral sense was put at ease by observing conduct reflecting concern with the general good, that is satisfying the benevolent sentiment of 'sympathy'.

It is also worth recalling Bentham's objection to what he refers to as Hume's 'few exceptions' to the utilitarian rule. By this he perhaps intended Hume's 'cases of less moment' (see Chapter 5, p. 121). Yet it is a fact that Bentham himself allowed at one point 'other considerations than those of utility [from which] we derive our notions of right and wrong', namely 'a moral sentiment' which is 'originally conceived from any other source than a view of utility' (Bentham 1982 [1789]: 28). Although he treated the allowance as a 'speculation', it would seem that – surprising though it may appear – he may himself have been skating rather close to the despised 'moral sense', since 'moral sentiment' as such figures large in his ethical system so that to describe it as merely as a speculative matter would scarcely be appropriate. I therefore find his remark puzzling.

Long is unconvincing when he charges Bentham with *distorting* Hume by attributing to him a utility perspective (Long 1990: 23–4). It would, however, be going too far to identify the two systems in all respects. Though there is common ground regarding the high weighting given to *benevolence* or *good-will* or *sympathy* in the moral hierarchy, for Hume the empirical significance of concern for the public interest is at least as powerful as self-interest (Hume 1927 [1777]: 214–18], whereas Bentham was less sanguine. Furthermore, a notion of 'fitness' (see Chapter 7, p. 166) is not to my knowledge expressed in so many words by Bentham. On the other hand, Hume incorporated within 'fitness' what he refers to as 'prudence and discretion', and Bentham certainly did recognize the moral approval attached to these qualities, expressed in the *Springs of Action* as 'prudence, circumspection, forecast, foresight' (Bentham 1843 [1815]: 204). Furthermore, whereas Hume focused on the social consequences of conduct for good or bad as evaluated objectively by a 'spectator' free of self-interested bias, Bentham provided (again, as far as I am aware) no formal discussion of the 'spectator', although disinterested evaluation is presumably always intended.

10.3 Bentham and Smith

Our concern next is with the Bentham–Smith relation, principally focusing on the *Theory of Moral Sentiments*. The extensive discussion in Chapter 7 allows me to make only brief comments here.

Bentham wrote reams on *The Wealth of Nations* but made no corresponding analysis of *TMS*. We may, however, take it for granted that he was familiar with this work. How he understood it is another matter.[8] If he had read *TMS* as opposing the utility principle would he not have addressed the matter in his lengthy note in *Morals and Legislation* enumerating objectionable positions? His silence leaves open the possibility that he perceived the 1759 text as *favouring* the principle of utility and therefore not requiring notice. This option is reinforced by the extensive evidence of close proximity between the Hume and Smith systems of ethical utilitarianism – confirmed by Hume's complimentary notice of *TMS* in the *Critical Review* of 1759 (above, pp. 157, 163) – and between the Hume and Bentham systems.

But this is presumptive. Whether Bentham indeed read *TMS* as in line with Hume cannot be answered with certainty. The observation in 1795 coupling Smith with Hume (above, p. 238) is suggestive but inconclusive since it extends too broadly. In particular, regarding Smith Bentham may have intended 'the art of legislation' rather than 'private ethics', with the *Wealth of Nations* in mind, although it might perhaps be said that this is unlikely since Bentham so much opposed the *Naturrecht* concept to be found in 1776: 'I leave it to Adam Smith, and the champions of the rights of man ... to talk of invasions of natural liberty, and to give as a special argument against this or that law, an argument the effect of which would be to put a negative upon all laws' (Bentham 1954 [1801]: 258). The matter at hand remains therefore in abeyance, as Rosen feared (Rosen 2003: 80).

Recall next how much is sometimes made of Smith's utility considerations, especially in the context of justice, as pertaining to *philosophical* interpretations of human morality and of relevance to an elite rather than the bulk of humanity (Chapter 7, pp. 153-4). It is certainly true that we encounter instances where Smith does specifically address politicians seeking to persuade the public regarding matters of policy, but this is no less the case with Bentham. Indeed, Viner cautioned that it was the ethics of moral leaders – attempting to influence legislation – rather than the ordinary man that mainly concerned Bentham and citing Bentham to the effect that '[t]he science whose foundations we have explored can appeal only to lofty minds with whom the public welfare has become a passion' (Viner 1958: 311–12). Leslie Stephen went yet further and dismissed Bentham's contribution to private ethics, writing of his reducing morality 'to a mere chaos of empirical doctrine' (Stephen 1902 1:126). Yet Bentham did at times write as if he were mainly concerned with private ethics, asserting for example, that '[t]here is no case in which a private man ought not to direct his own conduct to the production of his own happiness, and of that of his fellow-creatures', whereas 'there are cases in which the legislator ought not … to attempt to direct the conduct of the several other members of the community' (Bentham 1982 (1789): 285).[9] As for Smith, we have encountered his qualification to the exclusion of the 'bulk of mankind' from his ethical propositions, and his contention that a persuasive political campaign would culminate in explaining to the public 'their general subserviency to the happiness of society' (Chapter 7, p. 168). I conclude that to draw a sharp contrast between Smith and Bentham regarding the matters at hand is to be avoided.

One further feature of the Smith–Bentham *entente* – whether or not Bentham himself recognized the Smith branch – merits reiteration. I refer to Smith's application of the utilitarian maximand in *TMS* to justify population expansion and accordingly the '*real happiness of human life*' (see Chapter 7, p. 167). Bentham's counterpart reads thus: 'the encrease of abundance in point of population … encrease[s] the mass of comfort by encreasing the numbers of those who enjoy comfort' (Bentham 1954 [1801–4]: 310); or again: 'Encrease of population is desirable, as being an encrease of 1. the beings susceptible of *enjoyment*; 2. the beings capable of being employed as *instruments of defence*' (361). Hume in 'Populousness of Ancient Nations' (first published in 1752) describes the responsibility of government to adopt policies assuring 'the easy subsistence of men, and consequently … their propagation and encrease' (Hume 1994 [1777] 1994: 420), but does not justify increase of population in terms of increase in 'happiness' or 'enjoyment' in the Smith–Bentham manner, saying only that 'wherever there are most happiness and virtue, and the wisest institutions, there will also be most people' (382).

10.4 Bentham and Helvétius

Much of the evidence for Bentham's high appreciation of Helvétius appears in manuscript form (or, if printed by Bowring, not yet available to Mill when he composed his 'Bentham' (1838)). We have cited at the outset of the present chapter appreciations in 'Sundry Memoranda' of 1773–1774, in a memorandum of 1776, and in a draft letter to Voltaire of November 1776 where Bentham declared: 'I have built solely on the foundation of utility, laid as it is by Helvétius'. This is also true of Bentham's appreciation of Helvétius dating to the 1770s appearing in a planned project to be entitled *Elements of Critical Jurisprudence*: 'The present work as well as every other work of mine that has been or will be published on the subject of legislation or any other branch of moral science is an attempt to extend the experimental method of reasoning from the physical branch to the moral. What Bacon was to the physical world, Helvétius was to the moral. The moral world has therefore had its Bacon, but its Newton is yet to come' (Long 1988: 8 citing ms: UC clvii.32. de Champs 2011: 23n 14 refers to UC 69, f.17 on the authority of a Long lecture delivered in 2008).

Yet Bentham's perspective on Helvétius is not so easy to pin down, for there may be evidence of a dilution of enthusiasm over time. Thus Halévy cites the manuscript of the Preface to *An Introduction to Morals and Legislation*: 'To Helvétius I owe the principle of utility, the foundation of the work, to M. Beccaria the consideration of the ingredients in the value of a punishment, which put me upon extending the consideration of it to pain and pleasure' (Halévy 1995 (1901), vol. 1: 31, 201n87 citing Mss. Univ. Coll. 27: p. 109); but this commendation, written probably before 1780 (when a provisional version of the work was printed but not published), does not appear in any of the printed editions. Furthermore, Helvétius is not mentioned in an extract from the 1780s in Bentham's 'Commonplace Book' which cites Joseph Priestley as 'the first (unless it was Beccaria) who taught my lips to pronounce this sacred truth:— That the greatest happiness of the greatest number is the foundation of morals and legislation' (Bentham 1843 [1781–1785]: 142),[10] nor does he appear in the citation from 'Bentham's Conversations 1827–8' where Bentham claims priority for himself, limiting Locke's contribution to utilitarian ethics to a clearing of the ground. (above, p. 237). An informal note dated 29 June 1827 attributes the primary principle to Priestley and detailed applications to ethics for himself with only limited recognition allowed Helvétius: '*Greatest Happiness Principle.*–Priestley.–Applied to every branch of morals in detail, by Bentham: a part of the way previously by Helvétius' (Bentham 1843 [1827]: 561). And while the 'Article on Utilitarianism', referred to above with respect to Hume, recognizes *De l'esprit* as an advance respecting 'the application of the principle of utility to practical uses', and the connecting of the idea of 'happiness' to those of 'pleasure' and 'pain', the contribution failed to express adequately 'the various universally-experienced modifications of pain and pleasure' and, one is given to understand lacked force in application (Bentham 1983 [1829]: 290). 'A greater number of species … ranked under the two genera of pain and pleasure' were provided by David Hartley (1749) but even he was far from being 'all comprehensive' and thus falling short of what was required to 'giv[e] direction to human conduct in the several walks of life, public as well as private' (291). Again, as in earlier attributions, the precise phrase 'the greatest happiness of the greatest number' is attributed to Priestley, which constituted 'not only a rational foundation but the only rational foundation, of enactments in legislation and all rules and precepts destined for the direction of human conduct in private life'. Although, as noted above, the precise phraseology attributed to Priestley is not quite accurate, Priestley does emerge here as the author who most impressed Bentham.

Recall now from Chapter 6 Bentham's late expression of gratitude to Helvétius – and secondarily to Hartley – for instructing him to treat '*happiness*' as an 'aggregate or compound' of simple pleasures, however apparently irreducible the elements are to a common dimension. Specifically:

> Whether there ever were a time at which the word happiness failed of presenting to my mind the character of an aggregate, or compound, of which pleasures, and the exemption from corresponding pains, were the sole elements, is more than at present I can recollect. The satisfaction I remember to have experienced at the observation of this interpretation, as given to it in the first place by Helvétius [*De L'esprit*], and afterwards by Hartley [in Priestley's abridgement, Priestley 1775], affords some presumption of its being at the first of these times new to me. But perhaps the cause of that satisfaction was not the novelty of the notion in relation to my own conceptions, but the circumstance of seeing the confirmation given to them in these works.
>
> (Bentham 1843 (1827): 286)

Hartley's position may be illustrated by the proposition that '[t]he intellectual Pleasures and Pains are as real as the sensible ones, being ... nothing but the sensible ones variously mixed and compounded together. The intellectual Pleasures and Pains are also all equally of a factitious and acquired Nature. We must therefore estimate all our Pleasures and Pains equally, by their Magnitude, Permanency, and Tendency to procure others; and our Pains in like manner' (Hartley 1749: 83–4). And it is presumably the following characteristic Helvétius statements that attracted Bentham's attention, assuming that the desire of *happiness* is identified with maximizing pleasure and minimizing pain:

> I [God] place thee under the guardianship of pleasure and pain: both shall watch over thy thoughts, and thy actions; they shall beget thy passions, excite thy friendship, thy tenderness, thine aversions, thy rage; they shall kindle thy desires, thy fears, thy hopes, they shall take of the veil off truth; they shall plunge thee in error and after having made thee conceive a thousand absurd and different systems of morality and government, shall one day discover to thee the simple principles, on the unfolding of which depends the order and happiness of the moral world.
>
> (Helvétius 1759 [1758]: 161)

> I propose ... to follow the metamorphosis of the natural pleasures and pains, into the artificial pleasures, to shew, that in the passions, such as avarice, ambition, pride, and friendship, which seem least to belong to

the pleasures of sense, we always either seek pleasure, or shun natural pain.

(162–3)

But it is by no means clear what to make of Bentham's commendation. For Helvétius denied compounding at the aggregate level – entailing interpersonal comparison – on the grounds that 'there is properly none but [the individual] himself that can be the just appraiser of his own pleasure: that men being animated by different passions, the same objects cannot appear of the same value to different eyes; that sentiment alone can judge of sentiment; and that the desire of always citing to the tribunal of cold reason, is assembling the diet of the empire, in order to determine upon cases of conscience' (Helvétius 1759 [1758]: 317).[11] As for the individual, notwithstanding that Helvétius represents him as a 'just appraiser of his own pleasures', when discussing the behaviour of 'men of cold dispositions' he expressed small confidence in a *calculus* of pleasures and pains: 'But it ought not to be imagined, as their vanity would persuade them to believe, that before they take a resolution, they calculate the advantages and inconveniences of it: was this the case, these men would only be determined in their conduct by reflection; but experience informs us, that they are always moved by sensation, and in this respect, the men of cold dispositions are the same as the rest' (316). How far this passage should be generalized is unclear, for we have seen that only the genuine professional 'moralist' is granted the ability of making cost–benefit calculations regarding policy (see Chapter 6, p. 137).

Bentham's commendation may have related to *individual* 'happiness', for he himself denied aggregation maintaining, in a fragment headed 'Dimension of Happiness', that "Tis in vain to talk of adding quantities which after the addition will continue distinct as they were before. *One man's happiness will never be another man's happiness*; the benefit to one man is not the benefit of another' (cited Halévy 1995 [1904], vol. 3: 227; emphasis added). But we cannot be sure since he did adopt addibility as a counter-factual axiom required for practical purposes: 'This addibility of the happiness of different subjects, however, when considered rigorously, it may appear fictitious, is a *postulatum* without the allowance of which all political reasoning is at a stand' (emphasis added); and it is as an essential working rule that we may perhaps understand his allowances elsewhere for social aggregation, as in the unpublished *Institute of Political Economy* where he refers to 'what in every government ought to be, and is to a certain degree, the end or object aimed at – viz. the maximum of happiness with reference to the several members of the community taken together, and with reference to the whole expanse of time' (Bentham 1954 [1801–4]: 307).

Notes

1 To fully understand Bentham's, and also Hume's, perspective on Locke would require some consideration of their opposition to Lockean 'contractarianism', on which see Riley 2006: 355–8.
2 On this distinction as qualifying the egalitarian tone of the abbreviated formula, see Persky 2016: 28.
3 This contrast may lend support to a view of Hutcheson as engaged in 'a difficult task of reconciling rival sources' (Carey 2006: 157n).
4 We note by way of contrast Immanuel Kant's distinctive, and stricter, position that sympathy or benevolence, if a *natural* inclination, did not suffice to merit ethical commendation; only if an individual acts from *duty* 'has his action genuine moral worth' (Kant 1949 [1785]: 146). For recent expositions of Kantian ethics in relation to utilitarianism, see Frazer 2010, Timmermann 2014.
5 But for the contrary opinion, see Bagolini 1975: 109.
6 On this matter, see the instructive account by Sidgwick 1877: 648.
7 Strangely, Leslie Stephen makes no mention of Hume as listed by Bentham (Stephen 1900: 240).
8 See Rosen 2000: 100–1; 2003: 80 on this issue.
9 See on this, Hart: 'throughout his analysis [in his chapters on 'Human Actions in General'], Bentham adopts the viewpoint of a utilitarian legislator … But though this utilitarian and legislative viewpoint in some instances limits the general applicability of Bentham's analysis, there is still much of value to be learned … which is independent of this legislative viewpoint' (Hart 1982: lv). More generally: 'though legislation is the principal topic of *PML* the principle of utility requiring the maximization of the general welfare determines what ought to be done by individuals in the conduct of their own lives as well as what laws for the conduct of others ought to be enacted by the legislator' (xlix).
10 For Beccaria's formulation, see editorial note 4 to Bentham's 'Article on Utilitarianism' (1829) in Bentham 1983: 291n. (See also Harrison 1983: 115.) Priestley, in fact did not use the formula but rather wrote: 'The good and happiness of the members, that is the majority of the members of any state, is the great standard by which every thing relating to that state must be finally determined' (Priestley 1771: 13).
11 Helvétius however seems to imply some kind of aggregation when he writes: 'Every individual judges of things and persons, by the agreeable or disagreeable impressions he receives from them; and the public is no more than an assemblage of all the individuals; therefore it cannot fail of making its interest the rule of its decisions' (Helvétius 1759 [1758]: 24). But perhaps we should not read too much into this affirmation.

References

Bagolini, L. 1975. 'The Topicality of Adam Smith's Notion of Sympathy and Judicial Evaluations', *Essays on Adam Smith*, A.S. Skinner and T. Wilson, eds. Oxford: Clarendon Press: 100–113.

Bentham, J. 1843. Appendix on 'Logical Arrangements, or Instruments of Invention and Discovery employed by Jeremy Bentham', published from the mss. The *Works of Jeremy Bentham* 3, ed. John Bowring. Edinburgh: William Tait:285–295.

Bentham, J. 1982 (1789). *An Introduction to the Principles of Morals and Legislation*, ed. J.H. Burns and H.L.A. Hart. London and New York: Methuen.

Bentham, J. 1843 (1773–1774). 'Sundry Memoranda', *Works* 10, ed. John Bowring. Edinburgh: William Tait: 69–72.

Bentham, J. 1843 (1781–1785). 'Extracts from Commonplace Book', *Works* 10, ed. John Bowring. Edinburgh: William Tait: 141–147.
Bentham, J. 1843 (1827). 'Logical Arrangements', *Works* 10, ed. John Bowring. Edinburgh: William Tait: 560–561.
Bentham, J. 1843 (1827–1828). 'Bentham's Conversations', *Works* 10, ed. John Bowring. Edinburgh: William Tait: 581–588.
Bentham, J. 1843 (1776). *A Fragment on Government. Works* 1, ed. John Bowring. Edinburgh: William Tait: 221–295.
Bentham, J. 1843 (1815). *A Table of the Springs of Action. Works* 1, ed. John Bowring. Edinburgh: William Tait: 195–219.
Bentham, J. 1952 (1795). 'Supply Without Burthen'. *Jeremy Bentham's Economic Writings* 1, ed. W. Stark. London: George Allen and Unwin: 279–367.
Bentham, J. 1954 (1801). 'Defence of a Maximum', *Jeremy Bentham's Economic Writings* 3, ed. William Stark. London: George Allen and Unwin: 247–302.
Bentham, J. 1954 (1801–1804). ['Institute of Political Economy'], *Jeremy Bentham's Economic Writings* 3, ed. William Stark. London: George Allen and Unwin: 303–380.
Bentham, J. 1983 (1829). 'Article on Utilitarianism', *Deontology together with A Table of the Springs of Action and Article on Utilitarianism*. Oxford: Clarendon Press: ed. Amnon Goldworth. Oxford: Clarendon Press: 283–328.
Carey, D. 2006. *Locke, Shaftesbury, and Hutcheson: Testing Diversity in the Enlightenment and Beyond*. Cambridge: Cambridge University Press.
De Champs, E. 2011. 'Constitution and the Code: Jeremy Bentham on the Limits of the Constitutional Branch of Jurisprudence', *The Tocqueville Review / La revue Tocqueville* 32(1): 21–42.
Frazer, M. 2010. *The Enlightenment of Sympathy: Justice and the Moral Sentiments in the Eighteenth Century and Today*. Oxford: Oxford University Press.
Halévy, E. 1995 (1901). *La jeunesse de Bentham. La formation du radicalisme philosophiques* 1. Paris: Presses Universitaires de France.
Halévy, E. 1995 (1904). *Le Radicalisme Philosophiques. La formation du radicalisme philosophiques* 3. Paris: Presses Universitaires de France.
Harrison, R. 1983. *Bentham*. London: Routledge and Kegan Paul.
Hart, H.L.A. 1982. Introduction. *An Introduction to the Principles of Morals and Legislation*, edited by James H. Burns and H.L.A. Hart. London and New York: Methuen, xxxiii–lxx.
Hartley, D. 1749. *Observations on Man, His Frame, His Duty, and His Expectations*. London: Hitch and Austen.
Helvétius, C.A. 1759 (1758). *De L'esprit: or Essays on the Mind and its Several Faculties*, London: Dodsley.
Hume, D. 1927 (1777). *An Enquiry Concerning the Principles of Morals*, ed. L.A. Selby-Bigge.Oxford: Clarendon Press: 166–323.
Hume, D. 1994 (1777). 'On the Populousness of Ancient Nations' (first published in 1752). *Essays: Moral, Political, and Literary*, ed. Eugene F. Miller. Indianapolis: Liberty Fund: 377–464.
Hume, D. 1994 (1777). 'Of the Original Contract', *Essays: Moral, Political, and Literary*, ed. Eugene F. Miller. Indianapolis: Liberty Fund: 465–487.
Hutcheson, F. 1728. *An Essay on the Nature and Conduct of the Passions and Affections with Illustrations on the Moral Sense*. London: J. Darby and T. Browne.

Hutcheson, F. 1729. *An Inquiry into the Original of our Ideas of Beauty and Virtue in Two Treatises: Treatise* II: *An Inquiry Concerning Moral Good and Evil*. Third edition, corrected. London: J. and J. Knapton.

Hutcheson, F. 1755. *A System of Moral Philosophy*. London: Miller and Longman.

Hutcheson, F. 1769 (1742). *An Essay on the Nature and Conduct of the Passions and Affections with Illustrations on the Moral Sense*. ['The Third Edition'.] Glasgow: R. & A. Foulis.

Kant, I. 1949 [1785]. 'Metaphysical Foundations of Morals'. *The Philosophy of Kant: Immanuel Kant's Moral and Political Writings*, ed. C.F. Friedrich. New York: Modern Library: 140–208.

Long, D.G. 1988. 'Censorial Jurisprudence and Political Radicalism: A Reconsideration of the Early Bentham', *The Bentham Newsletter*, June (12): 4–23.

Long, D.G. 1990. '"Utility" and the "Utility Principle": Hume, Smith, Bentham, Mill', *Utilitas*, 2(1): 11–39.

Mill, J.S. 1969 (1832). 'Obituary of Bentham', *Collected Works* 10, ed. J M. Robson. Toronto: University of Toronto Press: 495–498.

Mill, J.S. 1969 (1838). 'Bentham', *Collected Works* 10. Toronto: University of Toronto Press: 75–115.

Persky, J. 2016. *The Political Economy of Progress: John Stuart Mill and Modern Radicalism*. Oxford: Oxford University Press.

Priestley, J. 1771. *An Essay on the First Principles of Government*, 2nd ed. London: J. Johnson.

Priestley, J. 1775. *Hartley's Theory of the Human Mind, on the Principle of the Association of Ideas*. London: J. Johnson.

Riley, P. 2006. 'Social contract theory and its critics', *The Cambridge History of Eighteenth-Century Political Thought*, ed. Mark Goldie and Robert Wokler. Cambridge: Cambridge University Press: 347–375.

Robbins, L.C. 1961. *The Theory of Economic Policy in English Classical Political Economy*. London: Macmillan.

Robbins, L.C. 1970. *The Evolution of Modern Economic Theory*. London: Macmillan.

Rosen, F. 2000. 'The Idea of Utility in Adam Smith's Theory of Moral Sentiments', *History of European Ideas* 26: 79–103.

Rosen, F. 2003. *Classical Utilitarianism from Hume to Mill*. London and New York: Routledge.

Sidgwick, H. 1877. 'Bentham and Benthamism in Politics and Ethics', *Fortnightly Review* n.s.21: 627–652.

Stephen, L. 1900. *The English Utilitarians* 1. London: Duckworth.

Stephen, L. 1902. *English Thought in the Eighteenth Century* 1. 3rd ed. London: John Murray.

Timmermann, J. 2014. 'Kantian ethics and utilitarianism, *The Cambridge Companion to Utilitarianism*, eds. Ben Eggleston and Dale. E. Miller. Cambridge: Cambridge University Press: 239–258.

Viner, J. 1958. *The Long View and the Short: Studies in Economic Theory and Policy*. Glencoe: The Free Press.

Part 5
Thomas Robert Malthus

11 Malthus and the utilitarians

11.1 Introduction

Malthus's role in building up the system of Classical economic thought, Lord Robbins opined nearly half a century ago, is 'a matter likely to arouse much more controversy than the answer to a similar question in the case of the other great Classical economists' (Robbins 1970: 86). This comment remains valid not only regarding economic theory and policy but also – and perhaps to a greater degree in the light of Malthus's status as a Church of England cleric – regarding ethical considerations. Most recently, in his *Utilitarianism and Malthus's Virtue Ethics* (2014) Sergio Cremaschi insists on a sharp contrast between Malthus and the secular Utilitarians (the Philosophical Radicals) rejecting interpretations which emphasize the coalescence of the Malthusian and Utilitarian perspectives. I welcome his book as providing an opportunity to clarify once again a central issue in intellectual history.

Professor Cremaschi has a powerful olfactory capacity, one which he generously attributes to others. In his opening chapter, 'Malthus the Utilitarian vs. Malthus the Christian moral thinker', he commends Ernest Albee (1901: xvii–ix) for having 'sensed that there was something stinking [sic] in [Leslie] Stephen's story of the utilitarian parson' (Cremaschi 2014: 8) – namely, Stephen's contention that Malthus 'was entirely at one with the Utilitarians proper, and seems to regard their doctrine as self-evident' (Stephen 1900 2: 157). (I am bemused by this attribution since nowhere in his book did Albee mention Malthus.) And he finds that Patricia James's 'pretty' biography of Malthus (1979) 'smells a little bit of "*surtout, pas d'idées*"' by 'leaving the reader with the impression that Malthus neither studied theology nor philosophy' (Cremaschi 2014: 9).

The original sin is traced to William Empson, whose obituary notice of 1837 represented Malthus 'in his views of life' as 'a utilitarian of the right sort [whose] quarrel with the followers of Bentham was only in their narrow conception of utility, and in their apparent ignorance of human nature' (cited Cremaschi 2014: 6). In his turn Bonar (1885) perceived Malthus as 'a Utilitarian on principle, even a more consequent Utilitarian than Bentham, but [who] adopted different views on such individual issues as moral motivation and the definition of virtue' (7); Plamenatz (1949) presumed that Malthus was 'another utilitarian clergyman' no different from the other great 'classical economists' Adam Smith and Ricardo (8); Robbins (1952) maintained that Malthus's attribution of 'disharmonies' to Divine Wisdom is 'extraneous to analysis and without influence on the theory of policy'(9, 194); and William Petersen (1999) represented Malthus as a 'wholehearted utilitarian' (9). While not characterized as malodorous – or, worse still, as 'pretty' – my own interpretation of Malthus (Hollander 1989, 1997) is taken to task as the latest in this misbegotten tradition. Winch (1987) by contrast comes out of all this smelling of roses, for he 'wisely reminds us that the depuration of science from theology, metaphysics and similar cant [sic] wished for by the Bonar–Robbins–Hollander alignment is a hasty enterprise since "Malthus should also be regarded as a seeker after scientific truth because of, rather than despite, his clear theological commitments"' (11). Professor Cremaschi might have mentioned Winch 1996 to similar effect (e.g., Winch 1996: 243).

The 'Robbins' view is in fact more widespread than Professor Cremaschi indicates (for a strong version, see Rashid 1984: 137), and may even be found expressed by commentators he classifies among the angels (see, for example, Winch 1983: 71, Waterman 1991: 136, 144–50.) But since amongst those he designates as 'cantists' I alone am still alive I shall take the opportunity to give my response.

Cremaschi makes life far too easy for himself by attributing a perception of Malthus as *secularist* to those who, like the present writer, emphasize his shared ground with the secular Utilitarians notwithstanding his unmistakable theological concerns. And in addition to tilting at windmills he adopts a simple-minded perspective of what Classical political economy entailed, ignoring the ethical component in 'Ricardian' policy prescription, by which I intend Ricardo himself and J.S. Mill. In any event, like the proverbial successful general, Cremaschi occupies all positions, making concessions at key junctures to the 'Bonar–Robbins–Hollander' perspective which are at times so disarming as to erase all differences. There is no purpose to responding to what Cremaschi perceives as 'cant' if we take seriously his assertion that 'whether theodicy is "extraneous to analysis" is probably an ill-framed question, since the answer is positive, but it is so by definition' (Cremaschi 2014: 197). In fact, some good arguments for the coalescence of the Malthusian and secular versions of utilitarianism can be garnered from this book.

As for Professor Cremaschi's primary objections to my own work, two passages from his introductory chapter specify my alleged *identification* of Malthus with 'the Philosophic Radicals, or the Benthamite[s], or later on, the Utilitarians', both in ethics and politics:

> Several … commentators – the most recent among them is Samuel Hollander – seem to believe that Malthus, who never met Bentham and apparently never read anything of his and had a rather distant and occasionally conflictive relationship with James Mill … was nonetheless simply a Utilitarian in ethics and politics. I believe that this sounds a bit strange to anybody who has any familiarity with the climate of opinion in early

nineteenth-century Britain ... [I]f the word Utilitarian denotes a follower of the family of doctrines that was being promoted by the group called the Philosophic Radicals, or the Benthamite[s], or later on, the Utilitarians, it is clear enough that Malthus was no Utilitarian and that he was precisely one of the enemies the Bentham–Mill coterie wanted to fight. In fact, this family of doctrines included democracy, atheism, psychological associationism, sociological individualism, *Laisssez-faire* economic liberalism somehow supported by a simplified version of Ricardianism, and the 'new morality', in turn consisting of hedonism, the harmony between self-interest and general interest, and the war on prejudice ... [T]he utilitarians in the first decades of the nineteenth century were the 'Philosophic radicals', and it is clear beyond any doubt that Malthus did not belong to this group.

(Cremaschi 2014: 2–3)

Samuel Hollander [1989, 1997] seems in his final outcome to coagulate the results of almost two centuries cross-purpose by adding the catalyst of the logical-empiricist dichotomy between science and ethics. He argues that Lionel Robbins had been right in claiming ... that 'Malthus's explanation of disharmony by reference to Divine Wisdom is extraneous to analysis and without influence on the theory of policy' [1989: 171], and that he was a Utilitarian in his appraisal of policies, albeit a Utilitarian afflicted with 'damaging vagueness'

(9)[1]

Cremaschi creates a straw man by asserting that I perceive Malthus 'simply [as] a Utilitarian in ethics and politics', for I nowhere dismiss Malthus's religious preoccupations. On the contrary, I refer to his continued efforts in the second and later editions of *The Essay on Population* to reconcile dogma and utility, despite the omission of the formal chapters on theology of 1798. Indeed, I maintain that Malthus's clerical status impeded his quest for solutions to burning social issues obliging him to *reinterpret* the scriptures appropriately. And I do not maintain an identity of position between Malthus and the secular Utilitarians extending to the whole slew of doctrinal elements (including atheism!) attributed by Cremaschi to the Philosophical Radicalism in his crash course on nineteenth-century intellectual history. My objective has been, and remains, to show that no good purpose is served by papering over the extent of shared opinion which is considerably greater than many of Malthus's contemporaries – and commentators to this day – ever realized. This commonality expanded radically with Malthus's adoption of the Ricardian prescriptions regarding commercial policy and critical attitude towards the landlord class in general. Certainly J.S. Mill applauded the reformist implications of Malthus's primary recommendations regarding population. And I will go on to show how close Malthus and Mill were even on Ireland.

Cremaschi's agreement that Malthus was indeed a utilitarian, we shall find, is expressed in a manner reflecting his vision of a horde of commentators denying

Malthus's clerical *persona*, and as a consequence he conveys the misleading impression that the 'greatest happiness' rule for Malthus differed somehow from that of the secular writers. I point out in this context that Malthus's adoption of the Ricardian industrialization programme in the mid-1820s was based almost entirely on an evaluation of altered empirical and legislative circumstances, theological matters not entering the picture. I then examine more generally how firmly based Malthus's reliance on theological sources was, taking into account his primary proposition that 'we should reason from nature up to nature's God, and not presume to reason from God to nature' – his 'natural theology' – and his remarkable interpretations of the scriptures along utilitarian lines to yield divine support for a reduced rather than an increased birth rate. Finally, I consider the ethics *vs.* happiness and the wealth *vs.* happiness dichotomies which Cremaschi believes distinguish Malthus from the secularists.

11.2 Malthus's theological utilitarianism

The key to an appreciation of Cremaschi's position lies in a brief remark asserting that 'ironically enough, utility … was itself the most markedly theological element in Malthus's system of ideas' (Cremaschi 2014:198). Repeatedly we find him emphasizing that Malthus was a utilitarian but a theologian, an insistence reflecting his mistaken belief that the 'cantists' identified Malthus as a *secularist*. Once this error is abandoned, the theological character of his utilitarianism becomes less of a crucial issue since no one questions the claim – provided always that it can be justified in the particular application under consideration. For a 'theological' no less than for a secularist utilitarian the point of reference in any particular application remains the 'greatest happiness' rule; meanwhile the secularist cannot dispense with value-judgment of some kind or other, as Bentham himself pointed out regarding the 'utility' reference point itself, and as we shall see is true of Ricardo and J.S. Mill.

I shall illustrate the pattern emerging from Cremaschi's criticism. He does not dispute Malthus's social reformism. In fact, a list of specific objectives properly ascribed to Malthus – 'equality, dignity, self-reliance, generalized education, higher wages, higher standards of consumption' (Cremaschi 2014: 154–5; see below Section 11.5) – could equally have been ascribed to John Stuart Mill. He also concedes that Malthus's proposal to evaluate policies 'with a view to the happiness of the great mass of society' (Malthus 1820: 522) 'was of a kind … shared with the Utilitarians' (Cremaschi 2014: 44); and of Malthus's plea for high wages (see Hollander 1997: 912) 'where the reason given is that a greater number of individuals would be happier', he says that it would 'no doubt …be plausible for a utilitarian' (Cremaschi 2014: 10). But he maintains that '[t]he points at which Hollander successfully singles out convergences between Malthus and the secular Utilitarian John Stuart Mill are in fact not points where the dogmatic divine gives way to the secular Utilitarian but those where a maximizing criterion' – presumably the plea for high wages – 'is fully justified for Malthus the theologian in his own terms'; furthermore, 'it is also

Adam Smith's argument, and it could be endorsed by thinkers of different descriptions since it needs no specifically utilitarian premise'. Unfortunately, Cremaschi's assurance of Malthus's theological terms of reference does not make the appeal to Greatest Happiness disappear. The response also begs the question of the Utilitarian component in Smith's work (regarding which the jury is still out).

The same pattern emerges regarding Malthus's privileging of labour on the grounds of 'Greatest Happiness' in justifying post-war agricultural protection. Here he represents the labouring classes as

> the foundation on which the whole fabric rests; and, from their numbers, unquestionably of the greatest weight, in any estimate of national happiness. If I were convinced, that to open our ports, would be permanently to improve the condition of the labouring classes of society, I should consider the question as at once determined in favour of such a measure. But I own it appears to me … that it will be attended with effects very different from those of improvement … It is very possible for a people to be miserably poor, and some of them starving, in a country where the money price of corn is very low.
>
> (Malthus 1986 [1815]: 162)

Cremaschi has read this passage, but asserts that 'Hollander [1997: 830] draws the wrong conclusions from his own findings when defining Malthus's policy advice as "utilitarian"' (Cremaschi 2014: 182). In this context, he also recognizes my discovery of Malthus's late abandonment of agricultural protectionism (Hollander 1992; 1995) but maintains in response that 'precisely a non-utilitarian distinction between considerations of justice and considerations of expediency lies constantly at the basis of Malthus's changing assessments' of trade policy'.

Here, once again, Cremaschi engages in comforting assurances forgetting that the devil lies in the details. Thus the 1815 text says not a word about justice but relates distinctly to 'national happiness' as reflecting the quantitative supremacy of the working classes. (Needless to say, it is possible to read into the text the notion that it is only 'just' to recognize the significance of numbers.) As for the policy transition of the mid-1820s, the argument turns on an objective evaluation of altered empirical and legislative conditions and the effect on welfare – and distribution – with the greatest-happiness principle extended to 'the commercial world in general': 'The most powerful of all the arguments against restrictions is their unsocial tendency, and the acknowledged injury which they must do the interests of the commercial world in general. The weight of this argument is increased rather than diminished by the numbers which may suffer from scarcity at the same time' (Malthus 1826 2: 209n). A 'moral' dimension is touched on only tangentially when Malthus writes to Thomas Chalmers in 1832: 'I quite agree with you in regard to the moral advantage of repealing the corn laws' (Hollander 1992: 272), Chalmers' position relates to the avoidance of 'the certain and urgent evil of a dissatisfied population, who feel, and perhaps with justice too, as if defrauded of their rights, by the compulsory restraints of the legislature on the importation of food' (Chalmers 1832: 533–4). There is nothing particularly 'theological' about this position, which is to be found in the *Wealth of Nations* in the context of working-class education and cited by Malthus in 1803 (Malthus 1803: 555–6).

It is pertinent to note here an alteration in Malthus's orientation not only regarding trade policy, but – at about the same time in *The Measure of Value* – also regarding the landlord class in general, taking him a further major step towards the Philosophical Radicals. The issue relates to a proposal to adjust contracts to the benefit of landowners at the expense of fund holders, which Malthus strongly rejected on moral grounds relating to 'fair play' – one might say 'justice' – but without formal theological underpinning:

> But whatever may have been the pressure on the owners of land since the peace, they cannot have the slightest plea for an attempt to indemnify themselves at the expense of the public creditor. In the turns of the wheel of fortune all parties should have fair play; no class of persons can be justified in endeavouring to lift themselves up by using unfair and dishonourable means to pull others down; and least of all ought such means to be thought of by the landlords of this country, who, whatever inconveniences they may have suffered latterly, have unquestionably altogether benefited much more largely from the alterations in the value of the currency, than the very persons who in their opinion should be made to relieve them from their embarrassment.
> (Malthus 1986 [1823]: 220–1)

Cremaschi, we have seen, places much weight on 'the distinction between considerations of justice and considerations of expediency' – or more generally between virtue and happiness – as a feature peculiar to Malthus. We shall presently see that this is in fact a distinction no less important for Ricardo and J.S. Mill.

11.3 Malthus's 'natural theology'

Professor Cremaschi, when comparing Paley and Malthus with respect to ethics, properly notes that the formal appeal to Natural Law should not be taken as a rejection of consequentialism: 'It is remarkable that Paley and Malthus argue following similar lines, that is, by proving that certain laws are "laws of nature" since, given certain factual data, if generally complied with, *they would produce positive consequences*' (Cremaschi 2014: 109; my emphasis). This brings us now to the central feature of Malthus's theological utilitarianism, that relating to so-called 'natural theology'. We have, for example, Malthus's definition of morality in the 1798 *Essay* which while citing both Godwin and Paley evidently prefers the latter: 'Morality, according to Mr. Godwin, is a calculation of consequences, or, as Archdeacon Paley very justly expresses it, "the will of God, *as collected from general expediency*"' (Malthus 1798: 213, my emphasis). This reflects the principle established at the outset of the first of two theological chapters concerned with the problem of understanding 'the constant pressure of distress on man from the difficulty of subsistence', namely: 'In all our feeble attempts ... to "find out the Almighty to perfection", it seems absolutely necessary, that we should reason from nature up to nature's God, and not presume to reason from God to nature' (Malthus 1798: 350). The 1803 edition similarly agrees with Paley that '[o]ur virtue ... as reasonable beings evidently consists in educing, from the general materials which the Creator has placed under our guidance, the greatest sum of human happiness' (Malthus 1803: 490–1); and, when elaborating the case for moral restraint, Malthus cites Paley to the effect that '[t]he method of coming at the will of God from the light of nature is to enquire into the tendency of the action to promote or diminish the general happiness' (501).

Cremaschi responds to my statement (Hollander 1989: 174n) that 'Malthus should have rejected "reliance upon the supernatural, revelation or scriptural authority"', with the 'obvious' objection 'that [Malthus] did have recourse to scriptural authority as late as 1824 in *A Summary View of the Principle of Population*' (Cremaschi 2014: 9–10).[2] I shall consider the substance of Cremaschi's response in Section 11.4, and here clarify that my formulation in 1989 maintains not that 'Malthus should have rejected' scriptural authority but rather that 'Malthus does not always live up to this perspective', referring specifically to the principle that 'it seems absolutely necessary, that we should reason from nature up to nature's God, and not presume to reason from God to nature'. Now it would have been open to Malthus to argue that where explicit scriptural ordinance is available this principle of 'natural theology' is no longer appropriate and we are then enjoined to reason from God to nature. (The context of the remarks in the *First Essay* suggests as much.) It is a contrast made early on by Paley who refers to 'two methods of coming at the will of God on any point: I. By his express declarations, when they are to be had; and which must be sought for in Scripture. II. By what we can discover of his designs and disposition from his works, or, as we usually call it, the light of nature' (Paley 1785: 54). As mentioned already, we shall find that Malthus goes a significant step further by maintaining that scripture itself cannot always be taken at face value, and may require interpretation taking consequences into account.

At this point I draw attention to Professor Cremaschi's concession that 'what matters for Paley are general consequences', while at the same time insisting on a sharp distinction between Paley and Bentham in this regard:

> [General consequences] matter only in so far as from an appraisal of consequences he comes back to a justification of natural law and innate rights, precisely those notions that for Bentham were the quintessence of obscurantism ... As a result, 'expediency' is merely the test of what should be expected as a law imposed by God, not a criterion on which we may decide the right course of action. It is true that Paley's consequentialism and Bentham's utilitarianism might seem to be almost equivalent 'extensionally' in so far as they approve or condemn the same acts ... but the difference is that, when considered 'intensionally', that is, by listing the

characteristics it needs to possess in order to qualify as such, Paley's right action is described in terms different from Bentham's namely those of an act conforming to a law described by God.

(Cremaschi 2014: 50)

Again, Cremaschi later reiterates in almost the same terms that Paley's description of 'the characteristics an act needs to possess in order to qualify as right, is quite different from Bentham's, that is, not that of a felicific act, but that of an act conforming to a law prescribed by God' (58). Now despite the repetition, all this tells us is that Paley was a believer – as if this were ever denied – whereas Bentham was not. The key point remains that, for Paley, an act is recognised as conforming to God's will *solely by dint of its desirable consequences* – 'what should be expected as a law imposed by God' – and Cremaschi agrees that as far as these are concerned there is no substantive difference between Paley and Bentham.

What Cremaschi says of Paley he extends to Malthus, referring to 'a point where Malthus apparently comes close to the Benthamite Utilitarians and actually does quote Paley approvingly. This point is the "test of Utility", or the role utility plays in deciding the right or wrong character of a line of conduct' (Cremaschi 2014: 49). And to reinforce his position he refers (153) to alterations made in the 1817 edition of the *Essay*: 'Though utility … can never be the immediate excitement to the gratification of any passion, it is the test by which alone we can know [1817: *independently of the revealed will of God*] whether it ought or ought not to be indulged; and is therefore the surest foundation of all morality [1817: *the surest criterion of moral rules*] which can be collected from the light of nature' (Malthus 1803: 560; 1817 3: 215). The alterations specify that utility is the proper court of appeal regarding moral conduct '*independently of the revealed will of God*' – implying instances where explicit scriptural direction is unavailable; and that even then utility is to be regarded as no more than the *criterion* or index, and not the *foundation* of morality.

The alterations of 1817 suggest to me that Malthus had become fearful lest readers obtain the impression of an excessively secular orientation.[3] Cremaschi's case is scarcely reinforced by the adjustments. In the first place, appeal to utility remains the only option where explicit scriptural authority is unavailable, Malthus simply *assuming* that 'the will of God' is revealed to us by consequences – the essence of his natural theology and in line with Paley's. But here we must note a suggestion that it is only a matter of high probability rather than absolute certainty that God's will is indeed reflected by appeal to consequences. Thus 'natural and moral evil', including poverty, are perceived as the outcomes of inadequate self-control, and '*seem* to be the instruments employed by the Deity in admonishing us to avoid any mode of conduct which is not suited to our being, and will consequently injure our happiness' (Malthus 1803: 484; emphasis added). The 'test of utility' is thus reinforced. Elsewhere the qualification is expressed as 'the *apparent* purpose of the Creator':

As animals, or till we know their consequences, our only business is to follow these dictates of nature; but, as reasonable beings, we are under the strongest obligations to attend to their consequences; and if they be evil to ourselves or others, we may justly consider it as an indication that such a mode of indulging these passions is not suited to our state, or conformable to the will of God. As moral agents, therefore, it is clearly our duty to refrain their indulgence in these particular directions; and by thus carefully examining the consequences of our natural passions, and frequently bringing them to the test of utility, gradually acquiring a habit of gratifying them, only in that way, which, being unattended with evil, will clearly add to the sum of human happiness, and fulfil the *apparent* purpose of the Creator.
(Malthus 1803: 559–60; 1817 3: 214–15; emphasis added)

Secondly, there is the fact that where biblical instruction is available, Malthus does not hesitate to interpret the texts appropriately in the light of expediential considerations should a clash with utility seem to exist. Utility is thus accorded absolute priority, justifying prudential population control albeit very much in opposition to a literal reading of the scriptures (see below, 11.5).

Regarding contraception within marriage, the matter is complex, Malthus expressing his strong opposition on *dual* grounds: 'I should always particularly reprobate any artificial and unnatural modes of checking population, both on account of their immorality and their tendency to remove a necessary stimulus to industry. If it were possible for each married couple to limit by a wish the number of their children, there is certainly reason to fear that the indolence of the human race would be very greatly increased' (Malthus 1817 3: 393). The presumption that contraception within marriage is 'immoral' is one of those instances where, as I phrased it earlier, Malthus does not always live up to his 'natural theology' or the principle that 'we should reason from nature up to nature's God, and not presume to reason from God to nature'. Here Malthus takes for granted that contraception by married couples is morally unacceptable even apart from consequences.[4] Cremaschi, strange to relate, asserts to the contrary that 'Malthus's argument is not that contraception is immoral and *besides* it discourages the virtues of sobriety, industry, independence and prudence, but that it is immoral precisely *because* it may be assumed to discourage those virtues' (Cremaschi 2014: 177, citing Malthus 1803: 557; see also 2014: 174). This reading actually weakens the case against the coalescence of Malthus's version and the secular version of utilitarianism. For my part, Malthus's explicit appeal to a presumed immorality of contraception within marriage (apart from its undesirable social consequences) renders his toleration of mere prudential restraint by the unmarried, where moral restraint cannot be relied upon, all the more remarkable.

******

On the subject of Malthus's natural theology I must protest Cremaschi's trashing of Leslie Stephen (above, p. 255). Let us try to read Stephen fairly.

To the question regarding Malthus's 'Moral Restraint': 'What ... is meant by "moral" in this connection?' (Stephen 1900: 156), Stephen responds: 'Malthus takes his ethical philosophy pretty much for granted, but is clearly a Utilitarian according to the version of Paley', citing those passages from the 1803 *Essay* provided above at the outset of Section 11.3. Stephen then notes an elaboration whereby our 'natural impulses are, abstractedly considered, good, and only to be distinguished by their consequences' (Malthus 1803: 491), and illustrates: 'Hunger he says [paraphrasing Malthus 1803: 487], as Bentham had said, is the same in itself, whether it leads to stealing a loaf or to eating your own loaf', whereas the former alone has dire social consequences. And after pointing to Malthus's citations of Godwin and Paley in the 1798 version he summarizes thus: 'Reason then regulates certain innate and practically unalterable instincts by enabling us to foretell their consequences. The reasonable man is influenced not simply by the immediate gratification, but by a forecast of all the results which it will entail. In these matters Malthus was entirely at one with the Utilitarians proper, and seems to regard their doctrine as self-evident' (Stephen 1900: 157). Here Stephen is evidently paraphrasing Malthus's comment that '[i]n the pursuit of every enjoyment, whether sensual or intellectual, Reason, that faculty which enables us to calculate consequences, is the proper corrective and guide' (Malthus 1798: 215–16). This principle defines of course the general argument of Chapter I, Book IV of the second *Essay* on 'moral restraint', the chapter commencing with a reference to the essential lesson of the first *Essay* that the check to population 'should arise from the foresight of the difficulties attending a family, and the fear of dependent poverty, [rather] than from the actual presence of want and sickness' (Malthus 1803: 484).

To Stephen's account Professor Cremaschi objects: 'the remark is in order here that Stephen, before baldly declaring that Malthus took his ethics "for granted" and that he had learned it from the Utilitarians, should have spent some time in reading chapters 1 and 2 in book IV of the second *Essay*, where Malthus presents his own ethics. In fact, 'Stephen's clumsy anachronism anticipates the birth of a Utilitarian school to the last decades of the eighteenth century' (Cremaschi 2014: 8).

This is an unfair response. (1) Stephen does not say that Malthus learned his ethics 'from the Utilitarians', but that he derived them from Paley. (2) As mentioned above, Stephen's discussion of Malthus's perception of 'virtue' relates specifically to the materials in Book IV, Chapter 1. (3) The charge of 'anachronism' is out of order. When Stephen writes: 'In these matters Malthus was entirely at one with the Utilitarians proper, and seems to regard their doctrine as self-evident' he is referring not to the perception of ethics but specifically to the proposition that 'the reasonable man is influenced not simply by ... immediate gratification' deriving from his conduct, but 'by a forecast of all the results which it will entail'. Stephen did not specify whom he had in mind by 'the Utilitarians proper' but Bentham is a likely candidate. – whether or not at first hand – since calculation of future consequences is implicit in Bentham's celebrated measurement of the 'value of a lot of pleasure or pain' taking account of 'propinquity or remoteness' (Bentham *Principles of Morals and Legislation*; 1982 [1789]: Chapter IV). Recall here Stephen's remark 'as Bentham had said' with regard to 'hunger' which evidently relates to an earlier work. Here too the *Principles* is probably intended, especially Chapters X and XI. And since the *Principles* – which was to become a bible for Bentham's early nineteenth-century disciples – appeared a decade before the *Essay on Population*, there is no '*anticipation*' by Stephen of 'the birth of a Utilitarian school to the last decades of the eighteenth century'. This is precisely when the Benthamite school first emerged.

11.4 Population control: 'moral restraint'

Professor Cremaschi puts great weight on the *Summary View* as disproving the Robbins position that Malthus's attribution of 'disharmonies' to Divine Wisdom is 'extraneous to analysis and without influence on the theory of policy'. In fact this work illustrates particularly well its *validity*. In the first place, the article constitutes a strictly objective theoretical and empirical analysis of the implications of resource scarcity, with an eye to the 'the happiness of society' – as expressed in the 1824 version (Malthus 1986 [1824, 1830]: 221) – and 'to promote the general good, and increase the mass of human happiness' in applications to property and poor relief in both the 1830 and 1824 versions (237–8). To this technical analysis is added a brief *coda* rejecting 'the objection which has been made by some persons on religious grounds … that a tendency in mankind to increase, beyond the greatest possible increase of food which could be produced in a limited space, impeaches the goodness of the Deity, and is inconsistent with the letter and spirit of the Scriptures' (239). This attempt at reconciliation in no way plays upon the *analysis* of the principle of population.

Secondly, the *coda* constitutes not a justification of unconditional population expansion by reference to the biblical injunction to be fruitful and fill the world – which would indeed sharply distinguish the policy position of Malthus from that of the Philosophical Radicals – but an attempt to reconcile the painful need to *restrain* population growth in conditions of land scarcity, painful because of the necessity for self-control, with the 'views of a benevolent Creator'. This Malthus does by maintaining that a 'virtue dictated to [individuals] by the light of nature, and sanctioned by revealed religion' (Malthus 1986 [1824, 1830]: 240) – that of self-control – has the beneficent consequence of increasing happiness, and this in the sense of *improving real income*, namely 'improv[ing] the condition, and increas[ing] the comforts', of individuals and therefore of society:

> First, it appears that the evils arising from the principle of population are exactly of the same kind as the evils arising from the excessive or irregular gratification of the human passions in general, and may equally be avoided by moral restraint … Secondly, it is almost universally acknowledged, that both the letter and spirit of revelation represent this world as a state of moral

discipline and probation. But a state of moral discipline and probation cannot be a state of unmixed happiness, as it necessarily implies difficulties to be overcome, and temptations to be resisted. Now, in the whole range of the laws of nature, not one can be pointed out which so especially accords with this scriptural view of the state of man on earth; as it … marks, in a more general and stronger manner, nationally, as well as individually, the different effects of virtue and vice, of the proper government of the passions, and the culpable indulgence of them. It follows, then that the principle of population, instead of being inconsistent with revelation, must be considered as affording strong additional proofs of its truth.

Lastly, it will be acknowledged, that in a state of probation, those laws seem best to accord with the views of a benevolent Creator, which, while they furnish the difficulties and temptations which form the essence of such a state, are of such a nature as to reward those who overcome them with happiness in this life as well as in the next … Each individual has the power of avoiding the evil consequences to himself and society resulting from [the law of population], by the practice of a virtue dictated to him by the light of nature, and sanctioned by revealed religion. And, as there can be no question that this virtue tends greatly to improve the condition, and increase the comforts both of the individuals who practise it, and through them of the whole society, the ways of God to man with regard to this great law are completely vindicated.

(Malthus 1986 [1824, 1830]: 240)[5]

The religious apologia is peculiar to Malthus, but the improvement in real income is precisely the justification for the policy of population control proposed by the secular Utilitarians.

Now Cremaschi is aware both that Malthus, while formally referring to biblical authority, recommends population *constraint* rather than unconditional expansion, and that the outcome of the divinely-inspired practise of self-control and 'relief from population pressure' would be a positive impact upon 'the general good' (Cremaschi 2014: 109). Since the primary policy recommendation resulting from the argument – the need for population restraint on welfare grounds in the light of land scarcity – was that of the secular writers, it is difficult to understand why Cremaschi refuses to accept the obvious conclusion that Malthus's attribution of 'disharmonies' to Divine Wisdom was *'without influence on the theory of policy'*.

11.5 Population control: 'prudence'

What now of policy in the event that 'moral restraint' – delayed marriage accompanied by abstinence – could not be relied upon as a practical prospect? Here there are indeed differences between Malthus and, pre-eminently, John Stuart Mill. But these differences are the opposite to those one might expect. For Mill's well-known hesitations regarding the practice of birth control by unmarried couples should be compared with the extraordinary courage of 'the parson Malthus' – Marx's derogatory term – who justified mere prudential control, or delayed marriage *unaccompanied* by sexual restraint, notwithstanding all its obvious implications, including implicitly the practice of birth control, should this prove necessary for the maintenance of wages. Cremaschi errs when he asserts that 'Malthus is at one with Paley regarding his recommendation of marriage with marital fidelity and pre-marital abstinence' (Cremaschi 2014: 109), overlooking Malthus's qualification when circumstances demanded it. To attribute to Malthus the view that concerning 'virtues' such as 'chastity, respect for rights, love for equality ... men have to comply with God's laws *in an unconditional way*' (10; emphasis added) is simply untenable. (See also Cremaschi 2014: 195 regarding other allegedly 'non-negotiable priorities'.) Malthus's position regarding chastity entails in fact an impressive balancing of consequential considerations both physical and 'moral', the latter including the effect of poverty on sexual and other forms of 'vice' relating to crime (robbery and murder) and not neglecting – in Benthamite fashion – punishment perceived as a 'painful' disutility (Hollander 1997: 874, 881–90; 2015: 442–3). Cremaschi is aware of this calculus (Cremaschi 2014: 12, 168), but fails to see how damaging it is for any notion of unconditional compliance with scriptural injunction.

A powerful statement first introduced in the *Essay* of 1803 summarizing the issue could not better convey the *effectively*, if unintended, secular character of Malthus's position. Malthus was prepared to take the risk to 'virtue' implied by delayed marriage:

> I should be most extremely sorry to say any thing which could either directly or remotely be construed unfavourably to the cause of virtue: but I certainly cannot think that the vices which relate to the sex, are the only vices which are to be considered in a moral question; or that they are even the greatest and the most degrading to the human character ... [T]here are other vices the effects of which are still more pernicious, and there are other situations, which lead more certainly to moral offences than the refraining from marriage. *Powerful as may be the temptations to a breach of chastity, I am inclined to think that they are impotent, in comparison to the temptations arising from continued distress.*
>
> (Malthus 1803: 489; emphasis added)

Equally forceful is the rejection in 1806 of Arthur Young's objection that in bringing 'moral restraint' into the picture Malthus had unrealistically assumed 'perfect chastity in the single state'.

> Whatever I may have said in drawing a picture *professedly* visionary, for the sake of illustration, in the practical application of my principles I have taken man as he is, with all his imperfections on his head. And thus viewing him, and knowing that some checks to population must exist, *I have not the slightest hesitation in saying, that the prudential check to marriage is*

better than premature mortality. And in this decision I feel myself completely justified by experience.

(Malthus 1806 2: 538, emphasis added; 'professedly' italicized in original.)

My case may be arrived at from another direction. We have seen that Malthus calls for *constrained* population growth, assuming land scarcity, in order to prevent the otherwise inevitable decline in living standards – an application of standard classical growth theory. But the other side of the same coin is the commendation of population growth whereby the resource-scarcity constraint can be overcome. Now it may be insisted that support for a growing population does after all have a biblical source. But what Malthus intends is that by *restricting the birth rate* a healthier population would result thereby raising productivity and also, by reducing mortality, would allow expansion of population consistently with constant, even increasing, wages (Hollander 1997: 875–80). (Life expectation is a key issue in the 1824 paper.) That population increase was to be achieved by a reduced birth rate is very much in conflict with the *literal* reading of the scriptures to be fruitful with its implication that God can be relied upon to provide.

That consequential considerations determine the appropriate reading of the scriptures is in line with the injunction that 'we should reason from nature up to nature's God, and not presume to reason from God to nature', the 'natural theology' discussed in Section 11.3. Here I note that Cremaschi himself makes precisely this point in discussing Malthus on benevolence, citing the passage we have already taken into account (Malthus 1803: 559–60; 1817 3: 214–15): 'Benevolence is, no less than the sexual drive, one of the basic impulses of our nature; both are "natural passions" and neither is good in an unqualified way or carries unfailingly good consequences. In so far as we are not only animals, but also reasonable beings, we must "attend to their consequences; and if they be evil to ourselves or others, we may justly consider it as an indication that such a mode of indulging these passions is not suited to our state or conformable to the will of God"' (Cremaschi 2014: 105). Unfortunately, Cremaschi's recognition that for Malthus the 'will of God' is indicated to us by consequences is not consistent with the position he also ascribes to Malthus that 'men have to comply with God's laws *in an unconditional way*'.

It is of high interest that Malthus's stance should coincide precisely with a general formulation of Bentham's in 1789 – the context relates to 'principles adverse to utility' – regarding the essential role of interpretation even where relevant scriptural texts can be adduced:

It may be wondered perhaps, that … no mention has been made of the *theological* principle; meaning that principle which professes to recur for the standard of right and wrong to the will of God. But the case is, this is not in fact a distinct principle … The *will* of God … cannot be his revealed will, as contained in the sacred writings; for that is a system which nobody ever thinks of recurring to at this time of day, for the details of political administration: and even before it can be applied to the details of private conduct, it is universally allowed, by the most eminent divines of all persuasions, to stand in need of pretty ample interpretations; else to what use are the works of those divines? And for the guidance of these interpretations, it is also allowed, that some other standard must be assumed ... We may be perfectly sure, indeed, that whatever is right is conformable to the will of God: but so far is that from answering the purpose of showing us what is right, that it is necessary to know first whether a thing is right, in order to know from thence whether it is conformable to the will of God.

(Bentham 1982 [1789]: 31)

Interpretation based upon 'some other standard' alludes of course to utility, and this we have shown is also the case for Malthus.

★★★★★★

A word next on the weak force attributed to 'moral restraint' in the program for a reduced population growth rate. Professor Cremaschi objects to my observations that Malthus had little confidence in such restraint in practise, contending 'that Malthus in 1803 did find not only a more orthodox, but also a more convincing answer to questions left open by his own theodicy by transforming it into a *social* theodicy' (Cremaschi 2014: 13). More specifically, whereas doubts with respect to moral restraints might cloud Malthus's evaluation of past experience this, he maintains, was not the case of future prospects:

> It is true that Malthus gives no great weight to moral restraint in terms of explanation of past phenomena (and here Hollander is right), but it is also true that moral restraint becomes the pivot around which his whole modified system now turns (and in this respect Hollander is wrong) in so far as (i) it allows for a satisfying theodicy and (ii) it allows for drawing a programme for a more happy, virtuous and less unequal society.
>
> (Cremaschi 2014: 59)

> ... Hollander is nearly right when he acknowledges that 'a theological dimension thus certainly remains in 1803 and thereafter [...]. Indeed, it is fair to say that the defence of the deity is reinforced – though only if limited to an ideal rather than the real world, considering the practical insignificance of [moral] restraint' [Hollander 1997: 919]. Or better, he *would* be *nearly* did he not miss one decisive point, namely that Malthus in 1803 still believed that the relevance of moral restraint *in the past* had been rather limited (which was contested by several of his critics including Chalmers), but his policy advice, namely equality, dignity, self-reliance, generalized education, higher wages, higher standards of consumption, pointed at a *possible*, not just *ideal*, world where the 'moral restraint' would

be practised, the lottery of society would yield further blanks, and this will allow for *respectability, virtue* and *happiness*.

(154–5)

Cremaschi even refers to 'Hollander's claim that according to Malthus moral restraint has not only played no relevant role in past history ... but also will play no relevant role in the future...' (162).

Now I have not 'claimed' Malthus's low estimate of the future likelihood of the general practise of moral restraint without documentation. Recall his response in 1806 to Arthur Young's objection that he had unrealistically assumed 'perfect chastity in the single state': 'whatever I may have said in drawing a picture *professedly* visionary, for the sake of illustration, in the practical application of my principles I have taken man as he is, with all his imperfections on his head' (see above, p. 267). This is a forward-looking declaration. And the 1824 paper 'Population' declares quite generally that prudential, not moral, restraint 'will be found to be the chief mode in which the preventive check practically operates' (1986 [1824, 1830]: 204; cited Hollander 1997: 890) which again has forward-looking implications. But the main point relates to the principle of the matter, which is unaffected by speculations regarding future prospects for moral restraint: In the event reliance could *not* be placed on the 'ideal' solution then simple 'prudential' control was yet advised on second-best grounds to assure the range of desirable ends listed in the second of Cremaschi's passages. These ends, as we have said, are almost identical to those famously championed by J.S. Mill.

So strong is Malthus's opposition to the expansion of population when not justified by ample resources that, while he distinguished Condorcet's 'unnatural' from Godwin's 'virtuous' scheme of communism incorporating a free-love component, he nonetheless neglected to appeal to the sanctity of the marriage institution when evaluating the Godwinian project. Indeed, Cremaschi himself recognizes that Malthus's primary objection turned on the probable social consequences, evidently consequences for 'human happiness': 'His main objection to such "virtuous free love" ... is that, once implemented, it would provide the conditions most favourable to [unwarranted] population growth, since some of the existing restraints on the decision of engaging in a stable partnership with a person of the other sex would be removed' (Cremaschi 2014: 110).

11.6 On happiness and virtue

We now put aside the second-best case justifying prudential control and attend to the ideal. This will allow us to focus upon Cremaschi's emphasis upon Malthus's dual ends of happiness *and* virtue. The position he attributes to Malthus is evident from the passages cited in the previous Section; and also in a complaint that even Winch (1987) 'does not go into a deep enough analysis of Malthus's own moral theory and he fails to clarify in detail how, for so-called theological utilitarians in general and Malthus in particular, the supreme criterion for judging individual actions and policies was the 'greatest surplus of virtue and happiness over vice and misery' (Cremaschi 2014: 11). Cremaschi's stance emerges particularly clearly in a passage on my 'Robbinsian' interpretation of Malthus's position regarding communism, where the former also alludes to a sharp contrast between Malthus and Bentham:

> [Hollander 1997] adds that Robbins was right in his claim that 'the test of policy is to be its effect on human happiness' and Malthus's discussion of policies concerning population is the best proof thereof, his case against communism showing a paramount case of adoption of 'the utilitarian perspective on social organization – the evaluation of institutions only by their consequences rather than as "good' or "bad" *per se*' [1997: 910]. [B]ut he adds also that communism was undesirable for Malthus because it would have implied legal limitations to individual freedoms which would be "unnatural, immoral, or cruel" (Malthus 1803 2: 285). I would have noted that Malthus writes 'unnatural, immoral or cruel', not 'un-felicific, un-felicific, un-felicific', and drawn the conclusion that such an argument, far from being utilitarian, implies adoption of a *pluralist* moral ontology incompatible with utilitarianism.
>
> (Cremaschi 2014: 9–10; see also 172)

Now Bentham famously expressed his gratitude to David Hume for teaching him 'that the foundations of all *virtue* are laid in *utility*' (including the unnecessary 'exceptions' Hume himself discerned) (Bentham 1843 [1776]: 268n). Cremaschi does not dispute that Bentham incorporated a virtue component within the utility maximand, but emphasizes that Bentham did so specifically as 'tending to felicific behaviour' whereas for Malthus *virtue* is *independent of consequences for happiness* as indicated by the contrast between 'misery and vice' and 'happiness and innocence' (Cremaschi 2014: 44–5; see also 10, 50). Similarly, Malthusian 'meta-ethics' is differentiated from the Benthamite variety in that the former alone 'includes virtue besides happiness into states of affairs to be appraised' (195). As we have seen (above, 11.2), Cremaschi also makes much of a contrast between '*strict justice*' against '*good policy*' – or 'rights-based reasons against expediency-based ones' – in the context of Malthus's changing position on agricultural protection (182).

Against this must be weighed the passage defining Malthus's 'natural theology' (above, 11.3) defining 'virtue' in consequentialist or 'happiness' terms: Our virtue, therefore, as reasonable beings, evidently consists in deducing, from the general materials which the Creator has placed under our guidance, the greatest sum of human happiness; and as all our natural impulses are abstractedly considered good, and only to be distinguished by their consequences, a strict attention to these consequences, and the regulation of our conduct conformably to them, must be considered as our principal duty (Malthus 1803: 490–1).

Cremaschi cites this passage (2014: 69) yet concludes, quite generally, that for Malthus virtue is an entity standing apart from consequences for happiness. To my mind, the declaration of confidence in the Creator's plan in establishing man's basic impulses – 'all our natural impulses are abstractly considered good' – is academic considering the insistence that virtuous conduct requires an evaluation of consequences.[6]

Cremaschi's indication that Malthus 'writes not "un-felicific, un-felicific, un-felicific"', in allegedly characteristic utilitarian fashion, but 'unnatural, immoral or cruel' seems rhetorical. Two considerations indicate the difficulty with any notion in this respect of a sharp discontinuity between Malthus and the secularists.

In the first place, for Malthus – as we have seen in the prime application relating to sexual conduct – welfare takes priority, since 'unchaste' conduct is perceived as the *consequence* of poverty: 'Powerful as may be the temptations to a breach of chastity, I am inclined to think that they are impotent, in comparison to the temptations arising from *continued distress*' (emphasis added). Equally significant, 'premature mortality' is represented as the worse possible option: 'knowing that some checks to population must exist, *I have not the slightest hesitation in saying, that the prudential check to marriage is better than premature mortality*', a perspective governing the appropriate *interpretation* of the biblical injunction to people the world – all this notwithstanding that deviation from a literal reading entails, formally speaking, 'unnatural' and 'immoral' behaviour. These qualifiers lose at least part of their negative connotation under certain empirical conditions, premarital sex in particular effectively shedding some of its 'immoral' character when worse sorts of sexual conduct, emanating from poverty, are taken into account.

The matter can be generalized, making use of Cremaschi's comments on 'politics as morality' where Malthus is shown to apply what is in effect the maximizing principle when denying absolute morality on the grounds that there can be too much of a good thing. 'Politics as morality', Cremaschi affirms, 'is not moralizing about public issues, since different moral objects should be balanced with each other on criteria dictated by prudence. Factors at play in human society are always variable and often unknown, and there is a point where one additional share of one factor starts yielding opposite effects. Thus the desirable amount of any factor has to be assessed on the basis of "general expediency". The overarching criterion for dealing with political issues is prudence' (Cremaschi 2014: 181). Cremaschi appears not to realize that this perspective is at odds with a genuine theological orientation where absolute moralities would be of the essence.

But secondly, while Malthus sometimes applied an 'absolutist' conception of virtue – as in the treatment of contraception by married couples – the secular writers, when identifying the ethical components they included within the utilitarian maximand, unhesitatingly perceived virtue independent of consequences for wealth and happiness. This is true of Ricardo and J.S. Mill as I shall show next.

11.7 Ricardo and J.S. Mill on virtue: a digression

I take note first of Ricardo's affirmation that '[m]y motto, after Mr. Bentham is "the greatest happiness to the greatest number"' (Ricardo to Maria Edgeworth, 13 December 1822; Ricardo 1952 9: 238–9). This all-inclusive definition is not however strictly adhered to, for elsewhere the utilitarian maximand runs in terms of 'the good of the whole' rather than 'happiness', thereby creating space for 'moral rights' in addition to the standard expediential components. This is the case in a discussion with Francis Place relating to private property, where Ricardo interprets Malthus to this effect notwithstanding Malthus's formal appeal to 'right' or 'laws of nature': 'By "right" and "law of nature" Mr. Malthus clearly means, 'moral right' 'utility' *the good of the whole*' or some equivalent expression. I am not defending the accuracy of Mr. Malthus's language on this occasion – I know it is not strictly correct, I as well as you am a disciple of the Bentham and [James] Mill school, but his meaning cannot be mistaken'. (Ricardo to Place, 9 September 1821; Ricardo 1952 9: 52; emphasis added).

Ricardo's insistence in the *Principles* upon an obligation to honour payment of interest on the National Debt turns on his appeal to moral rights as high-ranking constituents of 'utility' – evidently in the sense of 'the good of the whole' – strictly apart from expediential considerations relating to wealth, indeed apart from 'happiness':

> With a view to wealth only, it might be equally or more desirable that [a debtor] should or should not pay it; but the claims of justice and good faith, *a greater utility*, are not to be compelled to yield to those of a less … A debt guaranteed by the nation, differs in no respect from the above transaction. Justice and good faith demand that the interest of the national debt should continue to be paid, and that those who have advanced their capitals for the general benefit, *should not be required to forego their equitable claims, on the plea of expediency*.
>
> (Ricardo 1951 1: 245–6; emphasis added)

The incorporation within the Utilitarian maximand of both happiness and virtue and the treatment of the latter as an independent entity is similarly apparent in Ricardo's impressive representation when discussing James Mill's *History of British India* of the 'difficulty of the doctrine of expediency or utility', and his appeal to value judgment as proving, as far as he could see, the only possible solution. Ricardo's concern was the justification for increasing national happiness by means of 'unjust' measures, specifically the extension of British power by disregarding previous obligations to the native rulers and compelling their submission by force: 'Are we to fix our eyes steadily on the end, *the happiness of the governed, and pursue it at the expence of those principles which all men are agreed in calling virtuous?* … The difficulty of the doctrine of expediency or utility is to know how to balance one object of utility against another – there being no standard in nature, it must vary with the tastes, the passions and the habits of mankind. This is one of the subjects on which I require to be enlightened' (Ricardo to Mill, 6 January 1818; Ricardo 1952 7: 241–2; emphasis added).

Malthus, I conclude, cannot legitimately be set apart as differing from the secularists with regard to making allowances for virtue ethics divorced from happiness considerations.

A closely related consideration involving Ricardo requires further notice here. While Cremaschi concedes that 'the test of utility plays a central role in Malthus's meta-ethics', he distinguishes this role 'from the one played in Bentham's ethics', and this in part because 'Malthus's policy advice assumes a distinction between *wealth* and *happiness* as a starting point' (Cremaschi 2014: 195, emphasis added; see also 180). This distinction too is far from peculiar to Malthus. Ricardo drew this contrast in brilliant colours as the following three instances reveal. Firstly, regarding policy entailing depreciation, as raised in his correspondence of 1815: 'Depreciation of money may be beneficial because it generally favours that class which are disposed to accumulate, – but I should say that it augments riches by diminishing happiness…' (Ricardo to Malthus 27 June 1815; Ricardo 1952 6: 233). Secondly, again in the correspondence with Malthus, Ricardo discusses the case of New Spain where labourers chose to take advantage of high agricultural productivity in the form of leisure rather than real income, a principle applying to the desirability of development in the broad: 'Happiness is the object to be desired, and we cannot be quite sure that provided he is equally well fed, a man may not be happier in the enjoyment of the luxury of idleness than in the enjoyment of the luxuries of a neat cottage and good clothes' (Ricardo to Malthus, 4 September 1817; Ricardo 1952 6: 185). And thirdly, in the same letter, regarding a short crop: 'a bad harvest does not perhaps very much check the progress of wealth but it materially interferes with the general happiness' (4 September 1817; Ricardo 1952 7: 186).

******

I shall now bring John Stuart Mill into the picture. Bentham and the utility principle do not receive a good press in Mill's papers of the early 1830s which flirt with the notion of universally-held moral sentiments governing feelings of right and wrong independently of consequences. These doubts were more or less assuaged by the early 1850s. A growing ease with Benthamite doctrine as it relates to ethics – for Mill regretted till the end of his life an excessively narrow conception on Bentham's part regarding actual *motivation* – is spelled out in 'Whewell on Moral Philosophy' (1852) focusing on the perception of *intuition* as the origin of ethical sentiment: 'We are as much for conscience, duty, rectitude, as Dr. Whewell. The terms, and all the feelings connected with them, are as much a part of the ethics of utility as of that of intuition. The point in dispute is, what acts are the proper objects of those feelings; whether we ought to take the feelings as we find them, as accident or design has made them, or *whether the tendency of actions to promote happiness affords a test to which the feelings of morality should conform*' (Mill 1969 [1852]: 172; emphasis added).

Bentham, Mill affirmed, had well explained that those who tested right and wrong by reference to supposedly universal feelings in fact produced 'phrases which mean nothing but the fact of the approbation or disapprobation itself'; for 'all experience shows that those feelings are eminently artificial, and the product of culture' (178–9). A moralist can deduce from utility as a standard 'his whole system of ethics, without calling to his assistance any foreign principle' (194). *A System of Logic* closes with the affirmation that the 'ultimate principle of Morality ... is that of conduciveness to the happiness of mankind, or rather, of all sentient beings', referring readers in the 1865 edition for 'an express discussion and vindication of this principle [in] the little volume entitled *Utilitarianism*' (Mill 1973–4 (1843): 951). Furthermore, Mill in 1852 came readily to Bentham's defence against Whewell's strictures by rightly insisting that by the 'greatest happiness' principle Bentham intended 'the greatest happiness of mankind, and of all sensitive beings', not the self-interest of the agent; and, further, that Bentham did not intend, as the basis of morality, an appeal to 'public opinion' or the 'approbation of neighbours', but rather proposed popular sanction as a motive towards virtuous behaviour assuring that the self-interest of the agent coincides with the 'greatest happiness' rule (Mill 1969 [1852]: 183–4). In brief, popular sanction would keep 'the conduct of each in the line which promotes the general happiness' (185). It is the latter that Bentham identified with 'true morality', and the moral sentiments were ideally to be 'trained to act in this direction only'. Indeed, Mill reprobated Whewell's confusion of the 'Happiness theory of Morals with the theory of Motives sometimes called the Selfish System' (184n). Recall too that for Bentham *justice* – incorporating both 'individuality' and 'the purposes of benevolence' (see Chapter 9, pp. 216, 219) – occupied the highest rank in the utilitarian calculus.

J.S. Mill's reduction of all morality to considerations of 'general happiness' might be said to confirm a sharp distinction between the secularists and Malthus. But this conclusion would be premature on two grounds, one relating to the interpretation of Malthus, the other to that of Mill himself.

Regarding Malthus, we recall that he too linked morality to the 'general happiness' in the sense that consequential calculation relating primarily to welfare dictated for him the *interpretation* of seemingly unambiguous biblical injunctions such as that mere 'prudential' conduct – entailing sexual 'vice' – might be justified by taking into account a broad range of undesirable outcomes associated with poverty, including sexual misconduct and other vicious forms of conduct including crime.

As for Mill, his position in practice turns out to be more complex than his formal reduction of questions of morality to 'happiness' suggests. For he resolved Ricardo's 'difficulty' of 'balancing' different utilitarian objectives only by resort to subjective value judgment implicitly entailing an appeal to external considerations.[7] Beyond his recognition of animal rights in Benthamite fashion, there is in the constitutional context an extension of the greatest-good criterion to a national entity including an Irish component to be treated on equal terms with its British counterpart, for Westminster must 'legislate for Ireland rightly' or allow Irish members 'to transact the business of their own country mainly by themselves' (Hollander 2015: 416; also 398–9). Here there arises a variety of considerations including self-respect and conscience – extended in fact from the individual to the nation – unrelated to 'happiness' as such.

The context is Mill's recognition in *England and Ireland* of a 'desperate form of dissatisfaction, which does not demand to be better governed, which asks us for no benefit, no redress of grievances, not even any reparation of injuries, but simply to take ourselves off and rid the country of our presence' – that is a 'revolt of mere nationality' (Mill 1982 [1868]: 509–11). Mill could not have believed that the Irish situation had quite reached that stage since he put such weight on institutional reform as a last resort to save the Union. Only in its absence would Britain be forced, and rightly so, to abandon Ireland:

> It is not consistent with *self-respect*, in a nation any more than an individual, to wait till it is compelled by uncontrollable circumstances to resign that which it cannot in *conscience* hold. Before allowing its government to involve it in another repetition of the attempt to maintain dominion over Ireland by brute force, the English nation ought to commune with its *conscience*, and solemnly reconsider its position. If England is unable to learn what has to be learnt, and unlearn what has to be unlearnt, in order to make her rule willingly acceptable by the Irish people … are we the power which, according to the general fitness of things and the *rules of morality*, ought to govern Ireland? If so, what are we dreaming of, when we give our sympathy to the Poles, the Italians, the Hungarians, the Servians, the Greeks, and I know not how many other oppressed nationalities?
>
> (519–20; my emphasis)

The moral pressure Mill sought to exert is striking. That the issue reduces to one of *conscience* is the closing theme, Mill warning that without a solution to the land problem acceptable to the Irish tenantry, and should Britain nonetheless 'attempt to hold Ireland by force, it will be at the expense of all the character we possess as *lovers and maintainers of free government*, or respecters of any rights except our own' (1982 [1868]: 532; my emphasis). But even the wider international ramifications of such a course are expounded with an eye to ethics. For repression in Ireland:

> will most dangerously aggravate all our chances of misunderstandings with any of the great powers of the world, culminating in war; we shall be in a state of open revolt against the *universal conscience* of Europe and Christendom, and more and more against *our own*. And we shall in the end be *shamed*, or, if not shamed, coerced, into releasing Ireland from the connexion; or we shall avert the necessity only by conceding with the worst grace, and when it will not prevent some generations of ill blood, that

which if done at present may still be in time permanently to reconcile the two countries.

It should come as no surprise that by *applications* such as the foregoing, Mill undermined his formal declaration whereby a moralist can deduce from utility as a standard 'his whole system of ethics', since there surely is – as Ricardo suspected – no objective way of settling the 'grand difficulty of the utilitarian doctrine'. Furthermore, subjective secularist evaluations, Mill recognized, do not necessarily differ from those arrived at by adherents to Natural Law or religious doctrine (Hollander 2015: 33, 58–9, 84–7). Bentham himself insisted that the utility principle itself – and not only the constituent elements entering into the maximand, namely its extension to include allowance for animals and native peoples (see Bentham 1982 [1789]: 283n) – was a matter of value judgment or, as he expressed it, a 'postulate' (13).

11.8 Did Malthus strengthen the theological foundations of his work?

I turn finally to the main theme of Professor Cremaschi's concluding chapter: that '*malgré* Bonar and Hollander, what Malthus was doing step-by-step between 1803 and 1834 was not weakening, but instead strengthening the theological foundation of his work' as evidenced by the 'wider scope for morality and the related possibility of some kind of "worldly" harmonious design of human society' (Cremaschi 2014: 198). Cremaschi cites my position that 'Malthus's efforts to reconcile dogma and utility [was] a process involving effectively the undermining of the theological foundation' (194, citing Hollander 1997: 920–1) and objects: 'Malthus never attempted to reconcile "dogma" with "utility". Nor did he ever undermine any theological foundation he had laid before for his work. He just modified on a number of points his 1798 theological views, thus yielding different, albeit no less, and indeed even *more* theological views' (197–8).

The extract from my *Economics of Thomas Robert Malthus* provided by Cremaschi is garbled. The relevant sentence placed in context and with omissions corrected reads thus:

> Section II [in the chapter 'Utilitarianism in a Theological Context'], below, is devoted to the theological chapters of the 1798 version and the tension between them and the body of the work. Section III elaborates on the implicit secular or utilitarian orientation of the first *Essay* manifested particularly in recommendation of prudential control, despite the inevitability of 'vice'. The following section [IV] considers moral restraint within a utilitarian framework, and demonstrates Malthus's *continued efforts in 1803 and thereafter – despite the omission of the formal chapters on theology* – to reconcile dogma and utility, a process involving effectively the undermining of the theological foundation.
>
> (Hollander 1997: 920–1; the italicized words are omitted by Cremaschi)

Whereas Cremaschi represents me as maintaining a weakening on Malthus's part of the theological dimension of his endeavours, the unexpurgated exposition — which appears in a chapter entitled 'Utilitarianism in a Theological Context' — clearly proposes that despite the removal of the theological chapters of 1798, Malthus continued his efforts to 'reconcile' dogma and utility in 1803 and thereafter. That a weakening of the theological foundation was the *unintended consequence* of these efforts is also clearly intimated.

A subsequent elaboration — which must have passed Cremaschi by entirely — goes further by attributing to Malthus the *intention* to actually strengthen the theological foundation after 1798: 'Far from the theological concerns of Malthus diminishing between the first and second editions, the introduction of moral restraint evidently constitutes an attempt to *reinforce* the theological defence. Allusions to the training of 'mind' and character — the substance of the expunged theological chapters — re-emerge in 1803 in Book IV, on the obligation to practise the 'virtue' of moral restraint; various beneficial social effects to be expected therefrom; possible objections; and warnings against its avoidance' (Hollander 1979: 930).

But here I reiterate that 'Malthus, in 1803 and thereafter, effectively pulled the theological carpet from under his own feet'. A little later in my account I once again assert that the 'formal defence of the Deity in 1803 ... extends far beyond 1798' (936), and justify my belief that nevertheless Malthus effectively undermined the theological case when, for example, he argued that 'the source of virtue in a calculation of consequences is said to be common to both "heathen"' — it might be fair to understand him as silently including Benthamite secularists — 'and Christian moralists', namely the net balance of social good resulting therefrom:

> The difficulty of moral restraint, will perhaps be objected to this doctrine. To him who does not acknowledge the authority of the Christian religion, I have only to say, that, after the most careful investigation, this virtue appears to be absolutely necessary, in order to avoid certain evils which would otherwise result from the general laws of nature. According to his own principles, it is his duty to pursue the greatest good consistent with these laws; and not to fail in this important end, and produce an overbalance of misery, by a partial obedience to some of the dictates of nature while he neglects others. The path of virtue, though it be the only path which leads to permanent happiness, has always been represented by the heathen moralists, as of difficult assent.
>
> (Malthus 1803: 498–9)

Malthus would have had reason here, as elsewhere (above, 11.3), to be concerned that readers might come away with an impression of a totally secular orientation.

I am astonished by Cremaschi's assertion that 'Malthus never attempted to reconcile "dogma" with "utility"'. What of his deliberate quest, as expressed in

1824 (see above, 11.3), to reconcile the painful need on welfare grounds to *restrain* population growth in conditions of land scarcity – painful because of the necessity for self-control – with the 'views of a benevolent Creator'? Now this theme is to be found twenty years earlier in the 1803 *Essay* itself where the possibility of exercising moral restraint is said to assure that 'all apparent imputation on the goodness of the Deity [is] done away', there being 'no reason to impeach the justice of the Deity, because his general laws make this virtue necessary, and punish our offences against it by the evils attendant upon vice, and the pains that accompany the various forms of premature death' (Malthus 1803: 494, 502). I must say I am taken aback by Cremaschi's assertion since he himself insists (above, p. 269) 'that Malthus in 1803 did find not only a more orthodox, but also a more convincing answer to questions left open by his own theodicy by transforming it into a *social* theodicy'.

11.9 Conclusion

Provided we focus upon *intention*, Professor Cremaschi and myself are not perhaps so far apart regarding a strengthening of Malthus's theological concerns after 1798. But this common feature should not be exaggerated since I maintain that such 'strengthening' was in the nature of a rearguard action, Malthus having surrendered considerable ground to the secularists by his preparedness – in a manner which Bentham would certainly have approved – to interpret the scriptures in the light of consequentialist considerations as supporting a restricted birth rate, albeit directly opposed to the traditional reading. Malthus would have had reason to be concerned that he had at times expressed himself in a manner very much suggesting secularism. Equally pertinent is Malthus's abandonment of his agricultural bias in favour of the Ricardian vision of industrial development, almost entirely on the basis of perceived changes in the empirical and legislative environment. The same is true of his increasingly critical view of the landlords of his day with respect to fiscal policy.

All this should put paid to Professor Cremaschi's claim that his own 'reconstruction suggests a way out of familiar conundrums created *ex nihilo* by the Bonar–Hollander reading … How could Malthus be both a utilitarian and the target of Mill-and-co's condescension; how could an alleged utilitarian be biased in favour of established institutions on the ground of their being already there' (Cremaschi 2014: 198). I see no mystery whatsoever. The 'condescension' is easily understood as reflecting an unjustified perception of Malthus as an apologist for the landlord class. The hostility on the part of the Philosophical Radicals would have been transformed into admiration had his abandonment of agricultural protectionism – and indications of his growing impatience with the pretensions of landowners – been common knowledge, although even without such knowledge J.S. Mill applauded Malthus's vital contribution to the reform programme. Strange to relate, Cremaschi is apparently unaware that he has himself provided the appropriate response. Recall his own ascription to Malthus of the Mill-like social objectives 'equality, dignity, self-reliance, generalized education, higher wages, higher standards of consumption' (above, Section 11.5). And he has also rightly noted regarding Catholic Emancipation that: 'Malthus was decidedly on the side of the above alignment' – referring to a 'progressive' front of Whigs, Philosophic Radicals and Dissenters – 'something that was not so much a matter of course for a member of the clergy, who was supposed to belong automatically to the pro-establishment party' (184). Precisely.

I have also here shown, with particular reference to Ricardo and the younger Mill, that religious authority was not a necessary condition for adopting a perspective on ethical conduct apart from consequences relating to wealth and happiness. The common ground shared by the theological and secular utilitarians is greatly enhanced by this circumstance.

Notes

1 Cremaschi does not provide the source for 'damaging vagueness'.
2 Cremaschi might have said 'as late as 1830' since *A Summary View* is the title Malthus gave that year to a reduced-form version of the 1824 article entitled 'Population'.
3 On this matter, see James 1979: 119–20; Hollander 1997: 933n19; Cremaschi 2014: 53.
4 For recognition of the occasional designation of 'vice' as 'something bad in itself', see Stephen 1900 2: 158, Hollander 1997: 936–8.
5 On the 'state of probation', see Hollander 1997: 921–6.
6 Cremaschi cites a sermon of 1827 where Malthus 'makes important concessions to Evangelical views about the role of sentiment in religion' (2014: 71). The lesson is actually more general: 'Nothing great and arduous in action, nothing amiable and delightful in conduct, was ever accomplished without the aid of passions and affections' (Malthus 2004 [1827]: 16). The implications of this opinion for the character of 'virtuous conduct' are not clear, but it is of interest that David Hume had long before opined that the emotions must in practice be engaged, since 'reason' frequently did not suffice to assure action in the right direction (Hume 1751: 172–3).
7 See Hollander 2015: 64, 73.

References

Albee, E. 1901. *A History of English Utilitarianism*. London: Allen & Unwin.
Bentham, J. 1843 (1776). *Fragment on Government, Works* I, ed. John Bowring. Edinburgh: William Tait.
Bentham, J. 1982 (1789). *An Introduction to the Principles of Morals and Legislation*, ed. J.H. Burns and H.L.A. Hart. London and New York: Methuen.
Bonar, J. 1885. *Malthus and His Work*. London: Frank Cass.
Chalmers, T. 1832. *On Political Economy*. Glasgow: William Collins.
Cremaschi, S. 2014. *Utilitarianism and Malthus's Virtue Ethics: Respectable, virtuous and happy*. London and New York: Routledge.
Hollander, S. 1989. 'Malthus and Utilitarianism with Special reference to the Essay on Population'. *Utilitas* I: 170–210.

Hollander, S. 1992. 'Malthus's Abandonment of Agricultural Protectionism: A Discovery in the History of Economic Thought', *American Economic Review* 82: 650–659.
Hollander, S. 1995. 'More on Malthus and Agricultural Protection', *History of Political Economy* 27: 531–537.
Hollander, S. 1997. *The Economics of Thomas Robert Malthus*. Toronto: University of Toronto Press.
Hollander, S. 2015. *John Stuart Mill: Political Economist*. Singapore: World Scientific.
Hume, D. 1751. *An Enquiry Concerning the Principles of Morals*. Reprint (1927) from posthumous edition of 1777, ed. L.A. Selby-Bigge. Oxford: Clarendon Press.
James, P. 1979. *Population Malthus: His Life and Times*. London: Routledge & Kegan Paul.
Malthus, T.R. 1798. *An Essay on the Principle of Population*. London: J. Johnson.
Malthus, T.R. 1803. *An Essay on the Principle of Population*, 2nd ed. London: J. Johnson.
Malthus, T.R. 1806. *An Essay on the Principle of Population*, 3rd ed. London: J. Johnson.
Malthus, T.R. 1817. *An Essay on the Principle of Population*, 5th ed. London: John Murray
Malthus, T.R. 1820. *Principles of Political Economy*. London: John Murray.
Malthus, T.R. 1826. *An Essay on the Principle of Population*, 6th ed. London: John Murray.
Malthus, T.R. 1986 (1815). *The Grounds of an Opinion on the Policy of restricting the Importation of Foreign Corn*, *The Works of Thomas Robert Malthus* 7, eds. E.A. Wrigley and D. Souden. London: William Pickering: 147–174.
Malthus, T.R. 1986 (1823). *The Measure of Value stated and illustrated*, *The Works of Thomas Robert Malthus* 7, eds. E.A. Wrigley and D. Souden. London: William Pickering: 175–221.
Malthus, T.R. 1986 (1824, 1830). 'Population' (1824). *A Summary View of the Principle of Population* (1830); in *The Works of Thomas Robert Malthus* 4, eds. E.A. Wrigley and D. Souden. London: William Pickering: 177–243.
Malthus, T.R. 2004 (1827). 'Sermon', *T.R. Malthus: The Unpublished Papers in the Collection of Kanto Gakuen University* II, eds. J.M. Pullen and T.H. Parry. Cambridge: Cambridge University Press, 12–19.
Mill, J.S. 1969 (1852). 'Whewell on Moral Philosophy', *Collected Works* X, Toronto: University of Toronto Press: 165–201.
Mill, J.S. 1973–4(1843). *A System of Logic Ratiocinative and Inductive. Collected Works* Toronto VII–VIII. Toronto: University of Toronto Press.
Mill, J.S. 1982 (1868). *England and Ireland. Collected Works* VI. Toronto: University of Toronto Press: 505–532.
Paley, W. 1785. *The Principles of Moral and Political Philosophy*, 1st. ed. London: R. Faulder.
Petersen, W. 1999. *Malthus. Founder of Modern Demography*. New Brunswick, NJ: Transaction Books.
Plamenatz, J. 1949. *The English Utilitarians*. Oxford: Blackwell.
Rashid, S. 1984. 'Malthus' Theology: An Overlooked Letter and Some Comments', *History of Political Economy* 16: 135–138.
Ricardo, D. 1951 (1817). *Principles of Political Economy. Works and Correspondence of David Ricardo* I, ed. Piero Sraffa. Cambridge: Cambridge University Press.
Ricardo, D. 1952. *Letters: 1821–1823. Works and Correspondence of David Ricardo* IX, ed. Piero Sraffa. Cambridge: Cambridge University Press.
Robbins, L. C. 1952. *The Theory of Economic Policy in English Classical Political Economy*. London: Macmillan.
Stephen, L. 1900. *The English Utilitarians*. London: Duckworth.
Waterman, A.M.C. 1991. *Revolution, Economics, & Religion: Christian Political Economy 1798–1833*. Cambridge: Cambridge University Press.

Winch, D. 1983. 'Higher maxims: happiness versus wealth in Malthus and Ricardo', in Stefan Collini, Donald Winch & John Burrow, *That Noble Science of Politics*. Cambridge: Cambridge University Press: 63–89.

Winch, D. 1987. *Malthus*. Oxford: Oxford University Press.

Winch, D. 1996. *Riches and Poverty: An Intellectual History of Political Economy in Britain, 1750–1834*. Cambridge: Cambridge University Press.

12 Malthus, distributive justice and the equality issue

12.1 Introduction

This chapter focuses on Malthus's position regarding distribution, particularly equality and labour's welfare. Malthus described the first *Essay on Population* as proving 'the necessity of a class of proprietors, and a class of labourers', but proceeded immediately to the qualification 'that the present great inequality of property, is either necessary or useful to the society'. As for government, he later proposed an extension of the franchise to the end of according 'that respectability and importance, which are given to the lower classes by equal laws, and the possession of some influence in the framing of them', the hoped-for outcome being a reduction of the birth rate promising improved living standards even approaching those of the middle classes. But more is entailed than improved real wages assured by an appropriate adjustment of the labour supply, since the transfer of labour into the middle classes, enhanced equality, and consequently 'the sum of social happiness' are part of the picture.

A large middle class was particularly desirable from the perspective of aggregate demand while great inequality in the 'division of landed property' was perceived as constraining the market. Malthus favoured primogeniture on the grounds that, while it *restricted* the degree of equality in land distribution at the same time it *encouraged* professional and commercial activity on the part of younger sons, thereby undermining 'distinctions founded on rank and birth' while opening up those due to 'personal merit' and also encouraging the expansion of 'a very large class of effective demanders' with a positive effect on general wealth creation.

I supplement the account of desirable distribution by elaborating features of distributive justice emerging during the famous post-Napoleonic debates on trade regarding the effects of an altered price level on class distribution. The matter of 'fairness' also arises in the early 1820s when we are witness to a remarkable change in mood regarding Malthus's attitude towards landlords that may be understood as setting the stage for a subsequent abandonment of agricultural protectionism.

As noted, a case for greater equality turns on the economic importance of a strong middle class with an eye to the propensity to spend. But to this must be added Malthus's growing confidence in the potential of increased aggregate demand emanating from the *working classes* thus reinforcing the desirability of greater equality. This estimate, it will be suggested, may be accounted for by a reorientation regarding manufacturing in place of agriculture as the lead sector with positive implications for labour's real wages – subject always of course to enhanced population control by the exertion of 'prudence'.

Malthus's sympathy for labour is also apparent in his stance regarding poor-relief, an assertion requiring careful justification considering a broadly-held belief that Malthus revealed exaggerated harshness towards the poor. Malthus's enthusiasm for State-aided education programmes to inculcate the benefits to be expected from a reduced birth rate becomes a key consideration, while his celebrated 'plan' to abolish all relief but only after a certain period evidences concern to avoid short-term distress. A general preoccupation with the short-run implications of policy also emerges in a variety of contexts where Malthus recommends benefits to labour even should they be *impermanent*. The *Essay on Population* itself posits that though various alternatives to poor relief, such as land-renting schemes, might ultimately fail even if they were temporarily successful, we should not be deterred 'from making such experiments, when present good is to be obtained by them, and a future overbalance of evil not justly to be apprehended'. Similarly, despite general objections on demographic grounds, some plans for employing the poor 'at certain times and with proper restrictions, may be useful as temporary measures'. In brief, an excessive appeal to 'principle' was to be avoided.

We therefore take Malthus at his word when he declares that he would welcome significant income redistributions were it not that the unconditional guarantee of 'indiscriminate charity' promised to be disastrous from the perspective of the working classes it was ostensibly designed to help. In brief, the 'greatest happiness' rule broke down with a promise of open-ended population increase notwithstanding the depressing effects on *per capita* wages. Certainly, any serious attempt to understand Malthus requires attention to his inadequately-appreciated elaborations regarding welfare relief assuming that prudential population control was generally practised, elaborations extending to a justification of family allowances.

12.2 Income distribution and the equality issue

In the first (1798) edition of his *Essay on Population* Malthus described its 'principal argument' as proving 'the necessity of a class of proprietors, and a class of labourers', but proceeded immediately to a qualification which denied 'that the present great inequality of property, is either necessary or useful to the society. On the contrary, it must certainly be considered an evil, and every institution that promotes it, as essentially bad and impolitic' (Malthus 1798: 287n). Similarly: 'though in every civilized state, a class of proprietors and a class of labourers must exist; yet one permanent advantage would always result from a nearer equalization of property. The greater the number of proprietors, the smaller must be the number of labourers: a greater part of society would be in the happy state of possessing property; and a smaller part in the unhappy state of possessing no other property than their labour' (344–5). Further remarks introduced in the second edition of 1803, and remaining unchanged through all editions including the last of 1826, emphasize private property, the marriage institution, and general self-interest as providing the key to progress in working-class living standards: 'That the principal and most permanent cause of poverty, has little or no [*introduced in 1806*: direct] relation to forms of government, or the unequal division of property', followed 'from the principle of population' (Malthus 1826 2: 438). But this constraint did not preclude improvement and reform, including achievement of a more equable income distribution: 'The structure of society, in its great features, will probably always remain unchanged. We have every reason to believe, that it will always consist of a class of proprietors and a class of labourers; but the condition of each, and *the proportion which they bear to each* other, may be so altered, as greatly to improve the harmony and beauty of the whole' (441; emphasis added). Greater equality, achieved by raising working-class living standards, is thus stated to be a prime *desideratum*.

As for government, 'though it is comparatively impotent in its efforts to make the food of a country keep pace with an unrestricted increase of population, yet its influence is great in giving the best direction to those checks which in some form or other must necessarily take place' (Malthus 1826 2: 324). In addition to the positive effects of 'the perfect security of property' Malthus proposes an extension of the franchise to the end of according 'that respectability and importance, which are given to the lower classes by equal laws, and the possession of some influence in the framing of them' (325). 'If ... the representative system, by securing to the lower classes of society a more equal and liberal mode of treatment from their superiors, gives to each individual a greater respectability, and a greater fear of personal degradation; it is evident that it will powerfully co-operate with the security of property in animating the exertions of industry, and in generating habits of prudence; and thus more powerfully tend to increase the riches and prosperity of the lower classes of the community, than if the same laws had existed under a despotism' (325–6). (A late approving reference to the 1832 Reform Act, however, relates solely to middle-class representation.) Also proposed is a partially state-funded educational scheme along Smithian lines but with a curriculum including 'the frequent explanation of the real state of the lower classes of society, as affected by the principle of population, and their consequent dependence on themselves, for the chief part of their happiness, or misery' (353). Malthus here makes explicit his hope that the working classes would, in consequence, in some measure adopt behaviour patterns promising improved living standards *approaching those of the middle classes*: 'Besides explaining the real situation of the lower classes of society, as depending principally upon themselves for their happiness or misery, the parochial schools would, by early instruction and the judicious distribution of rewards, have the fairest chance of training up the rising generation in habits of sobriety, industry, independence and prudence, and in a proper discharge of their religious duties; which would raise them from their present degraded state, and *approximate them, in some degree, to the middle classes of society*, whose habits, generally speaking, are certainly superior' (359; emphasis added).[1] 'Harmony and beauty' are far from the whole story. Malthus formalizes the objective to be a system which perceives inequality as both essential and beneficial taking the force of emulation into account, *but only within limits*:

> It has been generally found that the middle parts of society are most favourable to virtuous and industrious habits, and to the growth of all kinds of talents. But it is evident that all cannot be in the middle. Superior and inferior parts are in the nature of things absolutely necessary; and not only necessary, but strikingly beneficial. If no man could hope to rise, or fear to fall in society; if industry did not bring with it its reward, and indolence its punishment; we could not expect to see that animated activity in bettering our condition, which now forms the master-spring of public prosperity.
>
> (Malthus 1826 2: 427–8).

The conclusion is unambiguous that ideally to be sought after is an increase in equality achieved by way of a relative increase in the 'middle parts': 'But in contemplating the different states of Europe, we observe a very considerable difference in the relative proportions of the superior, the middle and the inferior parts; and from the effects of these differences it seems probable, that *our best-grounded expectations of an increase in the happiness of the mass of human society are founded in the prospect of an increase in the relative proportions of the middle parts*' (428; emphasis added). Greater equality is thus recommended on the strict utilitarian grounds of 'greater happiness'.

More is entailed than improved real wages assured by an appropriate adjustment of the labour supply. Transfer of labour into the middle classes, and thus enhanced equality, is part of the picture. That this is so emerges strikingly in an analysis of a worst-case scenario entailing a *stationary* or *decelerating* growth rate of labour demand in consequence of labour-saving technological change.[2] Not only would the average wage be maintained 'if the lower classes of people had acquired the habit of proportioning the supplies of labour to a stationary or even decreasing demand, without an increase of misery and mortality, as at present' – more specifically, supposing 'the general prevalence of such prudential habits among the poor, as would prevent them from marrying, when the actual price of labour, joined to what they might have saved in their single state, would not give them the prospect of being able to support a wife and five or six children without assistance' – but new technology, accompanied by enhanced population control, could assure that the lowest ranks could be dispensed with: 'we might even venture to indulge a hope that at some future period the processes for abridging human labour, the progress of which has of late years been so rapid, might ultimately supply all the wants of the most wealthy society with less personal effort than at present; and if they did not diminish the severity of individual exertion, might, at least, diminish the number of those employed in severe toil' (Malthus 1826 2: 428). Malthus concludes that: 'If the lowest classes of society were thus diminished, and the middle classes increased,[3] each labourer might indulge *a more rational hope of rising by diligence and exertion into a better station*; the rewards of industry and virtue would be increased in number; the lottery of human society would appear to consist of fewer blanks and more prizes; and the sum of social happiness would be evidently augmented'; (emphasis added). But if a prospect of rising 'into a better station' is envisaged as a result of appropriate prudential conduct even when the growth rate of labour demand is declining such would *a fortiori* be the case under more usual, less restrictive, conditions as a result of real-wage increase.

The *Essay on Population* takes the case for enhanced equality yet further by disputing Paley's perception of desirable income distribution according to which 'the condition most favourable to the population of a country, and at the same time to its general happiness, is, "that of a laborious frugal people, ministering to the demand of an opulent luxurious nation"' (Malthus 1826 2: 425 citing Paley 1785 2: 359).[4] Malthus forcefully rejected Paley's case for extreme inequality:

> Such a form of society has not, it must be confessed, an inviting aspect. Nothing but the conviction of its being absolutely necessary could reconcile us to the idea of ten millions of people condemned to incessant toil, and to the privation of every thing but absolute necessaries, in order to minister to the excessive luxuries of the other million. But the fact is, that such a form of society is by no means necessary. It is by no means necessary that the rich should be excessively luxurious, in order to support the manufactures of a country; or that the poor should be deprived of all luxuries, in order to make them sufficiently numerous.
> (Malthus 1826 2: 426)

His case for greater equality turns partly on the importance of the working classes as a source of aggregate demand for manufactures, and will be elaborated presently. We have however seen that Malthus returns to focus on the middle classes when he formalizes the policy objective to be a system which perceives inequality as both essential and beneficial taking the force of emulation into account.

The utilitarian case for higher wages is also conspicuous in the *Principles*, with its emphasis on the quantitative superiority of the labouring class in standard classical fashion: 'It is most desirable that the labouring class should be well paid, for a much more important reason than any that can relate to wealth' – intending the increase in national product resulting from expenditure on the part of a well-paid workforce – 'namely, the happiness of the great mass of society' (Malthus 1820: 472; 1836: 405).[5] It would be an error to attribute to Malthus by this contrast between 'wealth' and 'happiness' the sort of issue raised by Adam Smith's contemplations in the *Theory of Moral Sentiments* regarding the happy beggar (see above, pp. 155, 182); Malthus never doubted that *ceteris paribus* a beggar would benefit from an increase in real income, insisting for example in the *Essay* that 'the country will evidently be the happiest, where the degree of distress at this point [the minimum of subsistence at which population growth ceases] is the least; and consequently, if the spread of luxury, by producing the check sooner, tend to diminish this degree of distress, it is certainly desirable' (Malthus 1826 2: 426n).

As for the landowning aristocracy, the *Principles* recognizes that the institution was – fortunately – not what it used to be insofar as that '[b]y the natural extinction of some great families, and the natural imprudence of some others, but, above all, by the extraordinary growth of manufactures and commerce, the immense landed properties which formerly prevailed all over the country have been to a great degree broken down, notwithstanding the right of primogeniture' (Malthus 1820: 435; 1836: 378–9), while the few remaining great land-owners Malthus adds, 'may perhaps be of use in furnishing motives to the merchant and master-manufacturer, to continue the exercise of their skill and powers till they have acquired large capitals, and are able to contend in wealth with the great landlords'; but this is an understatement, since so effective was the force of emulation that were primogeniture abolished, allowing only 'very inconsiderable' landed fortunes, 'it is not probable that there would be many large capitals among merchants' (436; 379). Nevertheless, Malthus cautioned against going too far by 'ventur[ing] upon any such [constitutional] change as would risk the whole structure, and throw us upon a wide sea of experiment, where the chances are so dreadfully against our attaining the object of our search' (437–8; 380). This concern did not prevent him in revisions for the second edition from reacting positively to the 1832 Reform Act, which – though it had been introduced prematurely by the force of circumstance – might turn out for the best by 'bring[ing] the practical working of the constitution nearer to its theory. And there is every reason to believe, that a great majority of the middle classes of society, among whom the elective franchise has been principally extended, must soon see that their own interests, and the interests and happiness of those who are dependent upon them, will be most essentially injured by any proceedings which tend to encourage turbulence and shake the security of property' (Malthus 1836: 380n). Indeed, the correction of unsightly defects in the system would remove excuses for 'discontents' which 'stir up the people [and] will place the British constitution upon a much broader and more solid base than ever'.

12.3 Distributive 'fairness'

I shall now supplement the account of desirable distribution by elaborating features of distributive justice emerging during the post-Napoleonic debates on trade regarding the effects of an altered price level on class distribution. The case against opening the ports for agricultural products in 1815 turned partly on the class gains and losses to be expected from generally lower prices in the presence of a significant *national debt*: 'I own it appears to me', Malthus wrote in 1815, 'that the necessary effect of a change in the measure of value on the weight of a large national debt is alone sufficient to make the question fundamentally different from that of a simple question about a free or restricted trade' (Malthus 1986 [1815] 7: 171). While the wartime inflation, brought about by an increase in paper money, had stimulated industry and accumulation by counteracting the 'prodigious' burdens of the national debt, to the advantage of the 'industrious classes' at the expense of stockholders – or fund-holders, referring to government creditors – a fall in general prices would provide an *'unfair'* advantage to stockholders with severe consequences for all other classes: 'If the price of corn were now to fall to 50 shillings a quarter, and labour and other commodities nearly in proportion, there can be no doubt that the stockholders would be benefited unfairly at the expense of the wealth and prosperity of the whole country' (169). Malthus would be prepared to tolerate 'this extraordinary generosity towards the stockholders', referring to the real increase in the interest rate, were it not that this 'can only be paid by the industrious classes of society and the landlords, that is, by all those whose nominal incomes will vary with the variations in the measure of value' (169–70).[6] More specifically: 'If we consider, with what an increased weight the taxes on tea, sugar, malt leather, soap, candles, etc., etc. would in this case bear on the labouring classes of society, and what *proportion* of their incomes all the active, industrious middle orders of the state, as well as the higher orders, must pay in assessed taxes, and the various articles of the customs and excise, the pressure will appear to be absolutely intolerable' (170). On balance, by opening up the ports 'very much the largest mass of the people, and particularly of the industrious orders of the state, will be more injured than benefited' (171). Although we see here, once again, the significance of the quantitative dimension for the estimate of the 'greatest good', the stockholding minority would not in fact be denied 'justice' at a high (protected) corn price of 80s. 'since the whole of the loans made during the war just terminated, will on average, be paid at an interest rate very much higher than they were contracted for'.[7]

The matter of 'fairness' also arises conspicuously in the early 1820s when we are witness to a remarkable change in mood regarding Malthus's attitude towards landlords that may be understood as setting the stage for the subsequent abandonment of agricultural protectionism. Thus, the *Measure of*

Value (1823) protests against proposals by landowners to adjust contracts to their own benefit at the expense of stockholders:

> But whatever may have been the pressure on the owners of land since the peace [agricultural prices in 1823 had not yet recovered from their collapse after the high wartime levels, notwithstanding protection, during the post-war deflation] they cannot have the slightest plea for an attempt to indemnify themselves at the expense of the public creditor. In the turns of the wheel of fortune, all parties should have fair play; no class of persons can be justified in endeavouring to lift themselves up by using unfair and dishonourable means to pull others down; and least of all ought such means to be thought of by the landlords of this country, who, whatever inconveniences they may have suffered latterly, have unquestionably altogether benefited much more largely from the alterations in the value of the currency, than the very persons who in their opinion should be made to relieve themselves from their embarrassments.
>
> (Malthus 1986 [1823] 7: 220–1)

'Fairness' also arises in the discussion of primogeniture, a practise that had been abandoned in France. Malthus favoured an institution which, while *restricting* the degree of equality in land distribution, had the effect of encouraging professional and commercial activity thereby undermining 'distinctions founded on rank and birth' while enhancing 'fairness' by opening up those due to 'personal merit':

> [I]t is certain that a very large body of what may be called the middle classes of society has been established in this country; while the right [1836] of primogeniture, by forcing the younger sons of the nobility and great landed proprietors into the higher divisions of these classes, has, for all practical purposes, annihilated the distinctions founded on rank and birth, and opened the fairest *arena* for the contests of personal merit in all the avenues to wealth and honours. It is probable that the obligations generally imposed upon younger sons to be the founders of their own fortunes, has infused a greater degree of energy and activity into professional and commercial exertions than would have taken place if property in land had been more equally divided.
>
> (Malthus 1820: 436; 1836: 379)

'Fairness' may perhaps also be said to enter the picture, at least implicitly, by the contention that 'the representative system ... [secures] to the lower classes of society a more equal and liberal mode of treatment from their superiors' (above, p. 285).

12.4 Distribution and aggregate demand: more on the equality issue

From the perspective of aggregate demand — the prime bone of theoretical contention between Malthus and Ricardo — 'the division of landed property' was accorded high significance by Malthus, who posited that great inequality constrained the market: 'A very large proprietor, surrounded by very poor peasants, presents a distribution of property most unfavourable to effective [1836: effectual] demand ... Thirty or forty proprietors, with incomes answering to between one thousand and five thousand a year, would create a much more effective demand for wheaten bread, good meat, and manufactured produce [1836: effectual demand for the necessaries, conveniences, and luxuries of life] than a single proprietor possessing a hundred thousand a year' (Malthus 1820: 429–30; 1836: 373–4). The general principle is extended beyond land distribution, with Malthus introducing the significance from the perspective of aggregate demand of a large middle class:

> no instance has ever been known of a country which has pushed its natural resources to a great extent, with a small proportionate body of persons of property, however rich and luxurious they might be. Practically it has always been found that the excessive wealth of the few is in no respect equivalent, with regard to effective [1836: effectual] demand, to the more moderate wealth of the many. A large body of manufacturers and merchants can only find a market for their commodities among a numerous class of consumers above the rank of mere workmen and labourers [1836: below the rank of the great proprietors of land].
>
> (431; 375)

For the British experience showed that the middle classes, who derived their purchasing power from the professions, commerce, manufactures, wholesale and retail trade, salaries of various kinds, and the interest of public and private debts, constituted a body of demanders 'likely, perhaps, to acquire tastes more favourable to the encouragement of wealth than the owners of the small properties on the land' (436–7; 379). Even so, Malthus insisted on an *optimal* degree of equality (applying in effect the so-called 'doctrine of proportions') that should not be surpassed: 'But though it is true that the division of landed property, and the diffusion of manufacturing and mercantile capital to a certain extent, are of the utmost importance to the increase of wealth; yet it is equally true that, beyond a certain extent, they would impede the progress of wealth as much as they had before accelerated it' (431; 375).

As we have already seen in the previous section, Malthus favoured an institution which *restricting* the degree of equality in land distribution while *encouraging* professional and commercial activity undermined 'distinctions founded on rank and birth' while opening up those due to 'personal merit'. A more specific consequence of primogeniture was that of encouraging the expansion of 'a very large class of effective demanders', and since this was to the benefit of wealth creation 'it might be rash to conclude that the nation would be richer if the right of primogeniture were abolished' (Malthus 1820: 437; 1836: 379). But even were this not the case, Malthus rejected the abolition of primogeniture since there were 'higher considerations ... than those which relate to mere wealth', alluding here to the importance of the British constitution based on a landed aristocracy which had assured 'better government, and more liberty to a greater mass of people for a longer time than any which history records' (437; 380). While such a consideration appears at first sight to clash with the immediately preceding downplaying of 'distinctions founded on rank and birth' in favour of the 'fairer' recognition of 'personal merit', we obtain a clearer view by recalling the estimate that the British aristocracy was no longer what it once had been.

The importance of a middle class from the perspective of aggregate demand dictated Malthus's attitude towards paying off the National Debt – one of Ricardo's strongest recommendations: 'If the *distribution* of wealth to a certain extent be one of the main causes of its increase, while it is inadvisable directly to interfere with the present division of land in this country, it may justly become a question, whether the evils attendant on the national debt are not more than counterbalanced by the distribution of property and increase in the middle classes' of society, which it must necessarily create ... By greatly reducing the national debt, if we are able to accomplish it, we may place ourselves perhaps in a more safe position, and this no doubt is an important consideration; but grievously will those be disappointed who think that, either by greatly reducing or at once destroying it, we can enrich ourselves, and employ all our labouring classes' (Malthus 1820: 507; 1836: 426–7). Again, it would be 'the height of rashness to determine, under all circumstances, that the [1836: sudden] diminution of the national debt and the removal of taxation must necessarily tend to increase the national wealth, and provide employment for the labouring classes' (482; 411). In 1820 Malthus summarized thus: 'Under the actual division of landed property which now takes place in this country, I feel no sort of doubt that the incomes which are received and spent by the national creditors are more favourable to the demand for the great mass of manufactured products, and tend much more to increase the happiness and intelligence of the whole society, than if they were returned to the landlords' (Malthus 1820: 483–4).[8]

The primary case for greater equality – from the perspective of positive economics –turns, on the evidence so far adduced, on the economic importance of a strong middle class with an eye to the propensity to spend. It is also intimated that any positive effect on wealth thus achieved raises the aggregate demand for labour (or its growth rate) – although, we should add, not necessarily the wage share in national income. But what, if anything, does Malthus have to say regarding at least the potential of increased aggregate demand emanating from the *working classes* thus reinforcing the desirability of greater equality from the perspective of purchasing power? Now at one point he does indeed posit that what was required to assure the sustainability of any investment programme yielding an increased aggregate supply was 'such a change in the tastes and habits of *the lower classes of people*, and such an alteration in the mode of paying their labour as would give them both the will and the power to purchase domestic manufactures and foreign commodities' (Malthus 1820: 400–1; emphasis added). A more equal social structure *including the wage share* is similarly rendered in a modification to this text for the second edition which reads that what is required is 'such a change in the tastes and habits of the lower classes of people, such an alteration in the mode of paying their labour and such an improvement in the structure of the whole society as would give *both the lower and middle classes* a greater will and power to purchase domestic manufactures and foreign commodities' (Malthus 1836: 350–1). The revised edition also inserts a note confirming that '[t]here is nothing so favourable to effectual demand as a large proportion of the middle classes of society', perhaps suggesting a degree of uncertainty regarding the treatment of labour; but against this we should note an alteration between editions already cited earlier – that whereas in the first edition Malthus writes: 'A large body of manufacturers and merchants can only find a market for their commodities among a numerous class of consumers *above the rank of mere workmen and labourers*', in the second this is modified to read '*below the rank of the great proprietors of land*' which goes so far as to treat the working and middle classes as one from the perspective of aggregate demand (see above, p. 291).[9]

The *Essay on Population* also argues for greater equality on the grounds of the importance of the working classes as a source of aggregate demand for manufactures, the full argument running thus:

> The best, and in every point of view the most advantageous manufactures in this country, are those which are consumed by *the great body of the people*. The manufactures which are confined exclusively to the rich are not only trivial, on account of the comparatively smallness of their quantity, but are further liable to the great disadvantage of producing much occasional misery among those employed in them, from changes of fashion. It is the diffusion of luxury among *the mass of the people*, and not an excess of it in a few, that seems to be the most advantageous, both with regard to national wealth and national happiness; and what Dr. Paley considers as the true evil and proper danger of luxury, I should be disposed to consider as its true good, and peculiar advantage.
>
> (Malthus 1826 2: 426–7; emphasis added)

Taken literally, this passage implies that the working classes constitute – assuming the spread of prudential habits to be partly stimulated by a taste for luxuries – the *prime* source of aggregate demand for manufacturers, superior even to the middle classes which are not even mentioned. If this indeed was Malthus's considered estimate it comes as a surprise. But we can by no means be sure that this is the weighting intended since in the next paragraph of the text the middle classes come back into their own (427–8).

12.5 Trade policy: implications for real wages

It seems fair to conclude from the texts thus far considered that Malthus was persuaded of the growing significance of the working classes as a source of increasing aggregate demand, implying thereby an extension of his case for greater equality to include the wage share. We have at hand a hypothesis to account for such a trend, namely a reorientation regarding manufacturing in place of agriculture as the lead sector with positive implications for labour's real wages, subject always of course to enhanced population control by the exertion of 'prudence'.

The reorientation in question entailed the abandonment of Malthus's original position favouring agricultural protection. For he had earlier, as in the post-Napoleonic years, supported high tariffs on the grounds that a system which depended in average years on foreign sources of supply subject to interruption constituted a threat to the 'happiness' of the working classes which he considered – as did all the classical economists – as 'the foundation on which the whole fabric rests; and, from their numbers, unquestionably of the greatest weight, in any estimate of national happiness' (Malthus 1986 [1815] 7: 162). 'If I were convinced, that to open our ports, would be permanently to improve the condition of the labouring classes of society, I should consider the question as at once determined in favour of such a measure'. But in 1815 he was unconvinced and based a case for protection on a perceived *advantage* to labourers – apart from the 'very poorest' – of a *high* corn price:

> [U]nder the same demand for labour, and the same consequent power of purchasing the means of subsistence, a high *money price* of corn would give the labourer a very great advantage in the purchase of the conveniences and luxuries of life. The effect of this high money price would not, of course, be so marked among the very poorest of the society, and those who had the largest families; because so very great a part of their earnings must be employed in absolute necessaries. But to all those above the very poorest, the advantage of wages resulting from a price of eighty shillings a quarter for wheat, compared with fifty or sixty, would in the purchase of tea, sugar, cotton, linens, soap, candles, and many other articles, be such as to make their condition decidedly superior.

Also taken into account here is the allegedly greater instability of corn prices under 'free trade' – the full case purports to demonstrate that a truly 'free' system was not in fact realistically conceivable – so that it would 'require a much greater increase in the demand for labour, than there is any rational ground for expecting, to compensate to the labourer the advantages which he loses in the high money wages of labour, and the steadier and less fluctuating price of corn' (164–5). In addition, the capitalists constituted after the labouring classes 'the next most important class of society' in terms of absolute numbers, one half of whom were farmers or dependent immediately on agriculture, and they would suffer at least temporarily from the opening of the ports (165). Capitalists engaged in foreign trade would benefit, but since these 'form but a very small portion of the class of persons living on the profits of stock, in point of number, and not probably above a seventh or eighth in point of property, their interests cannot be allowed to weight against the interests of so large a majority' (166).

A further feature governing Malthus's agricultural protectionism reflects a concern expressed in the *Principles* that prudential population control tending to raise the real wage might be disastrous in an economy dependent on manufacturing exports: 'woe will, I fear, befall us, greater than ever we have yet experienced, if the prosperity of our cotton trade should become necessary to purchase the food, of any considerable body of our people' (Malthus 1820: 236n). This note is absent in the second edition, an alteration among many indicating that Malthus finally threw in the towel and accepted Ricardo's position regarding the benefits of free trade in place of agricultural protection to assure balanced growth. Henceforth British development, Malthus conceded, should rely on industry as its lead sector.[10] What therefore requires exploration is Malthus's perception of the probable effects of such development on the condition of labour.

Recall his estimate of 1815 that it would 'require a much greater increase in the demand for labour, than there is any rational ground for expecting, to compensate to the labourer the advantages which he loses in the high money wages of labour, and the steadier and less fluctuating price of corn', and his contention, noted above, that '[i]f I were convinced, that to open our ports, would be permanently to improve the condition of the labouring classes of society, I should consider the question as at once determined in favour of such a measure'. By the mid-1820s the manufacturing sector was, on Malthus's revised view, proving itself adequate in that regard; indeed, a paper of 1824 explicitly refers to 'the happy opening of new and large channels of foreign commerce, combined with the improved views of our government in commercial legislation' – the Huskisson reforms – which had prevented 'great distress' and assured 'a renewed demand for labour' (Malthus 1986 [1824] 7: 287).

Consider also Malthus's protectionist or balanced-growth programme in the fifth (1817) edition of the *Essay on Population* to *counter* a natural trend to 'direct the greatest part of … new capital to commerce and manufactures' during the later stages of economic development – entailing growing land scarcity and an 'increasing taste for conveniences and luxuries' – partly because such development would not be to labour's advantage (Malthus 1817 3: 6). Compare this with the perception of the 'natural' course of development after adoption in the 1820s of the 'Ricardian' position that such a trend would be advantageous to labour, expressed in evidence before the Commons Select Committee on Emigration in 1827: '*the extent of the effectual demand for the manufactures and commodities consumed at home, depends essentially upon the good condition of the labouring classes'*, represented as always as '*the most important of all*' (Hollander 1997: 863; emphasis added). This declaration places the labouring classes even ahead of the middle classes insofar as concerns aggregate demand, implying a major extension of the case for greater equality outlined above. The disadvantage spelled out in 1820 that 'prudence' threatened the export industries by raising wage costs seems to have been retained, but the demand-side advantage flowing from good wages would be decisive. Thus responding to the view that low wages favoured trade and commerce, Malthus explained in his 1827 evidence: 'in one respect it is, and in one respect not; it may enable the capitalist to work up his commodities cheaper, and to extend his foreign trade, but certainly will have a tendency to diminish the home trade, and I think the home trade much more important than the foreign' (cited in Hollander 1997: 362).

In correspondence Malthus also confirms his new-found confidence in the advantage to labour promised by free trade. Thus a letter to Nassau Senior in 1829 forecasts improved real wages although with the important qualification that *permanent* advantage required increased prudential control: 'it follows from my principles, that if by a free trade, corn were obtained much cheaper, and a labouring family could really command a much larger quantity of it, population would unquestionably increase with greater rapidity than before, so as to reduce the increased corn wages; and that the final condition of the labouring classes would not depend on this change which had taken place in the law, but upon the greater or less prevalence of the moral checks to population after the peculiar stimulus to its increase had subsided', and such prevalence could not unfortunately be guaranteed (in Senior 1829: 84–5). Nonetheless, Malthus affirmed that 'the period during which the pressure of population is lightened, though it may not be of long duration, is a period of comparative ease, and ought by no means to be thrown out of our consideration' (85).

A letter to Jane Marcet of January1833 expressing a pessimistic view of the prospects for labour deriving from the abolition of the Corn Laws was written during a period of business depression, and directly reflects those special conditions:

> In the actual state of the redundancy of labour in this country, it appears to me scarcely possible to conceive that the money wages of labour will not fall nearly in proportion to the price of corn, and the labourers greatly disappointed. It will no doubt give a stimulus to foreign trade; but it must for a considerable time aggravate the redundancy of labour in country parishes; and during the process of the change, there will probably be more thrown out of work than in any other case of the restrictions of the freedom of trade, on account of the largeness of the concerns.
> (cited Hollander 1997: 855).

Furthermore, when writing to Thomas Chalmers the following month Malthus effectively reconfirmed his longer-term positive perspective, with a significant emphasis on the increased purchasing power of labourers deriving from manufacturing exports, for expenditure on agricultural produce:

> Do not manufactures and commerce increase the *Revenue* of a country, and enlarge the *returning power*? I own but I cannot but think that if the taste for luxuries and superior conveniences were at an end, the cultivation of the land would be essentially deteriorated, – at least under the present division of landed property. How could the actual number of labourers have an adequate demand for the produce of the soil, if commerce and manufactures were greatly to be diminished? What numbers would be out of work! What constant calls for an extension of Poor Laws, and of all public and private charities!
>
> (cited Hollander 1997: 862).

The emphasis in the foregoing statement is on the demand for food emanating from industrial workers under a free-trade regime. We recall too that Malthus, as in the later editions of the *Essay on Population* (above, p. 293), also recognised labour's demand for manufactures. But of course industrial capitalists constituted a further major source of demand as is clear from a comparison with the limited demand emanating from service labour employed by landlords expressed in a letter to Chalmers of 1832: 'The demand for useful and beneficial personal services is limited; and after all these have been fully paid, would it not be an impoverishing and very disadvantageous exchange to substitute for the rich capitalists and comfortable and independent traders living upon the profits of stock, a body of dependents upon the landlords?' (cited Hollander 1997: 861).

12.6 Poor relief

Much of the foregoing turns on positive rather than normative economics. I shall now elaborate Malthus's pervasive sympathy for labour from the latter perspective and with particular reference to poor-relief problems. This matter requires careful elaboration considering a firm belief held by both professionals and lay readers that Malthus revealed his harshness towards the poor by his declaration in the *Essay on Population* that 'no person has any claim of *right* on society for subsistence, if his labour will not purchase it' (Malthus 1826 2: 320). The second edition expresses this perspective even more sharply: 'A man who is born into a world already possessed, if he cannot get subsistence from his parents on whom he has a just demand, and if the society do not want his labour, has no claim of *right* to the smallest portion of food, and, in fact, has no business to be where he is. At nature's mighty feast there is no vacant cover for him. She tells him to be gone, and will quickly execute her own orders, if he do not work upon the compassion of some of her guests' (Malthus 1803: 531). The removal of this passage in later editions does not alter the warning that indiscriminate charity would encourage unlimited claimants until 'the plenty that before reigned is changed into scarcity'. As the matter is expressed in later editions:

> If all could be completely relieved, and poverty banished from the country, even at the expense of three fourths of the fortunes of the rich, I would be the last person to say a single syllable against relieving all, and making the degree of distress alone the measure of our bounty. But as experience has proved, I believe, without a single exception, that poverty and misery have always increased in proportion to the quantity of indiscriminate charity, are we not bound to infer, reasoning as we usually do from the laws of nature, that it is an intimation that such a mode of distribution is not the proper office of benevolence?
> (Malthus 1826 2: 369–70).

The concern, of course, was that the contemporary poor-laws 'tend in the most marked manner to make the supply of labour exceed the demand for it, their effect must be, either to lower universally all wages, or, if some are kept up artificially, to throw great numbers of workmen out of employment, and thus constantly to increase the poverty and distress of the labouring classes of society' (371).

There is no reason to question Malthus's declaration that he would welcome major income redistributions were it not that the unconditional guarantee of 'indiscriminate charity' would be disastrous from the perspective of the working classes it was ostensibly designed to help. Here we have an application of the 'greatest happiness' rule, one that makes no sense allowing for open-ended population increases regardless of the depressing effects on *per capita* income. The problem to be solved, therefore, as expressed in a criticism of Robert Owen's 'Systems of Equality' was: '*How to provide for those who are in want, in such a manner as to prevent a continual increase of their numbers, and of the proportion which they bear to the whole society*' (Malthus 1826 2: 395).[11] As for 'systems of equality and community of goods' such as Owen's, since self-interested calculation regarding the age of marriage were precluded, they would have to be replaced by legal constraints involving rigorous enforcement and punishment of an 'unnatural, immoral, or cruel in a high degree' (48). It is problematic that Malthus should have recommended that individuals in private-property systems be free to marry even without a prospect of maintaining a family, for although an 'immoral act, yet it is not one which society can justly take upon itself to prevent or punish; because the punishment provided for it by the laws of nature falls directly and most severely upon the individual who commits the act, and through him, only remotely and feebly, on the society' (339). This perspective, which plays down the social implications of irresponsible private behaviour, implies a failure to recognise the severe consequences of free-riding. Indeed, even assuming the success of an education system inculcating the principle that the wage depends on checks to the marriage rate, each self-interested individual has a motive to marry young if he believes others will behave responsibly and delay marriage. Nor is it the case that the responsible individual will 'reap the full fruits of his good behaviour 'whatever may be the number of others who fail', since his expectations of future earnings may be ruined by irresponsible behaviour by others.[12]

From this perspective we can appreciate Malthus's affirmation that without the Poor Laws, which encouraged irresponsible conduct enhancing population growth and abysmal living standards, 'though there might have been a few more instances of very severe distress, the aggregate mass of happiness among the common people would have been much greater than it is at present' (Malthus 1826 2: 86), which implies – *pace* Bonar (see below, p. 302) – that a smaller population receiving good average wages is preferable on utilitarian grounds to a larger population on low wages (such as Paley desired). This same estimate is also apparent in an exposition of the *conditional* desirability of population expansion, namely that an increasing population – not a large population as such – was desirable only insofar as such increase was in response to high standards. Malthus protested the misrepresentations of his position in this regard: 'as if any thing could be more desirable than the most rapid increase of population, unaccompanied by vice and misery' (450). The consistency of the *desiderata* of 'high' wages and population growth turns more specifically on the *quality* of the work force, specifically the greater potential of productivity increase in the case of a population with a high proportion of healthy adults. Thus Malthus estimated that the initial constraint on population growth *via* a reduced birth rate – the very objective of 'prudential' conduct – would, by altering the age distribution in favour of a 'larger share of adults', 'create fresh resources, and consequently … encourage a continued increase of *efficient* population' rather than the stunted variety encouraged by the existing Poor Law (470; emphasis added).[13]

It is held against Malthus that even 'after ten years of breathing space from war, Malthus had still nothing to offer insofar as concerned labour's welfare but deterrents to population – to England the refusal of poor relief after a certain date' (Fay 1950: 368). Fay cites the opinion given to the Commons Select Committee on Emigration in 1827, but the proposal appears in the *Essay on Population* itself: 'According to this plan, all that are already married, and even all that are engaged to marry during the course of the year, and all their children, would be relieved as usual; and only those who marry subsequently, and who of course may be supposed to have made better provision for contingencies, would be out of the pale of relief' (Malthus 1826 2: 458). Relief thereafter would become the responsibility of private charity. But to leave the matter here is to distort, for Malthus did not in fact expect or even recommend the wholesale abolition of poor relief. The population principle provided guidelines only, not a pretext for the abrogation of all responsibility for the poor by government. Thus he posited that 'the general principles on these subjects ought not to be pushed too far, though they should always be kept in view; and that many cases may occur, in which the good resulting from the relief of the present distress may more than overbalance the evil to be apprehended from the remote consequences' (Malthus 1826 2: 419). (This remark already appears in the second edition: Malthus 1803: 587.) Indeed: 'All relief in instances of distress, not arising from idle and improvident habits, clearly comes under this description; and in general it may be observed, that it is only that kind of *systematic* and *certain* relief, on which the poor can confidently depend, whatever may be their conduct, that violates general principles in such a manner as to make it clear that the general consequence is worse than the particular evil' (420). In his paper on 'Population' Malthus pointed out – very much in the manner later adopted by J.S. Mill – that much depended: 'upon the feelings and habits of the labouring classes of society, and can only be determined by experience. If it be generally considered as so discreditable to receive parochial relief, that great exertions are made to avoid it, and few or none marry with a certain prospect of being obliged to have recourse to it, there is no doubt that those who were really in distress might be adequately assisted, with little danger of a constantly increasing proportion of paupers; and in that case a great good would be attained without any proportionate evil to counter-balance it' (Malthus 1986 [1824] 4: 238).

Further qualifications arose from the practical manner in which poor relief was applied, implying the need for an intimate knowledge of administrative matters before any final conclusion could be reached; and in fact the precise manner of application modified the generally negative appraisal of the prevailing system as encouraging marriage, leading to the admission that '[s]hould this be true, some of the objections which have been urged in the Essay against the poor laws will be removed' (Malthus 1826 2: 468n; see Hollander 1997: 897n).

Particularly revealing of Malthus's overall welfare perspective is a response made to those who would object to plans for improving the cottages of the poor or enabling them to keep cows on the grounds that they would 'give them the power of rearing a greater number of children', namely that '[w]e cannot, in the nature of things, assist the poor in any way, without enabling them to rear up to manhood a greater number of children', while to reduce the mortality rate was precisely 'what we ought to aim at', to which there could be no objection provided 'we can impress these children with the idea, that, to possess the same advantages as their parents, they must defer marriage till they have a fair prospect of being able to maintain a family' (Malthus 1826 2: 424–5). Here Malthus's enthusiasm for State-aided education programmes (above, p. 284) becomes the key consideration.

★★★★★★

The 'plan' to abolish all relief only after a certain period, is evidence of a concern to avoid short-term distress.[14] A preoccupation with the short-run implications of policy also emerges in a variety of other contexts from the perspective of securing benefits to labour even if they should be *impermanent*. We have already encountered above Malthus' opinion that even the short-term advantages flowing from trade liberalization were not to be despised; indeed, he even suggested that 'the experience of such a period may sometimes operate in giving to the labouring-classes a taste for such a mode of living as will tend to increase their prudential habits' (to Senior 1829: 85–6). This same caution is implied by his support for state-aided emigration during periods of depression even if the benefits would be temporary in the light of unremitting population pressure: 'the immediate temporary relief … is a consideration not to be put out of the question' (letter dated 22 February 1830, to Wilmot Horton, cited Hollander 1997: 903). The *Essay on Population* itself posits that though various alternatives to poor relief, such as land-renting schemes, might ultimately fail even if temporarily successful, we should not be deterred 'from making such experiments, when present good is to be obtained by them, and a future over-balance of evil not justly to be apprehended. It should only make us less rash in drawing our inferences' (Malthus 1826 2: 464). Similarly, despite general objections on demographic grounds, some plans for employing the poor 'at certain times and with proper restrictions, may be useful as temporary measures', although Malthus reiterated that 'to prevent ineffectual efforts and continued disappointments' required an awareness 'that the permanent remedy which we are seeking cannot possibly come from this quarter' (407). This same concern with the short run from labour's perspective is also implied in the cautions against the excessive appeal to 'principle' in the context of poor relief itself, as we have already noted.

Any serious attempt to get Malthus right also requires an allowance for his position regarding welfare relief assuming that prudential population control is generally practised. With the removal of population pressure – implying incidentally a 'low' family size of about six children – the policy programme is transformed, public works, emigration, and insurance schemes coming fully into their own, supplemented even by a family-allowance scheme to help married couples who had more children than they could be expected to foresee: 'I do not think that any evil would result from making a certain allowance to every child above this number; not with a view of rewarding a man for his large family, but merely of relieving him from a species of distress which it would be unreasonable in us to expect that he should calculate upon. And with this view, the relief should be merely such as to place him exactly in the same situation as if he had six children' (Malthus 1826 2: 429). Some such arrangement 'might relieve particular individuals from a very pressing and unlooked for distress, without operating in any respect as an encouragement to marriage' (429–30). This proposal is by no means an afterthought, but appears as early as the second edition (1803: 595).

12.7 Summary and conclusion

The perspective on utilitarianism adopted by Malthus reflects his hostility to the upper-class, military, and Church ideology that rejected population control, our analysis confirming John Stuart Mill's representation of Malthus as a social reformer of the first order who identified 'the sole means of realizing that improvability [of human affairs] by securing full employment at high wages to the whole labouring population through a voluntary restriction of the increase of their numbers' (Mill 1981 [1873]: 108). Bonar does not convince when he writes that 'Malthus desired the great numbers as well as the great happiness, and was quite naturally led by his theological views to prefer a little happiness for each of many individuals to a great deal for each of the few' (Bonar 1924: 333).

Malthus's presumption regarding the probable permanence of a class-based society is less significant a difference with Mill's ruminations regarding the future than might at first sight appear since his estimate turns not on so-called 'natural law' but on a utilitarian calculus of the greatest happiness, with allowances made for greater equality and with labour's interests rated highest. In one respect Malthus may have even surpassed Mill, whose prime interest was with 'permanent' solutions to the labour problem, by allowing that 'the period during which the pressure of population is lightened, though it may not be of long duration, is a period of comparative ease, and ought by no means to be thrown out of our consideration' (see above, p. 296).

Notes

1 The 1803 edition adds a further remark to similar effect: 'These habits would be best inculcated by a system of general education and, when strongly fixed, would be the most powerful means of preventing their marrying with the prospect of being obliged to forfeit such advantages; and would consequently raise them nearer to the middle classes of society' (Malthus 1803: 557). It is not clear why this comment was excised from later editions.
2 For a brief technical account of Malthus's 'prudential wage path' entailing increasing *land scarcity*, rather than technical progress, as responsible for decelerating growth in labour-demand, (see Hollander 1992a: 202–5). In principle, the wage rate may even *rise* should the supply growth rate be reduced in greater proportion than that of demand.
3 Malthus merely asserts an increase in the middle classes.
4 Paley in *Natural Theology* sees Malthus's arithmetic and geometric rates as demonstrating the impossibility 'to people a country with inhabitants who shall be all in easy circumstances', leading him to justify 'the distinctions of civil life' (Paley 1803: 340–1).
5 Malthus continues, though none too clearly, that '[u]nder the habits of prudence, the whole of this vast mass [of wage earners] might be nearly as happy as the individuals of the other two classes, and probably a greater number of them, though not a greater proportion of them, happier' (1820: 423; 1836: 368).
6 The unfairness apparently reflects the relatively small size of the stockholding and other fixed-income classes and perhaps the circumstance that 'their interests are not so closely interwoven with the welfare of the state' as were those of the labouring classes and landlords (Malthus 1986 [1815] 7: 168).
7 This estimate does not seem to be confirmed in Homer and Sylla 1996: 195, Table 19: Prices and Yields of Long-Term British Government Securities: Nineteenth Century.
8 The removal of this passage for the second edition reflects an estimate that it nonetheless 'might be [1836: would be] desirable slowly to diminish the debt, and to discourage the growth of it in future, even though it were allowed that its past effects had been favourable to wealth, and that the advantageous distribution of produce which it had occasioned, had, under the actual circumstances, more than counterbalanced the obstructions which it might have given to commerce' (Malthus 1820: 485; 1836: 412).

9 Perceiving wages as a cost and not only a revenue, Malthus was exercised by the apparent problem that labour's expenditure could never provide an adequate stimulus for producers (Malthus 1820: 471–2; 1836: 404). His response to the dilemma was to suppose a preliminary rise in value from other sources in which case labour's consumption counts as an important supplement: 'When indeed this further value is created and affords a sufficient excitement to the saving and employment of stock [1836: capital] then certainly the power of consumption possessed by the workmen will greatly add to the whole national demand, and make room for the employment of a much greater capital' (472; 404–5).
10 A detailed demonstration of this theme will be found in Hollander 1997: 846–65, and a brief statement in Hollander 1992b.
11 It is a problem that similarly exercised and eluded Ricardo: 'No scheme for the amendment of the poor laws merits the least attention, which has not their abolition for its ultimate object; and he is the best friend to the poor, and to the cause of humanity, who can point out how this end can be attained with the most security, and at the same time with the least violence' (Ricardo 1951 [1817]: 107).
12 Malthus championed savings banks as 'the best' proposal in principle 'to effect a permanent improvement in the condition of the lower classes of society' by encouraging responsible family planning by each individual particularly when still in the single state and contemplating the future (Malthus 1826 2: 407–8). Now Malthus is clear that a desirable outcome with respect to population control assumes that savings banks 'should become general'. But in that case free riding would undermine the solution should an individual, assuming general responsibility regarding age of marriage, himself engage in irresponsible conduct calculating that any target income he may have in mind will nonetheless be achievable.
13 For an elaboration of the argument, see Hollander 1997: 875–80, 942–4.
14 Ricardo for his part affirmed that '[i]t is agreed by all who are most friendly to a repeal of these [poor] laws, that if it be desirable to prevent the most overwhelming distress to those for whose benefit they were erroneously enacted, their abolition should be effected by the most gradual steps' (Ricardo 1951 [1817]: 106).

References

Bonar, J. 1924. *Malthus and His Work*. 2nd edition. London: George Allen & Unwin.
Fay, C.R. 1950. *Great Britain from Adam Smith to the Present Day*. 5th edition. London: Longmans.
Hollander, S. 1992a. *Classical Economics*. Toronto: University of Toronto Press.
Hollander, S. 1992b. 'Malthus's Abandonment of Agricultural Protectionism: A Discovery in the History of Economic Thought', *American Economic Review* 82: 650–659.
Hollander, S. 1997. *The Economics of Thomas Robert Malthus*. Toronto: University of Toronto Press.
Homer, S. and R. Sylla, 1996. *A History of Interest Rates*. 3rd edition. New Brunswick: Rutgers University Press.
Malthus, T.R. (1798). *An Essay on the Principle of Population*. London: J. Johnson.
Malthus, T.R. (1803). *An Essay on the Principle of Population*. 2nd edition. London: J. Johnson.
Malthus, T.R. (1817). *An Essay on the Principle of Population* 3. 5th edition. London: John Murray.
Malthus, T.R. (1820). *Principles of Political Economy Considered with a View to Their Practical Application*. London: John Murray.

Malthus, T.R. (1826). *An Essay on the Principle of Population* 2. 6th edition. London: John Murray.

Malthus, T.R. 1836. *Principles of Political Economy Considered with a View to Their Practical Application*. London: William Pickering.

Malthus, T.R. 1986 (1815). *The Grounds of an Opinion on the Policy of Restricting the Importation of Foreign Corn*, The Works of Thomas Robert Malthus 7, eds. E.A. Wrigley and D. Souden. London: William Pickering: 147–174.

Malthus, T.R. 1986 (1823). *The Measure of Value stated and illustrated*, The Works of Thomas Robert Malthus 7, eds. E.A. Wrigley and D. Souden. London: William Pickering: 175–221.

Malthus, T.R. 1986 (1824) 'Political Economy' in *The Works of Thomas Robert Malthus* 7, eds. E.A. Wrigley and D. Souden. London: William Pickering: 255–297.

Malthus, T.R. 1986 (1824, 1830). 'Population' (1824). *A Summary View of the Principle of Population* (1830); in *The Works of Thomas Robert Malthus* 4, eds. E.A. Wrigley and D. Souden. London: William Pickering: 177–243.

Mill, J.S. 1981 (1873). *Autobiography*. Collected Works of John Stuart Mill 1. Toronto: University of Toronto Press: 1–290.

Paley, W. 1785. *The Principles of Moral and Political Philosophy*, 1st edition. London: R. Faulder.

Paley, W. 1803. *Natural Theology or Evidences of the Existence and Attributes of the Deity*, 2nd edition. London: R. Faulder.

Ricardo, D. 1951 (1817). *Principles of Political Economy. Works and Correspondence*, ed. Piero Sraffa. Cambridge: Cambridge University Press.

Senior, N. 1829. *Two Lectures on Population [with] a Correspondence between the Author and the Rev. T.R. Malthus*. London: Saunders and Otley.

Part 6
John Stuart Mill

13 Mill, distributive justice and reform

13.1 Introduction

Part VI comprises three chapters concerning J.S. Mill, the first devoted to Distributive Justice and reform.[1]

A celebrated lecture on 'The Economists and Equality' declares that 'the relative unimportance of the distribution of income to the classical economists is perhaps most eloquently and certainly most effectively shown simply by their neglect of the subject' (Stigler 1949: 1). Now it is scarcely helpful to assert a *neglect* of income distribution yet at the same time refer to its '*relative* unimportance', or to allow that '[f]rom Smith to Marshall greater equality of income was an objective, but it was one of the lesser objectives, of good social policy ... [T]hroughout the classical economics there runs a strong argument against assigning to greater equality of income a primary role in social ethics'. I show in this chapter that even the weaker version of the contention does not accurately portray Mill, who represented a greater equality of income as a *prime* consideration in social ethics. But Stigler goes further, denying that 'the ultimate utilitarian goal was maximum satisfaction [such] that greater output will lead to larger increases in satisfaction than will greater equality ... Most of the important classical economists explicitly rejected maximum satisfaction as a goal... not attach[ing] much importance to maximum output' (2). Adam Smith is cited to the effect that utility is independent of income; and so too is Mill, Stigler citing the chapter 'Of the Stationary State': 'I know not why it should be a matter of congratulation that persons who are already richer than anyone needs to be, should have doubled their means of consuming things which give little or no pleasure except as representative of wealth; or that numbers of individuals should pass over, every year, from the middle classes into a richer class, or from the class of the occupied rich to that of the unoccupied. It is only in the backward countries of the world that increased production is still an important object' (Mill 1965 [1848]: 755). If the classicals were nonetheless concerned to encourage work and saving – policies that maximize output – it was, so it is contended, to teach independence and self-discipline, reflecting a 'desire for better men, rather than for larger national incomes' (Stigler 1949: 4). Although Stigler alleged a disinterest in 'larger national incomes' his argument apparently extended to the *per capita* dimension.

All this was written some seventy years ago and conceivably the late lecturer had come to alter his interpretation. In any event, something akin to the Stigler version is suggested by a contention that Mill's stance regarding trade unionism demonstrates that he failed to accord 'social justice and concern for the poor … the highest priority' (West 1978: 584). Similarly, a contrast is made by Baum between the prioritizing of distributive justice in the manner of Louis Blanc, Saint-Simon, Fourier and the 1875 Gotha Programme, and Mill's co-operative market socialism designed to assure 'maximal individual economic freedom' rather than distributive justice as such – having in mind his justification of earning differentials reflecting innate natural differences (Baum 2007: 118–19).

Section 13.2 elaborates what Mill actually had to say in 'Of the Stationary State'. Amongst the advantages of stationariness he counted more effective population control precisely to the end of achieving higher *per capita* wages on standard 'classical' grounds of the numerical significance of the labouring class; and while higher average wages might be consistent with a reduced wage share in national income, *relative* wages were also intended. The above-cited passage relates specifically to the middle and upper classes rather than labour, undermining any notion of unconcern with distribution, while a continuation of the citation – which Stigler neglected to note – makes the latter point explicitly: 'It is only in the backward countries of the world that increased production is still an important object: in those most advanced, what is economically needed is a *better distribution*, of which one indispensable means is a stricter restraint on population' (Mill 1965 [1848]: 755; emphasis added).

Mill's concern with Distributive Justice is also strikingly apparent in general terms in his chapter 'Of Property' where the 'miseries and inequities of a state of much inequality of wealth' are related to the (unreformed) private-property institution (13.3). His discussions of the labour market – the wage structure, differential pay, and trade unionism (13.4) – reinforce our interpretation. We then turn to Mill's primary reform proposals which pertain to public finance, specifically *unearned* income (13.5), and land reform (13.6).

In an effort to arrive at a properly balanced overview of Mill, and proffer a friendly hand to the late author of 'The Economists and Equality', I close the discussion by attending to the limits to Millian reformism. These reflect a wish to avoid any extreme notion of 'equality' as constituting a threat to the private-property institution itself; the fact that to underscore a concern with income distribution is by no means to deny insistence also on 'better men' – or for that matter with 'maximal economic freedom' – for there were limits to what could be permanently accomplished by way of redistribution in the absence of responsible actors, particularly respecting population control. Beyond this, Mill was concerned lest an unenlightened public opinion would delay adoption of the full range of his proposals, particularly those relating to succession duties.

13.2 On distributive justice and the stationary-state analysis

We commence our discussion with a statement from 'Thornton on Labour and its Claims' expressing the 'Enlightenment' tradition of according prime ranking to working-class welfare on the grounds of labour's numerical preponderance. (Hume, Smith, Bentham, Malthus and Ricardo can all be cited to the effect that numbers count): 'Having regard to the greatly superior numbers of the labouring class, and the inevitable scantiness of the remuneration afforded even by the highest rate of wages which, in the present state of the arts of production, could possibly become general, whoever does not wish that the labourers may prevail' – alluding to the 'strife for wages between the labourers and the capitalists' – 'and that the highest limit, whatever it be, may be attained, must have a standard of morals, and a conception of the most desirable state of society, widely different from those of either Mr. Thornton or the present writer' (Mill 1967 [1869b]: 658). This strong declaration asserts not only the objective of higher wages but also that of a higher wage–profit ratio. This orientation may have been intended by Robson's contention that 'Mill's sympathy is with the labouring poor not because their immediate desires are more in accord with utility than those of the middle and upper classes, but because their share of the general interest has received less attention' (Robson 1968: 216), but it misleads in that Mill did believe working class desires to be 'more in accord with utility than those of the middle and upper classes', as we noted tangentially in 13.1 and will be confirmed when we take into account the 'marginalist' dimension.

It is certainly true, as Robson also insisted, that Mill was 'a friend of labour, but not an uncritical friend' (Robson 1968: 257). He placed the blame for low standards wherever he found it. First and foremost, the 'laws of production' had to be thoroughly understood; not all social ills could be blamed on governments or employers. It followed that *direct redistribution*, would not *by itself* provide a permanent solution to low wages. Thus Mill's appeal for 'a better distribution, of which one indispensable means is a stricter restraint on population' continues: 'Levelling institutions, either of a just or an unjust kind, cannot alone accomplish it; they may lower the heights of society, but they cannot, of themselves, permanently raise the depths' (Mill 1965 [1848]: 755). In his correspondence Mill put the matter thus: 'What does seem to me essential is that society at large should not be overworked, nor over-anxious about the means of subsistence, for which we must look to the grand source of improvement, repression of population, combined with laws or customs of inheritance which shall favour the diffusion of property instead of its accumulation in masses' (13 April 1847; Mill 1963: 713). By the 1860s Mill had come to believe that population pressure was much reduced (see Hollander 2015: 257–61), implying that greater weight might be placed on straightforward redistribution.

Secondly, Mill was troubled by the possibility that the majority, taking advantage by 'democratic' means of its numerical superiority would ride roughshod over a minority of property owners, and offered constitutional proposals to avoid such an outcome (see Hollander 2015: 374–84). A related concern was the possibility that good wages and short hours might be sought by fraudulent means, as is well clarified in *On Liberty* (Mill 1977 [1859]: 286). But the concern to eradicate fraud is not to denigrate the objective of improved working-class living standards, but to insist that more is required than mere redistribution if any advantage is to be *permanently* assured. As explained in the *Principles*, in addition to savings in resources with increased probity, in the industrial sphere there could be expected an 'immense increase of all kinds of labour, and saving of time and expenditure ... if the labourers honestly performed what they undertake' (Mill 1965 [1848]: 110). Mill evidently presumed that labour as a whole would benefit from the higher productivity resulting from honest effort. Indeed, as expressed more generally in his correspondence, the higher wages earned by free men with elevated standards was more promising than mere redistribution between classes – however desirable – as a permanent solution to inequality:

> It seems to me chiefly important to impress on [the working classes] – first, that they are quite right in aiming at a more equal distribution of wealth and social advantages; secondly, that this more equal distribution can only be permanently affected (for merely taking from Peter to give to Paul would leave things worse than even at present) by means of their own public spirit and self-devotion as regards others, and prudence and self-restraint in relation to themselves. At present their idea of social reform appears to be simply higher wages, and less work, for the sake of more sensual indulgence.
>
> (7 January 1852; Mill 1972: 81).[2]

★★★

Mill's primary objective was clearly a higher *per capita* income to assure that the masses were properly accommodated but also a higher wage share provided it was honestly come by. What then of the chapter 'Of the Stationary State' in Book IV of the *Principles*? A careless reading might suggest that Mill, by questioning the importance of the aggregate dimension of the economy – Stigler may have fallen into this trap – was denigrating rising wages and a higher wage share when in fact the very opposite is the case.

As in his earlier 'Claims of Labour' (Mill 1967 [1845]: 367–8), Mill rejected the aversion to stationariness expressed by members of the 'old school' of political economists – he cites Smith and McCulloch – who identified 'all that is economically desirable with the progressive state, and with that alone' (Mill 1965 [1848]: 752). He further objected to common misreadings of Malthus which ignored his demonstration that population growth is not a purely exogenous matter checked only by ultimate land scarcity, but is rather subject to human control, so that whether or not capital is growing, and at whatever rate, real wages will be high or low depending on the relative growth rate of population (753). Low standards were in brief compatible with rapid accumulation, and *high standards with stationariness*. But this is to understate the proposition. For the 'condition of society' which Mill favoured – one entailing a 'better distribution of property attained, by the joint effect of the prudence and frugality of individuals, and of a system of legislation favouring equality of fortunes, so far as is consistent with the just claim of the individuals to the fruits, whether great or small, of his or her own industry' – is not only perfectly compatible with the stationary state, but, it would seem, more naturally allied with that state than with any other (755). The encouragement of population control is here intended. Mill's objective is unmistakable: 'Under this two-fold influence' – of population control and a legislative programme of redistribution – 'society would exhibit these leading features: a well-paid and affluent body of labourers; no enormous fortunes, except what were earned and accumulated during a single lifetime; but a much larger body of persons than at present, not only exempt from the coarser toils, but with sufficient leisure, both physical and mental, from mechanical details, to cultivate freely the graces of life, and afford examples of them to the classes less favourably circumstances for their growth'. By his criticisms of 'progressive' society, of which so much was made by Stigler, Mill by no means rejected the objective of rising average wages and wage share but rather had in mind the ever-increasing incomes of the already well off, the middle classes included; indeed, 'the mere increase of production and accumulation' – 'the kind of economic progress which excites the congratulations of ordinary politicians' – were 'in themselves … of little importance, so long as either the increase of population or anything else prevents the mass of the people from reaping any part of the benefit of them'.[3]

That a notion of *diminishing utility* attaches to further increases of real income reinforced the case against a quest for expanded income specifically on the part of the middle and upper classes and, as we shall see in section 13.5, governed his case for the taxation of the so-called 'unearned increment', quantitative limitations on bequests – to which matter he reverts in the 'Stationary State' chapter – and the heavier *ad valorem* taxation of luxuries. The case for redistribution in labour's favour is amply confirmed. Any 'marginalist' reading of the text must of course be understood in strictly *qualitative* terms, entailing the moral perspective implied by what Mill, we shall see, designated as 'intrinsically worthless things' and by the contrast made between genuine 'needs for any personal purposes' and illegitimate purchases for 'ostentation or improper power'.[4]

Mill, however, was concerned not to push the objection to conspicuous consumption and the like too far, expressing concern that the democratic tendencies in the United States and 'the notion that the public has a right to a veto on the manner in which individuals shall spend their incomes' acted as 'a tolerably effectual sumptuary law', such that in places it was 'really difficult for a person possessing a very large income, to find any mode of spending it, which will not incur popular disapprobation' (*On Liberty*; Mill 1977 [1859]: 286). One had only 'to suppose a considerable diffusion of Socialist opinions', he warned, 'and it may become infamous in the eyes of the majority to possess more property than some very small amount, or any income not earned by manual labour' (286–7). Mill certainly championed greater diffusion of wealth but not when taken to an extreme.

Finally, a summary in the *Principles* of the objective of the chapter 'Of the Stationary State' provided at the outset of the chapter that follows – 'On the Probable Futurity of the Labouring Classes' – confirms that the principle of 'diminishing utility' (in Mill's sense) was not applied, assuming going conditions, to disparage further increases in *average wages*. His purpose insofar as it concerned 'the practical purposes of present times' had been the 'negative' one of casting doubt on 'a false ideal', the 'inordinate importance attached to the mere increase in [aggregate] production' on the part of the middle and upper classes precisely in order to focus attention on '*improved distribution, and a large remuneration of labour, as the two desiderata*' (Mill 1965 [1848]: 758; emphasis added), the dual *desiderata* we are insisting upon against the Stigler reading. Here we find confirmed all our primary themes: 'Whether the aggregate produce increases absolutely or not, is a thing in which, after a certain amount has been obtained neither the legislator nor the philanthropist need feel any strong interest: but that it should increase relatively to the number of those who share in it, is of the utmost possible importance; and this, (whether the wealth of mankind be stationary, or increasing at the most rapid rate ever known in an old country,) must depend on the opinions and habits of the most numerous class, the class of manual labourers'.

★★★

Mill's strategy in 'Of the Stationary State' was, we have concluded, to focus on the main policy objective, improved wages both absolutely and relative to property income, by deprecating that of mere expansion of aggregate output on the part of the middle and upper classes. But we cannot conclude from this that he actually recommended or hoped for a cessation of growth in going circumstances. While positive advantages attached to stationariness, a variety of strong counter arguments could not be ignored.

As for the perceived *advantages* of stationariness, population control is said to be more effective where there is no 'indefinite prospect of employment for increased numbers', so that it becomes evident to all that new entrants to the labour market are replacements for those who leave (Mill 1965 [1848]: 753). From this perspective, as we have earlier intimated, stationariness becomes the means to the end of high *per capita* earnings, reinforcing his observation that stationariness was not incompatible with high average wages. Beyond this, in a stationary state technical progress would result in advantage to the majority rather than merely to the middle classes: 'a stationary condition of capital and population implies no stationary state of human improvement ... Even the industrial arts might be as earnestly and as successfully cultivated, with this sole difference, that instead of serving no purpose but the increase of wealth, industrial improvements would produce their legitimate effect, that of abridging labour' intimating it appears increased leisure' (756). Matters as things stood were very different: 'Hitherto it is questionable if all the mechanical inventions yet made have lightened the day's toil of any human being. They have enabled a greater population to live the same life of drudgery and imprisonment, and an increased number of manufacturers and others to make fortunes. They have increased the comforts of the middle classes. But they have not yet begun to effect those great changes in human destiny, which it is in their nature and in their futurity to accomplish' (756–7). Mill then points to population control as well as institutional reform to assure the desired outcome: 'Only when, in addition to just institutions, the increase of mankind shall be under the deliberate guidance of judicious foresight, can the conquests made from the powers of nature by the intellect and energy of scientific discoverers, become the common property of the species, and the means of improving the universal lot' (757). It is all the more important then to recognise Mill's contention that stationariness would itself encourage restraint of population.

Now Mill pointed out that accumulation and population were currently proceeding apace, and that steady average real wages and a constant return to capital were achieved even without population control because of the extremely high rate of capital accumulation enabled by new technology (Mill 1965 [1848]: 742). Any argument for a stationary state was purely academic. But in addition to this empirical fact, stationariness might prove dangerous from a wide variety of perspectives, namely productivity improvement, labour-displacing technology, capital loss abroad, resource misallocation, and social conflict (Hollander 2015: 350–2). That class hostility would be aggravated in a stationary or slowly growing economy where upward mobility is impeded reflects Mill's low opinion of the working-class's status as such and his estimate that even should income distribution be altered in favour of labour as a result of 'just laws' and 'improved intelligence in the working-classes' – in themselves *desiderata* – workers would not be 'permanently contented with the condition of labouring for wages as their ultimate state' (Mill 1965 [1848]: 766). For 'they may be willing to pass through the class of servants in their way to that of employers', as in 'a new country, rapidly increasing in wealth and population, like America or Australia. But in an old and fully peopled country, those who begin life as labourers for hire, as a general rule, continue such to the end'.

Considering so many potential disadvantages attaching to stationariness within a capitalist environment what becomes of the objections to 'old school' champions of expansion noted above? Is there not evidence here of schizophrenia? I think not. For while continued accumulation might be necessary for the reasons we have given, at the same time there is no gainsaying a profound dislike of the behaviour patterns characterizing frenzied growth and the implied threat to amenity. Mill might perhaps have found acceptable a compromise entailing moderate growth. In any event, there remains his concern for high real wages and (*pace* Stigler) a fair (class) income distribution, to emphasize which he adopted a strategy in his chapter of condemning mere growth in the aggregate – even at unchanged, even reduced, wages – as an ideal.[5]

13.3 Of property, competition and income distribution

We turn next to Mill's analysis in the *Principles* of the private-property institution from the perspective of income distribution, entailing in particular a severe condemnation in the chapter 'Of Property' of the 'miseries and inequities of a state of much inequality of wealth' (Mill 1965 [1848]: 202). Such a deplorable state reflected in considerable part an arbitrary allocation of property, the accidental legacy of the past, which operated to assure an income distribution such that:

> the produce of labour was almost in an inverse ratio to the labour – the largest portions to those who have never worked at all, the next largest to those whose work is almost nominal, and so in a descending scale, the remuneration dwindling as the work grows harder and more disagreeable, until the most fatiguing and exhausting bodily labour cannot count with certainty on being able to earn even the necessaries of life … The social arrangements of modern Europe commenced from a distribution of property which was the result, not of just partition, or acquisition by industry, but of conquest and violence … and the system still retains many and large traces of its origin. The laws of property have made property of things which never ought to be property, and absolute property where only a qualified property ought to exist. They have not held the balance fairly between human beings, but have heaped impediments upon some, to give advantage to others; they have purposely fostered inequalities, and prevented all from starting fair in the race.
>
> (207)

Contemporary arrangements, thus governed by historical accident, failed even to satisfy those 'considerations of utility' which might to some degree justify the system (201). The later 'Thornton on Labour and its Claims' confirms the indictment:

> Landed property at least, in all the countries of modern Europe, derives its origins from force; the land was taken by military violence from former possessors, by those from whom it has been transmitted to its present owners … The sellers could not impart to others a better title than they themselves possessed. Movable property, no doubt, has on the whole a purer origin, its first acquirers having mostly worked for it, at something useful to

their fellow citizens. But, looking at the question merely historically, and confining our attention to the larger masses, the doctrine that the rights of capital are those of past labour is liable even here to great abatements.
(Mill 1967 [1869b]: p. 653)

Elsewhere Mill objected on grounds of justice to a defence of private property by Cardinal Newman: 'the distinction between rich and poor, so lightly connected as it is with merit and demerit, or even with exertion and want of exertion in the individual, is obviously unjust; such a feature could not be put into the rudest imaginings of a perfectly just state of society; the present capricious distribution of the means of life and enjoyment, could only be defended as an admitted imperfection, submitted to as an effect of causes in other respects beneficial' ('Newman's Political Economy'; Mill 1967 [1851]: 444).

Mill also declaimed against competition, alluding – with an eye to rivalry between workers in depressing wages – to 'the physical and moral evils which are not only consistent with, but directly grow out of the facts of competition and individual property' (Mill 1967 [1851]: 442), and to the 'arming one human being against another, making the good of each depend upon the evil to others, making all who have anything to gain or lose live as in the midst of enemies' (444). Here too Mill denies that the competitive wage can be identified with the 'just' wage because the outcome is biased against labour *based as it is on an unjust distribution of property*, though he admits no alternative assuming the private-property institution: 'Socialists do not say that competition can be dispensed with in society as it is. But they say it is a great defect in the constitution of society, that it can only work by such an instrument' (447).

Yet Mill also maintained in the same review that 'the benefits that flow from private property and competition are, like the evils, too obvious to be missed' (Mill 1967 [1851]: 442). And the 1852 and later versions of the 'Futurity' chapter in the *Principles* omit the comment regarding *hostile* competition between the parties in the criticism of the labour–capital relation; and introduce a strongly-worded case against the notion of competition as 'pernicious' in and of itself. Thus alluding to some form or other of cooperative arrangement he opined 'that the time is ripe for commencing this transformation, and that it should by all just and effectual means be aided and encouraged' while expressing his disagreement with Socialist writers regarding competition as such:

> They forget that wherever competition is not, monopoly is; and that monopoly, in all its forms, is the taxation of the industrious for the support of indolence, if not of rapacity. They forget, too, that with the exception of competition among labourers, all other competition is for the benefit of the labourers, by cheapening the articles they consume; that competition even in the labour market is a source not of low but of high wages, wherever the competition *for* labour exceeds the competition *of* labour, as in America, in the colonies, and in the skilled trades; and never could be a cause of low wages, save by the overstocking of the labour market; while,

> if the supply of labourers is excessive, not even Socialism can prevent their remuneration from being low.
>
> (Mill 1965 [1848]: 794–5)

Furthermore, the *dynamic* role of competition as a source of progress is now applauded considering 'the natural indolence of mankind; their tendency to be passive, to be the slaves of habit, to persist indefinitely in a course once chosen ... Competition may not be the best conceivable stimulus, but it is at present a necessary one, and no one can foresee the time when it will not be indispensable to progress' (795). And here the matter of distribution comes strikingly to the fore. Contemporary evils reflected not competition as such but 'the exploitation of labour by capital, and the enormous deduction made from the product by owners of instruments', while competition encouraged 'the development of individual faculties and the success of innovations'.

Mill, we conclude, perceived the general competitive wage as 'unjust' because the distribution of property governing the labour-market framework was inequitable rather than because of the workings of competition *per se*. His unhappiness with the dependency relationship characterizing capitalist organization would, one deduces, weaken to the extent that greater fairness in property distribution could be assured.

In 'Of Property' Mill also deplored that the 'generality of labourers in this and most other countries, have as little choice of occupation or freedom of locomotion, are practically as dependent on fixed rules and on the will of others, as they could be on any system short of actual slavery' (Mill 1965 [1848]: 209). Immobility distorting the wage structure under contemporary capitalist arrangement will be discussed in Section 13.4.

******

The posthumously-published 'Chapters on Socialism', commenced in 1869, merits particular attention as perhaps Mill's best-considered indictment of capitalism. Mill here confirms the evaluation of the *Principles* that the capitalism of his era was characterized by a severe failure of distributive justice, and this despite recent constitutional progress:

> Notwithstanding all that has been done, and all that seems likely to be done, in the extension of franchises, a few are born to great riches, and the many to penury, made only more grating by contrast. No longer enslaved or made dependent by force of law, the great majority are so by force of poverty; they are still chained to a place, to an occupation, and to conformity with the will of an employer, and debarred by the accident of birth both from the enjoyments, and from the mental and moral advantages, which others inherit without exertion and independently of desert.
>
> (Mill 1967 [1879]: 710)

Mill thus accepted the factual charge 'that the condition of numbers in civilized Europe, and even in England and France, is more wretched than that of most tribes of savages who are known to us' (713); and that poverty in no way reflected 'desert', rewards being divorced from merit or exertion, for it was not the case that everyone 'willing to undergo a fair share of ... labour and abstinence could attain a fair share of the fruits' (714). On the contrary – and as so often brought out in the *Principles* – 'the reward, instead of being proportioned to the labour and abstinence of the individual, is almost in an inverse ratio to it; those who receive the least, labour and abstain the most'. Birth, accident and opportunity were the ruling determinants, so that 'even the idle, reckless, and ill-conducted poor ... often undergo much more and severer labour, not only than those born to pecuniary independence, but than almost any of the more highly remunerated of those who earn their subsistence; and even the inadequate self-control exercised by the industrious poor costs them more sacrifice and more effort than is almost ever required from the more favoured members of society'. The general indictment, be it noted, refers to both the average wage and the wage structure. Also accepted is the Socialist contention that much 'crime, vice and folly' resulted from poverty (715).

Mill presents a remarkably severe condemnation of contemporary arrangements relating to worker efficiency, extending to restrictive practices by unions. The majority of wage earners 'being paid by fixed wages, are so far from having any direct interest of their own in the efficiency of their work that they have not even that share in the general interest which every worker would have in the Communistic organization' (Mill 1967 [1879]: 742). Indeed, 'the rules of some trade societies actually forbid their members to exceed a certain standard of efficiency, lest they should diminish the number of labourers required for the work; and for the same reason they often violently resist contrivances for economising labour'. Mill concludes that 'the change, from this to a state in which every person would have an interest in rendering every other person as industrious, skilful, and careful as possible (which would be the case under Communism), would be a change very much for the better'.

But the indictment is qualified. For Mill rejected the charge against contemporary competition ('individualism') that 'hardly any one can gain except by the loss or disappointment of one or of many others', a position leading Louis Blanc to 'predict' secularly falling real wages, and Considérant the Fourierist an increasing tendency towards concentration of wealth reflected in the failure of small firms. The charge Mill traced to 'ignorance of economic facts, and of the causes by which the economic phenomena of society as it is, are actually determined' (Mill 1967 [1879]: 727). Thus despite the earlier indictment in the same document of abysmal living standards, he yet allowed – consistently with his empirical estimate in the *Principles* (above, p. 313) – that even population pressure was no longer an 'irrepressible tendency' and an 'increasing evil', considering the acceleration of capital accumulation, easier emigration and – he now added – increased prudence (728). There was also no evidence of increasing monopolization (730). Mill summarized his position in a remarkable passage insisting not only on the fact of rising living standards, but also on the relatively limited effect which even a redistribution of income from capital to labour would have in raising the wages of the 'lower levels of remuneration':

> The present system is not, as many Socialists believe, hurrying us into a state of general indigence and slavery from which only Socialism can save us. The evils and injustices suffered under the present system are great, but they are not increasing; on the contrary, the general tendency is towards their slow diminution. Moreover the inequalities in the distribution of the produce between capital and labour, however they may shock the feeling of natural justice, would not by their mere equalisation afford by any means so large a fund for raising the lower levels of remuneration as Socialists, and many besides Socialists, are apt to suppose.
>
> (736)

This is not to reject the case for redistribution on grounds of justice but to warn against exaggerating the quantitative impact that could thereby be achieved by that alone, intimating once again the need for supplementary solutions – population control and responsible labour conduct.

13.4 The labour market and the role of the state

13.4.1 *The competitive wage structure*

The letter of 23 November 1861 rejects a proposal to rely on arbitration in determining the wages of particular categories of labours, and represents the competitive wage structure as strictly speaking *unjust* because of the distortions created by the very existence of 'past accumulations': 'The insuperable difficulty is that there being no *principle* of equity to rest the settlement upon, any decision must be arbitrary, dependent on the direction of the judge's sympathies' (Mill 1972: 749). Mill elaborates: 'I can conceive Socialism, in which the division of the produce of labour is made among all, either according to the rule of equality (Communism) or according to any other *general* rule which may be considered more just than absolute equality. But under a system of private property in past accumulations in which no general rule can be laid down, I think that to give any one the power of deciding according to his own views of equity without a general rule would only perpetuate & envenom instead of healing the quarrel between capital & labour'. Under these circumstances, the *market* provided the only practical solution: 'The only thing which people will in these circumstances submit to as final, is the law of necessity, that is, the demand & supply of the market, *tested* (when not otherwise known) by the result of a strike. All that I consider practical in the present state of society is to strengthen the weaker side in the competition, which can only be done by the prudence, foresight, wise restraint, & habit of cooperation, of the working people themselves'.

The reference to 'prudence' and 'foresight' has its counterpart in the *Principles* in the chapter 'Of Property'. Responsible behaviour by labour would of itself contribute towards the erosion of pay differentials and correspondingly towards greater fairness: 'In the existing system of industry these things do adjust themselves with some, though but a distant, approach to fairness. If one kind of work is harder or more disagreeable than another, or requires a longer practice, it is better paid, simply because there are fewer competitors for it; and an individual generally finds that he can earn most, by doing the thing which he is fittest for' (Mill 1965 [1848]: 977). Mill does not use this precise wording after the first two editions of 1848 and 1849 but there is no reason to believe that he had altered his position.

We also note the removal from the edition of 1852 of a statement lamenting the *injustice* of the current wage structure: 'I admit that this self-acting machinery does not touch some of the grossest of the existing inequalities of remuneration, and in particular the unjust advantage possessed by almost the commonest mental over almost the hardest and most disagreeable bodily labour. Employments which require any kind of technical education, however simple, have hitherto been the subject of a real monopoly as against the mass', while allowing better prospects in the light of the progress of 'popular instruction' (Mill 1965 [1848]: 977). Nonetheless, Mill retains the substance thereafter when he writes of 'the inequality and injustice with which labour (not to speak of remuneration) is now apportioned' (207). There is also a more optimistic prognosis appearing only in the first two editions: 'But as popular instruction advances, this monopoly is already becoming less complete, and every increase in prudence and foresight among the people encroaches upon it more and more'. But again, it is unlikely that Mill retracted this evaluation in 1852.

By 'prudence' Mill intended a population limitation on the part of the *lower-paid* workers in particular. It is essential to have in mind here the role accorded to the State in the matter of education (see Hollander 2015: 216–21), particularly the fact that the proposal extended beyond the elementary training required for the practise of any sort of skilled work to the inculcation of the advantages to be derived from 'prudential' restraint. *Reliance upon the market to assure an approach towards a just wage structure thus presumes government intervention.* Without this qualification, several of Mill's statements are easily misread as a simple-minded appeal to the market as providing the solution to the wage structure, if only for want of a better alternative.[6]

Mill's enthusiastic evaluation of the report upon which the Forster Educational Act of 1870 was based (see Hollander 2015: 364–7, 505–8) well summarizes his hopes at the end of the day for achieving a significant advance towards distributive justice within the capitalist-exchange system *via* state-supported universal education:

> The real hardship of social inequalities to the poor, as the reasonable among them can be brought to see, is not that men are unequal, but that they are born so; ... that the higher positions in life, including all which confer power or dignity, can not only be obtained by the rich without taking the trouble to be qualified for them, but that even were this corrected (to which there is an increasing tendency), none, as a rule, except the rich, have it in their power to make themselves qualified. By the proposal of the [Schools Enquiry] Commissioners [1867–68], every child of poor parents (for, of course, girls must sooner or later be included) would have that power opened to him, if he passed with real distinction through the course of instruction provided for all.
>
> (Mill 1967 [1869a]: 628)

The promised outcome was such that 'the feelings which give rise to Socialism would be in a great measure disarmed, in as much of them as is unreasonable or exaggerated, by this just concession to that in them which is rational and legitimate'.

******

As a minimum, we have seen, reform of the labour market was required to assure a tolerably 'just' wage structure. Now Mill introduces into the *Principles* an entirely original perspective on the linkage between macro- and microeconomics, for the popular Smithian analysis, which turned on the unjustified assumption that the *aggregate* labour market is in equilibrium, neglected the fact general unemployment distorted the differentials: 'when the supply of labour so far exceeds the demand that to find employment at all is an uncertainty, and to be offered it on any terms a favour, the case if totally the reverse. Desirable labourers, those whom every one is anxious to have, can still exercise a choice. The undesirable must take what they can get' (Mill 1965 [1848]: 383). For this reason, and also because of various 'natural and artificial monopolies', wage differentials were 'generally in the opposite direction to the equitable principle of compensation erroneously represented by Adam Smith as the general law to the remuneration of labour'.

The allusion to 'natural and artificial monopolies' attests to a second deviation from Smith, entailing Mill's celebrated *noncompeting industrial groups* reflecting social and financial obstacles to upward mobility (fortunately amenable to State action). For Smith's recognition of educational costs (even when reinforced by legal restrictions on mobility) failed to account for the ruling wage differentials, since the cost even of a minimal education and of maintenance during the training period excluded most workers from entering into competition with skilled labour and reducing its 'monopoly' return (Mill 1965 [1848]: 386). Notwithstanding broader educational opportunities currently available there remained 'a much greater disparity than can be accounted for on the principle of competition' (387). Various 'customary' expenses attaching to some trades, such as the cost of maintaining clothes and appearance, further hindered entry.

13.4.2 On 'natural' differences and differential pay

Mill maintained in the chapter 'Of Property' that 'the proportioning of remuneration to work done, is really just, only in so far as the more or less of the work is a matter of choice: when it depends on natural difference of strength or capacity, this principle of remuneration is in itself an injustice: it is giving to those who have; assigning most to those who are already favoured by nature' (Mill 1965 [1848]: 210). This affirmation might be read to imply that differential pay is *not* justified by differential ability. But this turns out not to be the case. When discussing distributive justice in the taxation context, proper policy is said it is true to entail 'redressing ... the inequalities and wrongs of nature' (808); and in 'Of Property' he similarly allowed that some compensation by the State might be made to 'the less robust members of the community' (201), intending those 'who were weakest in mind or body, either by nature or position ... those who are least capable of helping or defending themselves'. But he insists that the main concern is *unequal opportunity* and not unequal 'merit', so that impartial legislation 'would consist in endeavouring that [competitors] should all start fair, and not in hanging a weight upon the swift to diminish the distance between them and the slow' (811). Provided then that 'all were done which it would be in the power of good government to do, by instruction and by legislation, to diminish this inequality of opportunities, *the differences of fortune arising from people's own earnings could not justly give umbrage*' (emphasis added). Mill, in brief, did not recommend 'starting fair' in any extreme sense of that term, for that all should be 'on perfectly equal terms' was 'inconsistent with any law of private property' which permitted accumulations and corresponding inequalities arising not from historical accident but legitimately from 'unequal industry, frugality, perseverance, talents, and to a certain extent even opportunities' (207, 225). In fact, when evaluating the principle of wage *equality* notwithstanding the differential talent associated with some Communist schemes Mill in fact objected that '[t]he nominal equality of labour would be so great a real inequality that justice would revolt against its being enforced' (206; also 977).

While differential pay reflecting natural differentials 'could not justly give umbrage', there remains a sense in which such pay differentials do entail a deviation from the requirements of justice *in an ideal world* but which had to be tolerated as an expediential 'compromise with the selfish type of character formed by the present standard of morality, and fostered by the existing social institutions', and 'until education shall have been entirely regenerated ... far more likely to prove immediately successful, than any attempt at a higher ideal' (Mill 1965 [1848]: 210). For it would be foolhardy to neglect 'the strength of the incitement given to labour when the whole or a large share of the benefit of extra exertion belongs to the labourer' (204). This position is reflected in a protest of 1847 against the assumption 'that inequality is a thing which should actually be cultivated, that people should be educated with a view to a "just progression of nice distinctions of rank"' (to Arthur Helps; Mill 1972: 2002). For Mill, only 'as much inequality as necessarily arises from protecting all persons in the free use of their faculties of body & mind & in the enjoyment of what these can obtain for them, must be submitted to for the sake of a greater good: but I certainly see no necessity for artificially adding to it, while I see much for tempering it, impressing both on the laws & on the usages of mankind as far as possible the contrary tendency'.

13.4.3 On Trade Unionism

Mill raises the question in 'Thornton on Labour and Its Claims' of 'whether Unionists are justified in seeking a rise of wages for themselves, which in all probability produces a fall of wages, or loss of employment, to other labourers, their fellow-countrymen ... For (as Mr. Thornton recognizes) there is no keeping up wages without limiting the number of competitors for employment' (Mill 1967 [1869b]: 662). He then proceeds to a 'moral vindication' along Malthusian lines for exclusive unions as a protective device: '"As long as their minds remain in their present state", so the unionists might argue, "our preventing them from competing with us for employment does them no real injury; it only saves ourselves from being brought down to their level ... We do them no real wrong by intrenching ourselves behind a barrier, to exclude those whose competition would bring down our wages, without more than momentarily raising theirs, but only adding to the total numbers in existence". This is the practical justification as things now are, of some of the exclusive regulations of Trades' Unions' (664). This statement says nothing of a 'fall in wages, or loss of employment' of those excluded – the terms of Mill's initial query – for the justification applies specifically to an *existing* exclusive union on the grounds that permitting new entrants attracted by the higher wage would in the final resort, by adding to numbers, reduce the entire working-class body to the low level of the mass. He is certainly not arguing in favour of a newly-created union which, by forcing a wage increase, lowers employment opportunities for those excluded, resulting in an actual fall in their population as a consequence. Nevertheless, as noted at the outset of this chapter, one commentator, assuming otherwise, has entered a bitter protest: 'In all the literature of the effects of policy upon the poor, the statement ... that "our preventing them from competing with us for employment does them no real injury", must be the most astonishing. It is surely difficult, to say the least, to reconcile such words with an outlook that puts social justice and concern for the poor in the highest priority' (West 1978: 584). Indeed, West ascribed to Mill the position that social justice is served by a 'plan of social engineering' entailing the design of some future society populated with individuals who had been educated out of poverty, and away from their propensity to excessive reproduction, regardless of the implications for some of the existing poor

(585). As will be clear, rather than justifying dire consequences for the existing poor, Mill's case is simply that removing barriers to entry into an existing union would do no more than temporarily raise the newcomers' earnings but in the final resort reduce *all* to the same low level – scarcely a brutal position assuming the absence of prudential population control on the part of new entrants. And that Mill in his 1869 review perceived unions as an instrument to inculcate altered standards with respect to procreation (West and Hafer 1978: 616) can likewise be dismissed, for he intended organizations comprising individuals already practicing restraint and opposing encroachments by the irresponsible.

But beyond this, Mill's justification of exclusive unions is itself qualified. The 'practical justification' for exclusive unions applied only if unionists were *not* indifferent to the fortunes of those excluded. On this matter Mill expressed himself hopefully with particular reference to educational progress: 'It is a strong indication of a better spirit among them, that the operatives and artisans throughout the country form the main strength of the demand, rapidly becoming irresistible, for universal and compulsory education. The brutish ignorance of the lowest order of unskilled labourers has no more determined enemies, none more earnest in insisting that it be cured, than the comparatively educated workmen who direct the Unions' (Mill 1967 [1869b]: 665). The efforts by the union leaders to raise the standard of those excluded would, if successful, render their exclusionist practice unnecessary. In any event, the formulation of 1869 was rather in the nature of a theoretical justification, insofar as the 1852 and all later editions of the *Principles* applaud on-going improvements in the behaviour patterns of the poorest classes (see Hollander 2015: 356–9).

Further evidence of Mill's sympathy for the lowest paid is found at the conclusion to the chapter 'On the Probable Futurity of the Labouring Classes'. The passage in question, a powerful protest on behalf of the 'slopsellers', first appears in 1852 and is retained thereafter with minor variations only. The passage is preceded by a case for competition: 'Instead of looking upon competition as the baneful and anti-social principle which it is held to be by the generality of Socialists, I conceive that, even in the present state of society and industry, every restriction of it is an evil, and every extension of it, even if for the time injuriously affecting some class of labourers, is always an ultimate good' (Mill 1965 [1848]: 795). Accordingly:

> If the slopsellers and others, so unjustly and illiberally railed at – as if they were one iota worse in their motives or practices than other people, in the existing state of society – have lowered the wages of tailors, and some other artizans, by making them an affair of competition instead of custom, so much the better in the end. What is now required is not to bolster up old customs, whereby limited classes of labouring people obtain partial gains which interest them in keeping up the present organization of society, but to introduce new general practices beneficial to all; and there is reason to rejoice at whatever makes the privileged classes of skilled artizans feel that

they have the same interests, and depend for their remuneration on the same general causes, and must resort for the improvement of their condition to the same remedies, as the less fortunately circumstanced and comparatively helpless multitude.

(796)

This powerful defence of the slopsellers may be supplemented by the more general lament regarding the injustices to the *very poor* of the contemporary wage structure (documented above in Section 13.4.1) and the great concern expressed for the displaced cottiers and the unemployed in the Irish case (on which see Hollander 2015: 282–92). The charge that Mill turned his back on the *existing poor* in the Britain of his day may be confidently dismissed.

13.5 Reform proposals: public finance

I will not present here Mill's full position regarding public finance but will rather focus on the prime case for reform with an eye to the enhancement of distributive justice to which we have already briefly alluded, namely the taxation of the so-called 'unearned increment', quantitative limitations on bequests, and the heavier *ad valoram* taxation of luxuries.[7] But a preliminary word is required first to explain his general opposition to a progressive tax in the case of *earned* income.

13.5.1 The general case against progression

In the *Principles*, Mill adopted Adam Smith's celebrated canons, elaborating only the first, namely the equality of taxation, or taxation of the State's subjects 'as nearly as possible in proportion to their respective abilities, that is, in proportion to the revenue which they respectively enjoy under the protection of the state' (Mill 1965 [1848]: 805). This maxim Mill interpreted to mean an equality of *sacrifice*, such that each 'shall feel neither more nor less inconvenience from his share of the payment [towards the expenses of government] than every other person experiences from his', and this would be satisfied, at least in principle, by a system of *proportionate* income taxation (807). The notion of equality of *benefit* Mill rejected partly on the grounds that 'it is not possible to say that one person derives more benefit than another from the protection of the Government; it is necessary for all' ('The Income and Property Tax'; Mill 1967 [1852]: 495).

That the tax system should not deliberately be used to alter income distribution is maintained on the expediential grounds of avoiding disincentive; Mill opposed progression to satisfy the principle of equal sacrifice by assuring proportionality of income to effort and abstinence: 'I am as desirous as any one, that means should be taken to diminish … inequalities, but not so as to relieve the prodigal at the expense of the prudent. To tax the larger incomes at a higher percentage than the smaller, is to lay a tax on industry and economy; to impose a penalty on people for having worked harder and saved more than their neighbours' (Mill 1965 [1848]: 810–11). Public policy called only for 'impartiality between competitors ... endeavouring that they should all start fair, and not in hanging a weight upon the swift to diminish the distance between them and the slow' (811). It was *unearned* income – income from property – that required 'limitation'.[8]

Mill had warned in early editions of the *Principles* against 'opposing obstacles to the acquisition of even the largest fortune by honest exertion' (Mill 1965 [1848]: 811). Why this formulation was removed is unclear, since the general principle is retained throughout all editions, and is repeated without qualification in evidence given in 1861: 'I do not see how you can, either with justice or policy, tax a person more heavily because he earns more ... I do not think that you can lay a tax upon energy, or industry, or prudence. It seems to me that even upon the question of justice, apart from policy, there is no stronger or more valid principle than that of not giving any advantage to self-indulgence over industry and economy, even though the effect may be to give some advantage, or rather, not to interfere with the natural advantage of the rich over the poor' ('The Income and Property Tax'; Mill 1967 [1861]: 567). Again: 'I certainly do think it fair and reasonable that the general policy of the State should favour the diffusion rather than the concentration of wealth, but ... taxing people on a larger proportion of their income, because they are better off, does not hold the balance fairly between saving and spending; it is contrary to the canon of equity, and contrary to it in the worst way, because it makes that mode of employing income which it is public policy to encourage, a subject of discouragement' (569–70).

Mill rejected furthermore a claim that proportionate taxation in fact imposed a greater burden on lower income recipients: 'It may be said, indeed, that to take £100 from £1000 ... is a heavier impost than £1000 taken from £10,000 ... But this doctrine seems to me too disputable altogether, and even if true at all, not true to a sufficient extent, to be made the foundation of any rule of taxation' (Mill 1965 [1848]: 810). For all that, a degree of progression is justified by exemption limits allowed to low income recipients.

A contemporary objection to proportionate income taxation, that it bears more heavily upon middle-income compared with upper-income contributors by reducing them to a lower social status, is rejected on much the same grounds as the positive case advanced for restrictions on acquisition through bequests – abhorrence of conspicuous consumption: 'Government ought to set an example of rating all things at their true value, and riches, therefore, at the worth, for comfort or pleasure, of the things which they will buy: and ought not to sanction the vulgarity of prizing them for the pitiful vanity of being known to possess them, or the paltry shame of being suspected to be without them, the presiding motives of three-fourths of the expenditure of the middle classes' (Mill 1965 [1848]: 810). An objection to the very principle of income taxation itself, that it compels the revelation of contributors' pecuniary means, is rejected along the same lines: 'One of the social evils of this country is the practice, amounting to a custom, of maintaining, or attempting to maintain, the appearance to the world of a larger income than is possessed; and it would be far better for the interest of those who yield to this weakness, if the extent of their means were universally and exactly known, and the temptation removed to expending more than they can afford, or stinting real wants in order to make a false show externally' (831). This national characteristic reflected a 'debased state of mind', whereby 'respect (if such a word can be applied to it) is proportioned to what they suppose to be each person's pecuniary means'.

I turn to the support afforded to the heavier *ad valoram* taxation of luxuries, Mill's objection to conspicuous consumption implying raising 'as large a revenue as conveniently may be, from those classes of luxuries which have most connexion with vanity, and least with positive enjoyment; such as the more costly qualities of all kinds of personal equipment and ornament' (Mill 1965 [1848]: 870). The theme – which reappears in the case for heavy succession duties – is of the first importance:

> I disclaim all asceticism, and by no means wish to see discouraged either by law or opinion, any indulgence (consistent with the means and obligations of the person using it) which is sought from a genuine inclination for, and enjoyment of, the thing itself; but a great portion of the expenses of the higher and middle classes in most countries, and the greatest in this, is not incurred for the sake of the pleasure afforded by the things on which the money is spent, but from regard to opinion, and an idea that certain expenses are expected from them, as an appendage of station; and I cannot but think that expenditure of this sort is a most desirable object of taxation.
> (869)

Accordingly, taxation 'should rise very rapidly with the number of horses and carriages, and with their costliness' (870).[9]

13.5.2 Taxation of unearned income and income redistribution

Mill's opposition to using the tax system for redistribution explains his rejection of a progressive income tax and is also reflected in a general rule of non-discrimination, namely that government 'ought to make no distinction of persons or classes', a tax imposed specifically on any class constituting 'a violation of justice' amounting to 'partial confiscation' (Mill 1965 [1848]: 806–7, 826). But this relates to *earned* income. There were exemptions from this rule reflecting the 'better distribution of property attained, by the joint effect of the prudence and frugality of individuals, and of a system of legislation favouring equality of fortunes' (755; above, p. 311). That 'better distribution' recognized *formal* divergence from the principle of equality of taxation, though 'consistently with that equal justice which is the groundwork of the rule' (819). Such exemptions from the general rule played radically, and were intended to play, on income distribution.

Taxation of the unearned increment of future land values is one celebrated instance:

> It would be no violation of the principles on which private property is grounded, if the state should appropriate this increase of wealth, or part of it, as it arises. This would not properly be taking anything from anybody; it would merely be applying an accession of wealth, created by circumstances, to the benefit of society, instead of allowing it to become an unearned appendage to the riches of a particular class ... They grow richer as it were in their sleep, without working, risking, or economizing. What claim have they on the general principle of social justice, to this accession of riches?
>
> (819–20).

Similarly, rentals for houses 'of the favourite situations in large towns' are described as 'among the very few kinds of income which are fit subjects for peculiar taxation ... being the most gigantic example extant of enormous accessions of riches acquired rapidly, and in many cases unexpectedly, by a few families, from the mere accident of their possessing certain tracts of land, without their having themselves aided in the acquisition by the smallest exertion, outlay, or risk' (835).

Mill sought to avoid impingements on increases in rent due to the skill and expenditure of the landlord, and injustice to landowners who might legitimately claim a lack of 'faith' – that their lands had been purchased on the presumption that any impositions on rents would be no greater than on any other income – by proposing that 'all future increment of rent' beyond a specific date be subject 'to special taxation; in doing which all injustice to landlords would be obviated, if the present market-price of their land be secured to them; since that includes the present value of all future expectations' (Mill 1965 [1848]: 820–1). The foregoing proviso allows for State purchase of land since even 'a tax which, sparing existing rents, should content itself with appropriating a portion of any future increase arising from the mere action of natural causes ... could not be justly done, without offering as an alternative the market price of the land' (826). The precise extent of taxation of the unearned increment is left undecided.

Mill also justified an increase in the contemporary English land tax, albeit a *discriminatory* one, there being no counterpart in the case of other incomes. For this tax he interpreted as a reserve by the State of a certain portion of rent which had never belonged to the owner, constituting a feudal obligation ('The Income and Property Tax'; Mill 1967 [1852]: 479f). And he also insisted in the *Principles* upon public access to private land unless necessary for protection against damage to crops, denied that landowners had the right to do or abstain from doing anything inconsistent with the 'public good', and rejected any case for private property wherein land was not intended for cultivation, from which it followed that the public should at the very least suffer no inconveniences compared with their situation if the land was unappropriated (1965 [1848]:

232). By these proposals Mill sought to come to grips with the problem of justice in the special treatment of that class of income which had so troubled Ricardo. In his analysis of Leslie in 1870 the central issue is well stated: 'It is an acknowledged principle that when the State permits a monopoly, either natural or artificial, to fall into private hands, it retains the right, and cannot divest itself of the duty, to place the exercise of the monopoly under any degree of control which is requisite for the public good' ('Professor Leslie on the Land Question' Mill 1967 [1870]: 672).

Succession duties provide a second primary exemption from the rule of avoiding use of the tax system for redistribution purposes, again insisting that the *spirit* of a just system is satisfied since 'to guarantee ... the fruits of the labour and abstinence of others, transmitted to them without any merit or exertion of their own', is 'a mere incidental consequence' not the essence of the private-property institution (Mill 1965 [1848]: 208). From Mill's perspective (touched on earlier in 13.2 in the Stationary State context), limitations on the quantitative right of bequest to any one individual would scarcely be regarded 'as a burthensome restraint by any testator who estimated a large fortune at its true value, that of the pleasures and advantages that can be purchased with it: on even the most extravagant estimate of which, it must be apparent to every one, that the difference to the happiness of the possessor between a moderate independence and five times as much, is insignificant when weighed against the enjoyment that might be given, and the permanent benefits diffused, by some other disposal of the four-fifths' (225). What we have here is a condemnation of heaping 'to satiety those intrinsically worthless things on which large fortunes are mostly expended'. Likewise: 'if the restriction [on bequest] could be made practically effectual, the benefit would be great. *Wealth which could no longer be employed in over-enriching a few*, would either be devoted to objects of public usefulness, or if bestowed on individuals, would be distributed among a larger number. While those enormous fortunes which no one needs for any personal purpose but ostentation or improper power, would become much less numerous' (226; emphasis added). There is also a sharp complaint that 'the presiding motives of three-fourths of the expenditure of the middle classes' reflected 'pitiful vanity' (810).

More specifically, Mill recommended an absolute upper limit to sums received by legacy or gift, a limit which was apparently to apply to all categories of 'property': 'Each person should have the power to dispose by will of his or her whole property; but not to lavish it in enriching some one individual, beyond a certain maximum, which should be fixed sufficiently high to afford the means of comfortable independence ... I see nothing objectionable in fixing a limit to what any one may acquire by the mere favour of others, without any exercise of his faculties, and in requiring that if he desires any further accession of fortune, he shall work for it' (Mill 1965 [1848]: 225). Similarly: 'We may suppose ... a limitation of the sum which any one person may acquire by gift or inheritance, to the amount sufficient to constitute a moderate independence' (755). Restriction on what one may *acquire* not on what one may *bequeath* presumably reflects a wish to avoid interference with an individual's free use of his wealth (223).

Thus 'inheritances and legacies' – at least beyond a certain amount – were legitimate candidates to be taxed as heavily as was possible 'without giving rise to evasions by donation *inter vivos* or concealment of property, such as it would be impossible adequately to check. The principle of graduation ... seems to me, both just and expedient as applied to legacy and inheritance duties' (Mill 1965 [1848]: 811–12). Similarly, before an 1852 investigation regarding legitimate progression: 'there are no reasons of justice or policy against taxing enormously large inheritances more highly than smaller inheritances' (Mill 1967 [1852]: 491). Similarly, in the evidence of 1861: 'If the rich are to be subject to a greater proportionate amount of taxation than the poor ... succession duty is the most unobjectionable mode of doing it, because in that way it is confined to hereditary wealth' (1967 [1861]: 569).

Whereas in his evidence Mill was alert to the problem of double taxation, in the case of succession this was set aside entirely although both the property is taxed at succession and any income yielded thereby subsequently. The entire notion of 'equality of taxation' is said to be inapplicable. The statement encapsulates much of Mill's policy orientation:

> I do not think that the principle of equality of taxation has any application to the case of taxes on succession. It seems to me that taxes on succession stand on a different foundation from all other taxes, and that the State is entitled, in reference to them, to consider public policy and general morality, abstractedly from the special rule of equality of taxation. If a person is allowed by the State to succeed to that which he has not earned, but has obtained without any exertion, that is a privilege which he owes to the existence of law and society, to which the State is entitled to annex conditions, and if these conditions are just, when tried by a higher principle of morality, no general principle of equality of taxation has any application to them.
>
> (Mill 1967 [1861]: 566)[10]

13.6 Land reform

Mill's land reform programme focused, within a utilitarian framework, on the avoidance of excessive concentrations of wealth. First to consider here is the hostility towards primogeniture and legal restraints on the sale of property, feudal remnants designed 'to keep up large hereditary fortunes, and a landed aristocracy' (Mill 1965 [1848]: 888). Mill insists that 'unless a strong case of social utility can be made out for primogeniture, it stands sufficiently condemned by the general principles of justice; being a broad distinction in the treatment of one person and of another, grounded solely on an accident' (892). But importantly a yet 'deeper consideration' was the belief that 'the diffusion of wealth, and not its concentration, is desirable, and that the more wholesome state of society is not that in which immense fortunes are possessed by a few and coveted by all, but that in which the greatest possible numbers possess and are contented with a moderate competency, which all may hope to acquire' (891). Utilitarianism required its own set of value judgments defining the content of the greater good, and here we encounter one of the most outstanding.

Various defenses of primogeniture as stimulus to effort are rejected, including the argument by J.R. McCulloch (1843) whereby the expenses of the great landlords, though 'injurious to themselves', set a pattern for emulation by others or, as Mill paraphrased the argument, that 'the custom of primogeniture seems to render all classes more industrious, and to augment at the same time, the mass of wealth and the scale of enjoyment' (Mill 1965 [1848]: 889–90). Mill allowed only that 'a state of complete equality of fortunes would not be favourable to active exertion for the increase of wealth' (890). The 'industrial energy and ardour of accumulation' in the United States proved that differentials in *earned* income sufficed for the task.

The proposal regarding taxation of the unearned increment (above 13.5) was a key feature of the Programme of the Land Tenure Reform Association, an 'explanatory statement' for which was written by Mill in 1871. Here Mill declared that the contemporary Land Laws were designed 'to prop up a ruling class' – indeed, in the post-1867 world of a vastly broadened franchise, 'of all our leading institutions, none are more unsuited than the Land Laws' – for 'the land has been prevented, to a large extent, from passing out of the hands of the idle into those of the industrious, and its ownership has been retained as the privilege of a small and decreasing number of families' ('Land Tenure Reform'; Mill 1967 [1871]: 689). Mill alluded briefly to proposals to abolish entirely private property in land but hoped that all would go along with the milder measures of the Association.

The programme of the Land Tenure Reform Association regarding State acquisition, which Mill supported, goes beyond the formal argument of the *Principles*. For it is now firmly insisted that no *new* transfers from the public domain were to be permitted, Mill citing the practice whereby 'common lands' could, by Act of Parliament, be taken up for cultivation by their nominal owner – an 'iniquity', he charged, involving 'gifts' to the wealthiest class (Mill 1967 [1871]: 692–3). Similarly, land owned by public bodies and endowed institutions – much of London and the great towns – had to be regarded as public property (694).

Regarding the disposition of State property, the overriding consideration was the *general good*. The options listed are an important index of Mill's typical perspective. In the first place, in the case of State acquisition of wastelands, the property should 'either be kept open for the enjoyment of the people or cultivated for their use' (Mill 1967 [1871]: 693). Secondly, there is a perception of the general good with emphasis on amenity: 'The Society attach great importance to keeping open extensive tracts in a state of wild natural beauty and freedom; and a large portion of the waste lands of the country are of too poor a quality to be worth much for any other purpose'. And thirdly, the utilitarian maximand weighs the working-class component heavily: 'When the land is worth cultivation, and the wants of society require that it should be cultivated, the mode of bringing it into cultivation should be principally determined by the interest of the labouring classes'.

As for the latter, something akin to *peasant ownership* was one option: 'Were it desirable to give any further extension to private property in land, those classes would have a paramount claim to be admitted to a share in it, by the grant of the land in small parcels to respectable agricultural labourers at a fixed rent' (Mill 1967 [1871]: 693). But *public ownership* was more likely to be perceived by 'opinion' as preferable, and here Mill's concern with experimentation is conspicuous: 'these lands will remain with the State, or with local authorities, as a means of trying, with the greatest advantage and under every variety of circumstances, the modes in which land can be most successfully managed on the public account – whether by capitalist farmers, with stipulations for the benefit of the labourers, or by long leases on proper conditions to small cultivators, or, finally, by co-operative farming'.

In the context of State acquisition of lands from endowed institutions, we similarly encounter Mill's utilitarian standard, *the general good*, and an emphasis on experimentation: 'It may, without injustice or detriment to any one, make use of them for any well-considered social or philanthropic experiments' (Mill 1967 [1871]: 694). Large portions of the great towns, London included, were at stake, Mill enthusing regarding the opportunities created 'for promoting every improvement that tends to raise the condition of the people: sanitary works, improved dwellings, public gardens, co-operative buildings, co-operative agriculture, useful public institutions of every kind'. Since the endowed properties involved largely city areas, while fairness required that the proposed advantages should be enjoyed throughout the country, Mill further proposed that the State 'should purchase from private owners estates which are in the market, when such purchase is necessary for giving a fair trial in any neighbourhood to co-operative agriculture, or to a properly regulated system of small farming' (695).

******

What now, in summary, of Mill's specific preferences? In all editions of the *Principles* he recommends a wide diffusion of property in land amongst peasant and small-landed proprietors over the system of hired labour – at least 'in any form in which it exists at present' – from the perspectives of population control, 'security', and 'independence' (Mill 1965 [1848]: 767). But even this organization was far from ideal because it failed to take advantage of large-scale production and its related efficiencies. In any event, his extended demonstrations of the productive potential of peasant proprietorship and the metayer system in various European countries (see Hollander 1985: 238–44) were designed to counter those who exaggerated its defects, whereas he did not favour the actual introduction of such systems into a country already enjoying prudence in matters of population and institutional assurances against a skewed income distribution so that the benefits of high average productivity were broadly enjoyed.

A preference for maximum efficiency *provided labour benefited* is further confirmed in the present context thus: 'Labour is unquestionably more productive on the system of large industrial enterprises; the produce, if not greater absolutely, is greater in proportion to the labour employed: the same number of people can be supported equally well with less toil and greater leisure; which will be wholly an advantage, as soon as civilization and improvement have so far advanced, that what is a benefit to the whole shall be a benefit to each individual composing it'. (Mill 1965 [1848]: 768). But Mill in fact warned earlier in the *Principles* of the dangers of hastily replacing even an unproductive *metayer* system by that of 'money rents and capitalist farmers' on grounds of labour displacement: 'The enlargement of farms, and the introduction of what are called agricultural improvements, usually diminish the number of labourers employed on the land; and unless the growth of capital in trade and manufactures affords an opening for the displaced population, or unless there are reclaimable wastes on which they can be located, competition will so reduce wages, that they will probably be worse off as day-labourers than they were as metayers' (311).[11] But as for Ireland, efficiency might better be sacrificed for the sake of aggregate employment and various other objectives including population control and improved conditions for labour. (See Hollander 2015: 282–92 for an elaboration.)

13.7. Summary and conclusion

Mill's recommendation for state intervention in the capitalist-exchange system to the end of enhancing distributive justice contrasts radically with the position of his contemporary Karl Marx. For Marx objected to the focus on distributive justice in the Gotha Programme as conflicting with the principle that the pattern of distribution is the *necessary* outcome of the 'mode of production' rendering 'unfairness' an irrelevant consideration. (See Hollander 2008: 390–6.) Indeed, by ignoring the economic role of income inequality a redistributive programme implied the undermining of productive capacity and the very ability to produce a surplus. And it is Marx who strongly insisted on constraints imposed by the market system on income-redistribution proposals, such as that involving land taxation.

When we turn to the matter of the wage structure, we find the parties approaching each other in some respects. Relevant here are two Mill formulations regarding wage differentials reflecting differential talent: A declaration that 'it is an abuse of the principle of equality to demand that no individual be permitted to be better off than the rest, when his being so makes none of the others worse off than they otherwise would be' (Mill 1965 [1848]: 980); and his argument against schemes entailing wage equality notwithstanding differential talent: 'The nominal equality of labour would be so great a real inequality that justice would revolt against its being enforced' (above, p. 321). This position has an exact counterpart in Marx's insistence that natural differences between individuals with regard to 'talent', both physical and mental, would have to be recognized at least in the 'first phase' of a communist society emerging from capitalist society ('Critique of the Gotha Programme'; Marx 1989 (1875): 86–7). The Mill–Marx position precisely captures Hayek's insistence in the *Constitution of Liberty* that 'from the fact that people are very different it follows that, if we treat them equally, the result must be inequality in their actual position, and that the only way to place them in an equal position would be to treat them differently' (Hayek 2011 [1960]: 149–50). Hayek had no inkling of the pedigree of his remark.

Pace Stigler and others, Mill placed at the forefront of his programme redistribution designed to enhance distributive justice. But the matter is not yet quite settled. There were qualifications and these require attention if we are to get the picture just right.

Joseph Persky has recently pointed out that Mill considered the historical role of the system of industrial capital to be as yet unfulfilled, 'that private property in the form of industrial capital still had a historic role to play' (Persky 2016: 71). That this is indeed the case is reflected in Mill's concern that an 'unenlightened' working class might 'be tempted to throw all taxes on property – or even on realised property' (25 September 1865; Mill 1972: 1104); and in his representation – in the case of earned income – of a tax imposed specifically on any class as 'a violation of justice' amounting to 'partial confiscation', no less 'inexpedient and unjust' than Proudhonism (1 December 1871; Mill 1972: 1858–9). Consider also a statement in the *Principles* that captured the essential message of *On Liberty* from which perspective a communist arrangement is found to be defective, by 'plac[ing] every action of every member of the community under command' (Mill 1965 [1848]: 978), whereas any prospective advantages could be achieved under a *reformed* capitalism. In particular, under 'the Communistic scheme, supposing it to be successful, there would be an end to all anxiety concerning the means of subsistence; and this would be much gained for human happiness. But it is perfectly possible to realize this same advantage in a society grounded on private property; and to this point the tendencies of political speculation are rapidly converging. Supposing this attained, it is surely a vast advantage on the side of the individual system, that it is compatible with a far greater degree of personal liberty'. Similarly, Mill lamented the deficiencies of distributive justice for the majority of factory workers (above, pp. 316–17). The full range of defects when compared with the theoretical communist option is extensive: monotony, perhaps greater and longer monotony (and longer hours); small choice of occupation; restricted mobility; dependency 'on the will of others' no less than in 'any system short of actual slavery'; and little incentive in the case of day labourers or fixed-salary recipients who because they work 'for the gain of others, not for their own … have no interest in doing more than the smallest quantity of work which will pass as a fulfillment of the mere terms of their engagement' (Mill 1965 [1848]: 979). But as for the latter objection, a solution could be found in the extension of *piece-working* where technically practical, and of opportunities for promotion from the ranks even for day labourers who proved themselves meritorious. The other objections Mill conceded, although we should not overlook his hopes for the future *within capitalism* from extensions of 'popular instruction'. Mill, therefore, insisted on the continued relevance of the private-property institution – provided it is subject to reform – concluding in his correspondence of 1870 that 'the feeling of security of possession and enjoyment ... could not (in the state of advancement mankind have yet reached) be had without private ownership' (Mill 1972: 1739–40).

This takes us to the matter of population control which would be required to assure minimum standards – public regulation on the Communist scheme since there would be no motive for private prudential restraint (Mill 1965 [1848]: 979). But again, we find the same response – that with the same degree of restriction on numbers the lowest paid in a competitive system could enjoy these same standards as under communism, and this without precluding the further advance of individuals, in real earnings and in freedom, who exerted themselves differentially. Here indeed lay the advantage of capitalism: 'if we suppose an equal degree of regulation to take place under the present system, either compulsorily, or, what would be so much preferable, voluntarily; a condition at least equal to what the Communist [1848: Socialist] system offers to all, would fall to the lot of the least fortunate, by the mere action of the competitive principle. Whatever of pecuniary means or freedom of action any one obtained beyond this would be so much to be counted in favour of the competitive system' (980). Mill concludes with his striking formulation of his conception of what equality should and should not entail: 'It is an abuse of the principle of equality to demand that no individual be permitted to be better off than the rest, when his being so makes none of the others worse off than they otherwise would be'.

Finally, Mill distinguishes between landed property and capital, agreeing with Newman 'that property in land is essentially subordinate to public convenience; that the rights of the landed proprietor ought to be construed strictly; that the law ... should compel him to allow to others all such use as is not incompatible with the purposes for which he is permitted to exercise dominion over it; and, finally, that it may at any time, if the public interest requires, be taken by the legislature, on payment of compensation' ('Newman's *Political Economy*' Mill 1967 [1851]: 450–1). Apart from legitimizing such restrictions on ownership of landed property he also, of course, proposed taxation of the increase of land values generated by economic development. But for all that, he found sound expediential reasons for opposing the wholesale expropriation of land in the circumstances which then prevailed (Mill 1965 [1848]: 208), and indeed placed his immediate hopes upon capitalist farming, the farmer himself owning land or leasing it under conditions of secure tenure (767–8); even the efficacy of the traditional English landlords was increasingly seen in a favourable light (231n). This argument from expediency is reinforced by one from equity (a higher utility) namely respect for individuality itself. A concern not to go overboard by steps undermining the institution is manifest more specifically in

Mill's insistence on compensation rather than confiscation even where transfers of landed property to the State were fully justified.

Beyond all these cautions regarding the desirable extent of reform there were also practical limits to reform dictated by public opinion. Let us focus on a statement in his late correspondence: 'it is above all by succession duties that I wish to establish social justice' (to Costantino Baer, 22 September 1872; Mill 1972: 1905). More specifically: 'regarding successions, I recognize no moral right even of direct descendants beyond a sufficiency to assure them a good chance in life. If society permits inheritances beyond that limit it has a right to impose any conditions it pleases; and can use that right to the end of moderating inequality' (to Baer, 8 January 1873: 1932). As we know, both quantitative limits and progressive taxation of legacies and inheritances are amongst those conditions apart from progressive rates of indirect taxes. Here I call attention to a retrospect by Alexander Bain: 'what I remember most vividly of [Mill's] talk pending publication of the [*Principles*] was his anticipating a tremendous outcry about his doctrines on Property. He frequently spoke of his proposals as to Inheritance and Bequest, which if carried out would pull down all large fortunes in two generations. To his surprise, however, this part of the book made no sensation' (Bain 1882: 89). Now it is not at all clear that 'surprise' was a justified reaction, for − surprising though it may appear − a reader of the *Principles* might *not* in fact come away with an impression of urgency regarding the proposed redistributive measures. Consider the summary of the key clauses in the *Principles*:

> Freedom of bequest as the general rule, but limited by two things: first, that if there are descendants, who, being unable to provide for themselves, would become burthensome to the state, the equivalent of whatever the state would accord to them should be reserved from the property for their benefit; and secondly, that no one person should be permitted to acquire, by inheritance, more than the amount of a moderate independence. In case of intestacy, the whole property to escheat to the state: which should be bound to make a just and reasonable provision for descendents, that is, such a provision as the parent or ancestor ought to have made, their circumstances, capacities, and mode of bringing up being considered.
> (Mill 1965 [1848]: 887)

This is a fair summary of the main reform proposals. But this statement is immediately followed by an allowance that 'several phases of improvement' would be required 'before ideas so far removed from present modes of thinking will be taken into serious consideration'. To be noted is the fact that a compromise solution neglects entirely the proposal regarding quantitative limits: 'As an intermediate course, therefore, I would recommend the extension to all property, of the present English law of inheritance affecting personal property (freedom of bequest, and in case of intestacy, equal division): except that no rights should be acknowledged in collaterals, and that the property of those who have neither descendants nor ascendants, and make no will, should escheat to the state' (888). Expediential qualifications to the recommendation regarding restrictions of acquisitions by bequest may also be noted. Thus, in the sixth edition (1865) of the *Principles* Mill added that allowances might be made to prevent the break-up of single manufacturing and commercial enterprises or ancestral mansions and parks (225n). Again, in 'Leslie on the Land Question' Mill cites Leslie's proposal to limit the amount of land any single person could acquire by inheritance, and his belief that this would be so 'shocking to present proprietary sentiments' that 'only a violent revolution could at present accomplish it' (Mill 1967 [1870]: 681). Leslie accordingly limited his proposals to the removal of restrictions on land use as a means of increasing the supply of land in the market. Now while Mill did not think these proposals adequate to achieve their objective of raising rural living standards, he did not proceed to insist on an absolute upper limit to the inheritance of landed property. Once more we see that there were practical or expediential constraints on his radicalism.[12]

Mill is an artist who painted in shades of grey. There is no black and white with Mill. This imposes serious complexities for his interpreters. In the present instance, the contrast between our own and the Stigler readings is narrowed by Mill's wish to avoid going so far by redistributive reform as to threaten the private-property institution itself. Thus, for example, he championed a greater diffusion of wealth but not when taken to an extreme, his redistributive tax proposals were limited to *unearned* income specifically, and he rejected 'complete equality of fortunes' and 'starting fair' in any literal sense of the term as 'inconsistent with any law of private property'. There is too his recognition of the practical limits to the most radical of his proposals imposed by public opinion, namely those relating to bequest. And we must never lose sight of the fact that concern with income distribution does not exclude concern also with 'better men', as Stigler seems to have implied; to the contrary, little could be permanently achieved by redistribution in the absence of responsible conduct on the part of labour – particularly conduct respecting population control but also a range of restrictive practices. Finally, we recall that Mill even downplayed the quantitative advantages to labour of *mere* redistribution.

Notes

1 This chapter draws selectively on my researches first published in Hollander 1985 and, in a second edition, in Hollander 2015. Page references are provided throughout to elaborations of the present abridgement as they appear in the latter. A revised weighting of the issues, designed to bridge somewhat otherwise wholly divergent interpretations of Mill on distributive justice, will become apparent (see the Summary and Conclusion).
2 We might add that Mill takes the matter yet further by pointing out that a behavioural transformation as an essential pre-condition for any successful transition from capitalist to the preferable co-operative organization (see Hollander 2015: 138–48), a pre-condition far from satisfied as things stood: 'To be independent of master manufacturers, to work for themselves and divide the whole produce of their labour is a worthy object of ambition, but it is only fit for, and can only succeed with people who can labour for the community of which they are a part with the same

energy and zeal as if labouring for their own private and separate interest (the opposite is now the case)' (Mill 1972: 81). Yet more strongly, success required operatives 'who, instead of expecting immediately more pay and less work, are willing to submit to any privation until they have effected their emancipation'.

3 Mill's declaration in this same context that only in 'backward countries' was increased production 'still an important object' (cited above, p. 308) should, we conclude, be understood as a special case for increased aggregate output where unexhausted scale economies are potentially available, which would be consistent with the wherewithal to support increased wages. It is also true that Mill justified concern with the aggregative magnitude independently of implications for the wage rate from the perspective of national defence: 'For the safety of national independence it is essential that a country should not fall much behind its neighbours in these things' (Mill 1965 [1848]: 755).

4 As for ostentation, we may recall the famous declaration in *On Liberty*: 'It is desirable ... that in things which do not primarily concern others, individuality should assert itself. Where, not a person's own character, but the traditions or customs of other people are the rule of conduct, there is wanting one of the principal ingredients of human happiness, and quite the chief ingredient of individual and social progress' (Mill 1977 [1859]: 260).

5 There is an alternative possibility – that Mill's cogitations regarding the advantages of the stationary state were intended to apply less to the capitalist system than to an arrangement involving profit-sharing or, better still, co-operation. For it is unclear whether a condition of zero net accumulation, where productivity increases are entirely to the advantage of labour leaving the return on capital unaffected at its minimum to assure against expansion, is at all possible within capitalist arrangement. The profit rate (motivating innovation) is bound to increase and with it net accumulation. On such grounds it has been suggested that the stationary state for Mill implied a co-operative, rather than a capitalist, arrangement where incentives exist for the adoption of productivity-increasing technology even in the absence of ordinary profit calculation (Levy 1981: 278–9). And in fact the 'Futurity' chapter argues for technical progress and rising productivity provided institutional organization is such as to assure that 'what is a benefit to the whole shall be a benefit to each individual composing it', that is assuming arrangements whereby the gains are yielded 'without dividing the producers into two parties with hostile interests' (Mill 1965 [1848]: 768). It must be admitted that these propositions with respect both to stationariness and to co-operation, defining Mill's ideals for the future, are highly speculative.

6 Mill's general position also governs his approach in the *Principles* to women's earnings. It was the competitive market mechanism upon which he relied for at least part of the solution to relatively low women's earnings. For one of his concerns was the fact that 'occupations which law and usage make accessible to them are comparatively so few' (Mill 1965 [1848]: 395). 'For improving the condition of women, it should ... be an object to give them the readiest access to independent industrial employment, instead of closing, either entirely or partially, that which is already open to them' (953), alluding to restrictions on women factory workers. Again, reliance on the market *presupposed* State intervention.

7 For a comprehensive account entailing discussion of exemption limits, direct taxation and saving, income vs. capital taxation, indirect taxation and law taxes, see Hollander 2015: 292–310.

8 By the same token, Mill opposed the use of the tax system to treat extreme poverty – the modern negative income tax. Other solutions were preferable to him (Mill 1965 [1848]: 808).

9 The principle is extended to the 'stimulants' typically purchased by working-class consumers, 'because these, though in themselves as legitimate indulgencies as any

others, are more liable than most to be used in excess, so that the check to consumption, naturally arising from taxation, is on the whole better applied to them than to other things' (Mill 1965 [1848]: 871).
10 In his *Principles* Mill justified the further constraint that legators may not 'determine the person who should succeed to it after the death of all who were living when the will was made' (Mill 1965 [1848]: 895).
11 That labour-displacing technology was socially desirable only if the interests of those dismissed are taken into account is a position shared with Bentham; Ricardo apparently made no such condition (see Hollander 2019).
12 Were all Mill's proposals for a reform of the private-property institution put into effect the result would still fall short of the ideal, and for that reason be impermanent, the ideal being co-operation to be arrived at by way of an evolutionary transition from profit-sharing (see Hollander 2015: 138–43).

References

Bain, A. 1882. *John Stuart Mill, a Criticism: With Personal Recollections*. London: Longmans, Green.
Baum, B. 2007: 'John Stuart Mill and Liberal Socialism', in *J.S. Mill's Political Thought: A Bicentennial reassessment*, ed. N. Urbinati and A. Zakaras. Cambridge: Cambridge University Press: 98–123.
Hayek, F.A. 2011 (1960). *The Constitution of Liberty*. Chicago: University of Chicago Press.
Hollander, S. 1985. *The Economics of John Stuart Mill*. Toronto: University of Toronto Press.
Hollander, S. 2008. *The Economics of Karl Marx: Analysis and Application*. Cambridge: Cambridge University Press.
Hollander, S. 2015. *John Stuart Mill: Political Economist*. Singapore: World Scientific Press.
Hollander, S. 2019. 'Ricardo on Machinery', *Journal of Economic Perspectives*, 33(2), Spring 2019: 1–15.
Levy, M.B. 1981. 'Mill's Stationary State and the Transcendence of Liberalism', *Polity* 14: 273–293.
Marx, K. 1989 (1875). *Critique of the Gotha Programme. Marx–Engels Collected Works* 24, New York: International Publishers: 81–99.
Mill, J.S. 1963. *The Earlier Letters 1812 to 1848. Collected Works of John Stuart Mill (CWJSM)*. Toronto: University of Toronto Press.
Mill, J.S. 1965 (1848). *Principles of Political Economy*. *CWJSM* 2–3.
Mill, J.S. 1967 (1845). 'The Claims of Labour', *CWJSM* 4: 363–389.
Mill, J.S. 1967 (1851). 'Newman's Political Economy', *CWJSM* 5: 439–457.
Mill, J.S. 1967 (1852). 'The Income and Property Tax', *CWJSM* 5: 463–498.
Mill, J.S. 1967 (1861). 'The Income and Property Tax', *CWJSM* 5: 549–598.
Mill, J.S. 1967 (1869a). 'Endowments', *CWJSM* 5: 613–629.
Mill, J.S. 1967 (1869b). 'Thornton on Labour and Its Claims', *CWJSM* 5: 631–668.
Mill, J.S. 1967 (1870). 'Professor Leslie on the Land Question', *CWJSM* 5: 669–685.
Mill, J.S. 1967 (1871). 'Land Tenure Reform', *CWJSM* 5: 687–695.
Mill, J.S. 1967 (1879). 'Chapters on Socialism', *CWJSM* 5: 703–753.
Mill, J.S. 1972. *The Later Letters 1849 to 1873. CWJSM* 14–17.
Mill, J.S. 1977 (1859). *On Liberty. CWJSM* 18: 213–310.
Persky, J. 2016. *The Political Economy of Progress: John Stuart Mill and Modern Radicalism*. Oxford: Oxford University Press.
Robson, J.M. 1968. *The Improvement of Mankind: The Social and Political Thought of John Stuart Mill*. Toronto: University of Toronto Press.

Stigler, G.J. 1949. *Five Lectures on Economic Problems*. London: Longmans, Green.
West, E.G. 1978. 'J.S. Mill's Redistribution Policy: New Political Economy or Old?' *Economic Inquiry* 16: 570–586.
West, E.G. and R.W. Hafer. 1978. 'J.S. Mill, Unions. And the Wages Fund Recantation: A Reinterpretation', *Quarterly Journal of Economics* 92: 603–619.

14 Mill, ethical progress and personal liberty

14.1 Introduction

This brief chapter is devoted to two questions thus far left in abeyance yet pertinent to ethical utilitarianism. How did Mill evaluate the prospects for ethical progress – and accordingly for social progress – considering the admitted predominance of 'selfish' behaviour? And how does his position compare with that of Bentham, who – at least in the political context and tending somewhat to exaggerate the problem – cautioned against 'the chimerical' in reform programs and recommended that we 'seek only for what is attainable' (Chapter 9, p. 226). Mill, I shall show, is no less cautious, warning against 'overrat[ing] the ease of making people unselfish', and regretting that, in the state of advancement mankind have yet reached, private ownership was essential to assure 'the feeling of security of possession and enjoyment'.

Also considered is Mill on 'security' as including the *protection of personal liberty and individuality*, a notion already found in Bentham.[1] Here I take account of a recent criticism by Jonathan Riley (2016) of my own treatment of this issue (in Hollander 2015: 76). Riley persuades me to modify my account, although my charge against Mill of ambiguity when defining the 'border line' between the *self-* and *other-regarding* categories established in *On Liberty* survives intact, as does my position that Mill envisaged extreme circumstances justifying social constraint even when an action by an individual is strictly 'self-regarding', concerning 'the interests of no person but himself'.

14.2 Ethical progress: Mill and Bentham compared

I examined the prospects for ethical progress from Bentham's perspective in Chapter Nine and pointed to his caution against 'the chimerical' in reform programs. But there I suggested that in giving this warning he exaggerated the force of private selfishness when concerned with the reform of the British establishment, making use of any weapon at hand including exaggeration regarding 'the unchangeable constitution of human nature'. This reading is the one actually adopted by Mill, who reacted harshly in 1833 to the two passages from *The Book of Fallacies* as precluding all hope for ethical advance: 'By the promulgation of such views of human nature, and by a general tone of thought and expression perfectly in harmony with them, I conceive Mr. Bentham's writings to have done and to be doing very serious evil ... It is difficult to form the conception of a tendency more inconsistent with all rational hope of good for the human species, than that which must be impressed by such doctrines, upon any mind in which they find acceptance' (Mill 1969 [1833]: 15). The negative message conveyed by the passages is also alluded to in a qualification to the *defence* of Bentham against Whewell on the grounds of the allowance Bentham makes for ethical progress – namely, the 'large deficiencies and hiatuses in [Bentham's] scheme of human nature and life' (Mill 1969 [1852]: 174). For all that, Mill concluded regarding ethics that '[i]t is by his *method* chiefly that Bentham, as we think, justly earned a position in moral science analogous to that of Bacon in physical. It is because he was the first to enter into the right mode of working ethical problems, though he worked many of them, as Bacon did physical, on insufficient data'. And a further clarification is introduced in 1859 regarding ethics: 'not that his practical conclusions [1859: *in morals*] were often wrong' (173; emphasis added). It is indeed clear from the *System of Logic* – including the last edition of 1872 – that Mill's main concern pertained to the legislative implications flowing from Bentham's assumption that the actions of the *average ruler* are determined by his self-interest strictly interpreted (Mill 1974 [1843]: 889–91; see Hollander 2015: 61).

Even if there are limits to Bentham's allowances for ethical progress, as we have shown that there are, how far did Mill himself actually go with respect to the 'improvement of mankind', which demanded such progress? Relevant here is Mill's comment in the *Autobiography* explaining how he finally came 'to give a wider basis and a more free and genial character to Radical speculations; to shew that there was a Radical philosophy, better and more complete than Bentham's, while recognizing and incorporating all of Bentham's which is permanently valuable' (Mill 1981 [1873]: 221). Mill had not necessarily forgotten that in 1852 he himself had recognized Bentham's allowances for ethical progress, but was observing that Bentham had not gone far enough. Thus to the allowance by Benthamites even in early days for 'enlightening the selfish feelings' by way of education (referred to above) Mill appended the remark that '[a]lthough this last is prodigiously important as a means of improvement *in the hands of those who are themselves impelled by nobler principles of action*, I do not believe that any one of the survivors of the Benthamites or Utilitarians of that day, now relies mainly upon it for the general amendment of human conduct' (113–15; emphasis added). Mill too clearly had his own doubts concerning what could be achieved by education.

This conclusion may also be reached from another direction. We recall Mill's harsh verdict of 1833 that '[a]s an analyst of human nature (the faculty in which above all it is necessary that an ethical philosopher should excel) I cannot rank Mr. Bentham very high...' (Mill 1969 [1833]: 12). But Mill himself was preoccupied with the design of constitutional arrangements to protect minorities against people who are 'ignorant and unduly selfish'. And his concerns extended much more broadly. Thus he observed in the *Autobiography* that – when considering institutional arrangements in preparation for the *Principles* – he had taken into account the weakness of the motive force of 'interest in the common good', a deficiency reflecting 'the deep rooted selfishness which forms the general character of the existing state of society', which showed 'the folly of premature attempts to dispense with the inducements of private interest in social affairs, while no substitute for them has been or can be provided' (Mill 1981 [1873]: 241). This retrospect is confirmed by the affirmation in *Considerations on Representative Government* – it reads very much like Bentham! – that 'whenever it ceases to be true that mankind, as a rule, prefer themselves to others, and those nearest to them to those more remote, from that moment communism is not only practicable, but the only defensible form of society'– a condition thus far satisfied only by 'the *élite* of mankind' (Mill 1977 [1861]: 404–5). And in a letter to Harriet Taylor in 1849 Mill wrote: 'I cannot persuade myself, that you do not greatly overrate the ease of making people unselfish' (Mill 1972: 19). This muted view is reinforced by a denial in correspondence of 1870 'that, from the utilitarian point of view, the right of private property is founded *solely* on the motives it affords to the increase of public wealth; because independently of those motives, the feeling of security of possession and enjoyment which could not (in the state of advancement mankind have yet reached) be had without private ownership, is of the very greatest importance as an element of human happiness' (1739–40). The perspectives of Mill and Bentham regarding prospects for social progress are very similar, considering typical conduct in 'the state of advancement mankind have yet reached'.

14.3 The 'inviolability' of self-regarding actions

There remains to consider an objection by Jonathan Riley (2016) that I do not do justice to Mill's treatment in *On Liberty* of the contrast between *self-regarding* and *other-regarding conduct*. Thus Riley objects to my complaint of ambiguity (Hollander 2015: 76) regarding the 'two maxims which together form the entire doctrine of this essay' as summarized in the closing chapter (Mill 1977 [1859]: 292). He further asserts that Mill 'rejects the idea that others can legitimately exert "moral pressure" to discourage self-regarding behaviour. For him, their moral pressure is by definition coercive'.

Now Mill's summary does, in fact, justify what surely amounts to *moral coercion* even when the actions in question 'concern the interests of no person but himself': 'Advice, instruction, persuasion, and *avoidance by other people* if thought necessary by them for their own good, are the only measures by which society can justifiably express its dislike or disapproval of his conduct' (Mill 1977

[1859]: 292; emphasis added). For there is an obvious difference between 'advice, instruction, and persuasion', on the one hand, and 'avoidance' on the other since this last is a much stronger measure implying boycott, even excommunication, simply because people think it 'necessary ... for their own good'. However, Riley might rely upon an earlier statement of the object of the essay, to which I also refer, one specifying that only remonstration, reasoning, persuasion or entreaty *but not the 'moral coercion of public opinion'* – which is placed on a par with 'legal penalties' – can be warranted merely because it is deemed to be for 'his own good', that 'it will make him happier, because, in the opinion of others, to do so would be wise, or even right' (Mill 1977 [1859]: 223–4). Considering the contrast between the two formulations I would say that my charge against Mill of ambiguity survives intact.

Riley objects finally to my contention that the 'border line' between Mill's self- and other-regarding categories is 'defined by general utility' and so may vary across societies; that 'self-regarding conduct' may have 'nefarious social consequences'; and that 'the "inviolability" of self-regarding acts is by no means an absolute principle, wholly divorced from circumstances' (Riley 2016, citing Hollander 2015: 82, 433; for Riley's position on Mill and the self-regarding category, see also Riley 2015). I am led by Riley's objections to modify my position. I would no longer contend that Mill's observation that in contemporary Britain – unlike 'some early states of society' –the danger which threatens human nature is not the excess, but the deficiency, of personal impulses and preferences (Mill 1977 [1859]: 264), is inconsistent with, or in any way weakens, the contrast between the two behavioural categories since the irresponsible conduct of barbaric peoples entails *other-regarding* effects. Similarly, I erred by suggesting that since, under certain empirical conditions, Mill might have sided with Adam Smith in justifying usury laws, the 'inviolability' of self-regarding acts came into question (Hollander 2015: 433). This issue also falls within the *other-regarding* class, trade being for Mill 'a social act' (Mill 1977 [1859]: 293).

Nevertheless, I find that Riley goes too far. Mill himself asserts that '[t]he right inherent in society, to ward off crimes against itself by antecedent precautions, suggests the obvious limitations to the maxim, that purely self-regarding misconduct cannot properly be meddled with in the way of prevention or punishment' (Mill 1977 [1859]: 295). The border line is porous. But, more importantly, I have pointed to Mill's position regarding voluntary slavery which in most civilized countries, he maintained, is rightly to be treated as an 'exception' to the general rule that engagements should be kept even in cases where third parties are unaffected: 'an engagement by which a person should sell himself, or allow himself to be sold, as a slave, would be null and void; neither enforced by law nor by opinion' (299). Mill's rationale is of the first importance:

> The ground for thus limiting his power of voluntarily disposing of his own lot in life, is apparent, and is very clearly seen in this extreme case. The reason for not interfering, unless for the sake of others, with a person's voluntary acts, is consideration for his liberty. His voluntary choice is evidence that what he so chooses is desirable, or at the least is endurable, to him, and his good is on the whole best provided for by allowing him to take his own means of pursuing it. But by selling himself for a slave, he abdicates his liberty; he forgoes any future use of it beyond that single act ... *He therefore defeats, in his own case, the very purpose which is the justification of allowing him to dispose of himself.* He is no longer free; but is henceforth in a position which has no longer the presumption in its favour, that would be afforded by his voluntarily remaining in it. The principle of freedom cannot require that he should be free not to be free. *It is not freedom to be allowed to alienate his freedom.*
>
> (299–300; emphasis added)

Now Riley asserts that 'Mill's expressed disapproval of voluntary slavery ... does not imply that he prescribes coercion to prevent it', but only the 'non-coercive measure' of 'refus[ing] to enforce such contracts' (Riley 2016: 757). This affirmation understates Mill's position. Since the context relates to legal allowances for cases where changes take place in the 'will' of the parties to a contract, there is an implicit assumption that the 'voluntary slave' has changed his mind and wishes to be released. This, Mill points out approvingly, he may do since the contract is 'null and void' and will not be enforced either by law or opinion. The focus on a refusal to enforce contracts is easily understood by the context. But in the event that the law forbade release I strongly suspect that Mill would have spelled out explicitly his support for coercive means to prevent such contracts being entered into in the first place. The general logic of his case points directly to this conclusion, but so too do the specific formulations italicized in the main extract above. But the rationale offered in the case of voluntary slavery does, I still believe, imply that Mill would disallow suicide (Hollander 2015: 91, 170–1). For the issue of enforcing contracts is here irrelevant, and coercion can only mean forcible interference in a strictly self-regarding matter. If I am correct, we would find Mill directly at odds with David Hume (see his posthumously-published 'Of Suicide' (Hume 1994 [1777]).

Note

1 See also Rosen on 'the striking similarities between them in the way they conceived security in relation to liberty' (Rosen 1987: 121).

References

Hollander, S. 2015. *John Stuart Mill: Political Economist.* Singapore: World Scientific.
Hume, D. 1994 (1777). 'Of Suicide', *Essays, Moral Political and Literary*, ed. Eugene F. Miller. Indianapolis: Liberty Fund: 577–589.

Mill, J.S. 1969 (1833). 'Remarks on Bentham's Philosophy', *CWJSM* 10: 3–18.
Mill, J.S. 1969 (1852). 'Whewell on Moral Philosophy', *CWJSM* 10: 165–201.
Mill, J.S. 1974 (1843). *A System of Logic Ratiocinative and Inductive. CWJSM* 7–8.
Mill, J.S. 1977 (1859). *On Liberty. CWJSM* 18: 213–310.
Mill, J.S. 1977 (1861). *Considerations on Representative Government. CWJSM* 19: 371–577.
Mill, J.S. 1981 (1873). *Autobiography. CWJSM* 1: 1–290.
Riley, J. 2015. 'Is Mill an Illiberal Utilitarian?' *Ethics* 125: 781–796.
Riley, J. 2016. Review of Hollander 2015. *History of Political Economy* 48(4): 752–758.
Rosen, F. 1987. 'Bentham and Mill on Liberty and Justice', *Lives, Liberties, and the Public Good*, eds. G. Fever and F. Rosen. Basingstoke: Palgrave Macmillan: 121–138.

15 Mill and the 'moral sense': The return to Bentham (and Hutcheson)

15.1 Introduction

Chapter 15 concerns Mill's perception of the role played by the 'moral sense' in ethical evaluation and of its relation to the 'happiness' criterion identified with utilitarian ethics. In my *John Stuart Mill: Political Economist* (Hollander 2015) I described the transition from the 1830s and 1840s to that of the 1850s, as in Mill's 'Whewell on Moral Philosophy' (1852), as a 'Return to Bentham'. In a review of my book Professor Jonathan Riley (Riley 2016) sees eye to eye with me on matters relating to political economy but questions my perception of Mill as 'returning to Bentham's utilitarianism after adopting for a time a non-utilitarian approach in which secondary principles are grounded independently of the principle of utility'; and he denies that Mill ever relied on '"extra-utilitarian standards" to determine an optimal code of justice'. For support he cites the *Autobiography* where Mill maintains that he 'never ceased to be a utilitarian' (Mill 1981 [1873]: 185), and 'never, indeed, wavered in the conviction that happiness is the test of all rules of conduct, and the end of life' (145).

In the present study I confirm my conclusions on the basis of a closer analysis of alternative notions of the 'moral sense' in the Mill texts, and render the case for a 'return to Bentham' with greater precision, taking into account the abandoning in the early 1850s of the objections to Benthamite 'sympathy' which characterize the early years. This elaboration is especially called for since my critic has misunderstood me as maintaining that Mill returned to that version of 'Benthamite utilitarianism' which, based on the assumption that self-interest is 'a predominant motive', allows no more than 'external sanctions such as legal penalties and public opinion to encourage selfish agents to comply with reasonable legal and moral rules', thereby 'making the individual's self-interest accord with the general happiness principle' (Riley 2016: 756). This version Riley (quite rightly) rejects on the grounds that '[r]ational selfishness alone cannot explain why individuals will cooperate to construct a social code of equal rights instead of sacrificing one person's vital interests to promote the good of others...', and it creates the difficulty that one cannot understand what motivates reformers to pursue equal justice (755-6).

My present account differs from the original by demonstrating what until now had escaped me: that there were *two* distinct stages of the 'return to Bentham' each calling for a balance between 'feeling' and 'reason' depending on the circumstances. My argument regarding the duality in question emerges from an examination of Frederick Rosen's fine study, *Mill* (2013). Briefly stated, I find that whereas Mill in the 1830s called for a transition from the eighteenth to the nineteenth century (see Appendix), the latter entailing less reason and more feeling, by the early 1850s he had come to realize that *Bentham himself* had in fact diluted the ratiocinative dimension so that there was no need to escape the eighteenth century. Thus in 'Whewell on Moral Philosophy' (1852) we encounter the notion that *conscience* prioritizes other-regarding sentiment such that the dictates of conscience relate specifically to the intended consequences of actions for 'greatest happiness' rather than any other end. In effect, Mill engages in a reconciliation of utilitarianism with the moral sense.

By implicitly accepting the moral sense when the consequential condition is fulfilled Mill was *unwittingly* adopting the stance of Hutcheson, who specified 'the calm, stable universal good-will to all, or the most extensive benevolence' – benevolence understood as sympathy extended broadly – as 'the disposition ... which is most excellent, and naturally gains the highest moral approbation' (Chapter 4, p. 65). If the proximity of Bentham to Hutcheson – as argued in Chapter 10 – is accepted, then the Mill–Hutcheson linkage should come as no surprise. Hutcheson however serves for us as a stand-in for the other authorities that have appeared in our story – Locke, Shaftesbury, Hume, and Helvetius. Following Bentham, Mill read these 'moral sense' writers as opposed to utility whereas all were *effectively* utilitarians, the moral sense perceived by them as directing agents towards benevolent or other-regarding action in the interest of the general good.

I also draw on Mill's *Utilitarianism* (1861), 'Thornton on Labour and Its Claims' (1869), and the commentaries of 1869 on James Mill's *Analysis of the Phenomena of the Human Mind* and *Fragment on Mackintosh* to confirm the acceptance of the notion of a moral sense subject to its connection with benevolence and the greatest good. It should, however, be noted that the original *desideratum* that greater weight be placed on 'feeling' had in the 1860s been *reversed* to one of more reason and less feeling – implying in effect a plea to *return to the eighteenth century* – since feeling had been carried too far as manifested in Sir William Hamilton's enthusiasm for an 'intuitional metaphysics' which 'characterized the reaction of the nineteenth century against the eighteenth'. This is the second phase of the 'return to Bentham'. The reaction Mill once called for, he now feared, had gone too far.

Section 15.2 traces an evolution in Mill's perspective on the moral sense from his 'Remarks on Bentham's Philosophy' (1833a), 'Sedgwick's *Discourse*' (1835), and 'Bentham' (1838), through to 'Coleridge' (1840). This latter paper expresses a sharp criticism of Bentham regarding his perceptions of 'interest' and the 'general interest'. More generally, Bentham is here charged with falling short of his usual preoccupation with close analysis of concepts.

'Newman's Political Economy' (1851) and 'Whewell on Moral Philosophy' (1852), addressed in Section 15.3, reveal what Mill famously referred to in his *Autobiography* as a 'turn[ing] back from what there had been in excess in my reaction against Benthamism' (1981 [1873]: 236–7). It has been my contention (Hollander 2015: 56–64) that by the early 1850s Mill had 'returned to Bentham' by a new appreciation that Bentham himself had maintained a far broader perspective on utilitarianism than he had once believed, and by allowing in particular for ethical progress with respect to the sentiment of other-regarding *sympathy*. I also maintain that Mill retained his earlier emphasis on *conscience*, but with the crucial difference that what was 'moral' in the dictates of conscience is now said to turn specifically on prospective consequences for 'happiness' (including as always allowance for character formation) rather than some other end. There was, in the final analysis, no inconsistency in maintaining the existence of a moral sense (however it is designated) while adhering to the utilitarian principle.

The following two sections treat *Utilitarianism* (1861) and his *Commentaries* (1869) on James Mill's *Analysis of the Phenomena of the Human Mind* and *Fragment on Mackintosh*. These late contributions confirm his adherence to a moral sense governing ethical approval, taking account of the social significance of the consequences emanating (the 'general good') from the action in question, or more accurately expected to emanate from the action.

Section 15.6 introduces an important interpretation by Frederick Rosen whereby Mill's contrast between the eighteenth and nineteenth centuries essentially entails 'a struggle between a reliance on reason on the one hand and instinct (or feeling) on the other' (Rosen 2013: 22, 233–4). Now, in this context, the 'return' to Bentham is envisaged as entailing a new enthusiasm for 'reason', reflected in particular by the preparation of the *Principles* in the 1840s. It is this alleged indication that I find unconvincing. I argue that in a first stage, dating to the early 1850s, particularly in a study of Whewell, Mill recognised that he had exaggerated Bentham's stress on reason thereby distorting the character of the eighteenth-century doctrine. But Rosen's perspective is relevant to a *second stage* of the return entailing a protest against 'the intuitional metaphysics' characterizing the reaction of the nineteenth century against the eighteenth once applauded. In brief, as the century unfolded, 'feeling' in Mill's estimate had been carried too far at the expense of 'reason', justifying correction.

Section 15.7 underscores an effort at reconciliation between the utilitarian and the moral-sense perspectives apparent in the late 1860s both in a St. Andrews Address and an examination of Hamilton. This demonstration invites a reformulation in terms of a silent rapprochement by Mill towards the position of Hutcheson and other eighteenth-century moral philosophers, including Hume, Helvétius, and Shaftesbury, a reformulation which is undertaken in Section 15.8. A Conclusion draws the threads together by briefly reviewing the Mill–Locke and the Mill–Bentham linkages.

15.2 The 1830s: Mill's moral sense allowances

15.2.1 'Remarks on Bentham's Philosophy' (1833)

I turn first to Mill's affirmation in the 'Remarks on Bentham's Philosophy' (1833) that he found unacceptable Bentham's designation in *Principles of Morals and Legislation* (1789) of appeals to 'the phrases "law of nature", "right reason", "natural rights", "moral sense" ... as mere covers for dogmatism; excuses for setting up one's own *ipse dixit* as a rule to bind other people. "They consist all of them", says he, "in so many contrivances for avoiding the obligation of appealing to any external standard, and for prevailing upon the reader to accept the author's sentiment or opinion as a reason for itself"'. (Mill 1969 [1833a]: 5, with a reference to Bentham 1859 [1843]: 80). Now it may be said that Mill was here merely seeking to assure such contenders 'fair treatment', rather than necessarily himself expressing his own agreement with them – and he certainly complains that 'the greatest of Mr. Bentham's defects [was] his insufficient knowledge and appreciation of the thoughts of other men, [which] shows itself constantly in his grappling with some delusive shadow of his adversary's opinion, and leaving the actual substance unharmed' (6). According to Mill's own understanding of the moral-sense and related literature Bentham rejected, while 'the pursuit of happiness is natural to us', so too is 'the reverence for, and the inclination to square our actions by, certain general laws of morality', the moral sentiments – 'as much a part of the original constitution of man's nature as the desire of happiness and the fear of suffering' – reflecting universally-rooted human instincts rather than the unjustified personal feelings of particular individuals: 'No proof indeed can be given that we ought to abide by these [general] laws; but neither can any proof be given, that we ought to regulate our conduct by utility. All that can be said is, that the pursuit of happiness is natural to us; and so, *it is contended*, is the reverence for, and the inclination to square our actions by, certain general laws of morality' (emphasis added).[1] Nevertheless, I maintain that – notwithstanding 'it is contended' – Mill went further than attempting to fairly present the position of those Bentham opposed.

I note first Mill's more specific complaint against Bentham that he adopted too narrow a perception of the 'greatest-happiness principle' by identifying it in matters of practical ethics with 'specific consequences': '[Bentham] has practically, to a very great extent, confounded the principle of Utility with the principle of specific consequences, and has habitually made up his estimate of the approbation or blame due to a particular kind of action, from a calculation solely of the consequences to which that very action, if practised generally, would itself lead' (Mill 1969 [1833a]: 8). It is not that Mill here turns his back on consequentialism as such but rather that he insists on inclusion of the *effect of an action on character*, a condition that can be satisfied only when attention is properly focused on the *cause* of an action, and specifically on 'the relation of an act to a certain state of mind as its cause, and its connexion through that common cause with large classes and groups of actions apparently very little resembling itself'. In the absence of such an exercise, 'estimation even of the consequences of the very act itself, is rendered imperfect. For it may be affirmed with few exceptions, that any act whatever has a tendency to fix and perpetuate the state or character of mind in which itself has originated. And if that important element in the moral relations of the action be not taken into account by the moralist as a cause, neither will it be taken into account as a consequence'. [2]

The requirement for incorporation of the effects of actions on character, Mill regretted, had been beyond Bentham's competence: 'It is not considered (at least, not habitually considered) whether the act or habit in question, though not in itself necessarily pernicious, may not form part of a *character* essentially pernicious, or at least essentially deficient in some quality eminently conducive to the "greatest happiness". To apply such a standard as this, would indeed require a much deeper insight into the formation of character, and knowledge of the internal workings of human nature, than Mr. Bentham possessed' (Mill 1969 [1833a]: 8). Having said that, Mill withdrew the barb somewhat, though half-heartedly: 'Mr. Bentham is far from having altogether overlooked this side of the subject. Indeed, those most original and instructive, though, I conceive, in their spirit, particularly erroneous chapters, on *motives,* and on *dispositions,* in his first great work, the *Introduction to the Principles of Morals and Legislation,* open up a direct and broad path to these most important topics'. And he stood by his primary reservation: 'It is not less true that Mr. Bentham, and many others, following his example, when they came to discuss particular questions of ethics, have commonly, in the superior stress which they laid on the specific consequences of a class of acts, rejected all contemplation of the action in its general bearings upon the entire moral being of the agent; or have, to say the least, thrown those considerations so far into the background, as to be almost out of sight'.

'Happiness' may mean a variety of things, and 'extra-utilitarian' considerations are, as can be well understand from the foregoing texts, effectively brought into play relative to the narrower definition of general happiness Mill attributed to Bentham. Provided that the 'happiness' category is extended to incorporate the effect of actions on character we might be inclined to accept as accurate the retrospect of the *Autobiography* that Mill had 'never ceased to be an utilitarian', or 'wavered in the conviction that happiness is the test of all rules of conduct, and the end of life' (above, p. 346). But this is only part of the story and much more than a merely formal reconciliation of the facts with the retrospect is entailed. For there is a further complaint that whereas Bentham's 'list of motives' in his *Table of the Springs of Action* (1817) did include *sympathy* – or other-regarding motives – it omitted 'conscience, or the feeling of duty: one would never imagine from reading him that any human being ever did an act *merely because it is right,* or abstained from it merely because it is wrong' (Mill 1969 [1833a]: 13; emphasis added). That Mill subscribes to the notion of a moral sense yielding a verdict of what is right and wrong *independently of consequences of any kind* is confirmed when he describes the feeling in question as one 'which has no ulterior end, the act or forbearance becoming an end in itself' – an 'impulse' not subject to calculation in any strict sense of that term yet which defined 'virtuous' behaviour.

Benthamite 'sympathy' or 'benevolence' did not go far enough for Mill's taste, though he surmised that '[i]n Mr. Bentham's own mind, deeply imbued as it was with the "greatest-happiness principle", this motive' – conscience or feelings of moral obligation – 'was probably so blended with that of sympathy as to be undistinguishable from it' (Mill 1969 [1833a]: 13). 'Feelings of moral obligation', he cautions, are not to be *identified* with sentiments of 'benevolence' or 'sympathy' which underlie the end of 'happiness' for Bentham, who 'should have recollected that those who acknowledge another standard of right and wrong than *happiness*, or who have never reflected on the subject at all, have often very strong feelings of moral obligation; and whether a person's standard be happiness or anything else, his attachment to his standard is not necessarily in proportion to his benevolence. Persons of weak sympathies have often a strong feeling of justice; and others, again, with the feelings of benevolence in considerable strength, have scarcely any consciousness of moral obligation at all'. All this is not to deny outright the Benthamite perspective but to insist that it required major supplementation.

Mill's recognition of an extra-utilitarian ethical index governing the conduct of many in the 'Remarks on Bentham's Philosophy' is unmistakable. But here we face a dilemma. In the 'Death of Jeremy Bentham', from about the same time, Mill opines that while 'the doctrine of utility, as the foundation of virtue, [Bentham] himself professes to have derived from Hume', his 'real merit, in respect to the foundation of morals, consists in his having cleared it more thoroughly than any of his predecessors, from the rubbish of pretended natural law, natural justice, *and the like*, by which men were wont to consecrate as a rule of morality, whatever they felt inclined to approve of without knowing why' (Mill 1986 [1832]: 471; emphasis added). Now 'and the like' constitutes a catch-all encompassing 'whatever they felt inclined to' namely moral-sense feelings, or those 'feelings of moral obligation' the existence of which *he admits to* in the 'Remarks'. I can only suggest that when writing a death-notice of his father's close friend he allowed himself to be carried away, and if pressed would have been obliged to avoid gross self-contradiction by omitting 'and the like' or narrowing it down deliberately to exclude moral-sense notions.

There is a further complexity – that Mill goes on to assert a near identity of 'conscience' with 'social' or other-regarding or sympathetic interests. Thus he protested against 'the predominance of self-regarding interest over social interest' asserted in Bentham's *Book of Fallacies* (1824), on the grounds that '[t]here are, and have been, multitudes, in whom the motive of conscience or moral obligation have been … paramount'; and furthermore that '[t]he balance can be turned in favour of virtuous exertion, only by the interest of *feeling* or by that of *conscience* – those "social interests", the necessary subordination of which to "self-regarding" [Bentham] so lightly assumed' (Mill 1969 [1833a]: 15). Here we have a hint of the ultimate conciliation by Mill regarding the relationship between moral sense and utilitarianism – that conscience dictates approval of those actions which enhance the social interest. Mill himself thereby weakens the complaint that Bentham had allowed for sympathy but not conscience: 'one would never imagine from reading him that any human being ever did an act *merely because it is right*, or abstained from it merely because it is wrong'.

15.2.2 'Sedgwick's Discourse' (1835)

In his *Dissertations and Discussions* (1859) Mill cautioned that his paper on Sedgwick 'might give an impression of more complete adhesion to the philosophy of Locke, Bentham, and the eighteenth century, than is really the case, and of an inadequate sense of its deficiencies' (Mill 1969 [1859]: 494).[3] Unlike the paper of 1833 and those that were to follow in 1838 and 1840, the commentary on Sedgwick certainly presents utilitarianism in a good light, protesting against Sedgwick's simple-minded representation of ethical utilitarianism based on misreadings of Locke and Paley (Mill 1969 [1835]: 65). In particular, utilitarians never denied that 'it is a fact in human nature, that we have moral judgments and moral feelings. We judge certain actions and dispositions to be right, others wrong: this we call approving and disapproving them. We have also feelings of pleasure in the contemplation of the former class of actions and dispositions – feelings of dislike and aversion to the latter...' (50–1). But moral-sense theory maintained:

> that the distinction between right and wrong is an ultimate and inexplicable fact; that we perceive this distinction, as we perceive the distinction of colours, by a peculiar faculty; and that the pleasures and pains, the desires and aversions, consequent upon this perception, are all ultimate facts in our nature; as much so as the pleasures and pains, or the desires and aversions, of which sweet or bitter tastes, pleasing or grating sounds, are the object. This is called the theory of the moral sense – or of moral instincts – or of eternal and immutable morality – or of intuitive principles of morality'.[4]
>
> (51)

By contrast, according to the utilitarian view of morality,

> the ideas of right and wrong, and the feelings which attach themselves to those ideas, are not ultimate facts, but may be explained and accounted for; are not the results of any peculiar law of our nature, but of the same laws on which all our other complex ideas and feelings depend: that the distinction between moral and immoral acts is not a peculiar and inscrutable property in the acts themselves, which we perceive by a sense, as we perceive colours by our sense of sight; but flows from the ordinary properties

of those actions, for the recognition of which we need no other faculty than our intellects and our bodily senses.

(51)

As later neatly expressed: 'the capacity of perceiving moral distinctions [is] no more a distinct faculty than the capacity of trying causes, or of making a speech to a jury' (61).

There is a further detail to consider relating to 'the particular property in actions, which constitutes them moral or immoral, in the opinion of those who hold [the utilitarian] theory' (Mill 1969 [1835]: 51). The property in question is said to be 'the influence of those actions, and of *the dispositions* from which they emanate, upon human happiness' (emphasis added). This formulation of utilitarian doctrine establishes not only good *consequences* of actions but also good 'dispositions' directed to bring them about, namely other-regarding or *sympathetic motivation*. Similarly, to the question of 'what kind of acts and dispositions are the proper objects of those [moral] feelings' – the existence of which is not in any doubt for utilitarians – Mill responded that '[w]hether the ethical creed of a follower of utility will lead him to moral or immoral consequences, *depends on what he thinks useful*; – just as, with a partizan of the opposite doctrine – that of [1859, 1867: innate] conscience – it depends on what he thinks his conscience enjoins' (52; emphasis added).

Mill helpfully elaborates on this. With the exception of outliers such as Mandeville who perceived moral feelings as 'factitious and artificial associations, inculcated by parents and teachers purposely to further certain social ends, and no more congenial to our natural feelings than the contrary associations', '[n]obody ... says that moral feelings "come of mere teaching" ... The idea of the pain of another is naturally painful; the idea of the pleasure of another is naturally pleasurable. From this foundation in our natural constitution, arise all our affections both of love and aversion towards human beings, in so far as they are different from those we might entertain towards more inanimate objects which are pleasant or disagreeable to us. In this, the unselfish part of our nature, lies a foundation, even independently of inculcation from without, for the generation of moral feelings' (Mill 1969 [1835]: 60).[5] In the 1859 and 1867 editions Mill ascribes this position to 'the best teachers of the theory of utility'. Nevertheless, it is clear that the sentiment of sympathy and its intended effects on general welfare, the greater good, or 'happiness' is a 'foundation' only 'for the generation of moral feelings'. This suggests a frequent need to artificially reinforce the sentiment, at least for some individuals, and in fact Mill conceded perhaps more than he realized by admitting at this point that teaching was in reality 'the source of almost all the moral feelings which exist in the world'.

We return in the Conclusion to this chapter to consider the relationship of Mill's stance to the earlier authorities that have preoccupied us.

15.2.3 'Bentham' (1838)

Mill writes in his *Autobiography* that he did not regret the critical tone regarding Bentham which he adopted in the second of his Bentham papers – and in his 'Coleridge' (1840) – now that there was an undue swing back to him justifying notice of his defects (Mill 1981 [1873]: 227). In any event, he had provided appropriate balance in 1835 and 1852, on Sedgwick and on Whewell respectively.

Mill cites the passage in *The Introduction to the Principles of Morals and Legislation* regarding the moral sense, referred to in the first of the papers on Bentham in 1833: 'One man says, he has a thing made on purpose to tell him what is right and what is wrong; and that is called a "moral sense": and then he goes to work at his ease, and says, such a thing is right, and such a thing is wrong – why? "Because my moral sense tells me it is"' (*Works* I: 8; in Mill 1969 [1838]: 85). Now Mill applauds Bentham's reaction: that 'the phrases contain no argument, save what is grounded on the very feelings they are adduced to justify' was 'a truth which Bentham had the eminent merit of first pointing out' (86). But he immediately qualifies the commendation: 'Few, we believe, are now of opinion that these phrases and similar ones have nothing more in them than Bentham saw' [1867: Few will contend that [Bentham's] is a perfectly fair representation of the *animus* of those who employ the various phrases', such as 'moral sense', the 'law of nature', and 'natural justice']. And Mill commends (unnamed) Bentham 'disciples' for recognizing and offering a meaningful treatment of the moral sense: 'They may have followed him in his doctrine of utility, and in his rejection of a moral sense as the test of right and wrong: but while repudiating it as such, they have, with Hartley, acknowledged it as a fact in human nature; they have endeavoured to account for it, to assign its laws: nor are they justly chargeable either with undervaluing this part of our nature, or with any disposition to throw it into the background of their speculations' (1969 [1838]: 97; cited Chapter 6, p. 144).

The case for recognising a moral sense as a 'fact in human nature', to be taken seriously, is accompanied by a detailing of the simple proposition that 'general utility is the foundation of morality' – a proposition Mill regarded as due not to Bentham in particular but as of an ancient pedigree and derived by Bentham from Helvétius (Mill 1969 [1838]: 86). That formulation was too amorphous to be meaningful, so that Utilitarians were obliged in practice to seek supplementary principles to flesh out their theoretical doctrine and specify what precisely to include in any application within the 'general good'. These 'secondary ends' may turn out to be the first principles of their opponents:

> We think utility, or happiness, much too complex and indefinite an end to be sought except through the medium of various secondary ends, concerning which there may be, and often is, agreement among persons who differ in

their ultimate standard, and about which there does in fact prevail a much greater unanimity among thinking persons, than might be supposed from their diametrical divergence on the great questions of moral metaphysics ... Those who adopt utility as a standard can seldom apply it truly except through the secondary principles; those who reject it, generally do no more than erect those secondary principles into first principles.

(110–11)

Evidently it was Mill's wish in 1838 to avoid the impression of an irreconcilable conflict between moral-sense and utilitarian doctrines. Certainly the moral sense as 'the test of right and wrong' is unacceptable, as Bentham had always insisted; but – as Mill elaborates further – it is only those taking the moral sense *as such* as the test appealing to nothing more than 'vague feeling' and 'inexplicable internal conviction', who were beyond the pale, whereas '*the doctrine of rational persons of all schools*' took the matter further by positing some end 'to which morality should be referred':

Whether happiness be or not be the end to which morality should be referred – that it be referred to an *end* of some sort, and not left in the dominion of vague feeling or inexplicable internal conviction, that it be made a matter of reason and calculation, and not merely of sentiment, is essential to the very idea of moral philosophy; is, in fact, what renders argument or discussion on moral questions possible. That the morality of actions depends on the consequences which they tend to produce, is *the doctrine of rational persons of all schools*; that the good or evil of those consequences is measure solely by pleasure or pain, is all the doctrine of the school of utility which is peculiar to it.

(111; emphasis added)

This is a very different stance from that of 1833, when Mill himself allowed appeals to 'vague feeling' and 'inexplicable internal conviction'.

'Rational persons of *all* schools', taken literally, would include even moral-sense adherents provided they focus upon *some end* albeit unrelated to prospective consequences measured in terms of 'pleasure or pain', that is briefly stated in terms of *happiness*. But if Mill had in mind an eighteenth-century authority writing to this effect he does not say, and in fact we shall see that in 1852 he reiterated that '[d]uring the greater part of the eighteenth century, the received opinions in religion and ethics were chiefly attacked, as by Shaftesbury, and even by Hume, on the ground of instinctive *feelings of virtue*, and the theory of a moral taste or sense' (1969 [1852]: 170). Shaftesbury and Hume – there is no mention of Hutcheson – thus would not fit the bill.

It is possible to more precisely narrow down where Mill stood in 1838 regarding the moral sense, for the matter of *ends* appears conspicuously in the complaint that in Bentham's treatment of human motivation in *A Table of the Springs of Action* (1817): 'Man is never recognised ... as a being capable of pursuing *spiritual perfection as an end*; of desiring for its own sake, the conformity of his own character to his standard of excellence, without hope of good or fear of evil from other source than his own *inward consciousness*' (Mill 1969 [1838]: 95, emphasis added).[6] Bentham had in fact failed to recognise the *independent* status of 'conscience', apart that is from the religious motive or 'sympathy':

> Even in the more limited form of Conscience, this great fact in human nature escapes him. Nothing is more curious than the absence of recognition in any of his writings of the existence of conscience, as a thing distinct from philanthropy, from affection for God or man, and from self-interest in this world or in the next. There is a studied abstinence from any of the phrases which, in the mouths of others, import the acknowledgment of such a fact. If we find the words 'Conscience', 'Principle', 'Moral Rectitude', 'Moral Duty', in his *Table of the Springs of Action*, it is among the synonymes of the 'love of reputation'; with an intimation as to the two former phrases, that they are also sometimes synonymous with the *religious* motive, or the motive of *sympathy*. The feeling of moral approbation or disapprobation properly so called, either towards ourselves or our fellow-creatures, he seems unaware of the existence of; and neither the word *self-respect*, nor the idea to which that word is appropriated, occurs even once, so far as our recollection serves us, in his whole writings.
>
> (95)

Bentham's inadequate conception of 'sympathy' is firmly reiterated: 'Man, that most complex being, is a very simple one in his eyes. Even under the head of sympathy, his recognition does not extend to the more complex forms of the feeling – the love of *loving*, the need of a sympathising support, or of objects of admiration and reverence' (96).

The expressions '*conscience, as a thing distinct from philanthropy*', or 'inward consciousness', or 'the feeling of moral approbation ... properly so called', or 'the feeling of an approving or of an accusing conscience', indicate acceptance of the notion of a moral sense evaluating actions in terms of criteria other than consequences for 'happiness', always remembering that some 'end' must be specified or else we are in the realm of the *irrational* – this is in sharp contrast with the 1833 allowance for a 'feeling ... which has no ulterior end, the act or forbearance becoming an end in itself'. A summary affirmation that the 'morality of an action depends on its foreseeable consequences' (Mill 1969 [1838]: 112), may therefore be understood as allowing for consequences *in addition to* 'happiness'.

It is also worth keeping in mind the qualification already insisted on in 1833 and 1835, that 'utility' or 'happiness' must be interpreted broadly to include the consequences of actions for an agent's character, without which allowance a proper guide to 'practical ethics' was impossible:

In so far as Bentham's adoption of the principle of utility induced him to fix his attention upon the consequences of actions as the consideration determining their morality, so far at least he was in the right path [1867: so far he was indisputably in the right path]: though ... there was needed a greater knowledge of the formation of character, and of *the consequences of actions upon the agent's own frame of mind*, than Bentham possessed. His want of power to estimate this class of consequences ... render him, we conceive, a most unsafe guide on questions of practical ethics [1867: greatly limit the value of his speculations on questions of practical ethics].
(Mill 1969 [1838]: 111–12; emphasis added)

Now *sympathy* was 'the only disinterested motive which Bentham recognised' and even he had felt its 'inadequacy ... except in certain limited cases, as a security for virtuous action' (97). For sympathy alone:

will do nothing for the conduct of the individual, beyond prescribing some of the more obvious dictates of worldly prudence, and outward probity and beneficence. There is no need to expatiate on the deficiencies of a system of ethics which does not pretend to aid individuals in *the formation of their own character*; which recognises no such wish as that of self-culture, we may say no such power, as existing in human nature; and if it did recognise, could furnish little assistance to that grand duty of man, because it overlooks the existence of about half of the whole number of mental feelings which human beings are capable of, including all those of which the direct objects are states of their own mind.
(97–8; emphasis added)

All in all, Bentham had by his narrow perspective regarding relevant consequences disallowed an adequate treatment of 'properly ethical inquiry' (98).

I close by noting a more general complaint against Bentham as moralist rather than as utilitarian, said to be held in common with most other moralists, namely that he treated 'the *moral* view of actions and characters, which is unquestionably the first and most important mode of looking at them, as if it were the sole one: whereas it is only one of three', an action entailing a '*moral* aspect, or that of its *right* and *wrong*; [an] *aesthetic* aspect, or that of its *beauty*; [a] *sympathetic* aspect, or that of its *loveableness*' (Mill 1969 [1838]: 112). The moral aspect – more specifically – 'addresses itself to our reason and conscience', the 'morality of an action depend[ing] on its foreseeable consequences' (as we have noted earlier) – is the basis for approval or disapproval of actions and character. Bentham, runs the objection, set aside as meaningless both the *aesthetic* aspect – by which 'we admire and despise' – and the *sympathetic* aspect – by which 'we love, pity, or dislike', writing as if:

the moral standard ought not only be the paramount (which it ought), but to be alone; as if it ought to be the sole master of all our actions, and even of all our sentiments; as if either to admire or like, or despise or dislike a person *for any action which neither does good nor harm* ... were an injustice and a prejudice ... He thought it an insolent piece of dogmatism in one person to praise or condemn another in a matter of taste ... as if a person's tastes did not show him to be wise or a fool, cultivated or ignorant, gentle or rough, sensitive or callous, generous or sordid, benevolent or selfish, conscientious or depraved.

(113; emphasis added).

Apart from the overlapping of the second and third categories, Mill confuses by suggesting that 'sympathy' plays no part in determining the morality of actions whereas we have seen that in his 'Sedgwick' he had proposed that in 'the unselfish part of our nature lies a *foundation, even independently of inculcation from without, for the generation of moral feelings*', and in 'Bentham' itself the possibility is countenanced of a meaningful moral-sense perspective albeit one unrelated to prospective consequences for 'happiness' in any conventional sense of the term. In any event, as we shall now see, the linkage of the moral dimension and sympathy turns out to be essential to the discussion that followed.

15.2.4 'Coleridge' (1840)

To complete the picture of Mill's objections to Bentham, it is worth paying attention to his enthusiasm in 1840 towards Coleridge. Although Coleridge had scarcely broached a 'theory of government', Benthamite theory, Mill believed, could not 'stand a comparison with it as to its first principle' (Mill 1969 [1840]: 153). The concern relates to Bentham's simplistic treatment of 'interest' and 'general interest', specifically his failure to analyse these concepts appropriately. Thus he viewed 'interest' in terms of 'a calculating bystander, judging what would be good for a man during his own life' neglecting 'gratification of his present passions, his pride, his envy, his vanity, his cupidity, his love of pleasure, his love of ease' none of which was properly clarified (153–4).[7]

'General interest' in particular required proper analysis considering its extreme complexity. Mill concludes in markedly conservative terms, countenancing only marginal changes in constitutional arrangement: 'A government must be composed out of the elements already existing in society, and the distribution of power in the constitution cannot vary very much or long from the distribution of it in society itself. But wherever the circumstances of society allow any choice, wherever wisdom and contrivance are at all available, this, we conceive, is the principle of guidance; and whatever anywhere exits is imperfect and a failure, just so far as it recedes from this type' (Mill 1969 [1840]: 154). Coleridge had taken the matter of parliamentary representation further than Bentham by his analysis of 'the interests of society' in terms of 'the two antagonistic interests of Permanence and Progression':

Such a philosophy of government, we need hardly say, is in its infancy: the first step to it, the classification of the exigencies of society, has not been made. Bentham, in his *Principles of Civil Law*, [8] has given a specimen, very useful for many other purposes, but not available, nor intended so, for founding a theory of representation upon it. For that particular purpose we have seen nothing comparable as far as it goes, notwithstanding its manifest insufficiency, to Coleridge's division of the interests of society into the two antagonist interests of Permanence and Progression. The Continental philosophers have, by a different path, arrived at the same division; and this is about as far, probably, as the scheme of political institutions has yet reached.

(154–5)

Leslie Stephen represents the 'Coleridge' paper as the 'apogee' of Mill's hostility towards Bentham (Stephen 1900 2:377). Even so, we encounter the sort of difficulty so often created by Mill's qualifications, as in the present instance he introduces the qualification that although 'every Englishman of the present day is by implication either a Benthamite or a Coleridgian', Bentham nonetheless 'so improved and added to the system of philosophy he adopted, that for his successors he may almost be accounted its founder' (Mill 1969 [1840]: 121). Taken at face value this qualification regarding Bentham *almost* rules out meaningful doctrinal contrasts. Compounding the difficulty is a corresponding qualification regarding Coleridge:

> In the theory of ethics, he contends against the doctrine of general consequences, and holds that, *for man*, 'to obey the simple unconditional commandment of eschewing every act that implies a self-contradiction' – so to act as to 'be able, without involving any contradiction, to will that the maxim of thy conduct should be the law of all intelligent beings, – is the one universal and sufficient principle and guide of morality'. Yet even a utilitarian can have little complaint to make of a philosopher who lays it down that 'the *outward* object of virtue' is 'the greatest producible sum of happiness of all men', and that 'happiness in its proper sense is but the continuity and sum-total of the pleasure which is allotted or happens to a man'.

(159).

15.3 'Whewell on moral philosophy' (1852) and the return to Bentham

Professor Riley mistakenly attributes to me a Benthamism based on the assumption that self-interest is 'a predominant motive' and accordingly allows no more than 'external sanctions' to induce selfish agents to comply with reasonable legal and moral rules (above, p. 347). My argument, to the contrary, in fact turns on Bentham's allowances for the other-regarding motive of sympathy which Mill increasingly came to appreciate and clearly spelled out in his paper 'Whewell on Moral Philosophy'. The allowances to which I refer take account of possibilities for *progress* in the sentiment of sympathy. To avoid further misunderstanding I shall place my case in proper context.

Recall, firstly, Mill's affirmation in 1838 that there 'was needed a greater knowledge of the formation of character, and of *the consequences of actions upon the agent's own frame of mind*, than Bentham possessed. His want of power to estimate this class of consequences ... render him, we conceive, a most unsafe guide on questions of practical ethics' (Mill 1969 [1838]:111–12). Similarly, by omitting the consequences for *character formation* in evaluating the morality of actions, Bentham had disallowed 'properly ethical inquiry'. Here we emphasise the revision to the original 1838 text introduced in 1867 from the observation that by omitting the effects of actions on character Bentham provided a 'most unsafe guide on questions of practical ethics', to a more moderate charge that the restricted range of consequences he recognized 'greatly limit[ed] the value of his speculations'. Mill apparently remained troubled, albeit somewhat less so.

Secondly, recall the remark in 1833 that although Bentham had included *sympathy* – or other-regarding motive – in his 'list of motives' he omitted 'conscience, or the feeling of duty: one would never imagine from reading him that any human being ever did an act *merely because it is right*, or abstained from it merely because it is *wrong*'; or, as in 1838, that Bentham 'but faintly recognises, as a fact of human nature, *the pursuit of any ... ideal end for its own sake*' (above, p. 356, note 6). Again, *sympathy* was 'the only disinterested motive which Bentham recognised [but] felt the inadequacy of, except in certain limited cases, as a security for virtuous action' (357) whereas, Mill protested in 1838, there were other disinterested motives at play apart from sympathy yielding a verdict of what is right and wrong *independently of consequences for 'happiness'*.

As I shall presently explain, 'Whewell on Moral Philosophy' argues in favour of 'happiness' as the point of reference serving as a 'test' of what is ethical in recommendations deriving from conscience, thereby downplaying the *independent* role accorded to conscience and the pursuit of some ideal end for its own sake. (We should however recall that even in the 1830s we already encounter pointers in this direction.) Beyond this feature of the return to Bentham, the change in attitude reflects an altered view of Benthamite sympathy, one which accommodates potential ethical advance. My case for Mill's 'return to Bentham' requires therefore that we have on hand the earlier evidence provided of Bentham's position.

Although the paper on Whewell will be the primary concern in elaborating this case, an aside at the close of the *System of Logic* touching on 'the theory of the foundations of morality' serves particularly well as a preface to this discussion. Here Mill writes that: 'I shall content myself ... with saying, that the doctrine of intuitive moral principles, even if true, would provide only for that portion of the field of conduct which is properly called moral. For the remainder of the practice of life some general principle, or standard, must still be sought; and if that principle be rightly chosen, it will be found, I apprehend, to serve quite as well for the ultimate principle of Morality, as for that of Prudence, Policy, or Taste' (Mill 1974 [1843]: 951). Mill intends to affirm 'the general principle to which all rules of practice ought to conform, and the test by which they should be tried ... that of conduciveness to the happiness of mankind, or rather, of all sentient beings: in other words, that the principle of happiness is the ultimate principle of Teleology'. (The 1865 edition refers readers to *Utilitarianism* to support the foregoing observation. That benevolence, justice, truth, purity could all be derived from utility is indeed central to that work: 'The multiplication of happiness is, according to the utilitarian ethics, the object of virtue' (Mill 1969 [1861]: 220.)

In his correspondence from early 1849 the rejection of the moral sense *tout court* – as an instinctive sense of virtue independently of intended consequences – is reiterated, although with possible exception made for superior characters: 'I am convinced that competent judges who have sufficient experience of children will not ... agree that they have a natural idea of right and duty. I am satisfied that all such ideas in children are the result of inculcation & that were it not for inculcation they would not exist at all except probably in a few persons of pre-eminent genius & feeling' (Mill 1972: 30). At about this time Mill reaffirms his position without mention of an exception: 'How can morality be anything but the chaos it now is, when the ideas of right & wrong, just & unjust, must be wrenched into accordance either with the notions of a tribe of barbarians in a corner of Syria three thousand years ago, or with what is called the order of Providence' (22 November 1850; 53).

While Mill makes no formal mention of Bentham in 'Newman's Political Economy' (1851) he conveys a distinctly Benthamite flavour in a case made out against 'natural rights'. Mill, it must be said, does here allow that since some take 'natural rights' seriously, such 'supposed instincts' must be taken into account as a secondary consideration – secondary to the ultimate utilitarian ethical standard: 'So partial and imperfect are those supposed natural impressions of justice, that almost every disputed moral or social question affords them on both sides ... The question is a very complex one, into which the not offending these supposed instincts about rights, may be allowed to enter as one consideration, but not a principle one, of the many involved' ('Newman's Political Economy'; Mill 1967 [1851]: 443). Nevertheless, the 'ultimate standard' of ethical judgment remained the 'tendency of things to promote or impede human happiness', and it is at this point left unanswered whether Mill recognised a moral sense which perceived ethical merit with an eye to such utilitarian consequences. Thus the 1851 formulation raises the same issue encountered in our analysis of the 1835 contribution: Mill rejected a 'natural' moral sense *divorced from consequential considerations*, leaving open the possible existence of a 'natural' moral sense turning on the sympathy motive and according merit to conduct motivated by an intention to enhance the general good.

This matter arises in 'Whewell on Moral Philosophy' (1852) where Mill takes the *Lectures on the History of Moral Philosophy in England* to task for rejecting writers 'who derive their ethical conclusions, not from internal intuition, but from an external standard ... especially of utility, or tendency to happiness, as the principle or test of morality' (Mill 1969 [1852]: 169).⁹ Here we have it confirmed that Mill's objections were to versions of the moral sense entailing 'the doctrine of *a priori* or self-evident morality, an end in itself, independent of all consequences' (170) *but not necessarily to versions which took account of prospective consequences*. Also confirmed, as noted above (p. 355), is his erroneous attribution to Hume and the eighteenth century – without specific mention of Hutcheson – of the unacceptable version: 'During the greater part of the eighteenth century, the received opinions in religion and ethics were chiefly attacked, as by Shaftesbury, and even by Hume, on the ground of instinctive *feelings of virtue*, and the theory of a moral taste or sense. As a consequence of this, the defenders of established opinions, both lay and clerical, commonly professed utilitarianism' (emphasis added). We must take note of a quiet concession that Whewell and 'all other writers of the intuitive school of morals ... are none of them frankly and consistently intuitive ... [but] draw from a double fountain – utility, and internal conviction; the tendencies of actions, and the feelings with which mankind regard them' (Mill 1969 [1852]: 193–4). (Similarly, in 1833 moral-sense writers are said to have accepted that 'the pursuit of happiness is natural to us', but insisted in addition on 'the reverence for, and the inclination to square our actions by, certain general laws of morality' (Mill 1969 [1833]: 6). Yet this concession, although a step in the right direction, still does not go far enough towards an accurate statement of the utilitarian dimension to the eighteenth-century moral-sense writers, for whom the moral sense dictates conduct governed by utilitarian welfare consequences; for them it was not a matter of 'a double fountain – utility, and internal conviction'.

Most significant for our theme is the fact that in 1852 Mill formally comes to Bentham's defence and confirms a significant change in attitude compared with the often critical tone of the 1830s, maintaining now that a moralist can deduce from utility as a standard 'his whole system of ethics' (Mill 1969 [1852]: 194). I shall focus on three features of the altered perspective.

Firstly, Mill elaborates that feature of the 1835 paper – even hinted at in 1833 – which recognizes a moral sense incorporating *sympathy* or other-regarding motivation in according actions ethical approval. Thus while readily allowing a sense of morality – 'conscience', 'intuition', and 'feelings' – Mill posits that the *ethical status* of actions justified in such terms required that they be *directed towards enhancement of happiness*, that 'the feelings of morality should conform' to the promotion-of-happiness rule: 'We are as much for conscience, duty, rectitude, as Dr. Whewell. The terms, and all the feelings connected with them, are as much a part of the ethics of utility as of that of intuition. The point in dispute is, what acts are the proper objects of those feelings; whether we ought to take the feelings as we find them, as accident or design has made them, or whether the tendency of actions to promote happiness affords a test to which the feelings of morality should conform' (Mill 1969 [1852]: 172).¹⁰ All this illustrates Mill's 'turning back from what there had been in excess in my reaction against Benthamism' (see above, p. 348), for whereas the papers of the 1830s denied a peculiarly Benthamite contribution to ethics (see Hollander 2015: 59). Mill now reads Bentham as having established the utility principle as the *foundation* of so-called 'secondary or middle principles, capable of serving as premises for a body of ethical doctrine not derived from existing opinions, but fitted to be their test' (Mill 1969 [1852]: 173). *The moral sense is effectively allowed to take for granted that it recommends only those actions promising desirable utilitarian consequences.* It is however possible that the non-utilitarian ends emphasized in 1838 were not set aside in 1852 but rather assumed to be absorbed within the end of 'happiness'.

In defending Bentham's position, as he understood it, against Whewell's strictures later in his paper Mill confirms an allowance for a *natural* moral sense which commends actions by reference to their (intended) utilitarian consequences: 'There is no great stretch of hypothesis in supposing that in proportion as mankind *are aware* of the tendencies of actions to produce happiness or misery, they will like and commend the first, abhor and reprobate the second' (Mill 1969 [1852]: 184). 'Awareness' relates to a technical question regarding the tendencies of actions, whereas the mental approval of actions deemed to have desirable consequences is taken for granted as a *natural* phenomenon. Mill is in fact explicit regarding the natural character of the relevant sentiment – effectively that of disinterested sympathy – although he remains noncommittal regarding the moral character of such approval: 'How these feelings of *natural* complacency and *natural* dread and aversion directed towards actions, come to assume the peculiar character of what we term *moral* feelings, is not a question of ethics but of metaphysics, and very fit to be discussed in its proper place. Bentham did not concern himself with it. He left it to other thinkers. It sufficed him that the perceived influence of actions on human happiness is cause enough, both in reason and in fact, for strong feelings of favour to some actions and of hatred towards others' (184–5 emphasis added, 'moral' in original).

Yet for all that, if somewhat inconsistently, Mill does attribute an ethical stance to Bentham:

> Whether the greatest happiness is the principle of morals or not, people do desire their own happiness, and do consequently like the conduct in other people which they think promotes it, and dislike that which visibly endangers it. This is absolutely all that Bentham postulates. Grant this, and you have his popular sanction, and its reaction on the agent's own mind, two influences tending, in proportion to mankind's enlightenment, to keep the conduct of each in the line which promotes the general happiness. *Bentham thinks that there is no other true morality than this,* and that the so-called moral sentiments, whatever their origin or composition, should be trained to act in this direction only.
>
> (185; emphasis added).

At the end of the day, the natural character of the sentiments is not denied but in practice they are not to be relied upon without 'training'. I shall return to this requirement.

This brings us to a second outstanding feature of the revised orientation in 1852, namely the appreciation that *ethical progress* can be accorded to rather than conflicting with Benthamite utilitarianism as Mill had originally feared. I have in mind the defence of the utility principle of morals against Whewell's objections to those 'English writers on moral philosophy ... who derive their ethical conclusions, not from internal intuition, but from an external standard' – that of utility (Mill 1969 [1852]: 169).[11] Mill wrote severely that 'assaults on the only methods of philosophising from which any improvement in ethical opinions can be looked for, ought to be repelled ... When [Whewell] argues in condemnation of any external standard, and especially of utility, or tendency to happiness, as the principle or test of morality, it is material to examine how he gets on without it; how he fares in the attempt to construct a coherent theory of morals on any other basis'. Mill's defence – and it is Bentham that primarily concerns him, with Paley left to Whewell's 'tender mercies' (173) – turns on the affirmation that the utility standard alone allows for progressive morality: 'only methods of philosophising' based on 'utility, or tendency to happiness, as the principle or test of morality', could assure 'any improvement in ethical opinions'. Even stronger, Mill affirms that 'the contest between the morality which appeals to an external standard' – the utility standard – 'and that which grounds itself on internal conviction, is the contest of *progressive morality against stationary* – of reason and argument against the deification of mere opinion and habit' (179 emphasis added).

The charge against adherents of 'internal conviction' reflects his rejection of *simple-minded* moral-sense arguments reflecting wholly unreasoned prejudice. In brief, Mill's acceptance in 1852 of a moral sense incorporating *sympathy* or other-regarding motivation in according ethical approval to actions does not gainsay his conviction that Bentham had rightly rejected versions of the moral sense entailing 'the doctrine of á *priori* or self-evident morality, an end in itself, independent of all consequences' (Mill 1969 [1852]: 170), and accurately represented mere internal conviction, or 'instinctive feelings of virtue', as 'phrases which mean nothing but the fact of the approbation or disapprobation itself' (178). Shortly thereafter he firmly reiterated the charge that the notion of 'instinctive feelings of virtue' positively *hindered* 'the regeneration so urgently required, of man and society', when writing to Theodor Gomperz regarding the intention of the *System of Logic*. That work, Mill explained, 'was chiefly valued by me as a necessary means towards placing metaphysical & moral science on a basis of analysed experience, in opposition to the theory of innate principles, so unfortunately patronized by the philosophers of your country, & which through their influence has become the prevailing philosophy throughout Europe. I consider that school of philosophy as the greatest speculative hindrance to the regeneration so urgently required, of man and society; which can never be effected under the influence of a philosophy which makes opinions their own proof, and feelings their own justification' (19 August 1854; 1972: 239).

A third noteworthy feature of 'Whewell' is a clarification that, for Mill, *intention* matters for ethical evaluation of conduct rather than actual outcomes. He thus defends Bentham's doctrine that 'the increase of pleasure and the prevention of pain [are] the *proper ends* of all moral rules ...', referring to 'the pain or pleasure which an action or a class of actions *tends to produce*, as the criterion of morality' (Mill 1969 [1852]:176; emphasis added). 'Classes of actions', as distinct from individual actions, were in fact more easily accommodated since their tendencies in prospect are (statistically one supposes) more easy to calculate and it is this that matters in the 'establishment of moral rules' rather than 'calculation of the consequences of individual actions' which pertains to 'prudence' rather than morality (180).[12] It is difficult to imagine that Mill intended to renounce all concern with the morality of 'individual actions'; rather, his strategy in responding to Whewell is to focus on the *rules* of morality.[13] In any event, Mill responded quite generally to Whewell's objection that 'we cannot calculate all the consequences of any action, and thus cannot estimate the degree in which it promotes human happiness' by remarking: 'because we cannot foresee everything, is there no such thing as foresight? ... Uncertain or certain, we are able to guide ourselves by [consequences], otherwise human life could not exist'.

Illustrating this altered perception is the insistence that Bentham did not (as Whewell contended) base morality on the 'approbation of neighbours' or 'public opinion', namely 'popular sanction'; and furthermore, that by the 'greatest happiness' principle he intended the 'greatest happiness of mankind, and of all sensitive beings' to include animals – a 'noble anticipation' as Mill described this extension (Mill 1969 [1852]: 186) – and certainly not the self-interest of the agent (184). Accordingly: 'When [Bentham] talks of education, and of "the popular or moral sanction", meaning the opinion of our fellow-creatures, it is not as constituents or tests of virtue, but as *motives* to it; as means of making the self-interest of the individual *accord* with the greatest happiness principle'. Mill's reading is consistent with the Viner interpretation of Bentham whereby individuals are brought to '*spontaneously* associate the happiness of others with their own happiness' (see above, Chapter 9, p. 223). In effect, conduct is subject to progress whereby self-interest becomes, as it were, diluted by sympathy. Certainly, something more is envisaged here than inducements by the moral sanction of public opinion and legal sanction to *direct* self-interested individuals towards conduct appropriate for the general good. Indeed, something more is entailed than making the individual aware (through education) of the potential advantages to himself to be derived from taking into account the interests of others.

I return to the *training* of the 'moral sense' suggested by Mill's references to 'the tendency of actions to promote happiness afford[ing] a test to which the feelings of morality *should conform*' and designating those acts that 'are *the proper objects* of those feelings' (cited above, p. 362). Here again the 'natural' sense cannot, so to say, always – even perhaps usually – be relied on and those with a weak 'sympathetic' sentiment must be encouraged. That the empirical facts are pertinent is confirmed by the further declaration that 'all experience shows that [moral] feelings are eminently artificial, and the product of culture' (Mill 1969 [1852]: 179). This need not be understood as a wholesale abandonment of the notion of a natural sense designating what is ethically proper by reference to the promotion of happiness as the objective of conduct, but rather as an estimate that for most of mankind the moral sense in the raw does not operate effectively.[14] Mill's appreciation of an allowance by Bentham for moral training emerges during an elaboration of his factual *axiom* that 'people do desire their own happiness, and do consequently like the conduct in other people which they think promotes it, and dislike that which visibly endangers it' (Mill 1969 [1852]: 185). This, Mill insists, 'is absolutely all that Bentham postulates', and from it there followed Bentham's 'popular sanction, and its reaction on the agent's own mind, two influences tending, *in proportion to mankind's enlightenment,* to keep the conduct of each in the line which promotes the general happiness' (emphasis added). The point to note is that since the impact of popular sanction on the agent could not be taken for granted but depended on the state of 'enlightenment' there arose the possibility, even the necessity, of encouraging the social motive by *training* the moral sentiments to act appropriately: 'Bentham thinks that there is no other true morality than this, and that *the so-called "moral sentiments", whatever their origin or composition, should be trained to act in this direction only.* And Dr. Whewell's attempt to find anything illogical or incoherent in this theory, only proves that he does not yet understand it' (emphasis added).

When writing retrospectively in the *Autobiography*, Mill maintains that even during the 1830s an allowance had been made for an actual '*alteration of people's opinions*' reflecting an 'educated intellect, enlightening the selfish feelings':

> What we principally thought of, was to alter people's opinions; to make them believe according to evidence, and know what was their real interest, which when they once knew, they would, we thought, be the instrument of opinion, enforce a regard to it upon one another. While fully recognizing the superior excellence of unselfish benevolence and love of justice, we did not expect the regeneration of mankind from any direct action on these sentiments, but from the effect of educated intellect, enlightening the selfish feelings.
> (Mill 1981 [1873]: 113)

Perhaps the description here offered of the early days should not be taken at face value; for it scarcely accords with Mill's harsh accusation in the 1833 account itself that Bentham's perspective on human nature precluded *any* possibility of ethical progress. But even on the retrospective view the selfish feelings remain intact, albeit 'enlightened' through education to appreciate that neglect of the interests of other parties was not in fact in the agent's 'real interest'. An ethical standard of this order does not go as far as that attributed to Bentham in 1852 which extends to the training of the moral sentiments themselves.

15.4 *Utilitarianism* (1861)

We recall an aside in the *System of Logic* which might be seen as an introduction to the paper of 1852 on Whewell: 'the doctrine of intuitive moral principles, even if true, would provide only for that portion of the field of conduct which is properly called moral', Mill intimating that 'some general principle, will be found ... to serve quite as well for the ultimate principle of Morality, as for that of Prudence, Policy, or Taste', namely that 'conduciveness to the happiness of mankind, or rather of all sentient beings' (Mill 1974 [1843]: 951). The 1865 edition of the *Logic* refers readers to *Utilitarianism* in support of the foregoing observation, for it is indeed central to that work that benevolence, justice, truth, purity could all be derived from utility: 'The multiplication of happiness is, according to the utilitarian ethics, the object of virtue' (Mill 1969 [1861]: 220).[15]

For all that, the aforementioned summary rule is not intended as an outright *denial* of a moral sense. We may step back here briefly for perspective and consider a letter of November 1859 which explicitly recognises that there are those who possess 'a feeling of approving & condemning conscience', and that such moral feeling is conceived as traceable not (as James Mill had it) – at least in most cases – to a 'dread of disapprobation', but rather to 'the social nature of man', for 'a state of society is so eminently natural to human beings that anything which is an obviously indispensable condition of social life, easily comes to act upon their minds almost like a physical necessity', while 'that each shall pay regard to the other's happiness' constituted such a condition (Mill 1972: 649–50). In addition, there was 'a human creature's capacity of *fellow-feeling*' – Mill might have said *sympathy*. And on this dual basis 'the feelings of morality properly so called seem to me to be grounded & their main constituent to be the idea of punishment' (650). Mill informs his correspondent that his 'theory of our moral feelings' would be spelled out in his forthcoming *Utilitarianism*. And indeed, in *Utilitarianism* 'sympathy' figures large, designated as an 'instinct' or 'feeling'.

This is clear from Mill's response to the question as to 'whether the feeling, which accompanies the idea [of justice], is attached to it by a special dispensation of nature, or whether it could have grown up, by any known laws, out of the idea itself; and in particular, whether it can have originated in considerations of general expediency' (Mill 1969 [1861]: 248). Mill's response confirms the reality of a moral sense by allowing that the feeling of justice is indeed 'a special dispensation of nature', although specifically one which takes account of the 'general expediency' deriving from the actions under consideration. It is the latter that gives the sentiment of justice its ethical character: 'the sentiment itself does not arise from anything which would commonly, or correctly, be termed an idea of expediency; but ... though the sentiment does not, whatever is moral in it does'.[16] Again, the 'sentiment of justice' – reflected in the 'desire to punish' – 'has nothing moral in it; what is moral is, the exclusive subordination of it to the social sympathies, so as to wait on and obey their call. For the natural feeling [for retaliation] tends to make us resent indiscriminately whatever any one does that is disagreeable to us; but when moralized by the social feeling, it only acts in the directions conformable to the general good: just persons resenting a hurt to society, though not otherwise a hurt to themselves, however painful, unless it be of the kind which society has a common interest with them in the repression of' (Mill 1969 [1861]: 248–9). In brief, 'the sentiment of justice appears to me to be, the animal desire to repel or retaliate a hurt or damage to oneself, or to those with whom one sympathizes, widened so as to include all persons, by the human capacity of enlarged sympathy, and the human conception of intelligent self-interest'.[17]

Mill then appeals to readers to reject accounts of justice based on simple 'introspection' *divorced from utility*: 'If the preceding analysis, or something resembling it, be not the correct account of the notion of justice; if justice be totally independent of utility, and be a standard *per se*, which the mind can recognise by simple introspection of itself; it is hard to understand why that internal oracle is so ambiguous, and why so many things appear either just or unjust, according to the light in which they are regarded' (Mill 1969 [1861]: 251). The importance attached to his representation is also apparent from the closing paragraph of *Utilitarianism*, which asserts that '[i]t has always been evident that all cases of justice are also cases of expediency: the difference is in the peculiar sentiment which attaches to the former, as contradistinguished from the latter' (259). But the sentiment attached to justice was 'sufficiently accounted for', without calling in any special origin, if understood as 'simply the natural feeling of resentment, moralized by being made co-extensive with the demands of social good'. (As we have indicated, Mill treated *sympathy* as an 'instinct'. Accordingly, the term 'moralized' should not be understood as referring to artificial means of instilling sympathetic attitudes.) Mill accorded his solution, which focused on justice, high significance, thereby resolving 'the only real difficulty in the utilitarian theory of morals'.

Mill was evidently sensitive to the objections by Bentham, and indeed by himself over the decades, to raw notions of 'natural justice' and 'natural right' (see Robson 1968: 132). His point here is that one might accept a perception of 'natural justice' and 'natural right' subject to the condition that utilitarian consequences are assumed to be entailed by the action in question, in which case it is utility that assured its ethical character and not the *admitted* 'natural' sentiment. Robson leaves the impression that the solution was arrived at in the early 1860s, whereas our analysis of earlier documents confirm that Mill fairly represented his 'solution' as one he had long held. It is, however, fair to say that the precise formulation – reiterated in the letter to Thornton of 1863 – does help to elucidate his position entailing, in effect, a reconciliation of moral sense and utilitarian conceptions.

15.5 Commentaries on James Mill's *Analysis of the Phenomena of the Human Mind* and *Fragment on Mackintosh*

In his 1869 edition of his father's *Analysis of the Phenomena of the Human Mind* J. S. Mill represents the work as maintaining that 'disinterested love and hatred of actions, generated by the association of praise or blame with them, constitute ... the feelings of moral approbation and disapprobation', contrasting with 'the majority of psychologists' who 'refer to an original and ultimate principle of our nature' (Mill 1989 [1869]: 232). The majority view presumably refers to a source of ethical approval wholly disconnected from consequences, whereas James Mill has it that 'disinterested' moral evaluation derives from 'the association of praise or blame' perhaps implying that in and of itself sympathy is not an in-born component of human nature. Mill himself plays down the issue by referring to a 'correction' of James Mill proposed by Alexander Bain in Notes to the *Analysis*, which, while not positively excluding a 'natural force of sympathy', posits that even if not literally a natural feeling sympathy had the same force as if it were. The gloss proposes that the mere idea of pleasure and pain may be so powerful as to assure that 'care for others is, in an admissible sense, as much an ultimate fact of our nature, as care for ourselves; though one which greatly needs strengthening by the concurrent force of the manifold associations' insisted on by James Mill. Similarly, associations acquired by social connection made it possible 'that the moral sentiments, the feelings of duty, and of moral approbation and disapprobation, may be no original elements of our nature, and may yet be capable of being not only more intense and powerful than any of the elements our of which they may have been formed, but may also, in their maturity, be perfectly disinterested' (220).[18]

This gloss is one to which, Mill opines, his father 'would probably not have objected' and one which he seems to adopt as his own view subject, however, to the observation that Bain's reading 'is rather an account of disinterested Sympathy, than of moral feeling' (Mill 1989 [1869]: 232). Mill, however, proceeds immediately to insist on a tight linkage between sympathy and moral feeling while again playing down the issue of the '*natural*' character of sympathy: 'it is undoubtedly true that the *foundation* of the moral feeling is the adoption of the pleasures and pains of others as our own: whether this takes place by the natural force of sympathy, or by the association which has grown up in our mind between our own good or evil and theirs'. Mill elaborates that for 'this identification of the feelings of others with our own ... [t]o constitute a moral feeling, not only must the good of others have become in itself a pleasure to us, and their suffering a pain, but this pleasure or pain must be associated with our own acts as producing it, and must in this manner have become a motive, prompting us to the one sort of acts, and restraining us from the other sort' (232–3). This he adds 'is, in brief, the author's theory of the Moral Sentiments'.[19]

★★★★★★

His father's *Fragment on Mackintosh* (1835) is also the subject of Mill's commentary. Here the problem raised with respect to the *Analysis* regarding the 'natural' character of sympathy is no longer conspicuous. Indeed, we shall see that James Mill himself represented the other-regarding sentiment of sympathy as an 'active principle' of human nature no less than self-interest, albeit that the associationist requirement so central to the *Analysis* remains at play.

We first note that James Mill committed the same error as his son of disassociating eighteenth-century moral-sense doctrine from utility. This is clear from a passage in his *Fragment*, cited by J.S. Mill, which mentions Hutcheson and Hume as moral-sense adherents and takes Hume to task for inconsistency, presumably alluding to his well-known subscription elsewhere to the utility principle: 'they who ascribe the classification of acts, as moral, and immoral, to a certain taste, an agreeable or disagreeable sentiment which they excite (among whom are included the Scottish professors Hutcheson, and Brown, and David Hume himself, though on his part *with wonderful inconsistency*) – hold the same theory with those who say, that beauty is the source of the classification of moral acts' (James Mill 1835: 264; emphasis added. Cited in Mill 1989 [1869]: 237). That James Mill does not direct the charge of incoherence at Hutcheson may indicate a failure to appreciate that Hutcheson was in fact a utility adherent.

James Mill would have none of this. Representing beauty as a source of what is right was simply 'jargon' – although of course adherents did not see this – for 'what is the beauty of an act, detached from its consequences?' Similarly, classification in terms of 'fitness' meant 'either the goodness of the consequences, or … nothing at all'. 'Moral reason', on the other hand, albeit 'another name', was 'not a bad name, for the principle of utility' (James Mill 1835; 264–5; cited in Mill 1989 [1869]: 237). There was certainly, for James Mill, no such thing as an intuitive moral sense dictating what is right and wrong without reference to utilitarian consequences, but he did countenance a moral sense approving actions perceived to have 'good consequences' the contemplation of which *generates* 'the pleasurable feeling of moral approbation', as emerges from a discussion of the ethics of punishment. He provides an example of an impoverished poacher caught in the act:

> The act of which I have the idea, has two sets of consequences, one set pleasurable, another hurtful. I feel an aversion to produce the hurtful consequences. I feel a desire to produce the pleasurable. The one prevails over the other … Nothing in an act is voluntary but the consequences that are intended. The idea of good consequences intended, is the pleasurable feeling of moral approbation; the idea of bad consequences intended is the painful feeling of moral approbation. The very term voluntary, therefore, applied to an act which produces good or evil consequences, expresses the *antecedence of moral approbation or disapprobation*.
> (James Mill 1835: 377–8; cited in Mill 1989 [1869]: 238; emphasis added)

An 'antecedent' implies a sentiment motivating an act or directing moral evaluation of an observed act; and moral approbation, entailing the pleasure experienced by contemplating the expected desirable consequences of an act, implies the satisfaction of that sentiment. Now the sentiment in question relates to the 'active principles' of human nature including gratitude and generosity, James Mill forcefully denies that personal advantage was the only motive to action (James Mill 1835: 52; cited in Mill 1989 [1869]: 238). In brief, at play is the other-regarding sentiment of *sympathy*, represented as an 'active principle' of human nature no less than self-interest. James Mill explicitly posits that 'an action is stamped moral, or immoral, from the view of its consequences in the mind of the agent' (1835: 392). More elaborately:

> The idea, in the mind of the agent, of good to be obtained from his act, is ... the sole foundation of the favourable feelings we call moral approbation; it may be the idea of good to himself exclusively, if the prospect of evil to others is not conjoined; if the prospect of good to others is conjoined, though the motive be good to self, the act is still more virtuous; it is treated as entitled to the greatest praise, when good to others is the motive, and the prospect of nothing but what is good to them is conjoined.
>
> This is what is meant by those who say that utility is the principle of virtue. It is the expression of a matter of fact. Useful is the name for the cause of good. The actions which cause good to mankind, that is, which are useful, alone receive the appellation of virtuous.
>
> (394)

An associationist dimension nevertheless remains at play for James Mill, but it does not eradicate the notion of sympathy as a natural sentiment. This is seen clearly by Mill's citation of his father's defence of his position against Mackintosh who (as James Mill understood him) maintained that 'to trace up the motive affections of human nature to pain and pleasure, is to make personal advantage the only motive', or as paraphrased by the younger Mill against 'the very vulgar error, that to analyse our disinterested affections and resolve them into associations with the ideas of our own elementary pleasures and pains, is to deny their reality' (James Mill 1835: 51; Mill 1989 [1869]: 238). The point, as expressed by James Mill, is 'that [g]ratitude remains gratitude, resentment remains resentment, generosity in the mind of him who feels them, after analysis, the same as before'. Sympathy, we might say, remains sympathy as one of the 'constituent parts of human nature'.

The *Fragment* also insists against Mackintosh that there is no other 'original power or faculty in man', alluding to instinctive feelings of virtue (e.g., Mill 1835: 8). In his commentary J.S. Mill adopts this position as his own, and may be said to strengthen it against criticism by an application of Occam's razor: 'In the case ... of the moral sentiments, we have, on the one hand, a *vera causa* or set of causes, having a positive tendency to generate a sentiment of love for certain actions, and of aversion for certain others; and on the other hand, those sentiments of love and aversion, actually produced. This coincidence between the sentiments and a power adequate to produce them, goes far towards proving causation. That the sentiments are not obviously like the causes, is no reason for postulating the existence of another cause, in the shape of an original principle of our nature' (Mill 1989 [1869]: 239).

Mill is not, however, uncritical of his father. One issue involves James Mill's 'anticipation' in his *Fragment*, as J.S. Mill expressed it, of the position that some beneficial actions do not excite 'the moral sentiment of approbation' on the part of the observer, which circumstance is accounted for by the hypothesis that where sufficient (spontaneous) motives exist for a useful act to be undertaken supportive approbation is superfluous, or (again in J.S. Mill's terms) that 'we are made to have the feeling [of approbation], by a foresight that our having it will operate *usefully*' – rather than to no effect – 'on the conduct of our fellow-creatures' (Mill 1989 [1869]: 240; emphasis added).[20] Mill rejects this reading of his father, but in so doing reinforces his own support for 'a moral feeling in our minds':

> I cannot accept this explanation. It seems to me to explain everything about the moral feelings, except the feelings themselves. It explains praise and blame, because these may be administered with the express design of influencing conduct. It explains reward and punishment, and every other distinction which we make in our behaviour between what we desire to encourage, and what we are anxious to check. But these things we might do from a deliberate policy, without having any moral feeling in our minds at all. *When there is a moral feeling in our minds, our praise or blame is usually the simple expression of that feeling, rather than an instrument purposely employed to an end ... [N]o anticipation of salutary effects from our feeling will ever avail to give us the feeling itself*: except indeed, what may be said of every other mental feeling – that we may talk ourselves into it; that the habitual use of the modes of speech that are associated with it, has some tendency to call up the feeling in the speaker himself, and a great tendency to engender it in other people.
>
> (Mill 1989 [1869]: 240, emphasis added)

This text, especially the italicised section, it may be said, implies an instinctive feeling of virtue *unrelated to consequences*. But in that case Mill would be compromising his long-standing position to the contrary, established (as we have seen) in the article itself. If inconsistency of this order is ruled out, we are left with the recognition of 'a moral feeling in our minds' which approves only those actions directed towards the enhancement of the general good but without (necessarily) intending to *influence* such conduct. This is the added feature – nothing more is intended.

Mill goes on to amply confirm his acceptance of a moral sense – based on sympathy – as source of approval of those actions which are specifically intended to enhance the greater good. The associationist dimension is, as before, conspicuous compromising the 'natural' character of sympathy. The context entails the methodological requirement that differences in the significance of various categories of prospective beneficial effects must engender corresponding differences in the degree of approval accorded by the moral sense: the 'association theory of the moral sense ... must be required to show a corresponding difference in the antecedents' (Mill 1989 [1869]: 241). Drawing on the chapter in *Utilitarianism* 'On the Connexion between Justice and Utility'– to which we alluded in the preceding section – Mill accords acts entailing 'duties' first place in the ordering of the beneficial effects and relates them to differences in the degree of approval accorded by the moral sense:

> It will probably be admitted that beneficial acts, when done because they are beneficial, excite in us favourable sentiments towards the agent, for which the utility or beneficial tendency of the action is sufficient to account. But it is only some, not all, of these beneficial acts, that we regard as duties; as acts which the agent, or we ourselves if we are the persons concerned, are bound to do. This feeling of duty or obligation ... is a very different state of mind from mere liking for the action and good will to the agent ... I have ... endeavoured to shew what the association is, which exists in the case of what we regard as a duty, but does not exist in the case of what we merely regard as useful, and which gives to the feeling in the former case the strength, the gravity, and pungency, which in the other it has not.
> (Mill 1989 [1869]: 241)

The element in the association that distinguishes the feeling of duty or obligation is, Mill explains, the 'idea of Punishment', which comes into play when there is a threat to the 'vital interest of ourselves or of those we care for, (a category which may include the public, or the whole human race)' (242). 'This strong association of the idea of punishment, and the desire for its infliction, with the idea of the act which has hurt us, is not itself a moral sentiment ... [T]his impulse to self-defence by the retaliatory infliction of pain, only becomes a moral sentiment, when it is united with a conviction that the infliction of punishment in such a case is conformable to the general good, and when the impulse is not allowed to carry us beyond the point at which that conviction ends' (emphasis added). The 1869 contribution thus confirms the adherence to a moral sense governing ethical approval, taking account of the social significance of the consequences emanating (the 'general good') from the action in question, or more accurately expected to emanate from the action.

In his 'Thornton on Labour and its Claims' of the same year Mill reiterated his standard objection to intuitive or *a priori* theories of justice – intuitive theories *unrelated to consequences* – on the grounds that 'conclusions which seem to follow absolutely from an *a priori* theory of justice can be defeated by other deductions from the same premises' (1967 (1869): 654). Thus he recognized the strong popular appeal of a labourer's pay corresponding to 'his wants and his merits' but does not himself subscribe to it: '*If* justice is an affair of intuition – *if* we are guided to it by the immediate and spontaneous perceptions of the moral sense' (651; emphasis added).[21]

15.6 On Professor Rosen's *Mill* and the 'return to Bentham'

As Frederick Rosen expresses the matter in his recent *Mill*, the contrast between the 'eighteenth and nineteenth centuries' (see Appendix for an elaboration) entails 'a struggle between reliance on reason on the one hand and instinct (or feeling) on the other' (or one between the ascription of 'infallibility' to 'reason' and to 'instinct' respectively) (Rosen 2013: 22, 233–4).[22] Notwithstanding some hesitation in his account of the issue Rosen accepts the notion of a 'return to Bentham' after a period when Mill was attracted to 'nineteenth-century', particularly Comtiste, thinking. Thus Mill's 'emphasis on reason' constituted 'a reaffirmation of his return to the Enlightenment views of his father and Bentham', and an attempt 'to reintroduce the negative Enlightenment thought into his mature philosophy' on becoming aware of 'the despotic implications of Comte's position' (22, 112).

Similarly, and with an eye to 'the Germano–Coleridgian doctrine' expressing 'the revolt of the human mind against the philosophy of the eighteenth century' (Mill 1869 [1840] 125; see Appendix below), Mill sought to 'return those who acted, or believed they had acted, on instinct or feeling', to the standards of rationality enshrined in the eighteenth century, and, particularly, in Bentham and James Mill' (Rosen 2013: 234). At the same time, Rosen helpfully enumerates features of Mill's overall position which entail the continuation of the Benthamite tradition (270–1), and he opines that 'the so-called "return" was less a return and more a departure from Comte at the time when Mill made the decisive move in 1844 to write the *Principles*' (271). He nonetheless designates this 'change of focus from Comtean sociology to economics' as 'a return to Benthamism'.

I shall suggest that it is worth carefully distinguishing between two stages in the return to Bentham: first, that which is central to the paper on Whewell in 1852 which may be described as a recommendation for greater emphasis on feeling, and lesser on reason, reflecting an appreciation that this dimension had actually played a significant role in Bentham's *original* statements of doctrine; and secondly, that in the 1860s, in the light of experience, when Mill feared that nineteenth-century intellectual trends had gone too far in weighing feeling so that a rebalancing was in order. In effect, Mill *redefined* what precisely he intended by the 'eighteenth century' according to the ruling intellectual circumstances of the day.

I turn first to the details of Rosen's argument basing myself on Rosen 2013.[23] Rosen supports his case by citing 'The Subjection of Women' (1869), although the passage in question, I notice, is prefaced by a qualification casting doubt upon Mill's commitment to the contrast at that time, at least with regard to the alleged eighteenth-century component: 'It is one of the characteristic prejudices of the reaction of the nineteenth century against the eighteenth, to accord to the unreasoning elements in human nature the infallibility which the eighteenth century is *supposed* to have ascribed to the reasoning elements' (1984 [1869]: 263; emphasis added). Nonetheless, Mill's specific concern in 1869 is not in any doubt, since he continues: 'For the apotheosis of Reason we have substituted that of Instinct; and we call everything instinct which we find in ourselves and for which we cannot trace any rational foundation'. Also noteworthy is the account Mill provides in the *Autobiography* of the threat to political and religious reform posed by the 'intuitionists' against which he had cautioned in *An Examination of Sir William Hamilton's Philosophy* (1865), Hamilton engaging in 'the intuitional metaphysics which characterized the reaction of the nineteenth century against the eighteenth':

> There is ... a natural hostility between [the practical reformer] and a philosophy which discourages the explanation of feelings and moral facts by circumstances and association, and prefers to treat them as ultimate elements of human nature; a philosophy which is addicted to holding up favourite doctrines as intuitive truths, and deems intuition to be the voice of Nature and of God, speaking with an authority higher than that of our reason. In particular, I have long felt that the prevailing tendency to regard all the marked distinctions of human character as innate, and in the main indelible, and to ignore the irresistible proofs, that by far the greater part of those differences, whether between individuals, races, or sexes, are such as not only might but naturally would be produced by differences of circumstances, is one of the chief hindrances to the rational treatment of great social questions and one of the greatest stumbling blocks to human improvement. This tendency has its source in the intuitional metaphysics which characterized the reaction of the nineteenth century against the eighteenth, and it is a tendency agreeable to human indolence, as well as to conservative interests generally, that unless attacked at the very root, it is sure to be carried to even a greater length than is really justified by the more moderate forms of the intuitional philosophy. That philosophy, not always in its moderate forms, had ruled the thought of Europe for the greater part of a century.
>
> (Mill 1981 [1873]: 269–70)

This extract from the *Autobiography* confirms the contrast between reason and feeling, and also underscores the crucially important fact – it had escaped me until now – that whereas Mill in the 1830s called for a transition away from the eighteenth century in order to assure more feeling and less reason, by the 1860s the objective had been reversed to one of more reason and less feeling, in effect a return to the eighteenth century since feeling had been carried too far.[24] This feature proves highly pertinent in deciding whether and in what respects Mill may be said to have 'returned to Bentham' at some time after his reaction against Bentham in the 1830s. To this matter I turn next.

Rosen and I are therefore in general accord regarding a return by Mill to Bentham. But I am unconvinced that the writing of the *Principles* in particular signals such a 'return' since even at the height of his reaction against the eighteenth century, Mill had demonstrated his enthusiastic appreciation of 'ratiocination'. This is apparent from the flow of closely-reasoned technical papers dating from the late 1820s and the fact that several of the *Essays on Some Unsettled Questions of Political Economy* published in 1844 were written over the years 1829–1830. And, it may be added, little changed thereafter in this regard as is clear from the continuous flow of similar contributions throughout the 1850s and 1860s. All this does not gainsay the fact that Mill in the 1830s found *too little* allowance made for 'feeling' by Bentham and James Mill; but as for his subsequent 'return to Bentham', whereas Rosen focuses on a new reliance on 'reason' rather than 'feeling', as I read the evidence what was entailed was rather Mill's realization that there was considerably more to 'instinct' or 'feeling' in the original Benthamite utilitarianism and considerably less harshness than he had once discerned – 'hard' and 'stern' are the terms we encounter in the 1830s. An observation by Rosen regarding the move away from Comte is particularly pertinent here as it explicitly recognises the point I seek to emphasize. Where, Rosen writes, that move 'touched on fundamentals, it is to be found in Mill's insistence on the primacy of the idea of liberty', Mill's account representing 'a crucial "return" from the rigidity and despotism associated with Comtean positivism and the 19th cent. to the ideas of the Enlightenment *adopted by Bentham and embedded in the utilitarian tradition*' (Rosen 2013: 271; emphasis added). We are led, properly in my view, to conclude that the location of unacceptable harshness had been transferred from Bentham to Comte.

For the reasons given above, to envisage the return to Bentham in terms of a new enthusiasm for 'reason' as indicated by the preparation of the *Principles* in the 1840s is not, to my, mind convincing. On the other hand, Rosen's perspective is more relevant to *a second stage* in the return to Bentham implicit in the *Examination of Hamilton*, and surveyed in the *Autobiography*, entailing a protest against 'the intuitional metaphysics which characterized the reaction of the nineteenth century against the eighteenth'. In brief, as the century unfolded, 'feeling' in Mill's estimate had been carried too far at the expense of 'reason', justifying an appeal for 'a return to the eighteenth century' as a corrective. Here we may refer to Mill's Inaugural Address to the University of St. Andrews which weighed training in pure mathematics and 'ratiocinative' (as well as 'inductive') logic heavily as part of a proper 'intellectual education' (Mill 1984 [1867]: 235–7, 238–40). [25]

15.7 Utilitarianism and the moral sense reconciled

I am in accord with Professor Rosen's reading of Mill's general approach to method in social science whereby 'he attempted to identify polarities of thought that defined the transition from the eighteenth to the nineteenth centuries and sought to show how contrary positions could be reconciled to achieve improvements in thought and in practical politics' (Rosen 2013: 10); or again, that: 'Mill's approach to social science reflected his attempts to identify … polarities of thought in Bentham and Coleridge and to show how they might be reconciled and used to advance new thinking in this field' (65). More specifically, I have told the story in terms of a reconciliation between *utilitarianism* and the *moral sense* in the 1852 paper on Whewell in particular, correcting the earlier contrast made between the eighteenth and nineteenth centuries.

Reconciliation is in fact implicit in an essential feature of utilitarian doctrine, namely its basis in value judgment. Recall that the principle of utility itself is said by Bentham to be unsusceptible of direct proof: 'that which is used to prove every thing else, cannot itself be proved: a chain of proofs must have their commencement somewhere' (Chapter 9: p. 217).[26] Mill made the point early on that in practical application differences of basic principle fade away: 'We think utility, or happiness, much too complex and indefinite an end to be sought except through the medium of various secondary ends, concerning which there may be, and often is, agreement among persons who differ in their ultimate standard…' (Mill 1869 [1838]: 110). It would follow from this that the value judgment of a utilitarian might well correspond to positions maintained by 'moral rights' or 'natural law' writers. A striking instance is provided by Mill's own response to a presumptive interpretation of utilitarian doctrine as justifying the sacrifice of one individual to save the lives of several: 'Of course it is true that utilitarians … insist that "the good of the many" is what matters … It is better to save five people than to save the one' (Sunstein 2014: 14). This reading is precisely what Mill disclaimed – and in so doing was expressing a position effectively appealing to a moral sense – in considering 'the case of people required by a powerful enemy under penalty of extermination to surrender some distinguished citizen … Now in such a case as this I think there can be no doubt that the morality of utility requires that the people should fight to the last rather than comply with the demand', and this in part 'because of the special tie between the community & *each* of its members' (to W.T. Thornton, 17 April 1863;1972: 854; emphasis added). Here the quantitative dimension to the 'greatest happiness' formula gives way to the effectively incommensurable value ascribed to *every single individual*, amply confirming what I once proposed merely as a hypothesis (Hollander 2015: xv–xvi).

The 'reconciliation' at hand is in evidence in the Inaugural Address to the University of St. Andrews which recommends that the students draw what is best from the 'different standards of right and wrong which have been taken as the basis of ethics: general utility, natural justice, natural rights, a moral sense, principles of practical reason, and the rest', remarking that 'it is not so much the teacher's business to take a side, and fight stoutly for some one against the rest, as it is to direct them all towards the establishment and preservation of the rules of conduct most advantageous to mankind' (Mill 1984 [1867b]: 248). Throughout something akin to a moral sense is recognised taking into account its connection with benevolence and the greatest good: 'If you take an average human mind while still young, before the objects it has chosen in life have given it a turn in any bad direction, you will generally find it desiring what is good, right, and *for the benefit of all*; and if that season is properly used to implant the knowledge and give the training which shall render rectitude of judgment more habitual than sophistry, a serious barrier will have been erected against the inroads of selfishness and falsehood' (247; emphasis added). Reference is made to moral education as concerned with 'conscience and [the training] of the moral faculty' (251); similarly: 'It is quite possible to cultivate the conscience and the sentiments too. Nothing hinders us from so training a man that he will not, even for a disinterested purpose, violate *the moral law*, and also feeding and encouraging those high feelings, on which we mainly rely for lifting men above low and sordid objects, and giving them a higher conception of what constitutes success in life' (253; emphasis added).[27] The same spirit is apparent in *An Examination of Sir William Hamilton's Philosophy* where, in the course of a case made out to divorce the question of free will from that of 'moral distinctions', the 'nature or criterion' of such distinctions is dismissed as irrelevant:

> It matters not, for this purpose, whether the right and wrong of actions depends on the consequences they tend to produce, or on an inherent quality of the actions themselves. It is indifferent whether we are utilitarians or anti-utilitarians; whether our ethics rest on intuition or on experience. It is sufficient if we believe that there is a difference between right and wrong, and a natural reason for preferring the former; that people in general, unless when they expect personal benefit from a wrong, naturally and usually prefer what they think to be right: whether because we are all dependent for what makes existence tolerable, upon the right conduct of other people, while their wrong conduct is a standing menace to our security, or for some more mystical and transcendental reason.
>
> (Mill 1979 [1865]: 454).

The reality of moral distinctions, and the freedom of our volitions, are questions independent of one another. My position is, that a human being who loves, disinterestedly and consistently, his fellow creatures and whatever tends to their good, who hates with a vigorous hatred what causes them evil, and whose actions correspond in character with these feelings, is naturally, necessarily, and reasonably an object to be loved, admired, sympathized with, and in all ways cherished and encouraged by mankind ...: and this whether the will be free or not, and even independently of any theory of the difference between right and wrong; whether right means productive of happiness, and wrong productive of misery, or right and wrong are intrinsic qualities of the actions themselves, provided only we recognise that there is a difference, and that the difference is highly important. What I maintain is, that this is a sufficient distinction between moral good and evil: sufficient for the ends of society and sufficient for the individual conscience …

(456; paragraph added in third edition of 1867)

We are witness here to an effort at reconciliation between the utilitarian and the moral-sense perspectives, Mill leaving an impression, rather than making the point explicitly, that by a moral sense, or intuition, he intended to refer to the direction of conduct towards the advancement of the general good.

15.8 Mill and Hutcheson

John Stuart Mill shares with Bentham the distinction of making scarcely any mention of Francis Hutcheson. The latter's name is conspicuously absent from a summary statement in 'Whewell on Moral Philosophy' (1852) of eighteenth-century ethical writers.[28] Mill's startlingly restricted perspective on the eighteenth-century literature is apparent in 'Sedgwick's Discourses' (1835) where he challenged Sedgwick to show what rules of conduct were yielded by the 'moral sense' *understood simply as an intuitive capacity to discern what is right and wrong* (1969 [1835]: 64). Here we have an indication that Mill was unaware that Hutcheson – and also Hume, Shaftesbury and Helvetius – had represented the moral sense as specifically commending benevolence or motivation directed at enhancing general happiness, a neglect that cannot be excused by an allowance that '[w]hether the ethical creed of a follower of utility will lead him to moral or immoral consequences, depends on what he thinks useful;– just as, with a partizan of the opposite doctrine – that of innate conscience – it depends on what he thinks his conscience enjoins' (52). It does not help matters because Mill fails to see that what 'conscience enjoins' for the eighteenth-century writers is precisely *the greater good*. Whereas the 1838 contribution leaves the matter open, the erroneous view is explicitly expressed in 1852 when Mill writes that Shaftesbury and Hume opposed 'received opinions in religion and ethics' on the grounds of '*instinctive feelings of virtue*, and the theory of a moral taste or sense'.

In rejecting the moral sense as an instinctive index of what is right and wrong without reference to intended consequences – for only in 1833 is this strong position expressed – and in the acceptance of such a sense where the consequential condition *is* fulfilled – firmly stated in the paper on Whewell in 1852 though intimated earlier, especially in 'Sedgwick' – Mill was unwittingly adopting the stance of Francis Hutcheson who specified 'the calm, stable universal good-will to all, or the most extensive benevolence' – benevolence understood as sympathy extended broadly – as 'the disposition … which is most excellent, and naturally gains the highest moral approbation' (Chapter 4, p. 65). For, in a similar vein, 'Whewell on Moral Philosophy' posits that *conscience* prioritizes other-regarding sentiment such that the dictates of conscience relate specifically to the intended consequences of actions for the 'greatest happiness' rather than any other end. (We must though allow that the 'other ends' of 1838 entailing character formation were now assumed to be incorporated within 'happiness'.) Furthermore, Hutcheson's moral ranking is of the same order conveyed by Mill in his 1869 commentary. Also Hutchesonian is the allowance that the sympathetic sentiment comprising the moral sense might require encouragement by education and culture, which is of course the kingpin of Mill's life's work, the 'Improvement of Mankind'. We are witness to an unfortunate missed opportunity considering Hutcheson's campaign against the puritanical Presbyterian Church and its aggressive propagation from the pulpit of fear of God, a campaign opening the door, even if unintentionally, to a secular perspective toward social policy and doubtless would have pleased Bentham and both Mills had they not misunderstood the 'moral sense' writers as *opposed to* utilitarian consequentialism.

We have also established Mill's contrast between *sympathy* and *moral feeling*, as in 1835 when he represented 'the unselfish part of our nature' as a *'foundation'* for, rather than identifiable with, 'the generation of moral feelings' since a degree of training of the sympathetic component by education and culture is normally required (above, p. 353). And we recall that he accepted an interpretation by Alexander Bain of his father's *Analysis of the Human Mind* subject to the condition that Bain's reading was 'rather an account of disinterested Sympathy, than of moral feeling', although he recognized a strong connection between the two and downplayed the significance of the question of whether or not sympathy is an entirely natural sentiment taking into account the role of 'association' or the multifold bonds characterizing the social union. This orientation too is in line with Hutcheson having in mind his recognition of a need in practice to reinforce the 'natural' or 'instinctive' component of the moral sense, namely the sentiment of disinterested sympathy.

There is a further consideration. Hutcheson had made it clear that the utilitarian case for a morality based on consequences turns strategically on the *intention* ascribed to an agent rather than the actual outcome of the decision taken (Chapter 4, pp. 72-3), whereas Mill is sometimes ambiguous. Nevertheless, his frequent use of the term 'tendency' of actions to have certain effects imply *hoped for* rather than actual outcomes. As soon as we involve *actual* outcomes, we fall into the trap of asserting that moral merit attaches to the agent who has anti-social intentions in cases where the outcome happens to be socially desirable. And this Mill wanted to avoid.[29]

Mill might have missed the extensive common ground by an unquestioning acceptance of the interpretation of Hutcheson by Bentham and James Mill. Recall that he does refer to the latter though without comment (above, p. 370). But even were this the case, it remains difficult to comprehend why he neglected to discuss Hutcheson, even critically, anywhere in his extensive oeuvre. That this neglect reflects objections to Hutcheson's religious status can be ruled out since Mill did not refrain from treating the cleric Malthus with great respect. In any event, notwithstanding his own religious *bonâ fides* and despite the instinctive character of the moral sense that could only have been instilled by the Creator, Hutcheson insisted that 'particular Actions may be innocent, nay virtuous, where there is no actual

Intention of pleasing the Deity influencing the Agent' (Hutcheson 1728: 333). These remarks were directed against the puritanical Presbyterian Church and its aggressive propagation from the pulpit of the fear of God (see Buchan 2003), opening the door, even if unintentionally, to a secular perspective toward social policy, which would doubtless have pleased Bentham and both Mills had they not misunderstood the 'moral sense' writers as denying utilitarian consequentialism.

Our representation of Mill has focused on the shared ground with Hutcheson, albeit unrecognized by Mill himself, regarding a moral sense designating approval of actions governed by sympathy – subject to a qualification regarding the *natural* character of sympathy which Mill himself did not weigh heavily – and designed to enhance general happiness. But there is another component to Mill's thought entailing value judgment not strictly related to the 'happiness' maximand. A conspicuous instance is provided by an extension of the greatest-good criterion in the constitutional context to a national entity including an Irish component to be treated on equal terms with its British counterpart on grounds of self-respect and conscience, extended from the individual to the nation (Hollander 2015: 416; also 398–9).[30]

15.9 Summary and conclusion

The central theme of this chapter has been Mill's transition from reliance in matters relating to *personal* ethics on a moral sense (conscience) approving an action merely 'because it is right', to the proposition that the 'morality of an action depends on its foreseeable consequences' including *non-utilitarian* consequences such as 'spiritual perfection as an end', to a yet firmer conciliation of conscience with utilitarianism although I have been unable to establish with certainty that Mill in the final resort remained committed to incorporate ends such as 'spiritual perfection' within happiness.

The 'happiness' criterion governing ethical approval based on the moral sentiment of *sympathy or benevolence* is clearly discernible in Mill's critique of Sedgwick in 1835; and it is again intimated in 'Newman's Political Economy'; and given precedence in 'Whewell on Moral Philosophy' which prioritizes 'happiness' as the '*test*' of what is ethical in recommendations deriving from conscience. As for the formulation of utilitarian doctrine in 'Sedgwick', if Mill is understood to represent himself there as an adherent rather than a mere expositor – which seems to be the case, despite his admission of a possibly distorting bias in the presentation, considering reissues of the paper, and the ascription in the 1859 and 1867 editions of the position to 'the best teachers of the theory of utility' (above, p. 353) – then he is effectively retracting his approval two years earlier of the notion of a moral sense capable of adjudicating actions as *self-evidently* right or wrong, in favour of an orientation representing *sympathy* or other-regarding sentiment as 'a foundation … for the generation of moral feelings'. Such a view conveys (silently) the position of Hutcheson and also of Shaftesbury, Hume, and Helvétius, all of whom formally adopt the 'moral sense' but, as we have demonstrated in earlier chapters, enfeeble it by reducing it to an approval of sympathetic sentiment generating actions directed towards enhancing general 'happiness'. We must, however, take into account Mill's gloss that 'happiness' should be interpreted broadly to include the effects of actions on *character* (Mill 1969 [1835]: 55–6).

What though of Locke? Recall that Locke's rejection of a moral sense does not distinguish him from Hutcheson *et al* since his conception of what constitutes morality reduces to other-regarding conduct. This parallel holds good notwithstanding the possible need for the promise of worldly or other-worldly reward and punishment to encourage such conduct. In any event, even the rejection of belief in an after-life leaves untouched the Lockean proposition that other-regarding consideration constitutes the essence of ethical conduct; it merely weakens the *motive* for such conduct by placing reliance entirely on the worldly advantages promised thereby.[31]

As for the Mill–Bentham linkage, while at the end of the day it remained a lament that Bentham neglected the consequences of actions for character, Mill now recognized that Benthamite 'sympathy' was potentially open to ethical progress thereby reversing the dismissive, even hostile, view taken in some of his earlier papers. It is true that, as always, Mill found Bentham's estimate of the potential for such progress to be constrained by an unduly narrow reading of human conduct, but it is no less true that he had his own concerns considering the threat to 'the progress of mankind' emanating from an excessively strong tendency of mankind to selfishness. This matter has been further elaborated above, in Chapter 14.

Complexities also arise when we take account of Mill's personification of the nation, and correspondingly its 'conscience', a dimension to be taken seriously considering his great concern – no less than Bentham's – with the 'greatest happiness' principle as the relevant index for legislative purposes and the guidance of moral leaders. I have in mind his perception of Britain as '[o]f all countries which are sufficiently powerful to be capable of being dangerous to their neighbours … perhaps the only one whom mere scruples of conscience would deter from it', and his caution against endangering this moral superiority by actions such as the Suez Canal venture (Mill 1984 [1867a]: 115); or his assertion that 'the kind of advantage which we have had over many countries in point of morals – I am not sure that we are not losing it – has consisted in greater tenderness of conscience' (Mill 1984 [1867b]: 253). There is also a warning that without a solution to the Irish land problem which is acceptable to the tenantry, and should Britain nonetheless 'attempt to hold Ireland by force, it will be at the expense of all the character we possess as lovers and maintainers of free government, or respecters of any rights except our own'; indeed, repression would place Britain 'in a state of open revolt against the universal conscience of Europe and Christendom, and more and more against our own. And we shall in the end be *shamed*, or, if not shamed, coerced, into releasing Ireland from the connexion' (Mill 1982 [1868]: 532; emphasis added). Mill seems in much of this to come close to according *national* 'conscience' a life of its own, although it cannot be excluded that he silently included the effects of actions on the 'character' of the national entity *within* national 'happiness' as was his explicit practise in the case of individuals.

It remains to review Mill's stance on the 'natural' as distinct from the 'acquired' character of sympathy. In 1835 Mill affirmed 'that inculcation by teaching and culture was not the *sine qua non* of moral sentiment, our affections of love and aversion towards our fellows deriving from our 'natural constitution' which incorporates 'sympathy' or a concern for others and their welfare: 'the unselfish part of our nature [in 'sympathy'] lies a foundation, *even independently of inculcation from without*, for the generation of moral feelings' (above, p. 353). Nevertheless, since the natural sentiment of 'sympathy' was only a '*foundation*' for the generation of moral feelings there was a need to reinforce the moral sense artificially at least in some individuals. In fact Mill goes on to observe that teaching is in actuality 'the source of almost all the moral feelings which exist in the world'. Nearly thirty five years later Mill again distinguishes between 'disinterested Sympathy' and 'moral feeling', and – using a similar wording to the earlier statement – yet maintains that 'the *foundation* of the moral feeling is the adoption of the pleasures and pains of others as our own: whether this takes place by the natural force of sympathy, or by the association which has grown up in our mind between our own good or evil and theirs' (above, p. 369). Any doubt regarding the status of 'sympathy' is further mitigated by the insistence that, even if not literally a natural force, 'care for others is, in an admissible sense, as much an ultimate fact of our nature, as care for ourselves'. Recall too from *Utilitarianism* that it is sympathy or other-regarding sentiment, *whatever its origin*, that transforms the animal instinct for punishment into concern for the general good and thereby justifies the ethical designation attached to the sense of justice, a 'solution' resolving for Mill 'the only real difficulty in the utilitarian theory of morals' and also a confirmation in 1869 that even if there were no 'natural force of sympathy' – Mill does not positively exclude the possibility – the feeling of sympathy still had the same strength as if there were (above, p. 369).

In his account of Mill as moralist, John Robson recognized that moral excellence for Mill 'is founded ... on sympathy', but remained troubled by 'the difficulty aris[ing] over the "naturalness" of sympathy' in the light of statements focusing on sympathy as the result of education and circumstance (Robson 1968: 133 and note). I suggest here a simpler resolution of the perceived difficulty. That sympathy is a natural or instinctive feeling though frequently requiring artificial stimulus allows us to accommodate Mill's apparently contradictory statements by understanding them as entailing different evaluations at different times, and in different moods, of the natural and artificial components of the sympathetic sentiment. In any event, Robson himself downplayed the problem on the grounds that Mill's theory 'depends upon results and not upon origins ... [M]orality is connected with motivation *to action*; none of the utilitarians was apt to adopt a sentimental theory which ended in good feeling alone' (emphasis added).[32] I am unconvinced by this argument since while it is true that for the utilitarians 'morality is connected with motivation *to action*', it does not follow that [Mill's] theory 'depends upon results and not upon origins'. I shall explain.

It is true that in *Utilitarianism* Mill defended the doctrine on the grounds that its adherents 'had gone beyond all others in affirming that the motive has nothing to do with the morality of the action, though much with the morality of the agent' (Mill 1969 [1861]: 219; emphasis added). This is rather a superfluous affirmation since the entire ethical debate concerns 'the morality of the agent', or approval or disapproval of *conduct, ex ante* motivation being of the essence. (Hitler's impressive road-building program would scarcely merit *ethical* commendation, socially desirable though it might have been.) Here we step back to recall that Francis Hutcheson was both a moral-sense adherent and a utilitarian, the ethical status of motivation turning for him specifically on other-regarding or sympathetic or disinterested sentiment directed at the enhancement of the general good, the degree of merit turning on the extent of the enhancement '*expected* to proceed from the Action' (Hutcheson 1729: 179–80; emphasis added). Accordingly, should the intention of the agent be 'interested', his action would be morally defective, even when social advantage resulted therefrom (119). This position holds good also for Bentham – wholly unaware of Hutcheson's contribution – who proposed an 'order of pre-eminence among motives' (Bentham 1982 [1789]: 116). The ranking turns on 'the tendency which they appear to have to unite, or disunite an agent's interests and those of other members of the community', with 'good-will' ranked first considering that its 'dictates', or purposes, when taken in a general view, are surest of coinciding with those of the principle of utility; for the dictates of utility itself are perceived to be 'neither more nor less than the dictates of the most extensive and enlightened (that is *well-advised*) benevolence' (116–17). Benevolence means nothing if not proper motivation, and Bentham here posits that motivation is relevant even when the outcome is unsuccessful in terms of the effect on the general good. Bentham is equally clear that though 'antipathy' may be 'the cause of an action which is attended by good effects ... *this does not make it a right ground of action*' (32; emphasis added). James Mill implies as much in expounding 'the foundation of the moral feelings we call moral approbation' which excludes 'the prospect of evil to others' (see above regarding Mill's *Fragment*, 1835: 394). As for J.S. Mill, his frequent reference to 'feelings of morality' indicate that socially-desirable outcomes of actions *improperly* motivated would disallow according ethical credit to the agent.

Appendix: on Mill's eighteenth-nineteenth century contrast

At the time of his emotional reaction in the 1830s against his early upbringing, Mill objected to the 'old style of radical-utilitarianism' designated as *eighteenth-century* utilitarianism, in correspondence, in a series of journal articles and in his capacity as journal editor. He perceived this version to be based on narrow behavioural assumptions and excessive reliance on 'ratiocination' to the neglect of a broad range of human emotions, and correspondingly hostile to 'moral sense' and related 'naturalist' notions that fitted better (Mill then maintained) with the more humanistic perceptions of the early nineteenth century.[33] It is true that he claimed in the *Autobiography* that 'though, at one period of my progress, I for some time undervalued that great century, I never joined in the reaction against it, but kept as firm hold of one side of the truth as I took of the other' (Mill 1981 [1873]: 169). But this a matter of degree insofar as there were those who overstated the contrast, Mill describing 'the reaction against the eighteenth century' as 'the *great characteristic* of the first half of the nineteenth' (213). What his disclaimer tends to play down is the fact that in the 1850s he came to appreciate more clearly than he ever had in the past that Bentham had taken into account in his moral theorizing a range of behavioural traits according particularly high ranking to benevolent sentiment in ethical ranking, thereby in effect recanting the eighteenth–nineteenth century contrast. But we shall also see that this is not the end of the story, Mill fearing in the 1860s that 'feeling', and 'intuition', had been carried too far, the balance now necessitating proper allowance for Benthamite ratiocination. Mill was now calling for a return to the 'eighteenth century' thereby reversing his original stance.

More specifically, what is at stake in the early formulations is conveniently indicated in a description provided in the *Autobiography* of the 1828 and 1829 sessions of the London Debating Society (Mill 1981 [1873]: 133). At that time, 'the Coleridgians, in the persons of Maurice and Sterling, made their appearance ... as a second Liberal and even Radical party, on totally different grounds from Benthamism and vehemently opposed to it, bringing into these discussions the general doctrines and modes of thought of *the European reaction against the philosophy of the eighteenth century*' (emphasis added). As is clear from the 1829 correspondence, that by 'the European reaction' Mill intended in part Auguste Comte's *Système de politique positive* (1824) – written when Comte was a disciple of Saint-Simon (to Gustave d'Eichthal, 8 October 1829; 1963: 35).[34] A further letter to d'Eichthal elaborates that 'the proper mode of philosophizing & discussing for a person who pursues the good of mankind & and not the gratification of his own vanity, should be the exact opposite of the *philosophie critique* of the last century: it should consist, not in attacking men's wrong opinions, but in giving them that knowledge which will enable them to form right ones that will push off the wrong ones...' (7 November 1829; 42).[35]

The *Autobiography* also elaborates on Mill's connection to Sir William Molesworth's *London Review* founded in 1834 (renamed the *London and Westminster* in 1835) to be the representative of the 'philosophical radicals', 'with most of whom I was now at issue on many essential points' – James Mill had been initially the primary contributor – and over which he had little editorial control (Mill 1981 [1873]: 209). Because of his father's presence he was even unable to 'speak out [his] whole mind' in his own 'Sedgwick's *Discourse*' (1835) designed as part of his 'scheme of conciliation between the old and the new "philosophic radicalism"'. Correspondence of the 1830s and 1840s regarding his editorial functions provides brief expressions of hostility towards 'radical utilitarianism' perceived as a typically eighteenth-century phenomenon. A sampling will suffice to convey this perspective.

A letter to Bulwer in 1836 explains Mill's objective in returning after a break to the *London and Westminster Review*, where he expected to have 'through Molesworth's confidence in me, complete power over that review whenever I chuse to exercise it', and assures Bulwer that it will no longer be 'in the old style of radical-utilitarianism' (23 November 1836; Mill 1963: 311). He candidly admitted that the major changes in editorial policy had been made possible by the death of his father who had been the journal's 'most powerful writer, & the only one to whose opinions the editors were obliged to defer' (312). Those opinions reflected superannuated eighteenth-century doctrine: 'As good may be drawn out of evil ... that same event has made it far easier to do that, in the hope of which alone I allowed myself to become connected with the review – namely to soften the *harder* & *sterner* features of its radicalism and utilitarianism, both of which in the form in which they originally appeared in the Westminster, were part of the inheritance of the 18th century'.[36] As for radicalism: 'The Review ought to represent not radicalism but neoradicalism, a radicalism which is not democracy, not a bigoted adherence to any forms of government or to one kind of institutions, & which is only to be called radicalism inasmuch as it does not palter or compromise with evils but cuts at their roots'. As for utilitarianism, it should be:

> a utilitarianism which takes into account the whole of human nature not the ratiocinative faculty only – the utilitarianism which never makes any peculiar figure as such, nor would ever constitute its followers a sect or school – which fraternizes with all who hold the same *axiomata media* (as Bacon has it) whether their first principle is the same or not – & which holds in the highest reverence all which the vulgar notion of utilitarians represents them to despise – which holds Feeling at least as valuable as Thought, & Poetry not only on a par with, but the necessary condition of, any true & comprehensive Philosophy.
>
> (312)

The *Autobiography* refers to Mill's decision in 1840 to end his proprietorship of the *London and Westminster Review*: 'After the last hope of the formation of a Radical party had disappeared, it was time for me to stop the heavy expenditure of time and money which the Review cost me. It had enabled me to express in print, much of my altered mode of thought, and to separate myself in a marked manner from the narrower Benthamism of my earlier writings' (Mill 1981 [1873]: 227). Mill remarks here on his criticisms of Bentham in two articles for the *Review*, 'Bentham' (1838) and 'Coleridge' (1840), admitting that '[i]n both cases, the impetus with which I had detached myself from what was untenable in the doctrines of Bentham and of the eighteenth century, may have carried me, though in appearance rather than in reality, too far on the contrary side. But as far as relates to the article on Coleridge, my defence is, that I was writing for Radicals and Liberals, and it was my business to dwell most on that in writers of a different school, from the knowledge of which they might derive most improvement'.

A version of what Mill intended by the nineteenth century 'reaction' against the eighteenth is spelled out in 'Coleridge' subject to a qualification stipulating that doctrinal oscillations are (as economists would express it) 'damped' rather than 'explosive', that is tend towards an equilibrium: 'Thus every excess in either direction [in doctrine] determines a corresponding reaction; improvement consisting only in this, that the oscillation, each time, departs rather less widely from the centre, and an ever-increasing tendency is manifested to settle finally in it' (Mill 1969 [1840]: 125). The case at hand illustrated what Mill identified grandly as a 'general law of improvement':

> Now the Germano-Coleridgian doctrine is, in our view of the matter, the result of such a reaction.[37] It expresses the revolt of the human mind against the philosophy of the eighteenth century. It is ontological, because that was experimental; conservative, because that was innovative; religious, because so much of that was infidel; concrete and historical, because that was abstract and metaphysical; poetical, because that was matter-of-fact and prosaic. In every respect it flies off in the contrary direction to its predecessor; yet faithful to the general law of improvement last noticed, it is less extreme in its opposition, it denies less of what is true in the doctrine it wars against, than had been the case in any previous philosophic reaction; and in particular, far less than when the philosophy of the eighteenth century triumphed, and so memorably abused its victory, over that which preceded it.
> (Mill 1969 [1840] 125)

This version of the inter-century contrast creates some difficulty. For one thing, 'experimental' scarcely accords with 'abstract and metaphysical' as both characterising the eighteenth century. Moreover, the formulation does not specify what had been conspicuous in the letter to Bulwer of 23 November 1836 cited above, namely that eighteenth-century modes of thought took account only of 'the ratiocinative faculty' rather than 'the whole of human nature'. There is the further difficulty that later in his paper Mill undermines this contrast when he refers to Coleridge, in his capacity as conservative 'philosopher of the reactionary school' examining the institutional prerequisites of a stable society, as opposed to (unnamed) eighteenth-century French or Continental philosophers who put their trust in '*feeling*' even should all institutions be abandoned (1969 [1840]: 131, 138).[38] I return to Mill's journalism and a report to Aléxis de Tocqueville on 11 May 1840 that he had severed connection with the *London & Westminster*, and intended to commence reviewing for the *Edinburgh Review* (1963: 435). That periodical – 'the most perfect representative of the 18th century to be found in our day' and thus 'not the point of view for judging' *de la démocratie en Amerique* – had, not surprisingly, neglected to notice Part I, whereas 'I & some others who are going to write in the Ed. Review now, shall perhaps succeed in infusing some new blood into it'[39] In a similar tone Mill writes to Fox on 23 October 1842 of his forthcoming review of Michelet's *History of France* to appear in the *Edinburgh Review* 'unless Napier takes fright at some of the very heterodox things, in the eyes of an Edinburgh reviewer, still at the point of view of the 18th century, which the article contains' (1963: 602). Indicative of Mill's hostility at this time towards the 'eighteenth-century philosophy' is a slightly unpleasant comment regarding Salvador's *L'Histoire des Institutions de Moïse et du peuple hébreu* (1828): 'I could hardly help laughing at the manner in which he strains everything to recommend poor Moses to the Constitutional Opposition & to shew that the Jews were Liberals, political economists & Utilitarians, and that they had properly speaking no religion, or next to none, & were altogether à la hauteur de l'époque, worthy sons of the 18th century' (to Gustave d'Eichthal, 10 January 1842; 1963: 496).

At this time, in a first letter to Auguste Comte, Mill refers to the *Système de politiques positive* (see above, p. 385) as having been the determining cause behind his 'definitive departure from the Benthamite section of the revolutionary school in which he had been raised' (8 November 1841; 1963: 489). He then however admits that, for all that, he found in Benthamite procedure the best *preparation* available for Comtian 'positive method' as applied to social doctrine, intending primarily by such procedure, apart from its tight logic ('sa logique serréee'), its systematic opposition to all attempts at explaining phenomena of any kind by means of ridiculous metaphysical concepts ('des ridicules entités métaphysiques').

Shortly thereafter, and again to Comte, Mill indicates that one of the 'other causes' that had shaken his original Benthamism was the German philosophy represented by Kant and Hegel, and although his knowledge of these writers was acquired second-hand 'it had corrected what was excessively analytical in my mind, nourished as that had been by Bentham and eighteenth-century French Philosophy' (13 March 1843; 576). (Here Mill seems to reverse himself regarding the eighteenth-century French philosophers who in 'Coleridge' three years earlier he had represented as *excessively reliant* on feeling.) The German philosophy had also contributed 'sa critique de l'école négative' – Mill's standard designation of typical eighteenth-century *criticism* [40] – Hegel in particular having provided 'a real sense, albeit an incomplete one, of historical laws and the filiation of the various states of man and society'.

Mill was convinced that the development of the social sciences hinged upon an improved understanding of 'ethology', or the science of character formation, and shortly thereafter – commenting to Comte on biological studies – expressed regret that 'la réaction du 19me siècle contre la philosophie du 18me' had actually impeded such advance, that it had gone too far in the other direction 'tendant a faire aux diversités primitives une part trop large, et a dissimuler, sous plusiers rapports, leur vrai caractère' (30 October 1843; 605). That the reaction had gone too far, so much stressed in the Whewell paper of 1852, is thus already spelled out informally a decade earlier.

Notes

1 Mill does not mention the eighteenth-century British moral-sense writers here, but asserts, without supporting citation, that his rendition accurately reflected 'the ethical doctrines of the Reid and Stewart school, or of the German metaphysicians'.
2 Paley is also taken to task for the same deficiency: 'The recognition of happiness as the only thing desirable in itself, and of the production of the state of things most favourable to happiness as the only rational end both of morals and policy, by no means necessarily leads to the doctrine of expediency as professed by Paley; the ethical canon which judges of the morality of an act or a class of actions, solely by the probable *consequences* of that particular kind of act, supposing it to be generally practised. This is a very small part indeed of what a more enlarged understanding of the "greatest-happiness principle" would require us to take into account' (Mill 1969 [1833a]: 7).
3 In my earlier account (Hollander 2015: 48) I unduly played down the positive tone towards Bentham taken in 1835 and accordingly express surprise at the 1859 remark. The bias in question, Mill hastened to assure readers, was balanced by 'Bentham' (1838) and 'Coleridge' (1840) which – considered alone – 'would give just as much too strong an impression of the writer's sympathy with the reaction of the nineteenth century against the eighteenth', an exaggeration in turn corrected by 'the more recent defence of the "greatest happiness" ethics against Dr Whewell [1852]'.
4 In a lengthy footnote Mill protested Sedgwick's failure to distinguish between 'innate ideas' understood as 'ideas which exist in the mind antecedently to experience' – a notion long before effectively destroyed by Locke on the grounds that all knowledge depends upon experience – and a 'modern' version (Mill 1969 [1835]: 47n). That version – attributed to Hartley, James Mill, and 'even Hume, or Helvetius' – perceives ideas such as that of 'duty and the moral judgments and feelings' not as existing prior to experience – since 'impressions received from without, must precede the excitement of any ideas in the mind' – but as dependent upon experience only as a '*necessary condition*' for their existence. Mill apparently ascribes to Sedgwick the outdated version of the moral sense. The revised version Mill represents as a 'contention' only.
5 A 'foundation' rather than an identity, since 'affection or sympathy … are quite other feelings than those of morality' (Mill 1969 [1835]: 61), a caution also found in the 1833 critique of Bentham.
6 Mill also complained that in addition to overlooking 'the moral part of man's nature, in the strict sense of the term – the desire of perfection, or *the feeling of an approving or of an accusing conscience*', Bentham 'faintly recognises, as a fact of human nature, *the pursuit of any other ideal end for its own sake*' (emphasis added). He instances honour, personal dignity, beauty, order, power, action, finding that 'none of these powerful constituents of human nature are thought worthy of a place among the "Springs of Action"' (Mill 1969 [1838]: 96). It is not clear however whether these 'ends' are pertinent to the morality of an action.
7 Mill himself later distinguishes between the utility doctrine as such and the self-interest axiom (Mill 1969 [1852]: 170). And as a general rule he perceived Benthamite method as pre-eminently and characteristically analytical down to the last detail.
8 Mill intended *Principles of the Civil Code* (Bentham 1859 [1802]: 297–364).
9 Whewell's objections to Bentham are enumerated in Lecture XV where he insists on moral judgment as a 'universal property of human nature' (Whewell 1852: 223) and on 'an internal condition of morality', as opposed to Bentham's principle that 'we must aim at a certain *external* end; – at happiness…' (228–9). It is curious that Whewell should also have objected to the instinctive character of Hutcheson's Moral Sense as detracting from ethical merit albeit that it is an instinct 'which determines us to approve the actions which flow from the love of others', that is which flow from benevolent sentiment (94). It was essential, he there posits, to 'look to consequences'

(96). Also troublesome is his objection to the term 'Moral Sense' while he reamins receptive to 'a peculiar operation of our inward being' (101).

10 *Utilitarianism* later responds in similar terms in relation to justice.

11 Mill here remarks on a fundamental transition in the status of the utility doctrine commencing late in the eighteenth-century from the by-word of orthodoxy to 'heresy', and this as a consequence of unorthodox conclusions derived therefrom by French philosophers, by Godwin and by Bentham: Utility was now abjured as a deadly heresy, and 'the doctrine of *a priori* or self-evident morality, an end in itself, independent of all consequences, became the orthodox theory', the new orthodoxy based on an 'internal conviction' drawing in part from German metaphysics (Mill 1969 [1852]: 171). 'Dr Whewell … has done no little to impress upon the metaphysics of orthodoxy this change of character'.

12 On *rule* versus *act* utilitarianism, see Harrison 2011: 312–16.

13 The general rule against murder is a case in point. Such rules are subject to exceptions including suspensions 'partially against malefactors in private life … as far as is required by the peculiar nature of the case. That the moralities arising from the special circumstances of the action may be so important as to overrule those arising from the class of acts to which it belongs, perhaps to take it out of the category of virtues into that of crimes, or *vice versa*, is a liability common to all ethical systems' (Mill 1969 [1852]: 182).

14 Regarding Mill's perspective on the development of the social sentiments, see Stephen 1900 3: 314–15. On my reading, Stephen goes too far when he writes that for Mill '[s]ympathy is not an intrinsic part of human nature in its more advanced stages, but something artificial stuck on by indissoluble association'.

15 The theme that the sole criterion governing the morality of an action is utility itself, or the general good, is stated by Bentham himself (see, for example, Bentham 1817: 22).

16 This distinction is repeated in correspondence: 'I never contended that the feeling of justice originates in a consideration of general utility, though I think it is that consideration which gives it its binding, & properly moral, character' (letter to W.T. Thornton, 17 April 1863; 1972: 853–4).

17 Added in 1863: 'From the latter elements, the feeling derives its morality; from the former, its peculiar impressiveness, and energy of self-assertion' (1969 [1861]: 250).

18 On this matter, see Stephen 1900 2: 313. Recall that Hartley had adopted a similar stance with respect to the 'natural' sense of morality. J.S. Mill early on urged Robert Blakey 'to *read* Hartley [on 'association']; or a more recent work, which has done far more for Hartley's theory, than Hartley himself, Mr. Mill's *Analysis of the Human Mind*' (1969 [1833b]: 24).

19 Robson (1968: 133n), however, suggests that the clause beginning 'whether this takes…' is a modification by J.S. Mill.

20 Mill does not cite fully from the *Fragment*, but is apparently alluding to pp. 247–65, especially p. 249 (see Robson 1968: 130–1).

21 I erroneously suggested otherwise in Hollander 2015: 85.

22 Here we must emphasize that our concern throughout is *Mill's* perception in the light of a caution proposed by Jacob Viner: 'The eighteenth century is often termed the "Age of Reason", and it is correctly so termed if by the phrase is meant that it was the age in which philosophers held that the credibility of all things should be tested by reason. But from the point of view of its prevailing psychological doctrines, it could more properly be called the "Age of the Passions" because of its stress on the emotions and the instincts, the affections and the aversions, and its playing down of the role of reason in the behavior of the ordinary man' (Viner 1958 [1949]: 313).

23 For earlier investigations by Rosen of the Bentham–Mill relation, see Rosen 2003, 2011.

24 The generic term 'feeling' might be found misleading insofar as the lament of the 1830s related to inadequate *emotion* (including the poetic) relative to reason

whereas that of the 1860s related to excessive *intuition* relative to reason. But a note to Comte regarding Carlyle makes no such distinction: 'vous apprendrez peut être avec intérêt un rapprochement caractéristique qui a lieu entre vos idées et celles d'un de nos écrivains les plus remarquables ... M. Carlyle, qui bien que doué de facultés plutot esthétiques que scientifiques, et procédent par intuition beaucoup plus que par raisonnement, a souvent des éclairs de génie qui en font en quelque sort [sic] un prophète et précurseur du progrès social' (23 October 1842; 1963: 552).

25 A two-stage pattern is perhaps implied by the fact that the *Autobiography* describes 'the reaction against the eighteenth century' as 'the great characteristic of the first half of the nineteenth century' but also as ruling for 'the greater part of a century' (Mill 1981 [1873]: 213, 270).

26 Ricardo was sensitive to this characteristic subjectivity, and appealed to James Mill for advice regarding the 'difficulty of the doctrine of expediency or utility' which was 'to know how to balance one object of utility against another – there being no standard in nature, it must vary with the tastes, the passions and the habits of mankind' (Ricardo to Mill, 6 January 1818; Ricardo 1952 7: 242).

27 It is unclear what should be made of the ethical writers of the past that Mill cautiously recommended to students: 'There is even now no reading more profitable to students – confining myself to writers in our own language, and notwithstanding that so many of their speculations are already obsolete – than Hobbes and Locke, Reid and Stewart, Hume, Hartley, and Brown: on condition that these great writers are not read passively, as masters to be followed, but actively, as supplying materials and motives to thought' (Mill 1984 [1867b]: 243). Regrettably Mill did not expound further on the merits or defects of several of the authors that have interested us, in particular Hume, Hartley and Brown.

28 Elsewhere Mill lists Hutcheson amongst several treated by Blakey (1833) (Mill 1969 [1833b]: 21), and he cites a passage referring to Hutcheson from James Mill's *Fragment on Mackintosh*, as we shall see. When citing in his 1838 paper (1969 [1838]: 85) the Bentham passage on the moral sense from *Morals and Legislation* (above, p. 354). Mill neglects to mention the informal insertions made in 1819 indicating the culprits Bentham believed *opposed* the utility principle by appealing to a moral sense, including Hutcheson and Hume, although Mill might have known of those insertions since he was citing from the Bowring edition which made them public.

29 James Mill's perspective on morality also turned on the *anticipation* of beneficial consequences. There is a linguistic caution. James Mill insisted (with a credit to Bentham) 'that the morality of an act does not depend upon the motive' but 'on the intention' (Mill, 1835: 161). 'Motive' is here used in the sense of 'volition' such that every motive is necessarily, by definition, 'the desire of good; to the agent himself or to some one else', the action only becoming 'moral' when the agent anticipates 'beneficial consequences' (315–16). I use the term 'motivation' to encompass the intended consequences of actions.

30 This was Coleridge's perspective (Mill 1969 [1840]: 135n). I have implicitly touched on extensions of this order when noting the 'secondary' objectives recognized by Mill to be required by utilitarians when it comes to practice.

31 Locke's position contrasts with that of William Paley, at least if we follow Mill's interpretation: 'Paley not only represents the proposition that we ought to do good and not harm to mankind, as a mere corollary from the proposition that God wills their good, and not their harm – but represents the motive to virtue, and the motive which constitutes it virtue, as consisting solely in the hope of heaven and the fear of hell' (Mill 1969 [1835]: 53–4). That God wills conduct directed at enhancing the general good, thereby furthering happiness, is certainly an element in Lockean ethical doctrine; but his 'theological utilitarianism' had its limits and did not extend

to the second element of Mill's reading of Paley. (For insightful remarks on Paley's extremist stance, see Viner 1972: 73–4.)
32. See also Harrison: 'For a consequentialist ethics like utilitarianism, the important thing is that certain things are done, not why they are done' (Harrison 1983: 274).
33. On this contrast, see Harrison 2011: 306–8.
34. Even so, Mill noted a reservation that though it provided a sound '*partie critique*' of the eighteenth-century philosophy it failed 'to form the foundation of a *science positive*'.
35. Nevertheless, mere 'diffusion of knowledge among the labouring classes & the consequent improvement of their intellects' would not suffice as 'the grand instrument of the regeneration of mankind' (Mill 1963: 40) For Mill commends the objective behind the Saint-Simonian case for a *Pouvoir Spirituel* – while at the same time objecting strongly to anything like an *organized* institution – which was to assure that 'the body of the people, i.e. the uninstructed, shall entertain the same feelings of deference & submission to the authority of the instructed, in morals and politics, as they at present do in the physical sciences', and thus tend 'to protect us from many errors which the philosophers of the 18th century fell into'.
36. A comment in the *Autobiography*, while reiterating the standard location of James Mill in the previous century, is considerably milder than the 1836 letter to Bulwer: 'he was the last of the eighteenth century: he continued its tone of thought and sentiment into the nineteenth (though not unmodified nor unimproved), partaking neither in the good nor in the bad influences of the reaction against the eighteenth century, which was the great characteristic of the first half of the nineteenth' (1981 [1873]: 213).
37. Mill credited 'the great Germans of the latter part of the last century' as anticipating the essentials of Coleridge's doctrines (1969 [1840]: 121).
38. Mill commended Coleridge on Parliamentary reform for recognising both the importance of the landed interest to assure 'permanence'. While he rejected this 'as an universal principle' Mill thought it to be 'true of England' at that time – and of the capitalist class and of intellectuals to assure 'progression', concluding: 'How much better a Parliamentary Reformer, then, 'is Coleridge, than Lord John Russell, or any Whig who stickles for maintaining this unconstitutional omnipotence of the landed interest' (1969 [1840]: 150–3).
39. See Mill 1977 (1840).
40. Of Bentham's 'negativism' in the sense of pulling down and criticising, see 'Bentham' (Mill 1969 (1838): 80–1).

References

Bentham, J. 1817. *A Table of the Springs of Action*. London: Hunter.
Bentham, J. 1824. *The Book of Fallacies: From Unfinished Papers of Jeremy Bentham*. London: John and H.L. Hunt.
Bentham, J. 1838–43(1822). Extracts from Memorandum-Book, *Memoirs of Bentham, The Works of Jeremy Bentham* 10, ed. John Bowring. Edinburgh: William Tait.
Bentham, J. 1838–43(1827). *Rationale of Judicial Evidence*. In *The Works of Jeremy Bentham* 7, ed. John Bowring. Edinburgh: William Tait.
Bentham, J. 1859 (1843). *Essay on the Influence of Time and Place in Matters of Legislation. The Works of Jeremy Bentham* 1, ed. John Bowring. Edinburgh: William Tait: 169–194.
Bentham, J. 1859 (1802). *Principles of the Civil Code. The Works of Jeremy Bentham* 1, ed. John Bowring. Edinburgh: William Tait: 297–364.
Bentham, J. 1982 (1789). *An Introduction to the Principles of Morals and Legislation*. J.H. Burns and H.L.A. Hart eds. London and New York: Methuen.

Buchan, J. 2003. *Crowded with Genius: The Scottish Enlightenment.* New York: Harper Collins.
Harrison, R. 1983. *Bentham,* London: Routledge & Kegan Paul.
Harrison, R. 2011. 'John Stuart Mill, mid-Victorian', *The Cambridge History of Nineteenth-Century Political Thought,* ed. Gareth Stedman Jones and Gregory Claeys. Cambridge: Cambridge University Press: 295–318.
Hartley, D. 1749. *Observations on Man, His Frame, His Duty, and His Expectations.* London: Hitch and Austen.
Hollander, S. 2015. *John Stuart Mill: Political Economist.* Singapore: World Scientific Publishing.
Mill, James. 1835. *A Fragment on Mackintosh.* London: Baldwin and Cradock.
Mill, J.S. 1963. *The Earlier Letters 1812–1848. Collected Works of John Stuart Mill* 12–13. Toronto: University of Toronto Press.
Mill, J.S. 1967 (1851). 'Newman's Political Economy', *CWJSM 5.* Toronto: University of Toronto Press: 439–457.
Mill, J.S. 1967 (1869). 'Thornton on Labour and its Claims', *CWJSM 5*: 631–668.
Mill, J.S. 1969 (1833a). 'Remarks on Bentham's Philosophy', *CWJSM 10*: 3–18.
Mill, J.S. 1969 (1833b). 'Blakey's History of Moral Science', *CWJSM 10*: 19–29.
Mill, J.S. 1969 (1835). 'Sedgwick's Discourse', *CWJSM 10*: 31–74.
Mill, J.S. 1969 (1838). 'Bentham', CWJSM 10: 75–115.
Mill, J.S. 1969 (1840). 'Coleridge', *CWJSM 10*: 117–163.
Mill, J.S. 1969 (1852). 'Whewell on Moral Philosophy', *CWJSM 10*: 165–201.
Mill, J.S. 1969 (1859). Preface. *Dissertations and Discussions: Political, Philosophical and Historical,* CWJSM 10: 493–494.
Mill, J.S. 1969 (1861). 'Utilitarianism', *CWJSM 10*: 203–259.
Mill, J.S. 1972. *The Later Letters 1849–1873. CWJSM 14–17.*
Mill, J.S. 1974 (1843). *A System of Logic Ratiocinative and Inductive. CWJSM* 7–8.
Mill, J.S. 1977 [1840]. 'De Tocqueville on Democracy in America [II]'. *CWJSM 18*: 153–204. Mill, J.S.1977(1859). *On Liberty. CWJSM 18*: 213–310.
Mill, J.S. 1977 (1861). *Considerations on Representative Government. CWJSM 19*: 371–577.
Mill, J.S. 1979 (1865). *An Examination of Sir William Hamilton's Philosophy. CWJSM 9.*
Mill, J.S. 1981 (1873). *Autobiography. CWJSM 1*: 1–290.
Mill, J.S. 1982 (1868). *England and Ireland. CWJSM 6*: 505–532.
Mill, J.S. 1984 (1867a). 'A Few Words on Non-Intervention', *CWJSM 21*:109–124.
Mill, J.S. 1984 (1867b). 'Inaugural Address Delivered at the University of St. Andrews', *CWJSM 21*: 215–257.
Mill, J.S. 1984 (1869). 'The Subjection of Women', *CWJSM 21*: 259–340.
Mill, J.S. 1986 (1832). 'Death of Jeremy Bentham', *CWJSM 23*: 467–473.
Mill, J.S. 1989 (1869). 'James Mill's Analysis of the Phenomena of the Human Mind', *CWJSM 31*: 93–253.
Ricardo, D. 1952. *Letters 1816–1818. Works and Correspondence of David Ricardo,* ed. Piero Sraffa. Cambridge: Cambridge University Press.
Riley, J. 2015. 'Is Mill an Illiberal Utilitarian?' *Ethics* 125: 781–796.
Riley, J. 2016. Review of Hollander 2015. *History of Political Economy* 48(4): 752–758.
Robson, J.M. 1968. *The Improvement of Mankind: The Social and Political Thought of John Stuart Mill.* Toronto: University of Toronto Press.
Rosen, F. 1987. 'Bentham and Mill on Liberty and Justice', *Lives, Liberties and the Public Good,* G. Feaver and F. Rosen, eds. Basingstoke: Palgrave Macmillan: 121–138.

Rosen, F. 1996. New Introduction to *The Collected Works of Jeremy Bentham: An Introduction to the Principles of Morals and Legislation*, edited by J.H. Burns and H.L.A. Hart. Oxford: Clarendon Press, xxxi–lxix.

Rosen, F. 2003. *Classical Utilitarianism from Hume to Mill*. London: Routledge.

Rosen, F. 2011. 'From Jeremy Bentham's Radical Philosophy to J.S. Mill's Philosophic Radicalism', in *The Cambridge History Of Nineteenth-Century Political Thought*, eds., Gareth Stedman Jones and Gregory Claeys. Cambridge: Cambridge University Press: 257–294.

RosenF. 2013. *Mill*. Oxford: Oxford University Press.

Schofield, P. 2015. Editorial Introduction. *The Collected Works of Jeremy Bentham: The Book of Fallacies*. Oxford: Oxford University Press, xix–lxxxv.

Stephen, L. 1900. *The English Utilitarians*. London: Duckworth.

Sunstein, C.R. 2014. 'How Do We Know What's Moral?' *The New York Review of Books*, LXI, 24 April: 14–18.

Viner, J. 1958. *The Long View and the Short: Studies in Economic Theory and Policy*. Glencoe, Ill: The Free Press.

Viner, J. 1972. *The Role of Providence in the Social Order*. Philadelphia: American Philosophical Society.

Index

Agrarian laws 68, 105–9, 125, 127, 182–3 *see also* distributive justice; property
Albee, E 255
altruism *see* motivation (other-regarding)
Alvey, J.E. 156
association 83, 91, 144–7, 353, 369–75, 380, 383

Bain, A. 335, 369, 380
Bacon, C. 64
Bacon, F. 237, 238, 247, 341, 390
Baum, B. 308
Beccaria, C.B. 134, 238, 247
benevolence *see* moral sense; motivation (other-regarding)
Bentham, J. *and* Hartley 147; Helvétius 246–9; Hume 115, 116–18, 119, 120–1, 271, 242–5; Hutcheson 64–7, 89, 111, 238–41; Malthus 255–7, 262, 264–5, 267, 268–9, 271; Shaftesbury 38–9; Smith 245–6; *distributive justice and equality* 216, 228–33; and on individuality and personal liberty 215, 216, 227–8; on justice 219, 231, 234; *motivation*: altruistic 225–6; benevolent and sympathetic 216–21, 221–7, 239–40; interest and 'sinister' interest 221–3, 225–7; selfishness 215, 218, 220, 243, 340; *moral sense*: as arbitrary 20, 26, 216–17, 219, 223–4; as innate index of good and evil 38–9, 64, 73, 89, 223–4, 237, 238, 242–3, 244; as sympathy oriented 4, 92, 240, 242–3, 244; *utilitarian ethics*: 4, 215–16; and common Humean and Benthamite features 216, 242–5; and common Lockean and Benthamite features 26; and consequentialism 67, 218, 224; and ethical progress 223, 225–7; and the 'greatest happiness' principle 221–2, 224, 228, 230, 234, 239, 242, 247; natural rights 4, 234, 238; utility: aggregation 249; quantification; 224, 243
Blanc, L. 308, 317
Bonar, J. 31, 64, 115–16, 117, 120, 152, 157, 168, 182, 189, 255, 256, 277, 279, 299, 302
Bowring, J. 233–4, 246
Brown, J. defends utilitarian standard of virtue 49, 54–5, 61; moral sense as sympathy oriented 55–8; opposes Shaftesbury's alleged idealism 42; and selfishness 55–6, 58; theological utilitarianism 58–60
Burn, R. 195, 205
Burnet, G. 75, 82
Burnet, T. 20, 26

Campbell, T.D. 155–6
Cantillon, R. 200
Carey, D. 4, 11, 26, 32, 43, 44
Chalmers, T. 259–60, 269
Clarke, J. 66, 74, 77, 85, 109
Clarke, S. 11n5, 32, 110–11, 118
Coates, A.W. 128
Coleridge, S.T. 358–9, 377, 390–1
Colquhoun, P. 183, 198, 202
Comte, A. 374, 376, 389, 391–2
Condorcet, M. de 270
consequentialism *see* motivation (other-regarding); utilitarian ethics
Considérant, P.V. 317
Cremaschi, S. 255–72, 274, 277–80
Cudworth, R. 118
Cumberland, R. 77, 87

Deane, P. 195–6, 197–8
De Champs, E. 247

commutative justice 105
distributive justice 68, 70, 105–9, 124–9, 177, 216, 228–33, 258–90, 315–17 *see also* entries for individual authors

Eichthal, G. d' 389, 392
Empson, W. 255
equality 68, 82, 105, 125–7, 127, 216, 228–33, 285–7, 307, 332–4, 336 *see also* distributive justice

Fay, C.R. 176, 178, 180, 234, 299
Forget, E.L. 138
Fourier, F.M.C. 308, 317
Fraser, A.C. 4, 10
Frazer, M. 65

Godwin, W. 260, 264, 270
'greatest happiness' *see* entries for individual authors; *Lectures on Jurisprudence*; population; *Theory of Moral Sentiments*; utilitarian ethics; wealth

Haakonssen, K. 153–4
Hafer, R.W. 323
Halévy, E. 55, 146, 224, 247, 249
Hamilton, W. 347, 348, 375, 376, 378
Hanley, R.P. 155, 175, 177
Harris, I. 25–6
Harris, J. 200
Harrison, R. 222, 231, 233, 238
Hartley, D. ambiguous regarding the moral sense 144–5; on association 144–6; Bentham's commendation 132, 248; Mill's commendation 133, 354; theological features 146–7
Hegel, G.W.F. 392
Helvétius, C.A. and Locke 133–4; and Mill 133–4, 134–9; on the moral sense: as indolent 138, as sympathy oriented 138; on policy 139–41; on selfish interest 136–7, 139–41; and utilitarian ethics 134–6, 138, ethical progress 141–3
Herbert of Cherbury 17–18, 26
Himmelfarb, G. 202, 203
Hobbes, T. 25, 66, 68–9, 75, 89, 122–3
Hollander, S. 74, 156, 160, 168, 174, 176, 191, 206, 216, 256–9, 261, 267–71, 275–9, 296–7, 300, 301, 309–10, 313, 319, 323, 324, 331, 332, 340–4, 348, 363, 377, 381
Hont, I. 177, 203

Horton, W. 301
Hume, D. and Bentham 238, 240, 241–5; Hutcheson 64, 116, 121; Smith 151, 155, 156–9, 163, 245; Locke 4, 116, 122–3; *distributive justice* 124–9; and Agrarian laws 125, 127; and diminishing marginal utility 125; and education 116; and equality 125–7; and wage differentials 116, 125; and sympathy for labour 106n18, 126, 197, 203; on justice 121–2; *moral sense* as sympathy oriented 4, 26, 116–24; *utilitarian ethics* 4, 26, 116–24, 130; and 'fitness' 159, 166–7, 245; and priority of motivation over consequences 61, 156; and 'prudence' 130, 154, 156, 160–1; and self-satisfaction 35n3, 24–5, 61, 245
Huskisson, W. 295
Hutcheson, F. and Bentham 26, 64, 111, 221, 238–41; Burnet 75–6, 82; Hobbes 68, 69; Hume 64, 116, 121; Locke 66, 67, 68, 103–4, 109–11; Malthus 67; Mandeville 77, 79, 120; Mill 347, 348, 379–81; Shaftesbury 87; Smith 68, 105, 107–8, 111, 157, 163, 169, 182–3; commutative justice 105; *distributive justice* 68, 70, 105–9; and Agrarian laws 68, 105–9, 127, 182–3; and equality 68, 82, 105, 127; and excessive accumulation 105, 108–9; and sympathy for labour 106–8; theology 67, 82, 84–5, 90–1, 101–2, 103–4; *moral sense* 65, 66–7, 68, 71, 76, 80, 83–4, 91, 96, 111; and improvement potential 66–7, 91–2, 116, 241; and reason 76, 82, 104; as sympathy oriented 72–4, 78–9, 82–3, 89–90, 91–3, 116; motivation: altruism 66, 72–4, 77, 79, 241, benevolence 72, 73, 80, self-interest 64–6, 70–1, 73, 77–8, 109; *utilitarian ethics* 26, 32, 64–5, 115–16, 120, 152, 157, 182; and 'fitness' 91, 110, 111; and 'greatest happiness' formula 65–6, 72–4, 86, 146; and priority of motivation over consequences 64–5, 72–3, 80, 93, 94, 109, 116
Ignatieff, M. 177, 203
interest *see* motivation (self-regarding)

Jaffro, L. 266
James, P. 255
justice 121–2, 219, 231, 234, 260–71

Kant, I. 152, 392
Kaye, F.B. 31, 48, 50, 51, 53–4, 60–1
King, G. 197–8
Klein, L.E. 32, 57

labour: labour-market analysis *see* Mill, J. S.; *Wealth of Nations*; and working-class welfare *see* distributive justice; *Lectures on Jurisprudence*; Malthus, T.R.; Mill, J. S.; *Wealth of Nations*; utilitarian ethics
Lectures on Jurisprudence: Agrarian laws 127; distributive justice 177; equality 184–7; 'greatest happiness' 174; real wages 200–1; resistance to authority 190; unskilled labour 196; wealth and happiness 155, 182 *see also* Smith, A.
Leslie, T.E.C. 328
Levy, D. 174–5
Lindert, P.H. 195–6, 198
Locke, J. denies innate moral sense 14–22, 26; his hedonistic categories 5–9; and Hutcheson 66–7, 109–11; not strict theological utilitarian 4, 10–14; 'Of Faith and Reason' 3, 22–5; on property ownership 186n5, 188; his utilitarian ethics 4, 11, 22, 26; and altruism 12; and priority of motivation over consequences 11
Long, D.G. 238, 244, 247

Mackintosh, J. 347, 348, 368, 369, 371
Macpherson, C.B. 4
Macfie, A.L. 152, 153, 163
McCloskey, D.N. 154–5
McCulloch, J.R. 310, 330
Maine, H. 243
Malebranche, N. de 118
Malthus, T.R. and Bentham 255–7, 262, 264–5, 267, 268–9, 271; Mill 266, 274–5; Paley 260–2, 264, 267, 287, 299; *class distribution* and aggregate demand 284, 287, 291–4; *distributive justice*: enhanced equality via population control and labour transfer into middle classes 285–7; and 'fairness' 289–90; his policy proposals: the franchise 285; international trade 289–90, 294–7, 300; poor relief 284, 297–301; land ownership (primogeniture) 288, 290, 292; state-funded education 284, 285–6, 300, 384; state-funded emigration 301; population control: moral restraint 261, 264, 265–6, 267–8, 270, 288, 290, 292; prudential restraint 266–70; *theological utilitarianism* 258–60; and 'natural theology' 260–5, 268, 271, 277–8; *utilitarian ethics* 255–8, 266, 270–2, 273–7, 279–80; and benevolence 268; and consequentialism 260–5, 271–2, 275; and happiness and wealth 258, 272; and justice and expediency 260, 27; and labour's quantitative significance for 'greatest happiness' 284–9, 301–2
Mandeville, B. and Helvétius 141; Hume 120; Hutcheson 77, 79–80; Mill 353; Shaftesbury 47–8, 51–3, 61, 79–80; Smith 60–1; his rigourist perception of virtue qualified 5, 48–9, 51–2, 52–3, 60–2; his utilitarian ethics: consistent with Shaftesbury 51–3, 61, 79–80; and priority of motivation over consequences 51, 61; vindicates his '*Fable of the Bees*' 50, 54, 77, 141, 141n5
Marx, K. 125, 178, 180, 207, 267, 332–3
Massie, J. 198
Mautner, T. 11, 86, 89
Michelet, J. 391
Mill, J. 116–18, 216, 221–2, 226–7, 243, 256, 273, 347, 348, 351, 367, 368–74, 376, 380, 384, 385
Mill, J.S. and Bentham: early objections 274, 349–52, and return to 274–5, 346–7, 359–66, 374–6; and Brown 54–5, 56; Hartley 144–6; Helvétius 132, 133–4; Hume 132, 133; Hutcheson 347, 379–81, 384; Shaftesbury 54–5, 56, 61; *distributive justice*: his 'Chapters on Socialism' 316–17; and cooperation 315; and competition 315–16; and equality 307, 332–4, 336; and government support for education 319–20, and labour's quantitative significance 308, 309; and land reform 329–32, 334–5; and limits to land reform 308, 335–6; and the marginalist principle 309, 311; and population control 310–11, 313; and private property 308, 314–16, 333–4, 334–6; and public-finance reform 324–9, 335–6; and the stationary state 307, 310–12, 312–14; and trade unionism 308, 322–4; and the wage structure 178, 206–7, 308, 318–20, 320–1, 321–2; *moral sense*: 274, 349–58, 358–9, 359–66, 368, 381; and sympathy 359–63, 364–5, 368–71;

utilitarian ethics: and consequentialism 347–51, 353, 355–9, 360–2, 363–5, 368, 371, 379–84; and eighteenth-nineteenth century contrast 347, 348, 352, 362, 374–6, 384–8; and ethical progress 340–2, 364, 365–6, 380; on 'greatest happiness' and 'secondary' and 'middle' principles 176, 180; and 'inviolability' of self-regarding action 215, 227, 340, 342–4; and the nation 382; and natural rights 176, 180, 368; and priority of motivation over consequences 349, 364–5, 380, 383–4; and relation to moral sense 346–7, 351, 355, 368, 376–9 *see also* Mill, J.
Mingay, G.E. 183–4
Molesworth, W. 389
Montes, L. 152, 158
Montesquieu, C. de 238
Moore, J. 64
moral sense: as innate perception of right and wrong 5, 32–3, 38–9, 73, 89, 274, 348, 354, 364, 369, 381; as sympathy oriented 26, 31–2, 40, 44, 55, 64, 65, 66, 74–5, 76, 90, 101, 115, 117–21, 132, 138, 145, 151–2, 156–9, 162; *see also* motivation (other-regarding); utilitarian ethics
motivation (other-regarding) 32–8, 41; altruism 48, 49, 52, 65, 66, 225; benevolence and sympathy distinguished 65, 72, 78; and consequentialism 45, 51, 61, 64–5, 115, 120, 120–1, 123, 135–6, 156–9, 347–51, 353, 355–9, 360–2, 363–5, 368, 371, 379–84; and religion 3, 4, 18, 22–5, 40–2, 50, 59–60, 76, 85, 122–3, 143, 164, 218–19, 238–40, 265–6, 278, 355, 362, 379
motivation (self-regarding) 3–5, 11, 12, 35, 35n3, 53, 61, 66–7, 76–8, 79–80, 81–2, 86–9, 97, 98–100, 103–4, 109, 156–9; and selfishness 55–6, 58, 136–7, 139–41, 215, 218, 220, 243, 340
Mousourakis, G. 64
Muller, J.Z. 154, 156

natural rights 107, 176, 178, 180, 180–1, 206, 234, 238, 349, 361, 377
Newman, F.W. 315, 334, 348, 361, 381
Newton, J. 238, 247

Owen, R. 298

Paley W. 134, 238, 260–2, 264, 267, 287, 293, 299, 352, 364
Pascal, B. 4, 9, 25
Perkin, H. 183, 198, 202
Persky, J. 64, 169, 175, 178, 204, 206, 218, 239–40, 333
Petersen, W. 256
Plamenatz, J. 255–6
population: control *see* Malthus, T.R.; Mill, J.S.; and happiness *see* distributive justice; *Theory of Moral Sentiments*; utilitarian ethics; *Wealth of Nations*
Posner, R.A. 155
Priestley, J. 134, 146–7, 247–8
property *see* Agrarian laws; entries for individual authors; *Wealth of Nations*
Pufendorf, S. von 11, 68, 87

Rand, B. 44
Raphael, D.D. 153–4, 163, 165
Rashid, S. 256
Rasmussen, D.C. 175
Raynor, D.R. 155
Rawls, J. 155, 175
Ricardo, D. 74, 175, 255–6, 258, 260, 272, 273–7, 280, 291, 292, 295, 309, 328
Riley, J. 216, 227, 340, 342–4, 347, 359
religion *see* entries for individual authors; motivation (other-regarding); theological utilitarianism
Robbins, L.C. 124, 130, 152, 166, 176, 177–8, 180, 182, 189, 217, 224, 242, 243, 255–7, 265, 271
Robson, J.M. 215, 309, 368, 383
Rochefoucault, de La 137
Rosen, F. 65, 116, 156, 165, 227, 245, 347, 348, 374–6, 376–7
Rule, J. 202
rule versus act utilitarianism 365n12
Ryan, A. 25

Saint-Simon, L. de R. 308, 389
Salvador, J. 391
Schliesser, E. 177
Schneewind, J.B. 156
Schofield, J. 227
Schumpeter, J.A. 134–5, 137, 224
Scott, W.R. 175, 186, 189, 194, 199, 202
Sedgwick, A. 144, 347, 352, 354, 358, 379, 381, 389
selfishness *see* motivation (self-regarding)
Senior, N.W. 296, 301

Shaftesbury, Lord (A.A. Cooper) on *moral sense*: as sympathy directed 31–2, 39–44, weaknesses 42, 44; *motivation*: predominance of natural affection 35, 41; *utilitarian ethics*: consistent with Mandeville 51–3, 61, 79–80; and priority of motivation over consequences 45; public good as main end of virtue 32–8; on reason as harmonizing private advantage and public good 31, 40; unwittingly Lockean 31–2, 35, 44–5; and theological utilitarianism 43

Smith, A.: and Bentham 245–6; Hume 151, 155, 156–9, 159–63, 245; Hutcheson 62, 68, 105, 107, 157, 163, 169, 182; Mandeville 60; Shaftesbury 32–3, 37, 245 *see also Lectures on Jurisprudence; Theory of Moral Sentiments; Wealth of Nations*

Stark, W. 230–1
Stephen, L. 4–5, 64, 90, 97, 116, 122, 246, 255, 256, 263–5, 359
Stigler, G.J. 177, 307–8, 310, 311, 312, 314, 333, 336
Strasser, M.P. 64
Sunstein, C.R. 377
sympathy *see* moral sense; motivation (other-regarding)

Taylor, H. 342
theological utilitarianism: and Helvétius 133, 143, 144; Hutcheson 67, 109; Locke 3, 4, 13, 67, 109, 133, 143, 144; Malthus 258–60, 260–5; Shaftesbury 43

Theory of Moral Sentiments: moral sense as sympathy oriented 151–2, 156–9, 162, 164, 169; *utilitarian ethics* 151, 152–6, 156–9; and the Deity 165, 168; and 'greatest happiness' 166–8, 169; on happiness and population size 156, 167; on happiness and wealth 107, 155, 167, 182, 202, 288; and 'fitness' 159, 166–7, 245; and 'justice' 152, 163–5, 168; and 'natural liberty' 151; and 'propriety' 152, 159–63; and 'prudence' 130, 154, 156, 160–1; *motivation and consequentialism* 151, 156, 157–9, 19–63 *see also* Smith, A.

Thornton, W.T. 309, 314, 322, 347, 368, 373, 377
Tocqueville, A. de 391

Turco, l. 64, 74–5
Turgot, A.R.J. 133–4

utilitarian ethics 5, 10–11, 22, 234, 255–8, 270–2, 273–7, 279–80, 340–4; consistent with moral sense as sympathy directed 26, 31–2, 38–9, 44, 64, 65, 111, 115, 117–8, 151, 156–9, 159–63, 169, 346–8, 351, 354–5, 361–2, 363, 368, 373, 376–9, 381–4; and ethical progress 141–3, 146, 179, 193–4, 216, 225–7, 340, 340–2, 348, 364, 366, 382; 'greatest happiness' principle as axiomatic 66, 76, 91, 217–18, 238, 242, 244, 249, 366; and population size 156, 157, 167, 179, 193–4; and virtue 270–2, and wealth 107–8, 155, 182, 202, 288; and working-class welfare 174–5, 177; *see also* distributive justice; entries for individual authors; moral sense; motivation (other-regarding)

Viner, J. 3–4, 12, 14, 42, 44, 48, 54, 138, 140, 141, 193, 215, 221, 222–3, 225–7, 246, 365
Voltaire, F.M.A. de 238, 247

Waterman, A.M.C. 26, 256
wealth: and happiness *see Lectures on Jurisprudence*; Malthus, T.R.; *Theory of Moral Sentiments*; utilitarian ethics; *Wealth of Nations*

Wealth of Nations: *distributive justice*: and Agrarian laws 182; and class income distribution 178, 181–90, 204; and government 127, 177, 178, 179, 190–3, 203; and graded income differentials 178, 182, 183, 204, 205, 207, 233; and private property 179–80, 185, 187–8, 193, 204; and welfare of majority class 174–6, 204; and welfare of least advantaged 175, 196–203, 206; *equality* 176–7, 179–80, 194–6; useful versus oppressive 184–7, 204; and social investment 178, 184; significance of manufacturing sector 182–3, 205; productivity effects 185, 188, 204, 234; *utilitarian ethics* 174, 176, 181–90, 193–4, 206; and justice 234; and natural rights 176, 178, 180–1; on happiness and population size 181–2, 193–4; on happiness and wealth 181–2, 182, 189, 202; *the wage structure* 194–6, 205, 206–7; skilled versus unskilled

175–6, 179, 192–3, 194–6, 196–9, 199–203; comparisons with Marx and Mill 178, 206–7 *see also* Smith, A.
Wedderburn, A. 221
West, E.G. 308, 322–3
Whewell, W. 233. 274–5, 341, 348, 362–6

Williamson, J.G. 195–6, 198
Winch, D. 109, 127, 182, 186, 256, 270
Witztum, A. 151, 154, 166, 167
Wollaston, W. 32

Young, A. 201, 267–8, 270
Young, J.T. 151, 154, 166, 167, 175